TROUBLE IS THEIR BUSINESS

Garland Reference Library
of the Humanities
(Vol. 1151)

TROUBLE IS THEIR BUSINESS
Private Eyes in Fiction, Film and Television, 1927–1988

John Conquest

GARLAND PUBLISHING, INC. • NEW YORK & LONDON
1990

Library of Congress Cataloging-in-Publication Data

Conquest, John, 1943–
    Trouble is their business : private eyes in fiction, film, and television, 1927–1988 / John Conquest.
        p. cm. — (Garland reference library of the humanities; vol. 1151)
    Includes bibliographies and index.
    ISBN 0–8240–5947–6 (alk. paper)
    1. Detectives in mass media. I. Title. II. Series.
P96.D4C66 1990
016.30223'0883632—dc20   89–33039
                                                       CIP

Printed on acid-free, 250-year-life paper
Manufactured in the United States of America

CONTENTS

FOREWORD

Over sixty years ago Race Williams, Private Investigator, came through a door, a blazing .44 in each hand, and an epoch was born: Carroll John Daly's *The Snarl Of The Beast*, published in 1927, was the first true private eye novel. Robert A. Baker and Michael T. Nietzel, authors of the main survey of private eye fiction to date, believe that "the PI novel is the superior form of the mystery novel and . . . by far the most exciting and intriguing." It must be fairly obvious that I agree with them, for reasons which I hope are explained in the Introduction.

The purpose of this present survey is to expand upon Baker & Nietzel's pioneering work. Where they concentrated on selected and mainly hard to medium-boiled American writers, I have attempted to include all private eye writers and their creations published in English since 1927 plus films and television and radio shows in which PIs are the main characters; 952 authors, 176 feature films, 164 television series, pilots and films, 56 radio programs and a grand total of 1563 PIs are listed (including those to be found in the Stop Press section).

Inevitably there are omissions; many authors represented in my own collection are not mentioned in any reference or critical work. In seven cases they were not even listed in Hubin's bibliography. I must assume there are even more waiting to be discovered and would be very grateful to hear of any authors, PIs and titles that have not been included. For openers, I have included a section called Missing Persons that lists the particular titles which I know from reviews to be PI novels but whose heroes/heroines I have been unable to identify by name.

The private eye novel has accumulated a critical literature of its own, which is included in the bibliography. Much of the writing, particularly that of the academic community, I found tendentious and tedious to read, but I would like to acknowledge my debts to certain commentators whose insights influenced my own thinking, namely David Geherin, Robert A. Baker and Michael T. Nietzel and, invaluable on the subject of women detectives, Kathleen Gregory Klein.

However, all errors and misjudgments are mine alone. Since I evolved the idea of this work I have been the grateful recipient of many people's kindness, knowledge and patience; book stores that have been notably pleasant and rewarding to visit have been Compendium and Heroes, London; Rue Morgue, Boulder; Mystery Book Store, Fantasy Etc. and Elsewhere, San Francisco; Mitchell's Bookstore, Pasadena and The Book Treasury, Nashville. Among publishers in the field, Mysterious Press and Crossing Press alone provided any co-operation. If any current authors feel slighted, I refer them to their publishers' ill-named publicity departments.

Particular thanks go to Mike and Chris of Compendium, Alan of Heroes, Tom and Edith Schantz of Rue Morgue and Dick Stovall of Sierra Dynamics, Austin, Texas(for those interested, this book was prepared on a Macintosh + using MicroSoft File and WriteNow).

Finally, during much of the reading, digesting and writing involved in this work, I was supported and encouraged by my dear friend Fly, a cat born to be a writer's companion, to whom it is dedicated in loving memory.

London, England & Austin, Texas

INTRODUCTION

The mystery genre is a conglomerate of barely related forms, each with its own dedicated partisans. In their 'Aficionado's Guide to Mystery & Detective Fiction,' *1001 Midnights*, Bill Pronzini and Marcia Muller use twelve categories, and all convey essential information to mystery buffs.

Their distinction between Classic Sleuth and Private Eye mirrors the great divide between the cozy and the hardboiled. Private detectives have been around for at least a century, but nobody would call Sherlock Holmes, Private Inquiry Agent, a Private Eye; and PI fiction owes little to classic detective fiction, stemming rather from the frontier literature of James Fenimore Cooper and other early American writers and from the dime novel myths and legends of the West. The Private Eye as a discrete entity first saw the light of day in the May 15, 1923 issue of *Black Mask* with Carroll John Daly's short story "Three Gun Terry." However crudely, Terry Mack prefigured the hundreds of PIs who were to follow.

Daly and Dashiell Hammett were pioneers of the phenomenon Ron Goulart describes in *The Dime Detectives*, "The private eye could only have happened in those years after World War I, the years of Prohibition. There had always been aggressive, straight-shooting fiction heroes, but it took the mood of the Twenties to add cynicism, detachment, a kind of guarded romanticism, and a compulsion towards action. The disillusionment that followed the war and frustration over the mushrooming gangster control of the cities affected the detective story as much as they did mainstream fiction. The same things that were bothering the heroes of Hemingway, Dos Passos and Fitzgerald began to unsettle the private detectives. And the 1920s' preoccupation with the American language, the dissatisfaction with Victorian rhetoric and polite exposition, was nowhere more strongly felt than among the writers of pulp detective fiction."

American detective fiction had hitherto been dominated by the genteel, mannered, upper-class English mystery and imitated it slavishly, but the tough, realistic hardboiled style of the pulp magazines with its clipped syntax and relentless pace was visceral rather than cerebral, democratic rather than elitist, exploring fate, sex and the passions in the tenements, cheap hotels and barrooms of America. Taking murder out of the drawing room and putting it back into the alley, substituting passion for cold calculation, the means at hand for arcane poisons and comprehensible motives for intricate alibis, it gave murder back, as Chandler said of Hammett, to the kind of people who commit it for a reason, not just to provide a corpse. It was also, not to put too fine a point on it, better writing, or at least could be, though as Chandler pointed out in his seminal essay on this very subject, "The Simple Art Of Murder," it can be abused or faked.

Born in an age of institutionalized corruption, the fictional private eye became an enduring hero. The underlying message of the PI story was, and still is, that law and justice are two entirely different things. When the law fails the individual, whether through corruption, indifference, incompetence or inability, the PI is a Galahad for hire, confronting a violent, cruel and unjust world with an uncompromising code of honor. He, or she, cannot be bought off or bullied off. For the classical detective a crime was, and indeed still is, a problem to be solved, after which justice would automatically be done and the proper order of things restored. For the PI, justice, in an imperfect world, must be made to happen—by an act of will, not by reasoning. And the world would still be imperfect.

Raised to maturity in the pulp magazines of the 30s and 40s, notably *Black Mask* to which Hammett, Chandler and many other remarkable writers contributed, the private eye later found a natural vehicle in the paperback originals of the 40s, 50s and 60s with their garish, violent and erotic covers—icons of an age and a semiological treasure store. My personal feeling is that *all* PI novels should be in paperback.

In the 60s and 70s many critics and, indeed, some writers, notably Max Allan Collins, concluded that private eyes were anachronistic, in James Sandoe's words, "an endangered species." Seemingly outflanked as lone wolf heroes by secret agents and as instruments of justice by sensitive procedural policemen, private eyes, it was argued, no longer had a role as individual operators in an age of large, impersonal security corporations of which they would henceforth be employees and unsuitable subjects for fiction. There appears to be a flaw in this reasoning somewhere. The secret agent is still reeling from revelations about the illegality, incompetence and immorality of the CIA and MI5, while the realities of the police, overstretched, underpaid, often corrupt, frequently inefficient, racist, sexist, insensitive and crude, finally caught up with the police novel and made it into a very different thing.

The PI turns out, in fact, to be if not less at least no more of a fantasy figure than his rivals. Some of the best work ever produced in the field has appeared within the past few years from gifted young writers who recognize the characteristics that set the PI apart from all other fictional heroes. Sixty years may be a lifetime, but there is still wear left in that shabby old trenchcoat. An excellent analysis of the strengths of the PI is that of David Geherin, in *The American Private Eye*, who points to five characteristics of the genre (or sub-genre if you insist) that have contributed to its popularity and endurance.

The first, and most basic, of these strengths is that the PI is an archetypal hero. "Brave, courageous, resourceful, decisive, incorruptible, fiercely independent, he is a solitary figure, poor but honest, who follows the rigorous demands of his own personal code . . . as American society has grown increasingly industrialized and bureaucratized, the private eye has continued to celebrate the importance of the individual in mass society, and though he can never perhaps fully restore justice and order to a corrupt society, his actions proclaim the value of honorable behavior in a world which too often rewards dishonorable activities."

There is, of course, one major problem here, and in Chandler's famous "mean streets" passage, and that is the inherent sexism, once excusable, in practice if not principle, female PIs being exceptional enough to warrant being swallowed in phallocentric generalizations. Today, however, while their numbers are still very small, they constitute, in the work of Sara Paretsky and Sue Grafton alone, a significant force that cannot be ignored or passed over.

The second strength is a protean nature. PIs can be of either sex and of any age, even if 100+ (Barry Hughart's Li Kao) is unusual. They can be of any race, though it has to be acknowledged that they tend to be Irish or Jewish. They can subscribe to any creed, from Catholic to Zen Buddhist. They can come from any class, ghetto kid to millionaire semi-playboy. They can have any sexual orientation, though gay and lesbian detectives are still very rare. They can have handicaps or psychological problems. Their politics range from the extreme right to the radical left, and their philosophies from hedonist to stoic. They can be married or misogynist, celibate or sensuous, poets, princes(ses) or peasants.

Though many PIs graduated to the occupation and qualified for their licenses via police forces or the military police, an appreciable number, from Dr. Frederickson the dwarf to one-armed Dan Fortune, would never be accepted for uniformed service on physical grounds alone while many more, going all the way back to Terry Mack, are clearly temperamentally unsuitable—problems with authority figures, whether explicitly stated or simply implied, are a fundamental theme of private eye fiction.

This diversity clearly sets PIs apart from policemen, spies and other bureaucratic heroes, who must satisfy rigid physical, political and moral acceptability standards even in fiction. Another real distinction is the PI's geographical spread. Though Los Angeles, New York and, to a lesser extent, San Francisco, Chicago and London, still account for the vast majority of PI offices, a marked trend in modern PI fiction is the off-beat location. As will be seen in the Yellow Pages, PIs are to be found in every corner of America and many foreign cities and while their offices still tend to be in shabby buildings in the wrong part of town, the town can be Missoula, Barcelona or Sydney. The PI is, of necessity, an urban creature, cities, after all, are where their work is, though it seems that quite small urban areas generate sufficient crime to provide good plots.

Thirdly, from the very beginning the PI novel has been rooted in the vernacular, drawing authentically and colorfully from colloquial language, adapting with changes. Both the first person narrative, ideally suited to the PI's individualism and solo operation, and the third person, equally suited to the hardboiled ethos, have been staples of the genre, with tough, punchy language laced with slang, wisecracks and black humor. Both have proved remarkably flexible, embracing Hammett's terse, unadorned style, Chandler's elaborate use of simile, Macdonald's psychologising, Spillane's crudeness and Crumley's poetics.

Fourthly, the PI is socially mobile to an almost unique extent, moving freely between the offices and mansions of the rich and powerful, middle-class suburbs and the lowest socioeconomic depths. As Geherin puts it, "His investigations bring him into contact with characters that include bank presidents and dope pushers, housewives and hookers, saints and sinners." The PI is, therefore, an ideal vehicle for social comment.

Where the classic sleuth of the cozies lives in a hermetic and artificial world, the PI walks down Chandler's mean streets, observing and forming his or her own individual views and judgments on every aspect of society, the good, the bad and the ugly whether it be found among the wealthy, the poor or criminals. At the risk of sounding pompous, it is not going to far to say that, the Mike Hammers notwithstanding, the PI is essentially a progressive figure with, in Chandler's words, "a disgust for sham and a contempt for pettiness." Those who attack the PI as a vigilante, little better than the criminals he pursues, fail to see that while the PI may despise the letter of the law, nobody has more respect for its spirit. Born in a time when it was precisely duly appointed authority that put itself beyond the law, the PI has always been, and still is, an implacable foe of those people and organizations that regard the rule of law as something that does not apply to them, whether organized crime, corrupt officialdom, arrogant wealth, shadow government, sociopathic multinational companies or simply amoral individuals.

For, lastly, the genre is dynamic and responds to changing mores and social problems. Reflecting the world around them, private eyes encounter the real life issues of modern America or the other countries they operate in. From Prohibition gangsters and municipal corruption to religious cults, drugs, ruthless property developers, the sexual exploitation of children, lawyers and other unsavory modern evils, the PI has retained his essential nature, the Galahad for hire. Similarly PIs themselves have, as a general rule, been transformed from simple he-men, relying on guts, nerve and .45s to get them through, to professional experts in a craft with its own mysteries and methods. Their personal relationships have, by and large, undergone radical revision, the treatment of women in modern PI novels being in marked contrast to, particularly, those of the 60s.

To these points can be added a sixth; credibility. This is not to say that private eyes in fiction are necessarily realistic, far from it, but, to paraphrase Chandler, trouble is their business. Unlike those amateur sleuths for whom the word "homicidotropic" has been coined, it is in the very nature of their calling that private eyes should deal routinely with murder and other major crimes. The same is true, of course, for policemen but while law officers' personal views and moral judgements may well be interesting, they must always be irrelevant; their function is to solve crimes and apprehend the guilty regardless. The personal views and moral judgements of private eyes, on the other hand, are of the essence for, morally, they are free agents, answerable to nobody but themselves, though possibly taking their clients, the police and state licensing boards into consideration.

PI writers can, at their peril, take any conceivable liberty with these already elastic conventions. The genre has been mercilessly parodied, new elements are constantly being introduced and boundaries extended. As Chandler said, "To exceed the limits of a formula without destroying it is the dream of every magazine writer who is not a hopeless hack."

A crucial problem for the genre, trapping many writers who might otherwise receive wider acclaim, is the critical focus on Hammett, Chandler and Ross Macdonald who established the PI as a legitimate hero but unwittingly created a rigid mold of expectation that has all but eclipsed alternative visions. The archetype became a stereotype in one generation and all too often PI novels are reviewed with reference to the "Father, Son and Holy Ghost" as Michael Avallone dubbed them, mocking the critics. On the other side of the tracks, the sex-and-sadism school is dominated by the extraordinary power of Mickey Spillane.

Byrd, Estleman, Greenleaf, Hansen, Lewin, Lyons, Parker and Valin, to name only a few, have all been nominated as successors to the Holy Trinity. But the only realistic way to look at this is to identify those writers who have clearly redefined the genre as Hammett, Chandler and Macdonald did. To the qualities of naturalism, romanticism and psychology with which, respectively, they moved the genre forward in its evolutionary stages, can be added at least two other major contributions; Michael Collins (Dennis Lynds) made his books vehicles for sociological observation while James Crumley introduced empathy and poetry.

One obvious question is how does one define a private eye? Allen Hubin, in his series character chronology, has a very basic, even crude, definition under the heading 'Private': "an investigator who seeks clients and takes a fee," but this also includes lawyers. Much of the time, there is little problem. How many books open in a dingy office with "Private Investigator" in fading gilt letters on the door? But quite apart from a host of marginal figures, there are any number of unlicensed PIs, while others are, on paper, perfectly legitimate investigators, but belong to the alien cozy tradition which, almost from the beginning, has attempted to harness the PI's strengths without actually facing the PI's gritty world.

Jim Huang, writing about Jonathan Kellerman's hero in *Drood Review* remarked, "On the 'walks like a duck, talks like a duck, must be a duck' theory, Alex Delaware is a private eye. What does the average PI do that Delaware hasn't in his first three appearances? He's hired by clients, he breaks into buildings at night in search of evidence, he has physical confrontations with his adversaries, he pores over records in the library, he travels out of state with a weak cover story to learn about suspects' pasts, he has a friend on the police force who feeds him inside information, he continues to work on a case after the customary firing halfway into the book, and he even narrates in metaphor."

Delaware is, in fact, a retired child psychologist but he presents fewer obstacles to being labeled a PI than, say, Red Diamond, a cabdriver living a fantasy psychosis, department store, hotel and railroad detectives-employees, corporate troubleshooters, 'salvage' experts like Travis McGee and so on. Even more problematic are characters who have what musicians call 'day jobs,' earning their living, technically, in other ways. It may sound rather vague, but at the end of the day a PI is a PI is a PI, and I have employed the 'Duck' theory freely.

While it was easy to exclude all private detectives whose careers began before the appearance of Carroll John Daly's *The Snarl Of The Beast*, resulting, thankfully, in the elimination of such as Carolyn Wells and Lee Thayer, 1927 was not a clear-cut watershed, dividing Classic Sleuths and Consulting Detectives, on the one hand, from Private Eyes on the other. Without making frequent value judgments, often on the basis of minimal information, it was difficult to reject many post-1927 detectives completely, however cozy. Nero Wolfe is a good example of the problem. Pronzini & Muller label him, with good reason, a "Classic Sleuth," but, quite unlike the genuine Golden Age Classic Sleuth, who would spurn an offer of payment with loathing, Wolfe's fees are what put groceries on the table, for he has no other source of income. Similarly, Maud Silver is in it for money to augment her meagre pension. They may not be Sam Spade and V.I. Warshawski, but neither are they Philo Vance and Miss Marple.

Professionalism became the determining factor. The detectives in this guide exchange their services and skills, whether cerebral or physical, for money and in the private sector. Some inclusions may still raise the occasional eyebrow, but I felt it was safer, and fairer, to opt for a catholic definition of the private eye.

WHAT IS A PI? SOME QUOTES

CARROLL JOHN DALY

"I have a little office which says 'Terry Mack, Private Investigator' on the door; which means whatever you wish to think it. I ain't a crook, and I ain't a dick; I play the game on the level, in my own way. I'm in the center of a triangle; between the crook and the police and the victim. The police have had an eye on me for some time, but only an eye, never a hand; they don't get my lay at all. The crooks, well, some is on, and some ain't; most of them don't know what to think, until I've put the hooks in them. Sometimes they gun for me, but that ain't a one-sided affair. When it comes to shooting, I don't have to waste time cleaning my gun. A little windy that; but you get my game."

DASHIELL HAMMETT

"Your private eye does not want to be an erudite solver of riddles in the Sherlock Holmes manner; he wants to be a hard and shifty fellow, able to take care of himself in any situation, able to get the best of anybody he comes into contact with, whether criminal, innocent bystander or client. I see in him a little man going forward day after day through mud and blood and death and deceit—as callous and brutal and cynical as necessary—towards a dim goal, with nothing to push or pull him towards it except that he's been hired to reach it."

RAYMOND CHANDLER

"But down these mean streets a man must go who is not himself mean, who is neither tarnished nor afraid. The detective in this kind of story must be such a man. He is the hero, he is everything. He must be a complete man and a common man and yet an unusual man. He must be, to use a rather weathered phrase, a man of honor, by instinct, by inevitability, without thought of it, and certainly without saying it. He must be the best man in his world and a good enough man for any world. I do not care much about his private life; he is neither a eunuch nor a satyr; I think he might seduce a duchess and I am quite sure he would not spoil a virgin; if he is a man of honor in one thing, he is that in all things.

He is a relatively poor man, or he would not be a detective at all. He is a common man or he would not go among common people. He has a sense of character, or he would not know his job. He will take no man's money dishonestly and no man's insolence without a due and dispassionate revenge. He is a lonely man and his pride is that you will treat him as a proud man or be very sorry you ever saw him. He talks as the man of his age talks, that is, with rude wit, a lively sense of the grotesque, a disgust for sham, and a contempt for pettiness.

The story is this man's adventure in search of a hidden truth, and it would be no adventure if it did not happen to a man fit for adventure. He has a range of awareness that startles you, but it belongs to him by right, because it belongs to the world he lives in. If there were enough like him, I think the world would be a very safe place to live in, and yet not too dull to be worth living in."

DAVID GEHERIN

"For twenty-five dollars a day, for the gratitude of a beautiful woman, for revenge, or simply because it's his job, or he has given his word, or it's all he knows how to do."

MICKEY SPILLANE

"You're a cop, Pat. You're tied down by rules and regulations. There's someone over you. I'm alone. I can slap someone in the puss and they can't do a damn thing. No one can kick me out of a job. Maybe there's nobody to kick up a huge fuss if I'm gunned down, but then I still have a private cop's license with the privilege to pack a rod, and they're afraid of me."

THOMAS B. DEWEY

"I'm just a guy. I go around and get in jams and then try to figure a way out of them. I work hard. I don't make very much money and most people insult me one way or another. I'm thirty-eight years old, a fairly good shot with small arms, slow-thinking but thorough and very dirty in a clinch."

JAMES CRUMLEY

"For nearly eighty years the only way to get a divorce in our state was to have your spouse convicted of a felony or caught in an act of adultery. Not even physical abuse or insanity counted. And in the ten years since I resigned as a county deputy, I had made a good living off those antiquated divorce laws. Then the state legislature, in a flurry of activity at the end of a special session, put me out of business by civilizing those divorce laws. Now we have dissolutions of marriage by reason of irreconcilable differences. Supporters and opponents were both shocked by the unexpected action of the lawmakers, but not as shocked as I was. I spent the next two days sulking in my office, drinking and enjoying the view, considering the prospects for my suddenly very dim future."

RON GOULART

"They shared a distrust of politicians and the police. They could patiently collect evidence, but they could also cut corners the way the law couldn't. Yet they were linked with reality, with the real crimes of the urban world and the real smell and feel of the mean streets, and this put the best of them in a different class from the essentially adolescent phantom avengers and the earlier dime-novel sleuths with their upper-class values and methods. They were sometimes drunk, frequently broke. A private eye would always help someone in trouble, though he would downplay his compassion . . . Taking action was what was important, even when it wasn't well thought out. Though the operative wasn't always an optimist, he stuck to his word."

HOWARD BROWNE

"Private dicks had no business being married. Private dicks should live with nothing except a few books and a bottle or two on the pantry shelf and a small but select list of phone numbers for ready reference when the glands start acting up. Private dicks should be proud and lonely men who can say no when the hour is late and their feet hurt."

MICHAEL COLLINS

"Not that I investigate much that is big or dangerous. Some industrial work and some divorces. Armed guard jobs, and subpoenas for bread and butter. But mostly the personal problems of small people who want to apply a little pressure on someone but don't want the police. It's not work I especially like, but a man must eat, and it's work I know how to do. (Most men work at what they happened to learn how to do, not at what they wish they had learned how to do.) I'm my own boss, and I don't have to wear a white shirt or get up early. The work has one big drawback as far as Chelsea is concerned—it makes me a cop."

JAMES GRADY

"We created this 'New Wave' private investigator concept back in '79, remember? Our smart idea. Straight out of the D. C. experience, the investigative committees. Create a job for the right kind of person, somebody who knows his way round government and private institutions, somebody who can hunt through bureaucracies rather than bug some poor housewife who's getting a little on the side. Somebody who can sort through a complicated package and add up the real score. No domestic work: no child custody fights, no divorce. White collar crime and, yeah— we knew that spilled over into the organized boys, but no targeting mainline crooks, no hard-core criminal stuff. No tough guy nonsense. Political investigations, corporate wars."

SUE GRAFTON

"Cops and private eyes are always caught up in paperwork. Written records have to be kept . . . Since a private eye also bills for services, I have to keep track of my hours and expenses, submitting statements periodically so I can make sure I get paid. I prefer fieldwork. I suspect we all do. If I'd wanted to spend my days in an office, I'd have studied to be an underwriter for the insurance company next door. Their work seems boring 80 percent of the time while mine bores me about one hour out of every ten."

COMPARATIVE EYES

Comparing PI writers is fairly pointless—different aspects of different writers' work appeal in different ways to different readers. One has only to reflect that in 1930 *Black Mask* readers ranked Carroll John Daly over Erle Stanley Gardner and both some way ahead of Dashiell Hammett. However, three attempts to grade PI writers by quality and importance have been made and they are not without interest. One is David Geherin's choice of authors to illustrate the historical development of *The American Private Eye*. In chronological order, they are:

1 Carroll John Daly	14 Bart Spicer
2 Dashiell Hammett	15 Richard S. Prather
3 Raoul Whitfield	16 Mickey Spillane
4 Frederick Nebel	17 Ross Macdonald
5 George Harmon Coxe	18 Thomas B. Dewey
6 John K. Butler	19 William Campbell Gault
7 Norbert Davis	20 Michael Collins
8 Robert Leslie Bellem	21 Robert B. Parker
9 Jonathan Latimer	22 Bill Pronzini
10 Raymond Chandler	23 Michael Z. Lewin
11 Cleve F. Adams	24 Joseph Hansen
12 Brett Halliday	25 Arthur Lyons
13 Howard Browne	26 Lawrence Block

In 1983 Robert A. Baker and Michael T. Nietzel polled the PWA with a questionnaire involving six categories of evaluation of PI writers who had written novels, divided into two parts, 1920-1970 and 1970-present. With Geherin's selection I have little quarrel, but the PWA lists below seem to me to reflect very badly on that body's professionalism. One looks in vain for such names as Bart Spicer, Geoffrey Homes, Cleve F. Adams or William Ard, to mention only a few who, I would have thought, almost anyone would place well ahead of, say, Albert, Avallone or Fickling. Latimer's low position in the first list seems as extraordinary as Michael Collins' in the second (Elmore Leonard beat Latimer on the strength of one book that was published in 1977!), while anybody who has read Denbow's single PI novel, a candidate, indeed Baker & Nietzel's candidate, for all time worst, might reasonably ask whether the PWA was dealing from a full deck. Full details will be found in their book, but a simplified and, I hope, not distorted summary, looks like this:

1920-1970

1 Raymond Chandler
2 Dashiell Hammett
3 Ross Macdonald
4 Fredric Brown
5 John D. MacDonald
6 Rex Stout
7 John Evans
8 Thomas B. Dewey
9 William Campbell Gault
10 Ed Lacy
11 Talmage Powell
12 Elmore Leonard
13 Jonathan Latimer
14 George Harmon Coxe
15 A.A. Fair
16 Wade Miller
17 Brett Halliday
18 Marvin Albert
19 Stephen Marlowe
20 Curt Cannon
21 Mickey Spillane
22 Henry Kane
23 Richard S. Prather
24 Bill S. Ballinger
25 William F. Nolan
26 Carroll John Daly
27 Willis Todhunter Ballard
28 M.E. Chaber
29 G.G. Fickling
30 Frank Kane
31 Frank Gruber
32 Michael Avallone
33 John Jakes
34 Michael Brett

1970-Present (1983)

1 James Crumley
2 Stanley Ellin
3 Arthur Lyons
4 Tucker Coe
5 Timothy Harris
6 Lawrence Block
7 Michael Z. Lewin
8 Bill Pronzini
9 Joe Gores
10 Jonathan Valin
11 Mark Sadler (Dennis Lynds)
12 Joseph Hansen
13 Stephen Greenleaf
14 James Reasoner
15 Sara Paretsky
16 Andrew Bergman
17 Ed McBain
18 Loren D. Estleman
19 Roger L. Simon
20 Stuart Kaminsky
21 Robert B. Parker
22 Charles Alverson
23 Michael Collins (Lynds)
24 Marcia Muller
25 Ron Goulart
26 Pete Hamill
27 George Chesboro
28 William Hjortsberg
29 Ernest Tidyman
30 L.A. Morse
31 Robert J. Randisi
32 Max Byrd
33 Kin Platt
34 Andrew Fenady
35 Hamilton Caine
36 Ross H. Spencer
37 William Denbow

In *1001 Midnights*, Bill Pronzini and Marcia Muller discuss 199 of the titles listed in this work (making PI fiction almost exactly one fifth of the entire genre; the titles are marked in the main text) by 147 authors. Two, Chandler and Hammett, are recognized as 'Cornerstone' writers, while another 30 receive special commendation for "Titles that are especially good or interesting or that represent a particularly notable series or body of work." These authors are, in alphabetical order:

1 William Arden (Dennis Lynds)	17 Geoffrey Homes
2 Lawrence Block	18 Stuart Kaminsky
3 Fredric Brown	19 Baynard Kendrick
4 Howard Browne	20 Robert Kyle
5 Victor Canning	21 Ed Lacy
6 George Chesbro	22 Jonathan Latimer
7 Tucker Coe	23 Michael Z. Lewin
8 Michael Collins (Dennis Lynds)	24 David Linzee
9 James Crumley	25 John D. MacDonald
10 Thomas B. Dewey	26 Ross Macdonald
11 Stanley Ellin	27 David Marlowe
12 Dick Francis	28 Warren Murphy
13 William Campbell Gault	29 Bill Pronzini
14 Joseph Hansen	30 Bart Spicer
15 Bert & Dolores Hitchens	31 Mickey Spillane
16 Dolores Hitchens	32 Rex Stout

I append an alphabetical list of writers who should, I think, be considered in an update of the PWA's 1970-Present list. They are all at least as good, often much better, than many authors in that list.

1983-1989

1 Linda Barnes	11 Richard Hoyt
2 Robert Campbell	12 Rob Kantner
3 Stephen Dobyns	13 Jonathan Kellerman
4 Earl W. Emerson	14 Dick Lochte
5 Sue Grafton	15 T.J. MacGregor
6 Parnell Hall	16 Warren Murphy
7 Jeremiah Healy	17 Nick O'Donohoe
8 Carl Hiassen	18 Mark Schorr
9 Richard Hilary	19 Richard Stevenson
10 Doug Hornig	20 Andrew Vachss

WOMEN DETECTIVES

Of the 1530 PIs listed in this survey, 165 are women though 18 feature only as adjuncts to husbands and 13 appear only in anthologized short stories. This may well, of course, reflect the real world of private detection. In fact there are fewer female PI writers (116 at the most generous count, including co-writers and two dubious pseudonyms) than there are female PIs and many of the women listed wrote about male PIs. One has only to turn to such illustrious names as Leigh Brackett, Dolores Hitchens, Margaret Millar and Hilda Lawrence, not to mention Shelley Singer, Chris Wiltz and others. Many women, indeed, not only write about men but conceal their own sex, even in modern times, behind male pseudonyms or ambiguous initials—Jack Early (Sandra Scoppettone), M.V. Heberden, who also wrote as Charles L. Leonard, Paul Kruger (Roberta Sebenthal), M.R.D. Meek, J.M.T. Miller, Joe Rayter (Mary McChesney), L.J. Washburn and M.K. Wren (Martha Renfroe).

All but four of the '&' women were the creation of male authors, but Frances Crane's **Jean** (& Pat) **Abbott**, Gail Stockwell's **Sally** (& Kingsley) **Toplitt**, Sue MacVeigh's **Susie** (& Andy) **MacVeigh** and Atanielle Annyn Noel's **Gwen** (& Garamond) **Gray** differ little in their purpose from Dashiell Hammett's **Nora** (& Nick) **Charles**, Richard & Frances Lockridge's **Pamela** (& Jerry) **North**, Frank King's **Alice Faverden**, partner, fiancée and eventually wife of Clive Conrad, J.T. McIntosh's **Dominique** (& Ambrose) **Frayne**, Herbert Resnicow's **Nora** (& Alexander) **Gold**, Jack Foxx's **Hattie** (& Fergus) **O'Hara**, Ron Goulart's **Hildy** (& Jake) **Pace**, or James M. Fox's **Suzy** (& Johnny) **Marshall**. In each case the female partner is, in James M. Fox's phrase, "the little woman," with the male taking the initiatives and the woman making herself available for plot devices. They are all too often given to intuition and sometimes are secretly smarter than their partners, though rarely getting the credit. Exceptionally, Lewis Padgett's **Eve** (& Seth) **Colman** are used as a vehicle to comment on such pairings. TV adds **Connie** (& Adam) **Conway** of DETECTIVE'S WIFE, **Jane** (& Dick) **Starrett** of DICK & THE DUCHESS and **Amanda** (& Rick) **Tucker** of TUCKER'S WITCH, film **Dora** (& Dick) **Charleston** (parodying the Charleses), and radio **Debby** (& Jeff) **Spencer** (TWO ON A CLUE).

Of the women PIs created by male authors, there are three distinct classes; heroines, full partners and junior partners. In the first and largest category we find, in chronological order, E. Phillips Oppenheim's **Baroness Clara Linz** (1935) and ineffectual **Lucie Mott** (1936); Rex

Stout's **Theodolinda Bonner** (1937); Judson Philips' **Carole Trevor** (1938), given her agency by her wealthy ex-husband; James Rubel's **Eli Donovan**; Floyd Mahannah's floundering **Cassie Gibson**; Austin Lee's **Flora Hogg**; Henry Kane's 38-23-38 Miss America runner-up **Marla Trent**, the Private Eyeful; Fran Huston (actually Ron S. Miller)'s **Nichole Sweet**; James A. Yardley's erotic virgin **Kiss Darling**; Victor B. Miller's "liberated" **Fernanda**; James D. Lawrence's appalling black **Angela Harpe**; Arthur Kaplan's **Charity Bay**; Walter Wager's **Alison B. Gordon**; Karl Alexander's **Sara Scott**; David Galloway's lesbian **Lamaar Ransom**; Jim Conaway's joke feminist **Jana Blake**; W.R. Philbrick's well regarded (by a female critic) **Connie Kayle**; Max Allan Collins & Terry Beatty's comic strip heroine **Ms Michael Tree**; Richard Werry's **Jane Mulroy**; Robert Bowman's **Cassandra Thorpe**, Jerry Oster's **Eve Zabriskie** and Gerald Laurence's **Natalie Dauntless Fisher**.

The full partners begin in fact with two senior partners, though Stephen Ransome (Frederick C. Davis)'s **Jill Archer** (1939) pretends to be a mere secretary in the agency she actually owns, while A.A. Fair (Erle Stanley Gardner)'s **Bertha Cool** (also 1939) though nominally the boss is consistently sabotaged by her creator. Senior or full partners are Marvin Kaye's **Hilary Quayle**; Manly Wade Wellman's **J.D. Thatcher**; Patrick Buchanan's **Charity Tucker**; Brad Solomon's **Maggie McGuane**; Frank McConnell's **Bridget O'Toole** a n d Walter Satterthwait's **Rita Mondragon**. Reed Stephens' **Ginny Fistoulari**, technically the senior, license holding, agency owning partner is pushed into subordinate status, as is Carter Brown's dizzy **Mavis Seidlitz**, who actually gets spanked by her partner on one occasion.

David Linzee's **Sarah Saber** is lower on the organizational tree than her co-star and lover. Thomas Black's **Dolly Adams**, Robert George Dean's **Sue Barton**, Martin F. Freeman's **Mary Clerkenwell** and Daniel Estow's **Ann Lang** definitely play second fiddle, as do women's boxing champion **Angel Cantini** from Robert Eversz, Dick Lochte's **Serendipity Dahlquist**, admittedly only 14/15 years old, and William Babula's ex-cop **Mickey Farabaugh**, fired from the Ohio force for posing nude in *Playboy*. **Lynn McColl** runs her own agency but J.T. Morrow's male PI has to bail her out of trouble. **Pamela Yew** outsmarts Richard Hoyt's hero in one novel.

Turning to women created by women, we start in 1928 with Patricia Wentworth's cozy but professional **Maud Silver** and Kay Cleaver Strahan's 'crime analyst' **Lynn MacDonald**, followed by Hazel Campbell's **Olga Knaresbrook** and **Molly Kingsley** in 1933; Leslie

Ford's ladylike **Grace Latham** playing second fiddle except in one book of her own; Zelda Popkin's department store detective **Mary Carner** (1938); **Hilea Bailey**, doing the legwork for her crippled father in Hilea Bailey's books (1939) and (Marjorie) Torrey Chanslor's spinster sisters **Amanda & Lutie Beagle** (1940), the first female partnership.

Forties females were restricted to reluctant **Grace Pomeroy** from Anna Mary Wells (1943); **Pogy Rogers**, the brains of Z(ola) H(elen) Ross' mixed partnership (1946) and **Gale Gallagher**, one of whose two authors was Margaret Scott writing with Will Oursler as Gale Gallagher (1947). Nancy Spain's subversive quasi-lesbian duo **Miriam Birdseye** and **Natasha Nevkorina** filled the gap, apart from Bridget Chetwynd's Had-I-But-Known **Petunia Best** and Lois Eby & John C. Fleming's **Pat O'Leary**, until 38-22-36 sexbomb **Honey West**, the sexploitive creation of G.G. (Gloria & Forrest) Fickling in 1957 after which the female PI disappeared until P.D. James' **Cordelia Gray** in 1972. The arrival of the tough, autonomous woman was signaled by Lee McGraw's **Madge Hatchett** in 1976 but Baker & Nietzel were also baffled by the ambiguity of the author's name, in any case a pseudonym. The same year saw the arrival of Janice Law's ruthless **Anna Peters**, though she did not become a PI until 1980.

Though she has since been somewhat eclipsed, the modern era of the female PI opens with the 1977 publication of Marcia Muller's first book about **Sharon McCone**. In the same year M(ary) F. Beal produced the single feminist adventure of Chicana revolutionary **Kat Guerrera**. Eva Zaremba followed with lesbian Canadian **Helen Keremos** in 1978 and in 1979 Phyllis Swan "proved that a woman can write as badly as any man" (Baker & Nietzel) with preposterous **Anastasia Jugedinski**. In 1980, however, things began to look up with Liza Cody's first **Anna Lee** novel, followed in 1981 by Maxine O'Callaghan's **Delilah West** and then by the superlative Class of '82, the twin talents of Sara Paretsky, with **V.I. Warshawski**, and Sue Grafton, with **Kinsey Millhone**.

Since then Teona Tone has come up with proto-feminist **Kyra Keaton**; Hosanna Brown, a pseudonym I suspect conceals a male writer, with mulatto **Frank Le Roux**; Susan Steiner with **Alexandra Winter** and the exceptional T.J. McGregor with **Quin St. James**. A recent woman PI appears under an ambiguous byline—**Daisy Marlow** from D. Miller Morgan, who is in fact a woman; Patricia Wallace contributed the equally ambiguously named **Sydney Bryant** and Linda Barnes recently forsook her hero for **Carlotta Carlyle**. Elizabeth Atwood Taylor has **Maggie Elliott**; Dorothy Sucher has a female boss, **Sabina Swift**, while Carol

Jerina has an assistant to a male boss, **Jillian Fletcher**. Shelley Singer has a male hero but assisted by lesbian **Rosie Vicente** and Linda Grant a PI heroine, **Catherine Sayler**, with a PI boyfriend. Margaret Dobson's **Jane Bailey** helps out her PI boyfriend in a romance-mystery and **Guinevere Jones** is a solo PI in another. Dolores Komo's **Clio Brown** is a black woman who inherited her St Louis agency from her father. Gillian Slovo's **Kate Baeier**, Dolores Klaich and Diana McRae's very recent lesbians **Tyler Divine** and **Eliza Pirex**, Melisa C. Michaels' **Aileen Douglass**, Elizabeth Bowers' PI and mother **Meg Lacey** and Spanish feminist Maria-Antonia Oliver's **Lonia Guiu** are the latest additions.

Television's major contribution, to the numbers at least, is CHARLIE'S ANGELS' horde of plastic cuties, **Sabrina Duncan**, **Kelly Garrett**, **Jill** and **Kris Munroe**, **Tiffany Welles** and **Julie Rogers**. TV female bosses are **Judge Meredith** (The JUDGE & JAKE WYLER), **Judge Meredith Leland** (PARTNERS IN CRIME), **Laura Holt** (REMINGTON STEELE), **Maddie Hayes** (MOONLIGHTING), **Cassie Holland** (CASSIE & CO) and **Rose Winters** (BIG ROSE). PI heroines are limited to **Liz Stonestreet** (STONESTREET), **B.T. Brady** (THIS GIRL FOR HIRE) and **Carole Stanwyck** and **Sydney Kovak** (PARTNERS IN CRIME). **Contessa Caroline di Cantini** (The PROTECTORS), **Delia Langtree** (TRIPLECROSS), **Christina Towne** (DIAMONDS) and **Jane Watson** (The RETURN OF SHERLOCK HOLMES) have full partner status, but **Betty Jones** (BARNABY JONES), **Maggie Peters** (The INVESTIGATORS) and **Vanessa Smith** (The MOST DEADLY GAME) are strictly juniors, while **Janet Fowler** (SIMON & SIMON) was at the bottom of the tree.

Female PIs in films are a real rarity, with only **Stacey Hansen** (STACEY & HER GANGBUSTERS) and **Harriet Zapper** (BIG ZAPPER) as solo acts, but the former was played by a onetime *Playboy* Playmate, the latter featured in a sexploiter, while bill-collector **Rachel Dobs** (The SQUEEZE) was a mere wannabee. **Myra Winslow** (PRIVATE DETECTIVE) and **Nora O'Brien** (LEAVE IT TO THE IRISH) competed professionally but melted romantically with male co-stars, while **Nora Charles** (the 'THIN MAN' series) and **Dora Charleston** (MURDER BY DEATH) come from the '&' section.

In fact women did relatively better on radio than in any other medium. Starting with soap opera heroine **Kitty Keene**, of KITTY KEENE, INC., in 1937, there were twelve starring female parts, including the &s, **Nora Charles** (The ADVENTURES OF THE THIN MAN), **Jean Abbott** (ABBOTT MYSTERIES) and **Pamela North** (MR & MRS

NORTH) plus **Debby Spencer** (TWO ON A CLUE). Heroines were **Ann Scotland** (The AFFAIRS OF ANN SCOTLAND), **Candy Matson** (CANDY MATSON, YUkon 2-8209) and **Miss Pinkerton** (MISS PINKERTON INC.). **Theresa Travers** (RESULTS INC.) was a partner, while **Jerri Booker** (I LOVE A MYSTERY), **Claire Brooks** (LET GEORGE DO IT) and **Phyllis Knight** (MICHAEL SHAYNE) were sidekicks.

For a feminist critique of the female PI in fiction, analysing some of those mentioned above in considerable detail, the reader is referred to Kathleen Gregory Klein's *The Woman Detective* (1988), interesting, indeed fascinating, on the genre's consistent unwillingness to allow female PIs to succeed both as women and detectives—with women writers as guilty as their male counterparts—though I would like to think that Klein is over-pessimistic about future possibilities. PI fiction is, I hope, dynamic enough to respond to her call, echoing Carolyn Heilbrun on science fiction, to "deconstruct . . . the structures of the patriarchy." As things stand, Sara Paretsky is the only currently active PI writer of whom she approves in both genre and feminist terms.

ETHNIC DETECTIVES

I have been struck by an apparent predominance of Irish and Jewish PIs while the number of non-whites of any kind is very small—47 in fact, of whom three play secondary, basically non-PI roles. The most obvious American minority group, at least, that is poorly represented in PIdom is blacks. The first black PI, by many years, was Ed Lacy's **Toussaint Moore** who first appeared in 1957. Lacy (Leonard Zinberg) was himself white but married to a black woman. It was not until 1970 that Ernest Tidyman came along with **John Shaft**, the epitome of the proud, autonomous Black man. Since then there have been a number of black PIs, Ishmael Reed's very offbeat JuJu doctor **PaPa LaBas**, assisted in one book by **Black Herman**; Percy Spurlark Parker's **Big Bull Benson**, J.F. Burke's **Sam Kelly** and Nat Richards' **Otis Dunn** (all 1974); Eric Corder's Harvard graduate attack dog trainer **Wylie Lincoln** (1975); Kenn Davis' **Carver Bascombe** (1976); Mason Clifford's **Joe Cinquez** (1980) and Richard Hilary's **Ezell Barnes** (1987), all fully rounded characters. The most notable Black PI today is Gar Anthony Haywood's **Aaron Gunner**, whose debut won the second (1987) PWA Best First Novel contest.

Ralph Dennis' **Hump Evans**, the only one to live and work in the South, is a co-star, but Jerry Allen Potter's **Nicki Hill** and Richard Werry's

Ahmad Dakar only have supporting, non-professional roles. All three are characterized as football players (Browns, Cowboys and Dolphins respectively), ergo big and tough. A special case is **Hawk**, the much criticized creation of Robert B. Parker, who at best can only be described as a hired hand.

Finally there are two and a half black women PIs of whom the earliest, James Lawrence's unspeakable **Angela Harpe**, reflects little credit on either her sex or her race. However, Dolores Komo's **Clio Brown**, coming as she does from a woman writer and a feminist publisher, begins to redress the balance. Hosanna Brown's **Frank Le Roux** is a mulatto and, unfortunately, a lightweight.

Television adds only five more to the roster of black PIs, **Harry Tenafly** of the short-lived series TENAFLY, **E.L.** Turner from the equally transient TENSPEED & BROWNSHOE, **Larry Dean** from one failed pilot, TWO FOR THE MONEY, **Douglas Hawke** from another, SHOOTING STARS, and the eponymous **Sonny Spoon**. Joining John Shaft on the big screen were the eponymous **Truck Turner**, **Al Hickey** of HICKEY & BOGGS and **Hamberger** in DEADLY ILLUSION.

Native American Indians have a longer, if briefer, history in the genre but it is striking how seldom they are pure blooded. In fact there is only one full Indian, Gilbert Ralston's **Dakota** (1973) who is half Shoshone, half Piegan, though Seminole giant **Chief Moses** has a secondary, junior partner, role in a novel by William Babula.

Of the 'half-breeds,' the first (1938) was Geoffrey Homes' **Humphrey Campbell** who is part Piute. Hugh Lawrence Nelson's **Zebulion Buck** (1949) is part Indian, though of what nation I have been unable to determine. James Moffatt's **Johnny Canuck** (1966) is only a quarter Sioux, his grandfather having fled to Canada rather than surrender, but that blood seems to predominate in stereotyped ways. The appalling **Tony Garrity** (1969) books by Allan Nixon have a half Aztec hero, while the lame **Jerry Roe** (1975) novels by L.V. Roper make much of his half Cherokee heritage. M.K. Wren's **Conan Flagg** is half Nez Percé, but more sympathetically treated. Marcia Muller's **Sharon Cone** is Scotch-Irish-Shoshone. Warwick Downing's **Joe Reddman** was raised by a Cheyenne foster mother but is not himself of Indian blood.

Hispanic Americans have an even shorter record. In the 30s, Cleve F. Adams wrote short stories about Violet McDade that were narrated by her assistant **Nevada Alvarado**. In 1977 M(ary) F. Beal wrote one novel featuring Chicana ex-revolutionary and women's movement activist Maria Katerina Lorca Guerrera Alcazar, or **Kat Guerrera**. In 1987, Rider

McDowell featured Spanish Harlem PI **Willy Diaz** while Peter Israel's **Pablo Rivera**, in the same year, goes under the waspische name of Philip Revere, betraying a certain detachment from his roots. The latest addition is Bruce Cook's **Antonio Cervantes** in a book marred, according to one review, by stereotyped broken English. A forthcoming Ron Goulart novel features the likely sounding **Rudy Navarro**.

The rest of the world is represented by Poul Anderson's Norwegian-Japanese-Hawaiian **Trygve Yamamura** and Owen Park's half-Chinese, half-White Russian **Tommy Lee**. San Francisco's Chinatown was home to **Khan** in a TV series of the same name which was cancelled after four episodes and Hong Kong to **Joseph Wong** in a Cantonese comedy film, The PRIVATE EYES. Day Keene's **Johnny Aloha** is Irish-Hawaiian.

HOMOSEXUAL DETECTIVES

The predominant gay PI is, of course, Joseph Hansen's **Dave Brandstetter**, a purposefully didactic figure who first appeared in 1970 and was designed both to entertain in good stories and enlighten on the realities of homosexual life, and in both objects Hansen has been tremendously successful. The earliest gay I can discover is Lou Rand's **Francis Morley** from 1961, whom I am assured was a PI but whose one adventure I have been unable to obtain. Following very much in Hansen's footsteps, Richard Stevenson has broken into the mainstream market with **Don Strachey**, while Stephen Lewis' **Jake Lieberman**, published by a gay publishing house, has been aimed at a more specific audience, though his one story is by no means overtly sexual. **Derek Thompson** is a gay San Francisco PI in a book by Kelly Bradford put out by a small feminist house. The most aggressive lifestyle among gay PIs is that of Dan Kavanagh's British bisexual, **Nick Duffy**.

There are, in fact, rather more lesbians in the literature, though one of them, **Lamaar Ransom**, who has a gay, black secretary, was the creation of a male writer, David Galloway, while another, **Rosie Vicente**, takes only a secondary role in Shelley Singer's Jake Samson novels. M(ary) F. Beal's **Kat Guerrera** is a bisexual who prefers female partners and Eva Zaremba's **Helen Keremos** is a member of three different PI minority groups—a woman, a lesbian and a Canadian—but her sexuality is so low key that it's known from an author interview rather than from the text. A new book by Dolores Klaich features **Tyler Divine**, another by Diana McRae has **Eliza Pirex** and a short story in Zahava's WomanSleuth Anthology may be a debut for **Wiggins**. Knowledgeable readers could infer the sexual orientation of Nancy Spain's **Miriam Birdseye** and **Natasha Nevkorina** but it is never explicitly stated.

On the subject of homosexuality, a minor oddity is the genre's common misuse of the word "gunsel," which means a boy kept for immoral purposes. Joseph Shaw, editing *The Maltese Falcon* for serialization in *Black Mask*, misunderstood it as a variation of gunman (or he would have cut it out), in which error he has been followed by dozens of writers.

WOUNDED HEROES

The reader can reasonably expect the heroes or heroines of PI novels to have some individuality, an expectation that is not always rewarded, but many have a feature or characteristic that either dominates their entire persona or is a real and obvious physical handicap. Sometimes these complement personality, but all too often they substitute for it. In their pulp anthologies Gary Hoppenstand & Ray Browne call them Defective Detectives, but in most cases it is more positive to think of them as wounded heroes, a literary usage with a respectable history, even though, like any other usage, it is open to sensationalizing abuse or simplistic misuse.

The most exotic problems are, in fact, to be found in Hoppenstand & Browne's collections (see **ANTHOLOGIES: 7** and **8**) which include Edith & Ejler Jacobson's haemophilic **Nat Perry**, aka "The Bleeder," who could die from a scratch; John Kobler's **Peter Quest**, going blind from glaucoma; Nat Schachner's **Nicholas Street**, who is an amnesiac; Leon Bryne's stone-deaf **Dan Holden**; Warren Lucas' **Lin Melchan**, who has the opposite problem, hyperacute hearing; Russell Gray's **Ben Bryn**, stunted by polio as a child and Paul Ernst's **Seekay**, whose hideously mutilated face is hidden behind a plastic shield. Even in the shudder pulps, mainly *Dime Mystery*, these unfortunates would seem eminently unsuited to the life of a PI.

But the more respectable world of the PI novel can offer many equally unlikely heroes (well, almost). Of the physically handicapped PIs, there are several who lost a limb or its use. Michael Collins' **Dan Fortune** and Simon Ritchie's **John Kenneth Galbraith Jantarro** are both missing an arm; Dick Francis' **Sid Halley** lost a hand in a horseracing accident; Reed Stephens' **Ginny Fistoulari** lost hers holding a bomb out of a hospital window; Richard Deming's **Manville Moon** has an artificial leg; John Milne's **Jimmy Jenner** lost a foot and the hearing in one ear in a bomb outrage, and Jerry Allan Potter's **Samuel Clemens Tucker** left one of his feet and a testicle in Vietnam. Still there but effectively crippling them are the knees of Steve Knickmeyer's **Steve Cranmer**, Warren Murphy's **Steve Hooks** and John Lutz's **Fred Carver**, all three of whom got shot in that vulnerable place and reduced to canes, leg braces, physiotherapy or, in Cranmer's case, massive intakes of Demerol.

Not necessarily obvious are the two real sensory handicaps on record. Baynard Kendrick's **Duncan Maclain** is blind, but Kendrick, who worked with blind people, supplied him with both a seeing-eye dog and an attack-trained protector, a competent staff and careful research into the capabilities of blind people. Jack Livingston's **Joe Binney** is deaf, the result of an explosion when he was a Navy frogman, but this, in fact, is often an advantage as he can lipread (as can Dan Holden above). Paul Engleman's ex-baseball player **Mark Renzler** was blinded in one eye by a fastball but it seems to affect him not at all.

Equally unapparent is the fact that James Brendan O'Sullivan's debonair **Steve Silk** has only one lung, though it must slow him down a little as, more obviously, did the heart attack that Herbert Resnicow's **Alexander Gold** suffered, which retired him from engineering to become a cerebral detective. In this class we can also place the permanent insomnia of Robert Forward's **Alexandre L'Hiboux**, who perpetually roams the streets of Los Angeles, with no home, no car and no office.

The only other physical peculiarity on record is that of George Chesboro's **Dr. Robert 'Mongo' Frederickson** who is a dwarf, though John Jakes' **Johnny Havoc** and Ed Lacy's **Hal Darling**, both only 5'1", must be fairly noticeable. Apart from being over 100 years old, Barry Hughart's **Li Kao** only weighs 90 pounds and is carried by his assistant when speed is required.

On the psychological side, there are several traumatized women: Karl Alexander's **Sara Scott** and Maxine O'Callaghan's **Delilah West** are both obsessed by their husbands' murders. Patrick Buchanan's **Charity Tucker** and Phyllis Swan's **Anastasia Jugedinski** are both frigid as a result of rapes.

There *are* abstemious PIs (Geoffrey Homes' **Humphrey Campbell** drinks nothing stronger than milk) but far more problem drinkers. The most extreme case is that of Curt Cannon's **Curt Cannon**, who is not only an alcoholic, having pistol-whipped his adulterous wife and best friend and lost his license, but a homeless derelict in the Bowery. Combining steady drinking with a kind of quasi-respectable life are Lawrence Block's **Matt Scudder**, separated from his family and living in a hotel after quitting the NYPD when he accidentally killed a child, Reed Stephens' **Mick Axbrewder**, similarly plagued by his accidental shooting of his brother, and James Crumley's **C.W. Sughrue** and **Milo Milodragovitch**, both drowning existential guilt. Jonathan Latimer's **Bill Crane** simply enjoys booze, all the time, and Reed Harlan's **Dan Jordan** thinks of chucking PI work because it interferes with his drinking. This is merely the premier PI drinking league—most can deal with a bottle.

Guilt is also the problem for Tucker Coe's **Mitch Tobin**, an ex-cop who caused his partner's death, which he tackles by obsessively building a wall around his house in good symbolic fashion. Fear is what haunts John Lutz's **Alo Nudger**, who consumes handfuls of antacid tablets to try and calm his panic about almost everything. Sam S. Taylor's **Neal Cotten**, rather curiously for a hardboiled PI, is terrified of guns.

Eugene Franklin's **Berkley Hoy Barnes'** hypochondria is brought on by meeting strangers, so his assistant has to carry a pharmacy with him. But while Barnes' weakness is for prescription drugs, there are at least two notable drug abusers, James Crumley's **Milo Milodragovitch** who can virtually give the reader a contact cocaine high, and pill-popping **Dan Kruger**, a newcomer by Michael Cormany. Steve Knickmeyer's **Butch Maneri** is notably fond of marijuana while L.A. Morse's 78 year old **Jake Spanner** acquired a weakness for hash in the 20s.

The extreme psychological problems are those of Eric Bercovici's **Harold Shilling** and Louis Williams' **Bernardo Thomas**, both of whom are suicidal. Shilling went so far as to put a gun to his head and pull the trigger but his skull was so thick that the bullet bounced off. Thomas plays Russian Roulette and will, presumably, lose (or win, depending on the point of view) some day.

In the gimmicky world of television, the most outstanding problem of all must be that of **Marty Hopkirk** in MY PARTNER THE GHOST who is, of course, dead. **Mike Longstreet** of LONGSTREET was blind; **Mark Saber**, in his PI incarnation, The VICE and SABER OF LONDON, had only one arm and **Harry Orwell** of HARRY-O was seriously handicapped by the bullet lodged in his spine. **Arthur Boyle** in the television film GOODNIGHT, MY LOVE was a dwarf and Stephen Bochco, creator of *Hill Street Blues*, has aired a project for a series based on a *Hooperman* spinoff show with the well-known dwarf actor David Rappaport as sleazy, diminutive San Francisco PI **Nick Derringer**.

THE UNBAPTIZED PI

One minor, and, as far as I can tell, unique curiosity of the genre is the frequency with which PIs lack forenames. Indeed, in three noteworthy cases they lack a name of any kind—Hammett's **The Continental Op** (christened, in various film and television incarnations, Willy Bindbugel, Brad Runyan and Hamilton Nash), Bill Pronzini's **'Nameless Detective'** and Marc Behm's **The Eye**. Two are called after places, Gilbert Ralston's **Dakota** and William J. Reynolds' **Nebraska**, with J. Michael Reaves' **Kamus of Khadizar** as a special case.

This leaves, in non-significant alphabetical order, experimentalist writer Paul Auster's **Blue**; **Brody**, Vern Hansen's ersatz **Brody**; Andrew Vachss' urban survivalist **Burke**; Steranko's graphic novel hardboiled homage **Chandler**; Scottish dockyard 'tec **Clutha**, the work of Hugh Munro; James Reasoner's cult Texan **Cody**; A.E. Maxwell's Gold Coaster **Fiddler**; Glenn Cook's off-world **Garrett**; Conall Ryan's **Knightsbridge**; J.W. Rider's **Malone**, another Texan; W. Glenn Duncan's **Rafferty**; Les Roberts' **Saxon**; Robert B. Parker's **Spenser** and William Gibson's cyberpunk hero **Turner**. TV adds **Paladin** of HAVE GUN, WILL TRAVEL, **McGill** of MAN IN A SUITCASE, **Khan** of KHAN, **McGraw** of MEET McGRAW and **Shannon** of The D.A.'S MAN.

The overall impression is that the authors are attempting to create an immediate effect of autonomy and isolation, but often this effect does not match their characters' lives or lifestyles. A recent reviewer of a Les Roberts novel found Saxon's lack of a forename an increasingly irritating affectation and certainly it fails to ring true of an actor, even retired, and Californian who falls in love in every book. While it seems quite possible that Vachss' Burke or Gibson's Turner actually don't have forenames, and they certainly let no one close enough to use one if they do, it is difficult to imagine such prominent inamatora as Spenser's Susan Silverman or Fiddler's ex-wife murmuring endearments using surnames.

By way of contrast, five PIs lack a surname, though we do learn in the very last book that Thomas B. Dewey's famous **Mac** is called Robinson, but Samuel Fuller's **Sandy**, Marvin Kaye's **Gene** and Ishmael Reed's **Black Herman** remain informal while Victor B. Miller's **Fernanda** is the only woman in this section, her sole distinction.

ANIMALS; Bloodhounds & Others

The private eye is seldom encumbered with a wife let alone a pet, but the few that have been incorporated into the literature form an interesting footnote. The first, of course, was Nick and Nora Charles' famous Schnauzer **Asta**, the only film star in the pack. **Khan**, a Great Dane belonging to James M. Fox's Johnny & Suzy Marshall is clearly modeled on Asta though he is also quite a tough character. The most useful, however, must be Duncan Maclain's two German Shepherds, seeing eye **Schnucke** and attack-trained **Dreist**—Baynard Kendrick's Maclain was, it will be remembered, blind (see Wounded Heroes). William DeAndrea's Matt Cobb also has an attack-trained dog, a Samoyed called **Spot**, and Nigel Brent's Barney Hyde has his skin saved more than once by **Kurt**, "the best trained police dog in the world." Anne Nash's Mark Tudor has **Svea**, "the detecting dog," to help him. Another Schnauzer, **Isadore Goldberg**, raised by a rabbi client of Leo Rosten's Silky Pincus, only understands Yiddish and keeps kosher.

The only co-starring canine is **Carstairs**, a snooty Great Dane who regards his partner, Norbert Davis' Doan, who won him in a poker game, as being beneath his dignity. The most hardboiled beast in PI fiction is a title disputed between **Pansy**, a Neapolitan Mastiff which is part and parcel of the urban survivalist lifestyle of Andrew Vachss' Burke, and **Gaylord**, "a conglomerate of several man-eating species," which follows its own path in Conall Ryan's story about Knightsbridge.

Finally, the only cats I can find distinctive mention of are **Meg**, a blue-point Siamese which, appropriately enough, rules over Conan Flagg's Oregon bookstore in M.K. Wren's novels; **Marlowe**, Nathan Phillips' roommate in Nick O'Donohoe's novels and **Thomas C. Carlyle** (or Tom Cat) who inadvertently gets the FBI interested in Linda Barnes' Carlotta Carlyle. A very special case is **Manx McCatty**, a hardboiled feline PI in a parody by Christopher Reed.

UNAMERICAN ACTIVITIES

One aspect of this survey presents a special case: ersatz American PI novels. While there are some very competent writers of non-American PI novels, as we shall see, there are a number who wrote, and still write, books supposedly set in the US that range from the laughably inept to clever pastiche. It is not simply problems of language and geography; the fact is that the British and American experiences are so different that writing meaningful, or even readable, fiction about America is, if not impossible, beyond the competence of Carter Brown, Peter Chambers, Basil Copper and others. It can be argued that they are simply writing entertainments, with no literary presumptions, but I fail to see why 'mere' PI novels should be a license for third-rate hack work. I have, somewhat reluctantly, listed them for the sake of completeness, though many of their works appeared in very small hardback runs destined for public libraries and hardly ever become available except as library rejects.

After lack of talent, language is usually the most obvious pitfall. Writers like Carter Brown and James Hadley Chase relied on colloquial dictionaries, neither reliable nor current sources for American slang, and such artificial writing would occasionally supply outright *Gun In Cheek* gems such as Peter Cheyney's classic line "Lay the gat on the bonnet," bonnet being the British term for a car hood. Perhaps the absolute worst of all the ersatz writers (there are many contenders) is **W.B.M. FERGUSON**; but all are, at best, undistinguished.

A very striking feature of the ersatz is the fecundity of its main exponents. In this survey will be found one Australian and seven British authors who, between them, have written at least 421 PI novels—a brilliant illustration of the maxim "More means worse." Leading the field is, of course, **Carter BROWN** (78), trailed by **Harry CARMICHAEL** (65), **Neill GRAHAM** (65), **Basil COPPER** (62), **Bevis WINTER** (44), **Peter CHAMBERS** (34), **Hugh DESMOND** (33), and **Mark CORRIGAN** (30). A truly depressing thought is that Copper and Chambers are still actively churning out books that are even more worthless than Carter Brown's and the total has almost certainly risen already. Mercifully, John Creasey devoted little energy to his **Robert Caine FRAZER** PI series.

However, there are also some very fine writers in the field outside America who, it is very noticeable, chose without exception to write about their home ground. Britain offers better than average in **Peter CHEYNEY**, **Hugh MUNRO** and **Patricia WENTWORTH** (I do not count Victor Canning, P.D. James and Dick Francis as PI writers in the same sense) while seven British authors seem to me to belong firmly in The Rest of the World chart (below).

Australia has four alternatives to Carter Brown, but only **Peter CORRIS** (**Sidney J. BAKER**, **Hosanna BROWN** and **Richard CLAPPERTON** are the others) really excels. Canada, on the other hand, has produced four excellent writers (not counting Ross Macdonald), namely **Ted WOOD**, also writing as **Jack BARNAO**, Douglas

Sanderson writing as **Martin BRETT** and **Malcolm DOUGLAS**, **Howard ENGEL** and **Simon RITCHIE**.

The non-English-speaking world may well teem with untranslated PI writers, but so far only **Manuel Vazquez MONTALBAN** and **Maria-Antonia OLIVER** (Spain), **Attilio VERALDI** (Italy) and **Patrick MODIANO** (France) have surfaced in translation.

In my opinion, the 10 best non-American PI writers are, in chronological order:

1 Nancy Spain (UK)	6 Peter Corris (Australia)
2 Kevin O'Hara (UK)	7 Howard Engel (Canada)
3 P.B. Yuill (UK)	8 Dan Kavanagh (UK)
4 Manuel Vazquez Montalban (Spain)	9 John Milne (UK)
5 Liza Cody (UK)	10 Peter Whalley (UK)

THE SHORT STORY

The mountain of novels listed in this survey rests on a bedrock of short stories. Whether the PI novel would ever have emerged without the genre's gestation period in the pulp magazines is a very moot point. One need only follow Dashiell Hammett's creative development through his *Black Mask* stories, while it seems very unlikely that Raymond Chandler would have been able to write a whole novel from scratch at the outset of his career.

It's safe to say that all the PI writers of the late 20s, 30s and 40s wrote short stories for the pulp magazines, from *Black Mask* to *Spicy Detective*, few of which have ever been collected together except in the obvious cases of Hammett and Chandler. Some writers indeed were never published in book form at all, including such notables as John K. Butler, and many respected pulp PIs have been effectively consigned to oblivion apart from those few who have since resurfaced in anthologies. Recently the short story has made something of a comeback, while author collections from the pulps are becoming more common, thanks mainly to Mysterious Press.

Under **ANTHOLOGIES** in the main section will be found 30 collections ranging from the *Black Mask* omnibus assembled by its most famous editor, Joseph Shaw, whose dismissal led to the boycotting of that magazine by Chandler, Nebel and Lester Dent among others, to the rather clubby Private Eye Writers of America get-togethers. Diligent scouring of the various short story annuals and the recent proliferation of concept collections would doubtless turn up many more PI short stories but my rule of thumb was to include only anthologies with a reasonably high PI content (i.e. four or more stories).

Full details of the stories in these anthologies will be found under the author headings and I have listed those authors who have not appeared in book form on the grounds that the older, pulp, generation may yet attain due recognition, while the contemporary *New Black Mask/Matter Of Crime* writers are likely to produce books in the future, as, indeed, has already happened in the cases of Wayne D. Dundee and L.J. Washburn.

Having found considerable confusion, vagueness and inaccuracy in all sources, I have appended details of **Dashiell HAMMETT** and **Raymond CHANDLER**'s PI short stories to their main entries, an exercise that led me to wonder whether some of their many commentators bothered to read them before writing their biographies and critiques.

I leave it to some future hero of bibliography to fully chronicle the PI short story. William F. Nolan, in *The Black Mask Boys*, lists almost 100 pulp magazines with 'Detective' in the title!

THE GOLDEN AGES: The Period Eye

Since the mid-70s, a few writers have set PI books in the past, often over-parading their research and displaying a marked weakness for dragging in famous, but now safely dead, real-life personalities. The most articulate spokesman of this tendency is Max Allan Collins who commented (in Reilly), "I rejected the private eye because I could not find a way to write about him in the 1970s that didn't seem foolish to me—the private eye in the 1970s (and now 1980s) seemed an anachronism. Then it occurred to me that the private eye now existed in *history*—that Hammett had created archetypical P.I. Sam Spade in 1929—making Spade a contemporary of Al Capone's. From this starting point I developed the historical private-eye novel . . ."

Andrew BERGMAN, who set the whole thing off in 1974, has since departed the genre, but a number of writers are still committed to the historical PI, notably **Stuart KAMINSKY**, who has written 14 Toby Peters novels since 1977. **Harold ADAMS** began his Carl Wilcox series in 1981, **H. Paul JEFFERS** his Harry MacNeil novels in 1982, **Max Allan COLLINS**, a relative latecomer despite his epochal claims, produced his first Nate Heller book in 1983, **Gaylord DOLD** only started in 1987 but has four Wichita-set Mitch Roberts stories, while newcomers, **L.J. WASHBURN** and **Richard BLAINE**, seem series bent.

However, there is considerable disagreement as to exactly when the Golden Age was. The 1920s are supported by Washburn, who harks back to silent movies and Prohibition with her Lucas Hallam novel and stories, **Jeff ROVIN**, who moved forward to the earliest days of talkies for two dire 1927 Hollywood books, and **Joe GORES**, who plumped for 1928 for his selective portrait of Hammett.

Harold Adams, with indeterminate Depression dates, Collins, who started with 1933, and Jeffers, circa 1936, are the main 30s fans, seconded by **Brad LATHAM**, whose short series about Bill Lockwood started in 1938, and **Douglas HEYES**, who picked the same year for one novel about Ray Ripley.

The 1940s get slightly more support. Kaminsky has a permanent date of 1941, while 1942 was chosen by both **Richard BRAUTIGAN** and **David GALLOWAY** for superficial parodies. Bergman himself set his two books in 1944 and 1947, while **Barry FANTONI**, British author of two fine pastiches, and Richard Blaine both settled on 1948 Pennsylvania. **Gordon DeMARCO** explored McCarthyite politics from 1949.

The 1950s can only claim Dold and **William HJORTSBERG**, whose one horror-mystery novel opens with a 1959 Times Tower newsflash announcing Hawaii's admission to the Union.

To what extent Collins reflects the thinking of these writers is open to question, Kaminsky at least is less pretentious on the subject, but they too must have their reasons. Personally I feel that Collins' obviously faulty rationale tells us more about himself than about the truth of the matter, which is that many other, and better, writers, James Crumley, Loren D. Estleman, Sara Paretsky and Andrew Vachss to name only four who would not be called "foolish" by their harshest critics, are creating, and sustaining, 80s PIs in a genre that shows no sign of coming to a standstill. There is still more to life than *Moonlighting* and, indeed, the 80s are as much a PI 'Golden Age' as any other period since 1927.

The historical PI novel, in my view, sabotages the PI's historic, and still relevant, mission of social comment. As Geherin remarks, "Writers in the genre have aimed at depicting realistically the society in which they lived rather than follow the example of the classic whodunit tradition they rejected and create a safe cozy world that offers a temporary escape from reality and its actual concerns and problems." Readers would be better served by reprinting the all but unobtainable work of 20s, 30s and 40s writers rather than publishing what must be, in the very nature of things, inevitably ersatz recreations. The past itself is better served by writers like Mark Schorr, who acknowledge it without trying to reproduce it.

COVER ART or Eyes Front

However, one PI 'Golden Age' has passed and seems unlikely ever to be rivalled again, and that is the great era of paperback cover art in which, like other heroes of popular culture, the private eye was visually interpreted with vitality and panache. For about 20 years, roughly 1939, when Pocket Books went into business specifically to publish Pocket paperbacks, to 1959, when most paperback houses were swallowed by conglomerates, Books themselves becoming part of Gulf+Western, paperback cover art was, at its best, energetic, atmospheric, seething with erotic symbolism, often artistically daring and innovative. Even at its worst, it was rarely as banal or anemic as virtually all modern cover art.

Background can be found in O'Brien's *Hardboiled America* and Schreuders' *The Book Of Paperbacks* (see Bibliography). My personal all-time Top Ten most desirable PI paperbacks and the artists responsible, are, in chronological order:

Gerald Gregg	Leslie Ford: Ill Met By Moonlight (Dell 1943)
Leo Manso	Jonathan Latimer: The Lady in the Morgue (Pocket Books 1944)
Paul Kresse	Richard Ellington: It's A Crime (Pocket Books 1951)
Clyde Ross	Ross Macdonald: The Way Some People Die (Pocket Books 1952)
Denis Macloughlin	Fredric Brown: Compliments Of A Fiend (T.V. Boardman 1953)
Robert Maguire	Ed Lacy: Visa To Death (Perma Books 1956)
Walter Papp	Milton K. Ozaki: Dressed To Kill (Graphic 1956)
Robert Schulz	M.E. Chaber: The Splintered Man (Perma Books 1957)
Lou Marchetti	Ed Lacy: Invitation To Murder (Pocket Books 1957)
Robert E. McGinnis	Robert Kyle: Kill Now, Pay Later (Dell 1960)

FUTURE EYES; Down The Mean Spacelanes

While there is a small but definite PI/SF sub-genre (sub-sub-genre?), many writers of both PI stories and science fiction have never combined them. The two most notable names that do overlap them both did so for comic effect. **Ron GOULART**, who likes to "mix murder, bug-eyed monsters and satire," has two interplanetary agencies, one known, for reasons that chill a reluctant recruit's blood, as Suicide, Inc., and two Earth-based ones. **William F. NOLAN** placed Sam Space, great-grandson of his mundane PI Bart Challis, on Mars, where the beautiful woman who walks into his office has three heads. **Louis TRIMBLE** wrote two books about the Anthropol Detective Agency. **Lloyd BIGGLE Jr.** has had his future PI, Jan Darzek, who works for the Council of the Supreme, the ultimate galactic authority, catch up on him—the first story, published in 1963, was set in 1986.

Otherwise the future PI is the province of the straight SF writer. Off-planet can be found such characters as **Barney COHEN**'s Ascher Bockhorn, a sort of railroad detective of the future; ultra-high tech PI Stefan Vynalek in one of **A. Bertram CHANDLER**'s Rim World series; the rather limp satire of **Atanielle Annyn NOEL**'s old-fashioned interplanetary sleuths; the elliptical, somewhat impenetrable wanderings of **Alexei PANSHIN**'s Anthony Villiers and Torve the Trog; the competent and stylish investigations of **Jack VANCE**'s "effectuator" Miro Hetzel and, in my view, the best of this batch, the (wonderfully titled) adventures of **Michael J. REAVES'** Kamus of Khadizar, surely the only PI who is also a skilled swordsman.

On Earth, the emphasis is almost entirely on technological progress combined with social disintegration. Apart from **Gardner DOZOIS & George Alec EFFINGER**'s super-Aryan Karl Jaeger, the last PI on Earth who has to deal with invading aliens, future PIs live in a nightmare world. **Katherine MacLEAN**'s PI can only find people in a 1999 New York of two billion people because he's telepathic. In the same year, **David BEAR**'s last PI in New York lives in a slum—Park Avenue. **Philip K. DICK**'s Blade Runner, Rick Deckard, hunts rogue androids over in 2019 Los Angeles, or, as it's known in **John SPENCER**'s Charley Case books, LA Island City (since the Big One of '97).

Master of the 'cyberpunk' school, **William GIBSON**, has contributed one futuristic PI, Turner, who helps key personnel change jobs, a lethal proposition in a world ruled by jealous multinational companies. Cyberpunk pioneer **Mike McQUAY** wrote one of the very few PI/SF series about hardboiled 2083 PI Mathew Swain who lives in a very tough, lethal and still partly radioactive South Central Texas. **George Alec EFFINGER**'s cyberpunk effort featured rather ill-handled personality modifiers, with his hero at one point taking on Nero Wolfe's persona.

Fantasy has attracted only three writers to date, **Barry HUGHART**, whose Li Kao and Lu Yu operate in a mythical China of a thousand years ago, **Mike RESNICK**, whose hero is taken to an alternative New York to trace a stolen unicorn, and **Glen COOK**, whose hardboiled Garrett sleuths successfully on a planet where magic works.

TELEVISION DETECTIVES or Square Eyes

The private eye has been a television staple since the earliest days, **MARTIN KANE, PRIVATE EYE** going out first in September 1949, beating **MAN AGAINST CRIME** by a few weeks. Since then there have been a total of 114 private eye series, ranging from the two episodes (before cancellation) of **BIG SHAMUS, LITTLE SHAMUS** to the eight year runs of **BARNABY JONES, MANNIX** and **MAGNUM P.I.** The Golden Age was the period in 1959-60 when prime time offered **PETER GUNN, JOHNNY STACCATO, MARKHAM, RICHARD DIAMOND, PRIVATE EYE, PHILIP MARLOWE, HAVE GUN, WILL TRAVEL, SHOTGUN SLADE, 77 SUNSET STRIP** and **HAWAIIAN EYE**—among others! This feast was, however, soon followed by a unique famine. Between the close of **HAWAIIAN EYE** in September 1963 and the debut of **HONEY WEST** in September 1965 there were no original PI shows at all. Zip, zilch, zero, nada.

PI shows have, by and large, done poorly in ratings and the National Academy of Television Arts & Sciences has awarded them few of its Emmys. The first, in 1970, went to Gail Fisher for her supporting role as Peggy Fair in **MANNIX**. Anthony Zerbe, a Santa Monica cop in **HARRY-O**, won a Supporting Actor award in 1976. The outstandingly successful series in this context was **The ROCKFORD FILES**, voted Best Drama Series in 1978. James Garner won an Emmy in 1977 for his lead role, Stuart Margolin won two, in 1979 and 1980, for his support as Angel and Rita Moreno picked up one in 1978 for her performance in the episode "The Paper Palace." Tom Selleck received a lead role Emmy for **MAGNUM P.I.** in 1984, as did Bruce Willis for **MOONLIGHTING** in 1987, when John Hillerman of **MAGNUM P.I.** was voted Best Supporting Actor.

In the Top 100 TV shows, **HAVE GUN, WILL TRAVEL** is 40th, **MAGNUM P.I.** 48th, **SIMON & SIMON** 67th, **CHARLIE'S ANGELS** 68th and **BARNABY JONES** 97th. For clarity the year, ranking and ratings are shown below as a table:

1950/51:	**MARTIN KANE, PRIVATE EYE**	12th; 37.8
	MAN AGAINST CRIME	13th; 37.4
1957/58:	**HAVE GUN, WILL TRAVEL**	4th; 33.7
1958/59:	**HAVE GUN, WILL TRAVEL**	3rd; 34.3
	PETER GUNN	17th; 28.0
1959/60:	**HAVE GUN, WILL TRAVEL**	3rd; 34.7

	77 SUNSET STRIP	7th; 29.7
1960/61:	HAVE GUN, WILL TRAVEL	3rd; 30.9
	77 SUNSET STRIP	14th; 25.8
1970/71:	MANNIX	17th; 21.3
1971/72:	MANNIX	7th; 24.8
1972/73:	CANNON	14th; 22.4
1973/74:	CANNON	10th; 23.1
	BARNABY JONES	18th; 21.4.
1974/75:	ROCKFORD FILES	12th; 23.7
	MANNIX	20th; 21.6
	CANNON	21st; 21.6
1976/77:	CHARLIE'S ANGELS	5th; 25.8
1977/78:	CHARLIE'S ANGELS	5th; 24.4
	BARNABY JONES	22nd; 20.6
1978/79:	CHARLIE'S ANGELS	12th; 24.4
	VEGA$	23rd; 20.6
	BARNABY JONES	24th; 20.5
1979/80:	CHARLIE'S ANGELS	20th; 20.9
1980/81:	MAGNUM P.I.	14th; 21.0
1981/82:	MAGNUM P.I.	17th; 20.9
1982/83:	MAGNUM P.I.	4th; 22.6
	SIMON & SIMON	7th; 21.0
1983/84:	SIMON & SIMON	5th; 23.8
	MAGNUM P.I.	6th; 22.4
	RIPTIDE	18th; 18.8
1984/85	SIMON & SIMON	7th; 21.8
	RIPTIDE	14th; 19.2
	MAGNUM P.I.	15th; 19.1
	REMINGTON STEELE	24th; 17.0
1985/86	MOONLIGHTING	24th; 18.1
1986/87	MOONLIGHTING	9th; 22.4
1987/88	MOONLIGHTING	12th; 18.3

The history of PI television drama has largely been one of steady degeneration. The overwhelming tendency of American television has been towards glamorization and an emphasis on production values and this has militated particularly against the private eye, not essentially a glamorous figure, and, while there are rare, gritty exceptions such as **The LAW & HARRY McGRAW**, I find it hard to believe that shallow, glitzy programs like **MOONLIGHTING** or **PRIVATE EYE** attract true

PI fans. Generally speaking, American PI shows in recent times have not been able to rival those of Britain, where even the soap operas are working-class based, for realism and fidelity to the classic tradition, **PUBLIC EYE** and **HAZELL** particularly. Significantly, **PHILIP MARLOWE, PRIVATE EYE** was a Canadian production.

In surveying television PIs, it is interesting to see how few derive from the existing body of PI literature and how poorly programs based on even such well-known figures as Philip Marlowe, Michael Shayne, Lew Archer, Nero Wolfe, Travis McGee and Spenser have done. Of all the giants in the field, only Mickey Spillane can really be said to have made a successful jump to the small screen.

Also listed are 20 films, going back to the 1954 version of **The LONG GOODBYE** starring Dick Powell, and 28 pilot films for proposed PI series that never got off the ground, very few of which seem particularly more ridiculous or non-viable than series that did get made.

FILM DETECTIVES or Reel Eyes

Despite some fairly painstaking research, I was only able to identify some 175 feature films that warranted inclusion on the basis that they either had a PI as a lead character or were based on a PI novel—two very different things. This seemed to me to be a surprisingly low figure. The image of the PI in film is sharp enough to have inspired many parodies but, on closer examination, it almost appears that there are more spoofs of the PI film than there were PI films in the first place. The status of the PI in cinema history, and, it is fair to say, in popular culture, appears to depend on a mere handful of classic films; **The MALTESE FALCON** (1941), **The THIN MAN, MURDER, MY SWEET, The BIG SLEEP** (1946), **OUT OF THE PAST** and **KISS ME DEADLY**—all, it is interesting to note, based on novels by established masters in the field (cf. TELEVISION DETECTIVES above).

It should be noted that on occasion a PI novel was filmed with the main character being given a different occupation, most notably in the film of Dashiell Hammett's *Red Harvest*, **ROADHOUSE NIGHTS**, in which the hero was a journalist. Another scriptwriter's trick was renaming characters from books, most gratuitously in the case of **SATAN MET A LADY**, the second version of *The Maltese Falcon*, in which all the names were altered, Sam Spade becoming Ted Shayne, while Casper Gutman actually changed sex!

RADIO DETECTIVES or Vocal Eyes

The earliest PI radio program I located, **DETECTIVES BLACK AND BLUE**, started in 1931, the last, **HAVE GUN, WILL TRAVEL**, in 1958, though **YOURS TRULY, JOHNNY DOLLAR**, the last major dramatic series on network radio, ran until 1962. But the heyday of the radio PI was the five year period 1946-1950 when no less than 27 of the 56 series listed came on the air. As I was a toddler at the time, this section relies entirely on secondary sources.

Ken Crossen, in "There's Murder In The Air," an essay in Howard Haycraft's *The Art Of The Mystery Story* (1946), cited research showing that 10 million people listened to the 31 mystery shows broadcast in 1945, but this has not been seen as a phenomenon worth study. In marked contrast with the history of TV, none of the guides to radio programs are comprehensive and egregious errors can be found in all of them. When different sources do actually agree on the existence of a program, they invariably differ on titles, dates and cast details.

Among radio PIs were many familiar names. Hammett was particularly well represented with **The ADVENTURES OF SAM SPADE, The ADVENTURES (and NEW ADVENTURES) OF THE THIN MAN, The FAT MAN** and a one-off of **The MALTESE FALCON** with Bogart, Astor and Sydney Greenstreet. Greenstreet, of course, was the last radio Nero Wolfe. Stout, Chandler, Halliday, Frances & Richard Lockridge, Frances Crane, George Harmon Coxe, Henry Kane and Spillane all heard their main creations speak. Except for Crane and Kane, they were also to see them among the 12 radio shows that transferred to television as **BOSTON BLACKIE; CHARLIE WILD, PRIVATE DETECTIVE; CRIME PHOTOGRAPHER; The LONE WOLF; MAN AGAINST CRIME; MARTIN KANE, PRIVATE EYE; MICHAEL SHAYNE; MICKEY SPILLANE'S MIKE HAMMER; NERO WOLFE; PHILIP MARLOWE; RICHARD DIAMOND, PRIVATE EYE** and **The THIN MAN**.

Some names recur in PI drama. Gerald Mohr was heard as Michael Lanyard, Philip Marlowe, Archie Goodwin and Bill Lance; Santos Ortega as Hannibal Cobb, Peter Salem and Nero Wolfe; the inimitable Jack Webb as Jeff Regan, Johnny Modero and Pat Novak; Howard Duff as Sam Spade and Mike McCoy; Bob Bailey as George Valentine and Johnny Dollar. The versatile Dick Powell not only played Philip Marlowe on both film and TV but shone as Richard Diamond and Richard Rogue; Lloyd Nolan made seven films as Michael Shayne and went on to Johnny

Strange on radio and Martin Kane on both radio and TV. William Gargan also played Kane in both media as well as Ross Dolan and Barry Crane on radio and Jess Arno on film.

Well-known names such as Van Heflin (Philip Marlowe) and Jeff Chandler (Michael Shayne) are found only once, but others also recur. Edmund O'Brien tried to follow the radio Johnny Dollar with the TV Johnny Midnight; Glenn Ford went from Christopher London on radio to TV's Jarrett, Frank Sinatra from Rocky Fortune to two Tony Rome films; and Joan Blondell, Miss Pinkerton (her sister Gloria was in I LOVE A MYSTERY), had a role in TV's BANYON.

But perhaps the most dedicated radio thespian in the genre was Virginia Gregg who, as secretary-girlfriend-sidekick, tried unsuccessfully to snare PIs into matrimony in LET GEORGE DO IT, RICHARD DIAMOND, PRIVATE EYE and YOURS TRULY, JOHNNY DOLLAR. On top of which she was Hey Boy's girlfriend in HAVE GUN, WILL TRAVEL.

NOVELIZATIONS or Exploit Eyes

Many PI novels have, of course, been filmed or made the basis of TV series, notably the Philip Marlowe, Mike Hammer and Michael Shayne canons and Roy Huggins' *The Double Take* which, very loosely, became 77 SUNSET STRIP. There is, however, a small category of books based on TV series, though not, rather oddly, necessarily the best known or longest running. Most novelizations were the work of specialist hack writers such as Mike Jahn (The ROCKFORD FILES and SWITCH), William Johnston (BANYON and MY FRIEND TONY), Max Franklin, a Richard Deming pseudonym (CHARLIE'S ANGELS and VEGA$) and Richard Gallagher (CANNON and The MOST DEADLY GAME), with Paul Denver and Douglas Enefer also putting out CANNON books and Ed Friend doing another MOST DEADLY GAME title.

However, Lawrence Block's first novel was based on MARKHAM; Frank Kane, using his Frank Boyd pseudonym, wrote a good adaptation of JOHNNY STACCATO, and Henry Kane likewise did well by PETER GUNN. From Britain, Audley Southcott and Anthony Marriott gave acceptable renderings of the fine PUBLIC EYE, Bill Knox adapted four of Edward Boyd's Glasgow PI scripts The VIEW FROM DANIEL PIKE and Paul Ableman wrote two reasonable SHOESTRING books.

Other novelizations include those of BANACEK by Deane Romano; The BROTHERS BRANNIGAN by Henry Edward Helseth; GRIFF by

Robert Weverka; **HARRY-O** by Lee Hays; **HAWAIIAN EYE** by Frank
Castle; **McCOY** by Sam Stewart; **MAGNUM, P.I.** by both Roger
Bowdler and Dan Zadra; **MANNIX** by both Michael Avallone and J.T.
MacCargo; **MIAMI UNDERCOVER** by Evan Lee Heyman; **The
OUTSIDER** by Lou Cameron; **The PROTECTORS** by Robert Miall;
PRIVATE EYE by T.N. Robb, David Elliott and Max Lockhart and
SURFSIDE 6 by J.M. Flynn.

Film novelizations are, for no obvious reason, dominated by the
parodies with Robert Grossbach's adaptation of Neil Simon's screenplay
for **The CHEAP DETECTIVE**; Raymond Giles' book of **SHAMUS**;
Neville Smith's rewrite of his **GUMSHOE** script; Henry Keating's
version of **MURDER BY DEATH** and Alexander Edwards' that of **The
BLACK BIRD**. Otherwise there are only Philip Rock's book of
HICKEY & BOGGS and Malcolm Braly's of **LADY ICE**.

Edward S. Aarons, writing as Paul Ayres, novelized the radio show
CASEY, CRIME PHOTOGRAPHER, which was, of course, based on
the original work of George Harmon COXE.

HOW TO WRITE A PI NOVEL

DASHIELL HAMMETT

"It would be silly to insist that nobody who has not been a detective
should write detective stories, but it is certainly not unreasonable to ask
any one who is going to write a book of any sort to make some effort to
learn something about his subject. Most writers do. Only detective story
writers seem to be free from a sense of obligation in this direction and,
curiously, the most established and prolific detective story writers seem to
be the worst offenders."

RAYMOND CHANDLER

"When in doubt, have a man come through the door with a gun in his
hand."

HENRY KANE

"He drinks, drinks more, and more; flirts with women, blondes mostly,
who talk hard but act soft, then he drinks more, then, somewhere in the
middle, he gets dreadfully beaten about, then he drinks more, then he says
a few dirty words, then he stumbles around, punch-drunk-like, but he is
very smart and he adds up a lot of two's and two's, and then the case gets
solved."

FRANK GRUBER'S ELEVEN POINT FORMULA
1. A colorful hero
2. A theme that contains information the reader isn't likely to have
3. A villain more powerful than the hero
4. A colorful background for the action
5. An unusual murder method or unusual circumstances surrounding the murder
6. Unusual variations on the motives of hate and greed
7. A concealed clue
8. The trick that extricates the hero from certain defeat
9. Moving and carefully paced action
10. A smashing climax
11. A hero who is personally involved

STEVEN MARCUS

"What he (the detective) soon discovers is that the 'reality' that anyone involved will swear to is in fact itself a construction, a fabrication, a fiction, a faked and alternate reality—and that it has been gotten together before he ever arrived on the scene. And the Op's work therefore is to deconstruct, decompose, deplot and defictionalize that 'reality' and to construct or reconstruct out of it a true fiction, i.e. an account of what 'really' happened."

JOSEPH HANSEN

"Ideally, the reader will suspect A for a while, then switch his suspicions to B, then to C, then to D, and back again to A. If you're writing your book well, you'll keep the reader off balance this way most of the time . . . A, B, C and D, all, or each in turn, must appear to have had the opportunity, and motive. And means. For a time. That's the key phrase. For now, the logic of the structure you've set up takes over, and will complete your book for you. Only one suspect can be guilty. And with each suspect the detective rules out, he moves a step closer to the real murderer. First A, then B, then C, turn out to be wrong guesses. A, cornered, sweating, red-faced, blurts out that he was with E at the time of the victim's death; he's kept silent about this because E has a husband, perhaps the victim himself. B, grossly fat, could not have gone out on the rotting pier at the lake where the victim's body was dumped—the framework would have broken under his weight. And C? Suddenly C is found murdered. Which leaves the detective, the writer and the reader, with D."

MICHAEL COLLINS

"The detective story more than any other form focuses on human relations, on the human condition seen at naked moments. The detective story is told by an observer, a human 'eye' that watches and tries to understand what is happening and why. A detective seeks answers, asks questions . . . the immediate story ends, but the larger story goes on. The detective goes on. The questions go on. The search goes on. The attempt to understand."

LOREN D. ESTLEMAN

"As has happened with many of the Amos Walker novels and short stories, it began with a title . . . At that point I commenced writing with no clear idea of where the story was headed or how it would end. I'm told this is a very bad method of plotting fiction, but as it's seen me through fifteen books and a score of short stories I imagine it's too late to change."

REVIEWS & REVIEWERS

In compiling this survey, I read thousands of contemporary reviews. These served three purposes. First, they revealed countless PIs I was not aware of, either directly or from the critical literature; sleuths whose stories had appeared, sometimes to considerable acclaim, only to vanish both from secondhand bookstores and from, as it were, the collective consciousness of the genre. Secondly, they provided additional information and comment on novels which I knew of but had been unable to consult directly. Thirdly, they often persuaded me to reevaluate, positively or negatively, specific books and writers.

The most useful reviewer was, of course, Anthony Boucher—*San Francisco Chronicle* 1942-47, *Ellery Queen's Mystery Magazine* 1948-50 and 1957-68, and *New York Times Book Review* 1951-68. But, for all his undoubted merits, Boucher's exaggerated reverence for British mysteries and ingrained aversion to sex and violence, taken in concentrated doses, are extremely tedious. More to the point, he developed a hardline attitude to what he condemned, without specifics, as the clichés of PI literature which he reviewed less and less.

However, Isaac Anderson, his predecessor at the *New York Times*, manifested the same prejudices in far greater degree. While capable on occasion of pithy, revealing comments, Anderson regularly summarized plots while offering no opinions. A quote in the main text credited to *NYT* is usually Anderson, and usually damns with faint praise.

After Boucher's death, Allen J. Hubin maintained his standards for three years, but since then *NYT* has lost, or given up, its commanding position in mystery criticism.

Will Cuppy of the *New York Herald Tribune* was forthright in his views but covered less ground. James Sandoe, who took over his seat, rather oddly, considering the fame of his hardboiled check-list, rarely brought tough-guy novels to the attention of his readers, perhaps trimming his taste to his readership.

Far and away the most reliable, not to say pungent, source for the 30s, 40s and 50s is the uncredited Criminal Record column of *Saturday Review Of Literature* (from 1951 it carried the name of "Sergeant Cluff", actually 1966 Edgar winner John Winterich). Highly compressed, *SR*'s capsule reviews invariably convey more in 50 words than Anderson, Cuppy or, it must be said, Boucher, in four or five times that many. Over the years, however, the magazine showed less and less interest in crime fiction, dropping the column for weeks at a time and then completely.

In modern times, reviewers whom I have found consistently useful and credible have been the late Charles Willeford (*Mystery Scene*), virtually all the critics associated with *Drood Review*, Francis M. Nevins, Jr and the mystery reviewers of *Publisher's Weekly*.

RESEARCH MATERIALS

AMERICAN POLICE ACADEMY; Basic Course For Private Investigators (198?)

BLACKWELL, Gene; The Private Investigator (1979)

BLYE, Irwin & Ardy FRIEDBERG; Secrets Of A Private Eye or How To Be Your Own Private Investigator (1987)

GREENE, Marilyn & Gary PROVOST; Finder; The True Story Of A Private Investigator (1988)

KINCHUM, Moore K.; How To Become A Successful Private Eye (1982)

NOLAN, Frederick; Jay J. Armes, Investigator (1976)

PARKHURST, William; True Detectives; The Real World Of Today's Private Investigators (1989)

PILEGGI, Nicholas; Blye, Private Eye (1976)

SEDGWICK, John; Night Vision; Confessions of Gil Lewis, Private Eye (1983)

THOMPSON, Josiah; Gumshoe; Reflections In A Private Eye (1988, UK 1989)

BIBLIOGRAPHY

BAKER, Robert A. & Michael T. NIETZEL; *Private Eyes: One Hundred And One Knights; A Survey of American Detective Fiction 1922-1984* (Bowling Green, Ohio: Popular Press, 1985). Historical overview concentrating on major American authors with some idiosyncratic emphases but sound judgments.

BALL, John, ed. ; *The Mystery Story* (London: Penguin,1978). Contains an updated version of James Sandoe's 1952 pamphlet "The Hard-Boiled Dick; A Personal Checklist," misleadingly retitled "The Private Eye."

BARZUN, Jacques & Wendell Hertig TAYLOR; *A Catalogue of Crime* (NY: Harper & Row, 1974). 7,500 capsule reviews by establishment critics with no love for PI fiction, even less for hardboiled.

BOURGEAU, Art; *The Mystery Lover's Companion* (NY: Crown, 1986). 2,500 capsule reviews of favorites of the author, also a specialist bookstore owner, dividing the genre into American, English, Thriller and Police Procedural.

BROWNE, Ray B.; *Heroes & Humanities; Detective Fiction & Culture* (Bowling Green, Ohio: Popular Press, 1986). Includes essays on Peter Corris, Judson Philips, Ed Lacy, E.V. Cunningham, Thomas B. Dewey, Michael Z. Lewin, Jonathan Valin, George C. Chesbro.

GEHERIN, David; *The American Private Eye: The Image In Fiction* (NY: Ungar, 1985). A sober, essential work that concentrates on 26 PIs in six groupings—see Comparative Eyes above.

GEHERIN, David: *Sons Of Sam Spade; The Private Eye Novel In The 70s* (NY: Ungar, 1980). End of the decade assessment of Robert B. Parker, Roger L. Simon and Andrew Bergman, a selection Geherin may have come to regret.

GOULART, Ron; *The Dime Detectives* (NY: Mysterious, 1988). An overview of pulp magazine detectives, mostly PIs.

HUBIN, Allen J.; *Crime Fiction 1749-1980; A Comprehensive Bibliography* (NY: Garland, 1984). The 2nd edition adds not simply another five years'worth of books but other additions, corrections, a settings index and a detailed chronology of series characters which, unfortunately in this context, uses 'private' to include lawyers. The few titles unlisted in Hubin are specified in author entries.

HUBIN, Allen J.; *Crime Fiction Supplement 1981-1985* (NY: Garland, 1988). Adding some 6,900 titles to the above, additional information on 4,300 works, identifying 440 more series and 3,200 films.

KLEIN, Kathleen Gregory; *The Woman Detective; Gender & Genre* (Urbana & Chicago: University of Illinois Press, 1988). Trenchant feminist study of American, Canadian and British fictional female private detectives. I am indebted to Klein for many of her insights.

LANDRUM, Larry N.; Pat BROWNE & Ray B. BROWNE, eds.; *Dimensions of Detective Fiction* (Bowling Green, Ohio: Popular Press, 1976). Includes essays on Carroll John Daly's Race Williams, John B. West's Rocky Steele, Mickey Spillane, Ishmael Reed's HooDoo detectives, Ross Macdonald's Lew Archer and an interview with Macdonald.

LARKA, Robert; *Television's Private Eyes; An Examination of Twenty Years Programming of a Particular Genre, 1949 to 1969* (NY: Arno, 1979). A doctoral dissertation riddled with simple errors.

MARGOLIES, Edward; *Which Way Did He Go? The Private Eye in Dashiell Hammett, Raymond Chandler, Chester Himes and Ross Macdonald* (NY: Holmes & Meier, 1982). Academic and wishy-washy, skating very quickly over the fact that Himes did not write PI novels.

MEYERS, Richard; *TV Detectives* (San Diego & London: A.S. Barnes & Tantivy, 1981). Thorough, if uneven, chronological coverage of TV sleuths. Meyers is reportedly preparing a book on TV PIs.

O'BRIEN, Geoffrey; *Hardboiled America; The Lurid Years of Paperbacks* (NY: Van Nostrand Reinhold, 1981). Marginal but fascinating book that concentrates on cover artwork as much as text.

PENZLER, Otto; *The Private Lives Of Private Eyes, Spies, Crime Fighters & Other Good Guys* (NY: Grosset & Dunlap, 1977). Biographies and other background to Lew Archer, Nick & Nora Charles, Mike Hammer, Philip Marlowe, John Shaft, Sam Spade, Nero Wolfe, and their creators. Marginal.

PENZLER, Otto et al, eds.; *Detectionary; A Biographical Dictionary of Leading Characters in Detective & Mystery Fiction, including Famous and Little-Known Sleuths, Their Helpers, Rogues Both Heroic & Sinister, and Some of Their Most Memorable Adventures, As Recounted in Novels, Short Stories & Films* (Woodstock, NY: Overlook Press, 1977). Lacking any rigor of definition and often misleading.

PRONZINI, Bill; *Gun In Cheek; A Study of 'Alternative' Crime Fiction* (np: Coward, McCann & Geoghegan, 1982). Affectionate and satiric survey of Bad Writing in crime fiction with a chapter on PIs.

PRONZINI, Bill; *Son Of Gun In Cheek* (NY: Mysterious, 1987). Companion volume to the above.

PRONZINI, Bill & MULLER, Marcia, eds.; *1001 Midnights; An Aficionados' Guide To Mystery & Detective Fiction* (NY: Arbor House, 1986). If the editors, both PI writers, accurately reflect the field, then PI fiction, with 199 of the titles in this work discussed in depth (though some are not categorized as PIs), comprises almost exactly a fifth. See Comparative Eyes above.

REILLY, John M., ed.; *Twentieth Century Crime And Mystery Writers* (London: St James Press, 1985). The 2nd edition is a major improvement on the first, but it still fails to list many important writers while including others of marginal value. Some contributors are first rate, notably Francis M. Nevins, Will Murray and Carol Cleveland, but many seem dubiously qualified.

RUEHLMANN, William; *Saint With a Gun; The Unlawful American Private Eye* (NY: NYU Press, 1974). Attack on the genre as vigilante literature.

SCHREUDERS, Piet; *The Book of Paperbacks; A Visual History of the Paperback* (London: Virgin, 1981). Concentrates, like O'Brien, on artwork with a broader scope, lavish illustration, equally fascinating.

SKINNER, Robert E.; *The Hard-Boiled Explicator; A Guide To The Study of Dashiell Hammett, Raymond Chandler & Ross Macdonald* (Metuchen, NJ & London: Scarecrow, 1985). Bibliography of literature on the Holy Trinity.

SLUNG, Michele B., ed.; *Crime On Her Mind; Fifteen Stories of Female Sleuths from the Victorian Era to the Forties* (NY: Pantheon, 1975). Includes a patchy Chronological Survey that is less than precise or comprehensive.

STEINBRUNNER, Chris et al; *Encyclopedia Of Mystery & Detection* (NY: McGraw-Hill, 1976). Basic reference book with an emphasis that does not rate PI writers and their creations very highly.

TUSKA, Jon; *The Detective In Hollywood* (NY: Doubleday, 1978). Flagged "The Movie Careers of The Great Fictional Private Eyes and Their Creators" but this is grossly misleading. Some background to the Hammett, Chandler, Halliday and Ross Macdonald films, terminally etiolated by Tuska's admitted ignorance of the genre and stated preference for Van Dine and Stout.

METHOD: How To Use This Guide

To illustrate the various points in the entries:

Baker, Abel — CONQUEST, John
CONQUEST, John
British crime fiction critic and author of one book featuring ex-journalist, C&W fan and collector of PI fiction **Abel Baker**, who operates out of a houseboat on the Regent's Canal in North London. Semi-hardboiled with a parodic element as Baker models himself on different fictional PIs at different times. Conquest also wrote a book about Austin, Texas PI **Charlie Delta** as **Victor TANGO**, published in the UK under his own name. See **TV: ABEL BAKER, P.I.**
Baker: Diamond Hill* (UK 1986); as Bloodlines (1987)
Delta: Neon And Dust (UK 1988; as by **Victor TANGO** 1987)
Delta, Charlie — TANGO, Victor/CONQUEST, John
Foxtrot, Easy — TV: The EYE OF TEXAS
TANGO, Victor = CONQUEST, John
A British journalist who moves to Austin, Texas, **Charlie Delta**'s investigative experience is called on when he's hired as a troubleshooter by the local Musicians' Union. Interesting on the workings of the music business with some bizarre Texan and country music characters. A Delta short story, "Fair And Square" (*Dollar Detective* 1986) is in **A22**. As Tango, Conquest novelized the pilot film of **TV: The EYE OF TEXAS**, featuring good old boy San Antonio PI **Easy Foxtrot**. See **Films: LADIES OF THE NIGHT.**
Delta: Neon And Dust (1987; as by **John CONQUEST** UK 1988)
Foxtrot: Contrabandistas (1988)

Authors, films and radio and television programs are listed in **BOLD CAPITALS** except in the **ANTHOLOGIES** section and in passing references. Private eyes are listed in **Bold Upper & Lower Case.**
When the author's and hero's names are the same there is no cross-reference, otherwise all PIs are listed in the A-Z with cross-references except for the relatively few (21) whose names I was unable to determine (see Missing Persons). **TV:**, **Film:** and **Radio:** refer to the media sections following the A-Z, in which feature films and TV and radio programs are listed alphabetically by title. When a TV, film or radio PI subsequently appeared in a novelization, the cross-reference is to the original medium and title (as with **Easy Foxtrot**), with the novel/s cross-referenced under

that main entry. Abel Baker will further be found in the Yellow Pages under Great Britain: London and Charlie Delta under Texas: Austin.

An = sign refers back to a main entry under the author's true name or best known pseudonym if he/she has not written PI fiction under his/her own name (i.e. Dennis Lynds' main entry is as Michael Collins) and any other pseudonyms are cross-referenced.

Annotation are intended to give some idea of PIs' style and quality. I quote critics such as Boucher, Sandoe, Cuppy, Nevins, Baker & Nietzel and Klein, where appropriate, to provide diversification of opinion. When sharp disagreements occur, I have tried to quote both sides sufficiently to demonstrate this. On occasion I have had no information at all and been unable to obtain any of an author's books, and this is at least implied.

Short stories are listed only when they appear in one of the collections listed under **ANTHOLOGIES** in the main section. Each anthology has been given a number and is referred as shown (**A22**). Issue numbers are given for stories in *New Black Mask* and *Matter Of Crime*.

With rare exceptions, all books listed were published in America or Britain or both. A date on its own is always the first American edition, the first British is indicated by UK, Australia by Aus, Canada by Can, though Raven House's Toronto publications are treated as American. Alternative titles and pseudonyms are included and fully cross-referenced. An asterisk by a title indicates that the book is discussed at length in Pronzini & Muller.

In the title index only one short cut has been taken to save space. CoT = The Case Of The. The check list, however, has been ruthlessly pruned in order to make it as short as possible while still making every title, I hope, intelligible. > indicates more titles follow in the next column.

ABBREVIATIONS

LAPD	Los Angeles Police Department
MWA	Mystery Writers of America
NOPD	New Orleans Police Department
NYPD	New York Police Department
NYT	New York Times Review of Books
P&M	Pronzini & Muller (*1001 Midnights*, see Bibliography)
PWA	Private Eye Writers of America
SFPD	San Francisco Police Department
SR	Saturday Review of Literature
SS	Short stories

A-Z OF AUTHORS & EYES

ABBOTT, Keith
By alphabetical mischance, this survey opens with a piece of literary whimsy that has little to do with PI fiction other than the fact that the improbable heroes open a detective agency, Rhino Ritz, Troubleshooters. After Sherwood Anderson disappears and Gertrude Stein and Alice B. Toklas are kidnaped, **Ernest Hemingway** (Rhino) and **F. Scott Fitzgerald** (Ritz) launch their agency from an apartment at 314 Union Street, San Francisco. The author was once favorably compared to Richard BRAUTIGAN, who similarly exploited the genre without adding to it.

> Rhino Ritz; An American Mystery (1979)

Abbott, Pat & Jean — CRANE, Frances
Abilene, Cody — Films: MALIBU EXPRESS
ABLEMAN, Paul
Novelizations of the British **TV: SHOESTRING** featuring Bristol PI **Eddie Shoestring**.

> Shoestring (UK 1979, 1984)
> Shoestring's Finest Hour (UK 1980, 1985)

ABRAHAMS, Robert D.
Young, raw and ignorant but shrewd and ambitious, **Pete Taylor** featured in two novels, one of which was described by *NYT* in very Thurberish terms as "a crude little tale whose very unpretentiousness gives it a certain diverting appeal." Pronzini (*Gun In Cheek*) describes Taylor as having "all the wit and charm of Calvin Coolidge" and says of *Murder In 1-2-3*, "In no other mystery can you read until page 73, skip to page 203 and feel that you haven't missed a single plot thread."

> Death After Lunch (1941)
> Death In 1-2-3 (1942)

Ackroyd, Roger — FEIFFER, Jules

1

ACRE, Stephen = GRUBER, Frank
Heir to a detection correspondence school, energetic soldier of fortune **Joe Devlin** is drawn into a bizarre hunt. Described by *NYT* as "amusing and entertaining, a clever variation on the tough-and-funny type."
> The Yellow Overcoat (1942, UK 1945; as by **GRUBER** 1949);
> as Fall Guy For A Killer (as by **GRUBER** 1955)

ADAMS, Cleve F(ranklin) 1895-1949
After a varied career, including being a detective, Adams began writing for the pulps at 40. Often criticized as warmed over Hammett and second rate Chandler, Geherin and Baker & Nietzel praise him highly, while Nevins considers that "had he lived longer, he might have grown into a writer rivaling Chandler." Adams admitted that he was not much of a plotter and recycled character names, scenes and other elements, stealing the plot of Hammett's *Red Harvest* three times! His forte was characterization; **Rex McBride**, LA insurance specialist, was, in deliberate contrast to Chandler's white knight, coarse, racist, sexist, fascistic, hypocritical, an intemperate drinker, compulsive womanizer and pathological liar. As Nevins observes, his "apparent soft heart is itself a shell concealing a brutal and cynical core." Sandoe recommended *Sabotage*. Ex-LAPD Lieutenant **John J. Shannon**, making more money running his own agency, is a more positive character but still foul mouthed and alcoholic. **Stephen McCloud** is an insurance company's best detective and "what with killers, cops, drunks and the female of the species, he is in hot water all the time," as *NYT* put it. Of Adams' prolific pulp magazine output, the only story currently available (A3) is "Flowers For Violet" (*Clues Detective Stories* 1936), about **Violet McDade**, a "great lummox" with terrible clothes sense, who can fell a man with a blow, and her Hispanic narrator-partner **Nevada Alvarado**. See also **John SPAIN**.

McBride: And Sudden Death (1940)
            Sabotage (1940); as Death Before Breakfast (1942); as Death At The Dam (UK 1946)
            Decoy (1941)
            Up Jumped The Devil (1943); as Murder All Over (1950)
            The Crooking Finger (1944)
            Shady Lady* (1955). Completed by **Robert Leslie BELLEM & W.T. BALLARD.**
Shannon: The Private Eye (1942)
            No Wings On A Cop (1950). Expanded by **Robert Leslie BELLEM** from a novelet.
McCloud: What Price Murder (1942)

Adams, Dolly — BLACK, Thomas
Adams, Don — TV: CORONADO 9
ADAMS, Douglas
Famed for his *Hitchhiker's Guide to the Galaxy* series, Adams turned his comic attentions to the PI with novels about holistic detective **Dirk Gently** of 33A Peckender Street, London, N1, whose motto is "We solve the *whole* crime. We find the *whole* person. Phone today for the *whole* solution to your problem (Missing cats and messy divorces a specialty)." Strong SF and surrealist elements.

> Dirk Gently's Holistic Detective Agency (UK 1987, 1987)
> The Long Dark Tea-Time Of The Soul (UK 1989, 1989)

ADAMS, Harold
An interesting offbeat character in good stories, hobo come home **Carl Wilcox** graduated to being a PI because, as an ex-con, he was suspected of every crime in his 30s North Dakota home town of Corden and had to solve them to clear himself. Moving to the modern day, Adams created a more obvious PI in smart-mouthed **Kyle Champion**, who loses his job as a TV news anchorman and accepts an assignment from an old, now rich, flame to find her missing husband, getting attacked more often than most PIs in the process, once being left for dead.

Wilcox: Murder (1981)
           Paint The Town Red (1982)
           The Missing Moon (1983)
           The Naked Liar (1985)
           The Fourth Widow (1986)
           The Barbed Wire Noose (1987)
           The Man Who Met The Train (1988)
           The Man Who Missed The Party (1989)
Champion: When Rich Men Die (1987)

Adams, Squire — BROWN, Horace
Addison, David — TV: MOONLIGHTING
Ade, Thelma — HEALEY, Rose Million
ALBERT, Marvin
Under various names Albert has written mysteries, westerns, adventures and novelizations, with his PI novels written as **Anthony ROME** or **Nick QUARRY** among the better. Recently he returned to the genre with Franco-American PI **Pierre-Ange 'Pete' Sawyer**, living, like Albert himself, on the French Riviera and specializing, from his Paris office, in missing persons. His work permit replaces the usual PI license as authority's threat, part of the prevailing cultural dissonance.

Rome: Tony Rome (1967); as Miami Mayhem (as by **Anthony**
                     ROME 1961)
Sawyer: Stone Angel (1986, UK 1987)
                     Back In The Real World (1986, UK 1987)
                     Get Off At Babylon (1987, UK 1988)
                     Long Teeth (1987, UK 1988)
                     The Last Smile (1988)

Alder, Tom — GRUBER, Frank

ALEXANDER, David 1907-1973

Best known for his novels about *Broadway Times* columnist Bert Hardin,
Alexander also wrote two typically idiosyncratic books about NYC
private eye **Terry Rooke** and his 300lb boss, **Tommy Twotoes**, an
eccentric penguin fancier. An exasperated Boucher complained that
Alexander had too much originality, "What begins as the most hackneyed
of conventional private eye stories later starts blossoming into a mad
phantasmagoria," and he found the second book "purely preposterous,"
saying that Alexander suffered under the delusion that eccentricity is a
substitute for characterization.

                     Murder In Black And White (1951, UK 1954)
                     Most Men Don't Kill (1951, UK 1953); as The Corpse In My
                            Bed (1954)

ALEXANDER, Karl

Witness to her husband's murder, traumatized **Sara Scott** works as a PI's
secretary because she can't afford to pay him to investigate it, before
setting up on her own in Venice, California (Room 207, 71 Market
Street),   modeling herself   on   Jim   Rockford.   Overlong and
overwrought, replete with flashbacks and soliloquies, but ending on an
upbeat note when she reverts to her maiden name. See **TV: MISSING
PIECES.**

                     A Private Investigation (1980, UK 1981)

Allan, Cody — TV: RIPTIDE

ALLAN, Dennis (Elinore Denniston 1900-1978)

Well known as Rae Foley, the prolific Denniston wrote romantic
suspense novels, one, as Allan, featuring British PI **Bruce Carver**, sent
to New York to represent an insurance company. Cuppy remarked, "a
little on the goofy side, this may serve to entertain the less fussy
customers with its speed and surprises."

                     Brandon Is Missing (UK 1938, 1940)

ALLAN, Francis

Stilted and dated novel featuring NYC PI **John Storm**, whose first
entrance is a cliché classic: "In the first moment, his face seemed utterly

plain. Then it seemed to develop, though not a muscle moved. In the brown eyes there was keen intensity. Flecks of gray showed in the brown hair. A fragile vibrancy seemed to radiate, to stir restlessly beneath the calm surface of his features. Instinctively and at once Linda knew that this man was a stranger in her knowledge of men, and she could not draw her eyes from the flexible mask of his calm face."

> First Come, First Kill (1945, UK 1947)

ALLEGRETTO, Michael

Himself the son of a Denver police detective, Allegretto's **Jacob Lomax**, is a laconic, physically competent ex-cop with a dry wit, who retired after the gratuitous, unsolved rape-murder of his wife to set up as a Denver PI. The first book was nominated for 1988 PWA and Bouchercon Best First Novel awards.

> Death On The Rocks (1987, UK 1988)
> Blood Stone (1988)

ALLEN, Leslie = BROWN, Horace

His weakness for ice cream, of which he always eats at least three dishes, is such that **Napoleon B. Smith** almost let a criminal, who tried to bribe him with strawberry flavor, get away. Dismissed by Boucher because a sleuth who, we are told, can take in every detail of a scene at a single brief glance, fails to observe that the dead woman he finds has been killed with a bullet not a golf ball. *SR* thought it too dear at two bits.

> Murder In The Rough (1946; as by Horace BROWN UK
> 1948)

Allen, Pat — MURPHY, Robert

ALLEN, Steve

The famous entertainer wrote one book about educated, foppish, image conscious **Roger Dale** of Dale Security Agency, Suite C-7, Fairview Business Park, LA, who makes his living mainly by selling burglar alarms but is called in, due to a chance meeting with Steve Allen, when TV talk show guests start getting murdered on air. Compared to a hip Philo Vance, Dale makes *portraits parles*, or psychological profiles, of suspects. Witty parody with authentic background.

> The Talk Show Murders (1982)

Allen, Walter — TV: The CHEATERS

ALLYSON, Alan

British series featuring **Martin Ross** of which the only one published in the US was described by *Library Journal* as a stupid mishmash of clichés about a private eye in never-never land. *Bright As A Diamond* (UK 1973) may be another. >

Do You Deal In Murder? (UK 1972)
Don't Mess With Murder (UK 1972)
The Lady Said No (UK 1972, 1972)

Aloha, Johnny — KEENE, Day

Alvarado, Nevada — ADAMS, Cleve F.

ALVERSON, Charles

Fired from the SFPD for accidentally killing the mayor's cousin, **Joe Goodey** gets his PI license the very next day to help the police with an ultra-discreet inquiry into the murder of the mayor's mistress. In an homage to Chandler, Goodey is initiated into the PI code by retired Marley Phillips. Alverson says that Goodey is "me with more balls, Philip Marlowe with a receding hairline and no illusions," and that there won't be any more books because Joe can't stand the pace. Brutal, gun-happy **Alec Hoerner** failed to survive his one outing.

Hoerner: Fighting Back (1973, UK 1978)
Goodey: Goodey's Last Stand* (1975, UK 1976)
Not Sleeping, Just Dead (1977, UK 1978)

Ames, Russell — STEVENS, Frank

Ames, Sid — RODEN, H.W.

Anderson, Dick — KAUFMAN, Wolfe

ANDERSON, M.

From the Spillane school comes a title unlisted in Hubin featuring New York eye **Jason Marr** whose most obvious feature is a wide, ragged scar across his left cheek whose color, pale pink to deep purple, acts as a barometer of his emotions. Sex and sadism are brutally combined.

Her Mother's Husband (1960)

ANDERSON, Poul

The famous SF writer produced three novels about Norwegian-Japanese-Hawaiian judo expert, samurai sword connoisseur and cerebral San Francisco PI **Trygve Yamamura**, who is abstemious and happily married. A truly exotic PI who, like Anderson's SF heroes, is somewhat to the right of Attila the Hun.

Perish By The Sword (1959)
Murder In Black Letter (1960)
Murder Bound* (1962)

ANDREWS, L.M. — see KARLINS, Marvin & ANDREWS

Andrews, Russ — TV: The INVESTIGATORS

Angel, Harry — HJORTSBERG, William

Anglich, Pete — CHANDLER, Raymond

ANTHOLOGIES

Authors are listed (exceptionally not in bold), only when a story in an anthology features a PI. Details under author headings.

1 Bruccoli, Matthew J. & Richard Layman, eds.; *The New Black Mask Quarterly* (8 issues, 1985-1987; # 5 & 6 as *Crimewatch*, UK 1987). Paperbacks despite the title. Michael AVALLONE, Linda BARNES, David A. BOWMAN, R.D. BROWN, Mark COGGINS, Michael COLLINS, Clark DIMOND, W.S. DOXEY, Loren D. ESTLEMAN, Dashiell HAMMETT, Edward D. HOCH, Joseph LISOWSKI, John LUTZ, Arthur LYONS, Martin J. MILLER, William F. NOLAN, Sara PARETSKY, James Lee SNYDER.

2 Bruccoli, Matthew J. & Richard Layman, eds.; *A Matter Of Crime* (4 vols, 1987-1988). Michael AVALLONE, John Cabell CHURCH, Michael COLLINS, Loren D. ESTLEMAN, David GATES, Edward D. HOCH, Marcia MULLER, Josh PACHTER, Bill PRONZINI, James REASONER, D. RENEAU, Stephen A. RUDLOFF, L.J. WASHBURN.

3 Drew, Bernard, ed.; *Hard-Boiled Dames; Stories Featuring Women Detectives, Reporters, Adventurers and Criminals From the Pulp Fiction Magazines of the 1930s* (1986). Cleve F. ADAMS, Roswell BROWN, T.T. FLYNN, D.B. McCANDLESS, Frederick NEBEL, Theodore TINSLEY.

4 GORMAN, Edward, ed.; *The Black Lizard Anthology Of Crime Fiction* (1987). Max Allan COLLINS, Wayne D. DUNDEE, William Campbell GAULT, Edward GORMAN, Robert J. RANDISI, James REASONER.

5 GORMAN, Edward, ed.; *The Second Black Lizard Anthology Of Crime Fiction* (1988). Max Allan COLLINS, Wayne D. DUNDEE, Richard LAYMAN, Stephen MERTZ, Marcia MULLER, Robert J. RANDISI.

6 GOULART, Ron, ed.; *The Hardboiled Dicks; An Anthology And Study Of Pulp Detective Fiction* (1965, UK 1967). John K. BUTLER, Norbert DAVIS, Lester DENT, Raoul WHITFIELD.

7 Hoppenstand, Gary & Ray B. Brrowne, eds.; *The Defective Detective In The Pulps* (1983). Paul ERNST, Edith & Ejler JACOBSON, John KOBLER, Warren LUCAS, Nat SCHACHNER.

8 Hoppenstand, Gary; Garyn G. Roberts & Ray B. Browne, eds.; *More Tales Of The Defective Detective From The Pulps* (1985). Leon BRYNE, Russell GRAY, Edith & Ejler JACOBSON, John KOBLER.

9 Kittredge, William & Steven M. Krauzer, eds.; *The Great American Detective* (1978). Robert Leslie BELLEM, Raymond CHANDLER, Carroll John DALY, Brett HALLIDAY, Dashiell HAMMETT, Ross MACDONALD, Rex STOUT.

10 Morrison, Henry, ed.; *Come Seven, Come Death* (1965). Richard DEMING, Frank KANE, Henry KANE, Stephen MARLOWE, Richard S. PRATHER.

11 NOLAN,William F., ed.; *The Black Mask Boys; Masters In The Hard-Boiled School Of Detective Fiction* (1985). Paul CAIN, Raymond CHANDLER, Carroll John DALY, Dashiell HAMMETT, Frederick NEBEL.

12 Preiss, Byron, ed.; *Raymond Chandler's Marlowe* (1988). Chandler centennial collection of **Philip Marlowe** stories. Simon BRETT, Robert CAMPBELL, Raymond CHANDLER, Max Allan COLLINS, Robert CRAIS, Loren D. ESTLEMAN, Edward GORMAN, James GRADY, Joyce HARRINGTON, Jeremiah HEALY, Edward D. HOCH, Stuart KAMINSKY, Dick LOCHTE, Eric Van LUSTBADER, John LUTZ, Francis M. NEVINS, Jr., Sara PARETSKY, W.R. PHILBRICK, Robert J. RANDISI, Benjamin M. SCHUTZ, Roger L. SIMON, Julie SMITH, Paco Ignacio TAIBO II, Jonathan VALIN.

13 PRONZINI, Bill, ed.; *The Arbor House Treasury Of Detective And Mystery Stories From The Great Pulps* (1983). Robert Leslie BELLEM, Carroll John DALY, Norbert DAVIS, Dashiell HAMMETT, John JAKES, Frederick NEBEL.

14 PRONZINI, Bill & Martin H. Greenberg, eds.; *The Mammoth Book Of Private Eye Stories* (UK 1988, 1988). Robert Leslie BELLEM, Lawrence BLOCK, Fredric BROWN, Howard BROWNE, Raymond CHANDLER, Max Allan COLLINS, Michael COLLINS, Carroll John DALY, Loren D. ESTLEMAN, William Campbell GAULT, Edward GORMAN, Sue GRAFTON, Stephen GREENLEAF, Joseph HANSEN, Edward D. HOCH, Stuart KAMINSKY, Henry KANE, John LUTZ, Arthur LYONS, Ed McBAIN, Ross MACDONALD, Stephen MARLOWE, Marcia MULLER, Bill PRONZINI, Richard S PRATHER, Robert J. RANDISI.

15 RANDISI, Robert J., ed.; *The Eyes Have It; The First Private Eye Writers Of America Anthology* (1984). Lawrence BLOCK, Max Allan COLLINS, Michael COLLINS, Loren D. ESTLEMAN, Stephen GREENLEAF, Edward D. HOCH, Richard HOYT, Stuart KAMINSKY, Rob KANTNER, Michael Z. LEWIN, John LUTZ, Marcia MULLER, William F. NOLAN, Sara PARETSKY, Bill PRONZINI, Robert J.

RANDISI and L.J. WASHBURN.

16 RANDISI, Robert J., ed.; *Mean Streets; The Second Private Eye Writers of America Anthology* (1986). Max Allan COLLINS, Wayne D. DUNDEE, Loren D. ESTLEMAN, William Campbell GAULT, Sue GRAFTON, Stuart KAMINSKY, Rob KANTNER, John LUTZ, Arthur LYONS, Sara PARETSKY, Bill PRONZINI, Dick STODGHILL.

17 RANDISI, Robert J., ed.; *An Eye For Justice; The Third Private Eye Writers of America Anthology* (1988). George CHESBRO, Michael COLLINS, Max Allan COLLINS, Wayne D. DUNDEE, Loren D. ESTLEMAN, Sue GRAFTON, Rob KANTNER, John LUTZ & Josh PACHTER, Arthur LYONS, Bill PRONZINI, Robert J. RANDISI, James REASONER, L.J. WASHBURN.

18 Roberts, Garyn G., ed.; *A Cent A Story! The Best From Ten Detective Aces* (1986). Paul CHADWICK, Lester DENT, G.T. FLEMING-ROBERTS, Norvell PAGE, Emile C. TEPPERMAN.

19 Ruhm, Herbert, ed.; *The Hard-Boiled Detective; Stories From Black Mask Magazine 1920-1951* (1977, UK 1979). Raymond CHANDLER, Merle CONSTINER, George Harmon COXE, Norbert DAVIS, Lester DENT, Erle Stanley GARDNER, Dashiell HAMMETT.

20 Shaw, Joseph, ed.; *The Hard-Boiled Omnibus; Early Stories From Black Mask* (1946; shorter paperback 1952) Raymond CHANDLER, Norbert DAVIS, Ramon DECOLTA, Lester DENT, Dashiell HAMMETT. Not in the paperback: George Harmon COXE.

21 Zahava,Irene, ed.; *The WomanSleuth Anthology; Contemporary Mystery Stories By Women* (1988). Helen & Lorri CARPENTER, Rose Million HEALEY, Gerry MADDREN, Karen WILSON.

ANTHONY, David (William Dale Smith 1929-1986)
After a breakdown, Korean War vet **Morgan Butler** works for a San Francisco detective agency before becoming a farmer outside Jordan, Ohio and part time PI. **Stan Bass** does part time PI work in Las Vegas and California, basing himself in Hyde Street, San Francisco, because "it gave me some W2 forms to file, a must for a professional gambler." The books have good characters, plots and atmosphere; Hubin found *Midnight Lady* a "substantial debut," Marcia Muller calls it "a novel you won't want to put down," Bourgeau described *Blood On A Harvest Moon* as "a classic," but *NYT*'s Newgate Callendar thought it "so badly written that is unforgettable, ineffable." See **Films: The MIDNIGHT MAN.**
Butler: The Midnight Lady And The Mourning Man* (1969, UK 1970)
　　　Blood On A Harvest Moon (1972, UK 1972)
　　　The Long Hard Cure (UK 1979) >

Bass: The Organization (1970, UK 1971)
           Stud Game (UK 1977, 1978)
ANTHONY, Evelyn
One of Anthony's romantic suspense thrillers featured a wonderfully misconceived detective agency, Dunston Fisher, after six years in business, the biggest agency in Europe with offices in every capital and over 100 operatives. Trying to recover a stolen heirloom from a fugitive Nazi General, ex-reporter **Eric Fisher** is, in Anthony's stock motif, smitten with his daughter, while his ex-Interpol partner **Joe Dunston** resorts to duplicity, double-dealing and even murder.
           The Poellenberg Inheritance (UK 1971, 1971)
Anthropol Detective Agency — TRIMBLE, Louis
April, Danny — BALLINGER, Bill S.
April, Johnny — ROSCOE, Mike
Arcane, Ethan — TV: The MOST DEADLY GAME
Archer, Jill — RANSOME, Stephen
Archer, Lew — MACDONALD, Ross
Archer, Oceala — CARR, Joseph B.
ARD, William 1922-1960
Ignored by Geherin and passed over very briefly by Baker & Nietzel, Ard was praised by Boucher as "just about unmatched for driving story movement and acute economy," while Nevins calls him "one of the most distinctive voices in the history of the private eye novel." Carrying on the classic tradition during the Spillane-McCarthy era, and influenced by John O'Hara, Ard was an hardboiled romantic, his New York eyes **Timothy Dane**, based at Broadway & 44th, and **Lou Largo**, at Times Square, being decent, honest men capable of real human relationships. Indeed, the young, naive Dane is "tender with women, inept at machismo, incapable of escaping tight spots single-handed, resorting to violence rarely" (Nevins). Shaky on plots, Ard recycled character names over and over but blended "tough-guy elements with singular warmth and tenderness." Mike Fontaine, who featured in *As Bad As I Am* (1959), a reworking of *Hell Is A City*, was renamed **Danny Fontaine** in the paperback, *Wanted: Danny Fontaine* (1960) and resurfaced under that name as an amiable, overly attractive young novice PI with not too many brains whose troubles his partner, **Barney Glines**, who also appeared solo in a novel Ard published under the name **Thomas WILLS**, has to straighten out. The last four Largo novels were ghost-written. Sandoe recommended *The Diary*. See also **Ben KERR**.
Dane: The Perfect Frame (1951, UK 1953) >

.38 (1952); as You Can't Stop Me (1953); as This Is Murder (UK 1954)

The Diary (1952, UK 1954)

A Private Party (1953); as Rogue's Murder (UK 1955)

Don't Come Crying To Me (1954)

Mr. Trouble (1954)

Hell Is A City* (1955); as The Naked And The Innocent (UK 1960)

Cry Scandal (1956, UK 1960)

The Root Of His Evil (1957, UK 1958); as Deadly Beloved (1958)

Largo: All I Can Get (1959)

Like Ice She Was (1960)

Babe In The Woods (1961). By **Lawrence BLOCK**

Make Mine Mavis (1961). By **John JAKES**

And So To Bed (1962). By **John JAKES**

Give Me This Woman (1962). By **John JAKES**

Fontaine: When She Was Bad (1960)

Glines: You'll Get Yours (1960; as by **Thomas WILLS** 1952)

ARDEN, William = COLLINS, Michael

Distinguished from Lynds' work as **Michael COLLINS**, **John CROWE**, **Carl DEKKER** or **Mark SADLER** by their plain, economical third-person style, the Arden books feature hard-bitten **Kane Jackson** of Kane Jackson Associates, Industrial Consultants, Santa Barbara, a mercenary in corporate wars, who hides his skills at reading dubiously obtained business ledgers and records behind a seldom used PI license. As usual, excellent and thought provoking.

A Dark Power* (1968, UK 1970)

Deal In Violence (1969, UK 1971)

The Goliath Scheme (1971, UK 1973)

Die To A Distant Drum (1972); as Murder Underground (UK 1974)

Deadly Legacy (1973, UK 1974)

Argos, Malcolm — TV: SWITCH

Armismendi, Oscar — TV: LEGMEN

Arno, Jess — Films: NO PLACE FOR A LADY

ARRIGHI, Mel 1933-1986

Mystery writer Hank Mercer of West 11th Street, New York, wants to shed his popular hardboiled Hammeresque character **Biff Deegan** in favor of a smoother sleuth but finds that he's an invaluable, and increasingly visible, "partner" in a true life mystery. Billed as "A Hank & Biff Mystery," no others appeared.

   Alter Ego* (1983, UK 1984)

Arthur, Dr. — **DELANCEY, Roger**

ARTHUR, Robert (Robert Feder 1909-1969)

Feder's only book was a hardboiled Ace novel featuring half Swedish, half English PI **Max London** of Vista Beach, California, a former boxer, "attractive in a rugged way," looking as if he'd been in a lot of fights.

   Somebody's Walking Over My Grave (1961)

Asch, Jacob — **LYONS, Arthur**

Atwood, Sharon — **MICHAELS, Melisa C.**

Audran, Marid — **EFFINGER, George Alec**

Austen, Major Roderick — **PARMER, Charles**

AUSTER, Paul

"The case seems simple enough. White wants **Blue** to follow a man named Black and to keep an eye on him for as long as necessary. While working for Brown, Blue did many tail jobs, and this one seems no different, perhaps even easier than most . . . It is February 3, 1947. Little does Blue know, of course, that the case will go on for years." Blue features in Vol 2 of Auster's *The New York Trilogy*. In Vol 1, mystery novelist Quinn, writes about PI **Max Work** and lives his life after getting phone calls for Paul Auster of the Auster Detective Agency. The poet and essayist's work could be dismissed as literary conceit but Elmore LEONARD is enthusiastic about it: "uses the bare bones of a genre to get to the essence of good writing . . . mystery as metaphor."

Work: City Of Glass (1985); in The New York Trilogy (UK 1987)

Blue: Ghosts (1986); in The New York Trilogy (UK 1987)

AVALLONE, Michael

The prolific Avallone featured **Ed Noon**, initially a straightforward PI, with an office on Central Park West, New York, who later in his career became personal investigator for a disgraced ex-President and more James Bond than PI, in some 30 of his 200+ books, creating a "Nooniverse" of tortured syntax, mutilated metaphors, endless allusions to old movies and an unrestrained distaste for hippies, deviants, Commies, pacifists, dissidents, militant blacks, feminists, longhairs and eggheads. "A Bullet For Big Nick," the first Noon story, written in 1949, and "Walter Ego" are in **A1** #2 and **A2** #2. With seven titles (indicated with GiC, one is a non-Noon) in Pronzini's Alternative Hall of Fame (*Son Of Gun In Cheek*), Avallone ranks with Harry Stephen Keeler as a Grandmaster of Bad Writing. Avallone also novelized **TV: MANNIX. >**

Noon: The Spitting Image (1953, UK 1957)
         The Tall Dolores (1953, UK 1956)
         Dead Game (1954, UK 1959)
         Violence In Velvet (1956, UK 1958)
         The Case Of The Bouncing Betty (1957, UK 1959)
         The Case Of The Violent Virgin* (1957, UK 1960)
         The Crazy Mixed-Up Corpse (1957, UK 1959). GiC
         The Voodoo Murders (1957, UK 1959)
         Meanwhile Back At The Morgue (1960, UK 1961). GiC
         The Alarming Clock (UK 1961, 1973)
         The Bedroom Bolero (1963); as The Bolero Murders (UK 1972).
             GiC
         The Living Bomb (UK 1963, 1972)
         There Is Something About A Dame (1963). GiC
         Lust Is No Lady (1964); as The Brutal Kook (UK 1965)
         The Fat Death (UK 1966, 1972). GiC
         The February Doll Murders (UK 1966, 1967)
         Assassins Don't Die In Bed (1968)
         The Horrible Man (UK 1968, 1972)
         The Flower-Covered Corpse (UK 1969, 1972)
         The Doomsday Bag (1969); as Killer's Highway (UK 1970)
         Death Dives Deep (1971, UK 1971)
         Little Miss Murder (1971); as The Ultimate Client (UK 1971)
         Shoot It Again, Sam (1972); as The Moving Graveyard (UK
             1973)
         The Girl In The Cockpit (1972, UK 1974)
         London,Bloody London (1973); as Ed Noon In London (UK
             1974)
         Kill Her—You'll Like It! (1973, UK 1974)
         The Hot Body (1973). GiC
         Killer On The Keys (1973)
         The X-Rated Corpse (1973)
         The Big Stiffs (UK 1977)
         Dark On Monday (UK 1978)
         High Noon At Midnight (1988)
Mannix: Mannix (1968)
Axbrewder, Mick — STEPHENS, Reed
Axminster, Jake — TV: CITY OF ANGELS
AYRES, Paul = RONNS, Edward (Edward S. Aaarons)
Aarons used this name for a novelization of **Radio: CASEY, CRIME**

PHOTOGRAPHER based on the character of **Jack 'Flashgun' Casey** created by **George Harmon COXE**.
>   Dead Heat (1950)

BABULA, William
Disillusioned with bureaucracy, easy-going assistant San Francisco DA **Jeremiah St. John** quits and becomes a PI, assisted by **Michelle 'Mickey' Farabaugh**, an ex-Ohio cop fired for appearing nude in a *Playboy* spread about women in uniform, and **Chief Moses**, a giant Seminole Indian. A routine plot but good humor makes this a fine read.
>   St. John's Baptism (1988)

Baeier, Kate — SLOVO, Gillian
Bailey, Hilary & Hilea — BAILEY, Hilea
BAILEY, Hilea (Ruth Lenore Marting)
Effectively crippled by arthritis, private detective **Hilary Dunsany Bailey III** uses his daughter **Hilea Bailey** to do the leg work, often putting her into considerable danger. The uneven stories were described by Cuppy as "a disarming blend of deadly deeds and artless prattle."
>   What Night Will Bring (1939, UK 1940)
>   Give Thanks To Death (1940)
>   The Smiling Corpse (1941)
>   Breathe No More, My Lady (1946)

Bailey, Jane — DOBSON, Margaret
Bailey, Jeff — Films: OUT OF THE PAST
Bailey, Red — HOMES, Geoffrey
Bailey, Stuart — HUGGINS, Roy
BAKER, Sidney J.
Boucher described this Australian academic's novel as "a private eye toughie about dope running which also involves some near science-fiction about an unlikely sort of surgico-chemical personality alteration. It's fast and readable enough and gains in interest from its Australian settings of Sydney and the Great Barrier Reef."
>   Time Is An Enemy (1958)

Ballard, Larry — GORES, Joe
BALLARD, Willis Todhunter 1903-1980
After 10 years of producing short stories for the pulps, the prolific Ballard, who also wrote many Westerns, produced four novels about his long running *Black Mask* character **Bill Lennox**. Not technically a PI, Lennox was troubleshooter for General Consolidated Studios, Hollywood but the paperback blurb isn't far off calling him "the Rat-Pack Private Eye." Like all Ballard's characters, he's noteworthy for his immediacy.

Tough enough and cynical (he wanted to be a writer), he nonetheless respects women and is capable of warm relationships. Sandoe remarked that Lennox "doesn't have to flex his biceps to prove that he's strong" and recommended *Dealing Out Death*. A later Lennox novel appeared only under the name **John SHEPHERD**. Much later, Ballard, who also wrote a PI series as **Neil McNEIL**, wrote a single novel, set, like much of his work, in Las Vegas, about low key LA PI **Mark Foran** in a complex murder plot.

Lennox: Say Yes To Murder* (1942); as The Demise of A Louse (as
           by **John SHEPHERD** 1962)
           Murder Can't Stop (1946, UK 195?)
           Dealing Out Death (1948, UK 195?)
           Hollywood Troubleshooter (1984). SS
Foran: Murder Las Vegas Style* (1967)

BALLINGER, Bill S(anborn) 1912-1980
Before embarking on the split narrative novels for which he is best known, Ballinger wrote two conventional PI novels, the first clearly derivative of *The Maltese Falcon*, about logical Chicagoan **Barr Breed**, who has a staff of three operatives. Ballinger's prose is stilted, with occasional irrelevant purple passages, and both Barr books are essentially locked room puzzles. Boucher, who admired the first, thought the second was "a shabby museum of every cliché of plot, style and action." **Bryce Patch**, former Military Police officer, owns the Amsterdam Investigation Bureau, East 12th Street, New York and has a BA in criminology and a brass knuckle scar on his face. Rather marginal is **Danny April**, new owner of a small-time Chicago collection agency who falls in love with a photograph in the files and sets out on a puzzling and sinister search. See **Films: PORTRAIT IN SMOKE and TV: CANNON/MICKEY SPILLANE'S MIKE HAMMER.**

Barr: The Body In The Bed (1948, UK 1960)
       The Body Beautiful (1949, UK 1960)
Patch: Heist Me Higher (1969, UK 1971)
April: Portrait In Smoke* (1950, UK 1951); as The Deadlier Sex (UK
       1958)

Baltic, Gillian — CLARK, Dale
Banacek, Thomas — TV: BANACEK
BANDY, Eugene Franklin 1914-1988
A Psychological Stress Detector expert, NYC based sophisticate **Kevin MacInnes** is known as the "Lie King" but has a PI like way of rigging the results to suit his own moral code. Bandy indulges in a good deal of

brand name-dropping—clothes, food, wines, luxury hotels. The first book in the series won an MWA Edgar for Best Original Paperback, though Marcia Muller (P&M) thought 100 pages could have been cut. See also **Eugene FRANKLIN**.

> Deceit And Deadly Lies* (1978, UK 1979)
> The Blackstock Affair (1980)
> The Farewell Party (1980)

BANKS, Oliver

Detailed art world backgrounds and characterization, rather than plots, are the attraction in two stories about Boston art detective **Amos Hatcher**, reluctantly relocated in New York, an investigator on permanent retainer to the International Association of Art Dealers. Trained as an art historian, his specialty is Dutch baroque. Banks is a New York art consultant and critic and very good on the art world's skullduggery and backbiting.

> The Rembrandt Panel* (1980); as The Rembrandt File (UK 1984)
> The Caravaggio Obsession (1984, UK 1985)

BANKS, Raymond

Boucher calls the first novel "outrageously wild goings-on in a Wyoming hotel, revolving (well, spinning) around a slew of murders, $185,000 in missing cash and the love life of private eye **Sam King**. None too coherent but commendable for its avoidance of the expectable clichés and for its close-to-parody approach which is sometimes very funny." A Denver native, King's LA agency specializes in recovering stolen goods.

> Meet Me In Darkness (1961)
> The Computer Kill (1961)

Banks, Steve — TV: The INVESTIGATORS
Bannerman, Jim — FLYNN, Jay
Banning, Bill — EASTON, Nat
Bannion, Burns — NORMAN, Earl
Bannon, Tom — TV: LEGMEN
Banyon, Miles — TV: BANYON
BARNAO, Jack = WOOD, Ted

Toronto bodyguard, **John Locke**, a 1st Lt. in Britain's élite SAS after dropping out of both Cambridge and Harvard, advertises "Physical Assurance" on his cards, but his work involves more than strong-arm skills. In both books seemingly straightforward jobs have complex developments in fact-paced action stories.

> Hammer Locke (1986)
> Lockestep (1987)

Barnes, Al — HUGO, Richard
Barnes, Berkeley Hoy — FRANKLIN, Eugene
Barnes, Ezell — HILARY, Richard
Barnes, Gerry — BOWEN, Robert Sidney
BARNES, Linda (J.)
Independently wealthy Fayerwether Street, Boston, aristo **Michael Spraggue III** trained at London's Royal Academy of Dramatic Art, gave up acting in disgust at actors and agents and became a PI, turning in his license in equal disgust at the dirt involved, and became both part-time actor and PI, starring, in *Bitter Finish*, in a private eye film. Barnes scored with critics and award nominations for her first novel about a female PI, **Carlotta Carlyle**, a spirited 6'1" redheaded former cab-driver and cop who lists her phone number as T.C. Carlyle (her cat's name) and, when business is slow, actually reads the junk mail most PIs throw in the bin. Carlyle debuted in "Lucky Penny" (A1 #3) which won a 1985 Bouchercon Anthony as Best Short Story. See **TV: SPRAGGUE.**

Spraggue: Blood Will Have Blood (1982)
             Bitter Finish* (1983, UK 1983)
             Dead Heat (1984, UK 1984)
             Cities Of The Dead (1985)
Carlyle: A Trouble Of Fools (1988, UK 1988)
             The Snake Tattoo (1989)
Barnett, Mike & Pat — Radio: MAN AGAINST CRIME
BARNS, Glenn M.
Boucher found **Jonathan Marks** "one of the more nearly naturalistic private eyes" and commented that *Murder Is Insane* "provides easy narration, underplayed humor and plentiful action-excitement without violent excess."

             Murder Is A Gamble (1952, UK 1954)
             Murder Walks The Stairs (1954, UK 1955)
             Murder Is Insane (1956, UK 1958)
Barr, Ronald — MURPHY, Robert
Barrett, Dave — TV: MANHUNTER
Barrow, Jake — QUARRY, Nick
BARRY, Joe (Joe Barry Lake)
In *The Clean Up*, a mysterious client pays hardboiled Chicago private eye **Rush Henry** ten grand to clean up a vice-ridden Midwestern town, which results in much blood letting. *SR* commented "Implausible but swiftly moving and cadaver-sprinkled tale with dauntless hero, helpful gal and exceptionally well concealed *diabolus ex machina*." *NYT* remarked

that it was impossible to kill Henry because a couple of drinks would bring him back from the grave.

> The Third Degree (1943)
> The Fall Guy (1945)
> The Triple Cross (1946)
> The Clean Up (1947)
> The Pay-Off (1953)

Barth, Stephen — KETCHUM, Philip
Barton, Sue — DEAN, Robert George
Bascombe, Carver — DAVIS, Kenn
Bass, Stan — ANTHONY, David
Bay, Charity — KAPLAN, Arthur
Bayliss, Pete — TREYNOR, Blair
BAYNE, Spencer (Floyd A. & Paula Teresa Bayne Spencer)
The blurb to the first novel about private detective **Hendrik Van Kill** boasted that the author could speak eleven languages, to which *NYT* acidly responded; "yet he is unable or unwilling to tell a reasonably intelligible story in English." Van Kill is a savant sleuth whose publisher quotes an anonymous source as saying that he is "as distinctive and amusing as Philo Vance," no longer quite the boost it might have been.

> Murder Recalls Van Kill (1939)
> The Turning Sword (1941)

Bayne, Warren — BYERS, Charles Alma
BAYNES, Jack (Bertram B. Fowler)
The European-based unofficial counter-espionage operation for which tough two-fisted **Morocco Jones**—"A gun is nice too, but I like the personal touch"— worked is now an agency specializing in recovering stolen money and valuables. More than a match for both the Mafia and CIA combined, he litters Chicago with a record number of corpses. Boucher found the second novel offering "more fantastic fun than anything in book form since Howard SCHOENFELD's *Let Them Eat Bullets.*"

> Meet Morocco Jones (1956)
> Meet Morocco Jones In The Case Of The Syndicate Hoods
>   (1957)
> Hand Of The Mafia (1958)
> The Peeping Tom Murders (1958)
> Morocco Jones In The Case Of The Golden Angel (1959)

Beagle, Amanda & Lutie — CHANSLOR, Torrey
Beagle, Otis — BOSTON, Charles K. / GRUBER, Frank

BEAL, M(ary) F.

An explicitly feminist thriller featuring Maria Katerina Lorca Guerrera Alcazar, otherwise **Kat Guerrera**, bisexual and former revolutionary, still wanted on an outstanding midwest warrant, who has abandoned the male-dominated left for the women's movement and is hired to guard a feminist author and investigate her lethal problems. Deconstructionalist, positing that a radical feminist PI is a contradiction because PIs are still part of the (patriarchal) system, and discussed at length by Klein.

> Angel Dance (1977)

BEAR, David

One of the better efforts in a surprisingly large sub-genre combining PI and SF. **Jack Hughes** is the best, but then possibly the only, PI in the world, operating in a nightmare 1999 Manhattan, with his Park Avenue address conveying rather different connotations (it's a slum). Well plotted with good SF ideas well suited to a future tough sleuth.

> Keeping Time (1979)

Beaudine, Jackson — TV: I HAD THREE WIVES

BECK, K.K. (Kathrine Marris)

Hired by a beautiful professor to obtain a restraining order on a man who has been obsessed with her for 15 years and has threatened her fiancé, **Michael Caruso** features in a weakly characterized and implausibly motivated novel in which most actions and emotions are filtered through the dry proceedings of the trial that takes up most of the book.

> Unwanted Attentions (1988)

BEHM, Marc

The famous *noir* author wrote one extraordinary, not to say bizarre, anxiety-ridden, minimalist PI novel, rich in psychological suspense. An aging Watchmen Inc. operative, only referred to as **The Eye**, his personality boiled down to pure essence of "peeper," already obsessed by an old girl's school class photograph sent by his embittered ex-wife, taunting him to guess which is his daughter, becomes obsessed with a woman who murders the man he's been detailed to watch, and follows her around America, watching her and covering up for her as she murders thirty more men. See **Films: MORTELLE RANDONEE.**

> The Eye Of The Beholder (1980); in Thrillers; Four Novels (UK 1983)

BEINHART, Larry

Yale Law School drop-out and former prison officer turned NYC PI, **Tony Cassella** takes on a high-paying but legally dubious job helping a Wall Street law firm anticipate an official investigation in the first novel. Soundly written with sharp, often satirical insights into class, power and relationships. *No One Rides For Free* won an MWA Best First Novel Edgar.

No One Rides For Free (1986, UK 1988)

You Get What You Pay For (1988)

Bellamy, Nick — CHEYNEY, Peter
BELLEM, Robert Leslie 1902-1968

"Hollywood's hottest hawkshaw" was the famous, or infamous, **Dan Turner**, of whom Bellem wrote hundreds of stories in *Spicy Detective* and *Dan Turner, Hollywood Detective* magazines, of which the latter often featured as many as five Turner stories. Zany is the word most often used for Bellem's offbeat style, which took all the conventions of the hardboiled school and ran endless comic variations on them, so inventive in their language and use of idiom that they transcended parody or satire. In his famous essay on Bellem, *Somewhere A Roscoe*, S.J. PERELMAN called Turner "the apotheosis of the private eye." Two *Hollywood Detective* Turner short stories are in anthologies, "The Lake of the Left Hand Moon" (1943; A9) and "Diamonds of Death" (1950; A13 and A14) and a 1940 *Spicy Detective* story, "Death's Passport," is in Tony Goodstone: *The Pulps* (1970). Bellem never wrote a novel about Turner, instead creating another PI who could have been his brother, **Duke Pizzatello**, in a somewhat tamed down version of his usual manner. See **Cleve F. ADAMS** and **John A. SAXON** for ghost-written novels. Bellem wrote scripts for **TV: 77 SUNSET STRIP**.

Pizzatello: Blue Murder (1938)

Turner: Dan Turner, Hollywood Detective* (1983). SS

               Three Dan Turner Stories (1986)

BENJAMIN, Paul

New York PI **Max Klein** is in the classic mold, bright, tough, enterprising, down on his luck and appealing, with an office in an old, rundown West Broadway building. A Columbia University graduate and college baseball player, he gets involved with the political aspirations of a former baseball star.

Squeeze Play (1982)

Bennett, Fred — LEWIS, Elliott
Bennett, Jim — MARTIN, Robert
Bennett, Reid — WOOD, Ted
Benson, Big Bull — PARKER, Percy Spurlark
Benson, Karl — Films: MANHANDLED

BENSON, O.G.
Author of a single novel featuring Chicago PI **Max Raven** of which
Boucher remarked that the emphasis was less on the sexy (pornographic
pictures used for blackmail) and violent elements than on the interesting
people along the way and particularly Raven's attempts, as he unravels her
past, to understand the woman who is dominating his life.

       Cain's Woman (1960); as Cain's Wife (1985)

Bent, John — BRANSON, H.C.

BENTLEY, John
Howard Haycraft, in *Murder For Pleasure* (1968), brackets Bentley with
Peter Cheyney as "competent-or-better" British authors, "whose **Dick
Marlow** and Slim Callaghan work hard to prove themselves the British
equivalents of Nick Charles and Sam Spade." Pick the bones out of that.
See **Films: The NIGHT INVADER.**

       Dangerous Waters (UK 1939); as Mr. Marlow Takes To Rye
         (1942)
       Prelude To Trouble (UK 1939); as Mr. Marlow Chooses Wine
         (1941)
       Front Page Murder (UK 1940); as Mr. Marlow Stops For Brandy
         (1940)
       Rendezvous With Death (UK 1941)
       Macedonian Mixup (UK 1944)
       The Dead Do Talk (UK 1944)

Bentley, Steve — DIETRICH, Robert

BERCOVICI, Eric
Detectives are often thickheaded, but none more so than **Harold
Shilling**, down and out San Diego ex-cop, his skills rusty from disuse,
who attempts to commit suicide while depressed only to have the bullet
bounce off his skull. The novel was praised by Arthur LYONS as "a
tight, fast-moving book that took me right to the last page." See **TV:
ONE SHOE MAKES IT MURDER.**

       So Little Cause For Caroline (1980)

BERGER, Thomas
The best selling author wrote two parodies featuring New York ex-teacher
and PI **Russel Wren**, a seedy type who lives in his East 23rd office, on
which he owes the rent. Some may find them funny but many will agree
with Baker & Nietzel: "so murky and heavyhanded, so intellectually
postured, so supercilious and showy, it (*Who Is Teddy Villanova?*) winds
up for any reader familiar with the PI genre as merely unreadable and
silly." The second book satirizes spy novels. >

Who Is Teddy Villanova? (1977, UK 1977)

Nowhere (1985, UK 1986)

BERGMAN, Andrew

Before he disappeared into Hollywood scriptwriting, Bergman produced two excellent books featuring **Jack LeVine**, 1940s New York PI with an office at Broadway & 51st, overweight, sweaty, balding and Jewish. Though born in 1945, Bergman's detailed evocation of the period, with cameo appearances by, among others, Richard Nixon and Humphrey Bogart, is very convincing and he himself says that his books are historical novels. They are also well judged parodies and fine mysteries.

The Big Kiss-Off Of 1944 (1974, UK 1975)

Hollywood And LeVine (1975, UK 1976)

BERNARD, Trevor

In contrast to Bellem's flashy Hollywood detective, **Nathan Brightlight**, who has left the security of a big firm to set up on his own on Hollywood Boulevard, is low-key and ironic.

Brightlight (1977)

Bernhardt, Alan — WILCOX, Collin

Best, Petunia — CHETWYND, Bridget

BESTOR, Clinton

SR commented "Private operative and luscious red-head keep story moving through scenes that strain credibility to cracking point." The redhead is a taxi dancer whose colleague and roommate has been killed and who mixes wise-cracking romance and real excitement as she helps an ambitious young detective.

The Corpse Came Calling (1941)

Betts, Johnny — TV: PRIVATE EYE

BEYER, William Gray

The signpainter wanted too much money, so the office door reads simply "**Cornelius Duffy**, Private." Duffy has a "lightning left-hand draw" and boasts of having no clients, no cases and collecting no fees and is somewhat unconvincingly depicted as a latter-day Robin Hood.

Eenie, Meenie, Minie—Murder! (1945); as Murder By

Arrangement (UK 1946); as Murder Secretary (1948)

BIGGLE, Lloyd Jr.

This SF/PI series opens in the future—1986! **Jan Darzek** owns a New York agency but spends most of his time far from Earth working for the Council of the Supreme, the ultimate galactic authority. More Great Detective than PI, with strong comic elements. Biggle has also written a crafty, atmospheric novel about **Jay Pletcher** of Lambert & Associates,

Investigative Consultants, LA, in which a big city PI finds himself out of his depth in small town Sparta, Ohio.

Darzek: All The Colors Of Darkness (1963, UK 1964)
            Watchers Of The Dark (1966, UK 1968)
            This Darkening Universe (1975, UK 1979)
            Silence Is Deadly (1977, UK 1980)
            The Whirligig Of Time (1979)
Pletcher: Interface For Murder (1987)

BILGREY, Marc

Collection of thematic cartoons sufficiently described by the title. Personally I find them weak and superficial, obvious jests about a subject as perceived from without rather than as appreciated from within.

            The Private Eye Cartoon Book (1985)

BILLANY, Dan 1913-1945

Described by *The Times* as "unblushingly crooked," **Robbie Duncan** is a former private detective who went to prison for robbing a client of a large amount of money. Released, he is tutoring an opera singer friend's son, when a murder outside the friend's house, and more importantly the prospect of loot, awakens his dormant detecting instincts. *N Y T* commented "murders and murderous assaults come thick and fast and none of the gory details are omitted. Except for those who enjoy homicide for its own sake and in its most revolting forms, there is not much merit in the book." *SR*, however, enjoyed it a good deal, calling it "eminent."

            The Opera House Murders (UK 1940); as It Takes A Thief
            (1940)

Bindbugel, Willie — Films: ROADHOUSE NIGHTS
Binney, Joe — LIVINGSTON, Jack
Birdseye, Miriam — SPAIN, Nancy
BIRKETT, John

From the title it can be deduced that Louisville, Kentucky PI **Michael Rhineheart**, 38 year old widower, feels fairly isolated, though his first outing features his aging mentor Farnsworth and would-be PI secretary Sally McGraw. "A guy who made a couple of hundred a day when he worked and drove a twelve-year-old Maverick with a bad clutch. Someone who lived in a furnished apartment. Someone who drank too much and slept with a lot of waitresses," Rhineheart also runs a lot and is not good at being intimidated. The story is set against the Kentucky Derby but, unlike other horsey PI novels, the hero knows nothing about bloodstock.

            The Last Private Eye (1988)

Bishop, Paul — FARJEON, J. Jefferson

Bishop, Robin — HOMES, Geoffrey
Bix, Calvin — MALING, Arthur
Black — CAIN, Paul
Black — Radio: DETECTIVES BLACK & BLUE
Black Herman — REED, Ishmael
Black, Reginald — RONNS, Edward
BLACK, Thomas
When the founder of Chancellor City's Redman Detective Agency is killed in his office at the opening of the first novel, operatives **Al Delaney** and **Dolly Adams** take over. The intelligent Delaney detests violence but has a national reputation as being handy with a gun. Sandoe remarks "Familiar and competent pre-Spillane pyrotechnicality with an avoidance of incidental clichés. Irritating habit of referring to women as hairpins."
> The 3-13 Murders (1946)
> The Whitebird Murders (1946)
> The Pinball Murders (1947)
> Four Dead Mice (1954); as Million Dollar Murder (1956)

Black, Thomas — EMERSON, Earl W.
Blade, Joe — TV: BLADE IN HONG KONG
BLAINE, Richard
Set in Lancaster, Pennsylvania in 1948, with gangsters, molls, millionaires and more, LA PI **Mike Garrett**'s debut has too many coincidences but is fast paced, full of tricky surprises. Ultra-tough trenchcoated Garrett, a former cop asked to leave the force because of "an attitude problem" (did they have those in 1948?) drinks Old Kentucky bourbon, drives a rented DeSoto and charges $30 a day.
> The Silver Setup (1988)
> The Tainted Jade (1989)

Blair, Mike — SEARLS, Hank
Blake, Arthur — LEE, Edward
Blake, Jake — WILLEFORD, Charles
Blake, Jana — CONAWAY, Jim
BLAKE, William Dorsey
So-so SF/PI blend with **Reggie Moon** time-traveling back to 1846 where he must solve a murder and find a way back to the 20th century.
> My Time Or Yours (1979)

Blaney, Jim — WEST, Elliott
BLANKENSHIP, William D.
Commenting on his fee of $500 a day for a minimum of five days, *NYT*'s Newgate Callendar observed that **Michael Saxon** was the most

expensive PI in the business, getting far more than Nero Wolfe. Also reviewing an M.E. CHABER Milo March novel, Callendar found both readable, neatly constructed entertainments featuring big, tough wisecrackers who could hold liquor, enjoyed a tumble in the hay and could handle the more bruising aspects of the job.

> The Programmed Man (1973, UK 1973)

BLEECK, Oliver = THOMAS, Ross
Thomas' professional go-between **Philip St. Ives,** who acts as intermediary between thieves and kidnapers on the one hand and owners, relatives and insurance companies on the other, shares many of the important characteristics of the PI and can simply be regarded as an unusual specialist in a field that many PIs have been drawn into at one time or another. The novels have much of Thomas' customary irony and style but also a certain glibness. See **Films: ST. IVES.**

> The Brass Go-Between* (1969, UK 1970)
> Protocol For A Kidnapping (1971, UK 1971)
> The Procane Chronicle (1972); as The Thief Who Painted
>   Sunlight (UK 1972); as St. Ives (1976)
> The Highbinders (1974, UK 1974)
> No Questions Asked (1976, UK 1976)

Bleekman, Jack — DOXEY, W.S.
Blissberg, Harvey — ROSEN, R.D.
BLOCH, Robert
The master of the macabre, who once said "I have the heart of a small boy. I keep it in a jar on my desk," wrote one routine Hollywood PI novel, full of beatings, wenches and marijuana, "occasionally illuminated, according to Boucher, by Bloch's acute vision of the grotesque or his loving knowledge of the history of films."

> Shooting Star (1958)

BLOCHMAN, Lawrence G. 1900-1975
An MWA President, recipient of an Edgar and an MWA Special Award, Blochman is best remembered for his forensic procedurals featuring Indian pathologist Dr. Coffee. Of his many books set in India, one featured **Bill Gabriel** of the Five Continents Detective Agency whose client is killed before telling him why she wanted another American, also sought by the Indian CID, found. *NYT* commented "a curiously complicated story, involving as it does love, hate, greed, ambition and pure cussedness on the part of the various characters," which sounds fairly normal to me.

> Wives To Burn (1940, UK 1940)

BLOCK, Lawrence

The key word for Block is versatile; his range includes the grimly serious and the wildly comic, and his private eye work is no exception. His first book featured New Yorker **Ed London** and established him immediately, as Foul Play reasonably claim with their reprint, as a master of urban violence and suspense. In the same year he wrote a novelization, unlisted in Hubin or Reilly, of **TV: MARKHAM** starring Ray Milland as **Roy Markham**. His highly regarded series about **Matt Scudder** is a gripping depiction of guilt, remorse and redemption. An NYPD cop who quit after accidentally killing a small girl, left his family and became a steady drinker, if not actually an alcoholic, living in a West 57th hotel, Scudder, unlicensed, does occasional favors for friends, tithing 10% to the first open church he passes and sending most of the rest to his family. *Eight Million Ways To Die* won a PWA Best Novel award. Scudder short stories are "Out Of The Window" (*Alfred Hitchcock's Mystery Magazine* 1977; **A14**; also in Block's short story collection *Sometimes They Bite*, 1983) and "By The Dawn's Early Light" (*Playboy* 1984; basis of *When The Sacred Ginmill Closes*, winner of MWA and PWA Best Short Story awards, **A15**). At the other extreme are Rex Stout spoofs featuring **Leo Haig** as a fat, indolent, would-be Great Detective and **Chip Harrison** as his horny, street-wise Archie. See **Jeff JACKS** for speculation on another pseudonym, **William ARD** for a ghost-written novel and **Films: EIGHT MILLION WAYS TO DIE.**

London:	Death Pulls A Doublecross (1961); as Coward's Kiss (1987)
Markham:	Markham; The Case Of The Pornographic Photos (1961); as You Could Call It Murder (1987)
Scudder:	In The Midst Of Death (1976, UK 1979)
	Sins Of The Fathers (1977, UK 1979)
	Time To Murder And Create (1977, UK 1979)
	A Stab In The Dark (1981, UK 1982)
	Eight Million Ways To Die* (1982, UK 1983)
	When The Sacred Ginmill Closes (1986, UK 1987)
Haig:	Five Little Rich Girls (UK 1984); as Make Out With Murder (as by **Chip HARRISON** 1974)
	The Topless Tulip Caper (UK 1984; as by **Chip HARRISON** 1975)

Bloodworth, Leo — LOCHTE, Dick

BLOOMFIELD, Robert = EDGELY, Leslie

A week into a waitress's marriage to a millionaire drunk, murder takes place and she hires wrong 'un PI **Alva Yaeger**. "How was she to know that this action would precipitate a nightmarish procession of violence far beyond her wildest dreams?" asks the blurb. Boucher commented, "rather substandard skill in the fitting together of the cardboard pieces."

From This Death Forward (1952)

Blue — AUSTER, Paul

Blue — Radio: DETECTIVES BLACK & BLUE

Blue, Robert — SNYDER, James

BLUMENTHAL, John

"He's hard as rock, tough as nails and dense as concrete." **Mac Slade** is the nadir of the Manhattan (42nd & Lexington) detective, a man who once tailed the wrong car all the way to Phoenix, Arizona. Blumenthal's wonderful parody of the Spillane style is crammed with word play, puns and non sequiturs and takes off virtually every aspect of the tough detective. "Future Mac Slade Mysteries" include *Good Riddance, My Lovely*; *Tough Guys Don't Use Doilies*; *Scumbags Are Not Luggage* and *Corpses Make Strange Bedfellows*!

The Tinseltown Murders (1985)

The Case Of The Hardboiled Dicks (1985)

BOCCA, Al = WINTER, Bevis

British author Winter's American tough guy novels, featuring PI **Al Bocca**, San Francisco PI, are of that irritating variety where the language is never precise enough to convince the reader that the writer has even visited America, full of usages that are quite obviously British and clumsy enough even then. See also **Peter CAGNEY**.

Blonde Dynamite (UK 1950)
City Limit Blonde (UK 1950)
Curves For Danger (UK 1950)
A Dame Ain't Safe (UK 1950)
Dead On Time (UK 1950)
It's Your Funeral (UK 1950)
The Long Sleep (UK 1950)
She Was No Lady (UK 1950)
Sinner Takes All (UK 1950)
Slaughter In Satin (UK 1950)
The Coffin Fits (UK 1951)
Deadly Ernest (UK 1951)
Easy Come,Easy Go (UK 1951)
The Harder They Fall (UK 1951)
Let's Face It (UK 1951)
No Dice! (UK 1951) >

Sudden Death (UK 1951)
Wait For It, Pal (UK 1951)
Any Minute Now (UK 1952)
Dressed To Kill (UK 1952)
Black Morning (UK 1952)
A Gun For Company (UK 1952)
Let's Not Get Smart (UK 1952)
Sorry You've Been Shot (UK 1952)
All Or Nothing (UK 1953)
Double Trouble (UK 1953)
Requiem For A Redhead (UK 1953)
The Slick And The Dead (UK 1953)
Ticket To San Diego (UK 1953)
Trouble Calling (UK 1953)
A Corner In Corpses (UK 1954)
No Room At The Morgue (UK 1954)

Bockhorn, Ascher — COHEN, Barney
BOGART, William G. 1903-1977
Pulp writer Bogart was only a moderate novelist but his books about New Yorker **Johnny Saxon**, former "prince of the pulps" who quit writing and went back to being a PI, are filled with fascinating detail about the world of the pulp magazines. The first title refers to the pulps' payday.

Hell On Friday* (1941); as Murder Man (1941)
Murder Is Forgetful (1944)
The Queen City Murder (1946)

Boggs, Franklin — Films: HICKEY AND BOGGS
Bolt, Sam — TV: HONEY WEST
Bond, Marty — Lacy, Ed
Bone, Enoch — WILSON, Gahan
Bonner, Theodolinda — STOUT, Rex
BONNEY, Joseph L.
NYT remarked of **Simon Rolfe** that "he does his stuff by means of what he calls 'psychological logic', but you need not be alarmed by that rather high-flown term. It is just another name for sleuthing. Rolfe affects to pay little attention to tangible, physical clues, but when he finds one, he uses it just as any other good detective would." *NYT* liked the "deliberate and often amusing presentation of Rolfe as a successor-with-a-difference to Sherlock Holmes."

Death By Dynamite (1940)
Murder Without Clues (1940); as No Man's Hand (UK 1940)

Booker, Jerri — Radio: I LOVE A MYSTERY
Booker, Sam — ODLUM, Jerome
BOOTH, Louis F.
A specialist in larceny and confidence cases, inconspicuous **Maxwell Fenner** featured in two novels, both set in financial institutions. The second, which has brokers in a firm in post-Crash receivership still embezzling money and getting killed off, was described by *NYT* as having "a sensational conclusion which largely offsets the occasional stodginess which elsewhere slows up the action."
>   The Bank Vault Mystery (1933, UK 1933)
>   Brokers' End (1935, UK 1935)

Booth, Silas — LINKLATER, Joseph
Borbah, El — BURNS, Charles
Bordelon, Johnny — OGAN, George
Boston Blackie — Radio: BOSTON BLACKIE
BOSTON, Charles K. = GRUBER, Frank
Gruber, already writing the Fletcher & Cragg and Simon Lash series under his own name, used the Boston byline for the first of three books about **Otis Beagle**, "big, flashy—and phony" like his diamond ring, more conman than PI, and his tough little legman, long-suffering **Joe Peel**, together the LA Beagle Detective Agency.
>   The Silver Jackass (1941; as by **Frank GRUBER** UK 1952,
>   1973)

BOUCHER, Anthony 1911-1968
The famous crime critic, anthology editor and writer, the most influential, broad-minded and scrupulous of commentators (though his Catholic aversion to sex and violence can be somewhat trying) in whose honor the annual Bouchercon mystery fan conventions are named, also created a PI, **Fergus O'Breen**, a soft-boiled Irish egg, who favors loud clothes, limericks and a bright yellow roadster. Operating the O'Breen Detective Agency in LA, he believes that sugar catches more flies than vinegar. A blurb description says O'Breen is "cocksure and Irish, a moderately successful private detective, and a thoroughly nice young man."
>   The Case Of The Crumpled Knave (1939, UK 1939)
>   The Case Of The Solid Key (1941)
>   The Case Of The Seven Sneezes (1942, UK 1946)

BOWDLER, Roger
Novelization of **TV: MAGNUM P.I.** (see also **Dan ZADRA**) starring Tom Selleck as **Thomas Magnum** who lives in Hawaii.
>   Magnum P.I. (1981, UK 1985)

BOWEN, Robert Sidney 1900-1977
After two weeks of no business for the NYC detective agency he opened for fun, ex-OSS man **Gerry Barnes**, for whom money is no object, finds detective work is almost too exciting and takes a lot of punishment in rough and tumble stories.

    Make Mine Murder (1946)

    Murder Gets Around (1947)

BOWERS, Elizabeth
Sara PARETSKY welcomed Bowers as "the first mystery writer to use the themes of child pornography and sexual abuse believably. The characters are complex, credible and compelling." Paretsky looked forward to more books featuring Vancouver PI and mother **Meg Lacey**.

    Ladies' Night (1988)

BOWMAN, David A.
An off-beat story, "Pincushion," about tattooed **Foy Laneer** (A1 #4) with a note that the author was then (1986) working on a PI novel.

Bowman, Glenn — HOWARD, Hartley

BOWMAN, Robert
Former San Francisco public defender **Cassandra Thorpe** marks time as an unlicensed investigator in the sleazy South of Market district, waiting to join a quiet Santa Rosa probate practice, a wait interrupted by a friendly judge who sentences her to two years as a proper PI when the usual PI misdemeanors catch up with her. Interesting on San Francisco's "dumping ground for its bums and crazies." Thorpe is a likable control freak. Nominated for 1988 Bouchercon (Best First Novel) and PWA Shamus awards.

    The House Of Blue Lights (1988)

Boyd, Danny — BROWN, Carter

BOYD, Frank = KANE, Frank
Kane used the Boyd byline for non-Johnny Liddell books, including a novelization of **TV: JOHNNY STACCATO.**

    Johnny Staccato (1960, UK 1964)

Boyle, Arthur — TV: GOODNIGHT, MY LOVE

Boyle, Tony — WALL, William

Bozinsky, Murray — TV: RIPTIDE

BRACKEEN, Steve
Castile, Florida PI **Clay MacKinnon** gets involved with the deposed dictator of Santa Cruz via a neighbor. A routine if early use of Florida's Latin bad guys with some detailed and explicit violence.

    Delfina (1962, UK 1963)

Brackett, Hank — TV: BEARCATS!
BRACKETT, Leigh 1915-1978
Best known for her SF, Brackett's first book, often considered the best hardboiled PI novel written by a woman, though Pronzini (P&M) differs very sharply (see **Dolores HITCHENS**), so impressed Howard Hawks that he invited her to work with Faulkner on the script of Chandler's *The Big Sleep*, assuming she was a man. It features Vine & Hollywood Boulevard, LA, detective **Edmond Clive**. Sandoe commented "Chandleresque and a sound chase which bogs down somewhat in plot before it stops. It is worth adding that Chandler liked Brackett." So also did Boucher who called it one of the more effective hardboiled stories between Chandler and Ross Macdonald's debuts. See **Films: The BIG SLEEP / The LONG GOODBYE** and **TV: CHECKMATE**.
  No Good From A Corpse* (1944)
Brackett, Walter — MARLOWE, Derek
Brade, Simon — CAMPBELL, Harriette R.
Braden, Stan — USHER, Jack
Bradford, Hank — WARDEN, Mike
BRADFORD, Kelly
Gay San Francisco PI **Derek Thompson** is retained to find a missing infant the police assume is a divorce action pawn and stumbles onto a big-money baby market in a feminist/New Age "WomanSleuth Mystery."
  Footprints (1988)
Bradley, Jim — O'ROURKE, Frank
Bradley, Rupert — RONALD, E.B.
Bradshaw, Charlie — DOBYNS, Stephen
Bradshaw, Steve — PEPPE, Frank
Brady, B.T. — TV: THIS GIRL FOR HIRE
Bragg, Pete — LYNCH, Jack
Braid, Peter — GARRITY, Dave J.
BRALY, Malcolm 1925-1980
Novelization of a dull caper film featuring Donald Sutherland as insurance investigator **Andy Hammond**. See **Films: LADY ICE**.
  The Master (1973)
Brandon, Mark — WARREN, Vernon
BRANDON, William
Brandon's one novel, set in Vermont and featuring PI **Sam Ireland**, was described by *NYT* as having a "story sure enough to keep the reader guessing" and by *SR* as "effective."
  The Dangerous Dead (1943)

Brandstetter, Dave — HANSEN, Joseph
Brannigan, Mike & Bob — TV: BROTHERS BRANNIGAN
BRANSON, H(enry) **C.** c1905-1981
A physician by training, bearded **John Bent** drifted into PI work when he had to find out who was poisoning a patient in order to be able to cure him and no longer practices medicine. The general Michigan area he works in, and Bent's character, are left unspecified. We know he is observant, outspoken, a heavy smoker and drinker, but the stories, while well-crafted, are detached and emotionless.

> I'll Eat You Last (1941, UK 1943); as I'll Kill You Last (1942)
> The Pricking Thumb* (1942, UK 1949)
> The Fearful Passage (1943, UK 1950)
> Case Of The Giant Killer (1944, UK 1949)
> Last Year's Blood (1947, UK 1950)
> The Leaden Bubble (1949, UK 1951)
> Beggar's Choice (1953)

Brass, Pete — LOCKE, Robert Donald
BRAUTIGAN, Richard 1935-1984
The counter-culture writer of "gentle whimsy" wrote one PI novel in his series of unprovoked assaults on various genres. **C. Card** (as in S. Spade) is a day-dreaming 1942 San Francisco PI so down on his luck that his office is a phone box and he has to scrounge bullets for his gun. Moderately amusing in places, though hardly shining with comic invention as Susan Dunlap (P&M) claims.

> Dreaming Of Babylon* (1977, UK 1978)

Bray, Patrick — COBB, Irvin S.
Breed, Barr — BALLINGER, Bill S.
Brennan, Mike — ZACKEL, Fred
BRENT, Nigel (Cecil Gordon Eugene Wimhurst)
"A snappy dresser and a quick thinker," **Barney Hyde**, once a Scotland Yard CID Detective Sergeant, now London manager for Global Investigations, Inc. of New York, San Francisco and Paris, drives round in a cream Jaguar accompanied by a black and tan Alsatian, Kurt, one of the best trained police dogs in the world (just as well, Kurt saves his life more than once). His brief, meteoric police career ended with advice to resign because of his methods. Standard mid-Atlantic tough guy stuff.

> The Scarlet Lily (UK 1953)
> Blood In The Bank (UK 1954)
> Motive For Murder (UK 1954)
> Dig The Grave Deep (UK 1955) >

Murder Swings High (UK 1956)
The Leopard Died Too (UK 1957)
The Golden Angel (UK 1958)
Badger In The Dusk (UK 1959)
No Space For Murder (UK 1960)
Spider In The Web (UK 1960)

Bressio, Al — SAPIR, Richard
Brett, Alan — GARRETT, Robert
Brett, Brian — MONIG, Christopher
Brett, Chico — O'HARA, Kevin
BRETT, Martin (Douglas Sanderson)
Boucher described *Hot Freeze* as "wholly unsubtle but surprisingly entertaining," French-Irish Montreal PI **Mike Garfin**'s involvement with dope, blackmail, nightclubs, beatings, tortures and erotic activities banal to the point of parody, but conceded that he was likeable, the tempo fast and the wisecracks genuinely amusing. See **Malcolm DOUGLAS.**

Hot Freeze (1954, UK 1954)
The Darker Traffic (1954, UK 1954); as Blondes Are My Trouble (1955)
A Dum-Dum For The President (1961)

BRETT, Michael
Often confused with a Miles TRIPP pseudonym, Brett wrote about **Pete McGrath**, New York PI who talks to himself, loathes pollution and tries to work as little as possible, rarely visiting his 34th Street office. Veering between straight hardboiled action and near farce, Brett's books, with their wonderful titles, were not successful when they first appeared but are now much prized as fine entertainments. See **Films: CRY UNCLE!**

Kill Him Quickly, It's Raining (1966)
Dead, Upstairs In A Tub (1967)
An Ear For Murder (1967)
The Flight Of The Stiff (1967)
Turn Blue, You Murderers (1967)
We, The Killers (1967)
Another Day, Another Stiff (1968)
Death Of A Hippie (1968)
Lie A Little, Die A Little (1968); as Cry Uncle! (1971)
Slit My Throat Gently* (1968)

BRETT, Simon
British author of the much admired actor-detective Charles Paris series, onetime President of the Crime Writers Association (the British

equivalent of the MWA), who contributed a **Philip Marlowe** short story, "Stardust Kills," to **A12**.

BREWER, Mike

An investigator for a big insurance company until he saw how many robberies could be prevented by sensible precautions, **Brendan Wallace** sets up as a Security Consultant in Knightsbridge, London. Mostly it's a quiet, easy, safe sort of job though not in unaffectedly English titles unlisted in Hubin, who has only one Brewer title, *Man Against Fear* (1966) which may be a third book or, more probably, a US title.

    Man In Danger (UK 1961)
    Man On The Run (UK 1962)

Brice, Andy — ROBERTS, Lee
Brightlight, Nathan — BERNARD, Trevor
Brill, Mark — MEYER, Nicholas
Brimmer, Sam — GOULART, Ron
Brisbane, Jack — YOUNG, David
Briscoe, Sam — HAMILL, Pete
Britton, Rickard — HOLT, Deben
BROCK, Stuart = TRIMBLE, Louis

Trimble/Brock, specialized in Seattle PIs. Tall, urbane **Pete Cory** of Boldman Investigations is hardboiled but has feelings and, on one occasion, is reduced to tears. Of **Bert Norden** I can discover nothing. **Steve Rourke**, troubleshooter for a Washington lumber magnate, featured in a book described by *SR* as containing plenty of movement, two good characters and little else. *Bring Back Her Body* (1953) may also be a PI book.

Rourke: Death Is My Lover (1948)
Cory: Just Around The Coroner (1948)
Norden: Killer's Choice (1956)

Brockelman, Richie — TV: RICHIE BROCKELMAN,
   PRIVATE EYE
Broder, Paul — DOYLE, James T.
Brodsky, Arthur — Films: THEY ALL LAUGHED
Brodsky, Dan — ROSENTHAL, Erik
Brody — HANSEN, Vern
Brogan, Terry — Films: AGAINST ALL ODDS
Bronx, Chip — TV: TWO FOR THE MONEY
Brooker, Mike — Films: SCREAM IN THE DARK
Brooks, B.G. — TUCKER, Wilson
Brooks, Claire — Radio: LET GEORGE DO IT

BROWN, Carter (Alan Geoffrey Yates 1923-1985)
Australian Yates wrote hundreds of lightweight, disposable, massively popular entertainments in the "leer and lights out" tradition of *Spicy Detective*, featuring minimal plots, lots of action, slang, of which Yates had an uncertain grasp, and, above all, gorgeous girls. One of the most amply endowed was zoftig dizzy blonde **Mavis Seidlitz** of LA, the most improbable PI of all time, who has an off and on partnership with **Johnny Rio. Rick Holman** was the reductio ad absurdum of Hollywood detectives, with **Danny Boyd** in the same mold. **Max Royal** of the expensive Cranmer Detective Agency, appeared in at least one title. Boucher, who reviewed Brown regularly, quoted a blonde in *The Wayward Wahine* saying to Boyd, "There's a quality of crudeness about you I find fascinating in a repulsive kind of way," and commented "That pretty much expresses the way I feel about Carter Brown."

Seidlitz: Honey, Here's Your Hearse (Aus 1955)
   A Bullet For My Baby (Aus 1955, as by Peter Carter-Brown)
   Good Morning, Mavis (Aus 1957?)
   Murder Wears A Mantilla (1962, UK 1962) Revised edition
   The Loving And The Dead (1959, UK 1966)
   None But The Lethal Heart (1959, UK 1967); as The Fabulous
    (Aus 1961)
   Tomorrow Is Murder (1960)
   Lament For A Lousy Lover* (1960, UK 1968)
   The Bump And Grind Murders (1964, UK 1965)
   Seidlitz And The Super-Spy (1967); as The Super-Spy (UK
    1968)
   Murder Is So Nostalgic (1972)
   And The Undead Sing (1974)

Boyd: So Deadly, Sinner! (Aus 1959); as Walk Softly, Witch (1959,
   UK 1965)
   The Wayward Wahine (1960, UK 1966); as The Wayward (Aus
    1962)
   The Dream Is Deadly (1960, UK 1962)
   The Seductress (Aus 1961); as The Sad-Eyed Seductress (1961,
    UK 1962)
   The Savage Salome (1961). Revised edition of Murder Is My
    Mistress (Aus 1954)
   The Ice-Cold Nude (1962, UK 1962)
   Lover, Don't Come Back! (1962, UK 1963)
   Nymph To The Slaughter (1963, UK 1964) >

The Passionate Pagan (1963, UK 1964)
The Silken Nightmare (1963, UK 1964)
Catch Me A Phoenix! (1965, UK 1966)
The Sometime Wife (1965, UK 1966)
The Black Lace Hangover (1966, UK 1969)
House Of Sorcery (1967, UK 1968)
The Mini-Murders (1968)
Murder Is The Message (1969)
Only The Very Rich? (1969)
The Coffin Bird (1970)
The Sex Clinic (1972)
The Angry Amazons (1972)
Manhattan Cowboy (1973)
So Move The Body (1973)
The Pipes Are Calling (1976)
The Savage Sisters (1976)
The Rip-Off (1979, UK 1979)
The Strawberry Blonde Jungle (1979, UK 1979)
Death To A Downbeat (1980)
Kiss Michelle Goodbye (1981, Aus 1984)
The Real Boyd (Aus 1984)

Holman: Death Of A Doll (Aus 1960); as The Ever-Loving Blues (1961)
Zelda 1961 (UK 1962)
Murder In The Harem Club (Aus 1962); as Murder In The Key
　　Club (1962, UK 1962)
The Murder Among Us (1962, UK 1964)
Blonde On The Rocks (1963, UK 1964)
The Jade-Eyed Jinx (Aus 1963); as The Jade-Eyed Jungle (1963,
　　UK 1964)
The Ballad Of Loving Jenny (Aus 1963); as The White Bikini
　　(1963, UK 1965)
The Wind-Up Doll (1964, UK 1965)
The Never-Was Girl (1964, UK 1965)
Murder Is A Package Deal (1964, UK 1965)
Who Killed Dr. Sex? (1964, UK 1965)
Nude—With A View (1965, UK 1966)
The Girl From Outer Space (1965, UK 1966)
Blonde On A Broomstick (1966, UK 1966)
Play Now—Kill Later (1966)
No Tears From The Widow (1966, UK 1968) >

The Deadly Kitten (1967)
No Time For Leola (1967)
Die Anytime, After Tuesday (1969)
The Flagellator (1969)
The Streaked-Blonde Slave (1969)
A Good Year For Dwarfs? (1970)
The Hang-Up Kid (1970)
Where Did Charity Go? (1970)
The Coven (1971)
The Invisible Flamini (1971)
The Pornbroker (1972)
The Master (1973)
Phreak-Out! (1973)
Negative In Blue (1974)
The Star-Crossed Lover (1974)
Ride The Roller Coaster (1975)
Remember Maybelle? (1976)
See It Again, Sam (1979, UK 1979)
The Phantom Lady (1980)
The Swingers (1980)

Royal: The Myopic Mermaid (1961, Aus 1962). Rewritten reissue of A
         Siren Signs Off (Aus 1958)

Brown, Clio — KOMO, Dolores
BROWN, Fredric 1906-1972
Several critics have traced a conflict between the romantic and the
naturalistic in Brown's equally famous SF, fantasy and mystery writing,
and Ron GOULART spoke of "the gentle tough guy." These opposing
elements combine in his series about the uncle and nephew team of
pragmatic streetwise carnyman **Am** (Ambrose) and idealistic **Ed Hunter**,
the youngest operative of the Starlock Agency. Operating in Chicago, the
Hunters did not go into formal business together until the fifth novel
when the Hunter & Hunter Detective Agency opened its doors. An Ed &
Am short story, "Before She Kills," is in **A14**. Brown's trademark was an
easily readable style combined with complex, often bizarre themes. *The
Fabulous Clipjoint* won the 1948 Best First Novel Edgar.

         The Fabulous Clipjoint* (1947, UK 1949)
         The Dead Ringer (1948, UK 1950)
         The Bloody Moonlight (1949); as Murder By Moonlight (UK
         1950)
         Compliments Of A Fiend (1950, UK 1951) >

Death Has Many Doors (1951, UK 1952)
The Late Lamented (1959, UK 1959)
Mrs. Murphy's Underpants (1963, UK 1965)

Brown, Fritz — ELLROY, James

BROWN, Gerald

Persona non grata with the Chicago police, fastidious **Marmaduke 'Duke' McCale** moves to Boston and re-establishes himself there, getting embroiled in political ambitions and blackmail in the first novel, Boston blueblood family skeletons in the second. Staccato style.

Murder On Beacon Hill (1941)
Murder In Plain Sight (1945)

BROWN, Horace

In one action packed day, on which he is supposed to be getting married, **Squire Adams** must solve a murder before 5pm or lose his New York PI license. Clever and breakneck if clumsily written. As **Leslie ALLEN**, Brown wrote a novel about **Napoleon B. Smith** published under his own name in the UK.

Adams: The Penthouse Killings (1950)
Smith: Murder In The Rough (UK 1948; as by **Leslie ALLEN** 1946)

BROWN, Hosanna

"Investigating agent extraordinary, toast of the leaders of businesses and governments across five continents and despair of the men on whom she selectively bestowed her caresses," New Orleans mulatto beauty **Frank Le Roux** features in two "light-hearted romps," the second of which is mildly interesting on the plight of Australian Aborigines, Hosanna Brown being the pseudonym of an Australian academic (male?).

I Spy, You Die (UK 1984)
Death Upon A Spear (UK 1986, 1986)

BROWN, R(obert) D.

Reliant Securities executive **Cheney Hazzard**, who describes himself as "a security specialist, not a private eye. Industrial applications, not divorce work. Brains not brawn," buys his company's franchise in Brownsville, Texas. His boss calls him a thinker, not a doer, and at 37 he still gets asked for ID in bars, but he finds himself in a situation involving the local cross-border narcotics and prostitution boss and shows his innate toughness. An exceptional debût with a rather florid follow-up. A short story, "Frisbee in the Middle," about law-studying PI **Frisbee** appeared in **A1** #6.

Hazzard (1986)
Villa Head (1987)

BROWN, Roswell
House name used for a story by Jean Francis Webb, "Hit The Baby!" (*The Shadow* 1936; A3), features **Grace 'Redsie' Culver**, former newspaper "sob sister," whose desk at the Noonan Detective Agency, Hollywood, says "Secretary," but who is very handy with the gun she carries in a garter holster and more a partner to Big **Tim Noonan**.
Brown, Vee — DALY, Carroll John
BROWNE, Howard
A writer for the Ziff-Davis pulps, later managing editor of their SF and fantasy titles, Browne wrote hundreds of film, radio and TV scripts, including **TV: 77 SUNSET STRIP / SIMON & SIMON**, and, as **John EVANS**, three novels featuring considerate, sensitive Chicago PI **Paul Pine**. The 4th and belated 5th Pine titles appeared under his own name. The PWA bestowed a Lifetime Achievement award on Browne. A Pine short story, "So Dark For April," in **A14** is under Browne's name.
> Halo In Blood (UK 1988; as by **John EVANS** 1946)
> Halo In Brass (1988; as by **John EVANS** 1949, UK 1951)
> The Taste Of Ashes* (1957, UK 1958)
> The Paper Gun (1985)

BROWNE, Ray B. (ed) — see **ANTHOLOGIES: 6 / 7**
BROWNER, John
After putting an ad in the New York Yellow Pages under "X Yourself: Divorce," chubby ex-cabbie **Larry Hornblower**, a descendant of Steve Midnight and Jigger Moran, gets lots of calls from suspicious wives.
> Death Of A Punk (1980)

Browning, Benjamin — Films: OH HEAVENLY DOG
BRUCCOLI, Matthew J. & LAYMAN — see
> **ANTHOLOGIES: 1 / 2**

Bryant, Steve — GEORGE, Peter
Bryant, Sydney — WALLACE, Patricia
Bryn, Ben — GRAY, Russell
BRYNE, Leon
A respected PI, **Dan Holden** loses his hearing in a shoot-out but, swearing his doctors and nurses to secrecy, learns to lip-read and hides his secret so well that even his secretary doesn't suspect, though he mysteriously recovers it at the very end of "Society Of The Singing Death" (*Dime Mystery* 1939) in **A8**.
BUCHANAN, Patrick (Edwin Corley 1931-1981 & Jack Murphy)
Reactionary ex-cop **Benjamin Lincoln Shock** and beautiful blonde **Charity Tucker**, a former top TV news reporter, frigid after being raped

(Shock killed her attacker) are New York's unlicensed Shock & Tucker—Investigations. *NYT* called the first book "one of the year's ten best mysteries . . . The author ignites his story on page one and heaps fuel on it all the way to the end." See also **David HARPER**.

> A Murder Of Crows (1970, UK 1973)
> A Parliament Of Owls (1971, UK 1973)
> A Requiem Of Sharks (1973, UK 1975)
> A Sounder Of Swine (1974)

Buchet, Paul — TV: The PROTECTORS
Buck, Phineas — FORD, Leslie
Buck, Zebulion — NELSON, Hugh Lawrence
BUNN, Thomas
An operative for Albany, New York's Mackelroy Agency, **John Thomas Ross** is a PI in the Lew Archer mold, as the title indicates. The jacket claims the book to be "a fast-paced, witty and sophisticated detective thriller that introduces the most engaging private eye since Sam Spade. John Thomas Ross is unflappable, savvy and consummately droll." Unfortunately Bunn was given to creating idiosyncratic, and totally artificial, speech patterns for every character.

> Closet Bones (1977)

Burgess, Barney — QUEEN, Ellery
Burke — VACHSS, Andrew
BURKE, Jackson F.
Black, bald and fortyish, **Samuel Moses Kelly** is an ex-cop, part-time private eye and house dick of the Hotel Castelreagh, Verdi Square, on Manhattan's Upper West Side. Kelly is a snappy dresser with a Siamese cat called Baudelaire and a beautiful blonde ladyfriend who runs the city's most elegant cathouse across the road. New York is an essential part of his medium-boiled, evocative, funny and chilling adventures.

> Location Shots* (1974, UK 1974)
> Death Trick (1975, UK 1976)
> Kelly Among The Nightingales (1979)

BURKE, Richard
In the first three books, all ex-cop **Quinny Hite**, bounced from the NYPD Homicide Squad for arresting someone with political clout, now "Times Square's own sleuth," with a room in the Hotel du Nord, wants to do is marry his girlfriend Joan but he keeps being frustrated by murders and eventually she gives up. Influenced by the hardboiled without being hardboiled in any way. See **Films: DRESSED TO KILL**.

> The Dead Take No Bows (1941) >

      Chinese Red (1942)
      Here Lies The Body (1942)
      The Fourth Star (1946)
      Sinister Street (1948)

BURNS, Charles

With a robotic head atop the body and garb of a pro wrestler, comic book character **El Borbah** features in a collected series of spoofy, up-dated cases, dealing with bizarre characters in classic down on his luck, hardboiled gumshoe fashion.

      Hardboiled Defective Stories (1988)

Burns, Joe — JAFFE, Michael

BURNS, Rex (Raoul Stephen Sehler)

The creator of the Gabe Wager procedurals has added Stanford Law School drop-out, ex-secret service man **Devlin Kirk**, 28, to his Denver repertoire. Partner in an industrial security firm, Kirk is a technical expert but solves his first case, in Charles WILLEFORD's words, "by looking into the human heart," also learning about himself. *Drood Review* was disappointed by lack of detection, a solution that "sinks to the nadir of mystery writing" (a written confession), a stereotyped love life and a hero ten years too young to fit the personal history Burns has given him.

      Suicide Season (1987)

Burroughs, Julian — MURPHY, Warren

BUSBY, Roger & Gerald HOLTHAM

Described by Hubin as standard PI fare with a British accent, redeemed by persuasive sequences among the hippies. The hero is **Maxwell Daly**.

      Main Line Kill (UK 1968, 1968)

BUTLER, John K.

A former playboy whose father lost everything in the Depression, Steve Middleton Knight, known as **Steve Midnight**, supports his mother and sister by driving for the Red Owl Cab Company of LA. By circumstance he acts as a PI, his tenacity making him a natural. Highly regarded for plotting, characterization and detail, Butler's eight Midnight stories have never appeared in book form and only "The Saint In Silver." (*Dime Detective* 1941; A6) is available.

Butler, Morgan — ANTHONY, David

BYERS, Charles Alma

Summoned to Thor Castle, Hollywood, to guard a client who has received mysterious threats and had guard dogs die from no obvious cause, **Warren Bayne** is not enlightened as to the reasons. *NYT* commented "The author has seen fit to employ several of the outworn devices of early mystery fiction, but he has not succeeded in adding any new twists to them or in making them either interesting or convincing."

  The Inverness Murders (1935)

BYRD, Max

Though showing influences both of Chandler and Robert B. Parker, Byrd's books about transplanted Bostonian **Mike Haller**, operating in an edgy, violent and sleazy San Francisco, with an office on Market Street, are among the best of the contemporary California crop, particularly well received in Britain and the first won him an MWA Best Paperback Award. All three books involve missing persons, with the second taking Haller to London, of whose geography Byrd has a somewhat shaky grasp. Haller is a tough, wisecracking eye with a code that's "some inscrutable combination of New England Puritan and bleeding heart."

  California Thriller* (1981, UK 1984)

  Fly Away, Jill (1983, UK 1984)

  Finders Weepers (1983, UK 1985)

Cabot, Philip — McDOUGALD, Roman

Cadee, Don — DEAN, SPENCER

Cage, Benjamin Franklin — ISRAEL, Peter

Cage, Huntingdon — RIEFE, Alan

CAGNEY, Peter = WINTER, Bevis

More of Winter's competent, derivative, lightweight and humorless ersatz (see also **Al BOCCA**), this time featuring PI **Mike Strang**. Boucher, though only mildly critical, commented that *Hear The Stripper Scream* "reaches a new high in completely irrelevent titles."

  No Diamonds For A Doll (UK 1960, 1961)

  Hear The Stripper Scream (UK 1960, 1962)

  A Grave For Madam (1961)

CAIN, Paul

The author of the legendary *Fast One*, described by Chandler as "some kind of high point in the ultra hardboiled manner," wrote 17 stories for *Black Mask*, seven of which make up his only other book. "Murder Done In Blue" (1933; in **A11** as "Gundown") featured married ex-stuntman **Johnny Doolin**, who goes out looking for PI work rather than waiting for it to come to him; **Black**, the narrator of "Black" (1932), is a tough PI from St. Paul; an unnamed Chicago agency operative, somewhat like Hammett's, features in "One-Two-Three" (1933) and former judge turned "extra-legal attorney" **Druse** in "Pigeon Blood" (1933). See **Films: GRAND CENTRAL MURDER**.

  Seven Slayers (1946). Seven SS

CAINE, Hamilton T. = SMOKE, Stephen
Former professional guitarist turned LA PI, **Ace Carpenter** is the Lew Archer-like, Stolichnaya-drinking creation of *Mystery Magazine*'s editor.
  Carpenter, Detective (1980)
  Hollywood Heroes (1986)
Caine, Nick — ZOCHERT, Donald
CAKE, Patrick = WELCH, Timothy
Name under which Welch published the second of two books about **Dion Quince**, undercover PI, a "photo fiction" larded with actual, though irrelevant, pictures of the Bing Crosby National Pro-Am golf tournament.
  The Pro-Am Murders (1979)
Calder, David — PAGE, Marco
Calder, Keith — HAMMOND, Gerald
Calhoun, Barney — DEMING, Richard
Calhoun, Burt — DICKINSON, Weed
Calhoun, Cal — TV: BOURBON STREET BEAT
CALIN, Hal Jason
One of the best educated, most intellectual of all PIs, New Yorker **Edwin Green** travels to Paris and Monaco in his one adventure which, while well-told, has a derivative *Maltese Falcon* treasure hunt plot and ends with virtually everybody in the story, Green and the police apart, dead.
  Rocks And Ruin (1954); as Payoff In Blood (1955)
Callaghan, Slim — CHEYNEY, Peter
Callahan, Brock — GAULT, William Campbell
Callahan, Mike — Films: WORLD FOR RANSOM
Callender, Sam — TV: The CATCHER
Calso, Willy — TV: The GREAT ICE RIP-OFF
Cambert, Harry — McGOWN, Jill
Camelot, Charles — ISRAEL, Peter
CAMERON, Lou
Novelization of **TV: The OUTSIDER** featuring **David Ross**.
  The Outsider (1969)
CAMP, Joe
Novelization by the director of a children's film with adult humor. **Benjamin Browning** is a PI who reincarnates as a dog and investigates his own murder. See **Films: OH HEAVENLY DOG**.
  Oh Heavenly Dog (1980)
CAMPBELL, Harriette R.
An eccentric private detective, created by an American who lived, and set her books, in England. **Simon Brade** dislikes the work but knows no

other way of financing a passion for rare ceramics. His main eccentricity is a game he plays with little Chinese ivory cubes which give him the answers to each case. As *NYT* point out, it's easy to get tired of them.

The String Glove Mystery (1936, UK 1936)

The Porcelain Fish Mystery (1937); as The Porcelain Fish (UK 1937)

The Moor Fires Mystery (UK 1938, 1939)

Three Names For Murder (1940, UK 1940)

Murder Set To Music (1941)

Magic Makes Murder (1943)

Crime In Crystal (1946)

CAMPBELL, Hazel

An odd-sounding British novel in which **Olga Knaresbrook**, bored with small-town life, sets up as a private detective. Eventually her Watson, **Molly Kingsley**, actually a private investigator posing as a reporter, reveals that Knaresbrook, a drug addict, is herself committing the crimes she then pretends to detect. Discussed at length by Klein.

Olga Knaresbrook: Detective (UK 1933)

Campbell, Humphrey — HOMES, Geoffrey

Campbell, Pat — COLTER, Eli

CAMPBELL, Robert

Drood Review, no faint hearts, found the debût of down on his luck, likable and realistic LA PI **Whistler**, well written but "nothing can compensate for its subject matter and language . . . brutal descriptions of child pornography, sex and murder . . . If you have a strong stomach, and aren't offended by the worst types of violence towards children and women, this book is for you." Very stylish and very gruesome, though hardly to the extent *DR* implies. A near-PI is **Jake Hatch**, plainclothes railroad cop for the Burlington Northern, operating out of Omaha. *Rue Morgue* found Campbell faulty on Colorado geography and atmosphere. Campbell contributed a **Philip Marlowe** short story, "Mice," to **A12**.

Whistler: In La-La Land We Trust (1986, UK 1987)

Alice In La-La Land (1987, UK 1988)

Hatch: Plugged Nickel (1988)

Red Cent (1989)

Campbell, Sam — Films: CRIME BY NIGHT

Canilli, Bill — PETERS, Bill

CANNING, Victor 1911-1986

Best known for spy novels, Canning had at least three PIs. Shabby **Edward Mercer** goes to Italy to find a man; both Boucher and *SR* admired the evocation of Venice, *SR* adding "not a phony word or character anywhere." **Rex Carver**, of Carver & Wilkins, near Trafalgar Square, London, works both for himself and British Intelligence, often getting involved in international shenanigans. Placid, humdrum, impassive **James Helder** seems to be wooden and slow-thinking but is dead-straight and efficient. His card carries only an unlisted phone number and if he doesn't like a job or a client, wild horses won't budge him.

Mercer: Venetian Bird (UK 1951); as Bird Of Prey (UK 1951)
Carver: The Whip Hand (UK 1965, 1965)
           Doubled In Diamonds (UK 1966, 1967)
           The Python Project (UK 1967, 1968)
           The Melting Man (UK 1968, 1969)
Helder: A Fall From Grace* (UK 1980, 1981)

CANNON, Curt = McBAIN, Ed

Evan Hunter wrote one PI novel as **Ed McBAIN**, not near as good and tough as two as and about **Curt Cannon**, once the best licensed PI in New York, who became a derelict alcoholic after finding his wife and best friend in bed together and losing his license because of an ensuing assault with a deadly weapon charge (he pistol-whipped them). However, he is still capable of functioning effectively when required.

       I'm Cannon For Hire (1958)
       I Like 'Em Tough (1958). SS.

Cannon, Frank — TV: CANNON
Cantini, Angel — EVERSZ, Robert
Cantrell, Roman — CHASE, Elaine Raco
Canuck, Johnny — MOFFATT, James
Carbo — QUARTERMAIN, James
Card, C. — BRAUTIGAN Richard
Card, James — LYALL, Gavin
Cardby, Mick — HUME, David
Cardigan, Steve — NEBEL, Frederick
Cardula — RITCHIE, Jack
Carlin, Race — GRIBBLE, Leonard
CARLO, Philip

Jogging Manhattan PI **Frank De Nardo**, of West 87th Street, off Central Park West, has an advantage in tracking down a girl kidnaped in Italy who turns up in a kiddie-porn magazine—Mafia connections. Carlo's sincere hatred of that disgusting trade does not however offset clumsy dialogue and crude plot devices.

       Stolen Flower (1988)

CARLTON, Mitchell
Still limping from an Army training accident that left him with a steel splint in his leg, slum kid **Pat Doyle** dropped out of law school after two years to become a NYC PI. An old girl friend brings him to Dallas to investigate a multi-million dollar crude oil theft.
Hot Oil (1980)
Carlyle, Carlotta — BARNES, Linda
Carmady, Ted — CHANDLER, Raymond
Carmichael, Casey — DATESH, John Nicholas
CARMICHAEL, Harry (Leopold Horace Ognall 1908-1979)
If he was just an insurance assessor, **John Piper** would not be listed here and probably could not have featured in so many novels. A perfect gentleman, Piper, who occasionally hired out as a proper PI, often teamed with brash, obnoxious, boozy reporter Quinn, who gradually became the main detective, in late Golden Age stories of ratiocination, noteworthy for their pessimistic view of marriage, which usually provided the plotline. See also **Hartley HOWARD**. Under these two names, Carmichael is, after Carter Brown, the most prolific author listed here.
Death Leaves A Diary (UK 1952)
The Vanishing Track (UK 1952)
Deadly Night-Cap (UK 1953)
School For Murder (UK 1953)
Death Counts Three (UK 1954); as The Screaming Rabbit (1955)
Why Kill Johnny? (UK 1954)
Noose For A Lady (UK 1955)
Money For Murder (UK 1955)
Justice Enough (UK 1956)
The Dead Of Night (UK 1956)
Emergency Exit (UK 1957)
Put Out That Star (UK 1957); as Into Thin Air (1958)
James Knowland, Deceased (UK 1958)
. . . Or Be He Dead (1958, UK 1959)
Stranglehold (UK 1959); as Marked Man (1959)
The Seeds Of Hate (UK 1959)
Requiem For Charles (UK 1960); as The Late Unlamented (1961)
Alibi (UK 1961, 1962)
The Link (UK 1962)
Of Unsound Mind (UK 1962, 1962) >

Vendetta (UK 1963, 1963)
Flashback (UK 1964)
Safe Secret (UK 1964, 1965)
Post Mortem (UK 1965, 1966)
Suicide Clause (UK 1966)
Murder By Proxy (UK 1967)
Remote Control (UK 1970, 1971)
Death Trap (UK 1970, 1971)
Most Deadly Hate (UK 1971, 1974)
The Quiet Woman (UK 1971, 1972)
Naked To The Grave (UK 1972, 1973)
Too Late For Tears (UK 1973, 1975)
Candles For The Dead (UK 1973, 1976)
The Motive (UK 1974, 1977)
False Evidence (UK 1976, 1977)
A Grave For Two (UK 1977)
Life Cycle (UK 1978)

Carner, Mary — POPKIN, Zelda
Carpenter, Ace — CAINE, Hamilton
CARPENTER, Helen & Lorri
Mother and daughter writing team whose short story, "The Disappearing Diamond" (A21), features septuagenarian **Emma Twiggs** who assists, or, as her PI nephew **James Galveston**, has it, intervenes in cases, on this occasion showing him up. They are working on a Twiggs novel.

CARR, Joseph B.
A fat, jovial man who loves eating, **Oceala Archer** enjoys the confidence of the police to such an extent that they let him conduct cases pretty much as he pleases. *NYT* commented of the first, Massachusetts-set, book "well told with a plenitude of thrills and considerable humor, but there is a little too much of the secret-passage stuff."

Death Whispers (1933, UK 1933)
The Man With Bated Breath (1934, UK 1935)

CARR, Kirby = PLATT, Kin
Though a cool, suave investigator by day, a clutch of paperbacks were more concerned with **Mike Ross'** other, night-time, persona, when he wheeled out his "war wagon" and became The Hitman in an action series that was minor even compared to other trashomatic he-man psychopaths.

The Girls Who Came To Murder (1974)
Let Me Kill You Sweetheart! (1974)
Who Killed You, Cindy Castle? (1974) >

You Die Next, Jill Baby! (1975)
You're Hired; You're Dead (1975)
Don't Bet On Living, Alice! (1975)
They're Coming To Kill You, Jane! (1975)
Carr, Owen — WALKER, Walter
Carromond, Steve — Films: BERMUDA MYSTERY
CARSON, Robert 1909-1983
Thomas CHASTAIN found this novel about LA investigators **Warren Hearst** and **Harry Herbold**, "one of the most—if not the most—fascinating private eye novels ever written." Revolving round a double indemnity insurance policy, it is more procedural mystery than hardboiled story with two skip-tracers who are neither prescient or two-fisted but just trying to make a living.
The Quality Of Mercy (1954, UK 1955)
Carstairs — DAVIS, Norbert
Carter, Ken — PAGE, Norvell
Carter, Maxwell — Films: SECRET FILE; HOLLYWOOD
Caruso, Michael — BECK, K.K.
Carvalho, Pepe — MONTALBAN, Manuel Vasquez
Carver, Bruce — ALLAN, Dennis
Carver, Fred — LUTZ, John
Carver, Rex — CANNING, Victor
Case, Charlie — SPENCER, John
Casey, Al — TV: KING OF DIAMONDS
Casey, Jack — COXE, George Harmon
Cash, Steve — FRANCIS, William
Cashin, Carrie — TINSLEY, Theodore
Cassella, Tony — BEINHART, Larry
CASSIDAY, Bruce
New Yorker **Johnny Midas** is reputed the best skiptracer in the business. Hubin lists other novels but does not specify whether they feature Midas. Cassiday also wrote two books about **Cash Madigan**, a bonding investigator of the rough-tough-sexy school, commended by Boucher for showing some originality.
Midas: The Brass Shroud (1956)
Madigan: The Buried Motive (1957)
                 While Murder Waits (1957)
Cassidy, Lew — MAXWELL, Thomas
CASTLE, Frank
Novelization of TV: HAWAIIAN EYE featuring Hawaii-based PIs

Tom Lopaka, Tracy Steele and Greg MacKenzie.
>   Hawaiian Eye (1962)
CASTLE, Jayne
One of a fairly recent spate of romance novels in which the heroine, in this instance **Guinevere Jones** of Camelot Investigations, Seattle, is supposed to be a PI. The love interest is tall, dark and handsome PI **Zachariah Justis**. The names alone give an idea of the shallowness.
>   The Desperate Game (1986)
>   The Chilling Deception (1988)
Cat, Thomas Hewitt Edward — TV: T.H.E. CAT
Cates, Sam — ERNST, Paul
Caul, Harry — Films: The CONVERSATION
Cavanaugh, Mike — O'MALLEY, Frank
Cervantes, Antonio — COOK, Bruce
CHABER, M.E. (Ken Crossen 1910-1981)
Mixed series about tall, dark and handsome **Milo March**, a WW2 OSS officer and former CIA man who, licensed as a PI, works as an insurance investigator, first for Intercontinental Insurance then with his own company. Based first in Denver, he moves to New York during the series, but travels a good deal, being frequently recalled to the colors by his old CIA boss. As a result, rather confusingly, some of the books are straight PI yarns, others are espionage thrillers. Either way they are written to a sound formula, fast, jokey and entertaining. See **Richard FOSTER** and **Christopher MONIG** and **Films: The MAN INSIDE.**
>   Hangman's Harvest (1952); as Don't Get Caught (1953)
>   No Grave For March (1953, UK 1954); as All The Way Down
>   (1953)
>   As Old As Cain (1954); as Take One For Murder (1955)
>   The Man Inside (1954, UK 1955); as Now It's My Turn (1954)
>   The Splintered Man* (1955, UK 1957)
>   A Lonely Walk (1956, UK 1957)
>   The Gallows Garden (1958, UK 1958); as The Lady Came To
>   Kill (1959)
>   A Hearse Of Another Color (1958, UK 1959)
>   So Dead The Rose (1959, UK 1960)
>   Jade For A Lady (1962, UK 1962)
>   Softly In The Night (1963, UK 1963)
>   Six Who Ran (1964, UK 1965)
>   Uneasy Lies The Dead (1964, UK 1964)
>   Wanted: Dead Men (1965, UK 1966) >

> The Day It Rained Diamonds (1966, UK 1968)
> A Man In The Middle (1967)
> Wild Midnight Falls (1968)
> The Flaming Man (1969, UK 1970)
> Green Grow The Graves (1970, UK 1971)
> The Bonded Dead (1971, UK 1973)
> Born To Be Hanged (1973)

Chadwick, John — COBDEN, Guy
CHADWICK, Paul
Best known for *Secret Agent X*, Chadwick created, according to Garyn G.
Roberts, "one of the most popular, enduring characters ever to come from
a Wyn magazine." **Wade Hammond** was "a sort of Sam Spade/Richard
Wentworth (aka the Spider) conglomerate" featured in "Fangs Of The
Cobra" (*Ten Detective Aces* 1933; **A18**).
Challis, Bart — NOLAN, William F.
Challis, Nick — NOLAN, William F.
Chambers, Peter — KANE, Henry
CHAMBERS, Peter (Dennis Phillips)
British author Phillips, who annoyed Henry Kane and Boucher by using
the name of Kane's PI as a pseudonym, writes straight Chandler
imitations featuring **Mark Preston**, a "Monkton City," California, PI,
deliberately old-fashioned in terms of plots, violence and sex. Barzun &
Taylor commended him to "fastidious readers," which says it all.
Pointless and tedious to list. See also **Peter CHESTER**.

> Murder Is For Keeps (UK 1961, 1962)
> The Big Goodbye (UK 1962)
> Wreath For A Redhead (UK 1962, 1962)
> Down-Beat Kill (UK 1963, 1964)
> Lady, This Is Murder (UK 1963)
> Dames Can Be Deadly (UK 1963, 1963)
> Nobody Lives Forever (UK 1964)
> This'll Kill You (UK 1964)
> Always Take The Big Ones (UK 1965)
> You're Better Off Dead (1965)
> Don't Bother To Knock (UK 1966)
> No Gold When You Go (UK 1966)
> The Bad Die Young (UK 1967, 1968)
> The Blonde Wore Black (UK 1968, 1968)
> No Peace For The Wicked (1968, 1968)
> Speak Ill Of The Dead (UK 1968, 1968) >

They Call It Murder (UK 1973)
Somebody Has To Lose (UK 1975)
The Day Of The Big Dollar (UK 1979)
The Deader They Fall (UK 1979)
The Deep Blue Cradle (UK 1980)
Nothing Personal (UK 1980)
Beautiful Golden Frame (UK 1980)
Female—Handle With Care (UK 1981)
The Lady Who Never Was (UK 1981)
A Long Time Dead (UK 1981)
Murder Is Its Own Reward (UK 1982)
The Highly Explosive Case (UK 1982)
Dragons Can Be Dangerous (UK 1983)
Jail Bait (UK 1983)
Moving Picture Writes (UK 1984)
The Vanishing Holes Murder (UK 1985)

CHAMBERS, Whitman
NYT came up with a 30s reviewing gem when talking about private
detective **Simon Lake**, whose "real errand in the Raybourne household
provides some entertaining episodes in which the detective acquits himself
more creditably than one would expect of a man of his type." *SR* found a
novel featuring PI **Pierre O'Brien** "suavely hard-boiled with neat twists
to rather translucent plot, staccato dialogue and hair-trigger action." See
Films: MANHANDLED.
Lake: Dead Men Leave No Fingerprints (1935, UK 1935)
O'Brien: Dog Eat Dog (1938); as Murder In The Mist (UK 1938)
Champion, Kyle — ADAMS, Harold
Chandler — STERANKO
Chandler — Films: CHANDLER
CHANDLER, A. Bertram
Spaceman John Petersen, hero of the SF writer's Rim World series,
marooned on Carinthia, is recruited by local PI **Stefan Vynalek** in the
2nd volume. Carinthia was colonized by Czechs and Vynalek's ultra-high-
tech office is in the Heinlein Building, Masaryk Square, New Prague.
         Bring Back Yesterday (1961, UK 1981)
CHANDLER, Raymond 1888-1959
Comment on the British educated oil company executive who turned to
writing at 45 when he lost his job seems superfluous. A slow,
painstaking writer (he took five months to write his first story, the
18,000 word "Blackmailers Don't Shoot"), Chandler was far from prolific

and regularly cannibalized his short stories (see below) to construct his novels, objecting to their reissue in their original form. The various detectives in them, whether unnamed, **Mallory**, **Ted Malvern**, **Ted Carmady**, **John Dalmas**, **John Evans**, **Pete Anglich**, **Tony Reseck** or **Steve Grayce**, all contributed to the genesis of **Philip Marlowe**, the most famous of all private eyes, role model for countless others. As Pronzini says, Chandler is "certainly the most imitated writer in the genre and, next to Hemingway, perhaps the most imitated writer in the English language." Details of the stories are given below; note that the original name of the detective is often changed to Marlowe in collections. *Unknown Thriller* is the script of an unmade film, *Playback*, which Chandler used some elements of in the novel of the same title. Sandoe was embarrassed by the "awful cuteness" of *Farewell, My Lovely*, which Pronzini & Muller regard as a cornerstone work. Chandler spent some unhappy years in Hollywood, writing, among others, screenplays for *Double Indemnity* and *The Blue Dahlia*. His own books have had a very mixed run, starting strong and fading; see **Films: The FALCON TAKES OVER / TIME TO KILL / MURDER, MY SWEET / The BIG SLEEP** (1946 & 1978) **/ The LADY IN THE LAKE / The BRASHER DOUBLOON / MARLOWE / The LONG GOODBYE / FAREWELL, MY LOVELY**. See also **TV: The LONG GOODBYE / PHILIP MARLOWE / PHILIP MARLOWE, PRIVATE EYE, Radio: The ADVENTURES OF PHILIP MARLOWE** and **A11** for a centenary collection of Marlowe stories by various authors.

> The Big Sleep* (1939, UK 1939)
> Farewell, My Lovely* (1940, UK 1940)
> The High Window (1942, UK 1943)
> The Lady In The Lake* (1943, UK 1944)
> Five Murderers (1944). 5M
> Five Sinister Characters (1945). 5SC
> Fingerman And Other Stories (1946). FM
> Red Wind (1946). RW
> Spanish Blood (1946). SB
> The Little Sister (UK 1949, 1949); as Marlowe (1969)
> The Simple Art Of Murder* (1950, UK 1950); in 3 vols as Trouble Is My Business (1951), Pick-Up On Noon Street (1952), The Simple Art Of Murder (1953). 12 SS & an essay. SAM (TIMB/PNS/SAM)
> The Long Goodbye* (UK 1953, 1954) >

Smart-Aleck Kill (UK 1953). SS
Pearls Are A Nuisance (UK 1953). SS
Playback (UK 1958, 1958)
Raymond Chandler Speaking (1962). Contains the unfinished
  novel Poodle Springs
Killer In The Rain (1964, UK 1964). KR
The Smell Of Fear (UK 1965). SoF
The Midnight Raymond Chandler (1971)
Playback (1985, UK 1985). Screenplay
Unknown Thriller (1987)

CHANDLER, Raymond — The Short Stories

Mallory

"Blackmailers Don't Shoot" (*Black Mask* 1933) — 5M/RW/A11
"Smart-Aleck Kill" (*Black Mask* 1934) — FM/SAM (PNS)

Unnamed

"Finger Man" (*Black Mask* 1934) — FM/SAM (TIMB)
"Killer In The Rain" (*Black Mask* 1935) — KR/used in *The Big Sleep*
"Red Wind" (*Dime Detective* 1937) — 5SC/RW/SAM (TIMB)

Ted Malvern

"Guns At Cyrano's" (*Black Mask* 1936) — 5M/SAM (PNS)

Ted Carmady

"The Man Who Liked Dogs" (*Black Mask* 1936) — KR/A20/used in
  Farewell, My Lovely
"Goldfish" (*Black Mask* 1936) — 5M/RW/SAM (TIMB)/A19
"The Curtain" (*Black Mask* 1936) — KR/used in *The Big Sleep*
"Try The Girl" (*Black Mask* 1937) — KR/used in *Farewell, My Lovely*

Pete Anglich

"Noon Street Nemesis" (*Detective Fiction Weekly* 1936) — SAM (PNS)
  as "Pick-Up On Noon Street"

Johnny Dalmas

"Mandarin's Jade" (*Dime Detective* 1937) — KR/used in *Farewell, My
  Lovely*
"Bay City Blues" (*Dime Detective* 1938) — KR/used in *The Lady In
  The Lake*
"Trouble Is My Business" (*Dime Detective* 1939) — 5SC/SAM (TIMB)
  /A9
"The Lady In The Lake" (*Dime Detective* 1939) — KR/used in *The
  Lady In The Lake*

Steve Grayce

"The King In Yellow" (*Dime Detective* 1938) — SAM (SAM) >

Tony Reseck
"I'll Be Waiting" (*Saturday Evening Post* 1939) — RW
John Evans
"No Crime In The Mountains" (*Detective Story* 1941) — KR/used in
　　The Lady In The Lake
Philip Marlowe
"Marlowe Takes On The Syndicate" (*London Daily Mail* 1959) as
　　"Wrong Pigeon" (*Manhunt* 1961) A14 — SoF/A12 as "The
　　Pencil"
Chandler, Raymond — DENBOW, Richard / LARSEN,
　　Gaylord
Chaney, Ace — GARRISON, Christian
CHANSLOR, Roy 1899-1964
Hired to keep tabs on a woman, close-mouthed PI **Storm** falls in love
with her in a cheerful, wise-cracking screwball romance-mystery, described
by Edward D. HOCH as "first rate." See **Films: HAZARD.**
　　　　Hazard (1947)
CHANSLOR, (Marjorie) Torrey
Elderly, eccentric, but lively New England spinsters **Lutie** and **Amanda
Beagle** inherit their brother's business, The Beagle Detective Agency, of
New York, and, from a spirit of adventure (Lutie) and sense of obligation
(Amanda), take it over. Noteworthy as Klein points out, for being, the
first functioning all female partnership in private detective fiction, though
not, as she claims, the only one. She herself wrote at length about Nancy
SPAIN's Birdseye et Cie.
　　　　Our First Murder (1940)
　　　　Our Second Murder (1941)
Charles, Nick & Nora — HAMMETT, Dashiell
Charleston, Dick & Dora — Films: MURDER BY DEATH
Charlie's Angels — FRANKLIN, Max
Chase, Dennis — TV: 21 BEACON STREET
CHASE, Elaine Raco
A romance writer, Chase's first mystery novels is a love story as much as
a PI tale. Former soldier of fortune, Nebraska born **Roman Cantrell**
got into the business by tracking down his runaway younger brother and
has a 93% success rate finding missing persons. Based in Miami, he has
branch offices in Atlanta, LA and Manhattan. The rather overblown plot
is dominated by his spiky relationship with a tough female reporter.
　　　　Dangerous Places (1987)
　　　　Dark Corners (1988)

CHASE, James Hadley (Rene Brabazon Raymond 1906-1985)
Using encyclopedias, street maps and slang dictionaries, the British author wrote some 80 books set in an America he visited infrequently. A book wholesaler, he devised a formula based on knowledge of public demand, and, while phony, he can be fast-paced, intricate, colorful and hardboiled, though Boucher's contempt for him was almost total. **Dave Fenner** is a crime reporter turned PI, **Vic Malloy** an Orchid City, California PI. Other Chase PIs almost certainly exist but the only identities to hand are **Steve Harmas, Floyd Jackson** and the much later **Dirk Wallace**, operative of the Acme Detective Agency, Paradise City, Florida. See also **Raymond MARSHALL and Films: NO ORCHIDS FOR MISS BLANDISH / The GRISSOM GANG.**

Fenner: No Orchids For Miss Blandish* (UK 1939, 1942; rev. ed.
              UK 1961, 1961); as The Villain And The Virgin (1948)
              Twelve Chinks And A Woman (UK 1940, 1941); rev. ed. as
                 12 Chinamen And A Woman (UK 1950); as The Doll's
                 Bad News (1970)
Malloy: You're Lonely When You're Dead (UK 1949, 1950)
              Figure It Out For Yourself (UK 1950, 1951); as The
              Marijuana Mob (1952)
              Lay Her Among The Lilies (UK 1950); as Too Dangerous
              To Be Free (1951)
Jackson: You Never Know With Women (UK 1949, 1972)
Harmas: The Double Shuffle (UK 1952, 1953)
              There's Always A Price Tag (UK 1956, 1973)
              Shock Treatment (UK 1959, 1959)
              Tell It To The Birds (UK 1963, 1974)
Wallace: Hit Them Where It Hurts (1984)

CHASTAIN, Thomas
Best known for his guess-the-killer novelty work *Who Killed The Robbins Family?*, Chastain has a New York PI, **J.T. 'Jake' Spanner**, both of whose ex-wives work for him. Bizarre and deftly wrought plots are a major feature.

              Pandora's Box (1974, UK 1975)
              Vital Statistics (1977)
              High Voltage (1979, UK 1980)

CHESBRO, George
The most obvious distinguishing feature of **Dr. Robert 'Mongo' Frederickson** is that he is a dwarf. He is also a NYU professor of criminology, once a starring circus artist, a karate black belt and a licensed

PI practicing, of course, in New York where his normal sized brother is a cop. Psychic powers, witchcraft and international intrigue are common themes in a rather eccentric series that charms some, annoys others. A Mongo story, "Candala," appeared in **A17**.

> Shadow Of A Broken Man* (1977, UK 1981)
> City Of Whispering Stone (1978, UK 1981)
> An Affair Of Sorcerers (1979, UK 1980)
> The Beasts Of Valhalla (1985, UK 1986)
> Two Songs This Archangel Sings (1986)
> The Cold Smell Of Sacred Stone (1988)

CHESTER, Peter = CHAMBERS, Peter

Boucher described the title about an American PI, **Johnny Preston**, in London, as a routine toughie "written and plotted with the gentle competence of a minor British writer" and "surprisingly readable." That about **Johnny Vincent**, after some editorializing on the oddity of writers pretending to be of some other nationality when the smallest slip will show them up, as lightweight and moderately competent. There are three other titles, not published in the USA, listed in Hubin which may also be Preston or Vincent stories.

Preston: Killing Comes Easy (UK 1958, 1959)
Vincent: Murder Forestalled (UK 1960, 1961)

CHETWYND, Bridget

Klein's verdict on the British mismatch of silly, "Had-I-But-Known" **Petunia Best** and sensible **Max Freund** is "no one could be more ridiculous . . . their questioning is amateurish; their deduction or ratiocination limited or weak; and their charm insufficient."

> Death Has Ten Thousand Doors (UK 1951)
> Rubies, Emeralds And Diamonds (UK 1952)

CHEYNEY, Peter 1896-1951

Best known for his zany, Bellem-like novels about FBI-man Lemmy Caution, Cheney also wrote spare, effective, ersatz-Hammett books mostly about **Slim Callaghan**, which drew on journalistic knowledge and experience of London gambling clubs and crime. Jaguar-driving **Johnny Vallon** runs London's Chennault Investigations of Regent Street. Other detectives are **Nicholas Gale**, **Terence O'Day**, **Nick Bellamy** and **Cary Wylde O'Hara**. Cheyney, though he only visited America only once, late in his life, was a British pioneer in adopting American styles in their entirety, by legend as the result of a £5 bet that he could write an imitation, and still enjoys slightly grudging critical respect, though Boucher, who admired the later 'Dark' espionage novels, was constantly amazed by his reputation, particularly in France, as a master of the hardboiled, and enormous sales. There are many collections of Cheyney's short stories which may contain additional material. See **Films: CALLING MR. CALLAGHAN** and **Radio: The CALLAGHAN TOUCH.**

Callaghan: The Urgent Hangman (UK 1938, 1939)
              Dangerous Curves (UK 1939); as Callaghan (1973)
              You Can't Keep The Change (UK 1940, 1944)
              Mr. Caution—Mr. Callaghan (UK 1941). SS
              It Couldn't Matter Less (UK 1941, 1943); as Set-Up For
                  Murder (1950)
              Sorry You've Been Troubled (UK 1942); as Farewell To The
                  Admiral (1943)
              The Unscrupulous Mr. Callaghan (1943)
              They Never Say When (UK 1944, 1945)
              Uneasy Terms (UK 1946, 1947)
              Calling Mr. Callaghan (UK 1953). SS
              G Man At The Yard (UK 1953). Some Callaghan SS
Vallon: You Can Call It A Day (UK 1949); as The Man Nobody
                  Saw (1949)
              Lady, Behave! (UK 1950); as Lady Beware (1950)
              Dark Bahama (UK 1950, 1951); as I'll Bring Her Back
                  (1952)
O'Day: One Of Those Things (UK 1949, 1950); as Mistress Murder
                  (1951)
Wylde: Dance Without Music (UK 1947, 1948)
Gale: Try Anything Twice (UK 1948, 1948); as Undressed To Kill
                  (1959)
Bellamy: Another Little Drink (UK 1940); as A Trap For Bellamy
                  (1941); as Premeditated Murder (1943)

CHRISTOPHER, Constance
"A NY PI discovers the nude body of a young Oriental girl while jogging in the park; her investigation leads her to a child prostitution ring operating out of a wealthy family's residence" (*Drood Review* preview).
        Dead Man's Flower (1988)
Church, Harvey — KLEIN, Norman
CHURCH, John Cabell
Author of a story in A2 #3, "Road Kill," about an unnamed PI, just fired by Mid West Security & Investigations, meeting trouble while driving through the Deep South.

CHUTE, Verne
Caught in a frame, **Rocky Nevins** leaves San Francisco ahead of the
police and, after washing dishes in an LA beanery, is hired via a lawyer
friend in a case notable for ultra-fast switching of scene and action. Will
Cuppy remarked that "Rocky's boudoir adventures seem to be the main
return on your investment" and *SR* that "several uninhibited dames (add)
pugency to eventful if confused proceedings."
> Wayward Angel (1948); as Blackmail (UK 1951)

Cinquez, Joe — MASON, Clifford
Clancy, Mike — ROSTEN, Leo
CLAPPERTON, Richard
Observing that Sydney, Australia PI **Peter Fleck**, who "staggers from
beating to bullet wound to lights out," wasn't so much hardboiled as
resiliant, Boucher considered the first book improbable, "but Mr.
Clapperton's tongue-in-cheek style makes his concotion quite palatable."
Victims Unknown (UK 1970) may be another Fleck title.
> No News On Monday (UK 1968); as You're A Long Time Dead
> (1968)
> The Sentimental Kill (UK 1976)

Clare, Andrew — ROBINSON, David
Clark, Ben — Radio: SECRET CITY
CLARK, Dale (Ronal Kayser)
Returning home to Camino City after four years in the Army, PI
Gillian Baltic finds that there have been many changes, all for the
worse, and that he's persona non grata with the police, who are in the
pockets of racketeers, when he sets up in business again. Much violent
action though the plot loses coherence.
> The Red Rods (1946); as The Blonde, The Gangster And The
> Private Eye (1949)

Claw, Theodore — PARADIS, Vincent A.
Clay, George — KETCHUM, Philip
CLAYFORD, James
Publisher's house name under which a retitled reprint of a novel by
Arthur WALLACE, lampooned by Pronzini (*Gun In Cheek*),
featuring Manhattan PI **Val Vernon**, appeared.
> Man Crazy (1951); as Passion Pulls The Trigger (as by **Arthur**
> **WALLACE** 1936)

Cleary, Jack — TV: PRIVATE EYE
Clemons, Frank — COOK, Thomas H.
Clerkenwell, Mary — FREEMAN, Martin J.

Clift, Cornelius Jr. — HEATH, Eric
CLINE, Edward
Cline is working on athe official Ayn Rand biography, so it's hardly surprising that the hero of his pretentious attack on publishing, foundations, universities and the media is a complete Objectivist. Independently wealthy New York PI **Chess Hanrahan** (doesn't that forename hit the note!) has no time for modern manners or welfare. Wooden characterization and almost unbelievably stilted dialogue, or, as *Drood Review* put it, "overdone and dreadful and easy to dismiss."
>   First Prize (1988)

Clive, Donald — STAFFORD, Marjorie
Clive, Edmond — BRACKETT, Leigh
Cluer, Daniel J — FERGUSON, W.B.M.
Clutha — MONRO, Hugh
Cobb, Charlie — TV: CHARLIE COBB
Cobb, Hannibal — Radio: HANNIBAL COBB
COBB, Irvin S. 1876-1944
After retiring from the NYPD to become a Long Island chicken farmer, **Patrick Bray** gets bored and sets up as a private detective. *NYT* commented approvingly "There is no attempt on the part of the author to portray Bray as a superman. He is a good detective, better than the average sleuth in real life, but by no means infallible." Will Cuppy hailed the book as "A meaty, heartening, well-built and most ingenious item."
>   Murder Day By Day (1933, UK 1934)

Cobb, Matt — DeANDREA, William L.
COBDEN, Guy
British author of a standard UK style series about **John Chadwick** who runs a detective agency and the obligatory Jaguar which gets him into chance encounters. Not sure how he makes any money.
>   Murder Was My Neighbour (UK 1955)
>   My Guess Was Murder (UK 1956)
>   Murder Was Their Medicine (UK 1957)
>   Murder For His Money (UK 1959)
>   Murder For Her Birthday (UK 1960)
>   Murder Inherited (UK 1961)

Cody — REASONER, James
CODY, Liza
Young ex-policewoman **Anna Lee** works for Brierly Security in Kensington High Street, West London, "not big enough for banks, not cute enough for clubs and too cute for pubs," so she gets the missing

minors and scent-counter security jobs from her chauvinistic, jingoistic, all-round bigoted employer. The first book won the British Crime Writers Association John Creasey award and all have been well received for their tough, low-key approach and engaging heroine.

> Dupe* (UK 1980, 1980)
> Bad Company (UK 1982, 1983)
> Stalker (UK 1984, 1984)
> Head Case (UK 1985, 1986)
> Under Contract (UK 1986, 1987)

Coe, George — ORMEROD, Roger
COE, Tucker = WESTLAKE, Donald E.

Westlake used his own name mostly for zany caper stories often with criminal heroes, the Richard Stark hat for his super-tough, amoral Parker novels and the Coe pseudonym for his short series about **Mitch Tobin**, a character rather similar to Lawrence BLOCK's Matt Scudder. Thrown out of the NYPD for causing his partner's death, the guilt-ridden Tobin works on building a high wall round his house and as an unlicensed PI, being drawn successively into the outcast worlds of professional criminals, disaffected youth, the mentally ill and sexual deviants, and by the fifth book has come to terms with reality, is licensed and no longer obsessed by his wall.

> Kinds Of Love, Kinds Of Death (1966, UK 1967)
> Murder Among Children (1968, UK 1968)
> Wax Apple (1970, UK 1973)
> A Jade In Aries (1971, UK 1973)
> Don't Lie To Me* (1972, UK 1974)

COGGINS, Mark

The author of a short story, "There's No Such Things As Private Eyes," featuring Phoenix, Arizona PI **August Hammond**, in A1 #4, was reported there as planning to expand it into a novel.

COGGINS, Paul

Known as "Pretty Boy" in the Drug Enforcement Administration before he was fired, **Steve Dart** made his début in a Dallas underworld of drugs, dirty money, steamy sex and virtual lawlessness. The plotting is seriously flawed but the descriptions of Boston's Combat Zone and high and low life Dallas are well done.

> The Lady Is The Tiger (1987)

COHEN, Barney

MaxAmerica & Pacific, one of the Six Sisters of 2077 space travel, is so large and powerful that its Security is virtually a police force with **Asher**

Bockhorn a lowly Fleet Agent, considered too good at field work to be promoted. The SF is of the "hard" variety but so is the PI content, tough stuff in the great tradition in a believable setting with the future equivalent of a railroad detective.

>The Taking Of Satcon Station (1983, with Jim Baen)
>Blood On The Moon (1984)

COHEN, Stephen Paul

Young alcoholic **Eddie Margolis**, reformed in *Heartless* (1986), agreed to join ex-NYPD detective Charles Murphy's New York agency. Putting his life back together—the book opens on his first day at the agency—he finds, working on a big case in Murphy's absence, that he could be a real detective. Reputedly good at fast track New York, with a stunning climax and a complex, surprising hero.

>Island Of Steel (1988)

COLAN, Gene — see **McGREGOR, Don & Gene COLAN**

Colby, Al — **DODGE, David**

Cole, Elvis — **CRAIS, Robert**

COLE, G.D.H. & Margaret (1889-1959 & 1893-1980)

The prominent socio-economic historian and his wife co-authored a large number of leisurely, mediocre Golden Age novels including one in which Elizabeth Warrender second guesses her private detective son **James Warrender** who refers to her as "an incurably meddling old woman." The five novelets of *Mrs. Warrender's Profession* also appeared as pamphlets in 1945/1948.

>Mrs. Warrender's Profession (UK 1938, 1939). Five novelets
>Knife In The Dark* (UK 1941, 1942)

Cole, Marty — **GRANT, Ben**

Cole, Schyler — **DAVIS, Frederick C.**

Collins, Greg — Radio: **IT'S A CRIME, MR. COLLINS**

COLLINS, Max Allan

Collins considers PIs anachronistic, and his fact and fiction blends feature 1933 PI **Nathan 'Nate' Heller**, whose office is at Van Buren & Plymouth, Chicago. Hailed as the best historical detective novels ever written, *True Detective* winning a PWA Best Novel award, but, in my view, redundant when many fine 30s writers are all but unobtainable. Anthologized Heller short stories are "Scrap" (**A4**), "The Strawberry Teardrop" (**A14 & A15**), "House Call" (**A16**) and "Marble Mildred" (**A17**). Collins is a great admirer of Spillane and has written a study of Mike Hammer. He also contributed a **Philip Marlowe** short story, "The Perfect Crime," to **A12**. >

> True Detective* (1983, UK 1984)
> True Crime (1984)
> The Million Dollar Wound (1986)
> Neon Mirage (1988)

COLLINS, Max (Allan) & Terry BEATTY

A comic strip heroine who has made the transition to visual novel respectability, **Ms Michael Tree** (that's her own and her husband's forename) first appeared in *Eclipse* in 1981, then in a monthly comic of her own, anthologized in large format in 1985/6, finally coming out in paperback. A former policewoman and daughter of a cop (her maiden name was Friday!) she takes over her dead husband's detective agency, Tree Investigations Inc., in which she was executive secretary. The strip, full of in-jokes, has won praise from ESTLEMAN, LUTZ and KAMINSKY but never quite achieves the *film noir* look (cf STERANKO. A 1985 Ms Tree short story, as by Collins alone, "The Little Woman," is in **A5**.

> The Cold Dish (1985)
> The Files Of Ms Tree (1986)
> The Mike Mist Case Book (1986)
> Ms Tree (1988)

COLLINS, Michael (Dennis Lynds)

Lynds is best known for his Collins novels featuring one-armed, beret-and-duffle-coat-wearing drop-out **Dan Fortune** (originally Polish-Lithuanian Fortunowski) of New York's Chelsea district, 28th Street. Intricately plotted and socially conscious, their main strength is the personality of Fortune, one of the most clearly "wounded" heroes in the genre, who brings compassion, ambiguity, philosophy, intuition and complexity to the hardboiled tradition. "Collins" is particularly admired in West Germany, whose Crime Literature Society named Lynds the Best Suspense Writer of the 70s. He can be seen as a stage in the evolution of the genre, in Baker & Nietzel's words, "from the naturalistic Spade through the romantic Marlowe and the psychological Archer to the sociological Fortune." Fortune short stories are "A Reason To Die" (**A1** #2 and **A14**), "Killer's Mind" (**A1** #6), "The Motive" (**A2** #2), "Crime And Punishment" (**A2** #3), "Eight Million Dead" (**A15**), and "Black In The Snow" (**A17**). See also **William ARDEN, John CROWE, Carl DEKKER** and **Mark SADLER**.

> Act Of Fear* (1967, UK 1968)
> The Brass Rainbow (1969, UK 1970)
> Night Of The Toads (1970, UK 1972)
> Walk A Black Wind (1971, UK 1973) >

Shadow Of A Tiger (1972, UK 1974)
The Silent Scream (1973, UK 1975)
Blue Death* (1975, UK 1976)
The Blood-Red Dream (1976, UK 1977)
The Nightrunners (1978, UK 1979)
The Slasher (1980, UK 1981)
Freak (1983, UK 1983)
Minnesota Strip (1987)
Red Rosa (1988)
Castrato (1988)

Colman, Seth & Eve — PADGETT, Lewis
COLTER, Eli(zabeth)
Contemporary reviews of books featuring massive PI **Pat Campbell** are so lackluster as to give the impression of irredeemable mediocrity, *SR* remarking "commendable detecting and sufficient suspense."

The Gull Cove Murders (1944, UK 1946)
Cheer For The Dead (1947, UK 1949)

Conacher, Steve — KNIGHT, Adam
CONAWAY, Jim
Conaway had the temerity to create not just a female PI but a feminist one, with a Christopher Street office, who advertises her services in *NYT*, "for women only." With "top model" looks and, according to the cover artist, a penchant for wearing little under her trenchcoat, there's nothing anti-men about **Jana Blake**. Risible.

Deadlier Than The Male (1977)
They Do It With Mirrors (1977)

Condor, Bart — WRIGHT, Wade
Cone, Timothy — SANDERS, Lawrence
Congdon, Peter — WAUGH, Hillary
Conigliaro, Rocco — DeMARCO, Gordon
Conlon, Chris — Films: The SPIDER
Connell, Shean — TORREY, Roger
Connor, Carl — RANSOME, Stephen
Conrad, Clive — KING, Frank
Conroy, Barney — FRAY, Al
Considine, Steve — WILMOT, Robert Patrick
CONSTINER, Merle
Pulp writer represented by a single short story, "The Turkey Buzzard Blues" (*Black Mask* 1943; **A19**), featuring **Luther McGavock** of the Atherton Browne Detective Agency, Memphis, Tennessee.

CONTERIS, Hiber
With the permission of **Raymond   CHANDLER**'s estate, the
Uruguayan writer and intellectual wrote a loving pastiche with **Philip
Marlowe** investigating the alleged 1956 suicide of Chandler's literary
agent, Chandler himself being a suspect (the title is taken from Chandler's
bitter diatribe against the whole tribe of agents). The idea of a fictional PI
investigating his own creator is, admittedly a novel one.
>   Ten Percent Of Life (1987)

Continental Op, The — HAMMETT, Dashiell
Contini, Contessa Caroline di — TV: The PROTECTORS
Conway, Adam & Connie — TV: DETECTIVE'S WIFE
Conway, Jim — TV: INTO THIN AIR
COOK, Bruce
"Writes like a rebel angel and gives new voice to the poetry of the LA
private eye" says Robert B. PARKER about a cross-border drug tale
featuring Hispanic PI **Antonio 'Chico' Cervantes**, *contrabandistas*,
Federales and DEA agents.
>   Mexican Standoff (1988)

COOK, Glen
A very successful blending of two genres, PI and fantasy. Hardboiled
detective **Garrett** operates on a planet where magic works and a perpetual
inter-species war is taking place. His cases are related in a gritty, laconic,
realistic style which takes for granted such things as a girlfriend who's a
witch, a partner who has been dead for 400 years, a tough renegade half-elf
hired hand, a beautiful client who is a fairy and other fantasy elements.
>   Sweet Silver Blues (1987)
>   Bitter Gold Hearts (1988)
>   Cold Copper Tears (1988)

COOK, Thomas H.
Former Atlanta homicide detective **Frank Clemons**, moved to New
York after his partner was killed by a psycho and became a private
detective, mainly to fight boredom. *Booklist* called this novel "a
textured, brooding work about personal ethics, acceptance and, most of
all, forgiveness . . . A flawless 24-caret gem."
>   Flesh And Blood (1989)

Cool, Bertha — FAIR, A.A.
Cool, Jerry — MADDREN, Gerry
COOMBS, Murdo = DAVIS, Frederick C.
After his PI license is revoked, **Thackeray Hackett** works for a firm
that supplies information about celebrities, whom he despises and about

whom he knows more than his employers. Acid pictures of life among celebs, an interestingly hard-bitten sleuth and a grisly motive. *NYT* said "persons with queasy stomachs are advised not to read this book."

A Moment Of Need (1947)

COOPER, Will

Having let the 180,000 acre mountain valley ranch in an unnamed Western state (presumably New Mexico—it borders Mexico and Texas) his family has owned for 165 years revert to wilderness, **John T. McLaren**, not just a licensed PI but a justice of the peace and deputy sheriff, does high-priced part-time PI work to pay his taxes. Flagged as "the first in an unusual suspense series featuring an unusual detective," no more have appeared, possibly because the hero is a pompous, unengaging reactionary and the plot (saving democracy from Chicanos) ludicrous.

Death Has A Thousand Doors (1976)

Cooperman, Benny — ENGEL, Howard

Copp, Joe — PENDLETON, Don

COPPER, Basil

It is perhaps significant that the fatuous review in Reilly of this British author's LA PI series featuring **Mike Faraday** is written by an Australian, and moreover one to whom the concept of hardboiled appears new. Better known for fantasy, occult and macabre writing, Copper has written 60+ formula Faraday books with a light icing of gimmicks. Aspiring to mediocrity, they never quite achieve it.

The Dark Mirror (UK 1966)
Night Frost (UK 1966)
No Flowers For The General (UK 1967)
Scratch On The Dark (1967)
Die Now, Live Later (UK 1968)
Don't Bleed On Me (UK 1968)
The Marble Orchard (UK 1969)
Dead File (UK 1970)
No Letters From The Grave (UK 1971)
The Big Chill (UK 1972)
Strong-Arm (UK 1972)
A Great Year For Dying (UK 1973)
Shock-Wave (UK 1973)
The Breaking Point (UK 1973)
A Voice From The Dead (UK 1974)
Feedback (UK 1974)
Ricochet (UK 1974) >

The High Wall (UK 1975)
Impact (UK 1975)
A Good Place To Die (UK 1975)
The Lonely Place (UK 1976)
Crack In The Sidewalk (UK 1976)
Tight Corner (UK 1976)
The Year Of The Dragon (UK 1977)
Death Squad (UK 1977)
Murder One (UK 1978)
A Quiet Room In Hell (UK 1979)
The Big Rip-Off (UK 1979)
The Caligari Complex (UK 1980)
Flip-Side (UK 1980)
The Long Rest (UK 1981)
The Empty Silence (UK 1981)
Dark Entry (UK 1981)
Hang Loose (UK 1982)
Shoot-Out (UK 1982)
The Far Horizon (UK 1982)
Trigger-Man (UK 1983)
Pressure-Point (UK 1983)
Hard Contract (UK 1983)
The Narrow Corner (UK 1983)
The Hook (UK 1984)
You Only Die Once (UK 1984)
Tuxedo Park (UK 1985)
The Far Side Of Fear (UK 1985)
Snow Job (UK 1986)
Jet-Lag (UK 1986)
Blood On The Moon (UK 1986)
Heavy Iron (UK 1987)
Turn Down An Empty Glass (UK 1987)
House Dick (UK 1988)
Print-Out (UK 1988)

Corbo — QUARTERMAIN, James
CORDER, Eric (Jerrold Mundis)
Black Harvard graduate ex-cop **Wylie Lincoln** and tough ex-con **Russ Turner** of the Cerberus School For Dogs, 25th & 2nd, New York City, PIs as needs be and if the money is right, feature in a novel loaded with Wylie's sex life, Turner's hang-ups, attack dog lore and a complex case,

described by *NYT* as taut and well-plotted.

Reader (1975, UK 1976)

Corey, Don — TV: CHECKMATE

CORMANY, Michael

Joining Crumley's Milodragovitch in the substance-abuse stakes is pill-popping, hard-drinking Chicago ex-cop, retired after accidentally shooting a by-stander, ex-rock star PI **Dan Kruger** who doesn't carry a gun, is averse to violence and loses brawls. In his 30s, Kruger's idea of a good time is playing guitar while stoned on speed, grass or Valium. As so often with Chicago-set novels, the Windy City comes across better than most of the characters. Hardboiled with unusual twists.

Lost Daughter (1988)

Red Winter (1989)

Corrigan, Brick-Top — MARSHALL, Raymond

CORRIGAN, Mark (Norman Lee 1905-1962)

A British writer of ersatz tough Americana. The hero, also **Mark Corrigan**, from the wrong side of the tracks, served with US Army Military Intelligence in WW2, afterwards going private in Philadelphia. At some point he joined the US Counter-Espionage Squad and "quit the Private Eye game for good" (this quote is from *Love For Sale*). His adventures take him to shakily described exotic locales.

Bullets And Brown Eyes (UK 1948)

Sinner Takes All (UK 1949)

The Wayward Blonde (UK 1950)

The Golden Angel (UK 1950)

Lovely Lady (UK 1950)

Madame Sly (UK 1951)

Shanghai Jezebel (UK 1951)

Lady Of China Street (UK 1952)

Baby Face (UK 1952)

All Brides Are Beautiful (UK 1953)

Sweet And Deadly (UK 1953)

I Like Danger (UK 1954)

The Naked Lady (UK 1954)

Love For Sale (UK 1954)

Madam And Eve (UK 1955)

The Big Squeeze (UK 1955)

Big Boys Don't Cry (UK 1956)

Sydney For Sin (UK 1956)

The Cruel Lady (UK 1957) >

Dumb As They Come (UK 1957)
Honolulu Snatch (UK 1958)
Menace In Siam (UK 1958)
The Girl From Moscow (UK 1959)
Singapore Downbeat (UK 1959)
Sin Of Hong Kong (UK 1960)
Lady From Tokyo (UK 1961)
Riddle Of Double Island (UK 1962)
Danger's Green Eyes (UK 1962)
Why Do Women . . . ? (UK 1963)
The Riddle Of The Spanish Circle (UK 1964)

CORRIS, Peter

Australian author Corris has set his Sydney PI **Cliff Hardy** in an Australia that combines aspects of modern day Southern California lifestyles with political and municipal corruption and hypocrisy reminiscent of America in the 30s. A distinctively indigenous ambience that has built up a loyal readership even though Corris seems to slip through almost every critical net.

The Dying Trade (Aus 1980, UK 1986, 1986)
White Meat (Aus 1981, UK 1986, 1986)
The Marvelous Boy (Aus 1982, UK 1982, 1986)
The Empty Beach (Aus 1983, UK 1985, 1987)
Heroin Annie (Aus 1984, UK 1985, 1987)
Make Me Rich (UK 1982, 1987)
The Winning Side (Aus 1984)
The Big Drop & Other Cliff Hardy Stories (Aus, 1985, UK 1986, 1988)
Deal Me Out (UK 1986, 1987)
The Greenwich Apartments (Aus 1986, 1988)
The Cliff Hardy Collection (UK 1987). SS
The January Zone (Aus 1987, UK 1988, 1989)

Corsello, Nick — TV: The DEVLIN CONNECTION
Cory, Peter — BROCK, Stuart
Costaine, Tony — McNEIL, NEIL
Cotten, Neil — TAYLOR, Sam S.
COX, Irving E.

Boucher applauded the sound notion of pitting an intelligent young sheriff against a novel-writing and imitating PI and the well-observed Central California setting, but found the writing drab and the story confused.

Murder Among Friends (1957, UK 1957)

COX, William R.
Cox, described as "the classic pulp writer," wrote over 1000 weird mystery, sports, western and detective stories for, among many others, *Black Mask* and *Dime Detective*, with one of his characters, New York professional gambler and troubleshooter **Tom Kincaid**, being promoted to novel form. Sharply characterized, well-paced and humanitarian, they have nearly all the pulp virtues.

> Hell To Pay* (1958)
> Murder In Vegas (1960)
> Death On Location (1962)

COXE, George Harmon 1901-1984
Two of the many creations of the prolific *Black Mask* and *Dime Detective* contributor, the "professional's professional" as Boucher called him, had no pretense to being private eyes, but no survey of the genre would be complete without them. Both **Jack 'Flashgun'** (later Flash) **Casey** and **Kent Murdock** are newspaper photographers whose work brings them constantly into contact with crime, whereupon they behave exactly like PIs, naturally making much use of their cameras and photographic skills. Casey works first for the *Boston Globe*, then the *Boston Express*, is 6'2", weighs between 210 and 220 pounds and has an Irish temper. Unusually, Casey ages, and matures, during the series. He was the hero of a ten year radio series, novelized by **Paul AYRES**, and of a three-act play, *Crime Photographer*, by Stephen Bristol (1950). A short story, "Once Around The Clock" (*Black Mask* 1941) is in both **A19** and **A20** (hardback only). Murdock works for the *Boston Courier-Herald*, rising to be picture chief, and is a more sophisticated and better educated character, whose second wife, Joyce, whom he meets in the first book, is often his partner. **Jack Fenner**, a proper PI, appeared in several Murdock novels before his own, with Murdock in a minor role. **Max Chauncy Hale** is another Boston PI, a tough young man who speaks roughly as if ashamed of his inherited fortune and good education. **Leon Morley** was one of PIdom's rotten apples, with a commanding manner and keen mind but a larcenous heart. **Sam Crombie** is a plodding detective and one jacket makes a virtue of the fact that he features in formal detective stories as distinct from suspense or hardboiled thrillers. The Crombie Agency is on 7th Avenue, New York, in the forties. Coxe's work has little explicit violence and his style is deceptively simple as he spins webs of deceit. See **Films: WOMEN ARE TROUBLE / HERE'S FLASH CASEY, TV: CRIME PHOTOGRAPHER** and **Radio: CASEY, CRIME PHOTOGRAPHER. >**

Murdock: Murder With Pictures* (1935, UK 1937). Features **Fenner**
            The Barotique Mystery (1936, UK 1937); as Murdock's Acid
                Test (1977)
            The Camera Clue (1937, UK 1938). Features **Fenner**
            Four Frightened Women (1939); as The Frightened Women
                (UK 1939). Features **Fenner**
            The Glass Triangle (1940)
            Mrs. Murdock Takes A Case (1941, UK 1949)
            The Charred Witness (1942, UK 1949). Features **Fenner**
            The Jade Venus (1945, UK 1947)
            The Fifth Key (1947, UK 1950)
            The Hollow Needle (1948, UK 1952)
            Lady Killer (1949, UK 1952)
            Eye Witness (1950, UK 1953)
            The Widow Had A Gun (1951, UK 1954)
            The Crimson Clue (1953, UK 1955)
            Focus On Murder (1954, UK 1956)
            Murder On Their Minds (1957, UK 1958)
            The Big Gamble (1958, UK 1960)
            The Last Commandment (1960, UK 1961)
            The Hidden Key (1963, UK 1964)
            The Reluctant Heiress (1965, UK 1966)
            An Easy Way To Go (1969, UK 1969)
Hale: Murder For The Asking (1939, UK 1940). With **Murdock**
            The Lady Is Afraid (1940, UK 1940)
Casey: Silent Are The Dead (1942)
            Murder For Two (1943, UK 1949)
            Flash Casey, Detective (1946). Four 30s pulp novelets
            Error Of Judgment (1961, UK 1962); as One Murder Too
                Many (1969)
            The Man Who Died Too Soon (1962, UK 1963)
            Deadly Image (1964, UK 1964)
Morley: Alias The Dead (1943)
Crombie: The Frightened Fiancée (1950, UK 1953)
            The Impetuous Mistress (1958, UK 1959)
Fenner: Fenner* (1971, UK 1973). Features **Murdock**
            The Silent Witness (1973, UK 1974). Features **Murdock**
            No Place For Murder (1975, UK 1976)
Coyle, Joseph — TRIMBLE, Louis
Cragg, Sam — GRUBER, Frank

Craig, Robert — CULLEN, Carter
Craig, Steve — WINTER, Bevis
CRAIS, Robert
The debut of Jiminy Cricket quoting, Walt Disney memorabilia-collecting
Elvis Cole, literate West Hollywood, LA PI, was received with
rapturous applause particularly for the female characters and the humor.
Lawrence BLOCK ("far and away the most satisfying private eye novel in
years"), Stephen GREENLEAF, Ben SCHUTZ, Roger L. SIMON and
Sue GRAFTON heaped superlatives on a fast, funny, sexy and memorable
novel which won the 1988 Bouchercon Best First Novel Anthony. A
Vietnam vet, Cole is determined not to grow up, his ideal age being 14.
He and his survivalist sidekick Pike make up one of the most effective
partnerships since Spenser and Hawk. Crais contributed a **Philip
Marlowe** short story, "The Man Who Knew Dick Bong," to A12.
>   The Monkey's Raincoat (1987)
>   Hagakure (forthcoming)
**Crane, Barry — Radio: BARRY CRANE, CONFIDENTIAL
INVESTIGATOR**
Crane, Bill — LATIMER, Jonathan
CRANE, Frances
Starting as Had-I-But-Knowns, Crane's color-coded series about **Pat &
Jean Abbot** moved towards more conventional mysteries. Based in San
Francisco, the strong silent Pat, who is a licensed investigator, and
narrator Jean travel frequently. Crane was strongest on descriptive writing,
her secondary characters rely on gimmicks, the Abbots are resolutely
unengaging, and Pat's reasoning processes are a mystery throughout. See
Radio: ABBOTT MYSTERIES.
>   The Turquoise Shop (1941, UK 1943)
>   The Golden Box (1942, UK 1944)
>   The Yellow Violet (1942, UK 1944)
>   The Applegreen Cat (1943, UK 1945)
>   The Pink Umbrella (1943, UK 1945)
>   The Amethyst Spectacles (1944, UK 1946)
>   The Indigo Necklace (1945, UK 1947)
>   The Cinnamon Murder (1946, UK 1948)
>   The Shocking Pink Hat (1946, UK 1948)
>   Murder On The Purple Water (1947, UK 1949)
>   Black Cypress (1948, UK 1950)
>   The Flying Red Horse (1950, UK 1950)
>   The Daffodil Blonde (1950, UK 1951) >

Murder In Blue Street (1951); as Death In The Blue Hour (UK
    1952)
The Polkadot Murder (1951, UK 1952)
Murder In Bright Red (1953, UK 1954)
13 White Tulips (1953, UK 1953)
The Coral Princess Murders (1954, UK 1955)
Death In Lilac Time (1955, UK 1955)
Horror On The Ruby X (1956, UK 1956)
The Ultraviolet Widow (1956, UK 1957)
The Buttercup Case (1958, UK 1958)
The Man In Gray (1958); as The Gray Stranger (UK 1958)
Death-Wish Green* (1960, UK 1960)
The Amber Eyes (1962, UK 1962)

Crane, Steve — HERSHMAN, Morris
Cranmer, Steve — KNICKMEYER, Steve
Craven, Karl — LATIMER, Jonathan
Crawford, Ace — TV: ACE CRAWFORD, PRIVATE EYE
CREIGHTON, John (Joseph L. Chadwick)
Boucher found PI **Matt Reber**'s outing more restrained and believable
than earlier Creighton novels, though with a painfully clichéd ending.
After opening his agency, Edward J. Donovan & Associates, Investigators
to Commerce & Industry, in "Lanford," ex-cop **Ed Donovan** finds
himself blacklisted by the city's businesses thanks to his ex-wife's new
and powerful husband. He's let his operatives and secretary go when a
beautiful blonde arrives in time to save him from ending up as a skid row
bum or a member of Alcoholics Anonymous.
Reber: A Half Interest In Murder (1960)
Donovan: The Blonde Cried Murder (1961)

Cristoforou, Julian — Films: PUBLIC EYE
Crockett, Fred — LANG, Brad
Croft, Jonathan — TV: The MOST DEADLY GAME
Croft, Joshua — SATTERTHWAIT, Walter
Crole, Simon — FLEMING, Robert/LEITFRED, Robert H.
Crombie, Sam — COXE, George Harmon
CRONIN, George
One of New York PI **Virgil Fletcher**'s clients was led to believe on
inquiry that he was bright, discreet, and resourceful, though they've also
heard of his "wit." Routine.
Answer From A Dead Man (1978)
Death Of A Delegate (1978)

Cronyn, Dan — DOYLE, James T.
CROSBY, Lee (Ware Torrey 1905-1967)
In *Too Many Doors*, a title explained by a floor plan of a Connecticut mansion, the numerous Crane clan is being whittled down during a 1938 hurricane which devastated New England and which has isolated the house from the outer world. How fortunate that **Eric Hazard**, private detective, should be on the premises. He solves the case by means of graphs in what *NYT* called "a satisfying blend of mystery and horror" though finding the authoress' first book far-fetched.
> Terror By Night (1938)
> Too Many Doors (1941); as Doors To Death (194?, rev. ed. 1965)

Cross, Peter — THOMAS, Jim
Crow, Orville — THORNBURG, Newton
CROWE, John = COLLINS, Michael
Dennis Lynds used the Crowe byline for a series of books featuring Buena Costa County, California rather than a specific hero, with a shifting, overlapping cast of characters taking greater or lesser roles. One of the novels features San Vicente PI **Ed Gray**, from Montana via an LA agency, now running his own one-man operation, who is called in when a local resident has a valuable painting stolen but the police are concentrating on a WW2 light machine gun taken at the same time.
> Crooked Shadows (1975)

Crumb, Harry — Films: WHO'S HARRY CRUMB?
CRUMLEY, James
"On the basis of just three novels, James Crumley has become the foremost living writer of private-eye fiction." I concur wholeheartedly with Nevins' flat statement, as did Crumley's own peers in a PWA poll (see INTRODUCTION: Comparative Eyes). His two "heroes," both operating out of Meriwether (Missoula?), Montana, are **Chauncy Wayne Sugrue**, a Vietnam war criminal and one time Army spy on domestic dissidents, now an alcoholic, and **Milton Chester 'Milo' Milodragovitch**, a compulsive womanizer, alcoholic, cocaine addict and child of two alcoholic suicides, who is marking time until he inherits his family fortune at 52. And yet, as Nevins remarks, "these are two of the purest figures in detective fiction and the most reverent towards the earth and its creatures." Crumley has redefined the genre in a wacked-out post-Vietnam world of losers and outcasts and made forgiveness, not justice, the greatest aim and introducing a tough strain of poetry. As Nevins says, "Crumley has miminal interest in plot and even less in

explanation, but he's so uncannily skillful with characters, language, and incident thatt he can afford to throw structure overboard."

Milodragovitch: The Wrong Case (1975, UK 1976)
                  Dancing Bear (1983, UK 1987)
Sugrue: The Last Good Kiss* (1978, UK 1979)

Crystal, Larry — MILES, John
Cuddy, John Francis — HEALY, Jeremiah
CULLEN, Carter (Mildred & Richard Macaulay)

Tough **Robert Craig** goes as far as having himself committed to a mental hospital in a big case that will save his one-man New York agency. Unusually, he has no connections inside the police force and also has the sense to move to Oregon and retire on the dangerous reward money he gets.

The Deadly Chase (1957, UK 1958)

Cullen, Kirk — GUNN, James
Culver, Grace — BROWN, Roswell
CUNNINGHAM, E.V. (Howard Fast)

Fast is best known as Cunningham for his Masuto books, but **Alan Macklin** is a small-time investigator hired by a multimillionaire on the eve of the wedding to find out who his prospective bride really is. **Harvey Krim** is an insurance investigator, and, in his superior's words, "cynical, nasty and unreliable and utterly unprincipled. The only thing that can be said in your favor is that you have brains," and his style is very PI-like. See **Films: SYLVIA.**

Macklin: Sylvia (1960, UK 1962)
Krim: Lydia (1964, UK 1965)
           Cynthia (1968, UK 1969)

Custer, Rocky — Films: GRAND CENTRAL MURDER
Cutting, Richard — Films: ASSIGNMENT TO KILL
Dahlquist, Serendipity — LOCHTE, Dick
Dakota — RALSTON, Gilbert
Dale, Roger — ALLEN, Steve
DALE, William

When victims' hands are removed in a series of robbery-murders, **Del Skinner** assigns his ace operative, chronic grouch **Loopy Jones**, constantly threatening to quit the PI business because there's no money in it, to investigate. *NYT* remarked "He takes it on the chin and on other portions of his anatomy many times but in the end comes up with a neat solution of an utterly incredible case . . . not for the critically minded."

The Terror Of The Handless Corpse (1939)

Dalmas, John — CHANDLER, Raymond
DALY, Carroll John 1889-1958
Whatever may be said of Daly's melodramatic writing, described as "crude but effective" by Bill Crider and Bill Pronzini (P&M), to him goes the credit for the first hardboiled private eye story, in the May 15, 1923 issue of *Black Mask*, four months before the debut of Hammett's Continental Op, and the first novel, two years before Hammett. **Terry Mack**, hero of "Three Gun Terry" (**A11**), unlike the nameless hero of "The False Burton Coombs," an earlier soldier of fortune story favored by some commentators, establishes himself immediately in an office with "Private Investigator" on the door, and carries two .45s and a .25 in a sleeve holster. In the June 1, 1923 issue of *Black Mask*, with "Knights Of The Open Palm" (**A9** and **A13**) still ahead of Hammett, Daly introduced **Race Williams**, his main hero, who is the real prototype, a tough uncomplicated vigilante, clearly descended from the Western gunslinger, whose stories were worth 15% extra sales to *Black Mask*, whose readers voted him their favorite, well ahead of Erle Stanley Gardner and Hammett, in 1930. Another Williams story, "Not My Corpse" (*Thrilling Detective* 1948) is in **A14**. Other Daly heroes were less successful, though **Vee Brown**, a tough, two-fisted PI by day, a writer of popular sentimental songs by night, under his real name—Vivian!—living in a Park Avenue penthouse and riding round New York in a chauffeur-driven limousine, appeared in two novels and Terry Mack made one appearance in a novel.

Williams:	The Snarl Of The Beast* (1927, UK 1928)
	The Hidden Hand (1929, UK 1930)
	The Tag Murders (1930, UK 1931)
	Tainted Power (1931, UK 1931)
	The Third Murderer (1931, UK 1932)
	The Amateur Murderer (1933, UK 1933)
	Murder From The East (1935, UK 1935)
	Better Corpses (UK 1940)
	The Adventures Of Race Williams (1988). 5 novelets
Mack:	The Man In The Shadows (1928, UK 1929)
Brown:	Murder Won't Wait (1933, UK 1934)
	Emperor Of Evil (1936, UK 1937)

Daly, Maxwell — BUSBY, Roger & Gerald HOLTHAM
Dalzell, Clay — Film: STAR OF MIDNIGHT
Damian, Paul — WALSH, Paul E.
Dan Kearny Associates — GORES, Joe
Dancer, Joe — TV: JOE DANCER

Dancey, Elton — PHILLIPS, R.B.
Dane, Timothy — ARD, William
DANIEL, Roland 1880-1969
Florida raised British author who wrote UK and US set books in a bizarre mid-Atlantic compromise style. **Buddy Mustard**, ran The Mustard Investigations, Piccadilly, London, and **Michael Grant**, worked in Los Pagos, presumably California. Daniel was fond of Orientals speaking almost incomprehensible pidgin English, but even the English speakers' dialogue is quite extraordinarily stilted.

Mustard: The Crawshay Jewel Mystery (UK 1941)
             Evil Shadows (UK 1944)
             The Lady In Scarlet (UK 1947)
             A Dead Man Sings (UK 1949)
             Murder At A Cottage (UK 1949)
             The Arrow Of Death (UK 1950)
             Three Sundays To Live (UK 1952)
             The Murder Gang (UK 1954)
             The Man From Paris (UK 1958)
             The Missing Body (1961)
             The Big Shot (UK 1962)
             The Hangman Waits (UK 1963)
             The Gangster's Daughter (UK 1965)
Grant: Frightened Eyes (UK 1956)
             The Kidnappers (UK 1959)
             Brunettes Are Dangerous (UK 1960)
             Red-Headed Dames And Murder (UK 1960)
             Women—Dope—And Murder (UK 1962)
             Murder In Ocean Drive (UK 1964)

Daniels, Mohawk — ROHDE, William L.
Darlan, Al — HOCH, Edward D.
Darling, Hal — LACY, Ed
Darling, Kiss — YARDLEY, James A.
Darrow, Eddie — Films: FORBIDDEN
Dart, Steve — COGGINS, Paul
Darzek, Jan — BIGGLE, Lloyd Jr.
DATESH, John Nicholas
Big, tough **Casey Carmichael** paid for college and got a PI license, no questions asked, after two transfers following FBI arrests of student "communist" organizers. "I just handed over information of their activities, their causes and their friends. It was 20 years ago, or almost.

And it didn't bother me at all anymore. Not a bit." Based in the Haller Building, Pittsburgh, he had one convoluted case.

The Janus Murders (1979)

Davies, Lobo — JONES, James

DAVIS, Frederick C(lyde) 1902-1977

Davis wrote over 1000 stories for the better pulps, including *Black Mask*, and his style still reads well. **Cyrus Hatch**, son of New York's Police Commissioner, is a professor of criminology who gets involved in the real world of crime, assisted by his ex-boxer bodyguard **Danny Delevan**. Semi-hardboiled New York PIs, **Schyler Cole**, of the $50 a day Cole Detective Agency, Lexington Avenue, Manhattan, who finds himself playing Watson to his brighter assistant **Luke Speare**, prides himself on being both honest and sensible with it and figures a private op can make good money without dying of overwork. Most of Davis' books were published in the UK as by **Stephen RANSOME**, a name he also used in America. See also **Murdo COOMBS**.

Hatch: Coffins For Three (1938); as One Murder Too Many (UK 1938)
        He Wouldn't Stay Dead (1939; UK 1939)
        Poor, Poor Yorick (1939); as Murder Doesn't Always Out (UK 1939)
        The Graveyard Never Closes (1940)
        Let The Skeletons Rattle (1944)
        Detour To Oblivion (1947)
        Thursday's Blade (1947)
        Gone Tomorrow (1948)

Cole: The Deadly Miss Ashley (1950; as by **RANSOME** UK 1950)
        Lilies In Her Garden Grew (1951; as by **RANSOME** UK 1951)
        Tread Lightly, Angel (1952; as by **RANSOME** UK 1952)
        Drag The Dark (1953; as by **RANSOME** UK 1954)
        Another Morgue Heard From (1954); as Deadly Bedfellows (as by **RANSOME** UK 1955)
        Night Drop (1955; as by **RANSOME** UK 1956)

DAVIS, Gordon = HUNT, E. Howard

Hunt, CIA man of Watergate fame, wrote prolifically under a number of names, most successfully as **Robert DIETRICH**. One Davis novel featured Washington, DC hotel—the Tilden on K Street—detective **Pete Novak**, a none too bright tough guy who operates in standard Gold Medal PI style.

        House Dick (1961); as Washington Payoff (as by **E. Howard HUNT** 1975)

DAVIS, Kenn

Out of a Detroit ghetto, black Vietnam vet **Carver Bascombe** got a PI license in San Francisco on the strength of his Military Police experience and has an office on Fillmore Street, though he pretends it's only to support his half-hearted law studies. A colorful character, Bascombe drives a baby blue Jaguar XKE and lives high, thanks to his white millionairess girlfriend. Davis aims to set each book in a different sector of San Francisco's cultural world, art, opera, literature, sculpture and so on. Davis' plotting is weak but his hero disarms criticism.

> The Dark Side (1976, with John Stanley)
> The Forza Trap (1979)
> Words Can Kill* (1984)
> Melting Point (1986)
> Nijinsky Is Dead (1987)
> As October Dies (1987)

DAVIS, Means

"Chess plays a part in this story," remarked *NYT*, "but not nearly as important a part as the author would have us believe," and complained that "the story is told in a peculiarly roundabout way." **James Augustus 'Jag' Gibbs** "senses immediately that there is something not quite on the level about the man who engages his services, but he does not know the half of it until much later." *SR* was much harder—"amazing mixture of naive writing and silly sleuthing."

> The Chess Murders (1937)

Davis, Milt — McBAIN, Ed

Davis, Neil — Films: The KEYHOLE

DAVIS, Norbert 1909-1949

Regarded as one of the best and most original of the 30s pulp writers, Davis, a suicide at 40 because of personal problems, successfully combined hardboiled violence with farce in three novels about **Doan** and **Carstairs**. Doan is a chubby Bay City, California PI who acts half-witted but is very dangerous and the best PI west of the Mississippi, tolerated by his Severn International Detectives boss because he's responsible for the agency's record. An alcoholic, he manages never to suffer from hangovers. Carstairs is his sidekick, a Great Dane he won in a poker game, who regards Doan and his lifestyle as being beneath him. A Doan & Carstairs short story, "Holocaust House" (*Argosy* 1940) is in **A13**. A selection of Davis' highly regarded **Max Latin**, "the shamus with a shady rep," *Dime Detective* stories has appeared in book form, with another story, "Don't Give Your Right Name" (1941) in **A6**. Joseph

Shaw chose a story about **Ben Shaley**, "Red Goose" (*Black Mask* 1934) for **A20**, while Ruhm (**A19**) picked one about tough egg Hollywood troubleshooter **Mark Hull**, "Kansas City Flash" (*Black Mask* 1933).

Doan: The Mouse In The Mountain* (1943); as Dead Little Rich Girl
           (1945); as Rendezvous With Fear (UK 1944)
           Sally's In The Alley (1943, UK 1945)
           Oh, Murderer Mine (1946)
Latin: The Adventures Of Max Latin (1988). SS

DAVIS, Tech

"The more baffling a case, the better (**Aubrey Nash**) likes it." However, *NYT* thought Davis went too far, calling the second book, set on a snowbound train in Wyoming, "exceedingly complicated both in its essential elements and, even more so, because of the way in which it is told . . . foggy style." Pronzini (P&M), while finding Davis' prose overblown, said "the plot is tricky enough to keep one reading and guessing, and Nash's piecing together of the puzzle is logical and well clued. There are also some good characters, some witty dialogue and more action than you might expect in this type of whodunit."

           Terror On Compass Lake (1935)
           Full Fare For A Corpse* (1937)
           Murder On Alternate Tuesdays (1938)

Daymond, Fred — GORDON, Russell
Dean, Garry — WHELTON, Paul
Dean, Jeffrey — WARGA, Wayne
Dean, Larry — TV: TWO FOR THE MONEY
DEAN, Robert George

Both *NYT* and *SR* had bones to pick with Dean's series, featuring "effervescent" private detectives **Pat Thompson**, whose boss insists is better drunk than most men sober, and **Sue Barton**. *SR* disliked their "spurious ebullience—which other may think poifeckly gra-and. Smart-alecky." *NYT* took issue with Dean's sloppy use of pronouns, complaining it was impossible to make out who was speaking. A sucker for a pretty face and a dry martini, **Anthony Hunter**, who, with **Bill Griffith**, works for the Imperator Schmidt Agency, 49th Street, New York, keeps getting involved in cases his shrewder boss has decided not to take. Boucher admired Dean for restraint in matters of sex and violence.

Thompson: What Gentleman Strangles A Lady? (1936)
               Three Lights Went Out (1936)
               The Sutton Place Murders (1936, UK 1936) >

Hunter:
Murder On Margin (1937)
Murder Makes A Merry Widow (1938)
A Murder Of Convenience (1938)
Murder Through The Looking Glass (1940)
A Murder By Marriage (1940)
Murder In Mink (1941)
On Ice (1942)
Layoff (1942)
The Body Was Quite Cold (1951)
The Case Of Joshua Locke (1951)
Affair At Lover's Leap (1953); as Death At Lover's Leap (UK 1954)

DEAN, Spencer = STERLING, Stewart

Sterling (Prentice Winchell) created a number of off-beat specialist detectives including a fire chief, a hotel detective, harbor police and, as Dean, a department store detective, **Don Cadee**, of Amblett's, 5th Avenue, New York. The stories are more routine than the Sterling books, normally featuring a damsel-in-distress who Cadee first apprehends, then helps, but the background is interesting.

The Frightened Fingers (1954, UK 1955)
The Scent Of Fear (1954, UK 1956); as The Smell Of Fear (1956)
Marked Down For Murder (1956, UK 1957)
Murder On Delivery (1957, UK 1958)
Dishonor Among Thieves (1958, UK 1959)
The Merchant Of Murder (1959, UK 1960)
Price Tag For Murder (1959, UK 1960)
Murder After A Fashion (1960, UK 1961)
Credit For Murder (1961, UK 1962)

DeANDREA, William L.

As troubleshooter for a 6th Avenue, New York TV network, where illusion is the reality, **Matt Cobb** has to have a sense of humor just to get by, and DeAndrea successfully combines wit with ingenious clues and plot devices. Cobb's constant companion, an attack-trained Samoyed called Spot, is a star in its own right. DeAndrea won an Edgar for the first Cobb book and another for a novel set in Sparta, New York and featuring smart aleck PI **Ron Gentry**, tall, blond and athletic, who couldn't become a cop because of poor eyesight and received his unique training from Professor Bendetti, a would-be Great Detective.

Cobb: Killed In The Ratings (1978, UK 1979) >

> Killed In The Act (1981)
> Killed With A Passion (1983)
> Killed On The Ice* (1984)
> Killed In Paradise (1988)

Gentry: The HOG Murders* (1979)

Deckard, Kelly J. — SPENCER, Ross H.

Deckard, Rick — DICK, Philip K.

Decker, R.J. — HIASSEN, Carl

Decker, Tyger — RIEFE, Alan

Deco, Eddy — WILSON, Gahan

DECOLTA, Ramon = WHITFIELD, Raoul

Drawing on personal knowledge of the Philippines, Whitfield wrote, as Decolta, eight stories about Manila PI **Jo Gar** which Ellery Queen described as having "the best features of the hard-boiled manner: the aura of authenticity, the staccato speech, the restrained realism. The tales are lean, hard—and unforgettable." Never published together in book form, three, "Death In The Pasig" (*Black Mask* 1930; A20) "China Man" (*Black Mask* 1932; A6) and "The Black Sampan" (*Black Mask* 1932) in Pronzini & Greenberg, eds.; *The Ethnic Detectives* (1985), have been anthologized, the latter two as by **Raoul WHITFIELD**.

Deegan, Biff — ARRIGHI, Mel

Dekkar, Bill — Films: CHEAPER TO KEEP HER

Dekker, Jake — ELLIN, Stanley

DEKKER, Carl = COLLINS, Michael

NYT's Newgate Callendar, who admired Lynds' work as **William ARDEN**, **COLLINS**, **John CROWE** and **Michael SADLER**, found his Dekker title, featuring a stubborn, honest PI, professional enough in plotting and construction, "the trouble is that Dekker writes in all but Basic English. His characters are stereotypes, his dialogue is stiff and the whole ambience unconvincing."

> Woman In Marble (1972)

DEKKER, Johnny

Dekker, a British author (?—background information is non-existent), tries hard to write Runyonese and, to be fair, does quite a creditable job at it. **Johnny Dekker** of New York is a former light-heavyweight boxing champion turned PI.

> Dolls And Dollars (UK 1948)
> The Siamese Cat (UK 1948)
> Singapore Set-Up (UK 1948)
> Hex Marks The Spot (UK 1949) >

Manhunt In Manhattan (UK 1949)
Streetcar To Hell (UK 1949)

DELANCEY, Roger

Not the strong, silent type, leisurely investigator **Dr. Arthur** loves to talk. *NYT* complained that, while often interesting, Arthur's conversations made the story unnecessarily long; another critic, though thinking it "agreeably raffish," found the book "filled with erudition that has no possible bearing on the crime."

Murder Below Wall Street (1934, UK 1934)

Delaney, Al — BLACK, Thomas
Delaney, Bud — TV: LAST HOURS BEFORE MORNING
Delaney, Eddie — GRAHAM, Anthony
Delaware, Alex — KELLERMAN, Jonathan
Delevan, Danny — DAVIS, Frederick C.
Delvecchio, Nick — RANDISI, Robert J.

DeMARCO, Gordon

Political radical DeMarco spent the late 60s in San Francisco, the setting for his 50s PI **Riley Kovacs** who at one point gets involved with the young Richard Nixon, then with McCarthy's House UnAmerican Activities Committee. Another, modern day, San Francisco PI, **Rocco Conigliaro**, is in self-imposed exile, visiting relatives in the large Italian community in Edinburgh during the famous Festival, when a Chilean Marxist theater director is found murdered. DeMarco has a rather irritating habit of stressing how well he knows San Francisco/Edinburgh, but he does well at integrating left-wing principles with tough action.

Kovacs: October Heat (1984, UK 1984)
            The Canvas Prison (1984, UK 1984)
            Frisco Blues (1985, UK 1985)
Conigliaro: Murder At The Fringe (UK 1987, 1988)

DEMARIS, Ovid (Ovide E. Desmarais)

Demaris, a specialist in tough gangster stories, wrote at least one novel about PI **Vince Slader**, reluctant bodyguard to a callous, self-centred and eminently killable actor-singer. Overloaded with characters and confusing.

The Gold-Plated Sewer (1960)

DEMING, Richard 1915-1983

Though an artificial leg may seem like a gimmick, Deming's books about **Manville 'Manny' Moon**, who operates out of the El Patio Café, have powerful atmosphere, sharp dialogue and are well-paced. Their lack of success is, as Baker & Nietzel remark, "one of those baffling mysteries of the paperback market." A Moon short story, "The Shakedown," is in

A10. Anti-hero PI, **Barney Calhoun**, a big ex-cop from Buffalo, fails to commit the perfect crime. See also **Ellery QUEEN** for a ghost written novel and **Max FRANKLIN**.

Moon: The Gallows In My Garden (1952, UK 1953)

             Tweak The Devil's Nose (1953, UK 1953); as Hand-Picked To Die (1956)

             Whistle Past The Graveyard (1954, UK 1955); as Give The Girl A Gun (1955)

             Juvenile Delinquent (UK 1958)

Calhoun: Hit And Run (1960)

De Nardo, Frank — CARLO, Philip

DENBOW, Richard

For a systematic analysis of Denbow's novel featuring **Raymond Chandler** saving Dashiell Hammett, both of them hopeless alcoholics, from vengeful "wop" gangsters, the reader is referred to Pronzini's *Gun In Cheek*. A contender for all-time worst PI novel.

          Chandler (1977)

Denning, Ted — McGREGOR, Don & Gene COLAN

DENNIS, Ralph

Victim of unfortunate packaging, Dennis wrote an unconventional series about Atlanta-based **Jim Hardman**, a disgraced ex-cop working as an unlicensed PI, and his sidekick, black ex-football player **Hump Evans**. The characterization and interactions are very good, the writing is stylish and the action fast. Robert J. RANDISI (P&M) remarked "At its worst, Dennis's writing is well above that of run-of-the-mill men's adventure series; and at its best, it is a fine example of PI writing that depends little on the conventions of the genre."

          Atlanta Deathwatch* (1974)

          The Charleston Knife's Back In Town (1974)

          Down Among The Jocks (1974)

          The Golden Girl And All (1974)

          Pimp For The Dead (1974)

          Murder's Not An Odd Job (1974)

          Working For The Man (1974)

          The Deadly Cotton Heart (1976)

          Hump's First Case (1977)

          The One-Dollar Rip-Off (1977)

          The Last Of The Armageddon Wars (1977)

          The Buy Back Blues (1977)

Denson, John — HOYT, Richard

DENT, Lester 1905-1959

A consummate hack writer, who wrote some 200 Doc Savage novels as Kenneth Robeson, Dent consciously used a formula for his vast output but had a special reverence for *Black Mask* and has an acknowledged place in its history on the strength of only two stories (like Chandler and Nebel, he refused to contribute to it after Joseph Shaw was fired). Both are about very tall, thin **Oscar Sail**, who lives on an all-black 34 foot Chesapeake Bay bugeye, *Sail*, in Miami's City Yacht Basin and whose world is characterized by violence and deception. "Sail" (1936) is in Shaw's collection (**A20**) and "Angelfish" (1936) in both Goulart and Ruhm's (**A6 & A19**). Dent's scientific private detective, **Lee Nayce**, who had a snake-shaped scar on his forehead,from the hilt of a Chinaman's thrown knife, and looked like a minister, featured in "The Tank Of Terror" (*Ten Detective Aces* 1933; **A18**).

DENVER, Paul

With **Douglas ENEFER** and **Richard GALLAGHER**, Denver was one of the authors of novelizations of **TV: CANNON** featuring fattest-ever PI **Frank Cannon**.

> The Golden Bullet (1973)
> The Falling Blonde (UK 1975)

DE PUY, E(dward) Spence

In two California hospital set novels, **Sam Houston**, investigator for the National Society for Hospital Standardization, featured in what *SR* summarized as "clever conglomerate of hard-boiled talk and action, grisly background, sex intrigue and B-grade detecting."

> The Long Knife (1936)
> The Hospital Homicides (1937)

Derringer, Nick — TV: NICK DERRINGER, P.I.

Desmond, Brian — Lawrence, Kelly

DESMOND, Hugh

A prolific British "lending library" author whose books about **Alan Fraser**, once an "Ace" detective who runs a private inquiry agency, are often based on true life crimes. Desmond feels little need to explain the deductive process.

> The Hand Of Vengeance (UK 1945)
> The Viper's Sting (UK 1946)
> Death Walks In Scarlet (UK 1948)
> A Clear Case Of Murder (UK 1950)
> Calling Alan Fraser (UK 1951)
> A Pact With The Devil (UK 1952) >

Deliver Us From Evil (UK 1953)
The Night Of The Crime (UK 1953)
The Death Parade (UK 1954)
Destination—Death (UK 1955)
She Met Murder (UK 1956)
Appointment At Eight (UK 1957)
Lady, Where Are You? (UK 1957)
Poison Pen (UK 1958)
Doorway To Death (UK 1959)
In Fear Of The Night (UK 1960)
The Case Of The Blue Orchid (UK 1961)
Fanfare For Murder (UK 1961)
Stay Of Execution (UK 1962)
Bodies In A Cupboard (UK 1963)
The Silent Witness (UK 1963)
A Slight Case Of Murder (UK 1963)
Condemned (UK 1964)
Hostage To Death (UK 1964)
Someday I'll Kill You (UK 1964)
The Dark Shadow (UK 1965)
Murder Strikes At Dawn (UK 1965)
Not Guilty, My Lord (UK 1965)
The Lady Has Claws (UK 1966)
Murder On The Moor (UK 1967)
Horror At The Moated Mill (UK 1967)
Mask Of Terror (UK 1968)
We Walk With Death (UK 1968)

Detweiler, P.J. — Films: P.J.
Devitt, Mike — TV: DIAMONDS
Devlin, Brian — TV: The DEVLIN CONNECTION
Devlin, Chris — TV: CHECKMATE
Devlin, Joe — ACRE, Stephen / GRUBER, Frank
DEWEY, Thomas B(lanchard) 1915-1981
The much underrated and influential Dewey is best known for his
excellent series about a Chicago PI, off Michigan Avenue, known only as
Mac, though in the final book we learn that his last name is Robinson.
An ex-cop, Mac is intelligent, quiet and gentle, though tough when
required, a light drinker, modest and compassionate who usually finds
himself on the side of the underdog. The ultimate White Knight. Dewey's
other lighter and sexier eye is **Pete Schofield** of LA, who has three

things Mac lacks, a private life (unusually he's happily married, to the beautiful red-headed Jeannie), a sense of humor and a readiness with the wisecrack.

Mac: Draw The Curtain Close (1947, UK 1951); as Dame In Danger (1958)

Prey For Me (1954, UK 1954); as The Case Of The Murdered Model (1955)

The Mean Streets (1955, UK 1955)

The Brave, Bad Girls (1956, UK 1957)

You've Got Him Cold (1958, UK 1959)

The Case Of The Chased And The Unchaste (1959, UK 1960)

The Girl Who Wasn't There (1960, UK 1960); as The Girl Who Never Was (1962)

How Hard To Kill (1962, UK 1963)

A Sad Song Singing* (1963, UK 1964)

Don't Cry For Long (1964, UK 1965)

Portrait Of A Dead Heiress (1965, UK 1966)

Deadline* (1966, UK 1967)

Death And Taxes (1967, UK 1969)

The King-Killers (1968); as Death Turns Right (UK 1969)

The Love-Death Thing (1969)

The Taurus Trip (1970)

Schofield: And Where She Stops (1957); as I.O.U. Murder (UK 1958)

Go To Sleep Jeannie (1959, UK 1960)

Too Hot For Hawaii (1960, UK 1963)

The Golden Hooligan (1961); as The Mexican Slayride (UK 1961)

Go, Honeylou (1962, UK 1962)

The Girl With The Sweet Plump Knees (1963, UK 1963)

The Girl In The Punchbowl (1964, UK 1965)

Only On Tuesdays* (1964, UK 1964)

Nude In Nevada (1965, UK 1966)

DE WITT, Jack

Ex-New York cop turned PI **Clint Walsh** is persuaded to travel to an island off the coast of Florida to search for a missing fugitive from Nazi Germany and finds the locals more lethal than the creatures of the island's swamps and jungles.

Murder On Shark Island (1941)

Dexter, Charles — FREDMAN, John
Diamond, Red — SCHORR, Mark

Diamond, Richard — Radio: RICHARD DIAMOND, PRIVATE DETECTIVE
Diamond, Sam — KEATING, Henry
Diaz, Willy — McDOWELL, Rider
DiCHIARA, Robert
A role-playing book in which the reader, armed with a pair of dice, attempts to solve three cases, written in a mock hardboiled manner, scoring according to the various objectives he identifies and successfully completes. The dice throws are used in various encounters which can add or subtract points from the reader's Muscle, Moxie and Magnetism, the three ingredients with which he or she is armed. Some of the programmed possibilities are lethal.

> Hard-Boiled; Three Tough Cases For The Private Eye With Smarts (1985)

DICK, Philip K(endred) 1928-1982
The great SF writer created a futuristic version of bounty hunting— tracking down replicants, genetically engineered androids out-lawed from Earth, who succeed, because of their extraordinary abilities, in returning and passing as human. Ex-cop **Rick Deckard** is a leading Blade Runner, as these hunters are known, in a nightmare 2019 LA. A tremendous book, both as SF and PI pursuit. See **Films: BLADE RUNNER.**

> Do Androids Dream Of Electric Sheep? (1968, UK 1972); as Blade Runner (1982, UK 1982)

DICKENSON, Fred 1909-1986
"Multi-married millionaire slain on eve of sixth wedding after warning private eye (**Mack McGann**). Trail leads through bizarre scenes to spectacular finish. Not quite credible but good fun" (*SR*). "Heavy-handed plot but the dialogue is light and in spots amusing" (Cuppy).

> Kill 'Em With Kindness (1950)

DICKINSON, Weed
A wisecracking, hard-drinking. gossipy Hollywood press agent calls in New York PI **Burt Calhoun** but dominates the story. *SR* commented "Studio atmosphere, blackmail, flip dialogue (somewhat phony) and solution that may elevate experts' eyebrows. Medium," while *NYT* considered that "the story is not bad and it could have been made much better by eliminating some of Ed Haley's wisecracks."

> Dead Man Talks Too Much (1937, UK 1937)

DICKSON, Arthur 1888-1940?
NYT, in unusually definite mood, said that "to call this a second-rate mystery would be gross flattery." Private detective **Hamilton Yorke**

sees through an elaborate locked room murder but can't prove it.

Death Bids For Corners (1941)

DIETRICH, Robert = HUNT, E. Howard

The CIA man of Watergate notoriety used several pen names, including **Gordon DAVIS**. The Dietrich books are considered his best. **Steve Bentley** is a CPA, but the toughest accountant in history and effectively a wise-cracking PI. Based in Washington, DC—"a great city. All you need is money, endurance and powerful friends"—his adventures are fast moving with tough dialogue. Bill Crider (P&M), pointing out irrelevant homophobia, says "most of the tough narrative rings true . . . The Washington setting is described with easy familiarity and the characterization is adequate."

Murder On The Rocks* (1957, UK 1958)

The House On Q Street (1959)

End Of A Stripper (1959)

Mistress To Murder (1960)

Murder On Her Mind (1960)

Angel Eyes (1961)

Curtains For A Lover (1961)

Steve Bentley's Calypso Caper (1961)

My Body (1962; as by **E. Howard HUNT** 1973)

Dill, Hugo — Films: WHO DONE IT? (1956)

DILLON, Walter

Two *Drood Review*ers stopped after 20 pages of this episodic story about **Jack Hanigan** investigating blind dates arranged through a computer network. Retired from the NYPD (Homicide), Hanigan lives in Washington DC, sells equipment to police forces, lectures at the police academy and is hired after an accidental meeting by the father of one of the victims of The Computer Killer. Nothing special.

Deadly Intrusion (1987)

DiMarco, Jeff — DISNEY, Doris Miles

Dime, Mike — FANTONI, Barry

DIMOND, Clark

A real life New Jersey PI, Dimond drew on experience for a short story, "You Can't Fire Me For Doing My Job" (A1 #7) with a nameless hero.

Disbro, Gil — MARTIN, James E,

DISNEY, Doris Miles 1907-1976

It has been remarked of Disney's 47+ novels that she never wrote the same book twice. One featured young PI **Griff Hughes,** of the Hughes Agency, Worcester, Connecticut, called on to solve a 44 year old murder in a novel of pure deduction by research. One of her few series characters was insurance investigator **Jeff DiMarco**, a believable character who ages with the books.

DiMarco: Dark Road (1946, UK 1947); as Dead Stop (1956)
              Family Skeleton (1949)
              Straw Man (1951); as The Case Of The Straw Man (UK 1958)
              Trick Or Treat (1955); as The Halloween Murder (UK 1957)
              Method In Madness (1957); as Quiet Violence (UK 1959); as
                   Too Innocent To Kill (1959)
              Did She Fall Or Was She Pushed? (1959, UK 1962)
              Find The Woman (1962, UK 1964)
              The Chandler Policy (1971, UK 1973)
Hughes: Here Lies . . . (1963, UK 1964)

Divine, Tyler — KLAICH, Dolores
DKA (Dan Kearny Associates) — GORES, Joe
Doan — DAVIS, Norbert
Dobs, Rachel — FILMS: The SQUEEZE
DOBSON, Margaret
In at least one romantic-cum-mystery novel, bookstore owner **Jane Bailey** works for her PI boyfriend, and the book carries a pistol logo, but is too turgid and sloppy to inspire any but the most dedicated to check out the other titles in the series, *Touchstone*, *Primrose* and *Nightcap*.

              Soothsayer (1987)
DOBYNS, Stephen
An ex-cop in the famous American horse racing town of Saratoga Springs, middle-aged **Charlie Bradshaw** sets up as a PI in a town that seems to have little need of one. Well described by one critic as "a true detective of the heart," Bradshaw is an engaging, unassuming hero, other characters are finely wrought and the horsy backgrounds are well done.

              Saratoga Swimmer (1981, UK 1986)
              Saratoga Headhunter (1985, UK 1986)
              Saratoga Longshot (1984)
              Saratoga Snapper (1986)
              Saratoga Bestiary (1988)
Dodd, Elmer — MILLAR, Margaret
**Dodge, Dan — Radio: A CRIME LETTER FROM DAN
              DODGE**
DODGE, David
Travel writer Dodge drew on his knowledge of Central and South America for three far-ranging stories about **Al Colby**, a hardboiled, cynical,

tough-guy detective-adventurer based in Mexico City. In earlier days, Dodge was an accountant and used this experience for four very different books about **Whit Whitney**, a tax accountant whom Sandoe counts as a PI because of his reluctant involvement in various murders. Though they have plenty of action and a medium-hardboiled atmosphere, there's more witty dialogue and cocktails in the screwball comedy style. Both series have fine dialogue, fast pace and sound plotting. See **Films: PLUNDER OF THE SUN.**

Whitney: Death And Taxes (1941, UK 1947)
            Shear The Black Sheep (1942, UK 1949)
            Bullets For The Bridegroom (1944, UK 1948)
            It Ain't Hay (1946); as A Drug On The Market (UK 1949)
Colby: The Long Escape (1948, UK 1950)
            Plunder Of The Sun (1949, UK 1950)
            The Red Tassel (1950, UK 1951)

Dolan, Dan — TV: A MASTERPIECE OF MURDER
Dolan, Michael — TV: REWARD
Dolan, Ross — Radio: I DEAL IN CRIME
DOLD, Gaylord
1950s Wichita, Kansas is the unusual setting for the first tough story about Lincoln Street PI **Mitch Roberts** in which the summer heat of the plains is an omnipresent, oppressive force. The second maintains the seedy, small city atmosphere but thereafter the writing degenerates into florid purple prose—the owner of the San Francisco Mystery Bookstore is fond of reading selected passages aloud to customers.

            Hot Summer, Cold Murder (1987)
            Snake Eyes (1987)
            Cold Cash (1987)
            Bonepile (1988)

Dollar, Johnny — Radio: YOURS TRULY, JOHNNY DOLLAR
Donahue, Dick — NEBEL, Frederick
Donovan — SANDERS, Daphne
Donovan, Cole — TV: TRIPLECROSS
Donovan, Ed — CREIGHTON, John
Donovan, Eli — RUBEL, James L.
Doolin, Johnny — CAIN, Paul
DOUGLAS, John
The latest historical PI is 1923 college drop-out **William Edmondson** who joins a New York agency and starts learning about Warren Harding

era life when he's teamed with a veteran drinking, smoking and cussing PI to investigate a murder in a labor war West Virginia coal-mining town where his partner is promptly killed. Reviewed as absorbing, well-paced, with a strong sense of place, well-drawn characters and some surprises.

Blind Spring Rambler (1988)

DOUGLAS, Malcolm = BRETT, Martin

Canadian author Douglas Sanderson, who first wrote PI novels as Brett, wrote at least one excellent book about easy-going Montreal PI **Bill Yates** which is classic tongue in cheek, fast paced, wry, observant, a bit gaudy and with an edge of parody.

The Deadly Dames* (1956, UK 1961)

Douglass, Aileen — MICHAELS, Melisa C.

Down, Jerry — GREX, Leo

DOWNING, Warwick

Raised by a Cheyenne foster mother, **Joe Reddman** is not himself of Indian blood but absorbs so much tribal lore that some call him the last wild Indian, some The Player because of his Cheyenne name which means Man Who Plays Games, while the Denver, Colorado, police know him as Mr. Cool. Reddman is patient and stoical under pain and, as well as wilderness craft, he uses visions in his investigations. Despite rave reviews for the quality of his writing and storytelling, Downing has suffered from the reverse of the usual problem of PI authors in that he has only appeared in hardback. Reddman makes a brief appearance in Downing's second book *The Mountains West Of Town* (1974). Baker & Nietzel mention a third title, *My Brother The Buffalo*, as forthcoming but it appears not to have been published.

The Player* (1974)

The Gambler, The Minstrel And The Dance Hall Queen (1976)

DOXEY, W.S.

The author is quoted (1987), in introducing a short story, "Family Business" (A1 #8), about Atlanta, Georgia PI **Jack Bleekman** as having recently completed a novel with the same character which he hopes will be the first of a series.

DOYLE, James T.

60s radical **Dan Cronyn** winds up as a Washington, DC, PI operating in a murky world of influence peddlers and minor ambassadors. The plot is well structured but the writing stiff and routine with too much rhapsodizing about the good old days. Another book, featuring (Tampa?) ex-cop PI **Paul Broder** was described as contrived and lackluster with every PI cliché. >

Cronyn: Deadly Resurrection (1987)

Broder: Epitaph For A Loser (1988)

Doyle, Matt — GILBERT, Dale L.

Doyle, Pat — CARLTON, Mitchell

DOZOIS, Gardner & George EFFINGER

Invalided out of the Army Intelligence of the future, huge, super-Aryan **Karl Jaeger** works for the Southern European Police Group before setting up Jaeger Incorporated in Nurnberg, selling his services as the last private eye on Earth. Ruthless invading aliens become a problem.

Nightmare Blue (1975)

Draco, Pete — FOSTER, Richard

Dragovic, Frank — GRIGORICH, Barbara

Drake, Alan — Radio: SPECIAL AGENT

Drake, Eddie — TV: The CASES OF EDDIE DRAKE

Drake, Paul — GARDNER, Erle Stanley

Drake, Steve — ELLINGTON, Richard

DREW,Bernard (ed) — see ANTHOLOGIES: 3

Drum, Chester — MARLOWE, Stephen

Drum, Justus — LOGAN, Carolynne & Malcolm

Druse — CAIN, Paul

DUFF, James

Tough, laconic novels about **John P. Phelan,** Hollywood PI with a weakness for betting on the wrong horses, described by Boucher as standard but lively and competent.

Some Die Young (1956)

Who Dies There? (1956)

Duffy, Cornelius — BEYER, William Gray

Duffy, Nick — KAVANAGH, Dan

Duncan, Hugh — FIELDING, A.

Duncan, Jonas — GILLIS, Jackson Clark

Duncan, Robbie — BILLANY, Dan

Duncan, Sabrina — TV: CHARLIE'S ANGELS

DUNCAN, W. Glenn

Making up his rules as he goes along, tough, clever and cynical **Rafferty** was fired from the Dallas, Texas, police for not taking direction. Assisted in hard thinking by his sexy antique dealer lady friend and in tight corners by ultra-dangerous husband and wife freelancers Cowboy and Mimi, Rafferty features in books that are hard-nosed, violent and laced with ironic humor, though *Drood Review* regard him as yet another Spencer wannabee. >

Rafferty's Rules (1987)
Rafferty: Last Seen Alive (1987)
Rafferty: Poor Dead Cricket (1988)

DUNDEE, Robert (Robert R. Kirsch 1922-1980)
Fired for drunkenness "above and beyond the call of duty" first from the *LA Inquirer*, then the *LA Graphic*, **Johnny Lamb**, whose name is hideously inappropriate , dries out and sets up as a Temple Street PI to the sleazy night characters of Sunset Strip. Kirsch wrote one other book, *Inferno* (1962), which may also be a Lamb story.

Pandora's Box (1962)

DUNDEE, Wayne D.
As might be expected from *Hardboiled*'s editor, **Joe Hannibal** of Rockford, Illinois, is a tough guy and an engaging one though he does do some rather inexplicable things which mar the plotline. Good characterization and atmosphere and, as Gorman comments, the novels are "tough-guy in the venerable and honorable sense. They don't suffer from the cutes and they are proud (rather than ashamed or exploitative) of their working-class roots." Hannibal appears in four anthologized short stories, "Shooting Match" (**A4**), "Death Of An Iron Maiden" (*Hardboiled* 1985; **A5**), "Body Count" (**A16**) and "The Judas Target" (**A17**).

The Burning Season (1988)

Dunn, Jim — NELSON, Hugh Lawrence
Dunn, Micah — SHUMAN, M.K.
Dunn, Otis — RICHARDS, Nat
DUNNE, Colin
Still loosely connected to a "Unit in Whitehall" and a part-time SAS man (known in Britain as "hooligans"), **Joe 'High Risk' Hussey** works as a Muswell Hill, North London garage attendant as a front for his blend of PI and espionage work. Chandler crossed with Spillane, with wisecracks and mayhem in a fast, chilling and funny blend.

Ratcatcher (UK 1985, 1986)
Hooligan (UK 1987, 1988)

Dunne, Joe — RIFKIN, Shepard
Dunston, Joe — ANTHONY, Evelyn
Durgan, Leo — LAND, Myrick
Dust, Joe — GRAAF, Peter
Dwyer, Jack — GORMAN, Edward
Dyer, Henry — RING, Raymond H.
Earlstone, John — MONMOUTH, Jack

EARLY, Jack (Sandra Scoppettone)
After inheriting money and making a good investment, **Fortune Fanelli** left the NYPD and became a PI. Living in Thompson Street, in the SoHo district, where his first case takes place and in whose community he is actively involved, Fanelli is also raising two teenage children dumped on him by their career woman mother in an unusual subplot. His mother is the local butcher and the book is full of good characters. The PWA voted it Best First Novel.

> A Creative Kind Of Killer* (1984)

East, Mark — LAWRENCE, Hilda
Easter, Dyke — Radio: DYKE EASTER, DETECTIVE
EASTON, Nat
A thriller writer on the side, **Bill Banning** has a London private enquiry agency in books described by Boucher as "less than lightweight—bantam, perhaps, or even fly—but they have a certain amusing insouciance."

> Always The Wolf (UK 1957)
> One Good Turn (UK 1957)
> Bill For Damages (UK 1958, 1958)
> Mistake Me Not (UK 1958, 1959)
> A Book For Banning (UK 1959, 1959)
> Quick Tempo (UK 1960)
> Right For Trouble (UK 1960)
> Forgive Me, Lovely Lady (UK 1961)

Easy, John — GOULART, Ron
EBY, Lois & John C. FLEMING.
The "daddy of all private dicks" makes progress so slowly the heroine begins to doubt he really is the famous **Zachary Stone**. Her impatient fiancé thinks detecting is dangerous, but chance-taking sleuthess **Pat O'Leary** wants a last fling, closing out an outstanding and baffling case. Klein doesn't seem to have found this one, but I feel sure she would have hated it. Another Eby & Fleming novel, *The Velvet Fleece* (1947), is in Pronzini's Alternative Hall of Fame.

Stone: The Case Of The Malevolent Twin (1946); as The Case Of
               The Wicked Twin (194?)
O'Leary: Hell Hath No Fury (1947)

Eckenberg, Dennis — McRAE, Diana
EDGELY, Leslie
Some one is trying to either kill or drive Sharon Carlin mad and her one hope is San Francisco PI **Jay Rogers** whom she met after escaping from arrest for murder, but even he seems to fail her before the mounting

suspense moves on to what *NYT* calls "its thrilling climax." See also **Robert BLOOMFIELD**.

Fear No More (1946, UK 1948)

Edgarson, John — WESTLAKE, Donald E.

Edmondson, William — DOUGLAS, John

EDWARDS, Alexander

Novelization of the misconceived revamping of Hammett's *The Maltese Falcon* featuring **Sam Spade Jr.** See **Films: The BLACK BIRD**.

The Black Bird (1975, UK 1976)

EFFINGER, George Alec

Living in the Budayeen, an Arab city, **Marid Audran** is a "cyberpunk" hero, more of a strong-arm than a PI, in a near future dominated by multinational corporations, with such as things as plug-in data modules ("daddies") for instant learning and personality modifiers ("moddies"). Marid modifies himself into Nero Wolfe at one point, though normally preferring old-fashioned drugs and alcohol. The setting is little used, the technology is heavy-handed and the personality changes are superficial. See also **DOZOIS, Gardner & EFFINGER**.

When Gravity Fails (1987)

Elfoot, Miss — NEBEL, Frederick

ELLIN, Stanley 1916-1986

The famous short story writer created three PIs, all successful, selfish, ruthless businessmen with expensive tastes and no interest in the weak and innocent. He won an Edgar for a book about **Murray Kirk**, head of New York agency Conmy & Kirk, a tough investigator with ethical problems. **Jake Dekker** is an ice-cold freelance New York insurance investigator. **Johnny Milano** of New York's Watrous Associates made his first appearance in what has been described as an hardboiled Agatha Christie house-party mystery. The other, described as one of the most ambitious and disturbing novels in contemporary mystery fiction, concerns the passions raised by racism. All Ellin's books are suspenseful psychological studies, finely plotted and characterized. See **Films: SUNBURN**.

Kirk: The Eighth Circle (1958, UK 1959)
Dekker: The Bind (1970); as The Man From Nowhere (UK 1970)
Milano: Star Light, Star Bright* (1979, UK 1979)
         The Dark Fantastic* (1983, UK 1983)

ELLINGTON, Richard 1914-1980

Starting as an actor, like his creator, **Steve Drake**'s career as a New York PI is interrupted by the war, with the superior series starting with the ex-GI going back to his old trade. A wisecracker and brandy drinker, Drake charges $30 a day from his office on 44th between Broadway & 8th. Ellington was chief scriptwriter for a radio series created by Hammett, see **Radio: The FAT MAN.**

      Shoot The Works (1948, UK 1950)
      It's A Crime (1948, UK 1956)
      Stone Cold Dead (1950, UK 1952)
      Exit For A Dame (1951, UK 1954)
      Just Killing Time (1953, UK 1954); as Shakedown (1955)

ELLIOTT, David

Novelization of an episode of **TV: PRIVATE EYE** featuring '50s LA sleuth **Jack Cleary** and his assistant **Johnny Betts**. See **T.N. ROBB** and **Max LOCKHART** for others in the series.

      Blue Movie (1988)

Elliott, Maggie — TAYLOR, Elizabeth Atwood

Ellis, Tony — KOEHLER, Robert Portner

ELLROY, James

Noted for his extraordinary *noir* police thrillers, Ellroy started his career with a PI novel, and a very odd and exceptional one. **Fritz Brown**, 33 year old ex-cop and alcoholic is the king of the LA automobile repossessors, or repo men, who maintains his Brown Detective Agency's Rancho Park office as a tax write-off and somewhere quiet to read. In his first, and last, case in years, Brown emerges not just as a romantic but a Romantic in the German sense, a man who can embrace Brahms and brass-knuckles without contradiction.

      Brown's Requiem (1981, UK 1983)

EMERSON, Earl W.

Driving his red pickup around Seattle, Washington, ex-cop, with a fat pension, **Thomas Black** gets involved in interesting, fast paced cases with a fine sense of place. A non-drinker, Black has a running sub-plot in his platonic relationship with his beautiful lawyer lodger. *Poverty Bay* won a PWA Best Paperback Award. His customers "loved" *Rainy City*, but Bourgeau confesses to giving up on it.

      The Rainy City (1985)
      Poverty Bay (1985)
      Nervous Laughter (1986)
      Fat Tuesday (1987)
      Deviant Behaviour (1988)

Emory, Jason — KOOTZ

Endicott, Charles — RUDLOFF, Stephen A.

ENEFER, Douglas
All the women go for New York eye **Dale Shand**, a "big, handsome devil" as one calls him. The whisky drinking ex-reporter had a bigger, or more enduring, following in Britain than in the author's native America. The sex is more suggestive talk than action. Enefer also wrote two, both for British publishers, novelizations of **TV: CANNON** featuring fat **Frank Cannon**, others being written by **Paul DENVER** and **Richard GALLAGHER.**

Shand: The Deadly Quiet (1961, UK 1973)
               The Long Chance (1961, UK 1973)
               The Dark Kiss (1965, UK 1973)
               The Shining Trap (UK 1965)
               The Painted Death (UK 1966)
               The Long Hot Night (UK 1967)
               The Girl Chase (UK 1968)
               Girl In Arms (UK 1968)
               The Gilded Kiss (UK 1969)
Cannon: Farewell, Little Sister (UK 1978)
               Shoot-Out (UK 1979)

ENGEL, Howard
Part of the new Canadian crime wave with Ted WOOD and Eric Wright, Engel has elected to write about **Benny Cooperman**, nice guy Jewish PI in Grantham, Ontario. Intelligent and dogged, Benny isn't a tough guy but strong enough and compassionate. A classic North American sleuth— his first case opens with a beautiful woman coming through his St. Andrew Street office door—the plots are well-constructed and the characters, especially the regulars, are real.

        The Suicide Murders* (Can 1980, 1984, UK 1985)
        The Ransom Game (Can 1981, UK 1982, 1984)
        Murder On Location (Can 1982, 1983, UK 1985)
        Murder Sees The Light (Can 1984, 1985, UK 1986)
        A City Called July (Can 1986, 1986, UK 1987)
        A Victim Must Be Found (1988, UK 1988)

ENGLEMAN, Paul
A former minor league second baseman, **Mark Renzler**'s baseball career ended when a fastball blinded him in one eye. After two years as a New York cop, he set up as a PI on West 72nd. Set in 1961, he's still an avid baseball fan and the combination of his background and reputation brings him a baseball heavy case, followed by one set in the *Playboy* world and another in television. Witty and assured writing. The PWA voted *Dead In*

Center Field Best Paperback Original.
> Dead In Center Field (1983)
> Catch A Fallen Angel (1986, UK 1987)
> Murder-In-Law (1987)

Ericson, Steven — STARK, Michael

ERNST, Paul

A specialist in unsolvable crimes, **Seekay** of Chicago sits in dim light when he interviews clients because he has "a blank curve of something pink and softly shining, like celluloid, from his hairline to just under where a chin should be," instead of a face, though he has an artificial one he puts on when he goes out. "Madam Murder—And The Corpse Brigade" (*Strange Detective Mysteries* 1937) is in **A7**. Boucher admired a Lt. Jim Ryan book that also featured **Sam Cates** of Home Protection Insurance, New York, "a pro of the old school, competent, likeable, medium-tough, who can use both fists and brains." Originally an adjuster, the ex-Marine, whose knee has been rebuilt with a metal whose name ends in *-ium*, has an unclassified job after showing a flair for detection.

> The Bronze Mermaid (1952, UK 1954)

ESTLEMAN, Loren D.

Critics often (too often) talk about successors to Hammett, Chandler and Macdonald, and Estleman is a favorite candidate, particularly with British reviewers, on the strength of his books about Detroit PI **Amos Walker**, though Bourgeau, for one, dissents. A Vietnam vet and stateside Military Policeman with a BA in sociology, street-wise introvert Walker dropped out of police academy because of his distrust of authority. He lives in Hamtramck, has an office on West Grand River, drives a souped up Cutlass, in which he keeps a Luger, and charges $250 a day for putting his client ahead of the law, though not his principles. Detroit, where, in Estleman's words, "the American Dream stalled and sat rusting in the rain" is a vividly drawn and essential part of the books. *Sugartown* was voted Best Novel by the PWA. Anthologized Walker short stories, all of which are also in *General Murders*, are "Bloody July" (**A1** #1), "Blond And Blue" (**A1** #4 which also contains an interview with Estleman), "Bodyguards Shoot Second" (**A2** #1), "The Crooked Way" (**A2** #3), "The Prettiest Dead Girl In Detroit" (**A15**), "I'm In The Book" (**A16**) and "Greektown" (*Alfred Hitchcock's Mystery Magazine* 1983, **A14**), plus "State Of Grace" (**A17**) which introduced a new PI, **Ralph Poteet**. Estleman has a **Philip Marlowe** short story, "Gun Music," in **A12**.

> Motor City Blue (1980, UK 1982)
> Angel Eyes (1981, UK 1982) **>**

The Midnight Man (1982, UK 1983)
The Glass Highway (1983, UK 1984)
Sugartown* (1985, UK 1986)
Every Brilliant Eye (1986, UK 1986)
Lady Yesterday (1987, UK 1987)
Downriver (1988, UK 1988)
General Murders (1988). 10 SS

ESTOW, Daniel

In his first appearance, 6'3" 175 pound **William Schaefer** worked for the Worldwide Detective Agency in New York but met and went into independent partnership with **Ann Lang**. People make the mistake of thinking that he's younger, gentler and less determined than he is as he moves through a sordid and violent world.

The Moment Of Fiction (1979)
The Moment Of Silence (1980)

ETHAN, John B.

Listed in the New York phone book as a management consultant, **Victor Grant's** specialty is catching embezzlers. His operation, which includes four legmen in various parts of America, is small, but thriving. Ethan's writing is below average but the Big Business backgrounds are well done.

The Black Gold Murders (1959)
Call Girls For Murder (1960)
Murder On Wall Street (1960)

Evans, Hump — DENNIS, Ralph

EVANS, John = BROWNE, Howard

An investigator for the State Attorney General's office in Chicago, **Paul Pine** quits and gets his PI license, opening an office in the Clawson Building, East Jackson, a good deal better appointed than most. Dry martini drinking Pine is a considerate and sensitive man, but the appeal of his books lies mostly in Browne's fine writing. Lively and witty, Browne's style shines in his crackling use of metaphor, simile and nutshell description and, as Pronzini says (P&M), all three Evans titles are first rate. Two later books were published under Browne's own name.

Halo In Blood (1946; as by **BROWNE** UK 1988)
Halo For Satan (1948, UK 1949)
Halo In Brass (1949, UK 1951; as by **BROWNE** 1988)

Evans, John — CHANDLER, Raymond

EVERSON, David

Former minor league baseball player **Robert Miles** is chief investigator for the Mid-Continental Op & Associates of Springfield, Illinois, the state capital, where his chief source of income is his association with the Speaker of the Illinois House of Representatives who uses him as a political troubleshooter.

> Recount (1988)

EVERSZ, Robert

Tough-guy LA PI **Paul Marston**, former security director turned independent specialist in corporate crime, and his self-appointed assistant, smart, beautiful, Southern California women's boxing champion **Angel Cantini**, are the main attractions in a hardboiled story with plenty of action but uninteresting plot and secondary characters.

> The Bottom Line Is Murder (1988)

Eye, The — BEHM, Marc

FAIR, A.A. = GARDNER, Erle Stanley

In a very different vein from his Perry Mason books, Erle Stanley Gardner used the Fair byline for his series about Cool Confidential Investigations of LA, later Cool & Lam, combining intricate plots and humor. **Bertha Cool**, in her 60s, irascible, penny pinching, given to archaic slang and weighing over 200 pounds, inherited the agency from her husband. **Donald Lam**, a mere 127 pounds and 5'6", a shrewd disbarred attorney, does the legwork. Kathleen Gregory Klein (see Bibliography) is particularly interesting in her observations on Gardner's sabotage of his female creation. Many of the Fair books are dedicated to prison officers, part of Gardner's campaign for prison reform.

> The Bigger They Come (1939); Lam To The Slaughter (UK 1939)
> Turn On The Heat (1940, UK 1940)
> Gold Comes In Bricks (1940, UK 1942)
> Spill The Jackpot (1941, UK 1948)
> Double Or Quits (1941, UK 1949)
> Owls Don't Blink* (1942, UK 1951)
> Bats Fly At Dusk (1942, UK 1951)
> Cats Prowl At Night (1943, UK 1949)
> Give 'Em The Axe (1944); as An Axe To Grind (UK 1951)
> Crows Can't Count (1946, UK 1953)
> Fools Die On Friday (1947, UK 1955)
> Bedrooms Have Windows (1949, UK 1956)
> Top Of The Heap (1952, UK 1957)
> Some Women Won't Wait (1953, UK 1958)
> Beware The Curves (1956, UK 1957)
> You Can Die Laughing (1957, UK 1958) >

> Some Slips Don't Show (1958, UK 1959)
> The Count Of Nine (1958, UK 1959)
> Pass The Gravy (1959, UK 1960)
> Kept Women Can't Quit (1960, UK 1961)
> Bachelors Get Lonely (1961, UK 1962)
> Shills Can't Cash Chips (1961); as Stop At The Red Light (UK 1962)
> Try Anything Once (1962, UK 1963)
> Fish Or Cut Bait (1963, UK 1964)
> Up For Grabs (1964, UK 1965)
> Cut Thin To Win (1965, UK 1966)
> Widows Wear Weeds (1966, UK 1966)
> Traps Need Fresh Bait (1967, UK 1968)
> All Grass Isn't Green (1970, UK 1970)

FAIRLIE, Gerard 1899-1983

Himself the inspiration for Bulldog Drummond, Fairlie took over the series on Sapper's death and greatly improved it, toning down the racism and jingoism. Outside the Bulldog canon, Fairlie also wrote a series about London private investigator **Johnny Macall**, former police Superintendent, possessed of natural inquisitiveness and Scottish obstinacy. Also a fairly stiff upper-lip. Very English.

> Winner Take All (UK 1953, 1953)
> No Sleep For Macall (UK 1955)
> Deadline For Macall (UK 1956, 1956)
> Double The Bluff (UK 1957)
> Macall Gets Curious (UK 1959)
> Please Kill My Cousin (UK 1961)

FAIRMAN, Paul W. 1916-1977

A quick scan persuaded me that PI **Rick Mason**, who is blessed with "the lucrative Global Indemnity account," was too third rate to justify a high asking price. I may be wrong.

> The Glass Ladder (1950)

Falconer, Daniel — GAGE, Edwin
Fane, Angus — YARDLEY, James A.
Fanelli, Fortune — EARLY, Jack
Fannin, Harry — MARKSON, David
FANTONI, Barry

Two successful and subtle PI parodies were written by an Englishman. **Mike Dime** is a licensed PI in 1948 Philadelphia and has all the trappings. The style, plots and character are pure Chandler, with a keen wit taking the metaphors and similes to elaborate and hilarious heights. Rather charmingly, Baker & Nietzel think that *Private Eye*, the British satirical magazine on which Fantoni works, is the equivalent of *Armchair Detective*.

> Mike Dime (UK 1980, 1981)
> Stickman (UK 1982)

Farabaugh, Michelle — BABULA, William
Faraday, Frank & Steve — TV: FARADAY AND CO
Faraday, Mike — COPPER, Basil
Fargo, Neil — GORES, Joe
FARJEON, J. Jefferson 1883-1955
A prolific British author, known for his skill at plots, one of whose books opens with a judge's summing up, complete with lengthy quotations from testimony. When the judge is incapacitated before concluding the summary, and the trial is adjourned, **Paul Bishop** is called in to mount a last minute investigation.

> The Judge Sums Up (UK 1942, 1942)

Farland, William — ROTH, Holly
Farley, Tom — SILER, Jack
Farmer, Jack — PACHTER, Josh
Farrel, John — HITCHENS, Bert & Dolores
FARREN, Mick
Having rated highly in an unexplained test, 21st century "leisure-out" **Marlowe** is allowed to live as a make-believe 40s PI with money and space set aside for him and his like while an android takes his place in the workaday world. Then he's hired, by a beautiful female client, for a real case, finding her missing sister. Described by *Drood Review* as occasionally humerous but more thriller than mystery and not very successful at it, pulling too many rabbits out of the hat.

> The Long Orbit (1988)

Faverden, Alice — KING, Frank
FEIFFER, Jules
The famous cartoonist and humorist made one satirical incursion into the PI field with a take-off of Agatha Christie's *The Murder Of Roger Ackroyd*. Presented as the diary of young **Roger Ackroyd** who becomes increasingly and eventually totally involved in the life of one of his clients, it is tedious and incoherent with insufficient funny moments. As one critic remarked, it's like a bowl of soggy raisin bran with too few raisins.

> Ackroyd (1977, UK 1978)

FENADY, Andrew
After plastic surgery to make him the double of Humphrey Bogart, **Sam Marlow**, his name officially changed, sets up as an PI on Larchmont & Beverly, LA, complete with vintage 1939 Plymouth coupé, an office with a rolltop desk and a beautiful blonde secretary who looks like Marilyn Monroe and makes as much sense as Gracie Allen. Dedicated to Hammett, Chandler, Bogart and Dick Powell (Fenady is a film producer), the books' confusion of image and reality are enormous fun. Note that Marlow's name is persistently, and incorrectly, spelt Marlowe in secondary sources.
See **Films: The MAN WITH BOGART'S FACE.**
> The Man With Bogart's Face (1977)
> The Secret Of Sam Marlow (1980)

Fenner, Dave — CHASE, James Hadley
Fenner, Jack — COXE, George Harmon
Fenner, Maxwell — BOOTH, Louis F.
Ferguson, Jim — VAN ATTA, Winfred
FERGUSON, W(illiam) B(lair) M(orton) 1881-1967
Quite where Ferguson picked up his image of America and his concepts of speech patterns is difficult to imagine, but the British author's books about **Daniel J. Cluer**, boss of the Manhattan Investigation Bureau, are state of the art ersatz. The dialogue, particularly that of Cluer's ex-con sidekick Bodinsky, is unbelievably inept, challenging the reader to progress far enough to assess the plot.
> Escape To Eternity (UK 1944)
> The Shayne Case (UK 1947)

Fernanda — MILLER, Victor B.
Ferrell, Hank — HOLDEN, Genevieve
FICKLING, G.G. (Gloria Fickling & Forrest E. Fickling)
"The sexiest private eye ever to pull a trigger" is **Honey West**, 5'5" blonde with a 38-22-36 body obvious enough in the negligible clothing she wears and more so when she loses even that. Though sexploitative in the extreme, with footling plots, there is, as one critic remarked, a certain prefeminist charm in seeing the hardboiled Honey at work in a man's world. Late in her career, in tune with fashion, she moved from Long Beach, California, to New York to become an "international eye-spy" for the CIA. Honey appeared in the TV series *Burke's Law* and had a short series of her own, **TV: HONEY WEST. Erik March** is a Sunset Boulevard, LA, PI who calls himself a "corporation consultant-investigator, who sometimes doubles in brass, babes and bullets to make a buck." His fee is $1000 a day. >

West: This Girl For Hire* (1957)
         A Gun For Honey (1958)
         Girl On The Loose (1958)
         Honey In The Flesh (1959)
         Girl On The Prowl (1959)
         Kiss For A Killer (1960)
         Dig A Dead Doll (1960)
         Blood And Honey (1961)
         Bombshell (1964)
         Stiff As A Broad (1971). Features **March**
         Honey On Her Tail (1971)
March: Naughty But Dead (1962)
         The Case Of The Radioactive Redhead (1963)
         The Crazy Mixed-Up Nude (1964)

Fiddler — MAXWELL, A.E.

FIELDING, A. (Dorothy Feilding)
Among 20+ Inspector Pointer novels he appeared in one only long enough to turn a case over to British PI **Hugh Duncan** in what *SR* described as "slightly muddled but richly adventurous yarn of fabulous treasure . . . So-so." Nicholas Blake thought it was "written in a quiet, unpretentious but no less effective manner," and *The Times* commented on the "excellent background of the Suffolk marshes." Fortunately for him, Duncan drives a Rolls Royce equipped with bullet-proof glass.
         Murder In Suffolk (UK 1938; as by **A.E. FIELDING** 1938)

FINE, Peter
A Southern California Gloomy Private Eye, as William DeAndrea dubbed them, is **Harry Lake** in what Baker & Nietzel describe as a stylish but hackneyed novel. A former Vietnam PoW and ex-cop, Lake's Pacific Yacht Sales in LA is going broke and the book ends with a near-promise of reinstatement as a Beverly Hills Homicide detective.
         Troubled Waters (1981)

Firth, Ian — PETERS, Ludovic

FISCHER, Bruno
A popular pulp writer, as **Russell GRAY**, who made the transition to paper-back novels, Fischer described his usual writing manner as "movement and suspense with very little violence . . . ordinary people in extraordinary situations." His main character, pipe-smoking, happily married **Ben Helm**, once a promising Coast City police lieutenant forced to resign, now a compassionate New York PI who depends more on wits than fists, and writes and lectures on criminology. >

The Dead Men Grin (1945, UK 1947)
More Deaths Than One (1947, UK 1950)
The Restless Hands (1949, UK 1950)
The Angels Fell (1950, UK 1951); as The Flesh Was Cold (1951)
The Silent Dust* (1950, UK 1951)
The Paper Circle (1951, UK 1952); as Stripped For Murder (1953)

Fisher, Eric — ANTHONY, Evelyn
Fisher, Natalie Dauntless — LAURENCE, Gerald
FISHER, Steve 1912-1980
Reflecting both pulp roots and the fact, as Frank GRUBER remarked, that he "was never afraid to put his heart on a printed page," Fisher's 20 novels mix toughness and sentiment. For *Black Mask* he created an Hawaiian PI, Kip I. Muldane, but only one novel has a PI hero. **Johnny Ryan** is a failure, specializing in phony divorce cases and sharing a room and telephone in a shabby building with four other tenants. A shady deal, designed to free him from his financial and emotional problems rather improbably redeems him and everybody round him. See **Films: The LADY IN THE LAKE/ROADBLOCK/SONG OF THE THIN MAN** and **TV: BARNABY JONES/KING OF DIAMONDS**.
Winter Kill (1946)

Fiske, Lee — ROBERTS, Lee
Fistoulari, Ginny — STEPHENS, Reed
Fitzgerald, F. Scott — ABBOTT, Keith
Fitzgerald, Kevin — TOPOR, Tom
Flagg, Conan — WREN, M.K.
Flaherty, Tim — HURLEY, Gene
Flamond — Radio: The CRIME FILES OF FLAMOND
Fleck, Peter — CLAPPERTON, Richard
FLEMING, John C. — see EBY, Lois & FLEMING
FLEMING, Robert
After another PI, about to make accusations against the LAPD, is shot at a police banquet, **Simon Crole** investigates in a manner described by *NYT* at its most prissy as hop-skip-and-jump story-telling, complaining that the author "has thus succeeded in confusing the reader in a manner that is most annoying." *SR* called it "some very tough eggs capably dished up in agile yarn." **Robert H. LEITFRED** wrote three books featuring a PI by the same name in the 30s, and I rather assume he and Fleming are one and the same. >

Night Freight Murder (1942); as A Bullet In His Cap (1942); as
Murder Comes To Dinner (UK 1943); as And Death Drove
On (194?)

FLEMING-ROBERTS, G.T.
A prolific pulp writer, particularly for *Dime Detective*, with only one
anthologized story, "The Death Master" (*Ten Detective Aces* 1935;
A18), featuring **Jerry Thacker**, Cosmo Life Insurance, Indianapolis,
investigator. See **Films: FIND THE BLACKMAILER.**
Fletcher, Jillian — JERINA, Carol
Fletcher, Johnny — GRUBER, Frank
Fletcher, Virgil — CRONIN, George
Flute, Adam — LAUNAY, Droo
FLYNN, Jay / J.M. 1927?-1986
His real name is a secret revealed only to men he is about to kill. **Slim
Jim Bannerman** is an operative for the Rocky Mountain office of
Gallows Detective Agency, San Francisco, founded by ex- Pinkerton
agent Vernon Gallowes. Set in 1916, the twilight of the Wild West, the
stories avoid many, but by no means all, the usual Western clichés. As
J.M. FLYNN, the author wrote a novel described by Boucher as
"lightweight but fast and ingenious" featuring credible and likeable PI
Burl Stannard and novelized **TV: SURFSIDE 6** featuring Miami
Beach PIs **Ken Madison, Dave Thorne** and **Sandy Winfield III.**
Stannard: Terror Tournament (1959)
Bannerman: Bannerman (1976)
            Border Incident (1976)
Madison: SurfSide 6 (1962)
Flynn, Peter — KENNEALY, G.P.
FLYNN, T.T.
From *Detective Fiction Weekly* (1933; A3) comes a story, "The Deadly
Orchid," with a hero-narrator, rugged redhead **Mike Harris** of the Blaine
Agency, overshadowed by his female partner **Trixie Meehan**, "a little
frail slip of a thing with forget-me-not eyes, a knock 'em dead face and a
clinging vine manner that covered concentrated hell. She had a razor
tongue, muscles like steel springs, a brain that made me dizzy at times,
and absolutely no fear." Also in Tony Goodstone, ed.;*The Pulps* (1970).
Foley, John — WOODFIN, Henry
Fontaine, Danny — ARD, William
FOOTE-SMITH, Elizabeth
Not much of a writer, Foote-Smith's two romance-mysteries featured
gentlemanly PI **Will Woodfield** and his bright, attractive, modishly

cool female assistant, who talk about bed a good deal without actually doing much about it. Henri C. Veit (*Library Journal*) found the solution of *Never Say Die* involving "not one but a series of wilted clichés and jarring coincidences."

        A Gentle Albatross (1976)
        Never Say Die (1977)

Foran, Mark — BALLARD, Willis Todhunter
Forbes, Rusty — OZAKI, Milton K.
Ford, Ashton — PENDLETON, Don
Ford, Brad — HOBSON, Hank
FORD, Leslie (Zenith Jones Brown 1898-1983)
A marginal PI writer, Ford combined Had-I-But-Known with gentility. She herself said that she was only interested in "murders done by . . . people I might play bridge or dine with," i.e. the wealthy, urbane and educated. Retired Army Intelligence **Colonel John T. Primrose**, assisted by former Army Sergeant **Phineas Buck** and beautiful Georgetown widow **Grace Latham**, who also appeared in an adventure of her own, do the upper-crust necessary. Latham, oddly, is mainly used as a vehicle for anti-feminist polemics.

Primrose: The Strangled Witness (1934)
            Ill Met By Moonlight* (1937, UK 1937)
            The Simple Way Of Poison (1937, UK 1938)
            Reno Rendezvous (1939); as Mr. Cromwell Is Dead (UK 1939)
            False To Any Man (1939); as Snow-White Murder (UK 1940)
            Old Lover's Ghost (1940); as The Capital Crime (UK 1941)
            The Murder Of A Fifth Columnist (1941)
            Murder In The O.P.M. (1942); as The Priority Murder (1943)
            Siren In The Night* (1943, UK 1944)
            All For The Love Of A Lady (1944); as Crack Of Dawn (UK 1945)
            The Philadelphia Murder (1945, UK 1945)
            Honolulu Story (1946); as Honolulu Murder Story (UK 1947); as Honolulu Murders (1967)
            The Woman In Black (1947, UK 1948)
            The Devil's Stronghold (1948, UK 1948)
            Washington Whispers Murder (1953); as The Lying Jade (UK 1953)
Latham: Three Bright Pebbles (1938, UK 1938)

Fortune, Dan — COLLINS, Michael
Fortune, Rocky — Radio: ROCKY FORTUNE

FORWARD, Robert
Suffering from permanent insomnia, **Alexander L'Hiboux** prowls the
streets of LA. An unlicensed private eye, he's never left a case unsolved,
"and there have been a lot of cases. Enough to fill a cemetery." L'Hiboux,
French for The Owl, "a poetic coincidence" because he is a mix of
American Indian, Negro and Irish, has neither home nor car nor any
possessions that aren't in his pockets. Gritty and unsettling, in Bourgeau's
words, like *The Shadow* written by Cornell Woolrich.

> The Owl (1984)

FOSTER, Richard = CHABER, M.E.
New Yorker **Pete Draco** moves down to Miami Beach and opens
Undercover Inc. on 27th & Collins, which brings him a nice office, a
comfortable apartment, a well-stocked private bar, a white Cadillac and a
lot of trouble, mostly with corrupt and brutal backwoods Florida cops.
Tough, fast-moving and menacing.

> Bier For A Chaser (1959, UK 1960)
>
> Too Late For Mourning (1960, UK 1961)

Fowler, Myron & Janet — TV: SIMON & SIMON

FOX, James M. (Johannes Knipscheer)
Although he only came to America from Holland in 1946, Knipscheer's
semi-hardboiled books about **Johnny**, glib, savvy ex-Army Counter-
Intelligence Corps Major, now a PI (license #2952A) at 6130 North
Broxton Avenue, Westwood, LA, and **Suzy Marshall**, referred to as
"the little woman," are reasonable imitations of the Nick & Nora Charles
style, complete with dog, a Great Dane called Khan, though it should be
added that Boucher was a great admirer of Fox.

> The Lady Regrets (1947, UK 1947)
>
> Death Commits Bigamy (1948, UK 1950)
>
> The Inconvenient Bride (1948, UK 1951)
>
> The Gentle Hangman (1950, UK 1952)
>
> The Wheel Is Fixed (1951, UK 1952)
>
> The Aleutian Blue Mink (1951, UK 1952); as Fatal In Furs
> (1952)
>
> The Iron Virgin (1951, UK 1954)
>
> The Scarlet Slippers (1952, UK 1955)
>
> A Shroud For Mr. Bundy (1952, UK 1955)
>
> Bright Serpent (1953, UK 1956); as Rites For A Killer (1957)

Fox, Tecumseh — STOUT, Rex

Fox, Thomas — Films: FOXTRAP

FOXX, Jack = PRONZINI, Bill
Pinkerton agent **Fergus O'Hara** gets valuable assistance from his wife **Hatty**, "women being able to obtain information in places men cannot." Their adventure is set in San Francisco and on the Sacramento River steamer *Freebooty* in 1863. Full of engaging characters and blending historical fact with an entertaining plot.
      Freebooty* (1976)

FRANCIS, Dick
In almost 30 books, the famous horse racing thriller writer and ex-champion jockey has only used one hero twice, **Sid Halley**, a former champion steeplechase rider. Like all Francis' heroes, he starts off flawed, having lost a hand and his self-respect in a racing accident, and detached, finding himself through resolving intrigue and murder, with the inevitable torture thrown in, getting his training with the Radnor agency, then setting up on his own, specializing, of course, in racing cases. See **TV: The RACING GAME**.
      Odds Against* (UK 1965, 1966)
      Whip Hand (UK 1979, 1980)

FRANCIS, William (William Urell)
Handsome LA PI **Anthony Martin**, with an office in the Crail Building on Broadway, has to be ultra-tough as he works the sleazy side of town and is, but has a equally tough sentimental streak. Standard hardboiled fare but compellingly sordid—*NYT* complained about "unsavory episodes." **Steve Cash** was another LA shamus, tackling mobsters and municipal corruption. From Boucher's review *The Corrupters* (1953) sounds like another Cash title.
Martin: Rough On Rats (1942); as I.O.U.—Murder (1951)
        Kill Or Cure (1942, UK 1951)
        Bury Me Not (1943, UK 1950)
Cash: Don't Dig Deeper (1953)

FRANKLIN, Eugene = BANDY, Eugene Franklin
A corporation lawyer who turned to criminal law then to sleuthing, **Berkeley Hoy Barnes** of New York City is a hypochondriac and meeting strangers upsets his stomach. So his girl-chasing assistant **Larry Howe**, a one-time hippy, has to keep a pharmacopoeia on him to cope with Barnes' various medical requirements. Fast, sharp and funny.
      Murder Trapp (1971)
      The Money Murders (1972)
      The Bold House Murders (1973, UK 1975)

Franklin, Ken — TV: INTERNATIONAL DETECTIVE

FRANKLIN, Max = DEMING, Richard
Novelizations of **TV: CHARLIE'S ANGELS** featuring **Charles Townsend**'s Detective Agency with its unseen male boss and three female operatives, **Sabrina Duncan, Kelly Garrett** and **Jill Munroe**. Deming also novelized **TV: VEGA$**, featuring Las Vegas PI **Dan Tanna**.

Townsend: Charlie's Angels (1977, UK 1977)
Angels In Chains (1977, UK 1977)
Angels On A String (1977)
The Killing Kind (1977, UK 1977)
Angels On Ice (1978, UK 1978)
Tanna: Vega$ (1978)

Fraser, Alan — DESMOND, Hugh
FRAY, Al (Ralph Salaway)
A Las Vegas PI who specializes in exposing crooked gambling, **Barney Conroy** featured in a novel described by Boucher as pretty simple and oversexed but fast and entertaining.
The Dame's The Game (1960)

Frayne, Ambrose & Dominique — McINTOSH, J.T.
FRAZER, Andrew = MARLOWE, Stephen
Out of the Red Hook slums of Brooklyn, **Duncan Pride**, former All-American quarterback, drifts into becoming an LA PI specializing in sports cases, having lost his place in the LA Rams after being crippled for not obeying game-fixing instructions from gamblers to whom he owed money. Some vivid characterization and tough action.
Find Eileen Hardin—Alive (1959)
The Fall Of Marty Moon (1960)

FRAZER, Robert Caine (John Creasey 1908-1973)
A Briton working in America, **Mark Kilby** is an ultra-confident, self-assured investigator for Regal Investment Security Corporation in a series written under one of John Creasey's many pseudonyms. Even Boucher, a great admirer of Creasey, particularly as J.J.Marric, found them weak.
Mark Kilby Solves A Murder (1959); as R.I.S.C. (UK 1962); as The Timid Tycoon (UK 1965)
Mark Kilby And The Miami Mob (1960); as The Miami Mob (UK 1965, with Mark Kilby Stands Alone)
Mark Kilby And The Secret Syndicate (1960); as The Secret Syndicate (UK 1963)
The Hollywood Hoax (1961, UK 1964)
Mark Kilby Takes A Risk (1962) >

> Mark Kilby Stands Alone (1962, UK 1965 with The Miami
> Mob); as Mark Kilby And The Manhattan Murders (UK
> 1966)

Frederickson, Dr. Robert — CHESBRO, George

FREDMAN, John

NYT commented of the third novel about tough and cynical British PI
Charles Dexter, "sometimes a book is so bad it has a transcendent
charm of its own . . . He has devoured Hammett and got indigestion."

> The Fourth Agency (UK 1969, 1970)
> The False Joanna (UK 1970, 1971)
> Epitaph To A Bad Cop (UK 1973, 1973)

FREDMAN, Mike

Based at 39 King Street, in London's Covent Garden, **Willie Halliday**
doesn't smoke or drink, is a vegetarian, meditates and spends his spare
time working on a translation of a Bhutanese holy book. For all that he's
tough, though better at taking punishment than giving it, and a
wisecracker. The plots are English-style, with more talk than action, little
violence and slow-moving.

> You Can Always Blame The Rain (UK 1978, 1980)
> Kisses Leave No Fingerprints (UK 1979, 1980)

Free, Donald — Films: PRIVATE DETECTIVE 62

FREEMAN, Martin J.

Of the first of two novels featuring Chicago detective **Jerry Todd** and
his assistant **Mary Clerkenwell**, *NYT* observed "some of Todd's
deductions verge a little too much on the miraculous and his arrangements
for winding up the case are so hurried that it is only by good luck that
they succeed," but found it swift-moving and readable. Pronzini inducted
The Scarf On The Scarecrow into his Alternative Hall of Fame (*Son Of
Gun In Cheek*).

> The Case Of The Blind Mouse (1935, UK 1936)
> The Scarf On The Scarecrow (1938)

French, Chickie — KAYE, William

Freund, Max — CHETWYND, Bridget

FREY, James N.

A Rocky Marciano type slugger in an age of finesse, motorcycle riding
Sicilian **Joe Zanca**, a former heavyweight contender known as Zank the
Tank, works for The Agency, "helping desperate people." Living in a
one-bedroom apartment near Broadway & Polk, San Francisco, and
working his way through the *World Book Encyclopedia*, Zanca dreams of
running a training camp in the High Sierra. >

The Long Way To Die (1987)

A Killing In Dreamland (1988)

Friday, Captain Bart — Radio: ADVENTURES BY MORSE

FRIEND, Ed (Richard Wormser 1908-1977)

Novelization of **TV: The MOST DEADLY GAME** featuring criminologists **Ethan Arcane**, **Jonathan Croft** and **Vanessa Smith**. See **Richard GALLAGHER** for another.

The Most Deadly Game; The Corpse In The Castle (1970)

Frisbee — BROWN, R.D.

FRY, Pete (James King)

Of one of Fry's books about **Pete Fry**, ex-Fleet Street journalist, now a Covent Garden (Southampton Street and Maiden Lane), London, PI Julian Symons said "It has the negative virtue that it is not written in pseudo-Americanese and the positive one that the detective's actions are reasonably plausible." Hubin, in *NYT*, however, described *The Brown Suede Jacket* as "unnecessary" and Fry (the sleuth) as having "all the character of an adolescent jellyfish," while Fry (the scribe) "unable to resolve his plot, smothers it in boredom."

The Long Overcoat (UK 1957)

The Scarlet Cloak (UK 1958)

The Grey Sombrero (UK 1958, 1958)

The Black Beret (UK 1959, 1959)

The Purple Dressing Gown (UK 1960)

The Green Scarf (UK 1961)

The Red Stockings (UK 1962, 1962)

The Yellow Trousers (UK 1963, 1963)

The Thick Blue Sweater (UK 1964, 1964)

The Paint-Stained Flannels (UK 1965, 1966)

The Bright Green Waistcoat (UK 1967, 1967)

The Orange Necktie (UK 1968)

The Brown Suede Jacket (UK 1968, 1968)

The White Crash Helmet (UK 1969, 1969)

The Black Cotton Gloves (UK 1970)

Frye, Chip — TV: SMALL & FRYE

Fuller, Danny — HUGGINS, Roy

Fuller, Max — ULLMAN, James Michael

FULLER, Samuel

Hardly surprisingly, the famous film director's one PI novel, based on his 1972 German financed Euro-thriller film starring Glen Corbett, has a vivid, fast-paced, cinematic feel, particularly in the dialogue. Sandy, a

New Yorker whose second name we never learn, is in Bonn to investigate the murder of his partner. See **Films: DEAD PIGEON ON BEETHOVEN STREET.**

> Dead Pigeon On Beethoven Street (1974)

FURST, Richard

Ex-marijuana middleman, ex-Chinese restaurant owner **Roger Levin** is an occasional unlicensed PI in New York, or, as he describes it, "a freelance operative specializing in the disbursal of funds under vague circumstances, plus other services on a cost-plus basis," which loosely translates as bagman. Only marginally a PI, but exciting escapades with well-conceived villains.

> Your Day In The Barrel (1970)
> The Paris Drop (1980)
> The Caribbean Account (1981)

Fury, Jackson — JERINA, Carol

Fury, Johnny — WADE, Harrison

Gabriel, Bill — BLOCHMAN, Lawrence G.

GAGE, Edwin

Gage has written one highly successful polemical PI novel in which Phoenix, Arizona, PI **Dan Falconer** is hired as bodyguard to a construction millionaire whose life is mysteriously threatened and gets involved in the corruption and politics of the nuclear power industry. Gage tells a good, gritty story made more ominous than most by the reality of his grim messages, backed at opportune moments by documentary material on the fearful hazards of nuclear energy and nuclear waste and the slapdash, profit-orientated way in which the industry is run.

> Phoenix No More (1978)

Gage, Jack — TV: LEGMEN

Gahagan, Zeke — McCONNOR, Vincent

GAINES, Audrey (Audrey Gaines Schultz)

Rotund PI **Chauncy O'Day**, whose "stomach trembles," and his red-headed fiancée Cassie Storm, a fortyish nurse he meets in the first novel and who narrates, featured in comic mysteries of which *NYT* commented "some ingenious tricks and plenty of speed."

> The Old Must Die (1939)
> While The Wind Howled (1940)
> The Voodoo Goat (1942)

GAIR, Malcolm (John Dick Scott)

Scottish PI **Mark Raeburn**, ex-Argyll & Sutherland Highlanders Korean War veteran, ex-Metropolitan Police, "on nodding terms with half the crooks and half the tarts in (London's) West End" makes burglar alarms on the side. After walking out of a crooked agency, he sets up on his own. Honest and commonsensical, Raeburn is a believable character with no transatlantic affectations.

> Sapphires On Wednesday (UK 1957, 1957)
> A Long Hard Look (UK 1958)
> The Burning Of Troy (1958, UK 1959)
> The Bad Dream (UK 1960)
> The Schultz Money (UK 1960, 1960)
> Snow Job (UK 1962, 1962)

Gale, Nicholas — CHEYNEY, Peter

GALLAGHER, Gale (Will Oursler & Margaret Scott)

The Acme Investigating Bureau, 5th Avenue, Manhattan, is run by policeman's daughter **Gale Gallagher**, who people expect to be a fat and fifty police matron type, but is actually a resourceful and stylish young woman. One of the first tough female PIs, she specializes in skip-tracing, with the advantage, as she says that "I could be any of the women who work through the night in a big city—waitress, telephone operator, nurse, small-time entertainer . . . even a call girl."

> I Found Him Dead (1947)
> Chord In Crimson (1949, UK 1950)

GALLAGHER, Richard

Novelizations of **TV: CANNON** featuring fat PI **Frank Cannon** (others were by **Paul DENVER** and **Douglas ENEFER**) and of **TV: The MOST DEADLY GAME** (see also **Ed FRIEND**) featuring criminologists **Ethan Arcane, Jonathan Croft & Vanessa Smith**.

> Cannon: Murder By Gemini (1971)
>   The Stewardess Strangler (1971)
> Arcane: The One-Armed Murder (1971)

GALLISON, Kate

There can be few less romantic locations for a PI than Trenton, where **Nick Magaracz** is forced to do a revolting thing, take a job with the State of New Jersey. With the divorce business down because of new legislation, Nick is looking for credentials in industrial espionage. Good parodies of the genre, under-pinned by deft stories, using the oddball location and underscoring it by putting the PI in mundane office environments.

> Unbalanced Accounts (1986)
> The Death Tape (1987)

GALLOWAY, David
An arch parody of Chandler featuring lesbian private eye **Lamaar Ransom**, with a transvestite black male secretary, Lavender Trevelyan, and a beautiful Chicana girl-friend. The place is LA, with Ransom's office in the Cahuenga Building no less, the period 1942, the fee $25 a day, the patter smart-ass and the plot convoluted. Klein admires it considerably.
        Lamaar Ransom, Private Eye (1979, UK 1979)
Galt, Bradford — ROSS, Leonard Q. / ROSTEN, Leo
Galveston, James — CARPENTER, Helen & Lorri
Gant, Steve — LARIAR, Lawrence
Gar, Jo — DECOLTA, Ramon
GARDNER, Erle Stanley 1889-1970
The only current reminder of Gardner's early pulp writing days is a short story, "Leg Man" (*Black Mask* 1938), about tough, womanizing, lawyer's investigator **Pete Winnick** in A19. An essential, but secondary role was played by LA private investigator **Paul Drake** in the Perry Mason series. Gardner, of course, wrote a PI series as **A.A. FAIR**. See **Radio: CHRISTOPHER LONDON.**
Garfin, Mike — BRETT, Martin
Garnish, Harry — McCONNELL, Frank
Garrett — COOK, Glen
Garrett, Kelly — TV: CHARLIE'S ANGELS
Garrett, Mike — BLAINE, Richard
GARRETT, Robert
Orphanage and reform school raised Korean War vet and former hustler **Alan Brett** is clearly identified as a PI, but works for governments, British and French respectively. Choppy but unflagging thrillers replete with torture, beatings, murder, bombings and assorted mayhem.
        Run Down (UK 1970, 1972)
        Spiral (UK 1971, 1972)
GARRISON, Christian
After losing his job on the police force of an unnamed, old-fashioned New South city (*Snakedoctor*, 1980), good old boy **Ace Chaney** works for one of the smallest Paragon International Protective & Detective Corp's offices, making more but bored to death until a colleague gets murdered.
        Paragon Man (1981)
Garrison, Roger — ROVIN, Jeff
GARRITY, Dave J.
Bearing the imprimatur of Mickey Spillane ("Guts, action . . . the kind of stuff I like to read") and a photograph of the two authors together,

Manhattan PI **Peter Braid**'s only adventure, "a bristling sex-hot hunt for a killer named Cain," is more than just influenced by Spillane. Braid, ex-Marine WW2 veteran, holder of the Navy Cross and judo expert, spends much time on the phone to Mike Hammer, seeking advice, and the story is taken from a 1954 Mike Hammer comic strip. There is considerable confusion about the spelling of the author's name, but Dave J. Garrity is, in this context, correct—I have a copy before me as we speak.

> Dragon Hunt* (1967)

Garrity, Tony — NIXON, Allan

GAT, Dimitri

After a promising start, Gat's series, featuring Russian-American **Yuri Nevsky**, information specialist (he finds out things for money) of 138 Morlande Street, Pittsburgh, came to an abrupt halt when 60,000 copies of the second book had to be withdrawn after John D. MacDonald's publisher alleged 32 instances of copyright infringement. Gat admitted that his book was "modeled" on MacDonald's *The Dreadful Lemon Sky* and wrote a letter of apology. And that was the end of Nevsky.

> Nevsky's Return (1982)
>
> Nevsky's Demon (1983)

Gates, Ben — KYLE, Robert

GATES, David

Described by the author as "a dry run for a detective novel about the past inhabiting the present," Boston PI **Buddy Margolies** features in a short story, "China Blue" (A2 #1).

GAULT, William Campbell

Gault sold his first story in 1936 and is still active today, returning to detective fiction after a long gap in the 60s and 70s to produce some of his best work ever. His main PI, **Brock 'The Rock' Callahan**, is one of the most universally admired figures in the genre. A former All-American and LA Rams football player, the 220 pound Callahan became a PI, advertising "Discreet Investigations At Moderate Rates," with an office on South Beverly Drive, Beverly Hills. A normal, middle-class, regular guy, he gets on well with the police, refuses divorce work and, in Boucher's words, is "an honest man trying not merely to maintain his own integrity but to concede to others their right to their own wholeness." He is also capable of healthy relationships with women, as is **Joe Puma**, a hardboiled down-market PI, big and arrogant, not as well educated than Callahan and serving a lower-class clientele. Puma is as honest as necessary and finally comes to a sticky end, his murder being investigated by Callahan, retired on an inheritance but bored, in *The*

Cana Diversion. The later books feature Callahan's protegé **Corey Raleigh**. An earlier, 1952 Edgar winning Gault hero was Saroyan-loving ex-tailback **Pete Worden** who attributes his success to being "sensitive, intuitive and a reader of Chandler." Gorman remarked (**A5**) that "One could make the case that the 'I' in *Don't Cry For Me* is still one of the most unique voices in private eye history, and that the book is, as Raymond Chandler was obliging enough to note in a letter to Gault, major stuff indeed." Gault has been undeservedly neglected by publishers, and all his books are of great merit. The PWA has bestowed a Lifetime Achievement award on him and voted *The Cana Diversion* Best Paperback Original. The first Puma book was published as by **Roney SCOTT** and two Puma short stories, "Take Care Of Yourself" (*Murder* 1957; **A4**) and "Stolen Star" (*Manhunt* 1957; **A14**) and a Brock Callahan story, "April In Peril" (**A16**) are in anthologies.

Worden: Don't Cry For Me* (1952)
Callahan: Ring Around Rosa (1955, UK 1955); as Murder In The Raw
                  (1956)
          Day Of The Ram (1956, UK 1958)
          The Convertible Hearse (1957, UK 1958)
          Come Die With Me (1959, UK 1961)
          Vein Of Violence (1961, UK 1962)
          County Kill (1962, UK 1963)
          Dead Hero (1963, UK 1964)
          The Bad Samaritan (Canada 1982)
          The Cana Diversion (Canada 1982). Fetaures **Puma**
          Death In Donegal Bay* (1984)
          The Dead Seed (1985, UK 1986)
          The Chicano War (1986)
          Cat And Mouse (1988)
Puma: End Of A Call Girl (1958); as Don't Call Tonight (UK 1960)
          Night Lady (1958, UK 1960)
          Sweet Wild Wench (1959, UK 1961)
          The Wayward Widow (1959, UK 1960)
          Million Dollar Tramp (1960, UK 1962)
          The Hundred-Dollar Girl* (1961, UK 1963)

Gaylord, Joe — MARBLE, M.S.
GELLER, Michael
Likable, tough but tender Irish-Jewish PI **Mickey 'Slots' Resnick** moves through a New York peopled by varied characters. Washed up as a rising baseball star, where he got the nickname, at 19 with a broken

ankle, he joined the police, rising to become Chief of Detectives until the advent of a disciplinarian Commissioner. After a false alarm brush with death, Resnick is a free-wheeling character with a candy-apple red Porsche 928, license plate SLOTS, who lives and works in a 33rd Street brownstone.

> Heroes Also Die (1988)
> Major League Murder (1988)

Gene — KAYE, Marvin

Gentle, Peter — Radio: MYSTERY WITHOUT MURDER

Gently, Dirk — ADAMS, Douglas

Gentry, Ron — DeANDREA, William L.

GEORGE, Peter 1924-1966

Best known for *Dr. Strangelove*, George's first book was a competent tough PI novel about **Steve Bryant** who operates out of a sixth floor office in the Staten Building, Pacific City, California, a picture-postcard town with a corrupt administration and "modern, streamlined, commercialized sin."

> Come Blonde, Come Murder (UK 1952, 1952)

Gibbs, James Augustus — DAVIS, Means

Gibson, Cassie — MAHANNAH, Floyd

GIBSON, William

Gibson is the leading exponent of "cyberpunk" which fuses high-tech SF with hardboiled style and sensibilities, looking at the sleazy aspects of a future dominated by multi-national corporations, where nationality is a meaningless concept and biological and computer sciences reign supreme. **Turner** is a free agent hired by corporations to expedite defections of key personnel from rival, and lethally possessive, companies. The plot is intricate and adept, but Gibson's main appeal is in his punk aesthetic, some idea of which may be gathered from the fact that Turner is killed on the first page, before the action even starts—and it's not told in flashbacks!

> Count Zero (1987, UK 1987)

GILBERT, Dale L.

Wisecracking Chicago PI **Matt Doyle** is forced to leave town after a run-in with the Mob and sets up an agency in San Diego with former Secretary of State **Carter Winfield**. The Wolfe & Goodwin premise, the thinker and the tough-guy, is let down by corny plots and recycled hardboiled dialogue.

> The Black Star Murders (1988)
> The Mother Murders (1989)

GILES, Guy Elwyn
NYT complained that **Brice Kent** took too much time out for drinking and other questionable activities and that his language was not the sort your maiden aunt was accustomed to! Objecting to an over-ingenious alibi and over-long explication, it was conceded that once started Kent was not easily stopped.

> Three Died Variously (1941)
> Target For Murder (1943)

GILES, Raymond (John Robert Holt)
Novelization of a forgettable, forgotten, film with Burt Reynolds as New York pool-hustler PI, **Shamus McCoy**. See **Films: SHAMUS**.

> Shamus (1973)

GILLIGAN, Roy
Much painting but little detecting in a book featuring **Pat Riordan**, San Francisco PI relocated in Carmel. An emotional basket case, he keeps reminding the reader how confusing everything is and wanders around dark houses at night. Good evocation of Carmel but the characters fail to come to life.

> Chinese Restaurants Never Serve Breakfast (1986)

GILLIS, Jackson Clark
Retired LA homicide investigator **Jonas Duncan** moves to Puget Sound, Washington and gets involved in searching for a killer, moving between Seattle's Skid Row and a beautiful private island, having already annoyed the local police by helping somebody. Gillis won a 1974 Edgar for a *Columbo* script.

> The Killers Of Starfish (1977, UK 1979)
> Chain Saw (1988)

Ginley, Eddie — Films: GUMSHOE
Ginsburg, Moe — HURLEY, Gene
Gittes, J.J. — Films: CHINATOWN
GLAZNER, Joseph Mark
Up-dated Spillane-style series with New York tough guy **Billy Nevers**, described by Art Bourgeau as "good, fast time-passers."

> Smart Money Doesn't Sing Or Dance (1979, UK 1980)
> Fast Money Shoots From The Hip (1980, UK 1980)
> Dirty Money Can't Wash Both Hands At Once (1980)
> Big Apple Money Is Rotten To The Core (1981)
> Hot Money Can Cook Your Goose (1981)

GLICK, Carl 1890-1971
Boucher remarked that this novel "starts off with an amusing screwball

satire on private eyes and a writers' conference but bogs down in flat and unconvincing conventionalities on the Red Menace."

    Death Sits In (1954)

Glick, Murray — KATZ, Michael J.

Glines, Barney — WILLS, Thomas / ARD, William

Gold, Alexander & Norma — RESNICOW, Herbert

GOLDMAN, Lawrence

Investigator for Coastal Mutual Insurance, **Johnny Saturday** is a tough sleuth who has to deal with tough characters and violent action. The produce market background of *Tiger By The Tail* is well done and unusual and Boucher was fulsome in his praise of it: "There's not a mention of fascism nor any other word on politics in the book, but its healthy attitude of defense of human rights and its unstressed allegories on labor solidarity and racial equality make it as sane and sensible a political whodunit as has emerged in some time. Quite aside from which, it rates high honors as a fast, vigorous, hard-boiled opus."

    Fall Guy For Murder (1943, UK 1945)

    Tiger By The Tail (1946)

GOLDSBOROUGH, Robert

Generating predictable controversy, Goldsborough has attempted to take up the **Nero Wolfe** and **Archie Goodwin** baton from their creator **Rex STOUT**. Art Scott, reviewing the second book, concluded that Goldsborough is no mystery writer and though avoiding the egregious characterization errors that had outraged Stout fans in the first book, nonetheless "They are obvious impostors, assembled from Stout's blueprint with obvious affection and considerable skill, but lacking the spark that only Rex Stout could provide." Beth Thoenen of *Drood Review*, on the other hand, thinks the reproduction is "uncanny," saying that "Goldsborough's strength is his exquisite discretion; he breaks Stout's rules with a facility that only Stout himself could equal."

    Murder In E Minor (1986)

    Death On Deadline (1987)

    The Bloodied Ivy (1988)

Good, Carl — SABER, Robert O.

Goodey, Joe — ALVERSON, Charles

Goodwin, Archie — STOUT, Rex / GOLDSBOROUGH, Robert

Gordon, Alison B. — WAGER, Walter

Gordon, Lee — HEYES, Douglas

Gordon, Monte — ROTH, Holly

GORDON, Russell

Owner of a moribund detective agency, movie scriptwriter **Fred Daymond** doesn't want to do any sleuthing but is persuaded by a movie magnate to look into pornographic film-making, a dirty racket with people who play rough—but so does Fred. *NYT* commented "Had Fred but known, he would probably have chosen to remain a detective in name only. But then he would never have met the girl" and *SR* remarked "slugging, shooting, snuggling and surprises."

       Dead Level (1948); as She Posed For Murder (1950)

GORES, Joe

A prolific short story and TV drama writer, Gores was a private detective for 12 years and, at Boucher's suggestion, used his expertise for a quasi-procedural series about automobile repossessors, debt collectors and skip tracers **Dan Kearny Associates** (DKA), of Golden Gate Avenue, San Francisco, described by Ellery Queen as "authentic as a fist in your face," with realistic practice and a fine cast of characters with **Larry Ballard** as the nominal lead. **Neil Fargo** is a tough, shady PI in a novel described by Pronzini as "one of the toughest, most brutal novels published since the days of *Black Mask*—so hard boiled that some readers, women especially, find it upsetting. But its power is undeniable." Gores is best known for his least satisfactory book, starring another PI turned writer, **Dashiell Hammett**. 1928 San Francisco and the *Black Mask* style are well enough evoked, but the story is melodramatic and Gores clearly has no sympathy with Hammett's politics. See **Jack FOXX, TV: MAGNUM P.I / MICKEY SPILLANE'S MIKE HAMMER** and **Films: HAMMETT**.

DKA: Dead Skip* (1972, UK 1973)
           Final Notice (1973, UK 1974)
           Gone, No Forwarding (1978, UK 1979)
Fargo: Interface (1974, UK 1977)
Hammett: Hammett: A Novel* (1975, UK 1976)

GORMAN, Edward

Humor and snappy dialogue characterize Gorman's books about Cedar Rapids, Illinois, PI **Jack Dwyer**—ex-cop, part-time actor and, at one point, part-time security guard in a discount supermarket, something he preferred not to talk about. See **A4 & A5** for **Gorman**'s Black Lizard collections, the first which contains his short story, "Turn Away," about an aging PI, **Parnell** and **A14** for a Dwyer story, "The Reason Why." Gorman has a **Philip Marlowe** short story, "The Alibi," in **A12**.

       New, Improved Murder (1985) >

Murder Straight Up (1986)
Murder In The Wings (1986)
The Autumn Dead (1988)

Gossett, Malcolm — OPPENHEIM, E. Phillips

GOTTLIEB, Nathan

Retired Newark PI and one-time newspaperman **Nash Kanzler** is
dragged back into action to track down a missing reporter who may be
systematically killing off black leaders and Mafia bosses. Baker & Nietzel
describe the book as "funny and harrowing."

Stinger (1978)

GOULART, Ron

Goulart says he liked to mix "murder, bug-eyed monsters and satire." The
most outrageous mix of these is ex-lawman, ex-convict **Jared Smith**'s
very, very reluctant recruitment by the Whistler Interplanetary
Investigation Agency, better known as Suicide, Inc. Back on Planet Earth,
sort of, **Jim Haley** is an operative with the Private Inquiry Office in a
wacky, disintegrated future California. **Jake & Hildy Pace** are the 21st
century husband and wife team of Odd Jobs, Inc., Redding Ridge,
Connecticut, one of the top inquiry agencies in the galaxy that takes only
the most difficult and unusual cases, **Max Kearny** is an occult detective,
Sam Brimmer a "time detective." Shapechanger **Ben Jolson**, formerly
of the Chameleon Corps, is an antiques dealer and reluctant part-time
operative for Briggs Interplanetary Detective Service of Barnum. Goulart's
most straightforward contribution to the genre is **John Easy**, a Sunset
Strip, Hollywood PI who seems to specialize in missing persons, usually
beautiful women, but even then his Southern California is a little more
surreal even than the real thing. Recently he added **Rudy Navarro**, an
operative with an agency called The Ajax Novelty Co. Goulart has written
short stories parodying Chandler, Macdonald and others that have not been
collected. See **A6** for his pulp story collection and the Bibliography for
his book on pulp magazine detectives.

Haley:	After Things Fell Apart (1970, UK 1975)
Kearny:	Ghost Breaker (1971) SS
Easy:	If Dying Was All (1971)
	Too Sweet To Die (1972)
	The Same Lie Twice (1973)
	One Grave Too Many (1974)
Pace:	Odd Job #101 & Other Future Crimes And Intrigues (1975, UK 1976)
	Calling Dr. Patchwork (1978) >

Hail Hibbler (1980)

Big Bang (1982)

Brainz, Inc. (1985)

Brimmer: The Enormous Hour Glass (1976)

Smith: Suicide, Inc. (1985)

Jolson: Daredevils, Ltd. (1987)

Navarro: The Wisemann Originals (1989)

GRAAF, Peter (Samuel Youd)

Giuseppe Polvio was a promising young hood in Dutch Schultz's mob until he was involved in a gun battle in which three young children were killed. After five years in prison, he moved to London, changed his name to **Joe Dust** and set up the Medea Bureau of Missing Persons (geddit?) on the Belgravia-Pimlico border. The books are a confused blend of Brooklynese and English genteel, the psychology banal and the plots thin.

Dust And The Curious Boy (UK 1957); as Give The Devil His
     Due (1957)

Daughter Fair (UK 1958, 1958)

The Sapphire Conference (UK 1959, 1959)

GRADY, James

Washington and its networks of power, wealth and influence are the background for **John Rankin**, who cruises the DC streets in a dirty silver Porsche, rock & roll on the tape deck, and has an office in the Eclectic Building, Capitol Hill. Psychology, including Rankin's own, is aired at the expense of the plot. Grady contributed a **Philip Marlowe** short story, "The Devil's Playground," to **A12**.

Runner On The Streets (1984)

Hard Bargains (1985)

GRAFTON, Sue

C.W. Grafton used lines from a nursery rhyme as titles for a series of thrillers in the 40s. His daughter, who acknowledges a debt to Ross Macdonald, has undertaken an even more ambitious project in her alphabetical series about Santa Teresa (Santa Barbara?), California PI **Kinsey Millhone**, 32 years old, twice divorced, no children, who drives a VW, lives in a converted garage and is "not good at taking shit, especially from men." Millhone short stories are "The Parker Shotgun" (**A16**), "Non Sung Smoke" (**A17**) and "She Didn't Come Home" (**A14**). Like Sara PARETSKY, whose V.I.Warshawski is somewhat similar to Millhone, Grafton intended to write a female parody of Chandler. Both ended up with superior PIs who bring a real feminine sensibility to the genre. *B Is For Burglar* won PWA and Bouchercon Best Novel awards. >

A Is For Alibi* (1982, UK 1986)
B Is For Burglar (1985, UK 1986)
C Is For Corpse (1986, UK 1987)
D Is For Deadbeat (1987, UK 1987)
E Is For Evidence (1988, UK 1988)
F Is For Fugitive (1989)

Graham, Angel — RUSSELL, Richard

GRAHAM, Anthony

From the wrong side of the tracks of Toleda (sic), ex-cop **Eddie Delaney** has had 38 crowded, tough and bitter years. He lives in a hotel, drives a very old Buick, and owes money to a loan-shark for an LA agency that went bust. Now he works if and when he can. Cops don't come much more corrupt or brutal than Graham's. Very tough and remarkably authentic sounding for a British author.

No Sale For Halos (UK 1954)

GRAHAM, Neill (W. Murdoch Duncan 1909-1975)

Apart from a rather opaque rave in Reilly, British author Duncan's PI books as Graham and **Lovat MARSHALL** have made little impression on genre history. There is nothing special about ex-Commando, ex-wrestler, ex-CID sergeant **James 'Solo' Malcolm**, "the most rugged and scrupulously honest operator in the business."

Play It Solo (UK 1955)
Murder Makes A Date (UK 1955, 1956)
Say It With Murder (UK 1956)
You Can't Call It Murder (UK 1957)
Salute To Murder (UK 1958)
Hit Me Hard (UK 1958)
Murder Rings A Bell (UK 1959)
Killers Are On Velvet (UK 1960)
Murder Is My Weakness (UK 1961)
Murder On The 'Duchess' (UK 1961)
Make Mine Murder (UK 1962)
Label It Murder (UK 1963)
Graft Town (UK 1963)
Murder Makes It Certain (UK 1963)
Murder Made Easy (UK 1964)
Murder Of A Black Cat (UK 1964)
Murder On My Hands (UK 1965)
Murder Always Final (UK 1965)
Money For Murder (UK 1966) >

Murder On Demand (UK 1966)
Murder Makes The News (UK 1967)
Murder Has Been Done (UK 1967)
Pay Off (UK 1968)
Candidates For A Coffin (UK 1968)
Death Of A Canary (UK 1968)
Murder Lies In Waiting (UK 1969)
Blood On The Pavement (UK 1970)
One For The Book (UK 1970)
A Matter For Murder (UK 1971)
Murder, Double Murder (UK 1971)
Frame-Up (UK 1972)
Cop In A Tight Frame (UK 1972)
Murder In A Dark Room (UK 1973)
Assignment, Murder (UK 1974)
Murder On The List (UK 1975)
Search For A Missing Lady (UK 1976)
Motive For Murder (UK 1977)

GRANT, Ben (Marilyn Granbeck)
Chicago PI **Marty Cole** is a straightforward example of mid-70s leer-and-lights-out, with bosoms prominent below eyes that say "I want it." Odd that this primitive sexploiter should be the work of a woman author.

Alice Dies Twice (1975)

Grant, Clifford — WARREN, Vernon

GRANT, James Edward
"Among the first wave of thirties smart-asses was one named **Tip O'Neil**," as Pronzini says (*Gun In Cheek*), commenting on writers who thought the Chandler wisecrack was an essential for success. Pronzini also took exception to O'Neil's bolt of lightning method of solving crimes. The blurb makes a virtue of the fact that "the whole thing's a cock-eyed maze." See **Films: MUSS 'EM UP.**

The Green Shadow (1935)

GRANT, Linda
A Silicon Valley specialist in white-collar crime, classical guitar playing, upscale San Francisco PI **Catherine Sayler**, daughter of a cop and ex-wife of a homicide inspector, and her boyfriend, "people's PI" **Pete Harman**, an unreconstructed hippie, are caught up in a complex, fast-paced whodunit.

Random Access Murder (1988)

Grant, Michael — DANIEL, Roland

Grant, Victor — ETHAN, John B.
Gray, Cordelia — JAMES, P.D.
Gray, Ed — CROWE, John
Gray, Gwen & Garamond — NOEL, Atanielle Annyn
GRAY, Russell = FISCHER, Bruno
Under this name Fischer was a prolific contributor to the mystery-horror genre espoused by the "shudder" pulps. **Ben Bryn**, who, as a result of polio, is only 5'2" (mind you, Johnny Havoc and Hal Darling are even smaller), with withered legs but extraordinarily well-developed upper-body musculature with which he can literally tear people apart or strangle with one hand, appears in three stories in the second *Defective Detective* collection (A8), "The Dead Hand Horrors," "Flesh For The Monster" and "Prey For The Creeping Death" (all *Dime Mystery* 1939).
Grayce, Steve — CHANDLER, Raymond
Green, Edwin — CALIN, Hal Jason
Green, Gregory George Gordon — MANN, Jack
Green, Jeffrey — KEITH, Carlton
Green, Marcus — RUNYON, Charles
GREENBERG, Martin H. (ed) — see ANTHOLOGIES: 13
Greenleaf, Hank — TREAT, Lawrence
GREENLEAF, Stephen
A non-practicing lawyer, like his creator, **John Marshall Tanner** operates in the Bay Area from an office on Jackson Square, San Francisco and can advise clients to retain him as an attorney. In his 40s, Tanner finds PI work "short on glamour and long on ambiguity." He charges $200 a day, with hourly rates, drives a '71 Buick and could fit all his assets into carry-on luggage, "if he owned any carry-on luggage." Greenleaf is an admirer of Ross Macdonald and opinion is divided as to whether he is a mere imitator (Marcia Muller in Pronzini & Muller) or carry the tradition forward (Baker & Nietzel, supported by many critics including a clean sweep of the Big Apple—*NYT*, *The New Yorker* and *New York*). A Tanner short story, "Iris," is in both A14 & A15.
> Grave Error (1979, UK 1981)
> Death Bed* (1980, UK 1982)
> State's Evidence (1982, UK 1983)
> Fatal Obsession (1983, UK 1984)
> Beyond Blame (1986, UK 1987)
> Toll Free (1987)

Gregg, Avery — KOEHLER, Robert Portner
Gregg, Matt — GUY, David

GREGORICH, Barbara
Living in a Croatian area of Chicago, **Frank Dragovic** is a mixture of old and new, enlightened but old-fashioned, health-conscious and wise-cracking. Varied, interesting characters struggle with an over-complex plot and a clumsy resolution muddied by unclear motives.
    Dirty Proof (1988)

GREX, Leo = GRIBBLE, Leonard
Hired by an American capitalist living in an English country house as a bodyguard and snoop, Irish free-lance sleuth **Jerry Down** does not show to good advantage in a book *NYT* described as "flagrantly implausible."
    The Man From Manhattan (UK 1934, 1935)

GRIBBLE, Leonard 1908-1985
In one novel, "another of Leonard Gribble's assemblies from stock," as Sandoe put it, series character Superintendent Anthony Slade of Scotland Yard sends a wealthy client the way of ex-cop private detective **Race Carlin**, but soon gets involved when homicide occurs. *SR* remarked "characters in main not too credible. Spotty." See Leo **GREX**.
    Stand-In For Murder (UK 1957, 1958)

Griffin, Wade — TV: GRIFF
Griffith, Bill — DEAN, Robert George
Gronig, Hector — WALKER, Walter
Gross, Sam — WOHL, James P.
GROSSBACH, Robert
Novelization of Neil Simon's film satirizing *The Maltese Falcon*, with **Lou Peckinpaugh** of Peckinpaugh & Merkle, Private Investigators, San Francisco. See **Films: The CHEAP DETECTIVE**.
    The Cheap Detective (1978)

GRUBER, Frank 1904-1969
See Introduction: How To Write A PI Novel for Gruber's 11 point formula for mystery stories. In his heyday, he wrote a complete novel every 16 days as well as Westerns, screenplays, and serials, and hosted a radio show. Though his plots were thin and not properly developed, the stories were fast paced and peopled with unusual and engaging characters in odd settings. Gruber was fond of PI duos, creating three sets. **Johnny Fletcher**, the brains, and **Sam Cragg**, the giant brawn, are shiftless adventurers, whose only address is c/o 45th Street Hotel, New York, in turn booksellers, conmen and PIs. **Simon Lash**, whose assistant is **Eddie Slocum**, is a hardboiled veteran ex-lawyer and licensed PI, hostile and cynical, especially about women, though he loves books, which feature strongly in his cases, and operates out of an office-home on Harper

Avenue, Hollywood. **Otis Beagle**, head of the Beagle Detective Agency, Hollywood Boulevard, LA, is, as his small, wiry, inconspicuous legman **Joe Peel** says, like his diamond ring, "big, flashy—and phony." Both abhor violence. **Tom Alder** was an hardboiled specialist in tracing missing heirs in a novel Boucher described as sharply detailed and acutely written, dissolving into a soggy ending full of coincidences and Fine Writing. A hero after escaping from a Vietcong PoW camp, Lt-Commander **Sargent** is hired to investigate a millionaire's fiancée. Disbarred attorney **Tom Logan** works for the Boss Detective Agency of Beverly Hills, Gruber's interest in archaeology enlivening a routine plot. **Joe Devlin** was in a novel reissued as by Gruber See **Films: ACCOMPLICE/The FRENCH KEY/TWENTY PLUS TWO** and **TV: SHOTGUN SLADE.**

Fletcher: The French Key (1940, UK 1941); as The French Key Mystery
        (1942); as Once Over Deadly (1956)
        The Laughing Fox (1940, UK 1942)
        The Hungry Dog (1941, UK 1950); as The Hungry Dog Murders
        (1943); as Die Like A Dog (1957)
        The Navy Colt (1941, UK 1942)
        The Talking Clock (1941, UK 1942)
        The Gift Horse (1942, UK 1943)
        The Mighty Blockhead (1942, UK 1948); as The Corpse Moved
        Upstairs (1964)
        The Silver Tombstone (1945, UK 1949); as The Silver
        Tombstone Mystery (1959)
        The Honest Dealer (1947)
        The Whispering Master (1947)
        The Scarlet Feather (1948, UK 1951); as The Gamecock Murders
        (1949)
        The Leather Duke (1949, UK 1950); as The Job Of Murder
        (1950)
        The Limping Goose (1954, UK 1955); as Murder One (1973)
        Swing Low, Swing Dead (1964)
Devlin: The Yellow Overcoat (1949; as by **Stephen ACRE** 1942,
        UK 1945); as Fall Guy For A Killer (1955)
Lash: Simon Lash, Private Detective (1941); as Simon Lash,
        Detective (UK 1943)
        The Buffalo Box* (1942, UK 1944)
        Murder '97 (1948, UK 1956); as The Long Arm Of Murder
        (1956) >

Beagle: The Silver Jackass (UK 1952, 1973; as by **Charles K. BOSTON** 1941)

       Beagle Scented Murder (1946); as Market For Murder (1947)

       The Lonesome Badger (1954); as Mood For Murder (1956)

Alder: Twenty Plus Two (1961, UK 1961)

Sargent: The Gold Gap (1968, UK 1968)

Logan: The Etruscan Bull (1969, UK 1970)

Guard, Carl — OZAKI, Milton

Guerrera, Kat — BEAL, M.F.

Guild, John — HAMMETT, Dashiell

Guiu, Lonia — OLIVER, Maria-Antonia

GUNN, James

A love story than anything else, and an occult one at that. SF writer Gunn pitched nice-guy, ex-high school English teacher turned PI **Kirk Cullen**, down to his last quarter after his partner and girlfriend ran off together with the firm's assets, into a magicians' covention (sic) and a full-scale battle between Good and Evil.

       The Magicians (1976)

Gunn, Peter — TV: PETER GUNN

Gunner, Aaron — HAYWOOD, Gar Anthony

GUTHRIE, Al

Widowed industrial consultant **Walter 'Mac' McKenzie** holds a PI license because of the unsavory nature of some of his work, but it's curiosity and a beautiful accused sister that lead him to look into the killing of his next-door neighbor in a sleepy town outside Chicago.

       Private Murder (1989)

GUY, David

A former small town cop who moved to Pittsburgh, where the force wasn't hiring, for the sake of his counselor-therapist wife's career, **Matt Gregg** works as a private investigator from a more than usually shabby building in East Liberty. The one novel, involving a descent into the porno underworld, is more an exporation of relationships than a mystery, compared by the blurb writer to an Antonioni film.

       The Man Who Loved Dirty Books (1983)

Hackett, Thackeray — COOMBS, Murdo

Hadden, Michael — ROFFMAN, Jan

Hagen, Mort — MASTERSON, Whit

Hagen, Paul — TV: HAGEN

Haggerty, Leo — SCHUTZ, Benjamin M.

HAIBLUM, Isidore
Classical music buff **James Shaw**, ex-Military Intelligence (18 months), who, with his ex-social worker buddy, has taken over his uncle's debt-ridden PI agency, isn't as funny as Haiblum supposes. He's good on Manhattan and tells a story well in what has been described as "a competent essay in the tough-guy genre." Curiously, given the title, the standard Chandler wise-guy humor has next to no Jewish content.
Murder In Yiddish (1988)

Haig, Leo — BLOCK, Lawrence / HARRISON, Chip
Hale, Max C. — COXE, George Harmon
Haley, Jim — GOULART, Ron

HALL, Parnell
Down on his luck PI **Stanley Hastings** chases ambulances for a lawyer, signing up accident victims. He lists himself as a private detective on the lobby call board of his 47th Street, New York office, but "It never occurred to me someone would walk in off the street." Happily married and a father, he's basically non-aggressive. "I'm not really a detective, I don't do surveillance, I don't carry a gun. I couldn't fight my way out of a paper bag." But after a client he rejects turns up dead, he decides he must find out if he has what it takes. An Edgar nominee for 1988 by an author who himself moonlights as a PI.
Detective (1987)
Murder (1988)
Favor (1988)

HALLAHAN, William H.
Perhaps the most unpleasant character in the business, **Arthur Tank**, correspondence student of Chamber's International Course on Private Investigation, uses his studies to such effect that he is able to quit on Lesson #7. One of Hallahan's best books, of which Tank is not the hero.
The Ross Forgery* (1973, UK 1977)

Hallam, Lucas — WASHBURN, L.J.
Haller, Mike — BYRD, Max

HALLERAN, Tucker
Though he's a fan of Travis McGee, **Cam MacCardle** doesn't live on his boat but in a Fort Lauderdale, Florida house. An ex-Marine and former New York professional football player, retired because of knee injuries, he scouts for his old team and does part-time licensed PI work on retainer for a law firm. A bold, likable character, less ultra-white knight than McGee.
A Cool, Clear Death (1984)
Sudden Death Finish (1985)

Halley, Sid — FRANCIS, Dick
HALLIDAY, Brett (Davis Dresser 1904-1977)
Dresser joined the US Cavalry at 14, riding with Pershing against Pancho
Villa, was an oilfield roughneck and a deckhand before qualifying as a
civil engineer. It took him four years to find a publisher for a novel
featuring Flagler Street, Miami (for a while, New Orleans) PI **Michael
Shayne**. Dubbed by Baker & Nietzel "The Generic Private Eye," the
tough, Martell-drinking Irish redhead became one of the most popular of
all PIs in over 60 books, countless short stories, his own magazine, film,
radio and TV series. A two-fisted character who rarely used a gun, the
logical, straightforward Shayne did more actual detecting than most PIs in
complex stories whose action rarely took longer than a day or two,
Halliday's style basic but efficient. A short story, "The Reluctant Client"
(*Manhunt* 1955) is in A9. After 1958 the series was mainly the work of
Robert TERRALL (see **Robert KYLE**), a better writer than Dresser
who injected new life into one of the longest careers in the genre. See
**Films: MICHAEL SHAYNE, PRIVATE DETECTIVE /
SLEEPERS WEST / DRESSED TO KILL / BLUE, WHITE
AND PERFECT / The MAN WHO WOULDN'T DIE / JUST
OFF BROADWAY / TIME TO KILL / MURDER IS MY
BUSINESS / LARCENY IN HER HEART / BLONDE FOR
A DAY / THREE ON A TICKET / TOO MANY WINNERS,
TV: MICHAEL SHAYNE and Radio: MICHAEL SHAYNE.**
Dividend On Death (1939, UK 1941)
The Private Practice Of Michael Shayne (1940, UK 1941)
The Uncomplaining Corpses (1940, UK 1942)
Tickets For Death (1941, UK 1942)
Bodies Are Where You Find Them (1941); in Michael Shayne
Investigates (UK 1943)
Michael Shayne Takes Over (1941)
The Corpse Came Calling (1942); as The Case Of The Walking
Corpse (1943); in Michael Shayne Investigates (UK 1943)
Murder Wears A Mummer's Mask (1943); in Michael Shayne
Takes A Hand (1944); as In A Deadly Vein (1956)
Blood On The Black Market (1943); in Michael Shayne Takes A
Hand (1944); as Heads You Lose (1958, rev. ed.)
Michael Shayne Investigates (UK 1943) contains Bodies Are
Where You Find Them/The Corpse Came Calling
Michael Shayne Takes A Hand (UK 1944) contains Murder
Wears A Mummer's Mask/Blood On The Black Market >

Michael Shayne's Long Chance (1944, UK 1945)
Murder And The Married Virgin (1944, UK 1946)
Murder Is My Business (1945, UK 1945)
Marked For Murder (1945, UK 1950)
Dead Man's Diary + Dinner At Dupre's (1945)
Blood On Biscayne Bay (1946, UK 1950)
Counterfeit Wife* (1947, UK 1950)
Blood On The Stars (1948); as Murder Is A Habit (UK 1951)
Michael Shayne's Triple Mystery (1948) contains Dead Man's
    Diary/A Taste For Cognac/Dinner At Dupre's
A Taste For Violence (1949, UK 1952)
Call For Michael Shayne (1949, UK 1951)
This Is It, Michael Shayne (1950, UK 1952)
Framed In Blood (1951, UK 1953)
When Dorinda Dances (1951, UK 1953)
What Really Happened (1952, UK 1953)
One Night With Nora (1953); as The Lady Came By Night (UK
    1954)
She Woke To Darkness (1954, UK 1955)
Death Has Three Lives (1955, UK 1955)
Stranger In Town (1955, UK 1956)
The Blonde Cried Murder (1956, UK 1957)
Weep For A Blonde (1957, UK 1958)
Shoot The Works (1957, UK 1958)
Murder And The Wanton Bride (1958, UK 1959). Dresser's last
    book
Fit To Kill (1958, UK 1959). By Robert Terrall
Date With A Dead Man (1959, UK 1960). Expansion of Dead
    Man's Diary
Die Like A Dog (1959, UK 1961)
Target: Mike Shayne (1959, UK 1960). By Robert Terrall
Dolls Are Deadly (1960). By Ryerson Johnson
The Homicidal Virgin (1960)
Murder Takes No Holiday (1960). By Robert Terrall
The Careless Corpse (1961)
Killers From The Keys (1961). By Ryerson Johnson
Murder In Haste (1961, UK 1963). By Robert Terrall
Murder By Proxy (1962, UK 1968)
Never Kill A Client (1962)
Pay Off In Blood (1962) >

The Body Came Back (1963)
The Corpse That Never Was (1963)
Too Friendly, Too Dead (1963, UK 1964)
Michael Shayne's 50th Case (1964)
A Redhead For Mike Shayne (1964)
Shoot To Kill (1964)
Nice Fillies Finish Last* (1965). By Robert Terrall
The Violent World Of Mike Shayne (1965). By Robert Terrall
Armed . . . Dangerous . . . (1966). By Robert Terrall
Murder Spins The Wheel (1966). By Robert Terrall
Guilty As Hell (1967). By Robert Terrall
Mermaid On The Rocks (1967). By Robert Terrall
So Lush, So Deadly (1968). By Robert Terrall
Violence Is Golden (1968). By Robert Terrall
Lady Be Bad (1969). By Robert Terrall
Fourth Down To Death (1970). By Robert Terrall
Six Seconds To Kill (1970). By Robert Terrall
Count Backwards To Zero (1971). By Robert Terrall
I Came To Kill You (1971). By Robert Terrall
Caught Dead (1972). By Robert Terrall
Blue Murder (1973). By Robert Terrall
Kill All The Young Girls (1973). By Robert Terrall
At The Point Of A .38 (1974). By Robert Terrall
Last Seen Hitchhiking (1974). By Robert Terrall
Million Dollar Handle (1976). By Robert Terrall

Halliday, Willie — FREDMAN, Mike
Halsey, Mick — MARTELL, Charles
Halstead, Arthur — HAYES, William Edward
Hamberger — Films: DEADLY ILLUSION
Hamet, Barney — HOCH, Edward D.
HAMILL, Pete

In Baker & Nietzel's survey (see Introduction: Comparative Eyes), New York journalist Hamill's **Sam Briscoe** drew dissent as to whether he was actually a PI, as, however, did George Harmon Coxe's Kent Murdock and Jack Casey and Hammett's Nick Charles, but was better known than Loren D. Estleman's Amos Walker. Briscoe is a New York investigative journalist in his late 30s, retired from the *Post* and freelancing, who uses his contacts for his own ends and whose hardboiled investigative methods are more Race Williams than Carl Bernstein.

Dirty Laundry* (1978) >

The Deadly Piece (1979)
Guns Of Heaven (1983)

HAMILTON, Donald

In novels **Matt Helm** was a freewheeling, outdoorsy photographer-writer-hunter-fisherman-, recruited by a government agency to undertake secret missions. In films he was a spoof super-agent. In **TV: MATT HELM** he became a PI but is listed here only to mark the lack of connection between the three incarnations.

Hammer, Mike — SPILLANE, Mickey

HAMMETT, Dashiell 1894-1961

Hardboiled giant of all fiction (André Gide et al), all detective fiction (Robert Graves et al) and the PI genre in particular, the former Pinkerton man supposedly modeled **The Continental Op**, fat, forty, tough and shrewd, on his one time Baltimore boss James Wright, and his methods are based on actual practice, with the agency called, naturally, the Continental Detective Agency. Featuring in only one novel and three stories, **Sam Spade** of Spade & Archer, later just Samuel Spade, Sutter Street, San Francisco, is, of course, the prototype hardbitten loner whose license number, according to the radio series, was #137596. Many critics prefer to avoid mentioning **Nick & Nora Charles** (originally Charalambides,"Greek and unpronounceable") at all for they are the products of Hammett's success and phonies compared to the Op and Spade. A former Trans-American Detective Agency of San Francisco operative, married to a rich woman, Nick has a last fling at his old profession, accompanied, of course, by Asta. Hammett's original story for the second Nick & Nora Charles film "After The Thin Man" is in A1 #5 & 6. Don Herron (*Mystery* 3/2 1981) refers to an uncompleted 1930 draft of *The Thin Man*, featuring **John Guild**, published in a special Hammett issue of *City Of San Francisco* (Nov. 1975). Two other PIs, bumbling, egocentric pseudo-intellectual **Robin Thin**, whose father's agency finds embarrassing, and ugly ex-cop **Alexander Rush**, who left the force in disgrace, appeared only in short stories, a guide to which is appended below with titles of collections abbreviated as shown. Robert S. Powell (*Clues* 2/2 1981) argues convincingly that Hammett was preparing a collection of Continental Op stories, "Including Murder," in 1925 and the probable selection is marked §. Hammett wrote nothing of consequence during his last 27 years and his literary executrix, Lillian Hellman, has used, and, in my view, abused, her powers to bar republication of much of his early work. Spade and the Charleses were satirized in the film MURDER BY DEATH as Sam Diamond and Dick &

Dora Charleston. See **Films:** AFTER THE THIN MAN /
ANOTHER THIN MAN / The FAT MAN / The MALTESE
FALCON (1931 & 1941) / MR DYNAMITE / ROADHOUSE
NIGHTS / SATAN MET A LADY / SHADOW OF THE
THIN MAN / SONG OF THE THIN MAN / The THIN MAN
/ The THIN MAN GOES HOME, **TV:** The DAIN CURSE /
NICK AND NORA / The THIN MAN and **Radio:** The
ADVENTURES OF SAM SPADE / The ADVENTURES OF
THE THIN MAN / The FAT MAN / The MALTESE
FALCON / The NEW ADVENTURES OF THE THIN MAN.

Op: Red Harvest (1929, UK 1929)

       The Dain Curse* (1929, UK 1929)

       $106,000 Blood Money (1943); as Blood Money (1943); as The
         Big Knockover (1948). $BM

       The Continental Op (1945). SS. CO45.

       The Return Of The Continental Op (1945). SS. RCO

       Hammett Homicides (1946). SS. HH

       Dead Yellow Woman (1946). SS. DYW

       Nightmare Town (1948). SS. NT

       The Creeping Siamese (1950). SS. CS.

       The Dashiell Hammett Omnibus (UK 1950). All 5 novels + 4
         Op SS.

       Woman In The Dark (1951) SS. WD

       The Big Knockover; Selected Stories & Short Novels* (1966);
         as The Hammett Story Omnibus (UK 1966); as The Big
         Knockover + The Continental Op (2 vols, 1967) Edited by
         Lillian Hellman. BK

       The Continental Op (1974, UK 1975) CO

Spade: The Maltese Falcon* (1930, UK 1930)

       The Adventures Of Sam Spade & Other Stories (1944); as They
         Can Only Hang You Once (1949); as A Man Called Spade
         (1949 with 2 stories omitted) ASS

Charles: The Thin Man* (1934, UK 1934)

Thin: A Man Named Thin & Other Stories (1962) MNT

HAMMETT, Dashiell — The Short Stories

Continental Op

"Arson Plus" (*Black Mask* 1923) — WD/A13

§"Crooked Souls" (*Black Mask* 1923) — MNT/BK both as "The
    Gatewood Caper"

"Slippery Fingers" (*Black Mask* 1923) — WD >

"It" (*Black Mask* 1923) — not collected and disputed as an Op story

§"Bodies Piled Up" (*Black Mask* 1923) — **A11**/DYW as "House Dick"

"The Tenth Clew" (*Black Mask* 1924) — RCO/CO

§"Night Shots" (*Black Mask* 1924) — HH

§"Zigzags Of Treachery" (*Black Mask* 1924) — CO45

§"One Hour" (*BM* 1924) — RCO/in Tony Goodstone (ed); *The Pulps*
     (1970)

§"The House In Turk Street" (*Black Mask* 1924) — HH/CO

§"The Girl With The Silver Eyes" (*Black Mask* 1924) — HH/CO

§"Women, Politics And Murder" (*BM* 1924) — CO45 as "Death On
     Pine Street"

"Who Killed Bob Teal?" (*True Detective Stories* 1924) — DYW/rejected
     by *Black Mask*

§"The Golden Horseshoe" (*Black Mask* 1924) — DYW/CO

"Mike, Alec Or Rufus" (*Black Mask* 1925) — not collected

"The Whosis Kid" (*Black Mask* 1925) — RCO/CO

"The Scorched Face" (*Black Mask* 1925) — NT/BK

"Corkscrew" (*Black Mask* 1925) — NT/BK

"Dead Yellow Women" (*Black Mask* 1925) — DYW/BK

"The Gutting Of Couffignal" (*Black Mask* 1925) — RCO/BK/**A19**

"Creeping Siamese" (*Black Mask* 1926) — CS

"The Big Knock-Over" (*Black Mask* 1927) — $BM/BK

"$106,000 Blood Money" (*Black Mask* 1927) — $BM/BK

"The Main Death" (*Black Mask* 1927) — HH/CO

"The Cleansing Of Poisonville" (*Black Mask* 1927) — Used in *Red
     Harvest*

"Crime Wanted—Male Or Female" (*Black Mask* 1927) — Used in *Red
     Harvest*

"This King Business" (*Mystery Stories* 1928) — CS/BK

"Dynamite" (*Black Mask* 1928) — Used in *Red Harvest*

"The 19th Murder" (*Black Mask* 1928) — Used in *Red Harvest*

"Black Lives" (*Black Mask* 1928) — Used in *The Dain Curse*

"The Hollow Temple" (*Black Mask* 1928) — Used in *The Dain Curse*

"Black Honeymoon" (*Black Mask* 1929) — Used in *The Dain Curse*

"Black Riddle" (*Black Mask* 1929) — Used in *The Dain Curse*

"Fly Paper" (*Black Mask* 1929) — CO45/BK/**A20**

"The Farewell Murder" (*Black Mask* 1930) — CO45/CO

"Death And Company" (*Black Mask* 1930) — RCO

Robin Thin

"The Nails In Mr. Cayterer" (*Black Mask* 1926) — CS >

"A Man Named Thin" (*Ellery Queen's Mystery Magazine* 1961) — MNT
Alexander Rush
"The Assistant Murderer" (*Black Mask* 1926) — ASS
Sam Spade
"A Man Called Spade" (*American Magazine* 1932) — ASS
"They Can Only Hang You Once" (*Collier's* 1932) — ASS
"Too Many Have Lived" (*American Magazine* 1932) — ASS/A9
Hammett, Dashiell — GORES, Joe
Hammond, Andy — Films: LADY ICE
Hammond, August — COGGINS, Mark
HAMMOND, Gerald
Living near Newton Lauder on the England-Scotland Border, **Keith Calder** is a gunsmith (and poacher) who gets drawn reluctantly into investigative work in an area with few places for would-be clients to turn, even the police sending people to him. Solid, professional story-telling, stronger on craft than style.

> Fred In Situ (UK 1965)
> The Loose Screw (UK 1966)
> Mud In His Eye (UK 1967)
> Dead Game (UK 1979)
> The Reward Game (UK 1980, 1980)
> The Revenge Game (UK 1981, 1981)
> Fair Game (UK 1982, 1982)
> The Game (UK 1982, 1983)
> Cousin Once Removed (UK 1984, 1984)
> Sauce For The Pigeon (UK 1984, 1985)
> Pursuit Of Arms (UK 1985, 1986)
> Silver City Scandal (UK 1986, 1986)
> The Executor (UK 1986, 1987)
> The Worried Widow (UK 1987, 1988)
> Adverse Report (UK 1987)
> Stray Shot (UK 1988)

Hammond, Wade — CHADWICK, Paul
Hand, Christopher — PAGE, Stanley Hart
Hanigan, Jack — DILLON, Walter
Hannegan, Edge — LOVELL, B.E.
Hannibal, Joe — DUNDEE, Wayne D.
Hannigan, Nick — TV: DETECTIVE SCHOOL
Hanrahan, Chess — CLINE, Edward

HANSEN, Joseph
The most obvious thing about **Dave Brandstetter** is that he is homosexual and Hansen has stated his didactic purpose in writing thrillers that will make the reader keep turning pages while learning more about the realities of homosexuality. An insurance death claims investigator, first for his father's company Medallion Life, then, fired after his father's death, as a celebrated freelancer, Brandstetter works from his Horseshoe Canyon Drive, LA, home. Older then most PIs, approaching 60, he is rich, cultured and indulges himself in good things. Dealing realistically and empathetically with mundane aspects of homosexual life, the Gay Mafia connections are more probable sources of information than the standard PI's rarely justified, contacts. Hansen's prose style, with its jump cuts and subtle humor, is much admired, as is his plotting ability, with clues well placed. A Brandstetter short story, "Surf" (*Playguy* 1976) is in **A14** and *Brandstetter & Others*.

> Fadeout* (1970, UK 1972)
> Death Claims (1973, UK 1973)
> Troublemaker* (1975, UK 1975)
> The Man Everybody Was Afraid Of (1978, UK 1978)
> Skinflick (1979, UK 1980)
> Gravedigger (1982, UK 1982)
> Nightwork* (1984, UK 1984)
> Brandstetter & Others* (1984). SS, 2 featuring **Brandstetter**.
> The Little Dog Laughed (1986)
> Early Graves (1987)
> Obedience (1988)

Hansen, Stacey — Films: STACEY (AND HER GANGBUSTERS)
HANSEN, Vern
The title listed is a laughably inept British ersatz American PI novel featuring Times Square, New York detective **Brody**. Hubin lists another title, *Murder With Menaces* (UK 1962) that may be a Brody story.

> The Whisper Of Death (UK 1963)

Hardman, Jim — DENNIS, Ralph
Hardy, Cliff — CORRIS, Peter
Harley, John — TACK, Alfred
Harman, Pete — GRANT, Linda
Harmas, Steve — CHASE, James Hadley
Harpe, Angela — LAWRENCE, James D.
Harper — Films: HARPER / The DROWNING POOL

HARPER, David (Edwin Corley)
Forced to resign from an unpublicized, unadmitted CIA special forces squad, "after I helped blow the whistle on a little caper known as Watergate," **Warren Stone** compares himself to Travis McGee, except that he salvages towns, on a strictly illegal basis. "A few concerned citizens put up enough cash to lure me out of my Kentucky cabin . . . the next thing you know, newspaper headlines are reporting the suicide of a crooked mayor or the disappearance of a corrupt police chief." See **Patrick BUCHANAN.**

> The Hanged Men (1976)

HARRINGTON, Joyce
Edgar winning author, best known for macabre suspense stories, who contributed a **Philip Marlowe** short story, "Saving Grace," to **A12.**

Harris, Barney — LACY, Ed

HARRIS, Hyde = HARRIS, Timothy

Harris, Mike — FLYNN, T.T.

HARRIS, Timothy
Harris moved to screen writing (with at least one unfortunate result) after only two books featuring young widower and Vietnam vet **Thomas Kyd,** in which LA, "Mutant City," has a co-starring role. Callous, tough and sarcastic, Kyd is a Berkeley graduate, no longer a liberal and plagued with moral uncertainty. *Goodnight And Goodbye* is an unused Chandler title and Harris has said "It's an homage to Chandler and I don't want anyone to think it's an original. Any writer moving into the mystery field is doing something derivative," which undersells his hero. See **Films: CHEAPER TO KEEP HER.**

> Kyd For Hire (1978, UK 1981; as by **Hyde HARRIS** UK 1977)
>
> Goodnight And Goodbye* (1979, UK 1981)

HARRISON, Chip = BLOCK, Lawrence
Block wrote two sex romps featuring the adolescent **Chip Harrison,** at one point a deputy sheriff in a North Carolina whorehouse, and then had him answer an *NYT* ad placed by **Leo Haig** who wants an Archie Goodwin to immortalize his brilliance as a detective. Very funny pastiche/parodies with Haig as a fat, tropical-fish raising, would-be Nero Wolfe and Harrison as a horny, street-wise Goodwin trying to make Haig's West 20th Street home as famous as Wolfe's.

> Make Out With Murder (1974); as Five Little Rich Girls (as by **BLOCK** 1984, UK 1984)
>
> The Topless Tulip Caper (1975; as by **BLOCK** UK 1984)

Harrison, Clay — ROBBINS, Clifton
Hart, Kirby — ST. CLAIR, Dexter
Harwell, Bump — HIRSCHFIELD, Burt
Hastings, Stanley — HALL, Parnell
Hatch, Cyrus — DAVIS, Frederick C.
Hatch, Jake — CAMPBELL, Robert
Hatch, Sam — TV: PARTNERS IN CRIME
Hatcher, Amos — BANKS, Oliver
Hatchett, Madge — McGRAW, Lee
Havoc, Johnny — JAKES, John
Hawk, Nathan — McKNIGHT, Bob
Hawke, Douglas — TV: SHOOTING STARS
Hawkins, J.D. — PHILBRICK, W.R.
Hawkins, Sam — PAIRO, Preston
Hayes, Maddie — TV: MOONLIGHTING
HAYES, William Edward
Characterized by *SR* as an "amazingly casual private sleuth," **Arthur Halstead** is the man his New York agency sends when they get a wire asking for an operative "shrewd enough to deal with the devil himself."
>The Black Doll (1936)
>Before The Cock Crowed (1937)
>Black Chronicle (1938)
HAYS, Lee
Novelizations of TV: HARRY-O featuring **Harry Orwell**.
>Harry-O (1975)
>Harry-O #2 (1976); as The High Cost Of Living (UK 1978)
HAYWOOD, Gar Anthony
Winner of the 2nd (1987) PWA First Novel competition with a grim story about black LA PI turned electrician turned detective again **Aaron Gunner** who wants to quit the business but gets caught up in what appears to be a white racist attack on a black militant. Haywood has a good ear and conveys a bleak sense of the hopelessness of the oppressed.
>Fear Of The Dark (1988, UK 1988)
Hazard, Eric — CROSBY, Lee
Hazard, Norman O. — WALLACE, F.L.
Hazell, James — YUILL, P.B.
Hazzard, Cheney — BROWN, R.D.
HEALEY, Rose Million
Hardboiled, self-reliant New York PI **Thelma Ade** solves a case without even leaving her office in a short story, "A Neat Crime" (**A21**).

HEALY, Jeremiah
Rather bravely, Healy set **John Francis Cuddy** in Spenser-dominated Boston. An ex-Military Police Captain, and licensed PI head of the claims units of the Boston office of Empire Insurance until he refused to sign a dubious claim, Cuddy, a widower still mourning his young wife, opens an office on Park Street and Boston Common. Exceptionally well plotted, well written and with an intelligent, sensitive, ethical hero. Healy has a **Philip Marlowe** short story, "In The Line Of Duty," in **A12.**

> Blunt Darts* (1984, UK 1986)
> The Staked Goat (1986); as The Tethered Goat (UK 1986)
> So Like Sleep (1987, UK 1987)
> Swan Dive (1988, UK 1988)

HEARN, Daniel
Charles WILLEFORD described hardboiled New York ex-cop, ex-Pinkerton, Irish-Italian PI **Giovanni Alberto 'Joe' Noonan** as "reminiscent of a juggler who spins plates on sticks, rushing back and forth to keep all the plates spinning. His answering service, his health club and his ex-wife are demanding money he doesn't have." A part-time job as bouncer in a West Side bar gets him into even more trouble. "A compelling if visibly seamed novel that suffers from an excess of marginal incidents." AAAAA Private Investigations (a phone book ploy) operates out of a Chelsea pigeon coop on West 17th Street, just off 7th.

> Bad August (1987)

Hearst, Warren — CARSON, Robert
HEATH, Eric
Described by *NYT* as "a thorough, competent detective," **Cornelius 'Copey' Clift Jr.**'s cases, narrated by his capable assistant and, later, fiancée, **Winnie Preston**, were "mildly entertaining" and "fair to middling." Heath rewrote *Death Takes A Dive* as *Murder Of A Mystery Writer* (1953) with an amateur sleuth to whom Pronzini devotes several admiring pages of *Gun In Cheek.*

> Death Takes A Dive (1938)
> Murder In The Museum (1939)

HEBERDEN, M(ary) V(iolet)
Tall, husky, hard-bitten Irish redhead **Desmond Shannon** of Boothe & Shannon is reputed to be the highest paid PI in New York City, perhaps the entire country. Though a man of action, he's well-read, with an interest in philosophy, and violently anti-Communist (*They Can't All Be Guilty* is rather ludicrous on the subject of Communist "infiltration"). Ex-Naval Intelligence Commander **Rick Vanner** has

found that private enterprise pays better and specializes in foreign inquiries. Heberden also wrote a PI series as **Charles L. LEONARD**. She is one of the four women listed in Sandoe's check-list, *Murder Of A Stuffed Shirt* described as "competent and relatively restrained."

Shannon: Death On The Doormat (1939)
           Fugitive From Murder (1940)
           Subscription To Murder (1940)
           Aces, Eights And Murder (1941)
           The Lobster Pick Murder (1941)
           Murder Follows Desmond Shannon (1942, UK 1949)
           Murder Makes A Racket (1942)
           Murder Goes Astray (1943, UK 1951)
           Murder Of A Stuffed Shirt (1944)
           Vicious Pattern (1945, UK 1952)
           Drinks On The Victim (1947)
           They Can't All Be Guilty (1947)
           The Case Of The Eight Brothers (1948, UK 1949)
           Exit This Way (1950, UK 1954); as You'll Fry Tomorrow
              (1955)
           That's The Spirit (1950); as Ghosts Can't Kill (UK 1951)
           Tragic Target (1952, UK 1953)
           Murder Unlimited (1953, UK 1954)
Vanner: Murder Cancels All Debts (1946, UK 1947)
           Engaged To Murder (1949)

Hefferman, Hooky — MEYNELL, Laurence
Helder, James — CANNING, Victor
HELGERSON, Joel
Minneapolis firefighter turned detective **Chet Johnson** trades his services as a private eye for information on his own past.
           Slow Burn (1987)
Heller, Carl — RODERUS, Frank
Heller, Nate — COLLINS, Max Allan
Helm, Ben — FISCHER, Bruno
Helm, Matt — TV: MATT HELM
HELSETH, Henry Edward
Novelization of TV: The **BROTHERS BRANNIGAN** about Phoenix, Arizona, PIs **Mike & Bob Brannigan**.
           The Brothers Brannigan (1961)
Hemingway, Ernest — ABBOTT, Keith
Hendricks, Noah — TV: The CATCHER

Henry, Ben — WEISS, Mike
Henry, George Herbert — SHARKEY, Jack
Henry, Rush — BARRY, Joe
HERBER, William
Chicago plays a major, and seamy, role in two excellent, tough stories about Wabash Avenue PI **Jim Rehm**, a memorable character who gets on unusually badly with Chicago's hard-nosed brand of police who resent his successes.

> King-Sized Murder (1954, UK 1955); as Some Die Slow (1956)
> Live Bait For Murder (1955, UK 1956)

Herbold, Harry — CARSON, Robert
Herring, Freddie — LEWIN, Michael Z.
Hershey, Steve — HINKLE, Vernon
HERSHMAN, Morris
Korean War buddies and former NYPD detectives **Steve Crane** and Ben Verber go into the PI business together but Verber goes missing in a novel expanded from an *Alfred Hitchcock Presents* short story. Crane usually wears a black patch over an eye injured in the war, giving rise to many "private eye" quips. Routine.

> Guilty Witness (1964)

Hetzel, Miro — VANCE, Jack
Hewitt, Jefferson — REESE, John
HEYES, Douglas
One of 848 private detectives licensed and bonded by the State of California, and of 388 operating in LA, **Steve Mallory** and his partner Harry Jellison ran a five-man office in the Branch Building, Miracle Mile, and mostly it was a dull and tedious business. The exception is one case with a shock ending well described by a reviewer: "by the time you finish this chiller, you'll think the icebox is a place to warm up in." PI **Lee Gordon** investigated the murder of the mistress of one of world's wealthiest men (see also **TV: The LONELY PROFESSION**). Heyes returned to the genre with a savage tale of betrayal, set in 30s LA, about ex-cop self-employed PI **Ray Ripley**. See **TV: ARCHER**.

Mallory: The Kiss-Off (1951); as Goodbye Stranger (UK 1952)
Gordon: The 12th Of Never (1963, UK 1964)
Ripley: The Kill (1985)
HEYMAN, Evan Lee
Novelization of **TV: MIAMI UNDERCOVER** featuring **Jeff Thompson**.

> Miami Undercover (1961)

HIAASEN, Carl
At 5'10", 32 year old reporter turned Miami PI, with an office off SW 2nd Avenue, **Brian Keyes** looks younger and "somehow failed to exude the authority so necessary for survival in rough bars, alleys, police stations, jails and McDonald's drive-throughs . . . not slick enough to be a lawyer, not frazzled enough to be a social worker, and not old enough to be a private investigator." Keyes made his debut in a black, violent comedy about a group of wildly disparate terrorists scheming to drive tourists, retirees and developers out of Florida. Hiaasen's second book introduced ex-photographer, ex-con, ex-husband **R.J. Decker**, caught up in very competitive pro bass fishing.
Keyes: Tourist Season (1986, UK 1987)
Decker: Double Whammy (1988, UK 1988)
Hickey, Albert — Films: HICKEY AND BOGGS
Hicks, Alphabet — STOUT, Rex
HILARY, Richard
Newark, New Jersey is home to black ex-prizefighter, ex-cop **Ezell 'Easy' Barnes**, one of the best of the knights-errant of the decaying inner cities, who live inside and are part of the almost surreal lives and lifestyles that accompany urban decay. Barnes' office is in the city's heart, on Branford Place, Broad Street.
            Snake In The Grasses (1987)
            Pieces Of Cream (1987)
            Pillow Of The Community (1988)
HIMMEL, Richard
Though he has a law school diploma on his office wall, **John Patrick Aloysius 'Johnny' Maguire** is pure hardboiled PI. Born on the wrong side of the Chicago tracks, the one time street gang kid ends up on the right side of the law more by chance than anything else. As the Gold Medal blurb writer says, "Dangerous Johnny Maguire is back in a hurricane of guys, gals and guns."
            The Chinese Keyhole (1951, UK 1968)
            I Have Gloria Kirby (1951, UK 1953)
            Two Deaths Must Die (1954, UK 1957)
            Cry Of The Flesh (1955); as The Name's Maguire (UK 1963)
            I'll Find You (1950, UK 1958); as It's Murder, Maguire (1962)
            The Rich And The Damned (1958, UK 1960)
HINKLE, Vernon
Only 5'3", **Steve Hershey**, 23rd Street, New York, PI, wears elevator shoes and pumps iron at the YMCA. A muscle-bound co-pumper asks

him to check up on his girlfriend, mixing him up in rag trade industry intrigue and multiple murder.

> Murder After A Fashion (1986)

HIRSCHFELD, Burt

The bestselling author "turns his hand to the booming private-eye genre." **Bump Harwell**, 42nd Street, New York agency boss, prosperous but bored, traces Alena Verdugo from "the seamiest depths of the New York underworld to the fleshpots of Florida . . . to a steamy Caribbean island, where he finds himself caught in the crossfire between an iron-fisted dictator and a band of bullet-happy rebels . . . and it's a hundred to one shot that he'll get out alive." Opportunistic nonsense.

> The Verdugo Affair (1984)

HITCHENS, Bert & Dolores

The highly regarded mystery writer Dolores Hitchens (see below) and her ex-railroad policeman husband wrote about a group of railroad detectives in novels with outstanding, full-fleshed characterization, notably of hard-bitten, hard-drinking old pro **John Farrel, Michael Kernehan,** who distrusts anybody under 21 and is rarely given cases involving juveniles, **Chuck Reves** and eager beaver rookie **Vic Moine**. The railroad company police run on very similar lines to the regular police and the series has many procedural aspects, though, as Pronzini points out (P&M), they are not allowed to rule the stories. Farrel appears in most stories but the lead role varies.

> FOB Murder (1955, UK 1957)
> One-Way Ticket (1956, UK 1958)
> End Of The Line* (1957, UK 1958)
> The Man Who Followed Women (1959, UK 1960)
> The Grudge (1963, UK 1964)

HITCHENS, Dolores 1907-1973

Best known as D.B. Olsen, Hitchens wrote fine novels in many categories—whodunit, suspense, psychological suspense, police procedurals, neo-Gothics and Westerns—including two PI novels, featuring **Jim Sader** of Long Beach agency Sader & Scarborough, one of which, *Sleep With Slander*, Pronzini rates as "the best hardboiled private eye novel ever written by a woman—and one of the best written by anybody . . . better crafted, more compelling and ultimately more satisfying" than the rival work by **Leigh BRACKETT**, though he thought the first novel "marred by sentimentality and a shaky ending."

> Sleep With Strangers (1955, UK 1956)
> Sleep With Slander* (1960, UK 1961)

Hite, Quinny — BURKE, Richard
HJORTSBERG, William
An experimental writer who often mixes genres, once combining mountaineering and pornography, his single PI novel crosses the PI with the occult. **Harry Angel,** of the Crossroads Detective Agency, Times Square & 7th Avenue, New York, 1959, specializes in missing persons, but didn't bargain for what he was to find at the end of the search for one particular missing person. Stephen King said "I've never read anything like it. Trying to imagine what might have happened if Raymond Chandler had written *The Exorcist* is as close as I can come," while Stefano Tavi hails it as a "deconstructive anti-detective novel" in *The Doomed Detective; The Contribution of the Detective Novel to Postmodern American & Italian Fiction* (1984), though Max Allan Collins regarded it as "often labored and occasionally unpleasant . . . too literary." See **Films: ANGEL HEART.**
      Falling Angel* (1978, UK 1979)
HOBSON, Hank
The one-time commander of a WW2 security group known as The Suicide Mob, **Brad Ford** (!) is a London Private Enquiry agent with a Manchester Square, W1 office. After smoking marijuana—"you have to do all sorts of off-key things in my business"—he thinks he has "the toughness of Marlowe, the extra sensory perception of Vance, the courtliness of the Saint and the sagacity of Father Brown." Hobson is similarly confused.
      The Gallant Affair (UK 1957)
      Death Makes A Claim (UK 1958)
      The Big Twist (UK 1959)
      The Mission House Murder (UK 1959)
      Beyond Tolerance (UK 1960)
HOCH, Edward D.
One of the few surviving professional short mystery story writers, with over 650 and an Edgar to his credit, Hoch has published three non-PI SF mysteries and one mystery novel, which appropriately enough is set at the MWA's annual Edgar award ceremony. When the "Reader of the Year" is killed at the dais, ex-PI **Barney Hamet,** a successful mystery writer and MWA executive vice-president, turns sleuth again. Full of genre trivia and name-dropping, and a good, well-plotted story with fair clues. Hoch has written over 13 short stories about veteran PI **Al Darlan,** at least two of which, "The Other Eye" (A1 #4 and A14) and "The Rented Scar" (A15) feature his rookie partner **Mike Trapper.** The fourth story about

freelance female bodyguard **Libby Knowles**, "A Flash Of Red," is in
A2 #1. Hoch has a **Philip Marlowe** short story, "Essence D'Orient,"
in **A12.** See also **Ellery QUEEN** for a ghost-written novel.

   The Shattered Raven* (1969, UK 1970)

HODGES, Carl G. 1902-1964
Boucher approvingly noted that, despite shortcomings as a writer, Hodges
"manages the unexpected trick of coming up with a new plot for a private
eye novel." **Bob Ruff** of Chicago is a sensible professional who co-
operates with the authorities, "a dazzling enough departure," while
unfolding a complex, detailed and plausible tax racket.

   Murder By The Pack (1953)

Hoerner, Alec — ALVERSON, Charles
Hogan, Frank — TV: GOODNIGHT, MY LOVE
Hogg, Flora — LEE, Austin
Hoggett, Ron — MITCHELL, James
Holden, Dan — BRYNE, Leon
HOLDEN, Genevieve (Genevieve Long Pou)
Boucher commented that while the author "cannot plot for little green
apples, *Deadlier Than The Male* is better than her earlier books, with a
likeable private eye (**Hank Ferrell**) pursuing all over the South a
legendarily charming husband-poisoner."

   Deadlier Than The Male (1961)

Holgate, Peter — HOWIE, Edith
Holland, Bernard — SHELLEY, Mike
Holland, Cassie — TV: CASSIE & COMPANY
Holland, Pete — TAYLOR, H. Baldwin
Holman, Rick — BROWN, Carter
Holmes, Sherlock — TV: The RETURN OF SHERLOCK
      HOLMES
HOLT, Deben
Why he should be referred to on American TV as "the smartest private eye
in London" is a bit of a mystery itself. **Rickard 'Ricky' Britton** is
the clubland hero in PI guise, complete with Jeeves style batman. Light
and romantic, crossing an old-fashioned style rather uncomfortably with
semi-hardboiled concepts.

   Circle Of Shadows (UK 1957)

HOLT, Gavin (Charles Rodda)
Best remembered for his thriller partnership with Eric Ambler as 'Eliot
Reed', Rodda had two PIs, **Winton 'Ritzy' Tripp-Tyler**, commended
by *SR* as a clever and sardonically humorous sleuth, a connoisseur of

music, art, literature, wines, mixed drinks and American slang, and his boss, former Scotland Yard Inspector **Joel Saber**. *NYT* found *Begonia Walk* so baffling and suspenseful that it was inclined to forgive Rodda "for working his red herrings overtime," while *SR* found it crisply characterized and capitally plotted.

> The Theme Is Murder (UK 1938, 1939)
> Green For Danger (UK 1939)
> Swing It, Death (UK 1940)
> Give A Man Rope (UK 1942)
> Begonia Walk (UK 1946); as Send No Flowers (1947)
> Ladies In Ermine (UK 1947)

Holt, Laura — TV: REMINGTON STEELE
HOLTHAM, Gerald — see BUSBY, Roger & HOLTHAM
HOMES, Geoffrey (Daniel Mainwaring 1902-1978)
Mainwaring wrote many underappreciated books, well plotted, semi-hardboiled. realistic, fast paced, witty, with excellent dialogue and description. In his second novel about **Robin Bishop**, the reporter joins a shady private detective agency to make more money doing dirty but profitable work but his newshawk instincts about a case get the better of him and he goes back to journalism. **Humphrey Campbell**, 28, 6'1", part Piute Indian, who drinks nothing stronger than milk, is the unconventional, accordion-playing assistant to 65 year old **Oscar Morgan**, fat, lazy, liquor-drinking, easy-going, slightly corrupt boss of Morgan Missing Persons Bureau of LA. Campbell is chubby but it's all muscle and he knows how to use a .38. Mainwaring became a scriptwriter and adapted his own best book, a tight, suspenseful story full of mood and atmosphere about **Red Bailey**, a New York angle-playing PI who is destroyed by his own errors of judgment, as the 1947 *noir* classic *Out Of The Past*. See **Films: AGAINST ALL ODDS/CRIME BY NIGHT/NO HANDS ON THE CLOCK/OUT OF THE PAST /ROADBLOCK.**

Bishop: The Man Who Murdered Himself (1936, UK 1936)
Campbell: Then There Were Three (1938, UK 1945)
            No Hands On The Clock (1939)
            Finders Keepers (1940)
            Forty Whacks* (1941); as Stiffs Don't Vote (1947)
            Six Silver Handles (1944, UK 1946); as The Case Of The
                Unhappy Angels (1950)
Bailey: Build My Gallows High* (1946, UK 1988)
Hood, John — JAKES, John

Hooks, Steve — MURPHY, Warren
HOPKINS, A.T. (Annette Turngren 1902-1980)
Sandoe commented "This uproar involves a small Minnesota town possessed of a ruling family, an imminent division of estate, a putative heiress to be murdered if possible and a New York investigator who is remarkably susceptible on several scores. After a singularly unhelpful prologue, Mr. Hopkins keeps things hopping madly." *SR* remarked "one of those family affairs, nice but parlor too crowded."
  Have A Lovely Funeral (1954)
Hopkirk, Marty — TV: MY PARTNER, THE GHOST
HOPPENSTAND, Gary & BROWNE (eds) — see
  ANTHOLOGIES: 6
HOPPENSTAND, Gary et al (eds) — see ANTHOLOGIES: 7
Hornblower, Larry — BROWNER, John
Horne, Charles — TUCKER, Wilson
HORNIG, Doug
Operating in Charlottesville, Virginia, divorced Vietnam vet, unambitious **Loren Swift** loves the buzz but dislikes every other aspect of being a PI and was trying retire but doing a favor brought him so much publicity and police good-will that he's still in business. Hornig is an excellent writer and plotter, with fine dialogue, having cured a tendency to overdo the wisecracks, making good use of background tensions; New and Old South, black and white, rich and poor, liberal and conservative.
  Foul Shot* (1984)
  Hardball (1985, UK 1986)
  The Dark Side (1986, UK 1987)
  Deep Dive (1988)
Houston, Matt — TV: MATT HOUSTON
Houston, Sam — DE PUY, E. Spence
Howard, Anthony — McCUTCHEON, Hugh
HOWARD, Hartley = CARMICHAEL, Harry
British author Carmichael used the Howard name for a series of hardboiled imitations of the classic American private eye, featuring **Glenn Bowman**, "top flight New York private detective."
  The Last Appointment (UK 1951)
  The Last Deception (UK 1951)
  The Last Vanity (UK 1952)
  Death Of Cecilia (UK 1952)
  The Other Side Of The Door (UK 1953)
  Bowman Strikes Again (UK 1953) >

Bowman On Broadway (UK 1954)
Bowman At A Venture (UK 1954)
Sleep For The Wicked (UK 1955)
No Target For Bowman (UK 1955)
The Bowman Touch (UK 1956)
A Hearse For Cinderella (UK 1956)
The Long Night (UK 1957)
Key To The Morgue (UK 1957)
The Big Snatch (UK 1958)
Sleep, My Pretty One (UK 1958)
Deadline (UK 1959)
The Armitage Secret (UK 1959)
Fall Guy (UK 1960)
Extortion (UK 1960)
Time Bomb (UK 1961)
I'm No Hero (UK 1961)
Count Down (UK 1962)
Portrait Of A Beautiful Harlot (UK 1966)
Routine Investigation (UK 1967)
The Secret Of Simon Cornell (UK 1969)
Cry On My Shoulder (UK 1970)
Room 37 (UK 1970)
Million Dollar Snapshot (UK 1971)
Murder One (UK 1971)
Epitaph For Joanna (UK 1972)
Nice Day For A Funeral (UK 1972)
Highway To Murder (UK 1973)
Dead Drunk (UK 1974)
Treble Cross (UK 1975)
Payoff (UK 1976)
One-Way Ticket (UK 1978)
The Sealed Envelope (UK 1979)

Howe, Larry — FRANKLIN, Eugene
HOWIE, Edith
Though **Peter Holgate** is a PI, he features in a standard country house, in which Holgate and his wife take shelter from a blizzard, mystery with murders committed to the strains of "Danse Macabre." **Ross Langdon** is another unnecessary PI also with an invaluable female assistant.
Holgate: Murder For Christmas (1941, UK 1942)
Langdon: Cry Murder (1944, UK 1950)

Hoyt, Lester — TORREY, Roger
HOYT, Richard
Like Hoyt, Seattle PI **John Denson** was a journalist and intelligence officer. Now he's a softboiled (up to a point) sleuth who doesn't carry a gun and has his life saved by a woman in every story. Unpretentious, favoring screw-top wine and scruffy bars, he's a self-acknowledged flake, but "everybody underestimates a flake. I count on it. It's part of my act, has been for years. It's how I survive . . . Self-deprecation. That's the trick. Put yourself down . . . Lead with the obvious. Lulls 'em." Witty dialogue and twisting plots. In *Decoys* Denson makes, and loses, a high stakes wager with tough, stunning San Francisco PI **Pamela Yew**. A Denson short story, "Private Investigations," is in **A15**.

> Decoys (1980, UK 1982)
> 30 For A Harry* (1981, UK 1982)
> The Siskiyou Two-Step (1983, UK 1986)
> Siskiyou (1984). "Substantially different" from the above.
> Fish Story (1985, UK 1986)

Huggins, Barney — SHELLEY, Mike
HUGGINS, Roy
Renting desk space from a telephone answering service in the Pacific Building, downtown LA, **Stuart Bailey** is a sensitive Ivy League PhD, ex-OSS man who reads, collects folk music records, drives a pre-war car and charges modestly. Bailey later metamorphosed into a slick TV hero (see **TV: 77 SUNSET STRIP**). Hubin's annotation to *77 Sunset Strip* is incorrect—though Bailey is operating from that address, he is still a tough lone investigator. Another Huggins novel featured slimy, corrupt PI **Danny Fuller**, who is poisoned by the scheming woman he falls in love with and helps commit robbery and murder. See **Films: I LOVE TROUBLE / TOO LATE FOR TEARS**.

Bailey: The Double Take* (1946, UK 1947)
            77 Sunset Strip (1959). Three novelets
Fuller: Too Late For Tears (1947, UK 1950)

HUGHART, Barry
Operating from the Street of Eyes in a fantasy Peking, China of 1000 years ago, **Li Kao** is a former criminal who got bored and became a PI when he discovered that solving crime was more difficult than committing it. Aided by the immensely strong **Lu Yu**, known as Number Ten Ox, who carries the 90 pound, over 100 year old Li on his back when they're in a hurry, the mystery content is secondary to the stories, and stories within them. A son of Ernest Bramah's Kai Lung. >

Bridge Of Birds (1986)

The Story Of The Stone (1988)

Hughes, Griff — DISNEY, Doris Miles

Hughes, Jack — BEAR, David

HUGO, Richard 1923-1982

The great poet of the American wilderness and friend and mentor of James Crumley (*The Last Good Kiss* is a quote from Hugo) wrote one novel featuring a policeman, **Al Barnes**, who by leaving his jurisdiction is forced to act as a PI. Retired after 17 years on the Seattle force, Barnes is a deputy sheriff in western Montana. So warm and compassionate that he was known in Seattle as Mush-Heart Barnes, he doesn't like murder and was a successful homicide detective. People tell Barnes things, though he doesn't know why. Hugo pays more attention to plot than Crumley, while creating off-beat characters.

Death And The Good Life* (1981)

Hull, Mark — DAVIS, Norbert

HUME, David 1900-1945

With his ex-Chief Inspector father, **Mick Cardby** sets up a London private detective agency in books of which those few published in America were admired by *SR* for no very obvious reason.

Bullets Bite Deep (UK 1932)

Crime Unlimited (UK 1933, 1933)

Murders Form Fours (UK 1933); as The Foursquare Murders
(1933)

Below The Belt (UK 1934)

They Called Him Death (UK 1934, 1935)

Too Dangerous To Live (UK 1934)

Dangerous Mr. Dell (UK 1935, 1935)

The Gaol Gates Are Open (UK 1935); as The Jail Gates Are
Open (1935)

Bring 'Em Back Dead (UK 1936, 1936)

Meet The Dragon (UK 1936)

Cemetery First Stop! (UK 1937)

Halfway To Horror (UK 1937)

Corpses Never Argue (UK 1938)

Goodbye To Life (UK 1938)

Death Before Honour (UK 1939)

Heads You Live (UK 1939)

Make Way For The Mourners (UK 1939)

Eternity, Here I Come! (UK 1940) >

The Return Of Mike Cardby (UK 1941)
Destiny Is My Name (UK 1942)
Dishonour Among Thieves (UK 1943)
Get Out Of The Cuffs (UK 1943)
Mike Cardby Works Overtime (UK 1944)
Toast To A Corpse (UK 1944)
Come Back For The Body (UK 1945)
They Never Came Back (UK 1945)
Heading For A Wreath (UK 1946)

HUNT, E(verette) Howard

CIA man best known for his role in the Watergate burglary, Hunt wrote prolifically under a number of names, including **Robert DIETRICH** and **Gordon DAVIS**. One of his novels under the latter name, featuring Washington DC hotel detective **Pete Novak**, was later published under his own name.

Washington Payoff (1975); as House Dick (as by **Gordon DAVIS** 1961)

Hunt, Sonny — TV: MURDER IN MUSIC CITY
Hunter, Anthony — DEAN, Robert George
Hunter, Ed & Ambrose — BROWN, Frederic
Hunter, Ernie — WOLF, Gary
HUNTER, John 1891-1961

British author of many Sexton Blake novels and of one, listed in Hubin as a Blake title, featuring private detective **Bill Langley**. *NYT* chided him for errors in American slang and for the fact that Bill did little but fall in love with a suspect's daughter who, thanks to his carelessness, "falls into the hands of as ruthless a pack of scoundrels as ever appeared between the covers of a book . . . The story has bloodshed enough to make an exciting yarn but somehow it misses fire."

Three Die At Midnight (UK 1934, 1937)

Hunter, John — TV: The CHEATERS
Hunter, Pete — MARCUS, A.A.
Hunter, Sam — MORSE, Larry

HURLEY, Gene

A former crime reporter and PR man turned detective **Tim Flaherty** does all the sleuthing in one unremarkable book, his partner **Moe Ginsburg** playing virtually no part at all.

Have You Seen This Man? (1944)

Hussy, Joe — DUNNE, Colin

HUSTON, Fran (Ron S. Miller)
A cop's daughter, pretty, maladjusted **Nichole Sweet** follows in his footsteps by becoming a PI. Her one Southern California case was as a female Lew Archer. *NYT*, which accepted the author's sex at face value, found it competent but could have been better and complained about the clichés and creeping pace.

      The Rich Get It All (1973)

Hyatt, Dr. Carl — TV: CHECKMATE
Hyde, Barney — BRENT, Nigel
Hyde, John Baron — WOLFF, Benjamin
Hyer, Henry — STEEL, Kurt
Iovine, Alessandro — VERALDI, Attilio
Ireland, Sam — BRANDON, William
IRVINE, Robert R.
Irvine's Salt Lake City, Utah, PI is named after the angel who stands on top of the Mormon temple even though **Moroni Traveler Jr.** is not himself a Latter Day Saint. As in Gary STEWART's books, murder and Mormon heresy are mixed, together with sound plotting, local color, Mormon esoterica and vivid characters.

      Baptism For The Dead (1988)

ISRAEL, Peter (J. Leon Israel)
Israel once lived in Paris and moved cynical **Benjamin Franklin Cage** there after he cut a dangerous slice of the Cage Retirement Plan in LA. Cage's cards say "Public Relations" but his specialty is gathering and suppressing information with justice far from done in amoral stories with confusing, overcomplex plots and some disturbing racism. But the first book is a rough, tough mystery, the rest interesting on France's underworld. A Wolfe-Goodwin variant features arrogant, successful, happily married **Charles Camelot**, whose Manhattan home/office's top floor solarium is devoted to cocktail parties rather than orchids, and his cynical legman, **Philip Revere**, aka Pablo Rivera.

Cage: Hush Money (1974, UK 1975)
            The French Kiss (1976, UK 1977)
            The Stiff Upper Lip (1978, UK 1979)
Camelot: I'll Cry When I Kill You (1987)
            If I Should Die Before I Die (1989)

Ivey, Les — KOEHLER, Robert Portner
JACKS, Jeff
Speculating that "Jacks" might be **Lawrence BLOCK**, Pronzini draws parallels between the Scudder books and two featuring hard-drinking, ex-

cop PI **Shep Stone** in which New York's sleaze-charm is so well drawn that the city is a supporting character, "with an impact that's rare and wonderful." See **Films: BLACK EYE.**

> Murder On The Wild Side* (1971)
> Find The Don's Daughter (1974)

Jackson, Floyd — CHASE, James Hadley
Jackson, Kane — ARDEN, William
JACOBSON, Edith & Ejler
Husband and wife creators of a PI whom the editors of *The Defective Detective* regard as the *most* defective. **Nat Perry** is living on borrowed time; a haemophiliac, known to the underworld as "The Bleeder," he could die from a scratch. While being a PI might seem an odd career choice, he's pretty effective, with a very low profile—"most of those who had brushed against Nat Perry in his business capacity hadn't lived to give a description." He appears in "Dead Man-Killer" (**A7**) and "Funerals—C.O.D" (**A8**; both *Dime Mystery* 1939).

Jacoby, Miles — RANDISI, Robert J.
Jacoby, Quentin — SMITH, J.C.S.
Jacovich, Milan —ROBERTS, Les
JAEDIKER, Kermit c1912-1986
A New York society columnist is found skewered by blackmail-investigating (via burglary) PI **Louis Lait** who is, naturally, a little shy about reporting it. The plot dashes off on too many tangents but has meaty bits on typewriting, cryptograms, allergies and society high and low (*SR*). *NYT* remarked "the murderer is caught with the aid of a mouse which is, we believe, something new in the annals of crime. Aside from this the story is pretty run-of-the-mill."

> Tall, Dark And Dead (1947)

Jaeger, Karl — DOZOIS, Gardner & EFFINGER
JAFFE, Michael
Hired by friends of the accused in a murder trial, **Joe Burns** fails to solve the case in a novel mostly taken up by the trial.

> Death Goes To A Party (1942)

JAHN, Mike
Novelizations of **TV: The ROCKFORD FILES,** featuring James Garner as **Jim Rockford.** Jahn also novelized **TV: SWITCH** with **Frank MacBride,** a tough old retired bunco squad cop and ex-conman and crook **Pete Ryan.**

> Rockford: The Unfortunate Replacement (1975)
>   The Deadliest Game (1976)

MacBride: Switch (1976, UK 1976)
              Switch #2 (1976)

JAKES, John

Before his tedious bicentennial mega-series, Jakes wrote paperback originals of all kinds including three soft-core PI novels about unlicensed, handsome, libidinous, 5'1" **Johnny Havoc** who gets beaten up a lot, but finds solace in the arms of every babe to come along. Breezy, lightweight comedies in the Shell Scott mold. **John Hood** features in a short story, "The Girl In The Golden Cage" (*Thrilling Detective* 1953 as by Alan Payne) in **A13**. See **William ARD** for ghost-written novels.

 Johnny Havoc (1960)
 Johnny Havoc Meets Zelda (1962)
 Johnny Havoc And The Doll Who Had 'It'* (1963)

James, Mike — SCOTT, Denis

JAMES, P(hyllis) D(orothy)

Though without capital, qualifications or experience, 22 year old **Cordelia Gray** has become junior partner in Pryde's Detective Agency, Kingly Street, London, W1 and inherits the business when her partner commits suicide. Tough, intelligent, clear-eyed and independent, Gray was a fine creation and the first book is often regarded as James's masterpiece. The second title, ten years later, was a routine whodunit set on an isolated island. See **Films: An UNSUITABLE JOB FOR A WOMAN.**

 An Unsuitable Job For A Woman* (UK 1972, 1973)
 The Skull Beneath The Skin (UK 1982, 1982)

James, Walter — MILLER, Wade

Jantarro, John Kenneth Galbraith — RITCHIE, Simon

Jardinn, Ben — WHITFIELD, Raoul

Jarnegan, James — JENKINS, Will F.

Jarrett, Sam — TV: JARRETT

Jaworsky, Harry — TV: ROGER & HARRY

Jaxon, Wood — MICHEL, M. Scott

JEFFERS, H(arry) Paul

One of the writers of novels set in the past and featuring cameos of the famous of the time, in Jeffers case the late 30s. **Harry MacNeil**, who lives and works over a 52nd Street, New York, jazz club, is "an ex-cop who's now a private investigator who'd prefer nothing better than to play clarinet with a top jazz band and leave the detective work to better guys."

 Rubout At The Onyx Club (1982)
 Murder On Mike* (1984)
 The Rag Doll Murder (1987)

JENKINS, Will F. 1896-1975
Better known as Murray Leinster, Jenkins wrote one book about **James Jarnegan**, whose business Will Cuppy referred to as "confidential reports," while *NYT* noted that murder is out of his usual line, but both agree that he accepts a case in which violence is the main theme
      The Man Who Feared (1942).
Jenner, Jimmy — MILNE, John
JERINA, Carol
"One of the countless manuscripts spawned as a result of editors who wanted writers to submit *Moonlighting* clones," said *Rue Morgue*. Socialite **Jillian Fletcher** goes to work for Dallas PI and hunk **Jackson Fury**, "part comedy, part romance and part mystery and well short of the mark on all counts."
      The Tall Dark Alibi (1988)
      Sweet Jeopardy (1988)
JEROME, Owen Fox (Oscar J. Friend 1897-1963)
In what *NYT* described as "a whacky story if you ever read one," New York PI **George Robin** must deal with bodies disappearing and different bodies reappearing.
      The Corpse Awaits (1946, UK 1948); as Night At Club Baghdad
         (Can 1950)
Johnson, Chet — HELGERSON, Joel
JOHNSON, Philip
One of Pronzini's "truly memorable" Phoenix Press detectives (*Gun In Cheek*) was 5'2" **Blackie White**, "with a body like a tank and the eyes of a baby," who says things like "Holy suffering mother-in-laws" when he's excited.
      Hung Until Dead (1940)
JOHNSTON, William
Novelization of **TV: BANYON** about 30s PI **Miles Banyon**. Johnston also novelized **TV: MY FRIEND TONY** featuring UCLA criminology prof/PI **John Woodruff** and **Tony Novello**.
Banyon: Banyon (1971)
Woodruff: My Friend Tony (1968)
Jolson, Ben — GOULART, Ron
Jones, Barnaby — STOKES, Manning Lee
Jones, Barnaby, Betty & Jedediah Ross — TV: BARNABY
      JONES
Jones, Cosmo — Films: COSMO JONES, CRIME
      SMASHER

Jones, Guinevere — CASTLE, Jayne
JONES, James 1921-1977
The famous Big Novel writer strayed into the territory once with **Lobo Davies**, an American PI who goes to a Greek island populated by hippies, crooks, drug pushers, smugglers and decadent rich Americans in pursuit of embezzled money. A conventional, competent, well-plotted novel distinguished by, in the *New Yorker*'s words, "its almost breathtaking, red-hot hatred of the young."
  A Touch Of Danger (1973)
Jones, Jeffrey — TV: The FILES OF JEFFREY JONES
Jones, Kennedy — KLEIN, Norman
Jones, Loopy — DALE, William
Jones, Morocco — BAYNES, Jack
Jordan, Barry — MacKENZIE, Donald
Jordan, Dan — REED, Harlan
Jordan, Scott — MASUR, Harold Q.
Jugedinski, Anna — SWAN, Phyllis
Justis, Zachariah — CASTLE, Jayne
Kale, Connie — PHILBRICK, W.R.
KAMINSKY, Stuart M.
Think of anyone famous (but now dead) who was, or could have been, in LA in 1941 (the series' permanent date) from Mae West to Judy Garland, Joe Louis to Raymond Chandler, Errol Flynn to Al Capone, Howard Hughes to Bertolt Brecht, Chico Marx to Alfred Hitchcock, and sooner or later, they'll turn up in the life of Tobias Leo Pevsner, aka **Toby Peters**, ex-cop and security guard, now investigator to the stars. A naive, romantic dreamer, Peters, "the Dennis the Menace of private eyedom," who shares an office in the Faraday Building, Hoover, near 9th, with a dentist, lives on junk food and has a running feud with his Homicide Lieutenant brother. Comic nostalgia with a light parodic touch but sound, often very violent, Hollywood Babylon plots informed by Kaminsky's knowledge of Hollywood history. Two Peters short stories, "The Man Who Shot Lewis Vance" (**A15**; the basis for the novel) and "Busted Blossoms" (**A14** & **A16**) are in anthologies. Kaminsky contributed a **Philip Marlowe** short story, "Bitter Lemons," to **A12**.
  Bullet For A Star (1977, UK 1978)
  Murder On The Yellow Brick Road* (1978, UK 1979)
  You Bet Your Life (1979)
  The Howard Hughes Affair (1979, UK 1980)
  Never Cross A Vampire (1980) >

High Midnight (1981, UK 1982)
Catch A Falling Clown (1982)
He Done Her Wrong (1983)
The Fala Factor (1984)
Down For The Count (1985)
The Man Who Shot Lewis Vance (1986)
Smart Moves (1987)
Think Fast, Mr. Peters (1988)
Buried Caesars (1989)

Kamus of Kadizar — REAVES, J. Michael/SHIRLEY, John

KANE, Frank 1912-1968

Radio and TV scriptwriter Kane's **Johnny Liddell** novels have a cinematic quality with non-stop action and very little detection. A tough operative for the Acme Detective Agency in the early books, Liddell sets up on his own New York agency at 50 West 42nd in *Dead Weight*. Characterization is minimal and in 29 novels little about Liddell emerges, apart from his passion for redheads. Kane recycled entire scenes from previous books and each one has between two and ten killings, several fist fights and beatings, using every conceivable weapon, and a minimum of one kidnaping. Action is the thing and the writing is lean and vigorous, with an authenticity provided by Kane's New York policeman brother who was his technical advisor. A Liddell short story, "With Frame To Match," is in A10. See also **Frank BOYD, TV: MICKEY SPILLANE'S MIKE HAMMER / The INVESTIGATORS and Radio: The FAT MAN.**

About Face (1947); as Death About Face (1948); as The Fatal
    Foursome (1958)
Green Light For Death (1949, UK 1966)
Slay Ride (1950)
Bullet Proof (1951, UK 1969)
Dead Weight (1951)
Bare Trap (1952)
Poisons Unknown (1953)
Grave Danger (1954)
Red Hot Ice (1955, UK 1956)
A Real Gone Guy (1956, UK 1957)
Johnny Liddell's Morgue (1956, UK 1958). SS
The Living End (1957)
Trigger Mortis (1958)
A Short Bier (1960, UK 1964) >

Time To Prey (1960, UK 1964)
Due Or Die (1961, UK 1963)
The Mourning After (1961)
Stacked Deck* (1961, UK 1964). SS
Crime Of Their Life (1962, UK 1964)
Dead Rite (1962, UK 1968)
Ring-A-Ding-Ding (1963, UK 1964)
Johnny Come Lately (1963, UK 1964)
Hearse Class Male (1963, UK 1969)
Barely Seen (1964, UK 1964)
Final Curtain (1964, UK 1964)
Fatal Undertaking (1964, UK 1965)
The Guilt-Edged Frame (1964)
Esprit De Corpse (1965)
Two To Tangle (1965)
Maid In Paris (1966)
Margin For Terror (1967)

KANE, Henry
Kane's first novel about **Peter Chambers** was accepted by the first publisher he sent it to and the series ran for 25 years, though the debut was the only one in which Sandoe could discover any pleasure. Chambers describes himself as "A shamus, a private richard, a caper-kid. A wise guy private eye. Talks hard with the tough guys, purrs with the ladies. All the girls fall for him. You know, like what you read about." Written tongue firmly in cheek, with humor, wordplay, double entendres and wisecracks to the fore, they are often well plotted but Kanese either amuses or irritates. The later books are less frivolous and better written but pornographic passages were inserted in those with *Job* in the title. Chambers short stories, "The Memory Guy" and "Suicide Is Scandalous" (also in *Report For A Corpse*) are in **A10** and **A14. Marla Trent**, 38-23-38 Miss America runner-up, Vassar Phi Beta Kappa, Columbia PhD and ex-wife of the head of the NYPD Homicide Bureau, has a stylish office address, 527 Madison Avenue. Fiftyish, urbane, 6'3" former NYPD **Inspector McGregor**, rich through judicious investments and the most expensive PI in New York, is an older, wiser and slightly less libidinous version of Chambers, much preferred by Pronzini. Kane also novelized the quirky **TV: PETER GUNN**, for which he was a scriptwriter. See also **Radio: CRIME & PETER CHAMBERS**.
Chambers: A Halo For Nobody (1947, UK 1950); as Martinis And
          Murder (1956) >

Armchair In Hell (1948, UK 1949)

Report For A Corpse (1948, UK 1950); as Murder Of The Park Avenue Playgirl (1957). SS

Hang By Your Neck (1949, UK 1950)

A Corpse For Christmas (1951, UK 1952); as The Deadly Doll (1959); as Homicide At Yuletide (1966)

Until You Are Dead (1951, UK 1952)

My Business Is Murder (1954). Novelets

Trinity In Violence* (UK 1954; with different contents 1957). Novelets

Trilogy In Jeopardy (UK 1955). Novelets

Too French And Too Deadly (1955); as The Narrowing Lust (UK 1956)

The Case Of The Murdered Madame (1955); as Triple Terror (UK 1958, different contents)

Who Killed Sweet Sue? (1956); as Sweet Charlie (UK 1957)

Death On The Double (1957, UK 1958). Novelets

The Name Is Chambers (1957). SS

Fistful Of Death (1958); as The Dangling Man (UK 1959)

Death Is The Last Lover (1959); as Nirvana Can Also Mean Death (UK 1959)

Death Of A Flack (1961, UK 1961)

Dead In Bed (1961, UK 1963)

Death Of A Hooker (1961, UK 1963)

Kisses Of Death (1962); as Killer's Kiss (UK 1962) Features **Trent**

Death Of A Dastard (UK 1962, 1963)

Never Give A Millionaire An Even Break (1963); as Murder For The Millions (UK 1964)

Nobody Loves A Loser (1963, UK 1964)

Snatch An Eye (UK 1963, 1964)

The Devil To Pay (UK 1966); as Unholy Trio (1967); as Better Wed Than Dead (1970)

Don't Call Me Madame (1969)

The Shack Job (1969)

The Bomb Job (1970)

Don't Go Away Dead (1970)

Kiss! Kiss! Kill! Kill! (1970). Novelets

The Glow Job (1971)

The Tail Job (1971) >

　　　　　Come Kill With Me (1972)
　　　　　The Escort Job (1972)
　　　　　Kill For The Millions (1972)
Trent:　The Private Eyeful (1959, UK 1960)
Gunn:　Peter Gunn (1960)
McGregor:　The Midnight Man* (1965); as Other Sins Only Speak (UK
　　　　　　　1965)
　　　　　Conceal And Disguise (1966, UK 1966)
　　　　　Laughter In The Alehouse (1968, UK 1978)
Kane, Martin — Radio: MARTIN KANE, PRIVATE EYE
Kane, Sugar — MARSHALL, Lovat
KANTNER, Rob
Joining Estleman's Amos Walker in Detroit is Mustang-driving **Ben Perkins**, who got his arms and shoulders fitting doors on the Ford assembly line, before becoming union "liaison officer" doing discreet, sensitive and occasionally violent little chores. Out on the street after federal investigations and trials of union bosses, Perkins is rewarded for his refusal to give evidence with a job as head of maintenance, and later security, of Norwegian Wood, a Ford Lake, Bellevue, apartment block, which suits his predilection for putting things right, also exercised as a part-time PI, unlicensed though the Detroit police are pressing him to let them rubber-stamp an application. Gritty dialogue and very well-written. Perkins short stories, "The Rat Line," "Fly Away Home" and "Left For Dead," are in **A15, A16** and **A17**.
　　　　　The Back Door Man (1986)
　　　　　The Harder They Hit (1987)
　　　　　Dirty Work (1988)
Kanzler, Nash — GOTTLEIB, Nathan
KAPLAN, Arthur
Secretary to a stupid, sexist San Francisco PI, contentious and abrasive **Charity Bay** set up on her own in New York City, stealing her first client from her ex-boss. Good-looking, with world-wide contacts, Bay is so unpleasant, boasting, for instance, of not sending her parents Christmas cards, that her obnoxious personality overshadows her one powerful story.
　　　　　A Killing For Charity* (1976)
KARLINS, Marvin & L.M. ANDREWS
A PI of the future mentioned by Baker & Nietzel is **Victor Slaughter**.
　　　　　Gomorrah (1974)

KATZ, Michael J.

Chicago PI **Murray Glick** gets out of "hard-core, elbow-grease type cases" after being shot at and opens an office in a shopping mall. Refusing to investigate when a friend, sports commentator Andy Sussman, is accused of murder, he agrees to act as a consultant. "Murray's too slick to be a sleazebag. I think 'slimeball' would be more appropriate," says Andy's lawyer/girlfriend. A fine comic debut with offbeat characters and sharp dialogue. Glick and Sussman reappeared in a story about pro wrestling with a disappointingly implausible ending.

> Murder Off The Glass (1987)
> Last Dance At Redondo Breach (1989)

Kaufman, Philip — NEWMAN, Joel

KAUFMAN, Wolfe 1905-1970

Though he only drinks milk, quarts at a time, doesn't smoke and leaves swearing to others, **Dick Anderson** is a tough item who says of himself, "Unfortunately, headwork is not my strong suit. I just like to barge ahead and play my cards as they fall . . . I've trained myself not to think. I just follow my hunches." *NYT* found Kaufman "a decided find in the hardboiled whodunit field," with "murder, mayhem, unusual ladies and puzzle gambits" fighting for attention but *SR* thought he could do better.

> I Hate Blondes (1946)

KAVANAGH, Dan (Julian Barnes)

Forced to quit London's Metropolitan Police when his bisexuality is discovered and his superiors set him up, former detective-sergeant sharp, cynical **Nick Duffy** sets up Duffy Security, advising on protection for homes and offices and does a little freelance PI work on the side. Though using recurring stylistic tricks, the books feature dry humor, precise characterization of a host of London villains, policemen and citizens, gripping action and fine writing, as might be expected from Julian Barnes.

> Duffy (UK 1980, 1986)
> Fiddle City (UK 1981, 1986)
> Putting The Boot In (UK 1985)
> Going To The Dogs (UK 1987)

KAYE, Marvin

Unable and unwilling to qualify for a New York PI license, frustrated detective and arrogant show business PR woman **Hilary Quayle** makes her secretary **Gene**, the narrator, reactivate his license and act as legman for her deductive abilities. Quayle is insufferable but the series is entertaining and colorful.

> A Lively Game Of Death (1972, UK 1974) >

The Grand Ole Opry Murders* (1974)
Bullets For Macbeth (1976)
The Laurel And Hardy Murders (1977, UK 1978)
The Soap Opera Slaughters (1982)

Kaye, Simon — WAUGH, Hillary
KAYE, William
His real name is Charles, but because his little sister couldn't pronounce Chuck he became **Chickie French** and kept it because it attracted attention in the Yellow Pages of the unnamed city in which he runs a one-man office. A fat finder's fee for some recovered paintings paid for his one indulgence, a Porsche, though he uses less conspicuous cars for tailing people. Clever with a surprise twist at the end.

Wrong Target (1981)

Kearny, Dan Associates — GORES, Joe
Kearny, Max — GOULART, Ron
KEATING, Henry
Novelization of a mystery-comedy satirizing Sam Spade and Nick and Nora Charles as **Sam Diamond**, San Francisco's best known PI, and **Dick & Dora Charleston**. See **Films: MURDER BY DEATH.**

Murder By Death (1976)

Keaton, Kyra — TONE, Teona
KEENE, Day
A prolific pulp and paperback writer, Keene had, in Pronzini's words, "a strong sense of pace and narrative drive; he knew how to tell a story that gripped the reader immediately and held him to the end." Irish-Hawaiian **Johnny Aloha** was described by Boucher as "better company than many of fiction's private eyes."

Dead In Bed (1959)
Payola (1960)

KEENE, Kitty — Radio: KITTY KEENE, INC.
Keene, Max — SABER, Robert O.
Keene, Phil — OZAKI, Milton K.
KEITH, Carlton (Keith Carlton Robertson)
A handwriting expert by profession, **Jeffrey Green**, originally of South Dakota, then glorified messenger boy, now the entire firm of Monroe & Green, Examiners of Questioned Documents, NYC, behaves like a PI with his expertise called for in cases that take him as far afield as Zurich and Madrid.

The Diamond-Studded Typewriter (1958, UK 1960); as A Gem Of A Murder (1959) >

> Missing, Presumed Dead (1961)
> Rich Uncle (1963, UK 1965)
> The Crayfish Dinner (1966); as The Elusive Epicure (UK 1968)
> A Taste Of Sangria (1968); as The Missing Bookkeeper (UK 1969)

KELLERMAN, Jonathan

A child psychologist like his creator, **Alex Delaware**, burnt out in his mid-30s, is semi-retired, emerging occasionally from his Beverly Glen Drive, LA, home to appear as an expert witness in cases involving children. On the "Duck" principle (see Introduction) Delaware is a PI as he follows up requests for help from the police, medical friends and former patients, and Stephen King makes a reasonable point in saying that Kellerman has reinvented the private eye story. Full of insights, an edge of humor and very suspenseful. The first novel won an Edgar and a Bouchercon Anthony. See **TV: WHEN THE BOUGH BREAKS**.

> When The Bough Breaks (1985); as Shrunken Heads (UK 1985)
> Blood Test (1986, UK 1986)
> Over The Edge (1987, UK 1987)

Kelly, Sam — BURKE, Jackson F.

Kemp, Lennox — MEEK, M.R.D.

KENDRICK, Baynard 1894-1977

Blinded in WW1, ex-US Army Intelligence officer **Captain Duncan Maclain** is one of the most remarkable of the handicapped PIs, inspired by Ernest Bramah's Max Carrados but without the supersensory powers that Kendrick found incredible. Kendrick worked with the blind and ensured that everything Maclain did was authentic. Tall, dark, handsome and elegant, living in a luxury Manhattan penthouse on 72nd Street & Riverside Drive, Maclain is assisted by his partner Spud Savage, Spud's wife Rena and two German Shepherds, seeing-eye Shnucke and attack-trained Dreist. Maclain is a fascinating character and the books well plotted, though during the series shifting from detection to psychology. Earlier, Kendrick wrote three Florida-set novels featuring a gourmand who announces himself as "I'm **Miles Standish Rice**—The Hungry!" Rather oddly Rice, a deputy sheriff in his first appearance, *The Iron Spiders** (1936), is a Miami PI, referred to as a former Investigator for the State's Attorney, in the second. See **Films: EYES IN THE NIGHT / The HIDDEN EYE**.

Rice: The Eleven Of Diamonds (1936, UK 1937)
          Death Beyond The Go-Thru (1938)
Maclain: The Last Express (1937, UK 1938) >

The Whistling Hangman (1937, UK 1959)
The Odor Of Violets* (1941, UK 1941); as Eyes In The
    Night (1942)
Blind Man's Bluff (1943, UK 1944)
Out Of Control (1945, UK 1947)
Death Knell (1945, UK 1946)
Make Mine Maclain (1947) Three novelets
The Murderer Who Wanted More (1951)
You Die(t) Today (1952, UK 1958)
Blind Allies (1954)
Reservations For Death (1957, UK 1958)
Clear And Present Danger (1958, UK 1959)
The Aluminum Turtle (1960); as The Spear Gun Murders
    (UK 1961)
Frankincense And Murder (1961, UK 1962)

KENNEALY, G.P.

Former SFPD Inspector **Peter Flynn**, half his face rebuilt by plastic
surgery after an Iranian consulate bombing, sets up as a modern business-
style PI with a staff and office suite in the Golden Gateway Apartments.
His one adventure is standard contemporary (at the time) fare with drugs,
Mafiosi, homosexuals and girls. Kennealy was, possibly still is, a PI
himself and seems to have been reborn in the entry below.

Nobody Wins (1977)

KENNEALY, Jerry

Few PIs have been further down on their luck than **Nick Polo** of Green
Street, North Beach, San Francisco. Sprung out of Lompoc Federal
Prison mid-stretch by a powerful politician, Polo is offered his PI license
and, more important, his concealed weapons permit back in exchange for
undertaking a dangerous and secret case. Polo is a laid-back investigator,
the plots are well-constructed and the occasionally very violent action is
well-handled. See above entry.

Polo Solo (1987)
Polo, Anyone? (1988)
Polo's Ponies (1988)

KENNEDY, Elliot (Lionel Godfrey)

NYT described this British ersatz novel as "a stinker . . . all but a parody
of the tough-guy, private-eye species. The hero, an investigator in LA, is
one of the type who is always getting beat up. Every single cliché of the
style is harnessed up and proudly paraded. Dialogue and characterization
are rudimentary . . . sort of a collector's item." Hubin lists five other

titles, unpublished in the US, which sound (*Bullets Are Final*, etc.) as if they might be a series.

The Big Loser (UK 1972, 1972)

KENNEDY, Stetson

Based on his own experience as an undercover agent for the Georgia Bureau of Investigation, Kennedy's one novel is exceptional for its subject matter, the Ku Klux Klan, but, according to contemporary reviews, merges into an uneasy fusion of fact and fiction.

Passage To Violence (1954)

Kent, Brice — GILES, Guy Elwyn

Kent, Harry — LANDON, Christopher

KENT, Larry

The nadir of the private eye; Australian digest sized novelets, emblazoned "I Hate Crime," with a bathing beauty on the cover, promised "Thrills galore grip you as this unconventional detective plunges into tough, crime-busting adventures each one something new. That is why **Larry Kent's** popularity keeps on growing." Trash would be a compliment.

Keremos, Helen — ZAREMBA, Eva

Kernehan, Michael — HITCHENS, Bert & Dolores

Kernochan, Sam — ROCHE, Arthur Somers

KERR, Ben = ARD, William

Boucher admired Ard but found his pseudonymous Florida-set novel featuring PI **Johnny Stevens** "a mixture of clichés and chaos . . . the standard model, a little less sadistic and even more sexy than most."

Shakedown (1952)

KETCHUM, Philip

PI-phobic police suspect **Stephen Barth** of his foster-father's murder and obstruct his efforts to clear himself. *NYT* observed that "it would have helped if the author could have arranged to have more of his characters act like rational beings." **George Clay** undergoes more than usual physical punishment.

Barth: Death In The Library (1937)

Clay: Death In The Night (1939); as Good Night For Murder (1946)

Keyes, Brian — HIAASEN, Carl

Keyes, Jefferson — TV: COOL MILLION

Khan — TV: KHAN

Kilby, Mark — FRAZER, Robert Caine

Kildane, Eddie — Films: The RUNAROUND

Kilgerrin, Paul — LEONARD, Charles L.

Killian, Francis — PETERS, Ellis

Killian, Johnny — MARLOWE, Dan J.
Kincaid, John — SMITH, Richard N.
Kincaid, Tom — COX, William R.
KING, Frank 1892-1958
The Conrad Detective Agency, an admitted front for **Clive 'Dormouse'**
Conrad and his beautiful partner/fiancée/wife **Alice Faverden**, covers
up other things. Grudgingly admired (!) by the London police for the help
he gives them and for the fact that he takes lives and valuables from
"people who deserve to lose them," using brains not brawn, Conrad is a
rather tougher version of Raffles.

> Enter The Dormouse (UK 1936)
> The Dormouse—Undertaker (UK 1937)
> The Dormouse Has Nine Lives (UK 1938)
> The Dormouse—Peacemaker (UK 1938)
> Dough For The Dormouse (UK 1939)
> This Doll Is Dangerous (UK 1940)
> They Vanish At Night (UK 1941)
> What Price Doubloons? (UK 1942)
> Gestapo Dormouse (UK 1944)
> Sinister Light (UK 1946)
> The Catastrophe Club (UK 1947)
> Operation Halter (UK 1948)
> Operation Honeymoon (UK 1950)
> The Case Of The Strange Beauties (UK 1952)
> The Big Blackmail UK 1954)
> Crooks' Caravan (UK 1955)
> The Empty Flat (UK 1957)
> That Charming Crook (UK 1958)
> The Two Who Talked (UK 1958)
> The Case Of The Frightened Brother (UK 1959)

King, Jason — TV: KING OF DIAMONDS
KING, Rufus 1893-1966
Among King's Golden Age whodunits was **Cotton Moon**, whom
Boucher calls an "odd fish among fictional sleuths." A fanatic about edible
nuts. he charges $30,000 per case to support his yacht *Coquilla* on
which he roams the world looking for ever more exotic ones. The narrator
is his secretary, athletic Lower East Side ex-bartender **Bert Stanley**.
Cuppy, who called the book "a four star item from the Rufus King
workshop," wanted more but King does not seem to have obliged.

> Holiday Homicide (1940, UK 1941)

King, Sam — BANKS, Raymond
Kingsley, Molly — CAMPBELL, Hazel
KINGSLEY-SMITH, Terence
Though **Pete McCoy** is a contemporary LA PI, most of the action is recalled from 30s Hollywood events, attempting comic nostalgia in the KAMINSKY mode. Baker & Nietzel comment "The best that can said of this effort is that there a few scenes that may not annoy you."
      The Murder Of An Old Time Movie Star (1983)
Kinross, Dermot — Films: CITY AFTER MIDNIGHT
KINSLEY, Lawrence
Pornography on Boston University campus is **Jason T. O'Neil's** problem.
      The Red-Light Victim (1981)
Kirby, Birch — SPENCER, Ross H.
Kirk, Devlin — BURNS, Rex
Kirk, Murray — ELLIN, Stanley
Kirk, Peter — VANCE, William E.
Kirkwood, Bruce — TURNER, William Price
KITTREDGE, William & KRAUZER (eds) —see
      ANTHOLOGIES: 8
KLAICH, Dolores
An attempt to combine mystery and lesbian comedy, featuring Sapphic PI **Tyler Divine**, herself involved in the numerous gay and lesbian pairings during a murder investigation, described by a reviewer as a heavy-handed failure despite off-beat characters.
      Heavy Gilt (1988)
Klein, Max — BENJAMIN, Paul
KLEIN, Norman 1897-1948
Klein's specialty was Dixie detectives. **Kennedy Jones**, hired to protect a client from an unspecified (by the client) peril, is an uncouth roughneck from Missouri, made to feel very unwelcome by the rest of the household. **Harvey Church**, described by *NYT* as having "the unique distinction of being both gentle and hard-boiled," is a former Kentucky sheriff originally hired to guard the gifts at a fashionable Long Island wedding, then, by the bride, to clear her cousin of the murder of the Polish Prince groom. Klein had a choppy style and breathless pace.
Jones: The Destroying Angel (1933)
Church Terror By Night (1935)
Klick, Chris — McCALL, Wendell
Knaresbrook, Olga — CAMPBELL, Hazel

KNICKMEYER, Steve
Making more money betting on football games than as PIs, Oklahoma City good old boys **Steve Cranmer**, boss of Cranmer Investigations, Trinity Building, North May Avenue, and his dope-smoking assistant **Butch Maneri**, former pool shark, are a couple of wrecks. Cranmer gobbles Demarols for an injured knee and Maneri has gastritis. But they're tough enough to get through violent, action-packed cases. Double act comic dialogue and plots with plenty of twists and turns.

> Straight* (1976, UK 1977)
> Cranmer (1978, UK 1980)

KNIGHT, Adam = LARIAR, Lawrence
45th Street, New York, PI and specialist skip-tracer **Steve Conacher** is hard-fisted and pretty bone-headed. Plots keep moving only because he's always turning up late, jumping to conclusions and walking down dark passages. Racist and homophobic, with the classic "gunsel" error. See **LARIAR** (and also **Michael STARK**) for Boucher's low opinion of this series, though he found the comic-strip business detail in *I'll Kill You Next* interesting while still complaining about Conacher's conviction that the truth has to be beaten out of people.

> Murder For Madame (1951)
> Stone Cold Blonde (1951)
> The Sunburned Corpse (1952)
> Knife At My Back (1953)
> Kiss And Kill (1953)
> I'll Kill You Next (1954)
> Girl Running (1956)
> Triple Slay (1959)

KNIGHT, David = PRATHER, Richard S.
Prather originally published one **Shell Scott** title under this name.

> Pattern For Murder (1952); as The Scrambled Yeggs (as by
> Richard S. PRATHER 1958, UK 1962)

Knight, Phyllis — Radio: MICHAEL SHAYNE
Knightsbridge — RYAN, Conall
Knowles, Libby — HOCH, Edward D.
KNOX, Bill & Edward BOYD
Knox, author of the Thane-Moss Glasgow procedurals, adapted Boyd's scripts for **TV: The VIEW FROM DANIEL PIKE** about tough, pugnacious, slum-born Glasgow PI and debt collector **Daniel Pike**.

> The View From Daniel Pike (UK 1974, 1974) 4 SS

KOBLER, John
A notable *Defective Detective* is **Peter Quest** of New York who suffers from glaucoma. Not only is he going steadily blind but he's apt to lose his sight temporarily at inconvenient moments. As a result, he throws himself into the most dangerous cases, seeking death in action, and labels cases as failures because he lived through them. "The Brain Murders" and "Bubbles Of Murder" (both *Dime Mystery* 1939) appear in **A7** and **A8**.

KOEHLER, Robert Portner
Unemployed and hungover, **Les Ivey** takes a case more to keep his hand in than in any real expectation of profit, but ends up with the makings of many more hangovers. After the war, Major **Avery Gregg** and 2nd Lt **Tony Ellis**, co-workers in an hush-hush Intelligence unit, set up an LA investigation office that doesn't advertise, relying on referrals from a few law firms. The stories, set in New Mexico, Mexico and Central America, are heavy on clues and deduction.

Ivey: Corpse In The Wind (1944)
Gregg: The Road House Murders (1946)
         The Hooded Vulture Murders (1947)
         The Blue Parakeet Murders (1948)

KOMO, Dolores
Her father was the first black PI in St. Louis, possibly America, when he started his agency in 1947 and cop's widow **Clio Brown** inherited it, running it with the help of her mother, a 19 year old secretary, her bicycle-racing boyfriend and Pixie, a Yorkshire Terrier. A $10,000 retainer persuades her to break a rule not to get involved in family disputes in a "WomanSleuth Mystery."
        Clio Brown: Private Investigator (1988)

Kookson, Gerald Lloyd III — TV: 77 SUNSET STRIP

KOOTZ (Samuel Melvin 1898-1982)
Dizzy is the best word for two wild-eyed, occasionally quite funny and usually confusing books, centered on the art and fashion worlds, about pint-sized (5'4") Casanova and PI **Jason Emory**.
        Puzzle In Paint (1943)
        Puzzle In Petticoats (1944)

Kovacs, Riley — DeMARCO, Gordon
Kovak, Mike — TV: MAN WITH A CAMERA
Kovak, Sydney — TV: PARTNERS IN CRIME

KRAFT, Gabrielle
Operating in glitz and glamour high money California, ex-hippie, ex-con **Doyle Dean McCoy**, runs a guard dog hire company and operates as a

PI, teamed with lawyer and amateur sleuth Jerry Zalman and his clever girlfriend Marie Thrasher.

> Bullshot (1987)
> Screwdriver (1988)

Krajewski, Thaddeus — PRONZINI, Bill
Kramer, Phil — KRUGER, Paul
KRAUZER, Stephen M. (ed) — see **ANTHOLOGIES: 8**
Krim, Harvey — CUNNINGHAM, E.V.
Kruger, Dan — CORMANY, Michael
KRUGER, Paul (Roberta Elizabeth Sebenthal)
Operating somewhere in the Rockies, PI **Vince Latimer** featured in a tough actioner with a vintage finale. **Phil Kramer** is an "Astoria," Colorado, lawyer, but one who never goes to court, solving cases by legwork and detection, pre-empting charges against his clients by finding the real guilty parties, in PI style. Marcia Muller (P&M) thinks that Sebenthal does "a creditable job of creating an authentic male voice" in her first person narratives.

Latimer: A Bullet For A Blonde (1958)
Kramer: Weep For Willow Green (1967, UK 1971)
            Weave A Wicked Web (1967, UK 1971)
            If The Shroud Fits* (1969, UK 1971)
            The Bronze Claws (1972)
            The Cold Ones (1972)

Kyd, Thomas — HARRIS, Timothy
KYLE, Robert (Robert Terrall)
Terrall ghost-wrote the later **Brett HALLIDAY** books, but his finest work was as Kyle, a fresh inventive, wry, literate paperback series which, as Art Scott (P&M) remarks, got lost in the crowd. Rugged Manhattan PI **Ben Gates**, who has been compared to an older Archie Goodwin, working solo and less reticent about his many relationships with women.

> Blackmail, Inc. (1958)
> Model For Murder (1959)
> Kill Now, Pay Later (1960, UK 1965)
> Some Like It Cool (1962)
> Ben Gates Is Hot* (1964)

LA FRANCE, Marston
Anthony Boucher found the narrative sharply told in vivid prose, but thought that **Rick Larkan** of the Triangle Agency was even more implausible than most in his drinking and miraculous escapes.

> Miami Murder-Go-Round (1951)

LaBas, Papa — REED, Ishmael
Lacey. Meg — BOWERS, Elizabeth
LACY, Ed (Leonard S. Zinberg 1911-1968)
A white man married to a black woman, Zinberg is most noted for introducing the first black PI, **Toussaint 'Touie' Moore**, pipe-smoking, Jaguar-driving, 234 pound WW2 and Korean War vet, who shares a Harlem office-flat with a fireman and a photographer, with a sign saying "Private Investigator" in the window. Settling down after his first adventure, which won an Edgar, Moore became a postman but with a child on the way goes back to work, this time for the Ted Bailey Agency, Madison Avenue. Lacy also created five other, white, PIs. Ex-cop **Matt Ranzino**, back from Korea with TB, has to confront a reputation as the toughest guy in town and old enemies. Nimble witted **Hal Darling**, 5'1" is a boat-dwelling judo expert and former amateur flyweight boxer, hence Darling's Protective Agency. **Barney Harris**, 248 pound auto mechanic, who got into the business by tracing stolen cars, is a widower with a young daughter. Tough, bigoted, 54 year old ex-cop **Marty Bond**, thrown off the force for brutality, gets by as part-time house dick, grifter and pimp in a sleazy Manhattan hotel, in a grim book Pronzini rates as Lacy's best. Former amateur boxer **William Wallace** must come to terms with youthful heart attack, under doctor's orders to think like an older man. Lacy's hallmarks were compassion and sensitivity, to race and sexual orientation, combined with gritty hardboiled realism.

Ranzino:	Sin In Their Blood (1952); as Passport To Death (UK 1959)
Darling:	Strip For Violence (1953)
Harris:	The Best That Ever Did It (1955, UK 1957); as Visa To Death (1956)
Bond:	The Men From The Boys* (1956, UK 1960)
Moore:	Room To Swing* (1957, UK 1958)
	Moment Of Untruth (1964, UK 1965)
Wallace:	Bugged For Murder (1961)

Lait, Louis — JAEDIKER, Kermit
Lake, Harry — FINE, Peter
Lake, Simon — CHAMBERS, Whitman
Lam, Donald — FAIR, A.A.
LAMB, J.J.
Zach Rolf, or rather Zachariah Tobias Rolfe III, is a Las Vegas Gaming Consultant, who mainly works for the big casinos, catching the "cheats, thieves and crossroaders." A Porsche freak, like his creator. Lots of action and some nice off-beat automobile and driving lore.

Nickel Jackpot (1976)
The Chinese Straight (1976)
Losers Take All* (1979)
Lamb, Johnny — DUNDEE, Robert
Lance, Bill — Radio: ADVENTURES OF BILL LANCE
LAND, Myrick
Described by Boucher as "a study of a private detective (**Leo Durgan**)
who specializes in tracing embezzlers and of the case which leads him to
understand the private subconscious motivations behind his choice of
specialty."
Search The Dark Woods (1955); as The Search (1959)
LANDON, Christopher
Ex-British Military Police Special Investigation Branch Major, cab-driver
Bob Ross uses an inheritance to set up as a PI with no training, civilian
experience or contacts and investigates a Stock Market murder. Boucher
commented that a novel featuring London PI **Harry Kent** had "a certain
amount of literate readability and even charm in spots but not enough plot
and action to sustain a short story." *SR* however said "excellent pace,
some loose ends dangle. High grade."
Ross: Stone Cold Dead in The Market (UK 1955)
Kent: The Shadow Of Time (UK 1957); as Unseen Enemy (1957)
Laneer, Foy — BOWMAN, David A.
Lang, Ann — ESTOW, Daniel
LANG, Brad
Operating in a Michigan city, possibly Ann Arbor, **Fred Crockett** is a
young, hip, long-haired PI. How he manages to still be young with an
MA in Criminal Science, a stint as a policeman and a longer one as a
"private dick" is a minor puzzle. His office is in a musty old building
surrounded by hippies, secondhand stores, ethnic restaurants, bars and bead
shops and is decorated with rock posters. He gets a lot of business finding
runaways because "kids trust him." Shallow.
Crockett On The Loose (1975)
Brand Of Fear (1976)
The Perdition Express (1976)
Langdon, Ross — HOWIE, Edith
Langley, Bill — HUNTER, John
Langley, Tom — MONMOUTH, Jack
Langtree, Delia — TV: TRIPLECROSS
Lantz, Tony — MULLEN, Clarence
Lanyard, Michael — Radio: The LONE WOLF

Largo, Lou — ARD, William
LARIAR, Lawrence 1908-1981
Boucher said of a novel about PI **Mike Wells** shadowing a giant to New York on the Century, that "all the worst clichés of the private eye story turn up systematically . . . without a hint of distinction in plotting or style, it remains passably fast-paced and a trifle less revolting than the stories which Mr. Lariar turns out under the name **Adam KNIGHT**." New York PI **Steve Gant** is in the same mold. One novel featured a skip-tracer, chief suspect in the killing of his very unfaithful wife, of which *SR* said "frenetic little number which takes gradually anesthetized reader on Grand Tour of Manhattan dives. Nah!" Lariar also wrote a PI novel as **Michael STARK**.

?:   Friday Is For Death (1949, UK 1950)
Wells: You Can't Catch Me (1951)
Gant: Death Is Confidential (1959)

Larkan, Rick — LA FRANCE, Marston
Larkin, Chick — Films: WHO DONE IT? (1942)
LARSEN, Gaylord
A better attempt than DENBOW's to use **Raymond Chandler** as a hero, with the then Hollywood screenwriter getting into murky waters via a feud with Billy Wilder, whom, in real life, Chandler disliked.
          A Paramount Kill (1987)
LARSON, Russell W.
Boucher remarked that this was "not the most offensive, but may well be the most comprehensive anthology of private eye clichés in print; and its fourteen corpses in 37,000 words probably set a new record in carnage."
          Death Stalks A Marriage (1956)
Lash, Simon — GRUBER, Frank
Lassiter, Luke — SPENCER, Ross H.
LATHAM, Brad
Known as "The Hook" from WWI boxing exploits, **Bill Lockwood**, Columbia Law School graduate and investigator for Transatlantic Underwriters, New York, is a classy operator, a man-about-town with "a talent for violence and a taste for sex." Set in the late 30s with plenty of violence and graphic, steamy sex.
          The Gilded Canary (1981)
          Sight Unseen (1981)
          Hate Is Thicker Than Blood (1981)
          The Death Of Lorenzo Jones (1982)
          Corpses In The Cellar (1982)

Latham, Grace — FORD, Leslie
LATIMER, Jonathan 1906-1983
Though he doesn't drink that much more than most PIs, booze—and he'll drink anything—goes to **Bill Crane**'s head and he spends most of the time in an alcoholic haze or hungover. Second in command of Colonel Black's New York agency, Crane, whose motto is "I solve 'em, drunk or sober," usually has either **Doc Williams** or **Thomas O'Malley** or both along to lend brawn to his brains. Latimer wrote some of the most inventive and amusing of all PI novels, ranging from screwball humor and wisecracking to black comedy, using hardboiled characteristics with classic whodunit motifs, particularly locked rooms and final confrontation scenes. St. Louis PI **Karl Craven** appears in a hardboiled classic with a very odd publishing history and plot elements that include a religious cult, human sacrifice, grave-robbing, necrophilia, S&M, gangsters, crooked cops, knife fights and shoot-outs. Craven is a crude, tough Continental Op style investigator. Note that in the 1957 Dell edition of *Headed For A Hearse*, Latimer's comments on crime, the economy, capital punishment and other social issues were removed. Latimer wrote many great screenplays, notably the 1942 version of Hammett's *The Glass Key*, *The Big Clock* and *The Night Has A Thousand Eyes* but did not work on the three competent films based on his Bill Crane novels. See **Films: The WESTLAND CASE/The LADY IN THE MORGUE/The LAST WARNING/PLUNDER OF THE SUN.**
Crane: Murder In The Madhouse (1935, UK 1935)
            Headed For A Hearse (1935, UK 1936); as The Westland
            Case (1938)
            The Lady In The Morgue* (1936, UK 1937)
            The Dead Don't Care (1938, UK 1938)
            Red Gardenias (1939, UK 1939); as Some Dames Are
            Deadly (1955)
Craven: Solomon's Vineyard* (UK 1941, 1988; limited ed. 1982); as
            The Fifth Grave (1950, expurgated)
Latimer, Vince — KRUGER, Paul
Latin, Max — DAVIS, Norbert
LAUMER, Keith
The well-known science-fiction writer dedicated his one PI novel to Chandler and Marlowe. Los Angeleno **Joe Shaw** is a cynical, wisecracker in the Marlowe mold, with a Chandlerish plot. Flawed but well-written. See **Films: PEEPER.**
            Deadfall (1971, UK 1974); as Fat Chance (1975, UK 1975)

LAUNAY, Droo
Running his uncle Leopold's agency from a six room Bayswater Road, London apartment, where the receptionist illegally monitors police radio, **Adam Flute**, a nonchalant, quick-thinking fellow, has "a good jaw, which people like hitting". Smoothly written without trying to imitate American styles.

> She Modelled Her Coffin (UK 1961)
> The New Shining White Murder (UK 1962)
> A Corpse In Camera (UK 1963)
> Death And Still Life (UK 1964)
> The Two-Way Mirror (UK 1964)
> The Scream (UK 1965)

LAURENCE, Gerald
A Westlake-style caper novel told from two points of view, a small-time crook with a big-time plan and the PI, **Natalie Dauntless Fisher** of Milo Security, who "looks like fashion model, swears like a sailor," trying to catch him.

> One Bang-Up Job (1989)

Lavender, Jimmy — STARRETT, Vincent

LAW, Janice
Born in poverty, ruthless, ambitious, enterprising and unsentimental **Anna Peters** has blackmailed her way up corporate ladders to become a chief of security, before setting up as a Sarasota, Florida PI in her fourth adventure. Earlier thrillers were *The Big Payoff* (1976, UK 1976), *Gemini Trip* (1977, UK 1978) and *Under Orion* (1978, UK 1979).

> The Shadow Of The Palms (1980, UK 1981)
> Death Under Par (1981, UK 1982)

LAWRENCE, Hilda (Hildegarde Kronemiller)
Combining Manhattan PI **Mark East** with little old lady amateur sleuths New England spinsters Bessie Petty and Beulah Pond, Lawrence produced three chilling stories which juxtaposed several sets of opposites, most obviously male-female, young-old, hardboiled-cozy, native-outsider and urban-rural. Her specialty was to create a steadily increasing claustrophobic atmosphere.

> Blood Upon The Snow* (1944, UK 1946)
> A Time To Die (1945, UK 1947)
> Death Of A Doll (1947, UK 1948)

LAWRENCE, James D.
Born in Detroit to a junkie mother, Radcliff graduate, former fashion model, $1000 a night call-girl and NYPD policewoman, trained in

criminology, karate, flying, small-arms, electronics, gymnastics, Zen, yoga, lock-picking and scuba diving, black **Angela Harpe**, the "highest priced private eye in Manhattan," is known as The Dark Angel from her habit of sticking black angel decals on her victims' foreheads. Sex, normal and perverse, voluntary and involuntary, explicit violence and Bond style gadgets abound. Sadistic, pornographic, vicious, racist and sexist. Baker & Nietzel comment "You would say the style and characterization are wooden, except that gives wood a bad name."

> The Dream Girl Caper (1975)
> The Emerald Oil Caper (1975)
> The Gilded Snatch Caper (1975)
> The Godmother Caper (1975)

LAWRENCE, Kelly
Boston PI **Brian Desmond**, whose office is above Dimmy's Place on Hyde Park Avenue, reads Hammett for inspiration, Michener for sedation. Like many Boston writers, Lawrence is good at the nuances of that multi-ethnic city with an engaging, casual style though his use of metaphor is weak. The book features a particularly gruesome beating by Mob heavies and a critique of Robert B. Parker's version of the PI as social worker.

> The Gone Shots (1987)

LAYMAN, Richard — see ANTHOLOGIES : 1 / 2
LAYMON, Richard
Horror writer whose short story, "Eats" (A5), featuring PI **Duke Scanlon**, parodies a tough-guy gathering-the-suspects-together finale.
Le Roux, Frank — BROWN, Hosanna
Lee, Anna — CODY, Liza
LEE, Austin 1904-1965
Ex-school mistress turned professional PI, **Flora Hogg**, police superintendent's daughter, is very English. Middle-aged, wearing baggy tweeds and horn-rimmed spectacles, she won't tackle anything demeaning and describes her methodology as "inspired guessing."

> Sheep's Clothing (UK 1955)
> Call In Miss Hogg (UK 1956)
> Miss Hogg And The Brönte Murder (UK 1956)
> Miss Hogg And The Squash Club Murder (UK 1957)
> Miss Hogg And The Dead Dean (UK 1958)
> Miss Hogg Flies High (UK 1958)
> Miss Hogg And The Covent Garden Murders (UK 1960)
> Miss Hogg And The Missing Sisters (UK 1961)
> Miss Hogg's Last Case (UK 1963)

LEE, Babs (Marion van der Veer Lee)
Former fashion model Marion Lee had good if rather flossy, sometimes extraneous backgrounds to her stories about **Argus Steele**, PI turned mystery writer, who gets himself involved with a Russian Princess modiste, models, a millionairess or two, financiers, a man who used to sponsor Latin American revolutions and other up-market characters. Painfully witty dialogue and a tendency to leave the less believable details unexplained. In *Passport To Oblivion* Steele serves his country as a wartime spy in Portugal.

> A Model Is Murdered (1942)
> Passport To Oblivion (1943)
> Measured For Murder (1944, UK 1945). With Clare Castler Saunders

LEE, Edward (Edward Lee Fouts)
In the first book, young, unpolished Los Angeles PI **Arthur 'Red' Blake**, assistant to **Dan Wheeler** are involved in a lethal union-employers battle, aptly described as "cops and capitalists and Communists going round and round," with Fouts' sympathies clearly with the union. In the second they're employed to bodyguard a gambler and violent action ensues when he is killed in their presence. One reviewer commented of the conclusion—"Well now! Really!"

> The Needle's Eye (1941)
> A Fish For Murder (1944, UK 1947); as Death Goes Fishing (1944 abridged); as Lust To Kill (1955)

Lee, Steve — WELLS, Charlie
Lee, Tommy — PARK, Owen
Leidl, Constance — WILHELM, Kate
Leighton, Alex — SPARLING, Joyce
LEITFRED, Robert H.
Operating a small San Francisco agency with one operative and a secretary-receptionist, **Simon Crole** is harrassed by a DA in the second title, described by *NYT* as "not a very successful attempt at crime fiction in the hard-boiled manner," because the authorities don't have anything on him and can't believe a PI can be that honest. A PI with the same name appeared in a book by **Robert FLEMING**. I can't determine whether they are connected, but feel they are probably the same author.

> The Corpse That Spoke (1936, UK 1937)
> The Man Who Was Murdered Twice (1937)
> Death Cancels The Evidence (1938); as Murder Is My Racket (194?)

Leland, Joe — THORP, Roderick
Leland, Judge Meredith — TV: PARTNERS IN CRIME
Lennox, Bill — BALLARD, W.T. / SHEPHERD, John
LEONARD, Charles L. = HEBERDEN, M.V.
Pronzini much prefers "Leonard" to Heberden. Washington DC, based
Paul Kilgerrin, a specialist in espionage, described as having "a
powerful face, and its cold, contemptuous lines gave no indication
whether its power might be used for good or evil," is ruthless and amoral,
ready to use any methods, including cold-blooded murder, to get results.
Melodramatic, right-wing with painfully lame dialogue—as Pronzini
points out, she simply wasn't a very good writer—the main strength is
the action. Sandoe describes *The Stolen Squadron* as "wildly silly but so
rapidly managed from little excitements to large-scale ones that you're
sufficiently bound up with the personnel to gulp down the absurdities."

> The Stolen Squadron* (1942)
> Deadline For Destruction (1942)
> The Fanatic Of Fez (1943); as Assignment To Death (194?,
>   abridged)
> The Secret Of The Spa (1944)
> Expert In Murder (1945)
> Pursuit In Peru (1946, UK 1948)
> Search For A Scientist (1948, UK 1950)
> The Fourth Funeral (1948, UK 1951)
> Sinister Shelter (1949, UK 1951)
> Secrets For Sale (1950)
> Treachery In Trieste (1951)

LEONARD, Elmore
In *Swag* (1976) Detroiter **Frank Ryan** was a car salesman turned armed
robber. A year later he was a process server whose synopisis included
selling cars and insurance, construction work, truck driving, Teamster
"business manager," Chevrolet truck assembly and, when much younger,
breaking and entering, but not armed robbery. So good is Ryan at finding
people and serving papers on them that he's given the tough ones by court
officials and lawyers, eventually leading to a formal PI commission.
Alcoholic actor-PI, **Nolen Tyner**, of Marshall Sisco Investigations,
Miami, was a secondary character. PWA members voted Leonard, whose
first, non-PI novel appeared in 1969, 12th best (see Introduction:
Comparative Eyes) for 1920-1970. I find this extraordinarily annoying.
Ryan: Unknown Man #89 (1977, UK 1977)
Tyner: Cat Chaser (1982, UK 1986)

Leroy, J.R. — PEROWNE, Barry
Levin, Roger — FURST, Richard
LeVine, Jack — BERGMAN, Andrew
LEWIN, Michael Z(inn)
Though in the California mold, seedy, down at heel, wisecracking and short of clients, **Albert Sampson** actually plies his trade in Indianapolis. With a low, indeed non-existent, machismo level, Sampson, a college drop out briefly rich and famous for a book about his college days, advertises a 20% discount Gigantic Detective Sale, and does odd jobs on the side. Perennially broke, he works out of even less imposing, and more frequently changing, offices than most PIs and drives ancient old cars and trucks. Introspective, lacking heroism, refusing to carry a gun because of an incident in his days as a security guard, Sampson is, as Baker & Nietzel remark, "Average, but because of it, very special." Bruce Taylor feels (P&M) that Sampson is the best transplanted California PI and that "Anybody who can set a PI series in Indianapolis and make it work is a genius." In **A15** Lewin introduced **Freddie Herring**, an American lawyer who inherits a house in Frome, Somerset, England (Lewin's own home for 17 years), and sets up as a PI purely as a tax dodge, in "The Reluctant Detective." An unexpected, and unwelcome, client is deftly handled by his resourceful wife and in-laws.
> Ask The Right Question (1971, UK 1972)
> The Way We Die Now (1973, UK 1973)
> The Enemies Within (1974, UK 1974)
> Night Cover (1976, UK 1976)
> The Silent Salesman* (1978, UK 1978)
> Missing Woman (1981, UK 1982)
> Out Of Season (1984); as Out Of Time (UK 1984)
> And Baby Will Fall (1988)

LEWIS, Elliott
Working without office or license, **Fred Bennett**, dismissed from the LAPD, is an un-cop who maintains a working relationship with the force through his Captain of Detectives ex-partner, handling cases outside police jurisdiction or too sensitive for ordinary procedures. Nervy, unpredictable, isolated, divorced, living in a state of permanent personal crisis, driving a battered old Buick, "he'd stick pins in everyone connected with the case, anger and enrage them, until someone acted overtly, things were inadvertently said, promises were broken, anger was encouraged, confidences destroyed, all to bring the bugs out of the woodwork."
> Two Heads Are Better (1980) >

Dirty Linen (1980)
People In Glass Houses (1981)
Double Trouble (1981)
Here Today,Dead Tomorrow (1982)
Bennett's World (1982)
Death And The Single Girl (1983)

LEWIS, Stephen
With its peeling paint and Salvation Army furniture, **Jake Lieberman**'s Confidential Investigations Unlimited Vermont Avenue, LA, office is even more unprepossessing than most. Lieberman is homosexual and his one adventure was put out by a gay publishing company, but, that apart, is very routine, needing only minor rewriting to make it into a standard heterosexual romantic PI story.

Cowboy Blues (1985, UK 1986)

L'Hiboux, Alexander — FORWARD, Robert
Li Kao — HUGHART, Barry
Liddell, Johnny — KANE, Frank
Lieberman, Jake — LEWIS, Stephen
Lincoln, Wylie — CORDER, Eric

LINDSAY, R(obert) Howard
One of the items to be found in a plutocratic family's scavenger hunt is a PI. Thus dipso **McPherson** gets enmeshed in a weird and wacky murder investigation. Told in a modernistic manner, the author acknowledges debts to James Joyce, Eugene O'Neill, Hammett and Thorne Smith. The blurb advises "Take a dash of Dali, a jigger of Elliot Paul, a shot of Gertrude Stein, toss in Alfred Hitchcock for vermouth, shake vigorously and you'll get some idea of the effect."

Fowl Murder (1941)

LINGO, Ade E.
SR remarked "Newspaper owner shot as his oil-well gushes; town banker goes next. Girl reporter and private 'tec (**John Shields** from St. Louis) solve it. Malodorous mazes of small-town (Fordham, Texas) scandal form pungent background for quick-moving plausible yarn." *NYT* was less impressed but commented on the effective atmosphere.

Murder In Texas (1935)

LINKLATER, J(oseph) Lane (Alex Watkins)
A detective who'd rather be a blackmailer, if he can stay inside the law, **Silas Booth** of LA has a naturally suspicious nature that enables him to figure the angles on any situation. As one client says, "You—you unprincipled scoundrel!" Clumsily written with stilted dialogue. Some

titles were published as by **Joseph LINKLATER**.

> Black Opal (1947, UK 1949)
>
> Shadow For A Lady (1947, UK 1948)
>
> And She Had A Little Knife (1948); as She Had A Little Knife (UK 1950)
>
> The Bishop's Cap (1948); as The 'Bishop's Cap' Murder (UK 1949)
>
> Odd Woman Out (1955, UK 1959)
>
> The Green Glove (1959, UK 1960)
>
> A Tisket, A Casket (1959)

Linz, Baroness Clara — OPPENHEIM, E. Phillips

LINZEE, David

Compromising between advertising agency trendiness and law firm respectability, Inquiries, Incorporated, A Division of Securitco, One of the RGI Family of Service Companies, otherwise INQinc, or Inkwink, of Greenwich, Connecticut, employs **Chris Rockwell** and **Sarah Saber**, who spend much of their time filling out forms and satisfying corporate requirements. Discretion is the company's watchword, so that even though Chris and Sarah are lovers, they don't know what the other is doing. Nevins compares the books to the tone and mood of the lighter Hitchcock films such as *To Catch A Thief*.

> Discretion* (1977, UK 1981)
>
> Belgravia (1979, UK 1982)

LISOWSKI, Joseph

"An attempt to explore character in a short form of detective fiction" features **Wilcox**, a 50ish, 200 pound, 5'5" bookkeeper who pretends to be an investigator by running an ad in the paper, "Discreet Inquiries—reasonable rates" (A1 #8).

LIVINGSTON, Jack

A former US Navy underwater demolition man, **Joe Binney** lost his hearing in an accident, but that doesn't stop him being an effective New York PI, nor is it a gimmick as his disability remains in the background, sometimes a problem, as when he has to see people's faces to know what they're saying, sometimes an advantage, when he knows what people are saying if he can see their faces, and so on. Livingston has a distinctive style, wryly humorous and literate, combining action and characterization.

> A Piece Of The Silence* (1982, UK 1983)
>
> Die Again, Macready (1984, UK 1984)
>
> The Nightmare File (1986)
>
> Hell-Bent For Election (1988?)

LIVINGSTON, Nancy
Retired British Tax Inspector **G.D.H. Pringle** investigates as a hobby, charging a little to supplement his pension. He specializes, naturally, in fraud, but gets talked into more serious cases, usually by his companion, widow Mavis Bignall. A good deal of very arch satire and caricature rather than characterization.

> The Trouble At Aquitane (UK 1985, 1986)
> Fatality At Bath & Wells (UK 1986, 1986)
> Incident At Pargeta (UK 1987, 1988)
> Death In A Distant Land (UK 1988, 1989)

LOCHTE, Dick
As a practical joke, an LAPD officer sends precocious 14 year old space cadet **Serendipity (Sarah) Dahlquist** to middle-aged, grouchy, thrice-divorced **Leo Bloodworth** of South Figueroa for help in finding her missing dog. Brilliantly constructed as alternate chapters from Dahlquist and Bloodworth's "books" about a series of brutal murders, Lochte captures the shifting interplay between two very different characters and deftly interweaves their differing perceptions of events. A stunning, very funny debut. In the second book, Serendipity takes on one of Leo's cases while he's abroad on business, plunging them both into deep trouble. A **Philip Marlowe** short story, "Sad-Eyed Blonde," is in **A12.**

> Sleeping Dog (1985, UK 1986)
> Laughing Dog (1988, UK 1988)

Locke, John — BARNAO, Jack
LOCKE, Robert Donald
Durable and serviceable as his name **Pete Brass**, LA PI, appeared once only in a classic hardboiled tough-guy novel described by Frank Kane as "Strong stuff—I got a real belt out of private eye Pete Brass."

> A Taste Of Brass (1957)

LOCKHART, Max
Novelization of TV: PRIVATE EYE featuring 50s LA PI **Jack Cleary** and his assistant **Johnny Betts.** See also **T.N. ROBB** and **David ELLIOTT.**

> Nobody Dies In Chinatown (1988)

LOCKRIDGE, Richard (1898-1982) **& Frances** (1896-1963)
Far off the PI mainstream are **Jerry & Pamela North,** or, as the authors insist on calling them, and they were known in radio and TV serials, Mr. & Mrs. North. Jerry is a former PI turned New York publisher and the pair are really only amateur detectives. The books are characterized by Pamela's omniscient female intuition and her mandatory

pursuit by the murderer. There are 26 now seriously dated titles which will not be listed here. See **Radio: MR & MRS NORTH**.

Lockwood, Bill — LATHAM, Brad
LOGAN, Carolynne & Malcolm
Only seven men have keys to the room in which a dead man lies. They hire PI **Justus Drum** to find out which is guilty of murder and free the other six from suspicion. The dead man's character dominates the Logans' one book of which Boucher remarked "reasonably sound and ingenious story; but atmosphere of cultured sophistication rings spurious."

> One Of These Seven (1946, UK 1948)

Logan, Mark — PRATHER, Richard S.
Logan, Sam — TV: The MAN FROM BLACKHAWK
Logan, Tom — GRUBER, Frank
Lomax, Jacob — ALLEGRETTO, Michael
London, Christopher — Radio: CHRISTOPHER LONDON
London, Ed — BLOCK, Lawrence
London, Max — ARTHUR, Robert
Long, Doc — Radio: I LOVE A MYSTERY
Longstreet, Michael — TV: LONGSTREET
Lopaka, Tom — TV: HAWAIIAN EYE
LORE, Phillips (Terence Lore Smith)
Perhaps the most up-market PI of all is **Leo Roi**, of the Chicago law firm of Roi & Pine. Son of a French Baron who started as Al Capone's import supervisor then went into legal liquor and made millions, Roi went to law school but runs the investigative side of the business. Living in enormous luxury on the shores of Lake Michigan, his Bentley takes him to a Chicago Avenue, Evanston office decorated with pictures by Toulouse-Lautrec, Degas and Picasso. A far cry from the average PI. He and his elegant wife could be regarded as Nick and Nora Charles taken to the modern limit, but Lore manages to keep it just about believable.

> Who Killed The Pie Man? (1975)
> Murder Behind Closed Doors (1980)
> The Looking Glass Murders (1980)

LOUIS, Joseph
Thanks to successful PI novels and lucky investments, **Evan Paris**, once a drifter who discovered an aptitude for solving problems as a PI's researcher, took degrees in criminology and became a consultant on fraud and stock manipulation for corporations, is a multimillionaire. A recluse in his Santa Monica Mountains home since his wife's kidnaping and murder, Paris is drawn back to PI work when a therapist friend makes a

well calculated appeal to his ingrained inclinations.

> Madelaine (1987, UK 1987)
>
> The Trouble With Stephanie (1988)

LOVELL, B.E.

Black Irishman **Edge Hannegan** is a former big time gambler assigned to Army CID during WW2 under a San Francisco policeman who persuades him to set up as a PI in that city. The second book is a tough, edgy sermon on street gang violence—"they can kill me and it's only juvenile delinquency; but if I kill them, even in self defense, it's murder!"

> ... And Incidentally, Murder! (1952)
>
> A Rage To Kill (1957)

Lowell, A.Dunster — TV: A. DUNSTER LOWELL

Lu Yu — HUGHART, Barry

LUCAS, Warren

Considerably outweirded as a *Defective Detective* by most of his neighbors, **Lin Melchan** can only boast, or complain of, superacute hearing, his abnormally sensitive auditory system magnifying sounds so that he can hear the slightest whisper while loud noise causes him pain. "The Devil Beats Death's Drums" (*Dime Mystery* 1938) appears in A7.

Lujack, Jimmy — THOREAU, David

LUSTBADER, Eric Van

Cod-Japanese thriller writer who, for no apparent reason, was invited to contribute a **Philip Marlowe** short story, "Asia," to A12.

LUTZ, John

Starting as a varied and variable short story writer, Lutz branched out into almost every mystery genre as a novelist. His two PIs are **Alo Nudger**, a reluctant and cowardly but dogged St. Louis investigator who takes antacid pills like candy to help his nervous stomach and wishes he was in some other line of business, and **Fred Carver**, former Orlando, Florida detective sergeant, shot in the knee during a holdup, living on a disability pension and insurance settlement, and working intermittently as a PI, with former colleagues passing him work to keep him occupied. Both are finely wrought creations, and Lutz brings their backgrounds vividly to life, using precision skills honed in the short story format. Ed Gorman (A5) considers Nudger the best PI of the past decade and *Buyer Beware* the best PI novel of the 70s, views with which I cannot concur. Nudger short stories are "Flotsam And Jetsam" (A1 #8), "The Thunder Of Guilt" (A16), "DDS 10752 Libra" (co-authored with **Josh PACHTER**; A17), "Typographical Error" (A15) and "Ride The Lightning" (A14), which won an MWA Best Short Story Edgar. Lutz has a **Philip**

Marlowe short story, "Star Bright," in A12.

Nudger: Buyer Beware* (1976, UK 1977)
Nightlines (1984, UK 1986)
The Right To Sing The Blues (1985)
Ride The Lightning (1987)
Dancer's Debt (1988)

Carver: Tropical Heat (1986, UK 1986)
Scorcher (UK 1987, UK 1987)
Kiss (1988)

LYALL, Gavin
The British author of many excellent, literate thrillers has near-PI **James Card**, gun-wise former Military Intelligence interrogator and security advisor, taking a job bodyguarding a Lloyds marine insurance under-writer on a mysterious errand. When the client is killed, Card turns detective.

Blame The Dead (UK 1972, 1972)

LYNCH, Jack
Korean War vet **Peter Bragg** was a reporter in Seattle, Kansas City and finally San Francisco where he dropped out and worked in a bar in Sausalito, where he lives (Lynch did the reverse, first working in Sausalito's famous No Name Bar, then joining the *San Francisco Chronicle*). Working part-time for an old lawyer friend, he found he liked the PI business and set up an office at Market & Powell. A believable, competent hero with simple tastes, he appears in straightforward, no frills stories with good action sequences and sound, if rather extravagant, plots.

Bragg's Hunch (1981)
The Missing And The Dead (1982)
Pieces Of Death (1982)
Sausalito* (1984)
San Quentin (1984)
Monterey (1985)
Seattle (1985)

LYNNE, James Broome
Under the name **James QUARTERMAIN**, Lynne wrote about a PI involved in various aspects of the diamond business. Under his own name he has produced one international thriller featuring **Richard Walker**, investigator for the London-based Central Selling Organization, whose job is to police diamond trading.

Rogue Diamond (UK 1980, 1980)

Lyon, Anthony J. — Radio: JEFF REGAN, INVESTIGATOR

LYON, (Mabel) Dana 1897-1982
An ex-convict with no previous experience, **Jeff Miles** is employed by a California agency, running into an unusually clever criminal gang in his first case. He flubs the detecting and another detective finishes the job. *SR* found it "tough but not too credible . . . full of action and surprises."
  It's My Own Funeral (1944, UK 1948)

LYONS, Arthur
An LA reporter fired after being jailed for contempt for refusing to name a source, **Jacob Asch** turned PI and has had a noteworthy career. Starting in the Chandler school, Lyons created a diverse, satisfying series with geographical, sociological and psychological shifts. Asch travels widely round Southern California, and occasionally beyond, and has come into contact with many different classes and sub-cultures, including Satanists, a motorcycle gang, gays, music promoters, Jesus freaks and others, while different aspects of Asch's personality, his prison-induced claustrophobia, his Judeo-Episcopalian dichotomy, his latent violence, come to the fore. In the front tank of modern PI writers, combining hardboiled excellence with social comment, Lyons, owner of a Palm Springs restaurant, is talked of as Ross Macdonald's less pretentious heir. *Mystery Magazine* see him as "setting the standards for today's hard-boiled novel," though Art Scott (P&M) is very cool, seeing no more than "sufficient novelty." Asch short stories are "Trouble In Paradise," (**A1** #1 and **A14**), "Missing In Miami" (**A16**) and "Dead Copy," (**A17**). See **TV: SLOW BURN**.
  The Dead Are Discreet (1974, UK 1977)
  All God's Children (1975, UK 1977)
  The Killing Floor (1976, UK 1979)
  Dead Ringer (1977, UK 1983)
  Castles Burning* (1980, UK 1983)
  Hard Trade (1982, UK 1984)
  At The Hands Of Another (1983)
  Three With A Bullet (1984, UK 1987)
  Fast Fade (1987)
  Other People's Money (1989)

Mac (Robinson) — DEWEY, Thomas B.
Macadam, Philip — WAUGH, Hillary
Macall, Johnny — FAIRLIE, Gerard
MacAllister, Frank — PERRY, Ritchie
McBAIN, Ed (Evan Hunter)
Hunter, who wrote two PI novels as **Curt CANNON**, uses the McBain name mostly for his 87th Precinct procedurals but also for one PI novel.

Benjamin Smoke (of a Dutch family originally called Smoak) was an NYPD lieutenant retired because of boredom. 48 years old, 6'3", weighs 200 pounds, he neither has, nor expects to apply for, an investigator's license, prizing his gold lieutenant's badge much higher. Living comfortably on his pension and investments, his only regret is that he's never investigated a case he couldn't solve. Though the publisher intimated that it was the first of a series, only the one title has appeared. A short story, "Death Flight," in A14 (also in *The McBain Brief*, UK 1982, 1983) features **Milt Davis**.

> Where There's Smoke (1975, UK 1976)

McBain, Victor — ROBERTSON, Colin
McBride, Frank — TV: SWITCH
McBride, Rex — ADAMS, Cleve F.
McCale, Marmaduke — BROWN, Gerald
McCALL, John J.
Ex-Marine **Al Mooney** has been operating around LA since the war, at times a couple of jumps ahead. In a routine novel unlisted by Hubin his '56 Chrysler is about to be repossessed. Hubin lists one novel by McCall, *Downbeat On A Debutante* (1964), which may be another Mooney story.

> Is Money Everything? (1963, UK 1964)

McCall, Micah — QUEEN, Ellery
McCall, Norbert — MacNEIL, Neil
McCALL, Wendell
A rather different kind of skip-tracer is **Chris Klick** who tracks down vanished musicians in order to deliver outstanding royalty payments, collecting a percentage himself. On vacation, he finds his skills being solicited in a rather more desperate cause in a novel described as like a TV action film, redeemed by strong writing.

> Dead Aim (1988)

McCANDLESS, D.B.
McCandless wrote a series of short stories, one of which, "Cash Or Credit" (*Detective Fiction Weekly* 1933) is in A3, featuring "square and dusty" Mrs. **Sarah Watson**, who emerges "from any given fracas with somebody's goat and a substantial amount of dollars and cents," and her assistant **Ben Todd**, whom she usually keeps in the dark.

MacCardle, Cam — HALLERAN, Tucker
MacCARGO, J.T.
Novelizations of **TV: MANNIX** featuring **Joe Mannix**. See also **Michael AVALLONE**.

> The Faces Of Murder (1975) >

A Fine Day For Dying (1975)
Round Trip To Nowhere (1975)
A Walk On The Blind Side (1975)

McCatty, Manx — REED, Christopher
McCleary, Mike — MacGREGOR, T.J.
McCloud, Stephen — ADAMS, Cleve F.
McColl, Lynn — MORROW, J.T.
McCone, Sharon — MULLER, Marcia
McCONNELL, Frank
When her father falls ill, elderly ex-nun **Bridget O'Toole** takes over his Chicago detective agency, making a surprisingly good team with her foul-mouthed, smart-aleck, alcoholic, divorced chief op **Harry Garnish**. A real and fallible human being, Harry screws up, lies and hurts his friends. Norman Mailer thought it "fast-paced, funny, full of sting."

Murder Among Friends (1983)
Blood Lake (1987)

McCONNOR, Vincent
A former Pinkerton agent, **Zeke Gahagan** was trained by Dashiell Hammett himself. Now over 80, with a card that proclaims him to be "the world's oldest private eye," but still able to handle romance when it comes his way, one reviewer found him an appealing, resourceful, downright frisky hero, while describing his first appearance as badly underplotted with a surfeit of Hollywood history and Hammett references that grow tiresome quickly.

The Man Who Knew Hammett (1988)

McCoy — TV: McCOY
McCoy, Doyle Dean — KRAFT, Gabrielle
McCoy, Mike — Radio: The McCOY
McCoy, Pete — KINGSLEY-SMITH, Terence
McCoy, Shamus — Films: SHAMUS
McCURTIN, Peter
Apart from minor trashomatic series novels about The Assassin and The Marksman, McCurtin wrote one book about New York PI **Pete Shay**, according to Baker & Nietzel who give no other details.

Minnesota Strip (1979)

McCUTCHEON, Hugh
Generally disdainful of British ersatz, Boucher conceded that McCutcheon was "a clever eclectic," using selected elements from the American tough school, the British school of literacy and aristocracy (his PI, **Anthony Howard**, was an ex-Royal Navy officer and the son of a knight) to

produce "mildly readable" books.

> The Angel Of Light (UK 1951); as Murder At The 'Angel' (1952)
>
> Cover Her Face (UK 1954)

McDade, Violet — ADAMS, Cleve F.

McDermott, Mike — MILLER, Martin J.

MACDONALD, John — see MACDONALD, Ross

MacDONALD, John D(ann) 1916-1986

Opinions differ on MacDonald's famous "salvage consultant" **Travis McGee**; Baker & Nietzel embrace him wholeheartedly as a PI, Marcia Muller calls him a Classic Sleuth, Geherin passes. On the "Duck" principle (see Introduction), there is no problem, the big, rugged, ex-minor league football player, Korean War vet and Peter Pan is perhaps the foremost of all the unlicensed shamuses. Living on his luxurious boat, *The Busted Flush*, won in a poker game, at Slip F-18, Bahia Mar, Fort Lauderdale, Florida, McGee recovers stolen but legally irrecoverable goods and money for a 50% commission and is MacDonald's vehicle for a critique of modes of corruption in modern America. Towards the end of a long and illustrious career which began in *Black Mask* and other pulps, MacDonald increasingly editorialized on the state of Florida, America and the world, and on the destruction of the quality of life by greed and profiteering. McGee's repeated emotional salvaging of bruised ladies through therapeutic sex becomes somewhat tedious, but the stories are nearly always very fine. Just before McGee, MacDonald featured Florida private detective **Paul Stanial** in a novel which combined solid detection with MacDonald's realistic observation and suspense. See **Films: DARKER THAN AMBER** and **TV: TRAVIS McGEE.**

Stanial: The Drowner (1963, UK 1964)

McGee: The Deep Blue Goodbye (1964, UK 1965)
> Nightmare In Pink (1964, UK 1966)
> A Purple Place For Dying (1964, UK 1966)
> The Quick Red Fox (1964, UK 1966)
> A Deadly Shade Of Gold (1965, UK 1967)
> Bright Orange For The Shroud (1965, UK 1967)
> Darker Than Amber* (1966, UK 1968)
> One Fearful Yellow Eye (1966, UK 1968)
> Pale Grey For Guilt (1968, UK 1969)
> The Girl In The Plain Brown Wrapper (1968, UK 1969)
> Dress Her In Indigo (1969, UK 1971)
> The Long Lavender Look (1970, UK 1970) >

A Tan And Sandy Silence (1972, UK 1973)
The Scarlet Ruse (1973, UK 1975)
The Turquoise Lament (1973, UK 1975)
The Dreadful Lemon Sky (1975, UK 1976)
The Empty Copper Sea (1978, UK 1979)
The Green Ripper* (1979, UK 1980)
Free Fall In Crimson (1981, UK 1981)
Cinnamon Skin (1982, UK 1982)
The Lonely Silver Rain (1984, UK 1985)

MACDONALD, John Ross — see **MACDONALD, Ross**
MacDonald, Lynn — **STRAHAN, Kay Cleaver**
MacDonald, Paul — **WAUGH, Hillary**
MACDONALD, Ross (Kenneth Millar 1915-1983)

Boucher thought Macdonald a better novelist than either Hammett or Chandler, Sandoe regarded him as "a clever master of pastiche," calling *Blue Money* "a hardboiled phony" and the PWA bestowed a Lifetime Achievement award on him. Based at 8411 1/2 Sunset Boulevard, LA, **Lew Archer** is a deliberately shadowy figure, a camera for observing the human (or rather Californian) condition. We learn that he was a Long Beach policeman fired for not condoning corruption, is divorced from a wife who couldn't stand his work and was a wartime Intelligence officer. But Macdonald's main thrust goes into the psychology of Archer's clients, their families and other characters involved in his cases which invariably involve rich people and problems of identity. While not going as far as John Skow (*Time* 1973), who maintained that Macdonald wrote the same novel 18 times, I must admit I'm never quite sure which Archer books I've read and which I haven't. Archer short stories are "Midnight Blue" (*Ed McBain's Mystery Book* 1960; A9; also in Pronzini, Malzberg & Greenberg, eds: *Arbor House Teasury Of Mystery & Suspense*, 1981) and "Guilt-Edged Blonde" (*Manhunt* 1954; A14). See **Films: HARPER / The DROWNING POOL** and **TV: ARCHER**.

The Moving Target (as by John Macdonald 1949, UK 1951); as Harper (1966)
The Drowning Pool (as by John Ross Macdonald 1950; as by John Macdonald UK 1952)
The Way Some People Die (as by John Ross Macdonald 1951, UK 1953)
The Ivory Grin* (as by John Ross Macdonald 1952, UK 1953); as Marked For Murder (as by John Ross Macdonald 1953)
Find A Victim (as by John Ross Macdonald 1954, UK 1955) >

The Name Is Archer (as by John Ross Macdonald 1955). SS
The Barbarous Coast (1956; as by John Ross Macdonald UK
    1957)
The Doomsters (1958; as by John Ross Macdonald UK 1958)
The Galton Case (1959; as by John Ross Macdonald UK 1960)
The Zebra-Striped Hearse* (1962, UK 1963)
The Wycherly Woman* (1961, UK 1962)
The Chill (1964, UK 1964)
The Far Side Of The Dollar (1965, UK 1965)
Black Money* (1966, UK 1966)
The Instant Enemy (1968, UK 1968)
The Goodbye Look (1969, UK 1969)
The Underground Man (1971, UK 1971)
Sleeping Beauty (1973, UK 1973)
The Blue Hammer* (1976, UK 1976)
Lew Archer, Private Investigator* (1977). Contains all 14 SS

MacDONALD, William Colt

Special Investigator for the Texas Northern & Arizona Southern Railroad,
Gregory Quist has his office-cum-living quarters in the Pierson Hotel,
El Paso from which he travels to sort out latter day Wild West problems.

Law And Order, Unlimited (1953, UK 1955)
Mascarada Pass (1954, UK 1957)
Destination Danger (1955, UK 1957)
The Comanche Scalp (1955, UK 1958)
The Devil's Drum (1956, UK 1962)
Action At Arcanum (1958, UK 1961)
Tombstone For A Troubleshooter (1960, UK 1961)
The Osage Bow (UK 1964)

McDOUGALD, Roman

Detectionary calls **Philip Cabot** "something of an American Albert
Campion . . . an urbane, nimble-minded private detective who is on good
terms with both the rich and police." Not much of a recommendation.

The Deaths Of Lora Karen (1944)
The Whistling Legs (1945)
The Blushing Monkey (1953, UK 1953)

MacDOUGALL, James

Trained as a lawyer, widower **David Stuart** quit his father's Cleveland
law firm because he was more interested in the truth than judicial forms.
In the Lew Archer mold, Stuart is a philosophical, sensitive investigator
but his quest for moral certainties makes him humorless. Baker & Nietzel

observe that "Stuart sometimes flaunts his moral superiority. He's too preachy, too insistent on his distinctions." An intelligent writer with minimal action but well observed characterization.

> Weasel Hunt (1972)
>
> Death And The Maiden (1980)

McDOWELL, Emmett 1914-1975

Louisville, Kentucky PI **Jamie MacRae** reads a lot of novels and wonders why his life isn't like them. When he tries to live them out, reality keeps pulling hilarious switcheroos on fiction-based expectations.

> Switcheroo (1954)

McDOWELL, Rider

A hard-drinking, hard-playing ex-cop, **Willy Diaz** is a down and out private eye in Spanish Harlem in a bleak, compelling novel of unremitting violence featuring dangerous junkies, hustlers and a huge, retarded Vietnam vet.

> The Mercy Man (1987)

McGann, Mack — DICKENSON, Fred

McGavock, Luther — CONSTINER, Merle

McGee, Travis — MacDONALD, John D.

McGill — TV: MAN IN A SUITCASE

McGinty, Slade — PENDOWER, Jacques

McGIRR, Edmund (Kenneth Giles 1922-1972)

As McGirr, British author Giles wrote about American redhead **Jim Piron**, who runs the small London office of a giant American detective agency. Much of his work comes from the US Embassy or the British government. The stories, have lively characters and ingenious plots.

> The Funeral Was In Spain (UK 1966)
>
> The Hearse With Horses (UK 1967)
>
> Here Lies My Wife (UK 1967)
>
> The Lead-Lined Coffin (1968)
>
> An Entry Of Death (UK 1969, 1969)
>
> Death Pays The Wages (1970)
>
> No Better Fiend (UK 1971, 1971)
>
> Bardel's Murder (UK 1973, 1974)
>
> A Murderous Journey (UK 1974, 1975)

McGOWN, Jill

A former Detective Inspector, who resigned due to his legendary temper and turned reluctant London PI, **Harry Cambert**, smokes too much, drinks too often and doesn't eat often enough in a menacing British novel.

> An Evil Hour (UK 1986, 1987)

McGrath, Pete — BRETT, Michael
McGraw — TV: MEET McGRAW
McGraw, Harry — TV: The LAW AND HARRY McGRAW
McGRAW, Lee
Chicago ex-policewoman **Madge Hatchett**, aka Madge the Badge, the Black Widow or Bloody Madge, is the toughest female PI of all. When not beating people up or getting beaten up, she drives round in a Mercedes, lives in a luxury apartment and carries a Beretta on her tall, dark and voluptuous person. Possibly intended as a parody of Mike Hammer, but fine pulp pastiche anyway. The pseudonymous author (and his or her sex) seems not to have been identified.

> Hatchett (1976)

McGREGOR, Don & Gene COLAN
Described by Robert Randisi as "a solid private eye yarn with sparkling dialogue and two private dicks who care. If Culp and Crosby had been eyes instead of spies, this is what they would have been like." A three part "graphic mystery" in comic book form, Detectives Inc. consists of **Bob Rainier** (white) and **Ted Denning** (black), with writing and illustrations drawing from movie techniques such as cross cutting.

> Detectives Inc. (1986)

McGregor, Inspector — KANE, Henry
MacGREGOR, T(rish) J(aneschutz)
At the beginning of the first book Miami female PI **Quin St. James** is partner in Forsythe & St. James, Private Investigators, but by the end of it she's bought out Forsythe, who sailed too close to the wind trying to make money, and the firm becomes St. James & McCleary, Private Eyes, **Mike McCleary** being a Metro Homicide detective she meets in the investigation of her lover's murder. By the second book they've married. McGregor is a very fine writer whose specialty is the problem of being too close to a problem.

> Dark Fields (1986, UK 1988)
> Kill Flash (1987)
> Death Sweet (1988)
> On Ice (1989)

McGuane, Maggie — SOLOMON, Brad
McGuffin, Amos — UPTON, Robert
MacInnes, Kevin — BANDY, Eugene Franklin
McINTOSH, J.T. (James Murdoch MacGregor)
The agency is owned by **Ambrose Frayne** whose wife **Dominique** works as an investigator, secretary and typist, an arrangement which,

along with Dominique's adopting her husband's name, nationality, profession, values and judgement, is viewed with particular scorn by Klein, who sees the supposed partnership as an empty device in Ambrose dominated books. The first book was a novelization of Peter O'Donnell's play **TV: TAKE A PAIR OF PRIVATE EYES**.

       Take A Pair Of Private Eyes (UK 1968, 1968)

       A Coat Of Blackmail (UK 1970, 1971)

McIver, Houston — WOODY, William

Mack, Terry — DALY, Carroll John

McKain — WILLIAMSON, Chet

McKellar, Ross — PEEBLES, Nile

McKenna, Bugs — THOMPSON, Jim

McKenzie, Craig — MARBLE, M.S.

MacKENZIE, Donald

An operative for a shabby agency, **Barry Jordan** is hired by a Hollywood film director to get evidence of his wife's adultery. He falls for her and finds himself framed when she's murdered, spending a few years behind bars, planning his revenge in a low to medium key, but carefully orchestrated novel.

       The Kyle Contract (1970, UK 1971)

MacKenzie, Greg — TV: HAWAIIAN EYE

McKenzie, Walter — GUTHRIE, Al

MacKinnon, Clay — BRACKEEN, Steve

Macklin, Alan — CUNNINGHAM, E.V.

McKNIGHT, Bob

Running a one-man office in Sun City (St. Petersburg?), Florida, northern emigrant **Nathan Hawk** spends a lot of time taking cases, and friendly damyankee abuse, from Detective Lieutenant Tobias Duane, which he figures is good politics and might pay off. Serviceable stories, fast paced with few affectations or pretensions that move around interesting Florida locales.

       Downwind (1957)

       Murder Mutuel (1958)

       The Bikini Bombshell (1959)

       Swamp Sanctuary (1959)

       Kiss The Babe Goodbye (1960)

       Running Scared (1960)

       A Slice Of Death (1960)

       Drop Dead, Please (1961)

       The Flying Eye (1961) >

A Stone Around Her Neck (1962)
Homicide Handicap (1963)
Maclain, Captain Duncan — KENDRICK, Baynard
McLaren, John T. — COOPER, Will
MacLEAN, Katherine
Working with the Rescue Squad of 1999 New York, a city of over 2
billion people, **George Sandford** is a telepathic PI who finds people in
trouble by zeroing in on their mental distress signals.
Missing Man (1975)
MacNeil, Harry — JEFFERS, H. Paul
MacNEIL, Neil = BALLARD, Willis Todhunter
Specialists in business cases, with a going rate of $20,000 dollars plus
expenses, **Tony Costaine** and **Bert McCall** are New York's most
expensive PIs. Tough, smart, handsome womanizers who served together
in both the OSS and FBI, Dartmouth and Columbia Law School educated
Costaine is a tall, dark Latin type, McCall a 6'5", 265 pound bagpipe-
playing, bourbon-guzzling giant. Devil-may-care, dangerous men in Ivy
League suits, they are cool, cocky cut-ups with a witty line in repartee.
The books are intricately plotted and fine entertainment.
Death Takes An Option (1958, UK 1960)
Third On A Seesaw (1959, UK 1961)
Two Guns For Hire (1959, UK 1960)
Hot Dam (1960, UK 1960)
The Death Ride (1960, UK 1962)
Mexican Slay Ride (1962, UK 1963)
The Spy Catchers (1966)
McNEILE, H.C. — see SAPPER
McPherson — LINDSAY, R. Howard
McQUAY, Mike
A cyberpunk pioneer, combining hardboiled style with futuristic
technology and advanced social decay. **Mathew Swain** lives in an
unnamed South-Central Texas city whose Old Town is a quarantined
mutant ghetto on the site of a nuclear power station meltdown. In 2083
virtually every public service has broken down, the rich live in armored
fortresses and, with bodies usually collected by Meat Wagons and
immediately atomized, the police charge in advance to investigate crimes.
The series, dedicated to Chandler, is wryly witty, exciting tough-guy
stuff.
Hot Time In Old Town (1981)
When Trouble Beckons (1981)

> The Deadliest Show In Town (1982)
> The Odds Are Murder (1983)

McRAE, Diana

Dignified and savvy, lesbian **Eliza Pirex** runs her own Oakland, California agency with the help of her mentor **Dennis Eckenberg**, with whom she served the 2000 hour apprenticeship required by California law for a PI license, in an intricate story slowly and deftly unfolded.

> All The Muscle You Need (1988)

MacRae, Jamie — McDOWELL, Emmett

McSHANE, Mark

Retiring from the Birmingham (UK) police, ex-detective sergeant **Norman Pink** buys a partnership in Peerless Private Enquiry Agents Ltd. Known on the force as a hard case, Pink's soft side is revealed in an obsession with a nine year old girl he saw killed in an accident, whose body was never claimed or identified. Boucher commented, "the routine slogging of detection is carefully, plausibly, even lovingly depicted," and commended the second, carny-set, book for atmosphere.

> The Girl Nobody Knows (1965, UK 1966)
> Night's Evil (UK 1966, 1966)

MacVeigh, Andy & Susie — MacVEIGH, Sue

MacVEIGH, Sue

Hotshot investigator for the New York, Chicago & Western Railroad, Captain **Andy MacVeigh** is assisted by his narrator wife **Susie** in, judging by the first title, rather icky soft-boileds. See **Films: GRAND CENTRAL MURDER.**

> Murder Under Construction (1939)
> Grand Central Murder (1939)
> Streamlined Murder (1940)
> The Corpse And The Three Ex-Husbands (1941)

Madden, Con — WALSH, Maurice

MADDREN, Gerry

San Francisco PI **Jerry Cool** involves himself in one murder while drunk at a winery party and his VISA card is found near another body and he has to clear himself. The author's characterizations lack substance and she meanders rather than developing the plot. A short story in A21, "Fit For Felony," features a unique mother and daughter PI team, **Ivy Middaugh**, driven into it by her retired husband's TV sports and **Judith Perino**, who prefers J.D. According to the contributor notes, Maddren is working on a novel featuring two women detectives.

> The Case Of The Johannesberg Riesling (1988)

Madigan, Cash — CASSIDAY, Bruce
Madigan, Jocko — Radio: PAT NOVAK, FOR HIRE
Madison, Ken — TV: BOURBON STREET BEAT
Magaracz, Nick — GALLISON, Kate
Magnum, Thomas — TV: MAGNUM P.I.
Magnuson, Arnold — SMITH, Mark
Maguire, John Patrick Aloysius — HIMMEL, Richard
MAHANNAH, Floyd
Trying to keep her father's detective agency going, **Cassie Gibson** doesn't realize she's got a dead woman in her yellow Cadillac until she picks up hitchhiker Nap Lincoln. "Rough and tumble in the tradition of private eye yarns but the characters are warmer, more likeable and more credible than most," remarked *SR*. Characterization was also applauded in a novel featuring **Riley Waddell**, paid $13,000 to hide a woman even he thinks is guilty of murder for two weeks who falls for her and proves innocent in a romantic adventure.
Gibson: The Yellow Hearse (1950, UK 1951); as No Luck For A Lady
        (1951)
Waddell: The Golden Goose (1951, UK 1952); as The Broken Body (1952)
Mahoney, Terrence Aloysius — Films: PRIVATE EYES
Malcolm, James — GRAHAM, Neill
MALING, Arthur
The well-known suspense writer's 14th book features perhaps the first yuppie detective, **Calvin Bix**, a phenomenally successful Chicago ex-cop who quit the force to make money, losing his wife in the process ("Most women want their husbands to get ahead, but Phyllis had wanted hers to stay behind. Upward mobility scared her"). Bix is an unengaging fellow with no code of honor or philosophy, only a profit motive.
        Lover And Thief (1988)
Mallard, Eddie — TV: GOTHAM
Mallin, David — ORMEROD, Roger
Mallory — CHANDLER, Raymond
Mallory, Bert — REAMY, Tom
Mallory, James Maxfield — SMITH, Richard N.
Mallory, John Justin — RESNICK, Mike
Mallory, Mike — Radio: MIKE MALLORY
Mallory, Steve — HEYES, Douglas
Malone — RIDER, J.W.
Malone, Peter — TV: ACAPULCO
Malvern, Ted — CHANDLER, Raymond

MANDELKAU, Jamie
Before witnessing a top-level bribe, **Deuce Ramsey** was a motorcycle cop in Yellow, Texas. In forced retirement the six-foot, barrel-chested, tough, ugly, poetry-reading brute set up as a PI, working for either side in divorces or finding missing persons with single-track dedication and his fists, rarely using the police .38 he hung onto. Very funny, with weird characters and crisp dialogue.

      The Leo Wyoming Caper (1977)

MANER, William
Hubin describes the one story about public-relations expert cum PI **Parker Rowe** as "smooth and satisfying."

      The Image Killer (1968, UK 1970)

Maneri, Butch — KNICKMEYER, Steve

Manfred, Ben — TV: The FOUR JUST MEN

MANN, Jack (E. Charles Vivian 1882-1947)
Unable to stand the strict discipline, **Gregory George Gordon Green**, known as Gees, quits the British police force and offends his rich dignified father with advertisements reading "Consult Gees' Confidential Agency for everything from mumps to murder." After one fairly straightforward story, the series became supernatural, involving werewolves, ghosts, sorcery and avatars.

      Gees' First Case (UK 1936, 1970)
      Grey Shapes (UK 1937, 1970)
      Nightmare Farm (UK 1937, 1975)
      The Kleinart Case (UK 1938)
      Maker Of Shadows (UK 1938)
      Her Ways Are Death (UK 1939)
      The Ninth Life (UK 1939, 1970)
      The Glass Too Many (UK 1940, 1973)

Mannix, Joe — TV: MANNIX

MANOR, Jason (Oakley M. Hall)
Ex- Peninsula City, California policeman **Steve Summers** set up an agency and did well before coming into money and, deciding he'd rather deal with fish than people, retired and bought a fishing boat. Manor is good at small town corruption which Summers gets reluctantly involved with in the first book. Boucher was impressed by the "convincing and restrained toughness with an adroit plot" of the second in which Summers tackles a vicious right-wing organization, America Inc.

      The Red Jaguar (1954, UK 1955); as The Girl In The Red Jaguar
      (1955)

The Pawns Of Fear (1955, UK 1955); as No Halo For Me (1956)

Maquis, Johnny — WARREN, Vernon

MARBLE, M(argaret) S(harp)

Will Cuppy found a novel featuring PI with psychological tendencies **Craig McKenzie** "a casual, plain-speaking, fairly hard-boiled and teen-minded story with its typical emphasis on the sour and sordid." Boucher commented of *Die By Night*, featuring San Francisco PI **Joe Gaylord**, "some of the season's most agreeable writing wasted on one of the season's most incoherent plots."

McKenzie: Everybody Makes Mistakes (1946, UK 1947)

Gaylord: Die By Night (1947, UK 1948)

March, Erik — FICKLING, G.G.

March, Lester — Films: IT'S ONLY MONEY

March, Milo — CHABER, M.E.

March, Urgan — WHEELER, Benson & Claire Lee PURDY

MARCUS, A(rthur) A.

Routine, though fast, lively and economically told stories about **Pete Hunter**, PI in an anonymous corrupt small city. The third novel blatantly recycles the plot of *The Maltese Falcon*.

The Widow Gay (1948); as Post-Mark Homicide (1953)

Walk The Bloody Boulevard (1951)

Make Way For Murder (1955)

Margolies, Ben — GATES, David

Margolis, Eddie — COHEN, Stephen Paul

Marker, Frank — TV: PUBLIC EYE

Markham — REASONER, James

Markham, Roy — TV: MARKHAM

Marks, Jonathan — BARNS, Glenn M.

MARKSON, David

Greenwich Village, New York PI **Harry Fannin** has several .32 and .38 caliber bullets holes in various inconsequential portions of his anatomy, a knife wound in his right shoulder, shrapnel in his left, not to mention two broken noses and sundry other minor disabilities. The stories are as tough and gritty as he is.

Epitaph For A Tramp (1959); as Fannin (1971)

Epitaph For A Dead Beat (1961)

Miss Doll, Go Home (1965)

Marley, James — ROSS, Philip

Marlow, Daisy — MORGAN, D. Miller

Marlow, Dick — BENTLEY, John
Marlow, Sam — FENADY, Andrew
Marlowe — FARREN, Mick
MARLOWE, Dan J. 1914-1986
Tough semi-detective **Johnny Killian** who lives in New York's Hotel
Duarte is violent with mild flashes of sensitivity. Boucher found *Fatal
Frails* "crude and oversexed but with some originality," but admired
Shake A Crooked Town, in which Killian singlehandedly cleans up a
corrupt, upstate burg, for "pace and bite as convincingly hardboiled as any
toughie for some time."
> Doorway To Death (1959, UK 1959)
> Killer With A Key (1959)
> Doom Service (1960)
> The Fatal Frails (1960)
> Shake A Crooked Town (1961)

MARLOWE, Derek
Leaving England out of boredom, **Walter Brackett** wound up in San
Francisco, becoming a PI in the firm of Brackett & Kemble. At 53 he is a
widower, his partner reads comics in a rest home and business is non-
existent. Marlowe is also British but drew good American reviews for an
intricately plotted hardboiled story with some minor faults of geography,
but literate, enigmatic and sophisticated.
> Somebody's Sister* (UK 1974, 1974)

Marlowe, Philip —CHANDLER, Raymond / CONTERIS,
> **Hiber / A11 / Films: RADIOACTIVE DREAMS**

MARLOWE, Stephen (Milton Lesser)
Dubbed by Baker & Nietzel "The Peripatetic Knight," **Chester Drum**
must be the most widely traveled of all PIs. Ex-FBI, his Drum Agency is
on F Street, Washington, DC, and his extensive government connections
often involve him in espionage. Combining exotic locales with non-stop
action, Marlowe produced hardboiled international detective stories that
won considerable critical respect, Boucher remarking on his acute story-
telling and taut understatement of sex and violence. A collaboration with
Richard S PRATHER, bringing together Drum and **Shell Scott**,
defies description. Drum short stories, "Baby Sitter" and "Wanted—Dead
Or Alive," are in A10 and A14. See **Andrew FRAZER**.
> The Second Longest Night (1955, UK 1958)
> Mecca For Murder (1956, UK 1957)
> Killers Are My Meat (1957, UK 1958)
> Murder Is My Dish (1957) >

      Trouble Is My Name* (1957, UK 1958)
      Violence Is My Business (1958, UK 1959)
      Terror Is My Trade (1958, UK 1960)
      Double In Trouble (1959). With **Richard S PRATHER**
          featuring **Shell Scott**
      Homicide Is My Game (1959, UK 1960)
      Danger Is My Line (1960, UK 1961)
      Death Is My Comrade (1960, UK 1961)
      Peril Is My Pay (1960, UK 1961)
      Manhunt Is My Mission (1961, UK 1962)
      Jeopardy Is My Job (1962, UK 1963)
      Francesca (1963, UK 1963)
      Drum Beat—Berlin (1964)
      Drum Beat—Dominique (1965)
      Drum Beat—Madrid (1966)
      Drum Beat—Erica (1967)
      Drum Beat—Marianne (1968)

Marr, Jason — **ANDERSON, M.**

MARRIOTT, Anthony

Novelization of the fine British **TV: PUBLIC EYE** featuring Birmingham PI **Frank Marker**. See also **Audley SOUTHCOTT**.

      Marker Calls The Tune (UK 1968)

Marshall, Johnny & Suzy — **FOX, James M.**

MARSHALL, Lovat = **GRAHAM, Neill**

The Times Literary Supplement, never a good judge of crime fiction, called former military policeman and British Empire middleweight boxing champion turned Proud Lane, London, PI **Sugar Kane** "a hero of guts and probity . . . his simple but well-devised sagas can be widely recommended." Offhand racism.

      Sugar For The Lady (UK 1955)
      Sugar On The Carpet (UK 1956)
      Sugar Cuts The Corners (UK 1957)
      Sugar On The Target (UK 1958)
      Sugar On The Cuff (UK 1960)
      Sugar On The Kill (UK 1961)
      Sugar On The Loose (UK 1962)
      Sugar On The Prowl (UK 1962)
      Murder In Triplicate (UK 1963)
      Murder Is The Reason (UK 1964)
      Ladies Can Be Dangerous (UK 1964) >

Death Strikes In Darkness (UK 1965)
The Dead Are Silent (UK 1966)
The Dead Are Dangerous (UK 1966)
Murder Of A Lady (UK 1967)
Blood On The Blotter (UK 1968)
Money Means Murder (UK 1968)
Death Is For Ever (UK 1969)
Murder's Out Of Season (UK 1970)
Murder's Just For Cops (UK 1971)
Death Casts A Shadow (UK 1972)
Moment For Murder (UK 1972)
Loose Lady Death (UK 1973)
Date With Murder (UK 1973)
The Strangler (UK 1974)
Key To Murder (UK 1975)
Murder Mission (UK 1975)
Murder To Order (UK 1975)

Marshall, Nick — MITCHAM, Gilroy
MARSHALL, Raymond = CHASE, James Hadley
Like all his work, Chase's hardboiled, violent Marshall titles about
unscrupulous PI **Brick-Top Corrigan** were constructed from reference
books. Another PI, New Yorker **Marc Spencer**, is brought in to
investigate police inactivity in the cases of three missing blonde young
women in a small town where the police dislike PIs and the citizens are
afraid of the police. *NYT* remarked that Spencer's adventures were
"exciting enough but they do not make much sense."
Spencer: Blondes' Requiem (UK 1945, 1946)
Corrigan: Mallory (UK 1950)
            Why Pick On Me? (UK 1951)
Marshall, Steve — Films: GIRL IN ROOM 13
Marston, Paul — EVERSZ, Robert
MARTELL, Charles
Former Summer of Love hippie, Stanford drop-out, detective story writer
and SFPD cop **Mick Halsey** finally goads his millionaire father beyond
endurance by turning up to his mother's funeral stoned. But Halsey Sr. is
killed in a plane crash before he can cut Jr. out of his will. Halsey then
sets up as an over-priced San Francisco PI, not allowing work to cut too
far into his leisure.
            Halsey And The Dead Ringer (1988)
Martin, Anthony — FRANCIS, William

MARTIN, James E.
Young ex-cop, operating in Cleveland, **Gil Disbro** is asked to find a sick woman's biological mother. *Publisher's Weekly* said of this hardboiled debut, "while this mystery reveals more about Cleveland than some readers may wish to know, and its young hero speaks in a distinctly middle-aged voice, it is nonetheless well plotted and competently told."
> The Mercy Trap (1989)

MARTIN, Robert 1908-1976
The head of the Cleveland, Ohio branch of American-International Inc. is **Jim Bennett,** a solidly professional, indeed bourgeois, PI who plays poker and golf, hunts and fishes, drinks dry martinis and is engaged to his secretary. Martin is much admired by critics, Boucher commenting "I know few writers who can infuse into fictional murder so deep a sense of human sadness and pity," and called him hardheaded rather than hardboiled, though he thought that *A Key To The Morgue*, Martin's toughest, most hardboiled novel, was more Mike Hammer than Bennett, while Sandoe, who usually panned Martin, liked it a great deal! Normally Martin, a pulp writer who, like Chandler, later cannibalized many of his own stories, was low-key, with good plots, characterization, detection, suspense and emotion. He also wrote as **Lee ROBERTS.**
> Dark Dream (1951)
> Sleep, My Love (1953, UK 1955)
> Tears For The Bride (1954, UK 1955)
> The Widow And The Web (1954, UK 1956)
> Just A Corpse At Twilight (1955, UK 1957)
> Catch A Killer (1956, UK 1958)
> Hand-Picked For Murder (1957, UK 1958)
> Killer Among Us (1958, UK 1959)
> A Key To The Morgue (1959, UK 1960)
> To Have And To Kill* (1960, UK 1961)
> A Coffin For Two (UK 1962, 1972)
> She, Me And Murder (UK 1962, 1971)
> Bargain For Death (UK 1964, 1972)

Martin, Willard — Films: SUPER SLEUTH
MASON, Clifford
Cool Harlem Korean War veteran, fiftyish with a checkered past, **Joe Cinquez** couldn't get into officer training because despite his light skin and Caucasian hair, he's still black. Though unlicensed and unemployed, he gets work from a black Army buddy, now a successful lawyer. In the second book he moves to a Jamaican area of Brooklyn.

When Love Was Not Enough (1980)

Jamaica Run (1987)

Mason, Rick — FAIRMAN, Paul

Masters, J.C.K. — RUD, Anthony M.

Masters, Jacob — Films: CRY UNCLE!

MASTERSON, Whit = MILLER, Wade

Wade and Miller used this name for off-beat, non-series books, the first of which featured ex-Army Intelligence Captain **Mort Hagen**, divorced himself, who specializes in divorce investigations. He charges $50 a day for his services, a written report and court testimony if required and cultivates ordinariness down to his suit and car. Boucher, who admired other Masterson novels, said of this one, referring to the publisher's teaser, "I can't think of an established team who would construct quite so improbable a plot or relate it with so little action and suspense."

Dead, She Was Beautiful (1955, UK 1955)

MASUR, Harold Q.

As Art Scott points out (Reilly), though **Scott Jordan**, is a lawyer, he functions more as a private detective, active away from the office and courtroom. Masur conceived him to fall somewhere between Perry Mason and Archie Goodwin, hoping to combine Gardner's ingenious plots with Stout's dashing, insouciant PI. Less elaborate and unlikely than Gardner (Art Bourgeau regards Jordan as superior to Mason), Masur wrote tight, entertaining, well resolved books that hold up very well.

Bury Me Deep* (1947, UK 1961)

Suddenly A Corpse (1949, UK 1950)

You Can't Live Forever (1951, UK 1951)

So Rich, So Lovely, And So Dead (1952, UK 1953)

The Big Money (1954, UK 1955)

Tall, Dark, And Deadly (1956, UK 1957)

The Last Gamble (1958); as The Last Breath (UK 1958); as
    Murder On Broadway (1959)

Send Another Hearse (1960, UK 1960)

The Name Is Jordan (1962) SS

Make A Killing (1964, UK 1964) >

The Legacy Lenders (1967, UK 1967)

The Mourning After (1981, UK 1983)

MATHIS, Edward 1927-1988

The closest stoical, straightforward pickup driving Dallas-Fort Worth area, Texas, PI **Dan Roman** got to becoming a jet pilot, his secret dream, was a helicopter pilot in Vietnam, where he was taken prisoner. After quitting the local police force, he set up in private practice. Mathis evoked Texas and its people very well, and constructs good plots. Roman is a rather distant, if compassionate, figure and the series was very promising until cut short by the author's death.

> From A High Place (1985)
> Dark Streaks And Empty Places (1986)
> Natural Prey (1987)
> Another Path, Another Dragon (1988)

Matson, Candy — Radio: CANDY MATSON

MAXWELL, A.E. (Ann & Evan Maxwell)
After inheriting money from an uncle and having his investment banker wife work on it, Montana raised **Fiddler** ends up with "more money than you can count, an ex-wife, a numb butt and a desire to kill something." Boredom drives him give other people a hand, which gives him an extra crack in the skull, a rearranged nose and a few odd scars. Driving a Shelby Cobra round up-market Southern California, and living on the Gold Coast, in Crystal Cove, between Newport Beach and Laguna, he features in a hard-hitting, sexy and engaging stories.

> Just Another Day In Paradise (1985)
> The Frog And The Scorpion (1986)
> Gatsby's Vineyard (1987, UK 1988)
> Just Enough Light To Kill (1988)

MAXWELL, Thomas
In the second book about **Lew Cassiday**, who first appeared in *Kiss Me Once*, the former football star becomes partner in a detective agency with former Fordham sidekick Terry Leary and another ex-cop Harry Madrid. The time is 1945 and the plot, centered round an escape route for wanted Nazis, sounds more like a period thriller than straight PI material.

> Kiss Me Twice (1988)

Maynard, Garrett — SWIGGETT, Howard

Meehan, Trixie — FLYNN, T.T.

MEEK, M(argaret) **R**(eid) **D**(uncan)
Female author of two books about disbarred lawyer **Lennox Kemp** who works for McReady's Detective Agency, 110 Beaver Lane, Walthamstow, East London. The writing is affected and the plots uninteresting though the double meaning hidden in the first title is well executed. After the second book Kemp was reinstated at the bar and later titles concern his exploits as a practicing lawyer.

> Hang The Consequences (UK 1984, 1985)
> The Split Second (UK 1986, 1986)

Meiklejohn, Charlie — WILHELM, Kate
Melchan, Lin — LUCAS, Warren
Mercer, Edward — CANNING, Victor
Meredith, Judge — TV: The JUDGE AND JAKE WYLER
MERTZ, Stephen
Mertz, the actual author or co-author of many of The Executioner novels published as by Don PENDLETON, has a rather banal 1979 short story, "Death Blues," featuring PI **O'Dair** in A5.
MEYER, Nicholas
Famous for *The Seven-Per-Cent Solution*, a well received Conan Doyle pastiche, Meyer also wrote a novel about Westwood Village, LA, PI **Mark Brill** who, during the Watergate days, investigates the truth about an incident in Vietnam. Chilling and suspenseful
>   Target Practice (1974, UK 1975)
MEYNELL, Laurence
Operating out of a seedy Gerrard Mews office in London's Soho, **Hooky Hefferman** specializes in getting information in pubs, having mastered the casual bonhomie of male gossip. Amiable, forceful when pressed and possessing a direct cunning, Hefferman is, in H.R.F.Keating's words "charming and salty."
>   The Frightened Man (UK 1952)
>   Danger Round The Corner (UK 1952)
>   Too Clever By Half (UK 1953)
>   Death By Arrangement (UK 1972, 1972)
>   A Little Matter Of Arson (UK 1972)
>   The Fatal Flaw (UK 1973, 1978)
>   The Thirteen Trumpeters (UK 1973, 1978)
>   The Fairly Innocent Little Man (UK 1974, 1977)
>   Don't Stop For Hooky Hefferman (UK 1975, 1977)
>   Hooky And The Crock Of Gold (UK 1975)
>   The Lost Half Hour (UK 1976, 1977)
>   Hooky Gets The Wooden Spoon (UK 1977, 1977)
>   Papersnake (UK 1978)
>   Hooky And The Villainous Chauffeur (UK 1979)
>   Hooky And The Prancing Horse (UK 1980)
>   Hooky Goes To Blazes (UK 1981)
>   Silver Guilt (UK 1983)
>   The Open Door (UK 1984)
>   The Affair At Barwold (UK 1985)
>   Hooky Catches A Tartar (UK 1986) >

Hooky On Loan (UK 1987)

Hooky Hooked (UK 1988)

MIALL, Robert

Novelization of the glossy **TV: The PROTECTORS** featuring international PIs, American **Harry Rule, Contessa Caroline di Contini**, British widow of an Italian nobleman and Frenchman **Paul Buchet.**

The Protectors (UK 1973)

MICHAELS, Melisa C.

Library Journal found San Francisco PIs tough and shrewd **Aileen Douglass** and beauteous **Sharon Atwood** "insubstantial but likeable . . . a smoothly written romp round the bay." The novel features a wild auto chase and a violent, bloody finale.

Through The Eyes Of The Dead (1989)

MICHEL, M(ilton) Scott

NYT commented "The outstanding feature of (*The X-Ray Murders*) is that there is not a single character in it with whom one can feel any sympathy. That goes for the victims, the suspects, the police and most of all for **Wood Jaxon.** The author belongs in the Dashiell Hammett school of detective story writing, but down at the foot of the class." *SR* remarked "Pungent pabulum for readers who like their mysteries hard-boiled and, to say the least, unconventional—also pretty sordid." Tough, handsome lady-killing New Yorker Jaxon claims to use psychological methods, but there is little evidence of this in his procedure.

The X-Ray Murders (1942, UK 1945); as Sinister Warning (Can 1950)

Sweet Murder (1943, UK 1945); as House In Harlem (Can 1950)

Midas, Johnny — CASSIDAY, Bruce

Middaugh, Ivy — MADDREN, Gerry

Midnight, Johnny — TV: JOHNNY MIDNIGHT

Midnight, Steve — BUTLER, John K.

Milano, Johnny — ELLIN, Stanley

Miles, Gregg — TV: ACAPULCO

Miles, Jeff — LYON, Dana

MILES, John (John Bickham)

Dragged to Fenton, Oklahoma to provide protection for a fellow operative of a Kansas City detective agency, PI **Larry Crystal** featured in one tough, fast-moving story.

Dally With A Deadly Doll (1961)

Miles, Robert — EVERSON, David

Milgrim, Mervyn — Films: WHO DONE IT? (1942)
MILLAR, Margaret
Among many exceptional mysteries, Millar created three memorable PIs.
Self-made San Francisco PI **Elmer Dodd**, called by *SR* "a real find," is
a former New Jersey carpenter, Panamanian merchant seaman, MP in
Korea, bodyguard in Singapore and LA Bible saleman. **Steve Pinata**, an
orphan, probably of Mexican parentage, makes most of his living as a
bail bondsman as there isn't much call for a PI in San Felice, California,
where he has offices at 107 East Opal Street. **Joe Quinn** has a Nevada
detective's license and was working as a Reno casino security officer when
he mixed pleasure with business and had to leave town. En route to San
Felice he is hired by a religious cult after stopping to scrounge a meal.
Like all Millar's books these conjure up what Julian SYMONS called "an
atmosphere of uneasiness," with things never what they seem to be.
Dodd: The Listening Walls (1959, UK 1959)
Pinata: A Stranger In My Grave (1960, UK 1960)
Quinn: How Like An Angel (1962, UK 1962)
MILLER, Geoffrey
Hooked on Hammett and Chandler in his parents' bookstore, **Terry
Traven** joined the LAPD to gain the necessary hours to qualify for a
California PI license, resigned and opened The Black Mask Detective
Agency at Melrose & Citrus. Wearing 40s clothes, driving a restored '41
Buick and speaking in hardboiled style, he became a counterculture figure
and, through his contacts in the drug world, very successful at finding
runaways. His business began to decline in 1973 when he picketed Robert
Altman's house to protest his version of *The Long Goodbye*. When his
one modern LA hardboiled story opens he hasn't worked for 103 days.
        The Black Glove (1981)
MILLER, J.M.T.
Vietnam vet **Artie Weatherby** pulls himself out of alcoholism and
does well enough as a PI to run a BMW. Operating out of a quasi-LA, he
debuted in a novel described by James ELLROY as "crackerjack . . . with
a strong plot, great repartee and well-drawn characters." One feature is a
reprise of the Sternwood family of Chandler's *The Big Sleep*. The author,
a woman, lives in Honolulu.
        Weatherby (1987)
Miller, Larry — TV: The PIGEON
MILLER, Martin J.
A PI specializing in internal business crime, Miller's short story, "Telex"
(A1 #8), features **Mike McDermott**, one of the four partners in Quad

Investigations of Los Angeles, specializing, surprisingly enough, in business crimes.

Miller, Paul — Films: DUMB DICKS

MILLER, Victor B.

A beautiful woman PI specializing in women's cases, **Fernanda**, in Klein's words, "mouths the jargon of sexual liberation and plays 'blame the victim.' She trades on a climate of fear and shame by seeming to offer a woman's insight but then betrays that promise," at one point telling a prospective rape victim client who doesn't want to go to the police, "You weren't raped; you were taken up on your word," and refers to her as "a singles-bar neurotic and a pathetic tease."

       Fernanda (1976)

MILLER, Wade (Bob Wade & Bob Miller 1920-1961)

Wade and Miller, who also wrote as **Whit MASTERSON**, were one of the few really successful collaborative PI writing teams. Their first book featured **Walter James** of the Lantz-James Agency, Atlanta, whose partner's death brings him to Wade and Miller's hometown of San Diego. They then created **Max Thursday**, San Diego PI, who started as a drunken bum working as house dick in a cheap hotel, but developed into a tough, competent detective, though with a dangerous temper, until he becomes successful with four PIs working for him in his Moulton Building offices. The Thursday series and the James novel are underrated in the second line of hardboiled fiction though Sandoe dismisses them as "synthetic but effective." See **Films: GUILTY BYSTANDER.**

James: Deadly Weapon (1946, UK 1947)
Thursday: Guilty Bystander* (1947, UK 1948)
           Fatal Step (1948, UK 1949)
           Uneasy Street (1948, UK 1949)
           Calamity Fair (1950)
           Murder Charge (1950)
           Shoot To Kill (1951, UK 1953)

Millhone, Kinsey — GRAFTON, Sue

Millner, Mark — SHORE, Julian

Mills, Ed — TV: BIG ROSE

MILNE, John

A respected young British litterateur, winner of a major fiction prize, and one (short) time police constable, Milne created **Jimmy Jenner**, a Romford, Essex policeman who loses his foot and the hearing in one ear in a terrorist bombing. Rather than take a desk job, Jenner sets up as an investigator with an office in Canning Town, in London's dockland.

Milne himself comes from the East End and captures the feel and sound of a very different part of London.

    Dead Birds (UK 1986, 1987)
    Shadowplay (UK 1987);as The Moody Man (1988)
    Daddy's Girl (UK 1988)

Milodragovitch, Milton Chester — CRUMLEY, James

MITCHAM, Gilroy (William Newton)

In the first book, **Nick Marshall**, London PI, hits the trail after his partner's murder, with other corpses turning up. *SR* remarked "Many cigarettes are pressed out and hearts a-flutter; regular cops pretty sappy; petroleum consumption high. Pace variable. All corn and a yard wide."

    The Full Stop (UK 1957, 1957)
    The Man From Bar Harbour (UK 1958, 1958)
    The Dead Reckoning (UK 1960, 1960)

MITCHELL, James

The author of the Callan spy novels turned to the genre with smooth-talking, self-educated Londoner **Ron Hoggett** and his existentialist sidekick **Dave Baxter** Good dialogue and pace but the first novel is a male fantasy, complete with a brace of beautiful heiresses for the heroes, and a ludicrous ending. The second, over-complex book had a similar breezy tone and an obtrusive love affair sub-plot but one reviewer admired the "clever, flawed, endearing and resourceful" duo.

    Dead Ernest (UK 1987, 1987)
    Dying Day (UK 1988, 1988)

Modero, Johnny — Radio: JOHNNY MODERO, PIER 23

MODIANO, Patrick

His employer, the owner of a detective agency in Paris, France, gave him his name and when **Guy Roland** succeeds his benefactor at his retirement, he decides to devote the resources of the agency to discovering his true identity. A *roman á clef*—the PI as his own client—very literary and very Gallic.

    Missing Person (UK 1980)

MOFFATT, James

One quarter Sioux through his grandfather who fought with Sitting Bull, escaped to Canada and stayed there, **Johnny Canuck**'s Indian ancestry supposedly accounts for his hot blood. A expert at brawling (sic), judo and other forms of self-defense, Canuck is a tough, resourceful and somewhat exhibitionist fellow. The Canadian locale, a city called Balmoral, seems little different from American PI habitats. More acceptable pastiche than most. >

> Time For Sleeping (UK 1966, 1970)
> Blue Line Murder (UK 1965, 1970)
> Blood Is A Personal Thing (UK 1965)
> The Eighth Veil (UK 1965)
> The Twisted Thread (UK 1966)
> Curtain Of Hate (UK 1966)
> Course Of Villainy (UK 1966)
> Terror-Go-Round (UK 1966)

Moine, Vic — HITCHENS, Bert & DOLORES
Molloy, Vic — CHASE, James Hadley
Mondragón, Rita — SATTERTHWAIT, Walter
MONIG, Christopher = CHABER, M.E.
Boucher observed, reviewing books by Ken Crossen as both **M.E. CHABER** and Monig, in the same week, that "insurance adjuster **Brian Brett** seems cut from the same bolt of cloth as March." Of *Abra-Cadaver*, in which Brett solves the case "by the extreme method of making love to a spectacular blonde," Boucher remarked "high marks on ingenuity, liveliness and legitimate integration of sex and violence."

> The Burned Man (1956, UK 1957); as Don't Count The Corpses (1958)
> Abra-Cadaver (1958, UK 1958)
> Once Upon A Crime (1959, UK 1960)
> The Lonely Graves (1960, UK 1961)

Monk, Gus — TV: The MONK
MONMOUTH, Jack (William Pember)
Monmouth's strong suit is his depiction of Central London's then very seedy underworld areas of Covent Garden and Soho. **Tom Langley** was a series sleuth, at least once employed by a crusading newspaper to investigate drug-dealing, while **John Earlstone**, never cold-sober but never drunk either, once the highest-paid crime reporter in London makes more money as a Shaftesbury Avenue PI, playing his cards close to his chest. Tough with authentic London and period atmosphere.

Langley: The Donovan Case (UK 1955)
          Lonely, Lovely Lady (UK 1956)
          Sleepy-Eyed Blonde (UK 1957)
          Lightning Over Mayfair (UK 1958)
Earlstone: Not Ready To Die (UK 1960)

MONTALBAN, Manuel Vazquez
A journalist and member of the Catalan Communist Party, Montalban won a major Spanish literature prize and a Grand Prix De Roman Policier

(the French Edgar) for books about **Pepe Carvalho**, ex-communist, overweight bon viveur who lives on Barcelona's Los Ramblas. He has also written books on political theory and cookery, both of which feature strongly, Carvalho being perhaps the greatest gourmet in the genre. To date only two of the books have been translated into English. See **Films: ASESINATO EN EL COMITE CENTRALE.**
>   Murder In The Central Committee (UK 1984, 1985)
>   Southern Seas (UK 1986)

Moon, Cotton — KING, Rufus
Moon, Manville — DEMING, Richard
Moon, Reggie — BLAKE, William Dorsey
Mooney, Al — McCALL, John J.
Mooney, Jerry — O'NEIL, Kerry
Moore, Toussaint — LACY, Ed
Moran, Jigger — ROEBURT, John
Moran, Peter — WILDE, Percival
Moran, Terry — Films: LEAVE IT TO THE IRISH
MORGAN, D. Miller
Middle-aged, overweight, given to hard liquor, strong language in snarling one-liners and clichés, and designer lingerie, rude, unlikable widow **Daisy Marlow** blunders and bullies her way through her gory debut. The second book's plot is riddled with holes. The author is, in fact, a woman.
>   Money Leads To Murder (1987)
>   A Lovely Night To Kill (1988)

Morgan, Oscar — HOMES, Geoffrey
Morgan, Ruff — SHANNON, Jimmy
Morley, Francis — RAND, Lou
Morley, Leon — COXE, George Harmon
MORRISON, Henry (ed) — see **ANTHOLOGIES: 9**
MORROW, J.T.
State of the art industrial espionage isn't too much for the old-fashioned detective work of 16th Street, San Francisco PI **Jason Prophet**, whose ex-partner/ex-lover, **Lynn McColl**, runs into serious trouble with her Silicon Valley agency in a neo-hardboiled caper.
>   Prophet (1988)

MORSE, Larry
Morse created two very different LA PIs, getting very different reactions for them. **Jake Spanner** is 78 years old but still hard as nails. A widower, he lives on his dwindling savings, eats spicy food against his doctor's advice and smokes hash, a habit he picked up in the 20s. His last

hardboiled case was praised by Jon Breen for "a view of old age that manages to be unsentimental and uncompromising yet optimistic and good-natured." Baker & Nietzel rated Morse's books about **Sam Hunter** as "the modern nadir of private eye literature . . . its attitude goes far beyond hardboiled—charred is more like it . . . a man of such Neanderthal sentiments and ugly excesses that he makes Mike Hammer look cerebral." Pronzini agrees that the Hunter books work neither as straight novels nor parodies, though another critic claimed they were parodies of parodies!

Spanner: The Old Dick (1981, UK 1982)
Hunter: The Big Enchilada* (1982, UK 1983)
           Sleaze (1985)

Moseby, Harry — SHARP, Alan
Mott, Lucie — OPPENHEIM, E. Phillips
MULKEEN, Thomas P.
New York PI **Clem Talbot** has no money, no car, and, in one book, no permit for the gun he's shot a man with, and lives with his mother in two black comedies combining ghoulish subject matter (dismembering a corpse, embalming, etc) with a light touch á la Westlake.

        Honor Thy Godfather (1973)
        My Killer Doesn't Understand Me (1973)

MULLEN, Clarence
A complementary team, narrator **Eddie Wright** is assistant and body guard to PI **Tony Lantz**, in which capacity he may, in *NYT*'s words, "best be described as a shock absorber. Just about all he does is take a lot of punishment and come back for more, while his boss does the necessary brain work. Tony is as poorly equipped for physical combat as Eddie is for thinking. If mayhem and murder are your dish, draw up a chair."

        Thereby Hangs A Corpse (1946)
        A Good Place For Murder (1948)

MULLER, Marcia
A pioneer in the modern wave of women writers with female PIs, Muller's **Sharon McCone** is a normal, liberated woman who has been criticized as tepid for her lack of character definition. From department store management training, the Scotch-Irish-Shoshone Indian San Franciscan moved into security then to an agency from which she was fired for having too much integrity. She is retained by a legal services co-operative, the All Souls of Bernal Heights, and works in a realistic way, relying on her .38 rather than physical strength, trying to avoid antagonizing the police despite her problems with authority figures (a spiky affair with a police detective was a recurring sub-plot), and, above

all, being both a woman and a detective and not a caricature of either, though Henri C. Veit (*Library Journal*) thought the first novel was "like a Nancy Drew tale, only dumber." McCone short stories are "Deceptions" (**A2** #1), "Merril-Go-Round" (**A5**; also in Pronzini, Malzberg & Greenberg, eds.; *The Arbor House Treasury Of Mystery & Suspense*, 1982); "Wild Mustard" (**A15**) and "The Broken Men" (**A14**; also in Greenberg & Pronzini, eds.; *Women Sleuths*, 1985).

> Edwin Of The Iron Shoes (1977, UK 1978)
> Ask The Cards A Question (1982, UK 1983)
> The Cheshire Cat's Eyes (1983, UK 1983)
> Games To Keep The Dark Away (1984, UK 1985)
> Leave A Message For Willie* (1984, UK 1985)
> Double (1984). With **Bill PRONZINI** featuring **'Nameless'**
> There's Nothing To Be Afraid Of (1985)
> The Eye Of The Storm (1988)
> There's Something In A Sunday (1989)

MULLER, Paul (Albert King)
British author of pitifully inept American-set novels. **Paul Muller** is a PI in Anfield, which from internal evidence is somewhere in the Western USA. Muller drives a Jaguar, has no noticeable ethics or qualifications and, while talking tough, with possibly the least-funny wisecracks in the genre, has a "major-domo" instead of a secretary. Pathetic.

> Make Mine Mayhem (UK 1967)
> You Kill Me! (UK 1967)
> The Lady Is Lethal (UK 1968, 1968)
> Danger—Dame At Work (UK 1968, 1968)
> The Hasty Heiress (UK 1968, 1969)
> Finder, Losers (UK 1968)
> Slay Time (UK 1968, 1969)
> Why Pick On Me? (UK 1969)
> Goodbye Shirley (UK 1969)
> Don't Push Your Luck (UK 1970)
> Some Dames Don't (UK 1970)
> This Is Murder (UK 1971)
> The Wistful Wanton (UK 1971)
> The Friendly Fiends (UK 1972)

Mulroy, Jane — **WERRY, Richard R.**
MUNRO, Hugh
Barzun & Taylor note, of *Who Told Clutha?*, "**Clutha** is a private detective employed by a Glasgow shipyard and the story is a fair example

of the British hard-boiled school. The investigation of the killing of a workman is over-seasoned with love interest and gangsters." Sounds great. Boucher found it unclued and unlikely with a foolishly chaotic ending, but praised its vivid picture of Glasgow and the docks and found Munro's books, plots that would embarrass Edgar Wallace aside, "refreshingly real and unhackneyed with an authentically tough protagonist."

Who Told Clutha? (1958, UK 1958)
Clutha Plays A Hunch (UK 1959, 1959)
A Clue For Clutha (UK 1960)
Clutha And The Lady (UK 1973)
Get Clutha (UK 1974)

Munroe, Jill — TV: CHARLIE'S ANGELS
Munroe, Kris — TV: CHARLIE'S ANGELS
Murdoch, S.Michael — TV: GRIFF
Murdock, Kent — COXE, George Harmon
Murdock, Matt — RAY, Robert J.
Murphy, Daedelus — TV: MURPHY'S LAW
MURPHY, Robert 1902-1971

PI **Ronald Barr** and his sidekick **Pat Allen**, who is "all but irresistible to women" though, as *NYT* pointed out, "the resistance he encounters is scarcely worth mentioning," drew heavy fire from reviewers. *NYT* took exception to the dialogue; "All of them speak in riddles and half sentences that may mean anything or nothing. The reader is often completely in the dark . . . just a little too cryptic," while *SR* tersely summarized it as "exhausting."

Murder In Waiting (1938)

MURPHY, Warren

Co-author with **Richard SAPIR** of *The Destroyer* series, Murphy also created a discontinuous PI series. **Julian 'Digger' Burroughs** is an Irish-Jewish Las Vegas PI who works freelance for a 5' bureaucrat at Brokers Surety Life Insurance, carries a miniature tape recorder everywhere, has a beautiful Japanese-Italian girl friend, a vengeful ex-wife, two children referred to as "what's his name and the girl," and drinks a lot of vodka. He mysteriously metamorphosed into Jewish-Irish Las Vegas PI **Devlin Tracy** who works for a 5' bureaucrat at Garrison Fidelity Insurance, carries a miniature tape recorder everywhere, has a beautiful Japanese blackjack dealer/hooker girlfriend, an identical estranged family and drinks a lot of vodka. In *Getting Up With Fleas* Tracy and his girlfriend, who wants a gun permit, join his father's New York agency. Either way, Murphy's books are fast and funny. *Pigs Get Fat* won an

MWA Best Paperback Original Edgar. More serious, with thriller elements, is a novel that also won an MWA Best Paperback Original award. Using a cane and leg-brace, **Steve Hooks**, a Secret Service agent who got shot in the knee saving the President from assassination, opens an agency.

Burroughs:	Smoked Out (1982)
	Fool's Flight (1982)
	Dead Letter (1982)
	Lucifer's Weekend (1982)
Tracy:	Trace (1983)
	Trace And 47 Miles Of Rope* (1984)
	When Elephants Forget (1984)
	Pigs Get Fat (1984)
	Once A Mutt (1986)
	Too Old A Cat (1986)
	Getting Up With Fleas (1987)
Hooks:	The Ceiling Of Hell* (1984)

Mustard, Buddy — DANIEL, Roland
'Nameless' — PRONZINI, Bill
NASH, Anne
Flower-shop girls Dodo and Nell were teamed with PI **Mark Tudor**, owner of Svea, the "detecting dog," who tells them what their detecting really means. Cuppy commented, "Miss Nash flings her ingredients around with reckless hand—a touch of screwballism here, a hearty cry there and so forth without much rhyme or reason." Very softboiled.

> Said With Flowers (1943, UK 1953)
> Death By Design (1944, UK 1954)

Nash, Aubrey — DAVIS, Tech
Nash, Hamilton — TV: The DAIN CURSE
Navarro, Rudy — GOULART, Ron
Nayce, Lee — DENT, Lester
NEBEL, Frederick 1903-1967
Fired from the NYPD for raiding the wrong gambling joint, **'Tough Dick' Donahue** joined the Inter-State Agency. An unsentimental, hard-boiled sleuth, with has no illusions about his job he gets involved in cases, often bending the agency's rules (and the law). He appeared in 14 *Black Mask* stories, two of which, "Rough Justice" (1930; A11) and "Red Pavement" (1931; A13) are not in *Six Deadly Dames*. Nebel called Shaw's dismissal as editor of *Black Mask* a "damned outrage" and, like Chandler and Lester Dent, refused to contribute further to it, instead

creating hard-as-nails **Steve Cardigan**, of the Cosmos Detective Agency, for *Dime Detective*. Seven of the 44 stories have recently been collected. Another Cardigan short story, "Murder By Mail" (*Dime Detective* 1936; A3), is meant to highlight female colleague **Patricia Seaward** but shows tough, hard-hitting secretary **Miss Elfoot**, in a better light. Toughness was only part of Nebel's talent, he could also draw vivid pictures of New York, had a fine ear for the slang of the period and a rich vein of black humor. See **Films: SLEEPERS WEST.**

Donahue: Six Deadly Dames* (1950). Six SS
Cardigan: The Adventures Of Cardigan (1988). Seven SS

Nebraska — REYNOLDS, William J.

NELSON,Hugh Lawrence
The Pine Detective Agency of Denver consists of part-Indian **Zebulion Buck** and former Texan **Jim Dunn** whose cases take them all over Colorado. Though the outdoor and action sequences are well-done, Buck and Dunn are not particularly memorable characters and the plots are no more than adequate. Boucher, who reviewed all Nelson's books, excepted the third title from his usual criticisms.

   Ring The Bell At Zero (1949, UK 1950)
   Murder Comes High (1950, UK 1952)
   Gold In Every Grave (1951, UK 1953)
   The Season For Murder* (1952, UK 1956)
   The Sleep Is Deep (1953, UK 1955)
   The Fence (1953)
   Kill With Care (1953)
   Suspect (1954)

Nelson, Jerry — SCHOENFELD, Howard
Nevers, Billy — GLAZNER, Joseph Mark
NEVINS, Francis M.Jr.
Crime critic Nevins, like Boucher, also writes novels, two of them concerning con-man PI **Milo Turner** in a computer-cult mystery described by *NYT* as "artificial and hard to believe," though the writing is described as "smart, pert and moves very quickly." Nevins contributed a **Philip Marlowe** short story, "Consultation In The Dark," to A12.

   The 120-Hour Clock (1986)
   The Ninety Million Dollar Mouse (1988)

Nevins, Rocky — CHUTE, Verne
Nevkorina, Natasha — SPAIN, Nancy
Nevsky, Yuri — GAT, Dimitri

NEWMAN, G(ordon) F.
A British author well-known for books and TV plays about police corruption as a symptom of social decay. His one PI book involves middle-aged ex-FBI man **Jimmy Vanesco**, a New York PI specializing in missing persons, by chance, working mainly for Mafia bosses, who finds layer after layer of corrupt co-operative between criminals, government agencies and international financiers.

> The Men With The Guns (UK 1982)

NEWMAN, Joel
Library Journal commented that Montreal was an important and unusual setting for a novel featuring PI **Philip Kaufman**, "full of sex and violence, with a compelling urgency that carries over the sometimes awkward writing."

> Dead Man's Tears (1981)

Newman, Vic — SUCHER, Dorothy

NISBET, Jim
One of the few contemporary writers in Black Lizard's hardboiled list, Nisbet wrote a very bizarre, murky book, featuring San Francisco PI **Martin Windrow** and a gruesome fusion of sex, violence, love and murder. Ultra-tough.

> The Gourmet (1981); as The Damned Don't Die (1986)

NIXON, Allan
Half-Aztec, half-Irish **Tony Garrity** is an unlicensed LA PI, an attorney disbarred after killing two men (in self defense naturally), with a drinking problem and wracked by guilt and self-pity. Baker & Nietzel observe, "Written with about as little taste or virtue as you'll ever find."

> Get Garrity (1969); as Garrity (UK 1970)
> Goodnight Garrity (1969, UK 1971)
> Go For Garrity (1970)

NOEL, Atanielle Annyn
Apparently satirical, this SF/PI blend features second cousins **Gwen & Garamond Gray** as old-fashioned detectives in the distant future hired to recover a letter that can compromise an entire planet from an aristocratic Poe fanatic. Heavy on style, light on plot with hit-or-miss humor.

> Murder On Usher's Planet (1987)

NOLAN, William F.
Hardboiled, two-fisted **Bart Challis** works in LA's armpit, the wino country below Spring Street, drives a Chevy Corvair Sprint and drinks Black Label or Haig & Haig whiskey. Spare writing, quick action, clipped dialogue and a sharp, poetic evocation of a surreal, hyper-modern Southern

California. Challis' great-grandson, **Sam Space**, also a PI, has an office on Mars in affectionate parodies of Hammett. The beautiful woman who walks into Space's office has three heads! Wildly funny space operas. Nolan announced his intention of reviving the Challis series with Bart's younger half-brother **Nick Challis** and a short story about him, "The Pulpcon Kill," is in **A1** #1, while Bart made possibly his final bow in "A Long Time Dying" (**A15**). See **A10** for Nolan's own pulp collection.

Challis: Death is For Losers (1968)
       The White Cad Cross-Up (1969)
Space: Space For Hire (1971)
       Look Out For Space (1984)

Noon, Ed — AVALLONE, Michael
Noonan, Joe — HEARN, Daniel
Noonan, Mike — PERELMAN, S.J.
Noonan, Tim — BROWN, Roswell
Norden, Bert — BROCK, Stuart
NORMAN, Earl (Norman Thomson)
An American ex-GI living in Tokyo, **Burns Bannion**, Karate expert and student, becomes a PI by accident when he's mistaken for an LA sleuth and has a case and cash pressed on him. The Japanese talk pidgin English and the girls are top-heavy. Baker & Nietzel nominated Norman for Pronzini's *Gun In Cheek* as one of the best of the worst.

       Kill Me In Tokyo (1958)
       Kill Me In Shimbashi (1959)
       Kill Me In Yokohama (1960)
       Kill Me In Shinjuku (1961)
       Kill Me In Yoshiwara (1961)
       Kill Me On The Ginza (1962)
       Kill Me In Atami (1962)
       Kill Me In Roppongi (1967)

North, Jerry & Pamela — LOCKRIDGE, Richard & Frances
Novak, Pat — Radio: PAT NOVAK, FOR HIRE
Novak, Pete — DAVIS, Gordon / HUNT, E. Howard
Novello, Tony — TV: MY FRIEND TONY
Nudger, Alo — LUTZ, John
NYLAND, Gentry
Hired as a bodyguard, but not told why one is needed, **Joseph South** takes the job because he needs the money, and before he finds out what he's up against. Partial to the grape, he wakes from a drunken stupor to find himself #1 murder suspect. *NYT* commented, with unusual (for the

time), good humor, "The moral of the piece seems to be that if Joey had remained sober there might not have been any murders. But in that case there would have been no story, so there you are."

> Mr. South Burned His Mouth (1941); as Run For Your Money (UK 1941); as Hot Bullets For Love (1943)

O'Breen, Fergus — BOUCHER, Anthony
O'Brien, Nora — Films: LEAVE IT TO THE IRISH
O'Brien, Pierre — CHAMBERS, Whitman
O'CALLAGHAN, Maxine
After resigning from the LAPD to join her husband in the West & West Detective Agency, Orange County, California, widowed **Delilah West** is haunted by his murder. The style is realistic, though she breaks more laws than most PIs, suppressing evidence, breaking and entering, assaulting a police officer and stealing a car.

> Death Is Forever (1981)
> Run From Nightmare (1981)
> Hit And Run (1989)

O'Dair — MERTZ, Stephen
O'Day, Chauncy — GAINES, Audrey
O'Day, Terence — CHEYNEY, Peter
ODLUM, Jerome 1905-1954
A reporter in the first book, **John Steele** gets fired from his paper during the story. Tough, greedy, unscrupulous PIs **Sam Booker** and **Jimmy Webb** are hired over and over again by different men, all claiming to be her husband, to find the same woman. See **Films: NINE LIVES ARE NOT ENOUGH / A SCREAM IN THE DARK.**
Steele: Nine Lives Are Not Enough (1940, UK 1944)
> Night And No Moon (1942)
> The Mirabalis Diamond (1945)

Booker: The Morgue Is Always Open (1944)
O'DONOHOE, Nick
The series opened with young, poor and angry Minneapolis PI **Nathan Phillips** losing his senior partner in a car accident and having to prove that he could run the agency himself. Phillips has the soul of a poet, the eyes of a hawk and a cat called Marlowe. Very well written, with fine plots, dialogue, characterization, local atmosphere and pace, though the third book is confusing and has some odd temporal compressions.

> April Snow (1981)
> Wind Chill (1985)
> Open Season (1986)

OGAN, George
Cajun French New Orleans PI **Johnny Bordelon** ran out of money
during prelaw at Tulane University, joined the NOPD, made homicide
detective then quit to become a painter making a living from his cases.
Living in a studio apartment on Rampart Street, Bordelon is divorced, a
mean Cajun cook and a karate black belt. Good local color, average plots.
>   To Kill A Judge (1981)
>   Murder In The Wind (1981)
>   Murder By Proxy (1983)
O'Hara, Cary Wylde — CHEYNEY, Peter
O'Hara, Fergus & Hattie — FOXX, Jack
O'HARA, Kevin (Marten Cumberland 1892-1972)
Cumberland wrote intricate, challenging whodunits featuring French
Commissaire Saturnin Dax and, as O'Hara, medium-boiled, action packed
thrillers about red-haired, vermouth-drinking Irish-Spanish **Chico Brett**,
born in Argentina and operating as a PI from an office in Shepherd
Market, Mayfair, London and working on the seamy side of Soho
nightclubs. Good on 50s London atmosphere.
>   The Customer's Always Wrong (UK 1951)
>   Exit And Curtain (UK 1952)
>   Sing, Clubman, Sing! (UK 1952)
>   Always Tell The Sleuth (UK 1953)
>   It Leaves Them Cold (UK 1954)
>   Keep Your Fingers Crossed (UK 1955)
>   The Pace That Kills (UK 1955)
>   Women Like To Know (UK 1957)
>   Danger: Women At Work! (UK 1958)
>   Well, I'll Be Hanged! (UK 1958)
>   And Here Is The Noose! (UK 1959) >
>   Taking Life Easy (UK 1961)
>   If Anything Should Happen (UK 1962)
>   Don't Tell The Police (UK 1963)
>   Don't Neglect The Body (UK 1964)
>   It's Your Funeral (UK 1966)
O'Hara, Timothy — ROOS, Kelley
O'Keefe, Bill — TV: SHOOTING STARS
O'Leary, Pat — EBY, Lois & John C. FLEMING
OLIVER, Maria-Antonia
The second (see MONTALBAN) of Barcelona's PIs, in translation at least,
Spanish author Oliver's tough **Lonia Guiu** features in a novel first

published in Catalan and described by its feminist publisher as "a fast-paced, fast-talking thriller that raises important feminist issues."

> Study In Lilac (1988)

O'MALLEY, Frank = O'ROURKE, Frank

A noted Western writer, O'Rourke impressed *NYT* with his grasp of detective methodology and steady hand with dialogue plus touches of Stout, Gardner and Freud. "Jacinto City," Texas, PI **Mike Cavanaugh**, "scared of guns but not of women. He learned better," finds a routine tailing job complicated by a series of murders, a double suicide and a steady tattoo of flying fists and bullets.

> The Best Go First (1950, UK 1955)

O'Malley, Thomas — LATIMER, Jonathan

O'Neil, Jason T. — KINSLEY, Lawrence

O'NEIL, Kerry (John T. MacIntyre 1871-1951)

Billed as a Philadelphia Robin Hood, tough ex-cop **Jerry Mooney** has a wide circle of equally tough friends all with hearts of gold, and is distrusted by the local police, who believe, with good reason, that he takes liberties with the law. Poorly written, with trivial stories, the books occasionally have a good underworld flavor. *Death Strikes At Heron House* was the first Bonus Mystery, the publishers offering to refund the buyer's $2 if a seal round the last 80 pages was unbroken.

> Mooney Moves Around (1939)
> Ninth Floor: Middle City Tower (1943)
> Death Strikes At Heron House (1944)

O'Neil, Tip — GRANT, James Edward

OPPENHEIM, E. Phillips 1866-1946

"The Prince of Storytellers" sneaks in with three short story collections. **Malcolm Gossett** gave up a promising police career to specialize in cases involving innocent people in trouble through no fault of their own, getting well-heeled clients and more than his fair share of the breaks. **Baroness Clara Linz** operates Advice Limited, Adam Street, London and reveals little of either her character or methods. Naive, reckless dilettante **Lucie Mott**, advice columnist and owner of Mott's Enquiry Agency, is, in Klein's words, "morally culpable" for the murder of a man who threatens to expose an aristocratic criminal. "The illusion of a professional detective," she fails to solve eight of her ten cases.

Gossett: The Ex-Detective (UK 1933, 1933)
Linz: Advice Limited (UK 1935, 1936)
Mott: Ask Miss Mott (UK 1936, 1937)

ORMEROD, Roger
A British "fair-play" writer of traditional mysteries who often employed private detective **David Mallin** sometimes in harness with another, **George Coe**. According to Trevor Royle (Reilly), "As well as realism of background, Ormerod's writing is notable for its terse and natural dialogue and for an ability to switch the direction of the narrative." Personally, I find them tedious and unworthwhile.

> Time To Kill (UK 1974)
> The Silence Of The Night (UK 1974)
> Full Fury (UK 1975)
> A Spoonful Of Luger (UK 1975)
> Sealed With A Loving Kill (UK 1976)
> The Colour Of Fear (UK 1976)
> A Glimpse Of Death (UK 1976)
> Too Late For The Funeral (UK 1977)
> A Dip Into Murder (UK 1978)
> The Weight Of The Evidence (UK 1978)
> The Bright Face Of Danger (UK 1978)
> The Amnesia Trap (UK 1979)
> Cart Before The Hearse (UK 1980)
> One Breathless Hour (UK 1981)

O'ROURKE, Frank
A noted Western writer, O'Rourke was roughly handled by Boucher, who called a book featuring insurance detective **Jim Bradley**, stationed in a Mexican coast town to watch for clues to the loot from a $2 million robbery, "a meticulous exercise in the imitation of the imitators of Hemingway." Boucher found the plot loose and implausible and commented that "several over-neat sub-plots combine to illustrate generalizations on the Meaning of Life." See **Frank O'MALLEY**.

> High Dive (1954)

Orwell, Harry — TV: HARRY-O

OSTER, Jerry
New York freelance journalist and PI **Eve Zabriskie** investigates murders in a Western American upper-crust planned community whose cops drive, according to rank, BMWs, Volvos or Honda Accords. The dialogue is very readable though the plot is a little obvious. The paperback blurb located Rancho Maria in California (never specified) with policeman Sam Branch, the lead character.

> Rancho Maria (1986); as California Dead (1988)

O'SULLIVAN, James Brendan
Ex-prizefighter and unlicensed PI **Steve Silk** has only one lung but a big heart, a ready wit, a good wardrobe and an eye for the ladies. The dialogue is poor and clichéd, but O'Sullivan constructs good plots with attention-getting devices. Note his continuing popularity in Britain.

> Death Came Late (1945)
> The Death Card (1945)
> Casket Of Death (1946)
> Death On Ice (1946)
> Death Stalks The Stadium (1946)
> Nerve Beat (UK 1953)
> Don't Hang Me Too High (UK 1954, 1954)
> Someone Walked Over My Grave (UK 1954)
> The Stuffed Man (UK 1955)
> The Long Spoon (UK 1956)
> Choke Chain (UK 1958)
> Raid (UK 1958)
> Gate Fever (UK 1959)
> Backlash (UK 1960)

O'Toole, Bridget — McCONNELL, Frank
OZAKI, Milton K.
Three good Chicago PIs were tax accountant Ozaki's **Rusty Forbes**, **Carl Guard** and **Phil Keene**, the two latter, presumably because of contractual problems, being identical with Carl Good and Max Keene in novels under the pseudonym **Robert O. SABER**. Unfortunately I was unable to identify all the books with any degree of precision; *Never Say Die* (1956) and *Murder Doll* (1959) may also be PI titles.
Forbes: Dressed To Kill (1954)
Guard: Maid For Murder (1955)

Pace, Jake & Hildy — GOULART, Ron
PACHTER, Josh
Author of a short story in **A2** #3, "The Milky Way," about two PIs, **Jack Farmer** and **Jet Schilders**, one American, one Dutch, operating in Amsterdam. Pachter plans to feature the pair in a forthcoming novel, *Dutch T(h)reat*. Pachter also co-authored an **Alo Nudger** short story, "DDS 10752 Libra" with **John LUTZ (A17)**.

Packard, Jack — Radio: I LOVE A MYSTERY
PADGETT, Lewis (Henry Kuttner 1914-1958)
Kuttner hit a rather false note with his PI, **Seth Colman**, who owns a successful detective agency and makes good money but is, we are asked to

believe, reluctant to pry into other people's secrets unless persuaded by his wife **Eve**. Boucher, who called *The Brass Ring* an excellent psychology-cum-action whodunit with some shrewd commentaries on other husband and wife detecting teams, said "the top man in science fiction threatens in this debut to take over the mystery field with equal success."

The Brass Ring (1946, UK 1947); as Murder In Brass (1947)

PAGE, Marco (Harry Kurnitz 1907-1968)

Bruce Taylor (P&M) consigns the Page books into "more or less deserved obscurity," but Guy M. Townsend (Reilly) praises "remarkably adroit use of sprightly and highly amusing dialogue and . . . selection of gripping situations with convincing backdrops." Lawyer **Dave Calder** found he didn't enjoy either civil law or criminal and got a New York PI's license through Fidelity Casualty Insurance, by whom he's retained, after helping them with a loss.

The Shadowy Third (1946); as Suspects All (UK 1948)

PAGE, Norvell 1904-1961

As Grant Stockbridge, Page was the best and best known of the Richard Wentworth, aka the Spider, writers. A pulp story, "Satan's Hoof" (*Ten Detective Aces* 1933; A18), under his own name featured long, lean impatient **Ken Carter**, who had once been a professional juggler.

PAGE, Stanley Hart

Even the normally docile pre-Anthony Boucher *NYT* mystery reviewer found PI **Christopher Hand** hard to take, complaining of his Sphinx-like habit of keeping all the real clues to himself while letting everybody else in the book, and the reader, get by on ill-fitting false clues.

Sinister Cargo (1932, UK 1933)

The Resurrection Murder Case (1932, UK 1933)

Murder Flies The Atlantic (1933)

Fool's Gold (1933, UK 1934)

Tragic Curtain (1935)

Paget, Steve — STOKES, Manning Lee

Paige, Henry — STODGHILL, Dick

Paine, Jack — SARRANTONIO, Al

PAIRO, Preston III

An ex-PI, who left the business because there was too much danger and too little money and does better as a Palm Beach gigolo, **Sam Hawkins** is hired by a strange woman in a wheelchair to find her uncle in Antigua.

Razor Moon (1988)

Paladin — TV: HAVE GUN, WILL TRAVEL

Palladino, Nick — ROBINSON, Abby

PALMER, M. Earle
Operating in Gulfport on the Mississippi Gulf Coast, **Wayne Temple**
averages an instant seduction every chapter in a softporn novel in which
all the women have football (sic) sized breasts. Unlisted in Hubin.
>   Southern Exposure (1967)

PALMER, Stuart 1905-1968
The creator of the comic Hildegarde Withers novels also wrote two about
overweight, middle-aged, misogynist ex-journalist **Howie Rook**, a
Larrabee Street, West Hollywood, PI with a penchant for quotations.
Palmer, who at one time worked as an investigator for LA defense
lawyers, was once a clown with Barnum & Bailey's circus and draws on
that experience in the first Rook story.
>   Unhappy Hooligan (1956); as Death In Grease Paint (UK 1956)
>   Rook Takes Knight (1968)

PANSHIN, Alexei
Leisurely and elliptical investigators **Anthony Villiers**, Viscount
Charteris, and **Torve the Trog**, member of a Restricted Sentient species
barred from the Galactic Empire due to strange, unpredictable behaviour,
travel against a backdrop of massive bureaucracy, strange local customs,
galactic criminality and aristocratic wealth. A fourth book, *The Universal
Pantograph*, was announced but may not have been published.
>   Star Well (1968)
>   The Thurb Revolution (1968)
>   Masque World (1969)

Panzer, Saul — STOUT, Rex

PARADIS, Vincent
Jock PI-lawyer-special agent **Theodore 'Tut' Claw**, ex-boxer, wrestler,
baseball pitcher, Green Beret and karate teacher, is in two poorish books.
>   The Cocaine Caper (1978)
>   The Castilian Caper (1978)

PARETSKY, Sara
In the front rank of female and Chicago PIs, **V.I. Warshawski** allows
only a colleague of her dead policeman father, to call her Vicki, her friends
calling her Vic (her full name is Victoria Iphigenia). Polish on her father's
side, Italian-Jewish on her mother's, she worked as an attorney for the
Cook County public defender's office before taking out her PI license. Her
office is in the Loop in the Pulteney Building, Monroe & Wabash, and
she specializes in financial cases. A feminist, but not a radical one, she's
firmly independent, divorced from a lawyer who couldn't accept her as she
was. Skilled with firearms and at street fighting, she's not omnipotent and

takes several beatings. A tough and credible heroine in carefully researched and grippingly told stories set against various Chicago backgrounds—union pension funds, Great Lakes shipping, the Catholic Church and private medicine. Warshawski short stories are "Skin Deep" (A1 #8; also in Pronzini & Greenberg, eds.; *Homicidal Acts*, 1989), "Three-Dot Po" (A15) and "At The Old Swimming Hole" (A16). Paretsky has a **Philip Marlowe** short story, "Dealer's Choice," in A12.

> Indemnity Only (1982, UK 1982)
> Deadlock* (1984, UK 1984)
> Killing Orders (1985, UK 1986)
> Bitter Medicine (1987, UK 1987)
> Blood Shot (1988); as Toxic Shock (UK 1988)

Paris, Evan — LOUIS, Joseph
PARK, Owen
The only known Eurasian (father Chinese, mother White Russian) PI is **Tommy Lee**. After service in the Army Counter-Intelligence Corps in Vietnam, he worked under contract for the Defense Intelligence Agency and laid the foundations for East-West Investigations, based in San Francisco with offices in Hong Kong, Saigon, Manila, Bangkok, Singapore, Tokyo, Taiwan, Seoul, Vancouver and New York. At thirty, he's making well over $100,000 a year. The writing is average but the book is interesting on Sino-America and Chinese gangs.

> The Chinatown Connection (1977)

PARKER, Percy Spurlark
One of the few black writers of PI fiction who, unlike John B. WEST, created a black PI. **Big Bull Benson** owns a Chicago hotel and bar, which he won in a poker game, and works part time as a PI. A good mystery and a tough, tense and realistic picture of black urban America.

> Good Girls Don't Get Murdered* (1974)

PARKER, Robert B(rown)
Some people consider ultramacho Boston PI **Spenser** the successor to Marlowe and Archer, praising Spenser's developing relationship with Susan Silverman, the dialogue and moral code. Others, with Pronzini, find the books "underplotted, pretentiously literary, talky, excessively (and sometimes gratuitously) violent, fundamentally immoral . . . Spenser an overbearing tough with psychotic tendencies." Spenser is, undeniably, physically competent, and does manage, despite a professed aversion to violence, to kill and beat up a lot of people. Part weight-lifting jock, part gourmet, his aims in life are honor and autonomy. Another criticism is of series character Hawk, a black enforcer, but the Hawk/Spenser double act

has great moments. Beyond all praise and criticism, the Spenser books are pretty good reads. *Promised Land* won a Best Novel Edgar, not as undeservedly as Pronzini feels, and Spenser must be the only PI with his own fan club, The Judas Goats. See **TV: SPENCER; FOR HIRE.**

>   The Godwulf Manuscript (1973, UK 1974)
>   God Save The Child (1974, UK 1975)
>   Mortal Stakes (1975, UK 1976)
>   Promised Land* (1976, UK 1977)
>   The Judas Goat (1978, UK 1982)
>   Looking For Rachel Wallace (1980, UK 1982)
>   A Savage Place (1981, UK 1982)
>   Early Autumn (1981, UK 1985)
>   Ceremony (1982, UK 1983)
>   The Widening Gyre* (1983, UK
>   Valediction (1984, UK 1985)
>   A Catskill Eagle (1985, UK 1986)
>   Taming A Sea Horse (1986, UK 1987)
>   Pale Kings And Princes (1987, UK 1988)
>   Crimson Joy (1988)
>   Playmates (1989)

Parmalee, Bill — WILDE, Percival
PARMER, Charles
Parmer's only novel, featuring Kentucky State Racing Commission investigator **Major Roderick Austen**, was interesting in characters and atmosphere when it stayed in its original setting but weakened whenever it wandered away.

>   Murder At The Kentucky Derby (1942)

Parnell — GORMAN, Edward
Parnell, Tim — SMITH, Don
Patch, Bryce — BALLINGER, Bill S.
PAYNE, Laurence
Film stuntman, extra and then star Mark Sutherland gave up acting after a serious car crash, his actress wife's desertion and a bout of alcoholism. Reborn as **Mark Savage**, he runs a PI agency with an office near St. Paul's Cathedral, London, lives in Wimbledon, rides a motorcycle and still gets half-recognized. Payne has a penchant for whimsical dialogue and set piece encounters.

>   Take The Money And Run (UK 1982, 1984)
>   Malice In Camera (UK 1983, 1985)
>   Dead For A Ducat (UK 1985, 1986)

Vienna Blood (UK 1984, 1986)
Late Knight (UK 1987)

PECK, (Lady) Winifred 1882-1962

Involved in clan doings near Edinburgh, Scotland, private detective **Bob Stuart**, as *NYT* complained, learns the truth by heeding a hunch. *SR* thought it "best for its atmosphere. Better written and characterized than most," while *The Spectator* lauded it as "A perfect piece of detection. The whole episode, ghoulish as it may be, seems a genuine event."

The Warrielaw Jewel (UK 1933, 1933)

Peckinpaugh, Lou — GROSSBACH, Robert

PEEBLES, Nile

Two effectively authentic stories about aging New York PI **Ross McKellar** of whom Anthony Boucher remarked , "The publisher's blurb calls (him) hard-nosed but he comes across as far more human and introspective than that designation suggests . . . astute observation and graphic descriptions of New York . . . writes with humor and perception."

See The Red Blood Run (1968)
Blood Brother, Blood Brother (1969)

Peel, Joe — GRUBER, Frank / BOSTON, Charles K.

PENDLETON, Don

From the creator of The Executioner series comes PI **Ashton Ford**, genius, ex-Naval Intelligence officer, of independent means, good with his hands and guns and psychic. As *Drood Review* remarked, "pretty impressive credentials," adding, "Pendleton can't seem to make up his mind whether he's writing adventure or science fiction . . . a series to watch, cautiously, for the future." Also new is **Joe Copp**, an ex-policeman who boasts of a (much-needed) "neutral stomach," in violent, glossy LA, San Francisco and Hawaii capers. Both seem intended to show that Pendleton can create heroes who use their minds instead of just killing everything in sight. Still ultra-macho and superficial.

Ford: Eye To Eye (1986)
Ashes To Ashes (1986)
Mind To Mind (1987)
Life To Life (1987)
Heart To Heart (1988)
Copp: Copp For Hire (1987)
Copp On Fire (1988)

PENDOWER, Jacques 1899-1976

Prolific British author of undemanding books in any prevailing fashion. **Slade McGinty** works for the Karton Agency, mainly abroad, becoming virtually a secret agent. Not above faking or suppressing evidence, he is a very attractive 6'2" of bone and muscle with "a devil-may-care gleam in his large, bold eyes."

> The Perfect Wife (UK 1962)
> Operation Carlo (UK 1963)
> Master Spy (UK 1964)
> Sinister Talent (UK 1964)
> Traitor's Island (UK 1967)

PENFIELD, Cornelia 1892-1938

Five years after an unscrupulous financier's "accidental" death, the people who had been in his Connecticut home at the time are invited back, plus a PI "who has a better nose for liquor than for clues. His exploits supply a goodly part of the comedy in which this book abounds" (*NYT*).

> After The Widow Changed Her Mind (1933)

PEPPE, Frank

Appearing in at least one quite astonishingly inept book is **Steve Bradshaw** of London's Bradshaw Agency. Not listed in Hubin.

> The Riddle In Wax (UK no date)

PERELMAN, S(idney) J. 1904-1979

Two of the great humorist's best pieces were "Somewhere A Roscoe," a hymn of praise to *Spicy Detective* ("they have juxtaposed the steely automatic and the frilly panty and found that it pays off"), and more specifically to Robert Leslie BELLEM's Dan Turner, "the apotheosis of all private detectives," and "Farewell, My Lovely Appetizer," featuring **Mike Noonan**, perhaps the sharpest of all parodies of the hardboiled PI. Both are in *The Most Of S.J. Perelman* (1958).

Perino, Judith — MADDREN, Gerry

Perkins, Ben — KANTNER, Rob

PEROWNE, Barry (Philip Atkey)

Best known for reviving E.W. Hornung's A.J. Raffles, Atkey first wrote about PI **J.R. 'Rick' Leroy** and used him in neo-Raffles books. *They Hang Them In Gibraltar* appeared in Britain as *Raffles' Crime In Gibraltar* with Sexton Blake as the detective. *NYT* said of *I'm No Murderer*, "so many diverse elements come into it that the official police are content to leave it all to Leroy and take their orders from him . . . The not-too-critical reader will probably enjoy it."

> Arrest These Men! (UK 1932)
> I'm No Murderer (UK 1938, 1939)
> They Hang Them In Gibraltar (1939)
> Raffles And The Key Man (1940)

Perrin, Christopher — WAYE, Cecil
Perry, Nat — JACOBSON, Edith & Ejler
PERRY, Ritchie
The British thriller writer manages his usual quota of suspense as London
PI **Frank MacAllister** tracks down a case in Rio de Janiero.
>   Presumed Dead (1987)
Peters, Anna — LAW, Janice
PETERS, Bill (William P. McGivern 1922-1982)
McGivern's pseudonymous PI novel was roughly handled by Boucher,
who allowed the simplicity, brevity and fast tempo but found it "a
museum of banalities" with a Philadelphia PI, **Bill Canilli**, who "out-
Hammers Hammer, literally praying for opportunities to kill his enemies
before they can be arrested."
>   Blondes Die Young (1952, UK 1956)
PETERS, Ellis (Edith Pargeter)
Best known for her medieval Brother Cadfael mysteries, one of Pargeter's
series about policeman George Felse and his family is centred round a PI,
Francis Killian, hired by a beautiful, famous singer who is convinced
that she caused a man's death. While he searches for her real or imagined
victim, romance blossoms.
>   The House Of Green Turf (UK 1969, 1969)
Peters, Joe — Films: ROADBLOCK
PETERS, Ludovic (Peter Brent)
Former Inspector and Sergeant of the British Colonial Police in Africa,
Ian Firth and **John Smith**, partners in a struggling London detective
agency, spend much of their time on espionage cases together with
American **Godwin Stamberger**, either in unnamed communist
countries run by sadists and buffoons or in Capri, San Francisco or The
Riviera. Boucher admired Peters' novels for no very obvious reason.
>   A Snatch Of Music (UK 1962, 1962)
>   Tarakian (UK 1963, 1963)
>   Two Sets To Murder (UK 1963, 1964)
>   Out By The River (UK 1964, 1965)
>   Two After Malice (UK 1965, 1966)
>   Riot '71 (UK 1967, 1967)
Peters, Maggie — TV: The INVESTIGATORS
Peters, Toby — KAMINSKY, Stuart
Phelan, John J. — DUFF, James
PHILBRICK, W.R.
Karol Kay Hope (P&M) rates New Hampshire based Philbrick as one of

the few men who can write a believable modern female detective. **Connie Kale** returns to her small New England hometown after failing to make it on the women's pro golf circuit, and sets up as a PI, valued both for her knowledge of the community and absolute discretion. Philbrick turned to a male hero with wheel chair-bound Boston ex-cop **J.D. Hawkins** who writes mystery novels as well as sleuthing, drawing good reviews for characterization, suspense and atmosphere. He also writes about **T.D. Stash**, a down-market Travis McGee, living further south, on Key West, Florida, where he's a wharf rat who works erratically as a fishing guide and more so as an unlicensed investigator. Philbrick contributed a **Philip Marlowe** short story, "The Empty Sleeve," to **A12**.

Kale: Slow Dancer* (1984, UK 1986)
Hawkins: Shadow Kills (1985); possibly as Slow Grave (UK 1986)
           Ice For The Eskimo (1986)
Stash: The Neon Flamingo (1987)
           The Crystal Blue Persuasion (1988)
           Tough Enough (1988)

PHILIPS, Judson
Better known as Hugh Pentecost, two of Philips' earliest books featured lovely, clever **Carole Trevor** of the Old Town Detective Agency, given to her by her rich man about town, amateur sleuth ex-husband Maxwell Bythe who assists her. *SR* described the first book as "A-1 thriller."

        The Death Syndicate (1938, UK 1939)
        Death Delivers A Postcard (1939, UK 1940)

Phillips, Nathan — O'DONOHOE, Nick
PHILLIPS, R.B.
A "part time everything," actor, pianist, surfer and unlicensed LA PI, **Elton Dancey** errs classically in sleeping with a woman who has more problems than he does. Sharp writing, an interesting, funny hero but a ludicrous climax.

        Gun Play (1987)

Pierce, Jim — RING, Adam
Pike, Daniel — KNOX, Bill & Edward BOYD
Pinata, Steve — MILLAR, Margaret
Pincus, Sidney — ROSTEN, Leo
Pine, Paul — BROWNE, Howard / EVANS, John
Pink, Norman — McSHANE, Mark
PIPER, H(enry) Beam 1904-1964
A disciple of Count Korzybski, claiming to apply General Semantics to detection, licensed PI **Colonel Jefferson Davis Rand** is also an

expert on antique pistols and revolvers and the one case is most notable
for its acute grasp of collector psychology.

> Murder In The Gunroom (1953)

Piper, Peter — CARMICHAEL, Harry
Pirex, Eliza — McRAE, Diana
Piron, Jim — McGIRR, Edmund
Pizzatello, Duke — BELLEM, Robert Leslie
PLATT, Kin
Ex-Army CID officer and karate expert **Max Roper** works for EPT in
Santa Monica (the initials mean anything you want). He specialized, after
the first two books, in sports cases (horseracing, basketball, women's pro
tennis, bodybuilding/weightlifting, baseball), the different jargons and
ambiences well sustained. The books are curiously old-fashioned in tone,
the plots uneven. See **Kirby CARR**.

> The Pushbutton Butterfly (1970, UK 1971)
> The Kissing Gourami (1970, UK 1973)
> The Princess Stakes Murder (1973, UK 1977); as A Pride Of
> Women (UK 1974)
> The Giant Kill (1974, UK 1975)
> Match Point For Murder (1975)
> The Body Beautiful Murder (1975)
> The Screwball King Murder (1978)

Pletcher, Jay — BIGGLE, Lloyd Jr.
PLUM, Mary
Murder At The World's Fair finds detective **John Smith** employed to
protect the interests of a man involved in a killing at the Chicago Century
Of Progress Exposition. The novels were set variously in Chicago,
Illinois and Michigan. >

> The Killing Of Judge McFarlane (1930, UK 1930)
> Dead Man's Secret (1931, UK 1931)
> Murder At The Hunting Club (1932, UK 1932)
> Murder At The World's Fair (1933); as The Broken Vase Mystery
> (UK 1933)

Po, Henry — RANDISI, Robert J.
Polo, Nick — KENEALLY, Jerry
Pomeroy, Grace — WELLS, Anna Mary
Pope, Jake — THOMAS, Ross
POPKIN, Zelda 1898-1983
Though former hotel and agency detective **Mary Carner** works for
Blanchard's, a New York department store, and is married to her

supervisor, only the first of her cases is work-related, the others putting her in the unpaid, involved by chance, amateur class. Klein admires the books particularly for the husband's supportive role, treating Carner with personal and professional respect, a reversal of normal genre practice. He even minds their house and child while she's out on a case.

> Death Wears A White Gardenia (1938, UK 1939)
> Time Off For Murder (1940, UK 1940)
> Murder In The Mist (1940, UK 1941)
> Dead Man's Gift (1941, UK 1948)
> No Crime For A Lady (1942)

Poteet, Ralph — ESTLEMAN, Loren D.
POTTER, Jerry Allen
Ex-Marine and PoW **Samuel Clemens Tucker** came back from Vietnam minus his left foot and left testicle, which effectively ended his career as a golf pro. Assisted by his ex-Army psychiatrist wife Trudy and black Dallas Cowboys football player and former Marine Nicki Hill, he sets up as a Carmel, California PI. Well crafted, reasonable plots and some rather forced witty dialogue.

> A Talent For Dying (1980)
> If I Should Die Before I Wake (1981)

POWELL, Talmage
The agent in charge of the Southeastern Office of Nationwide Detective Agency in Tampa, Florida is former Jersey cop **Ed Rivers**, early 40s, living alone in Ybor City, the Cuban barrio, with distinctive looks, "women either get a charge from the face or want to run from it. Men fear it or trust it to the hilt." Equally competent with a .38 and the sheath-knife he carries round his neck, Rivers is tough but human, a man with feelings and problems and a memorable character. The plotting, suspense and characterization is excellent and Tampa well-evoked, especially in *Corpus Delectable*, set in the annual Mardi Gras celebrations.

> The Killer Is Mine (1959)
> The Girl's Number Doesn't Answer* (1960)
> With A Madman Behind Me (1962)
> Start Screaming Murder (1962)
> Corpus Delectable (1964)

Powers, Johnny — RAYTER, Joe
PRATHER, Richard S.
His Hamilton Building, Broadway, LA agency is called Sheldon Scott Investigations, but the 6'2", 205 pound, crew-cut white haired ex-Marine is always known as **Shell Scott**. In his over 35 year career he has

"handled half the crimes listed in the California Penal Code including 578 PC (issuing fictitious warehouse receipts) and 653 PC (tattooing of a minor)." Starting as a Spillane style writer, albeit with a light touch, Prather turned, with *Strip For Murder*, to a combination of hardboiled and knockabout farce. Scott is permanently addled, either from lusting after one of the plentiful supply of voluptuous babes in his books, from drink or from being sapped. Despite any shortcomings of plot, dialogue or writing, Prather's comic vitality made the Scott books the most popular of their kind ever and the PWA gave him one of their Lifetime Achievement awards. Shell Scott short stories, "The Guilty Party" and "Dead Giveaway" (also in *Three's A Shroud*) are in **A10** and **A14**. Prather also wrote one book about ex-GI **Mark Logan** who also works out of LA, with a Farnsworth Building, Spring Street office.

Scott: Case Of The Vanishing Beauty (1950, UK 1957)
  Bodies In Bedlam (1951, UK 1957)
  Everybody Had A Gun (1951, UK 1959)
  Find This Woman (1951, UK 1957)
  Way Of A Wanton (1952, UK 1958)
  Darling, It's Death (1952, UK 1957)
  Ride A High Horse (1953); as Too Many Crooks (1956, UK 1957)
  Always Leave 'Em Dying (1954, UK 1957)
  Strip For Murder* (1955, UK 1957)
  The Wailing Frail (1956, UK 1957)
  Have Gat—Will Travel (1957, UK 1958) SS
  Three's A Shroud (1957, UK 1973). Three novelets
  Slab Happy (1958)
  Take A Murder, Darling (1958, UK 1961)
  The Scrambled Yeggs (1958, UK 1961); as Pattern For Murder (as by **David KNIGHT** 1952)
  Over Her Dead Body (1959, UK 1960)
  Double In Trouble (1959). With **Stephen MARLOWE** featuring **Chester Drum**.
  Dance With The Dead (1960, UK 1962)
  Dig That Crazy Grave (1961, UK 1962)
  Shell Scott's Seven Slaughters (1961, UK 1962) SS
  Pattern For Panic (revised ed 1961, UK 1962). Published 1954 without Scott.
  Kill The Clown (1962, UK 1963)
  Dead Heat (1963)

Joker In The Deck (1964, UK 1965)
The Cockeyed Corpse* (1964)
The Trojan Hearse (1964, UK 1967)
Kill Him Twice (1965)
Dead Man's Walk (1965, UK 1968)
The Meandering Corpse (1965, UK 1967)
The Kubla Khan Caper (1966)
Gat Heat* (1967, UK 1968)
The Cheim Manuscript (1969)
Kill Me Tomorrow (1969)
The Shell Scott Sampler (1969). SS
Shell Scott's Murder Mix (1970). Omnibus
Dead-Bang (1971)
The Sweet Ride (1972)
The Sure Thing (1975)
The Amber Effect (1986)
Shellshock (1987)

Logan: Dagger Of Flesh (1952, UK 1961)

PREISS, Byron (ed) — see **ANTHOLOGIES: 11**
Prentice, Louis — **Films: RUNAROUND**
Preston, Johnny — **CHESTER, Peter**
Preston, Mark — **CHAMBERS, Peter**
Pride, Duncan — **FRAZER, Andrew**
Primrose, Colonel John T — **FORD, Leslie**
Prince, Hank — **WILLIAMS, Philip Lee**
Pringle, G.D.H. — **LIVINGSTON, Nancy**
Prior, Jeff & Lloyd — **TV: The INVESTIGATOR**
Proctor, Chad — **ROBERTS, Lee**
PRONZINI, Bill

When Pronzini's "biography of a detective" opens, the Everyman hero, whose name is never revealed and is usually referred to, though not by the author, as **'Nameless'** or the **Nameless Detective**, is 47. A San Francisco policeman for 15 years, he's Italian, large and a compulsive reader and collector of pulp magazines, owning some 6,500 30s and 40s titles. Deriving initially from The Continental Op and Thomas B Dewey's Mac, with some plots elements taken from Ross Macdonald, the series has a strong continuity, especially in the PI's fear of cancer and his relationship, versatile plots and a realism derived from the hero's sheer ordinariness. He's not a smart-aleck, rarely breaks the law, doesn't own a gun, and worries about his waistline, his health, his finances and his love life. His office is on Drumm Street. *Hoodwink* won a PWA Best Novel award. Pronzini has also written a historical PI novel as **Jack FOXX**, introduced a new San Francisco PI, **Thaddeus 'Bonecrack' Krajewski**, former Raiders football player, in a short story, "Smart Guys Don't Snore" (**A2** #2) and written many 'Nameless' stories, among them "Skeleton Rattle Your Mouldy Leg" (**A14** and **A15**), "Ace In The Hole" (**A16**) and "Incident In A Neighborhood Tavern," (**A17**). See also **A13** and **A14** for edited and co-edited anthologies.

>The Snatch (1971, UK 1974)
>The Vanished (1973, UK 1974)
>Undercurrent* (1973, UK 1975)
>Blowback (1977, UK 1978)
>Twospot (1978). With **Collin WILCOX**
>Labyrinth (1980, UK 1981)
>Hoodwink (1981, UK 1981)
>Scattershot (1982, UK 1982)
>Dragonfire (1982, UK 1983)
>Bindlestiff (1983, UK 1984)
>Casefile; The Best Of The 'Nameless Detective' Stories (1983)
>Cat's Paw (1983). Limited edition.
>Quicksilver* (1984, UK 1985)
>Nightshades (1984, UK 1986)
>Double (1984). With **Marcia MULLER** featuring **Sharon McCone**
>Bones (1985)
>Graveyard Plots (1985). SS, 3 featuring 'Nameless'
>Deadfall (1986)
>Shackles (1988)

Prophet, Jason — MORROW, J.T.
Prospero, William — Films: DETECTIVE
Puma, Joe — GAULT, William Campbell / SCOTT, Roney
Purdue, Chance — SPENCER, Ross H.
PURDY, Claire Lee — see WHEELER, Benson & PURDY
Quade, Marty — TEPPERMAN, Emile C.
Quarles, Francis — SYMONS, Julian
QUARRY, Nick = ALBERT, Marvin
With an office on New York's Times Square, **Jake Barrow** is right in the thick of things, and tends to be up to his ears in tough action. Albert's New York is an unromantic place where a PI can derive little satisfaction even from a successful case, knowing that villainy will be back to normal

almost immediately. Well paced, crisply told puzzle plots.

> Trail Of A Tramp (1958, UK 1960)
> The Hoods Come Calling* (1958, UK 1959)
> The Girl With No Place To Hide (1959, UK 1961)
> No Chance In Hell (1960, UK 1962)
> Till It Hurts (1960, UK 1962)
> Some Die Hard (1961, UK 1963)

QUARTERMAIN, James = LYNNE, James Broome
Hubin described the first book as "a steaming portrayal of a drug-driven, murder-minded search for vengeance," featuring British private detective **Corbo** who most commonly sells his soul to an agency. He's security officer for a diamond trading house in the second book which *NYT* admired but offered as a jumping off point for a PhD thesis on private eyes getting hit over the head.

> The Diamond Hook (UK 1970, 1970)
> The Man Who Walked On Diamonds (UK 1971, 1972)
> Rock Of Diamonds (UK 1972, 1972)
> The Diamond Hostage (UK 1975)

Quayle, Hilary — KAYE, Marvin
QUEEN, Ellery (Frederic Dannay 1905-82 & Manfred B. Lee 1905-71) The famous team had their hero, mystery writer and semi-amateur assistant to his New York policeman father **Ellery Queen**, set up shop, much to his own surprise, as Ellery Queen, Inc., Confidential Investigations, Times Square, in partnership with another policeman's son, **Beau Rummell**, in one novel But the second Queen period, following the pure deductions of 1929-35, is often very PI-like. Pocket Books refer to him as a Private Eye on the cover of *The Devil To Pay*, Pronzini & Muller label him a Classic Sleuth, Baker & Nietzel ignore him completely. Two professional PIs, **Barney Burgess**, a tough Chicago sleuth who models himself on Humphrey Bogart, and **Micah 'Mike' McCall**, troubleshooter for a Governor, also of Chicago, appeared in ghost-written books under the Queen byline. Baker & Nietzel think highly of the Burgess book.

Queen: The Dragon's Teeth (1939, UK 1939); as The Virgin
            Heiresses (1954)
Burgess: Kiss And Kill (1969)
McCall: The Campus Murders (1969)
            The Black Hearts Murder (1970) by **Richard DEMING**.
            The Blue Movie Murders (1972, UK 1973) by **Edward D HOCH**

Quentin, Roger — TV: ROGER & HARRY
Quest, Peter — KOBLER, John
Quill, Peter — Radio: PETER QUILL
Quince, Dion — WELCH, Timothy / CAKE, Patrick
Quinlan, Charlie — SOLOMON, Brad
Quinn, Joe — MILLAR, Margaret
QUINN, E(leanor) Baker
British author of two, possibly three (*The Dead Harm No One* UK 1938)
books featuring PI **James Strange**, the second, in which Strange gets
involved with the cracked inhabitants of a nursing home and their equally
demented minders, described by *NYT* as "one of the craziest crime
problems we have encountered."
        One Man's Muddle (UK 1936, 1937)
        Death Is A Restless Sleeper (UK 1940, 1941)
QUINN, Patrick
Five British novels featuring **Pete Riley** I can discover nothing about.
        Once Upon A Private Eye (UK 1968)
        Twice Upon A Crime (UK 1969)
        Thrice Upon A Killing Spree (UK 1970)
        The Fatal Complaint (UK 1970)
        The Big Game (UK 1970)
Quint, Hugh — SHERMAN, Steve
Quist, Gregory — MACDONALD, William Colt
Raeburn, Mark — GAIR, Malcolm
Rafferty — DUNCAN, W. Glenn
Rafferty, Neal — WILTZ, Chris
Raffigan, Pat — WHITTINGTON, Harry
Rainier, Bob — McGREGOR, Don & Gene COLAN
Raleigh, Corey — GAULT, William Campbell
RALSTON, Gilbert
Part Shoshone, part Piegan Indian **Dakota** is a licensed Nevada PI,
operating from the Dakota Ranch, Jacks Valley Road, Carson Valley, in a
linked series of poorly written books that fail even to take advantage of
the basic premises.
        Dakota Warpath (1973)
        Red Revenge (1974)
        Cat Trap (1974)
        Murder's Money (1975)
        Chain Reaction (1975)
Ramsay, Oscar — TV: The DUKE

Ramsey, Deuce — MANDELKAU, Jamie
Rand, Colonel Jefferson Davis — PIPER, H. Beam
RAND, Lou (Lou Rand Hogan)
I'm assured that **Francis Morley** is a gay PI but cannot confirm this.
    The Gay Detective (1961); as Rough Trade (1965)
Randall, Jeff — TV: MY PARTNER THE GHOST
Randall, Steve — TV: STEVE RANDALL
RANDISI, Robert J.
A co-founder of the PWA and editor of its three anthologies (A15, A16 & A17), Randisi has written some 50 books, mostly Westerns, but also PI novels with three different leading characters. **Henry Po**, special investigator for the New York State Racing Club, steady work after his one man agency, is a good looking fellow who does well with the ladies around his horse racing based story. **Miles Jacoby**, professional middleweight boxer, starts as part time assistant to a New York PI, taking over the agency when he's killed, operating out of the back of Bogie's, a New York bar much favored by the MWA. The second book revolves round the theft of a priceless collection of pulp literature and is full of PI in-jokes and cameo appearances. Jacoby featured in a short story, "Deathlist" (A15), Po in "The Equine Theft" (*Hardboiled* 1985; A5) and "The Nickel Derby" (A14), while Randisi's latest PI, **Nick Delvecchio**, another New Yorker, also appeared in two short stories, "A Matter Of Ethics" (A4) and "The Vanishing Virgin" (A17). Randisi has a **Philip Marlowe** short story, "Locker 246," in A12.
Po: The Disappearance Of Penny (1980)
Jacoby: Eye In The Ring (1982)
          The Steinway Collection (1983)
          Full Contact* (1984, UK 1986)
Delvecchio: No Exit From Brooklyn (1987)
Randolph, Rex — TV: BOURBON STREET BEAT
Rankin, John — GRADY, James
Ransom, Glen — WARREN, Vernon
Ransom, Lamaar — GALLOWAY, David
RANSOME, Stephen = DAVIS, Frederick C.
Much of Davis' work, notably the **Schyler Cole/Luke Speake** novels, was published in the UK as by Stephen Ransome, a name he used in America for non-series work and regularly after 1961. One novel featured the first hardboiled female PI, **Jill Archer**, who pretends to be secretary to Captain Wallace, nominal head of Secrets, Inc., which she actually owns, because she feels no one would entrust an important case

to a young woman, an idea already used by Theodore TINSLEY in his Carrie Cashin stories. A Lt. Lee Barcello story revolves round the killing of a Palmport, Florida (Gulf Coast) PI called **Carl Connor.**

Archer: A Shroud For Shylock (1939)
Connor: The Sin File (1965, UK 1966)
Cole: The Deadly Miss Ashley (UK 1950; as by **DAVIS** 1950)
          Lilies In Her Garden Grew (UK 1951; as by **DAVIS** 1951)
          Tread Lightly, Angel (UK 1952; as by **DAVIS** 1952)
          Drag The Dark (UK 1954; as by **DAVIS** 1953)
          Another Morgue Heard From (UK 1955); as Deadly Bedfellows
              (as by **DAVIS** 1954)
          Night Drop (UK 1956; as by **DAVIS** UK 1955)

Ranzino, Matt — LACY, Ed
Raven, Max — BENSON, O.G.
Raven, Schlomo — SUTTON, Tom & Byron PREISS
RAY, Robert J.
Austin, Texas, Vietnam vet **Clayton Yankee Taggert**'s one appearance is described by Baker & Nietzel as "an uneven amalgam of Ludlum, LeCarre, Ross Macdonald and Louis L'Amour—very good at times, very bad at others." **Matt Murdock** lives over Wally's Surf Shop in Newport Beach, California. T. Jefferson Parker found the first book "witty, sly and sneaky-fast . . . Murdock is a West Coast Travis McGee," while *Drood Review* found them neatly done and stylish, while pointing out that they read like California PI books written by an English professor, as indeed they are.

Taggert: Cage Of Mirrors (1980)
Murdock: Murdock For Hire (1987)
           Bloody Murdock (1987)
           Dial 'M' For Murdock (1988)

RAYTER, Joe (Mary F. McChesney)
Dorothy B. Hughes thought highly of Kearny Street, San Francisco PI **Johnny Powers**, not without reason. Sick of divorce work, Powers is thinking of talking his way into the warehouseman's union and making an honest living. Rather slow moving, with a great deal of detail and day to day incidentals, McChesney does a solid job with very little violence and no sex but patient detective work.

           The Victim Was Important (1954, UK 1954)
           Asking For Trouble (1955, UK 1957)

Reach, Johnny — TV: BEARCATS!

REAMY, Tom
Though Reamy wrote only one novel and a few short stories before his untimely death, on the strength of one of the stories, "The Detweiler Boy" (*Fantasy & Science Fiction* 1977), featuring hardboiled Hollywood PI **Bert Mallory**, he may well have been as great a loss to PI fiction as to SF in which he was a fast rising star. His mastery of the classic style, with no hint of parody or superciliousness, was complete.

San Diego Lightfoot Sue & Other Stories (1979)

Reardon, Rigby — Films: DEAD MEN DON'T WEAR PLAID

REASONER, James
The one poorly distributed novel featuring Fort Worth PI **Cody** has achieved cult status in the field and it will, apparently, be reissued in 1989. With a Lew Archer style premise, Reasoner, who wrote many 70s novelets for *Mike Shayne's Mystery Magazine*, plays new variations on a theme even Macdonald wore down. A well-educated man and connoisseur of Western art, his office decorated with Frederick Remington and Charlie Russell prints, Cody disdains Texan hyperbole, though he does wear boots and a denim jacket. Cody short stories are "The Safest Place In the World" (**A17**) and "In The Blood" (**A2 #3**). "Death And The Dancing Shadows," (**A4**) features Los Angeles PI **Markham**. Reasoner's wife Livia writes under the name **L.J. WASHBURN**.

Texas Wind (1980)

REAVES, Michael J.
"I'm not as casual about killing as are most people on my world; after all, a private eye should have a basic moral code." **Kamus of Khadizar**'s world is Ja-Lur, the Darkworld, where science and sorcery struggle for supremacy and Kamus, half-earthling, half-darkling, is the only PI. Tough, strong, a skilled swordsman, paranoid ("an occupational hazard"), he features in four separate but linked cases, "The Big Spell," "The Maltese Vulcan," "Murder on the Galactic Express" and "The Man with the Golden Raygun." Good entertaining fusion of SF and PI. See **John SHIRLEY**.

Darkworld Detective (1982)

Reber, Matt — CREIGHTON, John

Reddman, Joe — DOWNING, Warwick

REED, Christopher
Unique among hardboiled detectives is **Manx McCatty**, a San Francisco feline PI who prowls the foggy waterfronts and seedy alleys in his investigation of the ruthless mysterious criminal organization Gato

Nostra. A finely tuned parody with many good touches.

> The Big Scratch (1988)

REED, Harlan

Even for a PI, he most distinctive thing about **Dan Jordan** is his drinking. *NYT* remarked of the first title (which has nothing to do with the story) "so alcoholic in its content that it might fittingly be sold in barrooms rather than in bookstores . . . Dan Jordan is not merely hard-boiled; he is pickled." In the second, set in Seattle, he thinks being a farmer would interfere with his drinking less than detecting did. *NYT* said of it, "Those who like swing music and hard-boiled detectives will probably enjoy this book."

> The Case Of The Crawling Cockroach (1937)
> The Swing Music Murder (1938)

REED, Ishmael

Out on the far fringes of the genre, and indeed of literature generally, are two "HooDoo detective novels" featuring "extra-mundane Private Eye" **PaPa LaBas**, a Harlem Ju Ju man who sizes up his clients to fit their souls in his Mumbo Jumbo Kathedral "mind haberdashery," and, in the first novel, **Black Herman**, "the noted occultist," who "investigates questions which have long plagued mankind and New Yorkers too" during the Warren Harding administration. Reed was condemned, as the jackets proudly boast, by everybody from *NYT* ("propaganda") to *The Journal of Black Poetry* ("crazy").

> Mumbo Jumbo (1972)
> The Last Days Of Louisiana Red (1974)

Reed, James — SANGSTER, Jimmy

REESE, John

Bill Pronzini highly recommends a Westerns-cum-crime series featuring roving 1880s private detective **Jefferson Hewit**, based in Cheyenne, Wyoming, who travels the West in search of paying commissions for the Bankers' Bonding & Indemnity Co. of which he is a partner. Born in the Missouri Ozarks, he joined the Army at 15, went into the Pinkertons and is an excellent shot, knowledgeable about livestock, a natural portrait artist, can imitate any American regional accent and is an expert masseur.

> Texas Gold (1975)
> Sequoia Shootout (1977)
> Dead Eye (1978)

REEVES, Robert 1912-1945

Before his wartime death, Reeves contributed entertaining and offbeat hardboiled novelets to *Black Mask* and wrote three novels featuring

Cellini Smith. The first, set in New York, where Smith is employed by gangsters, is violent and less amusing than the other two in which he moves to LA to freelance. A rather incompetent screwball with a tendency to drink heavily at inopportune moments, he encounters many other screwballs in bizarre plots laced with wry wit. Boucher called Smith "unique among hardboiled private eyes in being admittedly an intellectual—and tough enough to get away with it."

> Dead And Done For (1939, UK 1940)
> No Love Lost (1941); as Come Out Killing (1953, abridged)
> Cellini Smith: Detective* (1943)

Regan, Jeff — Radio: JEFF REGAN, INVESTIGATOR
Rehm, Jim — HERBER, William
RENEAU, D.
Author of a story in A2 #4, "Overtime," featuring an unnamed PI in what he describes as "the kind of American irony represented by the original *Black Mask*."

Reno, Pete — ROSENBLUM, Robert
Rentadick Inc. — Films: RENTADICK
Renzler, Mark — ENGLEMAN, Paul
Reseck, Tony — CHANDLER, Raymond
RESNICK, Mike
Sitting in his New York office alone on New Year's Eve, drinking the bourbon his ex-partner left behind when he ran away with his wife, **John Justin Mallory** assumes he's hallucinating when an elf walks in and offers him $10,000 to find a lost unicorn. An unusual blend of fantasy and mystery with the mystery losing out, but an entertaining affectionate pastiche.

> Stalking The Unicorn; A Fable Of Tonight (1987, UK 1987)

Resnick, Slots — GELLER, Michael
RESNICOW, Herbert
Retired from engineering after a debilitating heart attack, **Alexander Gold** is a cerebral detective in the Nero Wolfe mode, his wife **Norma** doing the legwork round New York as they take on investigations to help the finances. A charming couple in smart, cheerful romps.

> The Gold Solution (1983, UK 1984)
> The Gold Deadline* (1984, UK 1985)
> The Gold Frame (1984, UK 1986)
> The Gold Curse (1986)
> The Gold Gamble (1988)

Revere, Philip — ISRAEL, Peter

Reves, Chuck — HITCHENS, Bert & Dolores
REYNOLDS, Mack 1917-1983
Boucher described the well-known SF author's first novel as improbable,
but had warm praise for the background, a National Science Fiction
Convention, where a PI, name unknown, investigates a spate of deaths
among SF fans.

> The Case Of The Little Green Men (1951)

REYNOLDS, William J.
Trying to get out of the PI business and be a writer, **Nebraska** finds
himself sucked back in by personal or financial pressures. Living on 45th
& Decatur, Omaha, Nebraska, with a chilling description of winter in the
second book, Nebraska is a sardonic character with all the tough-guy
ingredients, though rather charmingly he finds himself baffled by his
success with two women in the second story. High standard
entertainment.

> The Nebraska Quotient* (1984, UK 1986)
> Moving Targets (1986, UK 1987)
> Money Trouble (1988, UK 1988)

Rhineheart, Michael J. — BIRKETT, John
Rice, Miles Standish — KENDRICK, Baynard
RICHARD, Nat
A black, pint-sized former FBI man, **Otis Dunn** specializes in tracking
down criminals on the Bureau's Most Wanted list.

> Otis Dunn, Manhunter (1974)

Rickey, Jim — Films: PRIVATE DETECTIVE
RIDER, J.W.
While it's unnerving to learn that Frank Sinatra thinks Rider is "a helluva
writer," his debut is reminiscent of Gregory Macdonald or early Parker.
Ex-seminarian and former FBI man **Malone** specializes in homicides or
threats of homicide in Jersey City where a murder is committed every 23
minutes. Asked how he solves them with his attitude, he replies "I wear
them down." An intelligent, wise-cracking type, with some good lines,
also a grieving widower and a guilt-ridden Catholic.

> Jersey Tomatoes (1986)
> Hot Tickets (1988)

RIEFE, Alan
New York PI **Huntingdon Cage** has an identical twin, Hadley, a New
Jersey painter he contacts by secret signal, two tones sent by a specially
designed watch, so he can seem to be in two places at once. Another NYC
(54th & 8th) PI, **Tyger Decker** also has a twin who wants to be a PI

too but ends up a corpse. Baker & Nietzel comment, "pretty thin stuff."

Cage: The Lady Killers (1975, UK 1976)
             The Bullet-Proof Man (1976)
             The Conspirators (1975, UK 1976)
             The Killer With A Golden Touch (1975)
             The Silver Puma (1975)

Decker: Tyger At Bay (1976)

RIFKIN, Shepard

Rifkin wrote a savage, fascinating one-off about New York PI **Joe Dunne**, a very tough character who finds a downhill path of direct action takes him beyond the point of no return. Ferociously well-written with a shattering climax.

        The Murderer Vine (1970, UK 1973)

Riggs, John — TV: MARKHAM

RIGSBY, Howard

Anthony Boucher described San Francisco PI **Timothy Wilde** as sensitive, intelligent and professionally tough in an "unusually good" case.

        Kill And Tell (1951, UK 1954)

RILEY, Dick

Touted as a potential East Coast Ross Macdonald, Riley wrote one novel about New Jersey journalist and former PI **Tom Riordan**. Returned to journalism after his skip-tracer boss suggested that he wasn't suited to the work ("I'd met his wife and wouldn't send my worst enemy back to her"), one of his few successes catches up with him and he's asked to investigate the disappearance of a devout young Catholic girl. The plot relies on coincidences but the provincial newspaper, New Jersey Irish Catholicism, drug culture and characters are well done.

        Rite Of Expiation (1976)

Riley, Pete — QUINN, Patrick

RING, Adam (Blair Reed)

After Baltimore PI **Jim Pierce** finds a dead client outside his office door, "gangsters, hoods, sadistic torturers and fat and sinister emissary of a foreign power all make life tough and terrible for long-suffering sleuth" (*SR*). *NYT*, which lost count of the corpses, remarked, "the story is gory as all get out and that is about all that can be said for it," while the *San Francisco Chronicle* added "little liquor, no luscious ladies, just slug, sap and shoot."

        Killers Play Rough (1946)

RING,Raymond H.
A hardboiled-with-humor novel by an award winning Arizona journalist featuring 50ish loner detective **Henry Dyer**, who lives on a desert ranch and has a decrepit office in a condemned building over a shoeshine shop in downtown Tucson. *Drood Review* found the book self-conscious and formulaic, Dyer the latest post-Travis McGee noble soul, railing against the corruptions and shallowness of modern society, the dénouement fantastic and the epilogue ludicrous.
    Tulluride Smile (1988)

Rio, Johnny — BROWN, Carter
Riordan, Pat — GILLIGAN, Roy
Riordan, Tom — RILEY, Dick
Ripley, Ray — HEYES, Douglas
RITCHIE, Jack (John G. Reitci 1922-1983)
A regular contributor to *Alfred Hitchcock's Mystery Magazine* and others, and often found in anthologies, Reitci's macabre contribution was a vampire PI, **Cardula**, whose Yellow Pages display specifies that he can only be reached during night hours.
    A New Leaf & Other Stories (1971)

RITCHIE, Simon
Drood Review called Ritchie's first novel "flawed with exceptional strengths" but *The Armchair Detective* found it fast-paced, well-structured with a lively, humorous, reflective and resourceful hero. **John Kenneth Galbraith 'Cagey' Jantarro** is a tough, seasoned, one-armed Toronto detective, of Basque origin, who has a love-hate relationship with the law.
    The Hollow Woman (1987)

Rivera, Pablo — ISRAEL, Peter
RIVERA, William L.
One of Pronzini's more modern Bad Writers (*Gun In Cheek*), Rivera's "main attraction" is his own special brand of prose in a novel featuring San Francisco 'Investigative Consultant' **Arthur 'Turo' Bironico**.
    Panic Walks Alone (1976)

Rivers, Ed — POWELL, Talmage
Roach, Sampson — SQUERENT, William
ROBB, T.N.
Novelizations of **TV: PRIVATE EYE** featuring LA sleuth **Jack Cleary** and his James Dean-type assistant **Johnny Betts**. See also **David ELLIOTT** and **Max LOCKHART** for others.
    Private Eye (1988)
    Flip Side (1988)

ROBBINS, Clifton
American reviews of British author Robbins' books about **Clay Harrison** consistently found them both implausible and unexciting, though perhaps the worst blow he received was from the English *Times Literary Supplement*, never a good judge of mystery fiction, which praised his detective above all others because there was "none whose character is more consistently and likeably British." Pshaw!

> Dusty Death (UK 1931, 1932)
> The Man Without A Face (UK 1932); as The Mystery Of Mr. Cross (1933)
> Death On The Highway (UK 1933)
> Smash And Grab (UK 1934, 1934)
> Methylated Murder (UK 1935)

ROBERTS, Garyn G. (ed) — see **ANTHOLOGIES: 7 / 18**
ROBERTS, Lee = MARTIN, Robert
As Roberts, the highly regarded Martin wrote about three different PIs, **Andy Brice**, tired, sad, sympathetic **Lee Fiske** and likable **Chad Proctor**, tough but human. Unfortunately I have been unable to locate any of the titles and am relying entirely on secondary sources.
Brice: Little Sister (1952)
Fiske: The Case Of The Missing Lovers (1957)
Proctor: The Pale Door (1955)
ROBERTS, Les
The winner of the 1st PWA competition for Best First PI Novel introduced **Saxon**, an Easterner transplanted to LA, living in Pacific Palisades, who had some success as an actor but, tired of the rat race, became a PI. A stylish story, with an unlikely motive, revolves round an aging but still virile Spillane-style thriller writer, neatly contrasted with modish Saxon, and his daughter with whom Saxon falls headlong in love. Good characterization and writing running variations on old themes. Ex-military and civilian cop, football player and husband **Milan Jacovich** investigated murder among Cleveland advertising executives.
Saxon: An Infinite Number Of Monkeys (1987, UK 1987)
         Not Enough Horses (1988, UK 1988)
         A Carrot For The Donkey (1989)
Jacovich: Pepper Pike (1988)
Roberts, Mitch — DOLD, Gaylord
ROBERTSON, Colin
Immensely proud of his neon sign, though it doesn't attract much business, **Victor 'Vicky' McBain** of London is a "Specialist

Investigator" (the nature of his specialty never clearly revealed) who relies on contracted business from other agencies, law firms and insurance companies rather than private clients of whom he has a distinct shortage. McBain lingers on in large print reissues for the short-sighted.

> The Tiger's Claws (UK 1951)
> You Can Keep The Corpse (UK 1955)
> Venetian Mask (UK 1956)
> The Eastlake Affair (UK 1957)
> Who Rides A Tiger? (UK 1958)
> The Golden Triangle (UK 1959)
> The Threatening Shadows (UK 1959)
> Murder Sits Pretty (UK 1961)

Robin, George — JEROME, Oscar Fox
Rockford, Jim — TV: The ROCKFORD FILES
ROBINSON, Abby
Out of work NYC photographer and mystery buff Jane Myers jumps at the chance to work for a PI but is put out when **Nick Palladino** turns out to look like Ratso Rizzo in *Midnight Cowboy* in a powder blue polyester leisure suit. She also learns that surveillance and other PI work are mostly boredom. Very funny, erotic, fast, tough and wisecracking. One critic observed, "Don't compare Abby Robinson to anybody. She has invented a furiously funny hardboiled genre all her own."

> The Dick And Jane (1985)

ROBINSON, David
Hubin, in *NYT*, observed that this was "not really the story of a private eye and I am in two minds as to whether it should be reviewed here. It is a probing, if jerky and sometimes snail-paced, study of (**Andrew**) **Clare**, his marital disaster, his liaison with the secretary to the scheming lawyer for whom he works and his gradual realization that he has contributed nothing to the lives he's touched."

> The Confessions Of Andrew Clare (1968)

ROCHE, Arthur Somers 1883-1935
After losing his high-paying job for criticizing the acquittal of a young New York society woman accused of murdering her husband, drunken star reporter **Sam Kernochan** is hired by her to find the killer, accepting because he thinks he will prove her guilt. Inevitably, he falls for her, while still uncertain, in a romantic mystery described by *SR* as "Gunmen, chorines, society rotters and other Broadway mobsters career through super-speedy and smoothly sophisticated tale."

> The Case Against Mrs. Ames (1934, UK 1935)

ROCK, Philip
Novelization of a downbeat film featuring PIs **Al Hickey** and **Frank Boggs**. See **Films: HICKEY AND BOGGS.**
> Hickey And Boggs (1972)

Rockwell, Chris — LINZEE, David
RODEN, H(enry) W(isdom) 1895-1963
New York PI **Sid Ames**, based at 5th & Decatur, featured in four action-packed novels. 28 years old, 6' tall, 175 pounds but tough, with a homely face, friendly brown eyes, and ingratiating grin, a square chin, an unruly shock of brown hair, catholic taste in women, a fondness for rye and a hatred for all policemen.
> You Only Hang Once (1944, UK 1946)
> Too Busy To Die (1944, UK 1947)
> One Angel Less (1945, UK 1949)
> Wake For A Lady (1946, UK 1950)

RODERUS, Frank
Raising Texas Longhorns and Quarter Horses on his ranch north of Lake George, near Colorado Springs, **Carl Heller**, law school dropout, is known round certain circles in the South-West as a man with a talent for correcting wrongs and keeping his mouth shut afterwards, which provides him with the extra he needs, the ranch barely covering his taxes. Heller rides a BMW motorcycle and is a tough, hard-drinking, laid back maverick son of the New West, a sort of Travis McGee of the mountains and in some ways preferable, though Roderus appears to enjoy no critical support whatever.
> The Oil Rig (1984)
> The Rain Rustlers (1984)
> The Video Vandal (1984)
> The Turn-Out Man (1985)
> The Coyote Crossing (1985)
> The Dead Heat (1985)

Roe, Jerry — ROPER, L.V.
ROEBURT, John 1908?-1972
A disbarred attorney turned New York cab driver, **Jigger Moran** is the man to see when you can't go to the police, a lawyer or even a licensed PI. A dedicated craps player, he charges high but gets results, using his secretly owned Independent Feature News Service, 1501 Broadway as a front. Boucher described the Moran books as "a highly individual and effective variant on the hardboiled school," and the stories are intricately plotted, fast and breezy.

Jigger Moran (1944, UK 1948); as Case Of The Tearless Widow (1946); as Wine, Women And Murder (1958)

There Are Dead Men In Manhattan (1946); as Murder In Manhattan (1957); as Triple Cross (1962)

Corpse On The Town (1950); as Case Of The Hypnotized Virgin (1956, revised)

The Hollow Man (1954, UK 1955)

ROFFMAN, Jan (Margaret Summerton)

Donna Casella-Kern (Reilly) described mystery-romancer Summerton's Roffman books as "slow-paced mystery/suspense novels involving women in murder plots where they are accused and victimized." In one, PI **Michael Hadden** is hired by a murdered woman's husband after a year of police inactivity. Hubin thought it "well-told, if not first-told."

A Daze Of Fears (1968)

Rogers, Jay — EDGELY, Leslie

Rogers, Julie — TV: CHARLIE'S ANGELS

Rogers, Pogy — ROSS, Z.H.

Rogue, Richard — Radio: ROGUE'S GALLERY

ROHDE, William L.

As detective for the Atlantic & Northern Railroad based in Vicksboro, somewhere in New England, **Mohawk Daniels** is part policeman, part hotel dick, part PI in standard action packed Gold Medal fare.

High Red For Dead (1951, UK 1953); as Murder On The Line (1957)

Roi, Leo — LORE, Phillips

Roland, Guy — MODIANO, Patrick

Rolfe, Simon — BONNEY, Joseph L.

Rolfe, Zachariah — LAMB, J.J.

Roman, Dan — MATHIS, Edward

ROMANO, Deane

Novelization of TV: BANACEK featuring casual, capable and cool Polish-American insurance investigator **Thomas Banacek**.

Banacek (1973)

ROME, Anthony = ALBERT, Marvin

An inveterate gambler, Miami ex-police lieutenant **Tony Rome** won his 36' sport cruiser *The Straight Pass*, moored at Dinner Key, in a crap game and the Luger he carries, in addition to a .38 Police Special and a .22 in his jacket sleeve, at poker. Another weakness is girls. A tough, philosophical PI, he's used to unfinished dramas. See **Films: The LADY IN CEMENT / TONY ROME**.

Miami Mayhem (1960, UK 1961); as Tony Rome (as by
    Marvin ALBERT 1967)
The Lady In Cement (1961, UK 1962)
My Kind Of Game (1962)
RONALD, E.B. (Ronald Barker 1920-1976)
Apart from a passing reference to wartime service in the Military Police,
Ronald offers no background, credentials or rationale for the adventures of
Rupert Bradley, tough guy London PI. Though not having any
Americanesque pretensions, the books live rather unhappily in a dated and,
even when first published, already anachronistic post-war ethos.
The Cat And Fiddle Murders (UK 1954, 1954)
Death By Proxy (UK 1976)
A Sort Of Madness (UK 1958, 1959)
RONNS, Edward (Edward S. Aarons 1916-1975)
Best known for his Sam Durrell books, Aarons' non-series Ronns novels
included one about exceedingly tough PI **Reginald 'Beauty' Black**,
involved in rough and tumble sleuthing in a graft and murder ridden New
Jersey resort. *NYT* called it "a good enough yarn of the hard-boiled type,"
but Will Cuppy was taken by its "temperate ruthlessness," describing
Black as "a hard-boiled detective with charm, if you can believe it." It was
one of three titles Aarons refused to have reissued under his own name.
See also **Paul AYRES**.
The Corpse Hangs High (1939)
Rook, Howie — **PALMER, Stuart**
Rooke, Terry — **ALEXANDER, David**
ROOS, Kelley (Audrey & William Roos)
Because the agency think the case is hopeless, they send broken down
operative **Timothy O'Hara**, in his 60s, to help a woman clear her name
of a murder. High tension told from various viewpoints,
Murder On Martha's Vineyard* (1981, UK 1982)
ROPER, L(ester) **V.**
Half Cherokee, half Irish "and all man," **Jerry 'Renegade' Roe**, partner
in the Worth & Roe Detective Agency of New Orleans, has blue eyes,
shoulder length black hair, wears a headband and moccasins and drives a
Mustang. A compulsive girl chaser, Roe spends much of his time in a
double act with his Puritan partner, **Stuart Worth**. Roper also wrote
about Kansas City PI and Korean War vet **Mike Saxon**.
Roe: The Red Horse Caper (1975)
         The Emerald Chicks Caper (1976)
Saxon: Hookers Don't Go To Heaven (1976)

Roper, Max — PLATT, Kin
ROSCOE, Mike (John Roscoe & Michael Ruso)
As Max Allan Collins remarks (P&M), the books written by two real-life
PIs, who worked for Hargreave's Detective Agency in Kansas City, are
due for revival and reassessment, being among the best of the 50s PI
novels. **Johnny April** is also a Kansas City PI, based in the 10th &
Baltimore Building, and the first four of his five adventures are
distinguished by their razor-sharp, stripped-down leanness, tough, vivid
and evocative. Boucher remarked that April "is the only genuine private
eye I know." *Riddle Me This* is remarkable, in the 50s context, for its
toughness on racism.
>   Death Is A Round Black Ball (1952, UK 1954)
>   Riddle Me This (1952, UK 1955)
>   Slice Of Hell (1954, UK 1955)
>   One Tear For My Grave* (1955, UK 1956)
>   The Midnight Eye (1958)
ROSEN, R(ichard) **D**(ean)
After discovering a talent for investigation in his first appearance, center
field baseball player **Harvey Blissberg**, once of the Boston Red Sox,
quits the Providence (Rhode Island) Jewels and goes into business as a
Boston PI, with an office on Mount Auburn Street. Rosen writes
crackling dialogue but the basketball and TV backgrounds of the second
and third books lack the authenticity which made the first, which won an
MWA Best First Novel Edgar, so remarkable. Competent though, with
good characters. >
>   Strike Three, You're Dead* (1984),
>   Fadeaway (1986)
>   Saturday Night Dead (1988)
ROSENBLUM, Robert
Italian-American ex-NYPD Homicide Squad detective **Pete Reno**, fired
for deliberately killing two drug dealers he blamed for his girl friend's
death by overdose, runs the practical and investigative side of Total
Protection Services Inc. Through a friend in the priesthood, he's hired by
the Vatican to look into the inexplicable charitable largesse of a small
town Italian priest, raising numerous ethical questions and getting
involved with a Mafia princess.
>   The Good Thief (1974, UK 1975)
ROSENTHAL, Erik
Knowing a lot about bounded linear operators on a separable infinite-
dimensional Hilbert space doesn't do mathematician **Dan Brodsky** much

good as he doesn't want to leave Berkeley and his tennis and poker friends. Having paid his way through college by serving subpoenas, he takes out a PI license and uses his talent for tracking people down. A fine, well-written puzzler. The follow-up, in which he's giving a paper at an Oxford maths conference, is marred by a thin plot, homophobia and the depiction of mathematicians as drunken, wenching party animals.

> The Calculus Of Murder (1986, UK 1987)
> The Advanced Calculus Of Murder (1988)

ROSS, Albert (Arthur D. Goldstein)
Crippled by a gunshot wound, ex-NYPD **Ben Lomax** has a limp, a cane and a disability pension, Not sure that he wants to be a PI, he can't think of any other way of making a living. Usefully, when he's given a challenging case involving stolen art, his nubile (and cheap) secretary has a Master's in art history. *NYT* commented "enough action and coherency to make it palatable."

> If I Knew What I Was Doing . . . (1974)

Ross, Bob — **LANDON, Christopher**
Ross, David — **TV: The OUTSIDER**
Ross, Jack — **SCHOPEN, Bernard**
Ross, John Thomas — **BUNN, Thomas**
ROSS, Leonard Q. = **ROSTEN, Leo**
Framed by his ex-partner, **Bradford Galt** goes to jail and on his release find himself caught up in machinations surrounding the ex-partner's affair with a married woman. See **Films: The DARK CORNER.**

> The Dark Corner (1945; as by **Leo ROSTEN** UK 1946)

Ross, Martin — **ALLYSON, Alan**
Ross, Mike — **CARR, Kirby**
ROSS, Philip
Vietnam vet **James Marley** of Boston works with refugees for the American Friends Service Committee and becomes a Quaker international businessman's troubleshooter, undertaking PI-like odd jobs between assignments. The first novel is as much a romance as anything else, with confused motivations and a plot held together by unexplained actions. The second, in which he is a straightforward PI, is described by *Publisher's Weekly* as "a diverting, well-paced mystery with a tension-filled ending."

> Blue Heron (1985)
> White Flower (1989)

ROSS, Z(ola) **H**(elen)
The widow of the late Sim Rogers, **Pogy Rogers**, is the brains in the partnership of Reno private detectives with **Beau Smith** providing the

muscle. Their two cases are set, respectively in a Nevada ghosttown and a Nevada mountain camp and are variations on the country house murder.

> Three Down Vulnerable (1946)
> One Corpse Missing (1948)

ROSTEN, Leo

"Picture Sam Spade played by Groucho Marx" said one reviewer of Vietnam vet and ex-cop **Sidney 'Silky' Pincus**, partner in Watson & Holmes Inc., 60th & 1st, Manhattan. Chutzpah is Silky's main schtick (Rosten usefully provides a glossary for non-Yiddish speakers), though he's pretty lecherous too. His partner is roguish Irishman **Mike Clancy**, who's picked up more Yiddish than half the Jews in New York and he also has a dog, Isadore Goldberg, a Schnauzer raised by a rabbi, which only understands Yiddish and keeps kosher. A very funny variant on the wise-cracking PI; Baker & Nietzel remark, the novels "are like dry martinis: exciting, spirit-lifting and intoxicating." As **Leonard Q. ROSS**, Rosten wrote a book featuring PI **Bradford Galt**.

Pincus: Silky! (1979)
> King Silky (1980)

Galt: The Dark Corner (1945; as by **Leonard Q. ROSS** UK 1946)

Roth, Clay — Films: ARMED RESPONSE

ROTH, Holly 1916-1964

In a short career Roth became known for her skill at suspense and characterization, mainly in espionage novels. One novel featured unproduced playwright and licensed PI **William Farland** in a Gothic formal mystery. Her series character Inspector Medford shared the honors with PI **Monte Gordon** in one book.

Farland: The Crimson In The Purple (1956, UK 1957)
Gordon: Shadow Of A Lady* (1957, UK 1957)

Rourke, Steve — BROCK, Stuart

ROVIN, Jeff

In 1927, with the first all-talking picture being made, **Roger Garrison** is an expensive, accomplished Melrose Avenue, LA, PI much called upon by Hollywood studios. A published composer, he's acknowledged as "one of the world's most brutal men. The lawless feared his name with the same passion that patrons of the arts applauded it." Very clumsily written with far too much needless exposition about the period.

> Hollywood Detective: Garrison (1975)
> Hollywood Detective: The Wolf (1975)

Rowe, Parker — MANER, William
Royal, Max — BROWN, Carter

RUBEL, James L.
"Most detectives have angles, but here's one who has curves. She never asks any special favors from men—except that they be on the tall side, with muscles and a loving nature." A former Marine and policewoman **Eli Donovan**, LA private eye with mascara, is one of the earliest hard-boiled female detectives and Rubel actually does quite a good job of it.

    No Business For A Lady (1950, UK 1952)

RUD, Anthony M. 1893-1942
A favorite of Pronzini who lists all three books about Long Island "crime analyst" **J.C.K. 'Jigger' Masters** in his Alternative Hall of Fame the second and third commended as "alternative works of considerable stature." Rud specialized in eccentric and eccentrically named characters, many either blessed or cursed with strange powers, maladies and/or thought processes, eerie, *very* improbable plot situations, sinister private estates and architectural monstrosities, full of trap doors, secret passages and weird gadgets, and bizarre "impossible" murders. For a full critique see *Son of Gun in Cheek*. Though an obvious supersleuth, Masters is referred to as a private dick and can fight or shoot with the best.

    The Rose Bath Riddle (1934)
    House Of The Damned (1934)
    The Stuffed Men (1935, UK 1936)

RUDLOFF, Stephen A.
Korean War vet **Charles Endicott** featured in a well-drawn, down-beat period piece short story, "A Cup Of Coffee" (A2 #2).

Ruff, Bob — HODGES, Carl G.
RUHM, Herbert (ed) — see **ANTHOLOGIES: 17**
Rule, Harry — TV: The PROTECTORS
Rummell, Beau — QUEEN, Ellery
Runyan, Brad — Radio: The FAT MAN
RUNYON, Charles
A Chicago based undercover specialist, so much so that it's some time before the reader is sure that he is a PI, **Marcus Greene** was involved in at least one case with lashings of sex, considerable violence and some effective use of drugs, with a quite well done extended LSD experience.

    The Black Moth (1967)

Rush, Alexander — HAMMETT, Dashiell
RUSSELL, Richard
The very inaptly named **Angel Graham,** born Angelo Grammone, is a very tough character. An orphan who ran away from relatives, who beat him, when he was 11 and became a hobo and eventually a New York PI,

he featured in three very fast books peopled with people as incomplete as he, sociopathic and psychotic.

     Paperbag (1979)
     Reunion (1979)
     Point Of Reference (1979)

Russo, John — Films: THEY ALL LAUGHED
Rutledge, Charles — Films: THEY ALL LAUGHED
RYAN, Conall
The business affairs of Joe Venice Investigations are run from *La Vita Nuevo*, moored in Boston's Charles River. Vietnam vet operative **Knightsbridge** spends most of his time in "exile from everywhere," getting about in a bullet-scarred ex-Checker cab, and his first story took him to Sutter Springs Gap, Wyoming, in search of a missing urn. An extraordinary, not to say bizarre story dominated by Gaylord, one of the two most hardboiled dogs in literature (Andrew VACHSS' Pansy is the competitor), "a conglomerate of several man-eating species."

     Black Gravity (1985)

Ryan, Frank — LEONARD, Elmore
Ryan, Johnny — FISHER, Steve
Ryan, Pete — TV: SWITCH
Ryder, Nick — TV: RIPTIDE
Rye, William — SPAIN, John
Saber, Joel — HOLT, Gavin
Saber, Mark — TV: SABER OF LONDON
SABER, Robert O. = OZAKI,Milton K.
Tax accountant Ozaki's Chicago PIs **Carl Good** and **Max Keene** are, rather confusingly, presumably because of contractual problems, identical with Carl Guard and Phil Keene in novels under his own name. Unfortunately it has not been possible to identify all the books with any degree of precision; *Affair Of The Frigid Blonde* (1950), *The Black Dark Murders* (1949, as *Out Of The Night*, Canada 1954) and *No Way Out* (1952, UK 1952) may be PI titles. Good, short, dough-faced, slightly paunchy, and Keene both deal in a world of ganglords, strippers and corrupt cops with greed as the underlying element.

Good: The Dove (1951); as Chicago Woman (1953)
       The Deadly Lover (1951)
       The Scented Flesh (1951)
       Murder Doll (1952)
       Too Young To Die (1954)
       Sucker Bait (1965)

Keene: A Dame Called Murder (1955)
             A Time For Murder (1956)
Saber, Sarah — LINZEE, David
Sader, Jim — HITCHENS, Dolores
SADDLER, K. Allen (Ronald Richards)
Tongue in cheek British romps featuring **Dave Stevens** in a cross
between Raymond Chandler and Jerome K. Jerome, fast-paced stories told
in a comic manner.
             The Great Brain Robbery (UK 1966)
             Gilt Edge (UK 1966)
             Talking Turkey (UK 1968)
SADLER, Mark = COLLINS, Michael
Under this name Lynds, who also wrote as **John CROWE, Carl
DEKKER** and **William ARDEN**, created a modern professional PI,
Paul Shaw of Thayer, Shaw & Delaney—Security & Investigations,
New York and LA, with a Madison Avenue address, Danish modern
furniture, wall to wall carpet and Finnish blonde secretaries, just like the
clients' own offices. Ex-actor Shaw is married to a successful actress and
drives a Ferrari. In Francis M. Nevins' words, "no other private eye novels
capture the nightmare America of the Vietnam and Nixon years." The
Shaw books pit hippies, environmentalists, black militants and students
against brutal police, corrupt politicians and ruthless capitalists with
savage force and some editorializing.
             The Falling Man* (1970)
             Here To Die (1971)
             Mirror Image (1972)
             Circle Of Fire (1973)
             Touch Of Death (1981)
             The Deadly Innocents (1988)
ST CLAIR, Dexter = STERLING, Stewart
A Gold Medal original about New York ex-Marine, former Burns man PI
Kirby Hart of Probe Associates, with a reputation for getting to the
bottom of things, regardless of how tough the case may be. Hired by a
major company, which has the Pinkertons on contract, for a discreet
investigation, he finds himself a perfect patsy all set up for framing.
             The Lady's Not For Living (1963, UK 1964)
St. Ives, Philip — BLEECK, Oliver
St. Ives, Raymond — Films: ST. IVES
St. James, Quin — McGREGOR, T.J.
St. John, Jeremiah — BABULA, William

Sail, Oscar — DENT, Lester
Salem, Peter — Radio: The AFFAIRS OF PETER SALEM
Samson, Albert — LEWIN, Michael
Samson, Jake — SINGER, Shelley
Samson, John — TRIPP, Miles
Sands, Nick — SMOKE, Stephen
Sanders, Harry — Films: COAST OF SKELETONS
SANDERS, Daphne (Georgiana Ann Randolph Craig 1906-1972)
Better known as Craig Rice, Georgiana Craig wrote a New York City set
PI novel featuring **Donovan** described by *NYT* as "a wildly improbable
yarn not too skillfully told."
>   To Catch A Thief (1943)

SANDERS, Lawrence
Opportunism by an author of overblown thrillers. The blurb, "The
hardboiled private eye is back," falls apart the moment it's construed for,
apart from anything else, **Timothy Cone**, of John Street, New York,
detective agency Haldering & Co., is far from hardboiled, and Sanders
betrays no knowledge of or inclination for tough-guy writing. Smooth,
urbane, moderately suspenseful.
>   The Timothy Files (1987, UK 1987)
>   Timothy's Game (1988, UK 1988)

Sanderson, Ned — WISE, Arthur
Sandford, George — MacLEAN, Katherine
Sandusky, Nick — TV: LONG TIME GONE
Sandy — Films: DEAD PIGEON ON BEETHOVEN
>   **STREET**

SANGSTER, Jimmy
A Briton who lives in Hollywood and works in movies, Sangster's two
series are higher on gloss than grit. **John Smith** is a former agent of
The Service whose dossier on his ex-boss enables him to retire but whose
PI business, based in London's Soho, isn't successful enough to keep him
from refusing freelance work for his old firm. The two books are
essentially spy stories, both filmed for TV, see **TV: FOREIGN
EXCHANGE / The SPY KILLER. James Reed**, formerly of
Scotland Yard, now lives in a Malibu beach house, a gift from his screen
superstar ex-wife, and aspires to be a screenwriter. Barely a PI.
Smith: Private i (UK 1967, 1967)
>   Foreign Exchange (UK 1968, 1968)
Reed: Snowball (1986)
>   Blackball (1987)

SAPIR, Richard 1936-1987
The co-author, with **Warren MURPHY**, of *The Destroyer* series, wrote one tough, riveting book about **Alphonse Joseph 'Al' Bressio**, a New York Italian PI with Family connections who looks like a Mafia soldier. Carrying a .38 Police Special, Bressio is 5'9", weighs 240 pounds and has a dark craglike face and burning black eyes under fierce bushy brows, and takes the fighting desire out of almost everyone who sees him. "He looked as though he could throw a man through a wall, and want to." A sad, funny novel about ideals and realities in law.
> Bressio (1975, UK 1986)

SAPPER (Herman Cyril McNeile 1888-1937)
Rather annoyingly the creator of Bulldog Drummond (see **Gerard FAIRLIE**), arch chauvinist, racist, sexist and sadist, waited until after this work's cut-off date to create a more intellectual hero, independently wealthy private detective and first-class cricketer **Ronald Standish**, who only takes cases that "amuse" him. Standish is clearly modeled on Doyle rather than British, let alone American, contemporary practice and in three books co-star Drummond's fists rather than his brains are the key factor.
> Tiny Cartaret (UK 1930, as by **H.C. McNEILE** 1930)
> Knock-Out (UK 1933); as Bulldog Drummond Strikes Back (as
>   by **H.C. McNEILE** 1933)
> Ronald Standish (UK 1933). SS
> Bulldog Drummond At Bay (UK 1935; as by **H.C. McNEILE**
>   1935)
> Ask For Ronald Standish (UK 1936). SS
> Challenge (UK 1937; as by **H.C. McNEILE** 1937)

Sargent — GRUBER, Frank

SARRANTONIO, Al
Battling alcoholism, **Jack Paine** isn't helped when he finds his client an apparent suicide and an envelope he was to collect holding only photos of three unknown men. *Publisher's Weekly* detected Ross Macdonald influence but found the story original in concept and execution.
> Cold Night (1989)

SATTERTHWAIT, Walter
Local atmosphere is well evoked in a Santa Fe, New Mexico-set novel. **Rita Mondragón**, the brains behind legman **Joshua Croft** who loves her unrequitedly, runs her Mondragón Agency from a wheelchair. Good characterization, quick pace, illicit and kinky sex, Swiss bank accounts, Indian grave-robbing and an endangered species make a strong debut.
> Wall Of Glass (1988)

Saturday, Johnny — GOLDMAN, Lawrence
Savage, Mark — PAYNE, Laurence
Sawyer, Matt — Films: NINE LIVES ARE NOT ENOUGH
Sawyer, Pierre-Ange — ALBERT, Marvin
Saxon — ROBERTS, Les
SAXON, John A. 1886-1947
Saxon wrote only one book about **Sam Welpton**, of Lane & Welpton, LA, insurance investigators, but his hero had such an uncanny way of getting into hot water, with much shooting, lurid and bibulous ladies and furiously bubbling action, that Bellem himself was able to take over and ghost-write a second book commended by *NYT*: "variety enough to please the most exacting mystery fan."

> Liability Limited (1947); as This Was No Accident (UK 1949)
> Half-Past Mortem (1947, UK 1951). By **Robert Leslie BELLEM**

Saxon, Johnny — BOGART, William G.
Saxon, Michael — BLANKENSHIP, William D.
Saxon, Mike — ROPER, L.V.
Sayler, Catherine — GRANT, Linda
Scanlon, Duke — LAYMON, Richard
SCHACHNER, Nat
Named by a hospital after the place he was found lying with a vicious blow on the head, **Nicholas Street** is an amnesiac with no idea of his true identity and little hope of ever finding out in "The Flowering Corpses" (*Dime Mystery* 1938, A7).
Schaefer, William — ESTOW, Daniel
Schilders, Jet — PACHTER, Josh
SCHOENFELD, Howard
A pity there was only one book about Graybar Building, New York PI **Jerry Nelson** for, in Boucher words, it's "wondrously wild . . . liveliest new, tough storytelling in years . . . complete with gangsters, blackmail, corpses galore and a nympho-sadist with arrested development . . . the funniest caper since S.J. PERELMAN's *Farewell, My Lovely Appetizer*." After typing in the 4,000 odd titles listed in this guide, this remains my favorite.

> Let Them Eat Bullets (1954, UK 1955)

Schofield, Pete — DEWEY, Thomas B.
SCHOPEN, Bernard
Ross Macdonald scholar Schopen's first novel features uncommonly sensitive Reno, Nevada PI **Jack Ross**, untangling the lineages of three

families in a web of deceit and murder. Marilyn Staso (*NYT*) found the plot "incredibly convoluted" but praised well-sustained characterization and moodily evocative description of the Black Rock Desert.

      The Big Silence (1989)

SCHORR, Mark

New York cab-driver Simon Jaffe is 42 with a ghastly family and a depreciating house. All that keeps him sane is his pulp magazine collection, and when his wife sells them as junk, leaving only one, a story about Jaffe's favorite pulp hero **Red Diamond**,he loses his grip on reality and actually becomes Diamond, who can "outpunch Mike Hammer, outdrink Nick Charles, outsleuth Sam Spade, outshoot Race Williams, outwisecrack Philip Marlowe, outstud Shell Scott and out-bench press Spenser," going around the New York he knows every inch of, behaving totally in character. The style is a brilliant melange of 40s and 80s. Later he has an office in the Carlin Building, Hollywood Boulevard, LA. Parodies and great stories, filled with action, humor, nostalgia and sympathy.

      Red Diamond: Private Eye* (1983)
      Ace Of Diamonds (1984)
      Diamond Rock (1985)

SCHUMAN, M.K.

Capable New Orleans PI **Micah Dunn** is hired to find out why ancient Mayan artifacts are being smuggled *into* a museum, leading to five deaths and Dunn's arrest for one of them. *Publisher's Weekly* said "the conclusion to this impossibly tangled story is inept, lengthy and contrived."

      The Maya Stone Murders (1989)

SCHUTZ, Benjamin M.

That rare thing, a native son of Washington, DC, **Leo Haggerty** specializes in missing persons in neo-hardboiled novels that are gripping, fast paced, brilliantly characterized and very well written. Paul Bishop observed in *The Thieftaker Journals* that his debut, "immediately sank its barbs down my throat and into my heart . . . The writing is clenched teeth tough." Schutz contributed a **Philip Marlowe** short story, "The Black-Eyed Blonde," to **A12**.

      Embrace The Wolf (1985)
      All The Old Bargains (1985)
      A Tax In Blood (1986)
      The Things We Do For Love (1989)

Schuyler, Jim — Films: A LOVELY WAY TO DIE

Scotland, Ann — Radio: AFFAIRS OF ANN SCOTLAND
Scott, Robin — TV: CASE OF THE DANGEROUS ROBIN
SCOTT, Denis (Mary Means & Theodore Saunders)
"Not a superhuman clairvoyant sleuth but a good guy who sometimes
makes mistakes and has to backtrack as most of us do," is how the blurb
characterizes impulsive young Chicago PI **Mike James**, described by
Will Cuppy as "gay and thirsty," by *SR* as "lively" and by *NYT* as "so
busy consulting railway timetables that he scarcely has time to dodge the
bullets aimed at him." *NYT* also complained of Scott's hop-skip-and-
jump story telling.
> Murder Makes A Villain (1944, UK 1955)
> The Beckoning Shadow (1946, UK 1956)

SCOTT, Roney = **GAULT, William Campbell**
Gault used this name for his first **Joe Puma** book but reverted to his
own for the rest of the series.
> Shakedown (1953)

Scott, Sara — ALEXANDER, Karl
Scott, Shell — PRATHER, Richard S. / KNIGHT, David
Scotter, John — WARRINER, Thurman
Scudder, Matt — BLOCK, Lawrence
SEARLS, Hank
Collection of seven 1949-1950 hardboiled short stories, mostly from
Dime Detective, featuring San Francisco PI **Mike Blair**, who, as
Searls notes in his foreword, "gets beat up in almost every story I wrote."
> The Adventures Of Mike Blair (1988)

Seaward, Patricia — NEBEL, Frederick
Seekay — ERNST, Paul
Seidlitz, Mavis — BROWN, Carter
SEWARD, Jack
An American PI who works in Japan, and can translate "without
conscious effort," **Curt Stone**, who has, we're told, been called "a
combination of Mike Hammer and Travis McGee," can kill easily
"because he's done so much of it."
> The Cave Of The Chinese Skeletons (1964)
> Assignment: Find Cherry (1969)
> The Chinese Pleasure Girl (1969)
> The Frogman Assassination (1969)
> The Eurasian Virgins (1969)

Shackelford, Lyman — TV: CASSIE & COMPANY
Shaft, John — TIDYMAN, Ernest

Shaley, Ben — DAVIS, Norbert
Shamus — TV: A MATTER OF WIFE . . . AND DEATH
Shand, Dale — ENEFER, Douglas
SHAND, William
A Canadian working as a London PI , **William A. Tempest** featured in three books, *SR* remarking of the last "placidly active, with much bludgeoning."

> A Man Called Tempest (UK 1957)
> Tempest Weaves A Shroud (UK 1957)
> Tempest In A Tea Cup (UK 1958, 1959)

Shannon — TV: The D.A.'S MAN
Shannon, Desmond — HEBERDEN, M.V.
SHANNON, Jimmy
A Spillane imitation, featuring New York PI **Ruff Morgan**, that Pronzini calls remarkable in *Gun In Cheek*. "If he is not the least intelligent detective in private eyedom—alongside Morgan, Race Williams is a genius—he must surely be a close runner-up." Totally derivative without even the requisite sex and sadism.

> The Devil's Passkey (1952)

Shannon, Joe — TV: SHANNON
Shannon, John J. — ADAMS, Cleve F.
SHARKEY, Jack
His real vocation is composing less-than-deathless lyrics and not-so-popular tunes, but **George Herbert Henry**, Private Eye, Songs for all Occasions, pays the rent and the installments on his baby grand, usually by the skin of his teeth, by cerebral sleuthing. Softboiled and, in a dust jacket's blood-chilling word, "irrepressible."

> Murder, Maestro Please (1960, UK 1960)
> Death For Auld Lang Syne (1963)

SHARP, Alan
Hailed by Jerry Palmer in his opaque "contribution to the sociology of literature,"*Thrillers; Genesis & Structure of a Popular Genre*" (1979) as an anti-thriller, "collapsing the negative thriller down to the failure to solve conspiracies." Self-questioning, chess problem playing **Harry Moseby** is so concerned with solving his personal problems that when the actual crimes occur in the closing pages, his misunderstanding of the relationships between the people involved and clumsy, last-ditch attempt to be a "proper detective" leads to the death of all the people involved, himself included. Pretty bleak. See **Films: NIGHT MOVES**.

> Night Moves (UK 1975)

Shaw, James — HAIBLUM, Isidore
Shaw, Joe — LAUMER, Keith
SHAW, Joseph T. (ed) — see ANTHOLOGIES: 18
Shaw, Paul — SADLER, Mark
Shay, Pete — McCURTIN, Peter
Shayne, Michael — HALLIDAY, Brett
Shayne, Ted — Films: SATAN MET A LADY
SHELLEY, Mike
Perhaps the seediest of all PIs is **Barney Huggins**, Korean War Sergeant from Northern Ireland, who operates in and around London's Soho. Greedy, duplicitous, broke, with total disregard for the welfare of his associates, he spends much of his time in the hands of the rightly suspicious police. Huggins handrolls cigarettes and plays mandolin-banjo. Ex-British Intelligence officer **Bernard Holland's** Rapid Results Investigation Agency shares its Ormeau Road, Belfast premises, and indeed its proprietor, with an Import-Export company and an Introduction service. Some editing might have helped, though it's possible that these parodies, self-published by the author, are deliberately intended to be confusing.
Huggins: The Terror Of Her Ways (UK 1984)
                     Madame Eddie's Chamber Of Horrors (UK 1984)
Holland: The Last Private Eye In Belfast (UK 1984)
SHEPHERD, John = BALLARD, Willis Todhunter
Two of Ballard's books about **Bill Lennox** appeared under the Shepherd name, one a retitled reissue, the other an original.
             Lights, Camera, Murder (1960)
             The Demise Of A Louse (1962); as Say Yes To Murder (as by
                 Willis Todhunter BALLARD 1942)
SHERMAN, Steve
An ex-cop who originally trained as a philosopher, **Hugh Quint** has an ever-available and omniscient friend with whom he exchanges concepts on the telephone. Boiling maple syrup makes one of the most original murder weapons in history in a well-executed novel with a twist in its tail. The second book was described by *Publishers' Weekly* as amusingly wacky if lacking in suspense.
             The Maple Sugar Murders (1987)
             The White Mountain Murders (1989)
Sherwood, Ned — SYLVESTER, Robert
Shields, John — LINGO, Ade E.
Shilling, Harold — BERCOVICI, Eric

Shillman, Harold — TV: ONE SHOE MAKES IT MURDER
SHIRLEY, John
Using a character created by **J. Michael REAVES**, Shirley has written
a sequel to his book about Darkworld Detective **Kamus of Khadizar**.

The Black Hole Of Carcosa (1988)
Shock, Ben — BUCHANAN, Patrick
Shoestring, Eddie — TV: SHOESTRING
SHORE, Julian
Several reviewers commented on Shore's resemblance to Erle Stanley
Gardner, both *NYT* and *SR* calling the book "streamlined." A private
detective, **Mark Millner**, in a Western city finds himself acutely
involved in a murder he knows nothing about and wriggles smartly off the
hook. Rapid-fire dialogue and action with a shrewd plot and good
characters.

Rattle His Bones (1941)
SILER, Jack
San Francisco (Suite 1812, Fred Weik Building) PI **Tom Farley** looks
like an absent-minded professor or middle-level bureaucrat, 45 and stuck in
a rut, but is the best private arson investigator in the West, possibly in
America, combining flair, scientific knowledge and legwork. With so
much technical content as to qualify as a procedural, this story about "the
fastest growing crime in America" was described by John D.
MacDONALD as "a compelling, explosive story of an ultimate moral
dilemma" but some readers may find it over-written and simplistic.

Triangles Of Fire (1984)
Silk, Steve — O'SULLIVAN, James Brendan
Sills, Jed — TV: CHECKMATE
Silver, Maud — WENTWORTH, Patricia
Simon, Andrew Jackson & Rick — TV: SIMON & SIMON
SIMON, Roger L.
His debut won British and American awards and prompted Ross
MACDONALD to state that Simon was "the most brilliant new writer of
private detective fiction who has emerged in some years." At that point
LA PI **Moses Wine** was "the people's detective," a long-haired, dope-
smoking, political activist Berkeley graduate. While he changes with the
books, he is constantly encountering contradictions between his beliefs
and the real world. In the fourth he is security director for a Silicon Valley
corporation, Apple Computers thinly disguised. The wry Wine and
Simon's dialogue are the best feature of books that suffer from
improbabilities and clichés, the earlier of which have dated badly. Simon

has a **Philip Marlowe** short story, "In The Jungle Of Cities," in **A12**.
See **Films: The BIG FIX**.

> The Big Fix (1973, UK 1974)
> Wild Turkey* (1975, UK 1976)
> Peking Duck (1979, UK 1979)
> California Roll (1985)
> The Straight Man (1986)
> Raising The Dead (1988)

SINGER, Shelley (Rochelle Singer)
After quitting the Chicago police in the summer of 1968, jewish **Jake Samson** moved to Oakland, where Singer herself lives, and became a hippy before starting out as an unlicensed PI assisted by his tenant, **Rosie Vicente**, a lesbian carpenter with a flair for detection. Softboiled, with appealing characters and well-observed relationships, the series is particularly effective in its portrayal of the Bay Area and its sub-cultures.

> Samson's Deal (1982)
> Free Draw* (1984)
> Full House (1986)
> Spit In The Ocean (1987)
> Suicide King (1988)

Skinner, Del — DALE, William
Slade, Jim — Films: The MIDNIGHT MAN
Slade, Mac — BLUMENTHAL, John
Slade, Shotgun — TV: SHOTGUN SLADE
Slader, Vince — DEMARIS, Ovid
Slaughter, Victor — KARLINS, Marvin & ANDREWS
SLESAR, Henry
Concerned about the mental well being of an about to come of age orphan heiress New York's Fiduciary Bank hires PI **Steve Tyner** to investigate and protect her in a psychological suspense novel.

> The Thing At The Door* (1974, UK 1975)

Slocum, Eddie — GRUBER, Frank
SLOVO, Gillian
Slovo appears to have improved since her debut, one of the more right-on titles in a well-meaning but unreadable British left-wing political thriller series. Of her first PI novel, featuring **Kate Baeier** and classical music, one reviewer remarked that she does "a nice job of portraying the private and professional lives of a believable female private eye," which sounds like faint praise, but could be worse.

> Death Comes Staccato (1988)

Small, Nick — TV: SMALL & FRYE
Smith, Beau — ROSS, Z.H.
Smith, Cellini — REEVES, Robert
Smith, China — TV: CHINA SMITH
SMITH, Don
CIA agent **Tim Parnell** moves to Holland and sets up as a PI, specializing at first in aircraft related cases, his office in Amsterdam Airport. Parnell is a rather anonymous character but the stories are intricately plotted. In *Corsican Takeover*, Smith, born in 1909, betrays a total lack of familiarity with youth culture.

> The Man Who Played Thief (1969, 1971)
> The Padrone (1971, UK 1971)
> The Payoff (1973, UK 1974)
> Corsican Takeover (1974, UK 1974)

SMITH, J(ane) C.S.
After retiring from the New York Transit Police in which he was a Sergeant, 55 year old widower **Quentin Jacoby**, living in Co-op City, finds himself bored and at a loose end and becomes an unlicensed PI by accident. Down to earth narration, well paced and constructed.

> Jacoby's First Case (1980)
> Nightcap (1984, UK 1985)

Smith, Jared — GOULART, Ron
Smith, John — PETERS, Ludovic
Smith, John — PLUM, Mary
Smith, John — SANGSTER, Jimmy
SMITH, Julie
Burnt-out journalist **Paul MacDonald** writes mysteries that don't get published and prepares reports for a PI who drops dead in the kitchen of his Chenery Street home and turns out to have been murdered. MacDonald must find out who killed him to protect himself. Smith is herself a former reporter who once wrote client reports for a detective agency, and, as usual, has written a witty and gripping novel. She contributed a **Philip Marlowe** short story, "Red Rock," to A12.

> True-Life Adventures (1985)
> Huckleberry Fiend (1987)

SMITH, Mark
The biggest, most pretentious PI novel ever features **Arnold Magnuson**, ex-cop become famous head of a vast organization of uniformed private guards who.hunts a serial killer across Chicago during the Korean War period. Two separate *NYT* reviews, neither by a mystery

expert, raved about it, one comparing Smith to Charles Dickens, finding it full of allegorical significance.

> The Death Of The Detective (1974, UK 1975)

Smith, Mr. — Films: **The CARIBBEAN MYSTERY**

Smith, Napoleon B. — **ALLEN, Leslie / BROWN, Horace**

SMITH, Neville

Novelization of a 1971 British film about Liverpool bingo caller **Eddie Ginley**, acting out hardboiled PI fantasies. See **Films: GUMSHOE.**

> Gumshoe (UK 1971, 1972)

SMITH, Richard C.

The debut novel about Boston PI **James Maxfield Mallory** is described by Robert Campbell as "nicely cut to tradition while innovative touches make it sparkle." Mallory quit Harvard law school because he was interested in justice, "but they weren't teaching it" and Smith is notably cynical about the American legal profession. But then who isn't? A derivative but promising debut.

> A Secret Singing (1988)

SMITH, Richard N.

Referred to in a Boston area paper as a "Society Detective," **John Kincaid** gets involved in Marblehead high society and gangsters in his one competent outing.

> Death Be Nimble (1967)

Smith, Thaddeus — TV: **TURNOVER SMITH**

Smith, Tim — **WESTLAKE, Donald**

Smith, Vanessa — TV: **The MOST DEADLY GAME**

Smoke, Benjamin — **McBAIN, Ed**

SMOKE, Stephen

An 'holistic' San Francisco PI, **Nick Sands**, is hired by a beautiful woman to find God in a metaphysical novel, "somewhere between Mickey Spillane and Teilhard de Chardin . . . private eye soul food," according to another New Age writer. See **Hamilton T. CAINE.**

> Trick Of The Light (1988)

SNYDER, James

In an oddball variant on the theme of tracing a missing person, California PI **Robert Blue** is mainly motivated by a desire to see New Orleans in a short story, "Shopping Cart Howard," in A1 #5.

SOLOMON, Brad

Born in LA, "the city of rubber walls," **Charlie Quinlan** tried acting and still does some extra work for spare change, but, going nowhere decided to get out with his sanity. Now he operates as a PI well thought of by ex-clients and the police. He has a weakness for pretty receptionists, as does **Fritz Thieringer**, another LA PI in partnership with **Maggie McGuane**. Fritz is partial to hats, Coke and stealing small objects; Maggie reviews movies on the side. Solomon is good at LA's glitz and grunge contrasts and has an ear for dialogue. *NYT* remarked Solomon's "remarkable assurance," while *The Washington Star* went as far as to say "easily the best private eye novel in years."

Quinlan: The Gone Man (1977)
Thieringer: The Open Shadow (1978)
Sommers, Harry — WHALLEY, Peter
South, Joseph — NYLAND, Gentry
SOUTHCOTT, Audley
Novelization based on the excellent British **TV: PUBLIC EYE** about seedy, small time Inquiry Agent **Frank Marker** of Birmingham, England. The tone is well caught. See also **Anthony MARRIOTT**.
        Cross That Palm When I Come To It (1974)
Space, Sam — NOLAN, William F.
Spade, Sam — HAMMETT, Dashiell
Spade, Sam Jr. — EDWARDS, Alexander
SPAIN, John = ADAMS, Cleve F.
Troubleshooter for a California oil magnate and political power broker, **William Rye** is a PI on retainer, solving murders in both books to get his employer off dangerous hooks. *NYT* said that Bill "tries to keep within the law whenever that is practicable, which it seldom is. More often he has to resort to skulduggery and even violence," and described the first book as "a lively yarn with plenty of rough stuff," the second as "loosely constructed and has little to recommend it."
        Dig Me A Grave (1942)
        Death Is Like That (1943)
SPAIN, Nancy (1917-84)
Looking respectively like a witch and a tart, former revue artiste **Miriam Birdseye** and ex-ballerina **Natasha Nevkorina** are Birdseye et Cie., a detective agency whose only objective is to banish tedium. Dottiness and flamboyance are what counts and the inconsequential takes precedence over the pompous and sententious. Frivolous farces with much sly lesbian humor—a girls' school called Radcliff Hall, for instance. Asked by an admiring schoolgirl if they catch men, Birdseye replies "Oh dear no. My partner often catches women . . . or so she says." Klein, an American academic, misses the subversive point of these very clever, but very English anti-hardboileds. >

Poison For Teacher (UK 1949)
Death Goes On Skis (UK 1949)
Cinderella Goes To The Morgue (UK 1950)
R In The Month (UK 1950)
Out, Damned Tot! (UK 1951)
Not Wanted On Voyage (UK 1951)

Spanner, J.T. — CHASTAIN, Thomas
Spanner, Jake — MORSE, Larry
SPARLING, Joyce
Former cult deprogrammer turned PI, **Alex Leighton** undertakes to bring a young woman back from India and a Sikh guru for a hefty fee. In India, he finds she has disappeared, accused of stealing a Sikh holy book. One review commented that while India was movingly portrayed, the protagonists were unbelievable.

North Of Delhi, East Of Heaven (1988)

Speare, Luke — DAVIS, Frederick C.
Speer, Gil — TRACY, Don
Spencer, Jeff — TV: 77 SUNSET STRIP
Spencer, Jeff & Debby — Radio: TWO ON A CLUE
SPENCER, John
The Big One of '97 created LA Island City in which **Charley Case** lives and operates. Various cyberpunk aspects, hardboiled narrative and a songwriter's way with words make Spencer's books very readable, with some very well turned lines. The author is a much admired and respected British musician and songwriter.

A Case For Charley (UK 1984)
Charley Gets The Picture (1985)

Spencer, Marc — MARSHALL, Raymond
SPENCER, Ross H.
Much longer on style and humor than content, Spencer's first PI, Chicago-based **Chance Purdue**, of Room 506, Braddock Building, featured in stories that were told in one sentence paragraphs. Short sentences. With no punctuation except periods and question marks. And very little plot. Some people loved them, one critic calling Spencer "the Groucho Marx of detective fiction," and his one-liners can be very funny, but the overall effect is rather exhausting. Other Chicago PI books about **Kelly J.'Buzz' Deckard** of West Irving Park Road and **Luke Lassiter** based in the Peerless Building, West Adams Street, are more conventionally related but still very funny and still very short on plot. The CIA give middle-aged PI **Birch Kirby,** of KIRBY PRIVATE

INVISTEGETIONS, Diversey Avenue, Chicago, a job because "nobody can be as inept as (he) pretends to be, and they need someone with his imagination." 49 year old **Tuthill Willow** is "the easygoing, play-it-as-it-lies sort, rarely belligerent and never temperamental. He smoked too much, drank too much, ate too little and slept too late. He was Chicagoan, born and raised—therefore skeptical, closemouthed, wary-eyed and quick on his feet." Spencer's latest PI is **Lacy Lockington**, suspended from the Chicago force after a columnist dubs him kill-crazy, who goes to work for Duke Denny's agency and ends up protecting, and sleeping with, his nemesis.

Purdue: The DADA Caper (1978)
                 The Reggis Arms Caper (1979)
                 The Stranger City Caper (1980)
                 The Abu Wahab Caper (1980)
                 The Radish River Caper (1981)
Deckard: The Missing Bishop (1985)
Lassister: Monastery Nightmare (1986)
Kirby: Kirby's Last Circus (1987)
Willow: Death Wore Gloves (1988)
Lockington: The Fifth Script (1989)

Spenser — PARKER, Robert B.

SPICER, Bart

Two distinguishing characteristics of Philadelphia PI **Carney Wilde** are his taciturnity about himself and his success. A veteran, we learn little about his background, and between the first and last books, he rises from being a one-man agency to heading Wilde Protective Systems Inc., Maritime National Building, with 200 employees. Spicer is universally admired by critics and commentators, who all remark on his latter-day neglect. Boucher praised his work "as human and even tender as it is tough and hard," bracketing him with Ross Macdonald, Sandoe thought him "one of the more considerable writers in the vein," Art Scott (Reilly) calls the books "among the very best private eye novels." A noteworthy feature is the sensitive, but not over-done, incorporation of black people.

             The Dark Light* (1949, UK 1950)
             Blues For The Prince (1950, UK 1951)
             The Golden Door (1951, UK 1951)
             Black Sheep,Run (1951, UK 1952)
             The Long Green (1952); as Shadow Of Fear (UK 1953)
             The Taming Of Carney Wilde (1954, UK 1955)
             Exit, Running (1959, UK 1960)

SPILLANE, Mickey

Spillane started out writing comic strips and his **Mike Hammer** books are best seen as comic-book novels. A master storyteller, his vicious sadism and voyeuristic sex have brought him perhaps the worst press of any PI writer, Chandler remarking that "pulp writing at its worst was never as bad as this," Boucher thinking that *I, The Jury* read like "required reading in a Gestapo training school," while Julian Symons sums it up best, "the most nauseating, and clinically disquieting, thing about these books is that Mike Hammer is the hero." Spillane, who called his work "chewing gum" (his son called it "crap"), addressed this problem in *One Lonely Night*, where Hammer is accused of enjoying killing and of being as bad as the murderers he kills with such relish. Spillane's answer is that Hammer is "evil for the good." Regardless, the PWA gave Spillane one of its Lifetime Achievement awards and Ed GORMAN recently remarked, apropos "talent the critics failed to see" (A5), "Spillane is the most misunderstood and abused literary figure of his time, the Great American Primitive whose real talents got lost in all the clamor over the violence of his hero . . . He brought energy and a street-fighter's rage to a form grown moribund with cuteness and imitation Chandler prose." Max Allan COLLINS, who rates Spillane with Hammett, Chandler and Macdonald wrote *One Lonely Knight: Mickey Spillane's Mike Hammer* (1984). Hammer's office is Suite 808, Hackard Building, New York. See **Films: I, THE JURY** (1953 & 1982)**/KISS ME DEADLY/M Y GUN IS QUICK/The GIRL HUNTERS** and **TV: MICKEY SPILLANE'S MIKE HAMMER** (1957 & 1984) and **Radio: THAT HAMMER GUY.**

> I, The Jury* (1947, UK 1952)
> My Gun Is Quick (1950, UK 1951)
> Vengeance Is Mine! (1950, UK 1951)
> The Big Kill (1951, UK 1952)
> One Lonely Night* (1951, UK 1952)
> Kiss Me, Deadly (1952, UK 1953)
> The Girl Hunters (1962, UK 1962)
> The Snake (1964, UK 1964)
> The Twisted Thing (1966, UK 1966)
> The Body Lovers (1967, UK 1967)
> Survival . . . Zero! (1970, UK 1970)
> Tomorrow I Die (1984). SS with the Mike Hammer screen test.

Spoon, Sonny — TV: SONNY SPOON
Spraggue, Michael — BARNES, Linda J.

SPROUL, Kathleen
NYT commented of *Murder Off Key*, that the story was excellent and ingenious, "an acutely devised problem," despite the conscientious fumbling of **Dick Wilson**, who seems to fancy himself unduly in the role of Sherlock." *SR* remarked "though yarn becomes confused at times and outcome is slightly disappointing, suspense holds up satisfactorily."
> The Birthday Murder (1932)
> Death And The Professors (1933); as Death Among The
> > Professors (UK 1934)
> Murder Off Key (1934)
> The Mystery Of The Closed Car (1935)

SQUERENT, Will (Will Bradbury)
Baker & Nietzel call the one story about **Sampson Roach**, Madison Avenue, New York, PI who actually makes money, "excellent." A rip-roarer complete with a missing heiress (luscious of course), blood feuds, pornography, a champion poodle, hippies and mobsters.
> Your Golden Jugular (1970, UK 1971)

Staccato, Johnny — TV: JOHNNY STACCATO

STAFFORD, Marjorie
A published criminologist whose "financial reverses had obliged him to put his technical knowledge to practical use and become a sort of glorified private detective," **Donald Clive** featured in, as Boucher put it, an "exercise in tidy emptiness," investigating murder in high diplomatic circles. Literate and knowledgeable with no action whatsoever.
> Death Plays The Gramophone (1953)

Stamberger, Godwin — PETERS, Ludovic
Standish, Ronald — SAPPER

STANFORD, Donald K.
A Mustang fighter pilot in WW2, **Dallas Webster**, of Yavapai, Arizona, smokes hand rolled Bull Durham, wears cowboy boots and works part-time on a dude ranch. An easy-going, laconic and tough Westerner, he operates as a rather reluctant PI. Enjoyable reads.
> Slaughtered Lovelies (1950, UK 1957)
> Bargain In Blood (1951, UK 1958)

Stanial, Paul — MacDONALD, John D.
Stanley, Bert — KING, Rufus
Stannard, Burl — FLYNN, J.M.
Stanwyck, Carole — TV: PARTNERS IN CRIME
STARK, Michael = LARIAR, Lawrence
NYT observed of Lariar's one Stark novel, featuring **Steven Ericson,**

"lest the story (errant husband becomes a corpse with a roll of atomic secret film) become too scientific, the author has introduced several lush females who threaten at times to divert Steve's attention from physics to physical charms, but he has just enough will power to restrain himself until the case is solved."

Run For Your Life (1946, UK 1948); as Kill-Box (1954)

Starrett, Dick & Jane — TV: DICK AND THE DUCHESS

STARRETT, Vincent 1886-1974

Named after a Chicago Cubs pitcher of the 1910s, **Jimmie Lavender** is the creation of a well-known Holmesian scholar, and Doyle's influence shows in short puzzle stories. Starrett was not good at characters and Lavender's most notable feature, eliminated in later stories, are his different colored eyes.

The Case Book Of Jimmie Lavender* (1944). SS

Stash, T.D. — PHILBRICK, W.R.

STEEL, Kurt (Rudolf Kagey 1904-1946)

Born in Iowa and raised in Chicago, **Hank Hyer** moves to New York and sets up as a PI, operating out of his Bank Street, Greenwich Village apartment. He is very expensive, charging up to $10,000 a case. Kagey, a New York University philosophy professor, was an hardboiled admirer of Hammett and his books are notable for character development, pace and lively dialogue. Hyer has a marked aversion to amateur and cerebral detectives. See **Films: MURDER GOES TO COLLEGE / PARTNERS IN CRIME.**

Murder Of A Dead Man (1935); as The Traveling Corpses (1942 abridged)

Murder For What? (1936)

Murder Goes To College (1936)

Murder In G-Sharp (1937); as Strangler's Holiday (1942 abridged)

Crooked Shadow (1939, UK 1945)

Judas Incorporated (1939)

Dead Of Night (1940, UK 1944)

Madman's Bluff (1941, UK 1945)

Ambush House (1943)

Steele, Argus — LEE, Babs

Steele, John — ODLUM, Jerome

Steele, Remington — TV: REMINGTON STEELE

Steele, Rocky — WEST, John B.

Steele, Tracy — TV: HAWAIIAN EYE

STEINER, Susan
Qutting a bad marriage and boring job, **Alexandra Winter** becomes an operative for Abromowitz & Bailey Investigative Agency, or, as they answer the phone, "the agency with a heart." Klein is particularly terse on the superficial feminism, "Cleverly, Steiner plays Alex Winter against herself in the contest between old and new woman . . . she is a mixture of awareness and unanalytical naiveté . . . The conclusion returns to what seems the most important issue throughout: Winter's responses to men."
        Murder On Her Mind (1985)

STEPHENS, Reed
Permanently losing his license after accidentally, and drunkenly, killing his policeman brother, **Mick 'Brew' Axbrewder** still works, sobering up from his guilt induced alcoholism, discreetly for his former partner **Ginny Fistoulari**, the backbone and brains of Fistoulari Investigations, who lost her hand to a bomb. Axbrewder is a very big man, a .45 Magnum being the only gun that "doesn't feel like a toy in my hand" and Ginny is pretty tough too. She almost lost her own license when somebody broke her nose with a crowbar and she shot him three times in the face. Very hardboiled stuff, with riveting situations. Marcia Muller (P&M) thinks their base of Puerta del Sol is in California.
        The Man Who Killed His Brother* (1980)
        The Man Who Risked His Partner (1984, UK 1985)

STEPHENSON, Neal
New Age PI **Sangamon Taylor** works for the Group of Environmental Extremists, going after major corporations' illegal toxic waste dumping, in this novel a threat to the entire biosphere in Boston harbor. *Drood Review* complain about Stephenson's individually interesting digressions on toxic waste chemistry, the staging of media events, bike and boat navigation of Boston, complex versus simple drugs and other topics that "muddy an already murky plot . . . fascinating in parts, but it's too lumpy to be easily digestible."
        Zodiac; The Eco-Thriller (1988)

STERANKO
An accomplished teenage escapologist and close-up magician, Steranko revolutionized comic book art in the late 60s with his dazzling, innovative techniques, in a style he called Zap Art that combined Op Art, psychedelia and motion picture effects, for Marvel Comic's *Nick Fury, Agent of SHIELD*. His tribute to the hardboiled novel, for which he conceived and wrote the narrative and executed the over 200 color illustrations, is a tour de force, evoking the style and atmosphere of such

classics as *Out Of The Past*, *Laura* and *The Long Goodbye*. The hero's name, **Chandler** (no forename), is the only crude note.

>Red Tide (1976)

Sterling, Brad — WARREN, Vernon
STERLING, Stewart (Prentice Winchell)
Among Winchell's unusual specialist detectives are a fire marshal, New York harbor police, a department store detective (as **Spencer DEAN**) and, as Sterling, a hotel detective, **Gil Vine**. His stories usually begin with a corpse being found in a bed or closet of the Plaza Royale, New York and go full speed from there, with wise-cracking Vine, who has an eye for the ladies, trying to protect the hotel's reputation. See also **Dexter ST. CLAIR.**

>Dead Wrong (1947)
>Dead Sure (1949, UK 1951)
>Dead Of Night (1950)
>Alibi Baby (1955, UK 1955)
>Dead Right (1956, UK 1957); as The Hotel Murders (1957)
>Dead To The World (1958, UK 1959); as The Blonde In Suite 14 (1959)
>The Body In The Bed (1959, UK 1960)
>Dead Certain (1960). Two novelets

Stevens, Dave — SADDLER, K. Allen
STEVENS, Frank
Boucher remarked that the one novel featuring New York PI **Russell Ames**, "for certain fetishists, offers the most generous servings of raincoats, high heels and flagellation scenes that I've encountered in an unspecialized publication. I don't see that it has anything more to offer to anyone else."

>She Left A Silver Slipper (1954, UK 1955)

Stevens, Johnny — KERR, Ben
STEVENSON, Richard
The gay community in Albany, New York has its problems with the city's finest, but **Don Strachey** manages to make a living as a Central Avenue PI nonetheless. Fast, clever plotting, well-observed gay backgrounds, engaging characters, dry wit and a very human and likable hero.

>Death Trick (1981, UK 1985)
>On The Other Hand, Death (1984)
>Ice Blues (1986)

STEWART, Gary
Mormons are warned off Stewart's books about Salt Lake City PI

Gabriel Utley. Called home from his New York base in the first book, Utley has effectively relocated in the second, cashing in his return ticket and opening an office on the mezzanine of the New Ritz Hotel, South Main. Breakneck action, interspersed with enlightenment on the many obscure aspects of Mormonism and a harsh look at a state that has been called America's largest minimum security prison. For another PI knock on the Mormons see Robert R. IRVINE.

> The Tenth Virgin (1983)
> The Zarahemla Vision (1986)

STEWART, Sam
Novelization of the pilot for **TV: McCOY** series featuring Travis McGee-like "salvage expert," conman-PI **McCoy.**

> The Big Rip-Off (1976, UK 1976)

STOCKWELL, Gail (Grace Stockwell)
NYT called young private detective **Kingsley Toplitt,** who "has been making a great reputation for himself" and is on good terms with the DA, and his wife **Sally** "delightful characters" without further comment. *SR* remarked that the second book was "ably plotted and mystifying throughout."

> Death By Invitation (1937)
> The Embarrassed Murderer (1938, UK 1938)

STODGHILL, Dick
Stodghill has a short story, "Wrongful Death," featuring Akron, Ohio,PI **Henry Paige,** in **A16.** Five years a cop, another five with Pinkerton's, twenty operating his own agency, he gives up and goes to work as investigator for a law firm.

STOKES, Manning Lee
Steel City PI **Steve Paget** is broke, desperate and just turned 40 when he's offered "a proposition so vile that even the hard-boiled detective was shaken," with a fortune to gain if he makes the right choices. **Barnaby Jones** was a PI in two novels, more exciting than coherent. In *Murder Can't Wait*, described by Boucher as fast, complex, grisly, harsh and violent, a PI whose license has been suspended is hired to kill an heiress and must work out how to collect the money without commiting murder.

Jones: The Wolf Howls "Murder" (1945)
> Green For A Grave (1946)

Paget: The Crooked Circle (1951); as Too Many Murderers (1955)

?:   Murder Can't Wait (1955)

Stone, Curt — SEWARD, Jack
Stone, Shep — JACKS, Jeff

Stone, Warren — HARPER, David
Stone, Zachary — EBY, Lois & John C. FLEMING
Stoner, Harry — VALIN, Jonathan
Stonestreet, Liz — TV: STONESTREET
Storm — CHANSLOR, Roy
Storm, J.D. — Films: HAZARD
Storm, John — ALLAN, Francis
STOUT, Rex 1886-1975
Fat, egotistical, orchid-growing, beer-swilling, indolent, house-bound, neurotic, Montenegran born **Nero Wolfe**, West 35th Street, Manhattan, is a Classic Sleuth but his competent legman and assistant **Archie Goodwin** introduced a hardboiled element and both had to work for a living, often assisted by freelance PI **Saul Panzer**. In 41 years neither Wolfe nor Goodwin aged in an hermetic world that Stout, an MWA President, created in minute detail that has many devoted fans, of which this writer is not one. There is even a Wolfe "biography", W.S. Baring-Gould's *Nero Wolfe Of West 35th St.* (1969). A Wolfe short story, "Bullet For One," from, *Curtains For Three*, is in **A9**. An independent PI, **Theodolinda 'Dol' Bonner**, who flipped a coin to decide between landscape design and detection, the only career options that would let her be her own boss, appeared in Wolfe books, Goodwin disparagingly refers to her as a "she-dick," in a novel of her own and one of those featuring **Tecumseh Fox**, who looks more like a chess player than a PI. Somewhat ludicrous is disbarred attorney turned PI, **Alphabet Hicks** who plays letter games. See **Robert GOLDSBOROUGH, Films: MEET NERO WOLFE / The LEAGUE OF FRIGHTENED MEN; TV: NERO WOLFE and Radio: THE ADVENTURES OF NERO WOLFE / The AMAZING NERO WOLFE / The NEW ADVENTURES OF NERO WOLFE.**
Wolfe: Fer De Lance* (1934, UK 1935); as Meet Nero Wolfe (no date)
       The League Of Frightened Men (1935, UK 1935)
       The Rubber Band (1936, UK 1936); as To Kill Again (1960)
       The Red Box (1937, UK 1937); as Case Of The Red Box (1958)
       Too Many Cooks* (1938, UK 1938)
       Some Buried Caesar* (1939, UK 1939); as The Red Bull (1945)
       Over My Dead Body (1940, UK 1940)
       Where There's A Will (1940, UK 1941)
       Black Orchids (1942, UK 1943); as The Case Of The Black
          Orchids (1950). Two novelets
       Not Quite Dead Enough (1944). Two novelets

Cordially Invited To Meet Death (1945); as Invitation To Murder (1956)

The Silent Speaker (1946, UK 1947)

Too Many Women (1947, UK 1948)

And Be A Villain* (1948); as More Deaths Than One (UK 1949)

The Second Confession (1949, UK 1950)

Trouble In Triplicate* (1949, UK 1949). Three novelets

In The Best Families (1950); as Even In The Best Families (UK 1951)

Three Doors To Death (1950, UK 1950). Three novelets

Door To Death (1951). Novelet

Curtains For Three (1951, UK 1951). Three novelets

Murder By The Book (1951, UK 1952)

Triple Jeopardy (1951, UK 1952). Three novelets

Prisoner's Base (1952); as Out She Goes (UK 1953)

The Golden Spiders (1953, UK 1954)

The Black Mountain* (1954, UK 1955)

Three Men Out (1954, UK 1955). Three novelets

Before Midnight (1955, UK 1956)

Might As Well Be Dead (1956, UK 1957) >

Three Witnesses (1956, UK 1956). Three novelets

If Death Ever Slept (1957, UK 1958)

Three For The Chair (1957, UK 1958). Three novelets

And Four To Go (1958); as Crime And Again (UK 1959). 4 novelets

Champagne For One (1958, UK 1959)

Plot It Yourself (1959); as Murder In Style (UK 1960)

Too Many Clients (1960, UK 1961)

Three At Wolfe's Door (1960, UK 1961). Three novelets

The Final Deduction (1961, UK 1962)

Homicide Trinity (1962, UK 1963). Three novelets

Gambit (1962, UK 1963)

The Mother Hunt (1963, UK 1964)

A Right To Die (1964, UK 1965)

Trio For Blunt Instruments (1964, UK 1965). Three novelets

The Doorbell Rang (1965, UK 1966)

Death Of A Doxy (1966, UK 1967)

The Father Hunt (1968, UK 1969)

Death Of A Dude (1969, UK 1970)

Please Pass The Guilt (1973, UK 1974)

A Family Affair (1975, UK 1976)

Corsage (1977). Contains a 1940 novelet

Death Times Three (1985) Three novelets

Bonner: The Hand In The Glove (1937); as Crime On Her Hands (UK 1939)

Fox: Double For Death (1939, UK 1940)

Bad For Business (1940); in The 2nd Mystery Book (UK 1945)

The Broken Vase (1941, UK 1942)

Hicks: Alphabet Hicks (1941, UK 1942); as The Sound Of Murder (1965)

Strachey, Don — STEVENSON, Richard

STRAHAN, Kay Cleaver

Billed as a "crime analyst," red-haired **Lynn MacDonald**, played a minimal role, often not appearing until the last part of books often set in Oregon or Nevada. She refers once to an all-woman office, "the girls whom I have trained," and is reluctant to work with men because "consciously, or unconsciously they work against me, because I am a woman." Klein finds her habit of moaning about failure just as she is about to announce success particularly annoying. Hammett remarked in a review that *Death Traps* would have made a good short story.

The Desert Moon Mystery (1928, UK 1928)

Footprints (1929, UK 1929)

Death Traps (1930, UK 1930)

October House (UK 1931, 1932)

The Meriwether Mystery (1932)

The Hobgoblin Murder (1934, UK 1935)

The Desert Lake Mystery (1936, UK 1937)

Strang, Mike — CAGNEY, Peter

Strange, James — QUINN, E. Baker

Strange, Johnny — Radio: RESULTS, INC.

Street, Nicholas — SCHACHNER, Nat

Stryker, B.L. — TV: B.L. STRYKER

Stuart, Bob — PECK, Winifred

Stuart, David — MacDOUGALL, James

SUCHER, Dorothy

Part Cool & Lam, part Wolfe & Goodwin, Washington, DC PIs **Sabina Swift**, the boss, and **Vic Newman** sleuth around murder at a Lake Champlain Physics Institute gathering of Nobel Laureates and their guests. Psychology major and psychiatric nurse Newman got the job when he answered a *Washington Post* ad saying "Wanted: resourceful,

hardworking, intelligent, average-looking person in search of varied and
interesting work. Irregular hours, occasional danger." The publishers think
the book will appeal to readers of Sayers and P.D. James.

> Dead Men Don't Give Seminars (1988)

Sughrue, Chauncy Wayne — CRUMLEY, James
Summers, Steve — MANOR, Jason
**Sutter, Arnie & Max — TV: BIG SHAMUS, LITTLE
    SHAMUS**
SUTTON, Tom & Byron PREISS
From the same stable as STERANKO's hardboiled graphic novel came a
feeble parody featuring 3 foot tall detective, **Schlomo Raven**, complete
with tiny trenchcoat and snap-brim hat, which, for artwork, storyline and
jokes, would have been rejected by *Mad* in its heyday, though clearly
deriving from its epic, offbeat set pieces. See A12.

> Raven (1975)

Swain, Mathew — McQUAY, Mike
SWAN, Phyllis
Baker & Nietzel think Swan's series about "St. Mary" PI **Anastasia
Jugedinski** "proves that a women can write just as poorly as any man."
The bastard daughter of a police chief, and a former policewoman, she's
been frigid since she was raped at 13, still being taunted by her rapist, and
lives with a would-be incestuous brother. "If you find all that a little
improbable, wait till you try on the plots."

> Trigger Lady (1979)
> You've Had It Girl (1979)
> Find Sherri (1979)
> Death Inheritance (1980)

Sweet, Nichole — HUSTON, Fran
Swift, Loren — HORNIG, Doug
Swift, Sabina — SUCHER, Dorothy
SWIGGETT, Howard 1891-1957
The blurb compared the first book featuring Maryland lighthouse dwelling
PI **Garrett Maynard**, to a three ring circus, with Maynard as ring-
master. *NYT* found the comparison apt, the plot confusing, the writing
lacking clarity, the characters poorly differentiated and the author unfair in
withholding information. Christopher Morley in *SR* however thought it
"an admirable detective story which is witty, original and well-bred."

> The Corpse In The Derby Hat (1937); The Stairs Lead Nowhere
>   (UK 1937)
> Most Secret . . . Most Immediate (1944)

SYLVESTER, Robert 1907-1975
Unromantic, financially successful PI **Ned Sherwood** of 36th &
Lexington, New York, usually sticks to safe jobs, and admits he's out of
his depth when he accepts an assignment in Havana, Cuba. A parodic
edge, contrasting himself with 'fictional' PIs, and a very tough story. See
Films: The BIG BOODLE.
    The Big Boodle (1954); as A Night In Havana (UK 1958)
SYMONS, Julian
As a critic, Symons is not partial to PIs who get short shrift in his genre
study *Bloody Murder* (1985, UK 1985). As an author he created large,
dandyish, deceptively languorous **Francis Quarles**, working as a PI
shortly after WW2.
    Murder! Murder! (UK 1961). SS
    Francis Quarles Investigates (UK 1965). SS
TACK, Alfred
Of the last title, the only one published in the US, *SR* commented
"Much slugging, chit-chat . . . Timekiller." Hubin lists other UK titles,
at least four of which may also feature London eye **John Harley.**
    Selling's Murder! (UK 1946) >
    Interviewing's Killing (UK 1947)
    The Prospect's Dead (UK 1948)
    Death Takes A Dive (UK 1950, 1957)
Taffle, Elliot — TV: TRIPLECROSS
Taggert, Clayton Yankee — RAY, Robert J.
TAIBO, Paco Ignacio II
Leading Mexican mystery writer with a **Philip Marlowe** short story,
"The Deepest South," in A12.
Talbot, Clem — MULKEEN, Thomas P.
Tank, Arthur — HALLAHAN, William
Tanna, Dan — TV: VEGA$
Tanner, John Marshall — GREENLEAF, Stephen
Taylor, David — TV: LEGMEN
TAYLOR, Elizabeth Atwood
Attending a 15th reunion at Vassar, intelligent, good-humored, somewhat
reckless newly licensed San Francisco PI **Maggie Elliott** investigates a
schoolmate's murder in an absorbing, if rather romantic story. She first
appeared as a young widow and newly reformed alcoholic investigating her
sister's death in *The Cable Car Murder** (1981, UK 1983).
    Murder At Vassar (1987)

TAYLOR, H. Baldwin = WAUGH, Hillary
Seven weeks after Aabco Private Investigation Services (the name chosen to be at the head of telephone directory listings, when the new books came out that is), above Papa Parma's Restaurant on 48th Street, New York, opened, **Pete Holland**, ex-Army Intelligence, started his first case going undercover as chauffeur to a wealthy family. Routine.

> The Trouble With Tycoons (1967); as The Missing Tycoon (UK 1967)

Taylor, Pete — ABRAHAMS, Robert D.
TAYLOR, Sam S.
NYT found the first novel about **Neal Cotten** who, while hardboiled, is afraid of guns, limping from one stock situation to another until the halfway point when it swung into considerable originality. Taylor tapped an occasionally glib vein of screwball and gallows humor with a lively pace that carried his predictable plots and stock characters. The jacket of *No Head For Her Pillow* boasts that it's "a fast, exciting mystery that is almost as tough as a 40¢ steak."

> Sleep No More (1949, UK 1951)
> No Head For Her Pillow (1952, UK 1954)
> So Cold, My Bed (1953, UK 1955)

Taylor, Sangamon — STEPHENSON, Neal
Tempest, William A. — SHAND, William
Temple, Wayne — PALMER, M.Earle
Tenafly, Harry — TV: TENAFLY
TEPPERMAN, Emile C.
Straightforward hardboiled PI, **Marty Quayle**, a brusque, tough-talking sort, lived at the Hotel Baltic, New York and featured in a short story, "Killers' Club Car" (*Ten Detective Aces* 1936; **A18**).

Thacker, Jerry — FLEMING-ROBERTS, G.T.
Thatcher, J.D. — WELLMAN, Manly Wade
Thieringer, Fritz — SOLOMON, Brad
Thin, Robin — HAMMETT, Dashiell
Thomas, Bernado — WILLIAMS, Louis
THOMAS, Jim (Thomas B. Reagan)
A New York PI, **Peter Cross** is a nosy fellow in one undistinguished book that came off very badly when compared to a Mark SADLER novel reviewed in the same week by *NYT*.

> Cross Purposes (1971)

THOMAS, Ross
Raised in backwoods West Virginia, **Jake Pope**, tall, impossibly good-

looking, quick-witted and restless, went to LA, answered an ad for a "young Southern gentleman of good moral character" and became a fast rising star in a hotshot investigative agency. When his heiress wife died in a car crash, he inherited $19 million and retired, coming back to his Washington, DC penthouse in The Simmie-Lee, 23rd & P, which he owns and is named after his hillbilly mother, to investigate the death of an old friend. Thomas always writes brilliant, witty, knowledgeable books and this is no exception. See **Oliver BLEECK**.

The Money Harvest (1975, UK 1975)

Thomas, Shep & Tony — TV: TWIN DETECTIVES
Thompson, Derek — BRADFORD, Kelly
Thompson, Harry — WAINWRIGHT, John
Thompson, Jeff — TV: MIAMI UNDERCOVER
THOMPSON, Jim 1906-1977

A major cultural hero in France, Thompson was one of the most hardboiled of all the tough guy writers, his novels frequently narrated by their psychopathic protagonists. The closest he came to the PI field was in a book featuring **Bugs McKenna**, ex-con become house dick of a West Texas oil town hotel. Trapped by his own stubborn integrity, McKenna is manipulated by others, including, in a cameo appearance, the most notable of all Thompson's killers, good old boy deputy sheriff and psychopath Lou Ford of *The Killer Inside Me*.

Wild Town (1957)

Thompson, Pat — DEAN, Robert George
Thompson, T.N. — Films: MR. DYNAMITE
THOREAU, David

A possible murder two years ago multiplies into a bloody power struggle between rival hoods as **Jimmy Lujack**, ex-LAPD vice squad detective turned bookie and full-time PI, investigates pro football chicanery where it's not whether you win or lose but whether you make the point spread. Classic, even formula ingredients, handled with wit and street smarts.

The Good Book (1988)

THORNBURG, Newton

Among Thornburg's intricate California novels is one in which the hero, tough, rootless Crow, finds purpose when his ex-cop turned PI father, **Orville Crow**, Sr gets murdered in a novel about money and power and their effects on people who witness things they don't understand and get killed simply for being in the wrong place at the wrong time. A suspenseful morality play, very well-written.

Dreamland (1983)

Thorne,Dave — TV: SURFSIDE 6
THORP, Roderick
USAF flying hero and former career cop **Joe Leland** of Leland
Associates, Manitou, is hero of what must be the longest PI novel of all,
over 500 pages of complex characterization that, in one reviewer's words
"combined the techniques of both the police procedural and private eye
novel with the domestic realism of a John O'Hara novel." It was also one
of the few non-Spillane PI books to make the bestseller lists. In the
second book Leland is a police consultant and SWAT tactics expert. See
Films: The DETECTIVE.
> The Detective (1966, UK 1967)
> Nothing Lasts Forever (1979)

Thorpe, Cassandra — BOWMAN, Robert
Thorton, Cory — Films: ARMED RESPONSE
Thursday, Max — MILLER, Wade
TIDYMAN, Ernest
As violent as Mike Hammer but more sophisticated and intelligent, big,
bold, black and bad **John Shaft** was raised in Harlem, enlisted in the
Marines, and came back from Vietnam a hero. After dropping out of law
school he joined a big agency, then went into business on his own on
46th Street, just south of Times Square. Tough enough for anything, he
hates injustice and is straight out of *Black Mask*. See **Films: SHAFT
/ SHAFT'S BIG SCORE / SHAFT IN AFRICA** and **T V:
SHAFT.**
> Shaft (1970, UK 1971)
> Shaft Among The Jews (1972, UK 1973)
> Shaft's Big Score (1972, UK 1972)
> Shaft Has A Ball (1973, UK 1973)
> Goodbye,Mr. Shaft (1973, UK 1974)
> Shaft's Carnival Of Killers (1974, UK 1975)
> The Last Shaft (UK 1975)

TINSLEY, Theodore
Heroine of 38 pulp stories, **Carrie Cashin** let people think her assistant
Aleck was head of her Cash & Carry Detective Agency because "most
clients had no faith in the ability of girl detectives." A Cashin story,
"Riddle In Silk" (*Crime Busters* 1938), is in **A3.**
Tobin, Mitch — COE, Tucker
Todd, Ben — McCANDLESS, D.B.
Todd, Jerry — FREEMAN, Martin J.
Tolefree, Philip — WALLING, R.A.J.

TONE, Teona
An historical PI who is also a woman, **Kyra Keaton** had a progressive father who foresaw women's emancipation and ensured she received a proper education. Running an 1899 agency from her Broad Street, Philadelphia mansion, young, beautiful, wealthy Keaton is a feminist, sexually emancipated, confident and capable, with a far-flung reputation and a network of street urchins. Tone was an investigator for an LA agency and writes well with good plot twists.

> Lady On The Line (1983)
> Full Cry (1985)

Toplitt, Kingsley & Sally — STOCKWELL, Gail
TOPOR, Tom
Tough, cynical and resourceful **Kevin Fitzgerald** is a New York PI, the son of a cop who committed suicide. Topor is excellent at characterization and establishing mood.

> Bloodstar (1978)
> Coda (1984)

TORREY, Roger
A *Black Mask* contributor, Torrey wrote short stories about a host of Irishmen but only one made it into book form. **Shean Connell** is a piano-playing San Francisco PI, with a 19 year old assistant **Lester Hoyt**, whose one ultra-hardboiled adventure is set in wide-open Nevada, complete with gangsters, white slavers, dope runners and blistering pace.

> 42 Days For Murder (1938)

Torve the Trog — PANSHIN, Alexei
Towne, Christina — TV: DIAMONDS
Townsend, Charles — TV: CHARLIE'S ANGELS
Tracy, Devlin — MURPHY, Warren
TRACY, Don
After a five book career as a US Army Military Police undercover agent, Master Sergeant **Gil Speer** retired from the service and went into private practice in Washington, DC, losing his special interest status in the process. Henri C. Veit (*Library Journal*) called the PI incarnation "mindless semi-macho," though *Publisher's Weekly* thought *High, Wide And Ransom* a "good yarn."

> Flats Fixed—Among Other Things (1974)
> High, Wide And Ransom (1976)
> Death Calling—Collect (1976)
> The Big X (1976)

Trapper, Mike — HOCH, Edward D.

Traveler, Moroni Jr. — IRVINE, Robert R.
Traven, Terry — MILLER, Geoffrey
Travers, Theresa — Radio: RESULTS, INC.
Trayne, Nick — Films: The LIVING GHOST
TREAT, Lawrence
While using his familiar policemen Bill Decker, Mitch Taylor and Jub Freeman, Treat, considered by many to be the father of the police procedural, made a PI, **Hank Greenleaf**, described by Boucher as realistically credible, and a patrolman, both of whom have good reason to suspect the other of murder, and the curious duel between the two men, the focus of one novel.

     Lady, Drop Dead (1960, UK 1960)
Tree, Ms Michael — COLLINS, Max Allan & BEATTY
Trees, D.L. — Films: FIND THE BLACKMAILER
Trent, Marla — KANE, Henry
Trevor, Carole — PHILIPS, Judson
TREYNOR, Blair
Picking up where he left off before he went to Korea, recently discharged Air Force Major **Pete Bayliss** looks for PI work in LA. Boucher described the book as "all pretty wild and lurid but a great deal of fun."

     Widows's Pique (1956, UK 1958)
TRIMBLE, Louis
Normally a marine insurance investigator would be pushing the limits of the definition of PI, but Trimble managed to pack sexy wenches and violent action galore into **Martin Zane**'s life. Another PI, **Joseph Coyle**, investigated murder and fraud in an Arizona-Mexico border trucking concern in what Boucher described as "a fast story, with fair avoidance of private eye clichés." Ace author Trimble, who also wrote as **Stuart BROCK**, wrote two SF novels about the **Anthropol Detective Agency** but I have been unable to locate either.

Zane: Cargo For The Styx (1959)
         The Dead And Deadly (1963)
Coyle: Love Me And Die (1960)
Anthropol: Anthropol (1968)
         The Noblest Experiment In The Galaxy (1970)
TRIPP, Miles
A private detective by chance, **John Samson** inherited a debt-collecting agency in South London. Still tracing missing persons and collecting divorce evidence, he also advises on security and does background investigations on prospective employees. Overweight, with a secretary,

Sandy, who nags him about it, he's well able to take care of himself or others. Tripp has been writing crime fiction for over 30 years, planting characters rather than clues. Note that although **Michael BRETT** is a Tripp pseudonym, the one listed above is not him.

> Obsession (UK 1973)
> The Once A Year Man (UK 1977)
> The Wife-Smuggler (UK 1977)
> Cruel Victim (UK 1979, 1985)
> Some Predators Are Male (UK 1985, 1986)
> The Frightened Wife (UK 1987, 1988)
> Death Of A Man-Tamer (UK 1987, 1987)

Tripp-Tyler, Winton — HOLT, Gavin
TROY, Simon = WARRINER, Thurman
Boucher, noting attempts by "third-rate British novelists" to imitate the American PI novel, found Warriner, as Troy, "unique, so far as I know, in successfully creating not an imitation but a translation of Spade, Marlowe and the rest," and thought London operative **Lee Vaughan**, while very British, was as unorthodox, tough-minded and yet humanely sympathetic as Carney Wilde. Called to a seaside hamlet by a woman whose husband planned to destroy a local paradise, *SR* found this early environmental story "not too convincing . . . amiably preposterous" but Boucher remarked on its "fine brooding sense of evil."

> Road To Rhuine (UK 1952, 1952)

Tucker — Films: PEEPER
Tucker, Amanda & Rick — TV: TUCKER'S WITCH
Tucker, Charity — BUCHANAN, Patrick
Tucker, Samuel Clemens — POTTER, Jerry Allen
TUCKER, Wilson
Boone, Illinois is a large town or small city, depending on state of mind and personal opinion, but it supports **Charles Horne**, Confidential Services, on Wisley Street, though the Union Workman's Mutual of Chicago makes a big difference with its insurance investigations. A very oddball specialty is that of **B.G. Brooks** who is investigator for the Association of American Memorial Parks or, as Boucher dubbed him, a cemetery-detective, in a scantily plotted but macabre delight. Tucker is one of the hardboiled writers much admired by the French, but unmentioned in any American context.

Horne: The Chinese Doll (1946, UK 1948)
> To Keep Or Kill (1947, UK 1950)
> The Dove (1948, UK 1950)

The Stalking Man (1949, UK 1950)
Red Herring (1951, UK 1953)
Brooks: The Man In My Grave (1956, UK 1958)
Tudor, Mark — NASH, Anne
Turner — GIBSON, William
Turner, Dan — BELLEM, Robert Leslie
Turner, E.L. — TV: TENSPEED AND BROWN SHOE
Turner, Milo — NEVINS, Francis M. Jr.
Turner, Nick — TV: DETECTIVE IN THE HOUSE
Turner, Russ — CORDER, Eric
Turner, Skip — Radio: ADVENTURES BY MORSE
Turner, Truck — Films: TRUCK TURNER
TURNER, William Price
British ex-mercenary soldier and assassin **Bruce Kirkwood**, cynical and wise but a failure at life and broke, works as a PI, following an errant husband on behalf of a selfish, egotistical bitch. Narrated in alternate chapters by the detective and his client, the novel stresses character as much as plot.
Another Little Death (UK 1970, 1971)
Tuttle, Albert — Films: ONE BODY TOO MANY
Twiggs, Emma — CARPENTER, Helen & Lorri
Twotoes, Tommy — ALEXANDER, David
Tyner, Nolen — LEONARD, Elmore
Tyner, Steve — SLESAR, Henry
ULLMAN, James Michael
His license has been suspended nine times and nearly revoked twice, the price **Max Fuller** pays for being the only honest PI in an unnamed Mid-West city in an Inner Sanctum Mystery Contest Award winner.
The Neon Haystack (1963, UK 1964)
UPTON, Roger
Still perceiving his duty with "something of the innocent clarity of a romantic youth," **Amos McGuffin** became a San Francisco PI mainly because of reading pulps when he was an impressionable youth and is still waiting for a platinum blonde, naked under a chinchilla coat, to come into his office. Live-in security officer of an old ferryboat, *Oakland Queen*, converted into offices on the Embarcadero by Ghiradelli Square, Amos is a dedicated drinker except when he's working, at which point he becomes totally dedicated, stops drinking completely and doggedly pursues the case to the bitter end. Witty and assured.
Who'd Want To Kill Old George? (1977)

Fade Out* (1984)
Dead On The Stick (1986)
The Fabergé Egg (1988)

USHER, Jack

A sharpster who has never been quite honest or quite criminal, **Stan Braden** hires out as a detective to find a lost girl. Boucher, who found Braden believably tough, commented that while the ingredients, dope, smuggling, pornographic pictures and blackmail, were overfamiliar, "it's related with unfamiliar competence, vigor and conviction."

The Fix (1959); as The Girl In The White Mercedes (UK 1960)

Utley, Gabriel — STEWART, Gary

VACHSS, Andrew

The ultimate urban survivalist, **Burke** is as tough as they come, a neo-hardboiled New York hustler who works every angle there is as he cruises round the lower depths in a handbuilt Plymouth 70 designed to be the ultimate New York cab, while Pansy, a Neapolitan mastiff and perhaps the most hardboiled dog ever (see Conall RYAN for the only competitor), guards his fortress home-cum-office. Extraordinary, violent and very impressive, with some of the most lurid characters ever created. Cyberpunk set in the present.

Flood (1985, UK 1986)
Strega (1987, UK 1988)
Blue Belle (1988)

Valentine, George — Radio: LET GEORGE DO IT

Valiant, Eddy — WOLF, Gary

VALIN, Jonathan

A military policeman in Vietnam, 6'3", 215 pound hunk **Harry Stoner** worked for the Pinkerton Agency and the DA's office before setting up as a PI in the Riorley Building, Cincinnati. In his 30s, Stoner is a child of the 60s but shares his home town's innate Puritanism. His nail-biting, truly scary explorations of flawed and lethal extended families show the festering corruption of social decay in the very heartland of America but do so in a natural, unforced way, his narrative voice being perhaps his greatest strength, though he also writes good dialogue, multi-faceted plots and memorable characters. Baker & Nietzel object strongly to his tendency to end books with a shoot-out. Valin has a **Philip Marlowe** short story, "Malibu Tag Team," in **A12**.

The Lime Pit (1980, UK 1981)
Final Notice (1980, UK 1981)
Dead Letter (1981, UK 1982)

Day Of Wrath (1982, UK 1983)
Natural Causes* (1983, UK 1984)
Life's Work (1986)
Fire Lake (1987)
Extenuating Circumstances (1989)
Vallon, Johnny — CHEYNEY, Peter
VAN ATTA, Winfred
Blacklisted in his beloved profession after causing a policeman's death, journalist **Jim Ferguson** finds work with a New York firm of management consultants which wants someone with investigative experience who can write reports. *NYT* called the novel "a well-integrated tale of high finance, conspiracy and detection."

A Good Place To Work And Die (1970, UK 1971)
VANCE, Jack
One of the foremost stylists in science-fiction, Vance wrote two typically surreal and linguistically off-beat stories about subtle, resourceful and competent "effectuator" Vv **Miro Hetzel** (Vv indicates an Ordinary of the Legion of Truth, a low-grade honorific used to address a person lacking aristocratic distinction).

Galactic Effectuator (1980). Two novelets
VANCE, William E. 1911-1986
Boucher described the one novel as "a mildly entertaining quickie; there's nothing startling in private eye **Peter Kirk**'s involvement with gangsters and beautiful twins in a Mississippi town but for all the routine violence and sex-teasing, Vance shows some likeable individuality in minor touches."

Homicide Lost (1956)
Vanesco, Jimmy — NEWMAN, G.F.
Van Kill, Hendrik — BAYNE, Spencer
Vanner, Rick — HEBERDEN, M.V.
Vaughan, Lee — TROY, Simon
VERALDI, Attilio
Operating out of a Naples, Italy, bar **Alessandro 'Sasa' Iovine** is neither PI nor lawyer, though he calls himself both, but a halfway house between crooks and cops, a fixer and odd job man. Violent and, in an Italian way, quite funny. See **Films: La MAZETTA**.

The Payoff (UK 1978, 1978)
Vernon,Val — WALLACE,Arthur
Vicente, Rose — SINGER, Shelley
Villiers, Anthony — PANSHIN, Alexei

Vincent, Johnny — CHESTER, Peter
Vine, Gil — STERLING, Stewart
Vynalek, Stefan — CHANDLER, A. Bertram
Waddell, Riley — MAHANNAH, Floyd
WADE, Harrison
Boucher described the one novel featuring PI **Johnny Fury** as "cheap and oversexed but agreeably competent and experienced."
      So Lovely To Kill (1956)
WAGER, Walter
Ex-CIA agent, cool, professional, well-connected, .357 Magnum packing **Alison B. Gordon**, owner of a $500-a-day Wilshire Boulevard, Beverly Hills, agency and "the best-looking 35 year old woman she knew, and she knew half the major actresses and sex symbols in Hollywood," sounds like a sexploiter blueprint, but Marcia Muller calls the books well-plotted thrillers with plenty of action and an appealing heroine. Klein disagrees radically; "a cartoon figure engaged in exploits which are difficult to take seriously." Certainly for a mere PI on a missing person case to foil an attempted right-wing takeover of America with hundreds of casualties does put the emphasis on thriller. Baker & Nietzel compare the style to "a gossip columnist with commando training."
      Blue Leader (1979, UK 1980)
      Blue Moon (1980, UK 1981)
      Blue Murder* (1981, UK 1984)
WAINWRIGHT, John
A former Yorkshire, England policeman and prolific, very uneven, expert in intricate police procedurals for twenty years, Wainwright finally turned to the PI novel with **Harry Thompson**, failed investigative journalist and husband, in a routine story set in the fictitious seaside resort of Rogate-on-Sands, somewhere in North West England.
      Blind Brag (UK 1988)
Walker, Amos — ESTLEMAN, Loren D.
Walker, Richard — LYNNE, James Broom
WALKER, Harry = WAUGH, Hillary
Very obscure Waugh novel, reviewed only by *SR* who said "New York op earns board at wife's cousin's Conn. farm by tracing hired hand. Many fenders dented but pace is nowhere over-hot."
      The Case Of The Missing Gardener (1954)
WALKER, Walter
A simple, unpleasant, but supposedly very well-paying job of motel room photography plunges Market Street, San Francisco PI **Hector**

Gronig into a frantic downward spiral with bodies piling up round him and the police looking at him in a nasty way. Taking more lumps than most PIs, Gronig features in a tight, humorous, well-paced story with vivid vignettes of San Francisco life. Walker has also written a novel of observation in which disreputable **Owen Carr**, a veteran PI whose card boasts "Never A Day Off Since 1949," doggedly traces the minutest clues and evidence to locate not a murderer but the victim, so that he can persuade the family to bring a civil damages suit against the killer.

Gronig: The Two Dude Defense (1985)
Carr: The Rules Of The Knife Fight (1986)

WALL, William
One cover of the only story featuring 6'3", 200 pound, two-fisted **Tony Boyle** shows a yacht, *Sea Urchin*, behind a half-naked man with marine cap and pistol putting an arm-lock on a half-naked girl. This is a little odd as there's no water at all in the very simplistic story, not even in the drinks, and the cover actually belongs to a marine adventure, *Logan* by Alan Joseph. Not quite bad enough for *Gun In Cheek*, but close.

Wake Up Dead (1974); as Quiet Terror (1980)

WALLACE, Arthur
Pronzini (*Gun In Cheek*) found one short-lived publisher who tried to translate the 'Spicy' magazine story into novel form, with Manhattan PI **Val Vernon** and "a plot with threads of seduction, sin and sanguinary murder . . . Time and again, the lure of the flesh almost proves his undoing. Lust is matched against cunning and the thrill battle rages until the last page." But, Pronzini tells us, Val never does get laid.

Passion Pulls The Trigger (1936); as Man Crazy (as by **James CLAYFORD** 1951)

Wallace, Brendan — **BREWER, Mike**
Wallace, Dirk — **CHASE, James Hadley**

WALLACE, F(loyd) L.
Boucher commented "I can't think of anyone, save possibly Bill Gault, who has written Southern California more as it is and less like the accepted detective-story myth. With nice integration the plot could have happened nowhere else," and described PI **Norman O. Hazard** as likeably medium-boiled.

Three Times A Victim (1957)

WALLACE, Patricia
Despite the ambiguous name, **Sydney Bryant** is a female PI. "Occasionally, it worked to her advantage to catch someone off-guard." Set in and around San Diego, the publishers, who specialize in horror

novels, flag it "in the best-selling tradition of Mary Higgins Clark. A spine-tingling novel of riveting suspense!" Actually, it's a bit slow.

>Small Favors (1988)

Wallace, William — LACY, Ed

WALLING, R(obert) A(lfred) J(ohn) 1869-1949

As Pronzini (P&M) so rightly says, Walling wrote some of the dullest mysteries ever committed to paper and his private inquiry agent, **Philip Tolefree**, who operates out of his London apartment, is a twit. Symons puts them both into his Humdrum School. More omniscient Classic Sleuth than PI.

>The Fatal Five Minutes (UK 1932, 1932)

>Follow The Blue Car (UK 1933); as In Time For Murder (1933)

>VIII To IX (1934); as The Bachelor Flat Mystery (1934)

>The Tolliver Case (UK 1934); as Prove It, Mr. Tolefree (1933)

>The Cat And The Corpse (UK 1935); as The Corpse In Green Pajamas (1935) >

>The Five Suspects (UK 1935); as Legacy Of Death (1934)

>The Corpse In The Crimson Slippers (UK 1936, 1936)

>The Corpse With The Dirty Face (UK 1936, 1936); as The Crime In Cumberland Court (UK 1938)

>Mr. Tolefree's Reluctant Witnesses (UK 1936); as The Corpse In The Coppice (1935)

>Bury Him Deeper* (UK 1937); as Marooned With Murder (1937)

>The Mystery Of Mr. Mock (UK 1937); as The Corpse With The Floating Foot (1936)

>The Coroner Doubts (UK 1938); as The Corpse With The Blue Cravat (1938)

>More Than One Serpent (UK 1938); as The Corpse With The Grimy Glove (1938)

>Dust In The Vault (UK 1939); as The Corpse With The Blistered Hands (1939)

>They Liked Entwhistle (UK 1939); as The Corpse With The Red-Headed Friend (1939)

>Why Did Trethewy Die? (UK 1940); as The Spider And The Fly (1940)

>By Hook Or By Crook (UK 1941); as By Hook Or Crook (1941)

>Castle-Dinas (UK 1942); as The Corpse With The Eerie Eye (1942)

>The Doodled Asterisk (UK 1943); as A Corpse By Any Other Name (1943)

The Corpse Without A Clue (UK 1944, 1944)

The Corpse With The Missing Watch (UK 1949)

Walsh, Clint — DE WITT, Jack

WALSH, Maurice 1879-1964

Taking up a cold murder case on behalf of a man still under suspicion, Irish PI **Con Madden** sifts the stories and alibis of nine suspects in Scotland. "Good characterizations, alluring background, plenty of red herrings and sufficiently baffling puzzle. Top drawer" (*SR*).

The Man In Brown (UK 1945); as Nine Strings To Your Bow (1945)

WALSH, Paul E.

Boucher described a novel about **Paul Damian** of Brooklyn as confused and unlikely in spots but told in a straightforward and likeable manner, free of clichés.

The Murder Room (1957)

WARDEN, Mike

After his partner is killed, the widow holding him responsible, **Hank Bradford** quits the Seattle police force and becomes a part-time teacher of Criminal Justice Planning and, more or less accidentally, a PI.

Death Beat (1980)

Dead Ringer (1980)

Bitter Homicide (1980)

Model For Murder (198?)

The Topless Corpse (1981)

WARGA, Wayne

Far be it from me to quarrel with the PWA and if it wants to honor **Jeffrey Dean**, ex-foreign correspondent and CIA courier turned LA rare book dealer, as a newcomer PI (Best First Novel award), so be it, but the second book strains the most generous definition even more than the first.

Hardcover (1987)

Fatal Impressions (1989)

WARREN, Charles Marquis

An amnesiac with a valuable secret is "needled all round Baltimore by thugs, private eye and two beautiful gals. Tough, hardboiled, speedy and fantastic. Christmas Eve party on chief thug's Maryland estate is high point. Raw meat" (*SR*). *NYT* gave it a seen-it-all-before review.

Deadhead (1949, UK 1950)

WARREN, James

Characterized by Boucher as second or third string British imitation, Warren's **James Weston** is a London ex-cop PI. Sandoe remarked "upper second-rate English mysteries which seem designed for performance by a competent provincial stock company." Other titles listed in Hubin may also be Weston novels.

> The Runaway Corpse (UK 1957); The Disappearing Corpse (1958)
> Cold Steel (UK 1957)
> Brush Of Death (UK 1958)

WARREN, Vernon (George Chapman)
British author of ersatz American-set hardboiled PI novels, most featuring **Mark Brandon** of Chicago. Others include Makkerline Building, 196B East 10th Street, New York, eye **Glen Ransom**, generic **Brad Sterling** and **Johnny Maquis** and Seattle based **Clifford Grant**. The books are much sought after by British collectors for their dust jacket artwork feature lots of violence, minimal sex and a more than usually shaky grasp of locale and language.

Brandon:	Brandon Takes Over (UK 1953)
	Brandon In New York (UK 1953)
	Brandon Returns (UK 1954)
	Brandon:The Blue Mauritius (UK 1954)
	No Bouquets For Brandon (UK 1955)
	Bullets For Brandon (UK 1955)
Ransom:	Appointment In Hell (UK 1956)
Maquis:	Back-Lash (UK 1960)
Sterling:	Farewell By Death (UK 1961)
Grant:	Invitation To Kill (UK 1963)

Warrender, James — COLE, G.D.H. & Margaret
WARRINER, Thurman
British author with an unusual, and very English, blend of do-gooders; **John Cornelius Franklin Scotter**, a brash, outspoken PI, Mr. Ambo, a very proper wealthy bachelor, and devil-fearing Archdeacon Toft. Warriner's interests in music, book collecting and ecclesiastical architecture and history get roped in. See also **Simon TROY**.

> Method In His Murder (UK 1950, 1950)
> Ducats In Her Coffin (UK 1951)
> Death's Dateless Night (UK 1952)
> The Doors Of Sleep (UK 1955)
> Death's Bright Angel (UK 1956)
> She Died, Of Course (UK 1958)
> Heavenly Bodies (UK 1956)

Warshawski, V.I. — PARETSKY, Sara

WASHBURN, L(ivia) J.
Set in Hollywood and LA during Prohibition and silent movie days, **Lucas Hallam**, who gained a reputation as a gunfighter in 1890s Texas and New Mexico, then was a lawman, a Federal Marshal and a Pinkerton agent, works as a film extra while his Los Angeles detective agency isn't doing business, resisting offers to make him a star. Hallam short stories are "On The Prod" (**A2** #2), "Hallam" (**A15**) and "Hollywood Guns" (**A17**). The author's husband is **James REASONER**.
> Wild Nights (1987)

Watson, Jane — TV: The RETURN OF SHERLOCK HOLMES

Watson, Sarah — McCANDLESS, D.B.

WAUGH, Hillary
Best known for his procedurals featuring Chief Fred Fellows, Waugh did not do so well with PI novels, though he started his writing career with them. **Sheridan Wesley**, who has a personal fortune that enables him to turn down cases that don't interest him; youngish, goodlooking **Peter Congdon**, required by the Brandt Detective Agency of Philadelphia to dress like a banker; **Simon Kaye** and **Philip Macadam** are all in the Marlowe mold. Kaye's specialty is damsels in distress. One book features a retired PI turned Texan oil tycoon (name unknown) who reactivates his old profession when his wife gets involved in a New York murder. See also **H. Baldwin TAYLOR** and **Harry WALKER**.

Wesley:	Madam Will Not Dine Tonight (1947, UK 1959); as If I Live ToDine (1949)
	Hope To Die (1948, UK 1949)
	The Odds Run Out (1949, UK 1950)
?:	Rich Man, Dead Man (1956); as Rich Man, Murder (UK 1956); as The Case Of The Brunette Bombshell (1957)
Macadam:	The Girl Who Cried Wolf (1958, UK 1960)
Congdon:	Run When I Say Go (1969, UK 1969)
Kaye:	The Glenna Powers Case (1980, UK 1981)
	The Doria Rafe Case (1980, UK 1982)
	The Billy Cantrell Case (1981, UK 1982)
	The Nerissa Claire Case (UK 1983)
	The Veronica Dean Case (UK 1984)
	The Priscilla Copperwaite Case (UK 1986)

WAYE, Cecil
I have been unable to locate any of the books about British detective **Christopher Perrin** but glowing contemporary reviews make them

sound like standard, tedious fare from the last days of the Golden Age when a generation of writers tried to adjust to the (then) new wave. Perrin is one of those sleuths to whom Scotland Yard seemed endlessly willing to turn for help when baffled.

> Murder At Monk's Barn (UK 1931)
> The Figure Of Eight (UK 1931, 1933)
> The End Of The Chase (UK 1932)
> The Prime Minister's Pencil (UK 1933, 1933)

Weatherby, Artie — MILLER, J.M.T.
Webb, Jimmy — ODLUM, Jerome
Webster, Dallas — STANFORD, Donald K
WEISS, Mike
Weiss, a San Francisco journalist, won a non-fiction Edgar for *Double Play: The San Francisco City Hall Killings* in 1984. His San Francisco PI **Ben Henry** is an ex-newspaperman, forced off the *Courier* for probing too deeply into police corruption, and making do as a cab driver.

> No Go On Jackson Street (1987)

WELCH, Timothy
To the world **Dion Quince** is a famous, award-winning writer, but he is also an undercover, secret PI employed by Univest, the world's biggest agency. Personally I find Quince unbearable but Baker & Nietzel describe him as smooth and skillful, the book as taut and gut-gripping. For no obvious reason another Quince story appeared as by **Patrick CAKE**.

> The Tennis Murders (1976)

Welles, Tiffany — TV: CHARLIE'S ANGELS
WELLMAN, Manly Wade 1903-1986
An SF writer who did some research, unlike most raiders on the genre, to produce one PI novel, featuring **Stonewall Jackson Yates**, who gets a job with beautiful **J.D. Thatcher** by beating up another applicant who's making a nuisance of himself. Full of incident and narrow escapes and described by Baker & Nietzel as "very good," the hero "well-drawn."

> Find My Killer (1947, UK 1948)

WELLS, Anna Mary
When her employer enters the armed forces, psychiatric nurse **Grace Pomeroy** joins the Keene Detective Agency but shows little enthusiasm for her new job; "on the whole she rather thought she preferred to lose it if every case was going to prove as harrowing as this of the Osgoods." When responsibilities conflict, she reverts to being a nurse.

> Murderer's Choice (1943, UK 1950)

WELLS, Charlie
Dubbing Memphis PI **Steve Lee** "the year's most incompetent private detective," Boucher advised that "addicts of Spillane, under whose aegis the book was written, may find it worthwhile groping through all of Lee's fumbling misdetection to read the final scene, a loving slice-by-slice description of a girl being cut into small pieces by an airplane."
>   The Last Kill (1955)

Wells, Ira — Films: The LATE SHOW
Wells, Mike — LARIAR, Lawrence
Welpton, Sam — SAXON, John A.
WENTWORTH, Patricia 1878-1961
A retired teacher, **Maud Silver** augments her small, fixed income as a private investigator, operating out of her Marsham Street, London sitting room. Though often compared to Miss Marple, Silver is a true professional, even to breaking and entering in search of evidence and especially in getting paid, often very well. Her hats and knitting are deliberate camouflage to disarm attention and her clients are usually young couples from good families. Classically plotted and competently written cozies that vary between straight detection and romantic danger.
>   Grey Mask (UK 1928, 1929)
>   The Case Is Closed (UK 1937, 1937)
>   Lonesome Road (UK 1939, 1939)
>   In The Balance (1941); as Danger Point (UK 1942)
>   The Chinese Shawl (UK 1943, 1943)
>   Miss Silver Deals With Death (1943); as Miss Silver Intervenes
>   (UK 1944)
>   The Key (1944, UK 1946)
>   The Clock Strikes Twelve (1944, UK 1945)
>   She Came Back (1945); as The Traveller Returns (UK 1948)
>   Pilgrim's Rest (1946, UK 1948); as Dark Threat (1951)
>   Latter End (1947, UK 1949)
>   Wicked Uncle (1947); as Spotlight (UK 1949)
>   The Case Of William Smith (1948, UK 1950)
>   Eternity Ring (1948, UK 1950)
>   Miss Silver Comes To Stay (1949, UK 1951)
>   The Catherine Wheel (1949, UK 1951)
>   The Brading Collection (1950, UK 1952)
>   Through The Wall (1950, UK 1952)
>   Anna, Where Are You? (1951, UK 1953); as Death At The Deep
>   End (1963)

The Ivory Dagger (1951, UK 1953)
The Watersplash (1951, UK 1954)
Ladies' Bane (1952, UK 1954)
Vanishing Point (1953, UK 1955)
Out Of The Past (1953, UK 1955)
The Benevolent Treasure (1954, UK 1956)
The Silent Pool (1954, UK 1956)
Poison In The Pen* (1955, UK 1957)
The Listening Eye (1955, UK 1957)
The Gazebo* (1956, UK 1958); as The Summerhouse (1967)
The Fingerprint (1956, UK 1959)
The Alington Inheritance (1958, UK 1960)
The Girl In The Cellar (UK 1961)

WERRY, Richard R.
Operating from Woodward Avenue, Birmingham, near Detroit, **Jane Mulroy** is "your average Vic Tanny model—give ten pounds and two inches—123 pounds, five foot five, Irish black hair, eyes so blue they're almost black," who carries a snub-nosed .32 in her purse and relies on former Miami Dolphins tight end and black belt karate instructor Ahmad Dakar for the rough stuff. Funny and violent.

Casket For A Lying Lady (1985, UK 1985)

Wesley, Sheridan — WAUGH, Hillary
West, Delilah — O'CALLAGHAN, Maxine
WEST, Elliott
15 years an LA PI, after a WW2 captaincy, stints as an insurance investigator, Burns man and LA County DA's legman, **Jim Blaney** is pushing 50, divorced, tough and worldly-wise. He can't take punches the way he used to but he's got nerves of steel. Robert B. PARKER described the book as "powerful, human and exciting as hell," while *Kirkus Review* found it "fast and zigzaggy with many reverses to keep you in high gear." It's also a bit talky.

The Killing Kind (1976, UK 1986)

West, Honey — FICKLING, G.G.
WEST, John B. ?-1960
A 6'3", 198 pound ex-prize fighter and WW2 commando with a Manhattan office for Steele Special Services, a sexy karate expert secretary, a .45 automatic and a Cadillac, Aloysius Algernon **'Rocky' Steele**, a cross between Mike Hammer and Shell Scott, filled the gap when Spillane stopped writing at one point, In Max Allan COLLINS' words (P&M), West's strengths are "energetic pulpiness of the plots and

confident, tin-ear tough-guy dialogue." West was black, a specialist in tropical medicine and prominent in Liberia where he lived.

> An Eye For An Eye* (1959)
> Cobra Venom (1959)
> A Taste For Blood (1960)
> Bullets Are My Business (1960)
> Death On The Rocks (1961)
> Never Kill A Cop (1961)

WESTLAKE, Donald

The versatile Westlake has written everything from ultra-tough capers to pure farce, including PI novels as **Tucker COE**. His second book under his own name, featuring **Tim Smith**, the only PI in Winston, New York, has been compared to Hammett's *Red Harvest* and has a climax every bit as bloody. On the farce side, one of the novelets in *Enough!*, "A Travesty," features **John Edgarson** of Tobin-Global Investigations Service—Matrimonial Specialists, blackmailing the movie critic hero, who accidently killed the girl friend for whose husband the agency is working, and causing as much trouble dead as alive.

> Killing Time (1961, UK 1962); as The Operator (1964)
> Enough! (1977, UK 1980) Two novelets

Weston, James — WARREN, James
Weston, John — WILSON, Gahan
WEVERKA, Robert

Novelization of TV: **GRIFF**, featuring retired LAPD Captain **Wade Griffin** who opens a PI office with assistant **S.Michael Murdoch**.

> Griff (1973)

WHALLEY, Peter

Many PIs have been behind bars, but easy-going **Harry Somers** may be the only rightly sentenced ex-con in the business. After a second stretch in Her Majesty's Prison Wormwood Scrubs, Somers answers an ad and finds himself working for the tinpot Coronet Private Detective Agency, above a dry cleaners in Bethnal Green, East London. When the boss drops dead, his secretary-mistress inherits the business and makes Somers a partner. Good seedy plots, earthy dialogue and realistic characters.

> Robbers (UK 1986, 1987)
> Bandits (UK 1986); as Crooks (1987)
> Villains (UK 1987); as Rogues (1988)

WHEELER, Benson & Claire Lee PURDY

Authors of a single melodrama in which PI **Urgan March** is called to Zombi Island, South Carolina, so-called from its voodoo history, to determine which of seven guests to the only house murdered the hostess. *NYT* remarked "It is not difficult to guess who did the killing and one feels that March is no great shakes as a detective, else he might have prevented some of the bloodshed, but the story will please those who like a macabre tale in a setting made for mystery."

The Riddle Of The Eighth Guest (1936)

Wheeler, Dan — LEE, Edward

WHELTON, Paul
A reporter for the Belle City *Press-Bulletin*, **Garry Dean** is, on at least one occasion, hired as a PI because of his known penchant for crime investigation. There are 5 other Dean titles. Standard 40s tough-guy stuff.

Call The Lady Indiscreet (1946, UK 1946)

Whistler — CAMPBELL, Robert

White, Blackie — JOHNSON, Philip

White, Lance — TV: The ROCKFORD FILES

WHITFIELD, Raoul 1898-1945
An erratic writer, Whitfield's 100+ *Black Mask* stories varied between stock action yarns and superlative hardboiled masterpieces. One of his three novels features Hollywood Boulevard PI **Ben Jardinn** in a complex tale that E.R. Hagemann (Reilly) thinks is Whitfield's best, though Baker & Nietzel dismiss it as "a cynical distrusting hardboiled in the Chandler tradition." Unfortunately it was written two years before Chandler even submitted his first short story and Sandoe considered its toughness more compelling than *Farewell, My Lovely*. Whitfield also wrote short stories as **Ramon DECOLTA**, two, "China Man" (*Black Mask* 1932; **A6**) and "The Black Sampan" (*Black Mask* 1932; in Pronzini & Greenberg: *The Ethnic Detectives*), appearing in anthologies as by Whitfield.

Death In A Bowl (1931)

Whitney, Lionel — TV: TENSPEED AND BROWN SHOE

Whitney, Whit — DODGE, David

WHITTINGTON, Harry
One of the best, most inventive and fast-paced writers of paperback originals in the 50s and 60s, Whittington, whom French connoisseurs bracket with James M. Cain, wrote at least one PI novel featuring tall, distinguished looking **Pat Raffigan** of Indigo City.

The Lady Was A Tramp (1951)

Wiggins — WILSON, Karen

Wilcox — LISOWSKI, Joseph

Wilcox, Carl — ADAMS, Harold

WILCOX, Collin
Author of well-known San Francisco procedurals (see **Bill PRONZINI** for a co-authored book co-starring 'Nameless' and Lt. Hastings) Wilcox turned to actor-playwright **Alan Bernhardt**, a freelancer for San Francisco's Dancer Ltd., run by ruthless, Jesuitical Hubert Dancer. A routine missing person case explodes when Bernhardt discovers that he's working on behalf of a hitman. A nerve-wracking climax.
> Bernhardt's Edge (1988)

Wild, Charlie — Radio: CHARLIE WILD, PRIVATE DETECTIVE
Wilde, Carney — SPICER, Bart
WILDE, Percival 1887-1953
An apprentice PI studying with the Acme International Detective Correspondence School of South Kingston, New York, **Peter Moran**, a Wall Street tycoon's chauffeur who lives in a Connecticut village, isn't doing very well at it. He stumbles across crimes but invariably "deducts" wrong, though somehow coming out on top. Ellery Queen thought Moran the best comic detective of his era and Pronzini (P&M) concurs heartily. Rascally **Bill Parmalee** specializes in gambling cases.
Parmalee: Rogues In Clover (1929). SS
Moran: P. Moran, Operative* (1947, UK 1947). SS
Wilde, Timothy — RIGSBY, Howard
WILHELM, Kate
The eminent SF writer, like many others, turned her attention to the PI with ex-NYPD **Charlie Meiklejohn** and his former psychology professor wife-partner **Constance Leidl**, now living in upstate New York, who first investigate a double murder in a small theater company during a hard Oregon winter. Strong characterization and intricate plotting, with the second book described as a taut, high-tech mystery abounding with ingenuity.
> The Hamlet Trap (1987, UK 1988)
> Smart House (1989)

WILLEFORD, Charles 1919-1988
In 1949 a professional soldier on weekend leaves wrote a novel in a sleazy Powell Street, San Francisco hotel, that launched a remarkable, if belatedly recognized, literary career. Willeford wrote many more tough, gritty, hardboiled novels but never had a PI hero again. Amoral **Jacob C. 'Jake' Blake**, whose office is in the undesirable mezzanine of the King Edward Hotel, San Francisco, where he also lives, is hired to shake off two goons who are following the beautiful, insane young wife of a

socially prominent, elderly architect, becoming entangled in a web of deception, intrigue and multiple murder, ending up as the fall guy.

> Wild Wives (1956 with High Priest Of California, author's name misspelled as Williford)

Williams, Doc — LATIMER, Jonathan

WILLIAMS, Louis
Baker & Nietzel award Williams' one book the title The Best Unread PI Novel of the Past Decade. Set in Punto Fijo, Venezuela, whence **Bernado Thomas**, son of a Venezuelan whore and a drowned American tramp ship's captain, raised by relatives in the American South and trained as a lawyer, has returned. Drinking heavily, depressed, plagued by existential crises, he plays Russian roulette until hired in a case with a body count so high the priest and gravediggers lose track. "A novel with a Crumley style . . . leaves you feeling like Thomas feels at the end—(like) you have given the party of your life and all the guests have gone home."

> Tropical Murder (1981)

WILLIAMS, Philip Lee
The first Atlanta, Georgia PI since Jim Hardman is former baseball player **Hank Prince**. Literate, flip and often drunk, his habit of quoting from movies is engaging enough to carry an overloaded and uninteresting plot.

> Slow Dance In Autumn (1988)

Williams, Race — DALY, Carroll John

WILLIAMSON, Chet
Known only from a *Mystery Scene* ad, unreviewed anywhere and seemingly unavailable in bookstores, is a novel about **McKain**, who "has two adversaries—his conscience and his disease—either of which could kill him" and who covers up evidence that a client, also dying, is guilty of murder. Claimed to be "a killer cocktail mix with twists of Fleming, Robert Bloch and Mickey Spillane."

> McKain's Dilemma (1988)

Willow, Tuthill — SPENCER, Ross H.

WILLS, Thomas = ARD, William
Ard used this name for a novel about **Barney Glines**, New York PI at 49th & Madison, who also appeared in a novel under Ard's own name.

> You'll Get Yours (1952; as by **William ARD** 1960)

WILMOT, Robert Patrick
Owning 10% of Confidential Investigations, Manhattan, among the largest, most successful agencies in the world, **Steve Considine** specializes in recovering stolen property. Happily married, both he and his smooth boss **Mike Zacharias**, an iron hand under a silk glove, not

above slipping brass knuckles on under the silk if necessary, have a fine sense of humor. Boucher regarded *Blood In Your Eye* as the "most genuinely Hammett-like book which this column has covered for years."

Blood In Your Eye (1952, UK 1954)
Murder On Monday (1953, UK 1954)
Death Rides A Painted Horse (1954, UK 1955)

Wilson, Dick — SPROUL, Kathleen
Wilson, Donald — Films: DUMB DICKS
WILSON, Gahan
Billed as Humor/Science Fiction, the *New Yorker* illustrator and *Playboy* writer wrote a "hilarious, affectionate, illustrated parody" of the classic 30s and 40s hardboiled detective novel featuring **Eddy Deco**. Play fair clues in the text and 100+ drawings are meant to provide a well-turned mystery in its own right as well as featuring fairly obvious insider references, but the climax is from another genre. A heavy, complicated, pastiche features ex-Government agent **John Weston** playing hardboiled Archie Goodwin to his former superior turned ace detective, **Enoch Bone**, as they pursue an evil genius bent on taking over America.

Deco: Eddy Deco's Last Caper (1987)
Bone: Everybody's Favorite Duck (1988)

WILSON, Karen
A short story in **A21**, "Hot As A Pistol," concerns the first real caper in the young detecting career of cool LA lesbian PI **Wiggins**.

WILTZ, Chris(tine)
The fourth generation of a family of cops, **Neal Rafferty** has to quit the New Orleans Police Department when he tangles with a powerful politician and becomes a PI based in the Jesuit Fathers Building. Very well written with a strong sense of place, but rather flat characterization.

The Killing Circle (1981, UK 1987)
A Diamond Before You Die (1987, UK 1988)

Windrow, Martin — NISBET, Jim
Wine, Moses — SIMON, Roger L.
Winfield, Carter — GILBERT, Dale L.
Winfield, Sandy III — TV: SURFSIDE 6
Winnick, Pete — GARDNER, Erle Stanley
Winslow, Myra — Films: PRIVATE DETECTIVE
Winter, Alexandra — STEINER, Susan
WINTER, Bevis
British author who obviously read a lot of PI fiction. Santa Monica (?) PI **Steve Craig** is a reasonable imitation of run of the mill, second-rate

American writing. Winter's books as **Al BOCCA** and **Peter CAGNEY** are much the same.

> Redheads Cool Fast (UK 1954)
> Darker Grows The Street (UK 1955); as A Noose Of Emeralds (1956)
> The Dead Sleep For Keeps (UK 1955)
> Next Stop—The Morgue (UK 1956) >
> Let The Lady Die (UK 1957)
> The Night Was Made For Murder (UK 1957)
> Sleep Long, My Lovely (UK 1958)
> Blondes End Up Dead (UK 1959)
> The Dark And Deadly (UK 1961)

Winters, Rose — TV: BIG ROSE; DOUBLE TROUBLE

WISE, Arthur

An investigator for a London agency, **Ned Sanderson** finds himself lost in the provincial wilderness, bored by a dull industrial espionage case. Reads like a PI novel written by Jean-Paul Sartre.

> The Death's-Head (UK 1962)

WOHL, James P.

Ex-lawyer and insurance investigator **Sam Gross** works for an insurance company in the first of two novels, freelances, though somewhat of an industry pariah after getting fired, in the second. Wohl alternates between the hero's point of view and the villains' in complicated big money fraud scams.

> The Nirvana Contracts (1977)
> The Blind Trust Contracts (1978, UK 1980)

Wolfe, Nero — STOUT, Rex / GOLDSBOROUGH, Robert

WOLF, Gary

A bizarre attempt to write a surreal Lewis Carroll style PI novel; **Eddie Valiant** is hired by a cartoon character to find out why its contract is being terminated. Neither parody nor satire, it's very hard to read. Another Valiant title, *Who Ordered Donald Duck?*, and a straightforward PI novel, *What's Left Of Alice Withers?*, featuring **Ernie Hunter**, were planned, according to Baker & Nietzel, but I can find no evidence of them. See **Films: WHO FRAMED ROGER RABBIT?**

> Who Censored Roger Rabbit? (1981)

WOLFF, Benjamin

Highly decorated in Vietnam, **John Baron Hyde** buries himself in teaching karate in LA and working part time for a PI until he realizes and accepts that he's in love with danger. The first book was competent

California hardboiled, the second an over-written international thriller.

    Hyde And Seek (1984)

    Hyde In Deep Cover (1985)

Wong, Joseph — Films: The PRIVATE EYES

WOOD, Ted

One of the leading lights of the renaissance (naissance?) of the Canadian crime novel, Woods' series character Vietnam vet **Reid Bennett**, chief of police of Murphy's Harbor, undertakes private assignments during vacations, once helping a friend with Toronto construction site security problems and again in a straight action-adventure novel set in the Canadian wilderness. See also **Jack BARNAO**.

    Live Bait (1986)

    When The Killing Starts (1988)

Woodfield, Will — FOOTE-SMITH, Elizabeth

WOODFIN, Henry

Wooden and dated novel, opportunistically "contemporary" with "freaked-out hippies, drug heads and dangerous radicals," including black activists, on campus. **John Foley** is a caricature—he goes through flimsy tail shaking motions on his way to meet his client for the first time.

    Virginia's Thing (1968)

Woodruff, James — TV: MY FRIEND TONY

WOODY, William

El Paso detective **Houston McIver** has a Siamese cat as a Watson in a story reputed to be better than its title suggests, with well realized border locales.

    Mistress Of Horror House (1959)

Worden, Pete — GAULT, William Campbell

Work, Max — AUSTER, Paul

Worth, Stuart — ROPER, L.V.

WREN, M.K. (Martha K. Renfroe)

Rich, handsome, half-Irish, half Nez Percé Indian, ex-Intelligence officer **Conan Flagg** owns a bookstore, ruled by Meg, a blue-point Siamese cat, in Holliday Beach, Oregon and keeps quiet about being a licensed PI. Predictable plots but the characters and setting are well drawn.

    Curiosity Didn't Kill The Cat (1973, UK 1975)

    A Multitude Of Sins (1975, UK 1976)

    Oh, Bury Me Not (1976, UK 1978)

    Nothing's Certain But Death* (1978, UK 1978)

    Seasons Of Death (1981, UK 1984)

    Wake Up, Darlin' Corey (1984, UK 1985)

Wren, Russel — BERGER, Thomas
Wright, Eddie — MULLEN, Clarence
WRIGHT, Wade (John Wright)
A British author writing ersatz hardboiled American-set PI novels, this time about **Bart Condor** of New York and with rather more pace and toughness than usual.

> Blood In The Ashes (UK 1964) >
> Suddenly You're Dead (UK 1964)
> A Hearse Waiting (UK 1965)
> Until She Dies (UK 1965)
> Blonde Target (UK 1966)
> Shadows Don't Bleed (UK 1967)
> Two Faces Of Death (UK 1970)

Wyler, Jake — TV: The JUDGE & JAKE WYLER
Wyman, Press — TV: DETECTIVE IN THE HOUSE
Yaeger, Alva — BLOOMFIELD, Robert
Yamamura, Trygve — ANDERSON, Poul
YARDLEY, James A.
Naive, virginal **Kiss Darling** works for **Angus Fane**, who plans her seduction while interviewing her. In Klein's words, "she is merely a plot device to generate two exotic and erotic cartoon-like adventures," though conceding that they occasionally seem to be tongue-in-cheek with genre mocking excess.

> Kiss The Boys And Make Them Die (UK 1970, 1970)
> A Kiss A Day Keeps The Corpses Away (UK 1971, 1971)

Yates, Bill — DOUGLAS, Malcolm
Yates, Jackson — WELLMAN, Manly Wade
Yew, Pamela — HOYT, Richard
York, Reggie — Radio: I LOVE A MYSTERY
York, Simon — Films: LOCKER SIXTY-NINE
Yorke, Hamilton — DICKSON, Arthur
YOUNG, David
A Kafkaesque experimental novel, seasoned with grim humor. **Jack Brisbane** investigates a missing person case against a backdrop of the Bureau, a vast Canadian organization, constantly assessing and restreaming its various facets, cagily surviving the periodic circulation of his file while colleagues and friends get cold feet during policy swings, accepting voluntary reassignment or leaving.

> Agent Provocateur (Can 1976)

YUILL, P.B. (Gordon Williams & Terry Venables)
Perhaps the best of all British PIs is cocky Londoner, ex-copper and cured alcoholic **James Hazell**, a cheerful, tough East Ender in whose wryly humorous cases the city is a living, realistic setting, the rhythms and modes of language are caught with force and accuracy, the plots are convincing and unpretentious, the dialogue is earthy and witty and there is a light touch of moral comment on class distinctions. Like Kevin O'HARA's Chico Brett, Hazell has a Shepherd Market, Mayfair, office. "Yuill" teamed novelist Gordon Williams and soccer club manager Terry Venables, whose streetwise input was clearly vital to the powerful realism. The character was well translated in the British **TV: HAZELL.**
> Hazell Plays Solomon (UK 1974, 1975)
> Hazell And The Three Card Trick (UK 1975, 1975)
> Hazell And The Menacing Jester (UK 1976)

Zabriskie, Eve — OSTER, Jerry
Zacharias, Mike — WILMOT, Robert Patrick
ZACKEL, Fred
Carrying Ross Macdonald's imprimatur, "Powerful . . . I recommend it with pleasure," Zackel's first book is very much in the Macdonald mold, a little too literary for its own good. San Franciscan **Michael 'Mike' Brennan** has been fired by the Pacific Continental agency and is waiting for his PI license to expire when a $1000 bill from a dead man puts him back in business. Depressed, divorced and drawing unemployment benefit, Brennan is cynical, self-pitying and dogged. See **TV: COCAINE AND BLUE EYES.**
> Cocaine And Blue Eyes* (1978)
> Cinderella After Midnight (1980)

ZADRA, Dan
Novelization of **TV: MAGNUM P.I.** featuring Tom Selleck as Hawaiian eye **Thomas Magnum**. See also **Roger BOWDLER.**
> Magnum P.I. (1985)

ZAHAVA, Irene (ed) — see **ANTHOLOGIES: 19**
Zanca, Joe — FREY, James N.
Zane, Martin — TRIMBLE, Louis
Zapper, Harriet — Films: BIG ZAPPER
ZAREMBA, Eva
A member of three PI minorities, **Helen Keremos** is Canadian, a woman and a lesbian (though this last is known from an author interview rather than the text). A Navy veteran operating out of a second-floor walk-up in Vancouver's China town, she's tough, savvy, hardboiled and

somewhat brusque with clients. The plot has several twists and turns with Canadian atmosphere well incorporated. Klein disliked the first book (at least) with some passion.

A Reason To Kill* (1978)

Work For A Million (1987)

ZELAZNY, Roger

An independent contractor associated with Walsh's Private Investigations, the third largest detective agency in the world, Zelazny's future hero worked on the setting up of the world's Central Data Bank, but as his own records are not included, as far as the computers are concerned, he doesn't exist. For each of the three assignments in this book, he taps into the Data Bank and creates an entirely new paper identity.

My Name Is Legion (1976, UK 1979). Three novelets.

ZOCHERT, Donald

A Denver PI with a murky past and a long list of prejudices, **Nick Caine** appears in two hardboiled books whose style Baker & Nietzel find affected though they have high praise for the opening chapter of the first, Montana-set, novel, of which Stanley ELLIN said, "Powerful and totally engrossing from start to finish."

Another Weeping Woman (1980, UK 1983)

The Man Of Glass (1982, UK 1983)

MISSING PERSONS

On 22 occasions I was unable to determine the name of the PI character in a book. Any information on the books, films and radio programs below would be gratefully received.

BAKER, Sidney J.; Time Is An Enemy (1958)
BESTOR, Clinton; The Corpse Came Calling (1941)
BLOCH, Robert; Shooting Star (1958)
CHRISTOPHER, Constance; Dead Man's Flower (1988)
COX, Irving E.; Murder Among Friends (1957)
DEKKER, Carl; Woman In Marble (1972)
GLICK, Carl; Death Sits In (1954)
HOPKINS, A.T.; Have A Lovely Funeral (1954)
KENNEDY, Elliot; The Big Loser (1972)
KENNEDY, Stetson; Passage To Violence (1954)
LARIAR, Lawrence; Friday Is For Death (1949)
LARSON, Russell W.; Death Stalks A Marriage (1956)
PENFIELD, Cordelia; After The Widow Changed Her Mind ((1933)
REYNOLDS, Mack; The Case Of The Little Green Men (1951)
WALKER, Harry; The Case Of The Missing Gardener (1954)
WARREN, Charles Marquis;Deadhead (1949)
WAUGH, Hillary; Rich Man, Dead Man (1956); as Rich Man, Murder
        (UK 1956); as The Case Of The Brunette Bombshell (1957)
Films; NIGHTKILL, SKIP TRACER, PINK CHIQUITAS
Radio; BIG GUY, EASY MONEY

TELEVISION

A. DUNSTER LOWELL (1960). Eccentric, rather ludicrous sounding series starring Robert Vaughn as **A. Dunster Lowell**, a gentleman detective with Peter Gunn length hair, Ivy League clothes, a 1948 Jaguar convertible, a terrier, a New England agency and, best of all, extra-sensory perception. The show may possibly have never been aired.

ACAPULCO (February-April 1961). Somewhat marginal as the two heroes, **Gregg Miles** (James Coburn) and **Peter Malone** (Ralph Taeger), Korean War veterans turned girl-chasing Acapulco beachcombers, were mainly bodyguards to a retired criminal lawyer, Mr Carver (Telly Savalas), but the work took them into PI areas as they protected their boss from attempts at revenge by underworld characters and looked after his business interests. Operating out of Bobby's Place, a bistro, they traveled around by motor scooter.

ACE CRAWFORD, PRIVATE EYE (March-April 1983). Comedy show featuring Tim Conway as hard-nosed, trench-coated but bumbling **Ace Crawford** whose extraordinary luck and blind chance had given an undeserved reputation, much to the chagrin of the incredulous police, making him irresistible to women. He hung out at The Shanty, a sleazy wharfside club where his not-quite girlfriend Luana was a singer accompanied by blind jazz-great Bill Henderson.

ADVENTURES OF McGRAW = MEET McGRAW

AFFAIRS OF CHINA SMITH = CHINA SMITH

ANATOMY OF A CRIME = The OUTSIDER

315

ARCHER (January-March 1975). The 1974 pilot, a TV film of **Ross MACDONALD**'s novel **The UNDERGROUND MAN**, directed by Paul Wendkos with a faithful script by **Douglas HEYES**, was ruined by the miscasting of Peter Graves as **Lew Archer**. Brian Keith, complete with wig and face-lift, starred in the sophisticated TV series which was true to the original. At a time when all other PI shows had at least one gimmick, Archer was the antithesis of the slick, sexy, superefficient hero, using deduction to solve his cases.

B.L. STRYKER (February 1989-?). A rotating segment of the ABC *Monday Mystery Movie* featuring Burt Reynolds as retired NOPD homicide detective **Bobby Lee Stryker** who moves back to his native Palm Beach, Florida, living on a dilapidated houseboat, and starts a new career as a PI.

BANACEK (September 1972-September 1974). Cool, smooth, shrewd Polish-American freelance insurance investigator **Thomas Banacek** (George Peppard) was successful enough at collecting 10% rewards to be able to live in Boston's exclusive Beacon Hill area. Polish proverbs were used liberally and the show's positive image made it very popular with groups like the Polish-American Congress, which gave it an award. Novelization: **Deane ROMANO**.

BANYON (September 1972-January 1973). A period series set in 30s LA with Robert Forster as **Miles C. Banyon**, a tough, honest PI who would take any case for $20 a day. Joan Blondell was the head of a secretarial school in the same building, the Bradbury, who provided him with a new free secretary each week, ranging from sexpots to country girls. Novelization: **William JOHNSTON**.

BARNABY JONES (January 1973-September 1980). After a long, successful career as a PI **Barnaby Jones** (Buddy Ebsen) retired, leaving his Los Angeles agency to his son Hal. When Hal was murdered on a case, Jones came out of retirement to help his widowed daughter-in-law **Betty Jones** (Lee Meriwether) track down the killer. Betty became his assistant when he decided to keep the business going. A keen analytic mind, backed by a home crime lab, was disguised by a homespun exterior. In 1976 a young cousin, **Jedediah Romano (J.R) Jones** joined the team. There were occasional crossovers between the series and CANNON. Steve **FISHER** wrote scripts for the show.

BEARCATS! (September-December 1971). Operating in the 1914 Southwest, **Hank Brackett** (Rod Taylor) and **Johnny Reach** (Dennis Cole), who traveled around in a Stutz Bearcat complete with a Gatling gun, would ask for a blank cheque rather than setting a fee and would fill it in for what they thought their work had been worth. Launched by an April 1971 pilot entitled **POWDERKEG**.

BIG BLACK PILL = JOE DANCER

BIG RIP-OFF = McCOY

BIG ROSE: DOUBLE TROUBLE (1974). Pilot for a prospective series with Shelley Winters as brash PI **Rose Winters** and Barry Primus as her young assistant **Ed Mills**.

BIG SHAMUS, LITTLE SHAMUS (September-October 1979). House dick of the Ansonia Hotel, Atlantic City, **Arnie Sutter** (Brian Dennehy) had to cope with brand new problems when gambling was legalized in the resort as well as raising his 13 year-old son, and assistant, **Max** (Doug McKeon). Despite the fine Dennehy, the poorly produced show was received with such indifference that it was canceled after two episodes.

BLADE IN HONG KONG (1985). Pilot for a proposed action-adventure series featuring Terry Lester (soap star of *The Young & The Restless*) as **Joe Blade**, an American adopted by a wealthy Chinese merchant (Keye Luke, #1 Son in the *Charlie Chan* movies). Trained in criminology at UCLA, he became a PI in Hong Kong which critics agreed was the real star of the film.

BOSTON BLACKIE (September 1951-1953). The incorrigible, intellectual jewel thief of Jack Boyle's *Boston Blackie* (1919) and seven silent films, turned wisecracking adventurer in 14 B-movies, came over from radio as a PI, moving from New York to LA. Kent Taylor starred in the 58 episodes, with Lois Collier as assistant-girlfriend **Mary Wesley**. See **Radio: BOSTON BLACKIE**.

BOURBON STREET BEAT (October 1959-September 1960). A New Orleans variant of *77 Sunset Strip*, with two mature PIs, **Rex Randolph** (Richard Long) and **Cal Calhoun** (Andrew Duggan) with **Kenny Madison** (Van Williams) as the handsome, young, youth-appeal rookie. The show premiered with a straight lift from *The Maltese Falcon*. When it folded, Randolph went to join **77 SUNSET STRIP** as the fourth partner while Madison was promoted to full partner of a new team at **SURFSIDE 6**.

The BROTHERS BRANNIGAN (Syndicated 1960). Partners in a Phoenix, Arizona agency dealing with insurance fraud, theft, divorce and murder, **Mike & Bob Brannigan** (Mark Roberts & Steve Dunn), were contrasted characters in standard TV fashion. Mike quoted poetry and fell in love, Bob was the serious, business-like one who had to rescue him. Some sibling rivalry, family jokes, fraternal bonding and an unusual locale did not help the series survive its one season. Novelization: **Henry Edward HELSETH.**

CALL MR D = RICHARD DIAMOND, PRIVATE DETECTIVE

CANNON (September 1971-September 1976). Balding, middle-aged and portly, indeed fat, **Frank Cannon** (William Conrad) stood out from the run of TV PIs straight away. With expensive tastes—haute cuisine and a Continental which took a lot of damage in car chases—Cannon was more often ruled by his pocketbook than his conscience. Like **BARNABY JONES,** with whom he occasionally interlinked, he rarely used a gun. In 1980 Conrad starred in a TV movie **The RETURN OF FRANK CANNON** while ruling out another series. **Bill S. BALLINGER** wrote scripts for the show. Novelizations: **Paul DENVER, Douglas ENEFER** and **Richard GALLAGHER.**

The **CASE OF THE DANGEROUS ROBIN** (Syndicated 1960). Freelance international insurance investigator **Robin Scott** (Rick Jason) and his secretary-fiancée Phyllis Collier (Jean Blake) were always about to leave for a vacation when the phone rang, sending Scott off in pursuit of the villains who would stoop so low as to try and swindle an insurance company. A karate expert, Scott never used a gun. 38 episodes were made. Also known as **DANGEROUS ROBIN.**

The **CASES OF EDDIE DRAKE** (March-May 1952). Each of the 13 (nine were filmed in 1949 but not shown until 1952) episodes opened in the office of a female psychiatrist writing a book on criminal psychology based on the adventures of LA PI **Eddie Drake** (Don Haggerty), told in flash-backs. Another show, **The FILES OF JEFFREY JONES,** was a spinoff.

CASSIE & COMPANY (January-August 1982). Angie Dickinson reprised her *Police Woman* role as **Cassie Holland,** a former policewoman turned PI, taking over the business of retired **Lyman 'Shack' Shackelford** (John Ireland) whose help she would seek in tough cases, who used her looks and sex appeal as well as her skills. Her ex-husband, rather usefully, was the District Attorney.

The **CATCHER** (1972). Unmemorable pilot for a proposed series featuring Seattle ex-cop **Noah Hendricks** (Michael Witney) and Harvard graduate **Sam Callender** (Jan-Michael Vincent) as specialists in locating missing persons.

CHARLIE COBB; NICE NIGHT FOR A HANGING (1977). Pilot for a prospective series featuring Clu Gulager as 1870s Western PI **Charlie Cobb.**

CHARLIE WILD, PRIVATE DETECTIVE (December 1950-June 1952). Modeled directly on **Sam Spade**, tough New York PI **Charlie Wild**, played first by Kevin O'Morrison, then John McQuade, was obliged to deliver Wildroot Cream Oil commercials, even if it meant pausing during a chase scene. Cloris Leachman played his secretary Effie Perrine (cf Effie Perine of *The Maltese Falcon*). See **Radio: CHARLIE WILD. PRIVATE DETECTIVE.**

CHARLIE'S ANGELS (September 1976-August 1981). Promising more in the way of sex than it ever delivered, the long running, but always declining, series about the Charles Townsend Detective Agency, which consisted of the unseen **Charles Townsend** (the voice of John Forsythe) and three luscious female operatives originally featured **Sabrina Duncan** (Kate Jackson), **Kelly Garrett** (Jaclyn Smith) and **Jill Munroe** (Farrah Fawcett-Majors). Carried away by the success of her hair-do and cheesecake publicity pictures, Fawcett-Majors quit in 1977 and was replaced by her 'sister' **Kris Munroe** (Cheryl Ladd). Jackson left in 1979, replaced by **Tiffany Welles** (Shelly Hack), daughter of a Connecticut police chief, in turn replaced by street-smart **Julie Rogers** (Tanya Roberts) in 1980. The scripts, which called for maximum bikini wearing, were always dire, with atrocious dialogue, and there was less and less action as the series progressed. Novelizations: **Max FRANKLIN.**

The CHEATERS (Syndicated 1961). John Ireland starred as **John Hunter**, insurance fraud investigator for Eastern Insurance, with Robert Ayres as his associate **Walter Allen**, in this English made series.

CHECKMATE (September 1960-September 1962). The characters, created by Eric Ambler, of the expensive Checkmate firm, whose mission was to "Thwart crime and checkmate death," i.e. preventive detection, were **Don Corey** (Anthony George) and neophyte **Jed Sills** (Doug McClure), aided by their teacher, bearded and British graphologist and criminology professor **Dr. Carl Hyatt** (Sebastian Cabot). Another investigator, **Chris Devlin** (Jack Betts) was added in 1962. The show used guest stars from Broadway stage shows as victims, with Charles Laughton making his last TV appearance and Cyd Charisse her first. One of the scriptwriters was **Leigh BRACKETT.**

CHINA SMITH (1952-1955). Set in Singapore, Hong Kong and other Oriental locales, **China Smith** (Dan Duryea) was a wisecracking, girl-chasing soldier of fortune, opportunistic adventurer and sometime PI who talked with an Irish accent and was as athletic as Douglas Fairbanks Jr. 52 episodes were made, the second 26 syndicated as **The NEW ADVENTURES OF CHINA SMITH** and also known as **The**

AFFAIRS OF CHINA SMITH. Duryea starred in a 1954 film (see **Films: WORLD FOR RANSOM**) that reprised the character in all important details, an unusual reverse spinoff.

CITY OF ANGELS (February-August 1976). Set, obviously enough, in Los Angeles, in the 30s, this summer season replacement inspired by Roman Polanski's film *Chinatown* featured **Jake Axminster** (Wayne Rogers), an often broke but always free-wheeling PI who trusted nobody, not even his attorney. Notable mainly for its period sets, cars and clothes, and its "convoluted, disconnected bad story-telling," as the star subsequently put it, this rehash of **BANYON**, down to the Bradbury Building office and sardonic voice-over narration, was soon canceled.

COCAINE AND BLUE EYES (1983). Pilot for a proposed series based on **Fred ZACKEL**'s novel, with O.J. Simpson as **Mike Brennan**. Described as average.

COOL MILLION (October 1972-July 1973). A former CIA agent, **Jefferson Keyes** (James Farentino) was so successful as a PI that he could demand a million dollars, in advance, for his services. Based in Lincoln, Nebraska, because the phone lines were always open, he flew his own executive jet. He was also in demand as a raconteur. The pilot was subtitled **MASK OF MARCELLA** and also shown under that title.

CORONADO 9 (Syndicated 1960). Retired naval officer **Don Adams** (Rod Cameron) found new challenges as a San Diego PI for one season, the title taken, in the *77 Sunset Strip/SurfSide 6* mode, from his telephone exchange.

The **COUNTRY MUSIC MURDERS = MURDER IN**
          MUSIC CITY

CRIME PHOTOGRAPHER (April 1951-June 1952). After many novels and stories, a radio show and two films, **George Harmon COXE**'s Jack 'Flashgun' Casey was brought to TV, though only lasting one season. Moved to the New York *Morning Express*, and hanging out at The Blue Note Café, Casey was played first by Richard Carlyle then Darren McGavin. See **Radio: CASEY, CRIME PHOTOGRAPHER**.

The **D.A.'S MAN** (January-August 1959). Hired by the New York District Attorney's office as an undercover investigator and bodyguard for the DA, **Shannon** was played by John Compton. Most of his work involved sources of Mob income—narcotics, prostitution etc.

The **DAIN CURSE** (1978). Shown as a feature film in Europe and as a three part mini-series in the US, this complex, faithful version of **Dashiell HAMMETT**'s novel won the MWA's TV Edgar. James

Coburn, in his first TV appearance in 14 years, starred as **Hamilton Nash** (physically, a very remodeled Continental Op), in a strong, honest, well-acted period piece whose weaknesses were those of Hammett's original story, which he himself called silly, and which has three seperate plots and over 30 characters.

DANGEROUS ROBIN = CASE OF THE DANGEROUS ROBIN

DETECTIVE IN THE HOUSE (March-April 1985). Amiable light comedy about an engineer, **Press Wyman** (Judd Hirsch) who quit his career to try to establish himself as a freelance PI, for reasons never touched on. Jack Elam featured as **Nick Turner** a somewhat confused retired PI who acts as Hirsch's mentor. Good-natured sitcom stressing the normality of the PI's home situation.

DETECTIVE SCHOOL (ONE FLIGHT UP) (July-November 1969). Situation comedy with James Gregory as **Nick Hannigan**, a down-at-heels PI reduced to opening a shabby PI night school and getting involved in the cases of his motley collection of students.

DETECTIVE'S WIFE (July-September 1950). Though only wanting to run a quiet agency, **Adam Conway** (Donald Curtis) got so much publicity from solving a murder that all the cases he gets are homicides. His wife **Connie Conway** (Lynn Bari), getting more involved in these affairs than either she or her husband would like, was, naturally, the main character. Summer replacement for MAN AGAINST CRIME.

The DEVLIN CONNECTION (October-December 1982). Suave, debonair, independently wealthy **Brian Devlin** (Rock Hudson) had retired from his successful career as a PI to become director of the Los Angeles Cultural Arts Center when his long-lost son, coarse, impetuous **Nick Corsello** (Jack Scalia), a would-be tough-guy PI, turns up in his life. The two worked together in their different ways with the father keeping an eye on the son and helping him out, preferably without his knowledge and without damaging the Mercedes.

DIAMONDS (September 1987-?). A late-night show, wrong-footed with poor production, featuring **Mike Devitt** (Nicholas Campbell) and **Christine Towne** (Peggy Smithhart) as a married couple whose TV private eye series is canceled. They get divorced and go into the real PI business as Two Of Diamonds.

DICK AND THE DUCHESS (September 1957-May 1958). A carbon of *The Thin Man* that led one critic to comment that the only way the comedy-mystery team of **Dick Starrett** (Patrick O'Neal), a Yank insurance investigator based in London, and his aristocratic, mystery-writing British wife **Jane** (Hazel Court) could be told apart from Nick & Nora Charles was by the absence of Asta.

The **DOORBELL RANG** = NERO WOLFE

DOUBLE TROUBLE = BIG ROSE

The **DUKE** (April-May 1979). At 38, prizefighter **Oscar 'Duke' Ramsay** (Robert Conrad, who was once a professional boxer) lost a fight to a man half his age and decided it was time to quit and concentrate on his other interests such as Duke & Benny's Corner, a Chicago bar and grill. When his manager, partner and friend Benny gets killed, Duke tracks down the murderer and finds himself with a new career as a PI using fighting days contacts on both sides of the law.

FARADAY AND COMPANY (September 1973-August 1974). After 25 years in a South American jail, PI **Frank Faraday** (Dan Dailey) found himself in a changed world that included an illegitimate son by his secretary, born after he went to prison, now a PI himself. After tracking down and bringing to justice the man who really committed the crime for which he had been sentenced, Frank and **Steve Faraday** (James Naughton) operated an LA agency, with the two men in sharp contrast, Frank belonging to an old-style physical force school, Steve aware of the new technological and legal sophistication of criminals.

The **FILES OF JEFFREY JONES** (Syndicated 1952). An ex-GI working his way through law school by working part-time as a New York PI, **Jeffrey Jones** (Don Haggerty) spent most of his time, though a teetotaler, in the Golden Bubble Café which he used as an office. Haggerty came to the show, which ran for 39 episodes, from **The CASES OF EDDIE DRAKE**.

FOLLOW THAT MAN = MAN AGAINST CRIME

FOREIGN EXCHANGE (1969). TV film based on **Jimmy SANGSTER**'s novel of the same title, featuring Robert Horton as London PI and reluctant intelligence agent **John Smith**. A sequel to the equally convoluted and would-be cynical **The SPY KILLER**.

The **FORTY-EIGHT HOUR MILE** = The OUTSIDER

The **FOUR JUST MEN** (Syndicated 1959). British series loosely based on Edgar Wallace's 1905 novel. Four WW2 veterans are reunited at the deathbed of their former commander who asks them to band together to fight evil. The four consisted of British PI **Ben Manfred** (Jack Hawkins), American journalist Tim Collier (Dan Dailey), French lawyer Jeff Ryder (Richard Conte) and Italian hotel owner Ricco Poccari (Vittorio De Sica). The series was more popular in Britain than America where it lasted only one season.

GOODNIGHT MY LOVE (1972). Spoof TV movie set in the seamy underworld of 1946 Los Angeles with Richard Boone as seedy down and out PI **Frank Hogan**, Michael Dunn as his erudite dwarf partner **Arthur Boyle**. Described by Leonard Maltin as above average, if not the *Maltese Falcon* take-off it claimed to be, with an offbeat point of view, timeless atmosphere and good direction.

GOTHAM (1988). With a title designed to evoke both New York and the Gothic, this supernatural PI film, featuring Tommy Lee Jones as basic, hard-up, hardboiled NYC gumshoe **Eddie Mallard**, hired to rid a client of his late wife's ghost, veered between melodrama and comedy. Assuming that a fool and his money are soon parted, Mallard discovers that the ghost is all too unreal and falls for her.

The GREAT ICE RIP-OFF (1974). Light-hearted suspense and chase TV film featuring Lee J. Cobb as **Willy Calso**, dogged, grumpy retired cop pursuing a gang of jewel thieves across country by bus. Described by Leonard Maltin as above average.

GRIFF (September 1973-January 1974). Retiring, over a matter of principle, after 30 years, veteran LAPD Captain **Wade Griffin** (Lorne Green) became a Westwood PI assisted by young **S. Michael 'Mike' Murdoch** (Ben Murphy), tackling the usual murders, kidnappings, extortion schemes, etc., in a very short run. Oddly, the pilot, MAN ON THE OUTSIDE, was not shown until more than a year after the series ended. Novelization: **Robert WEVERKA**.

HAGEN (March-April 1980). Mismatch teaming of outdoorsy **Paul Hagen** (Chad Everett), a hunter and skilled animal tracker, who became an investigator for sophisticated San Francisco attorney Carl Palmer (Arthur Hill).

HARRY-O (September 1974-August 1976). An ex-Marine and ex-cop, retired after getting a bullet in his back too close to the spinal cord to be removed, **Harry Orwell** (David Janssen) lived a Bohemian life in a San Diego (later Santa Monica) beach shack, often having to use the bus instead of his old, unreliable car. He augmented his pension by working as a PI, his cases often involving pretty girls (his neighbor on the beach was an infrequently seen Farrah Fawcett), to whom he paid little attention. The pilot was shown as **SMILE JENNY, YOU'RE DEAD**. Novelizations: **Lee HAYS**.

HAVE GUN, WILL TRAVEL (September 1957-September 1963). Cultured, West Point graduate **Paladin** (Richard Boone), went to San Francisco after the Civil War where, based at the Hotel Carlton, he offered his professional black-garbed troubleshooting services, as detective, bodyguard or courier, throughout the Old West, with his famous business card which showed a white chess knight with the message "Have Gun, Will Travel. Wire Paladin, San Francisco." The series was by far the most successful of those listed in this section. See **Radio: HAVE GUN, WILL TRAVEL** for an unusual reverse spin-off.

HAWAIIAN EYE (October 1959-September 1963). Using the *77 Sunset Strip* format, the Hawaiian Eye Organization consisted of **Tom Lopaka** (Robert Conrad), **Tracy Steele** (Anthony Eisley) and, from December 1960, **Greg MacKenzie** (Grant Williams), assisted by Kazuo Kim (Hawaiian actor Poncie Ponce), a zany cabdriver with relatives usefully scattered round the islands, and night club singer and photographer Cricket Blake (Connie Stevens). **Stuart Bailey** from 77 SUNSET STRIP made occasional visits and Troy Donahue, a PI in SURFSIDE 6, played a resort hotel's special events director, thus starring in two PI shows simultaneously. Novelization: **Frank CASTLE**.

HAZELL (1977-1979). The best British PI series, adapted from the best British PI novels so far, by **P.B. YUILL**. Faithful to the books, **James Hazell** (Nicholas Ball) was a tough nut ex-copper with a sharp, street-wise sense of humor, working in a recognizable London, peopled by genuine Londoners, like Hazell himself. The series was especially strong on villains and had strong stories, one of which, "The Deptford Virgin," was a loving parody of *The Maltese Falcon* with Charles Gray in the Sidney Greenstreet role.

HOLLYWOOD OFF-BEAT = STEVE RANDALL

HONEY WEST (September 1965-September 1966). The sex-bomb in a trenchcoat PI **Honey West** (Anne Francis) first appeared in an episode of *Burke's Law*, then in a series which featured gadgets like tear gas earrings, lipstick-cum-radio transmitter and a high-tech van used as a traveling office. Adept at karate and judo, Honey also had a partner, **Sam Bolt** (John Ericson), to help with the rough stuff. Set in Los Angeles, the modishly dressed Honey posed as a model as a cover for her real work. Adapted from **G.G.FICKLING**'s novels.

I HAD THREE WIVES (August-September 1985). Summer replacement show featuring LA PI **Jackson Beaudine** (Victor Garber) who has a very chummy and fruitful relationship with his two ex-wives, an attorney and a martial arts expert actress, while his current wife was a journalist with a keen analytical mind and useful contacts. Light-hearted.

I LOVE A MYSTERY (1973). Send-up of the famous radio show, made six years before it was finally shown, starring Les Crane as **Jack Packard**, David Hartman as **Doc Long** and Hagan Beggs as **Reggie**

York, insurance investigators in an over-the-top caper, co-starring Ida Lupino, Terry-Thomas and Don Knotts. Described by Leonard Maltin as depressing, a waste of a good cast and below average. See **Radio: I LOVE A MYSTERY**.

INTERNATIONAL DETECTIVE (Syndicated 1959). British made series supposedly based on the files of the William J. Burns Agency, with Arthur Fleming as Burns agent **Ken Franklin**.

INTO THIN AIR (1985). Factually based TV film about a dogged retired detective, **Jim Conway** (Robert Prosky) who agrees to help the obsessed mother of a Canadian boy who disappeared on his way to Colorado summer school. Described by Leonard Maltin as above average.

The **INVESTIGATOR** (June-September 1958). Filmed live in New York, swinging **Jeff Prior** (Lonny Chapman) was a master of disguise when tracking suspects, helped by his retired newspaperman father **Lloyd Prior** (Howard St. John) from whom he learnt his detecting skills. Henry **KANE** wrote the stories.

The **INVESTIGATORS** (October-December 1961). Based in New York, on the fashionable East Side, but traveling widely, **Russ Andrews** (James Franciscus) **Steve Banks** (James Philbrook) and their secretary and occasional undercover operative **Maggie Peters** (Mary Murphy), Investigators Inc. were insurance detectives who tracked down fraud schemes that inevitably involved murder. **Frank KANE** produced and **James GUNN** was one of the script writers.

JARRETT (1973). Pilot film with Glenn Ford as **Sam Jarrett**, a sophisticated PI who specialized in cases involving fine art.

JIM ROCKFORD, PRIVATE INVESTIGATOR = The ROCKFORD FILES

JOE DANCER (1981). Conceived as part John Garfield, part Dick Powell, part Humphrey Bogart, hardboiled LA PI **Joe Dancer** was created and performed by actor Robert Blake who also produced the three pilots, The **BIG BLACK PILL**, also shown simply as **JOE DANCER**, **MONKEY MISSION** and **MURDER 1 DANCER 0**. Fluctuating between casual brutality, forced humor and self-conscious pathos, the character came across as rather incompetent and pitiable.

JOHNNY MIDNIGHT (Syndicated 1960). A one season syndicated filler starring screen veteran Edmond O'Brien as New York PI **Johnny Midnight** in a series reminiscent of *Johnny Staccato*.

JOHNNY STACCATO (September 1959-September 1960). A cult series, originally entitled **STACCATO**, **Johnny Staccato** (John Cassavetes) was a poorly-paid jazz pianist who made his living as a

Greenwich Village PI. Usually found at Waldo's, a MacDougal Street jazz club where he checked his coat and .38 in the cloakroom, which took telephone messages for him and where he usually met clients. A major feature, contributing to the series' enduring appeal, was the appearance of top jazz players including Barney Kessel, Shelly Manne, Red Mitchell, Red Norvo, Johnny Williams and others in the cast, playing with Pete Candoli's Combo, the house band. Novelization: **Frank BOYD**.

The JUDGE AND JAKE WYLER (1972). A lighthearted whodunit pilot starring Bette Davis as hypochondriac retired lady jurist **Judge Meredith** and Doug McClure as her charming ex-convict legman **Jake Wyler**. Exactly the same situation was tried again two years later, as **PARTNERS IN CRIME**, with no greater success.

KHAN (February 1975). Canceled after only four weeks, *Khan* was unusual in having ethnic actors playing ethnic roles. **Khan** (Khigh Dhiegh) was a PI based in San Francisco's Chinatown who, with the help of his children Anna (Irene Yah-Ling Sun), a criminology Ph.D. student, and Kim (Evan Kim) solved mysterious crimes in contemporary Charlie Chan style, using both traditional and modern methods.

KING OF DIAMONDS (Syndicated 1961-2). Security chief for Continental Diamond Industries, **Jason King** (Broderick Crawford) and his assistant **Al Casey** (Ray Hamilton) had international responsibility for diamonds in transit, with their main foe being something actually called the Illegal Diamond Buyers' Syndicate! A violent series in which King was as likely to beat up a female criminal as make a pass at her. **Steve FISHER** wrote for this show of which 39 episodes were made.

LAST HOURS BEFORE MORNING (1975). A TV film with atmospheric '40s setting featuring ex-cop **Bud Delaney** (Ed Lauter) as a hotshot house detective who moonlights by chasing dead-beats. Described by Leonard Maltin as average with an interesting performance by Lauter in a rare starring role.

The LAW AND HARRY McGRAW (September 1987-?). The basic premise of The JUDGE & JAKE WYLER and PARTNERS IN CRIME finally found a winning combination, reminiscent of Spencer Tracy and Katherine Hepburn's, in the teaming of tough, seedy, misanthropic Boston PI **Harry McGraw** (Jerry Orbach) with his office neighbor, classy Boston blueblood and recently widowed criminal lawyer Ellie McGinnis (Barbara Babcock, who stole many episodes of *Hill Street Blues* as Sgt Phil Esterhaus' lover Grace). A spin-off from *Murder She Wrote* in episodes of which Orbach appeared as a McGraw.

LEGMEN (January-March 1984). Two Southern California students, **Jack Gage** (Bruce Greenwood) and **David Taylor** (J.T. Terlsky), working their way through college, start out repossessing cars and process-serving, but soon find themselves involved in dangerous cases involving bullets and beautiful woman. Their first employer was seedy **Oscar Armismendi** (Don Calfa), replaced after a few episodes by the more demanding **Tom Bannon** (Claude Akins).

The **LONE WOLF** (1954). A continuation of the radio series featuring loner gumshoe **Michael Lanyard**, a reformed thief played by Louis Hayward.

The **LONELY PROFESSION** (1969.) A busted pilot adapted by **Douglas HEYES** from his novel *The 12th Of Never*, featuring Harry Guardino as no-nonsense PI **Lee Gordon**. Described by Leonard Maltin as a brave attempt at painting a complete view of a realistic PI with good results by any medium's standards and above average.

The **LONG GOODBYE** (1954). A TV film of **R a y m o n d CHANDLER**'s novel presented on the drama series *Climax!* Dick Powell played **Philip Marlowe**, as he had in the 1944 film of *Farewell, My Lovely* (see **Films: MURDER MY SWEET**), with Teresa Wright and Cesar Romero in support.

LONG TIME GONE (1986). Pilot for a proposed series, described by Leonard Maltin as a slightly off-center tale of a divorced, down on his luck (because of horse racing) gumshoe, **Nick Sandusky** (Paul LeMat), who suddenly has to take care of a young son he hardly knows (Wil Wheaton) who turns out to be a better detective than his father.

LONGSTREET (September 1971-August 1972). While working for New Orleans-based Great Pacific Casulty, insurance investigator **Mike Longstreet** (James Franciscus) was blinded and had his wife killed. Refusing to quit the business, Longstreet acquired a seeing-eye German Shepherd, Pax, and an electronic cane that enabled him to judge distances, and remained remarkably successful, his disability sharpening his other senses and his wits. Bruce Lee appeared in the show as Longstreet's self-defence instructor. **Howard BROWNE** wrote scripts for the show.

LOVE FOR RANSOM = ROGER & HARRY

McCOY (October 1975-March 1976). More Travis McGee-like 'salvage expert' than proper PI, **McCoy** (Tony Curtis) was an inveterate gambler and conman who sustained his luxurious life-style by working elaborate cons on conmen, taking a large cut before returning money to their victims. Only four episodes were shown before cancellation. The pilot for the series was **The BIG RIP-OFF**. Novelization: **Sam STEWART**.

MAGNUM P.I. (December 1980-1988). When *Hawaii Five-O* was taken off the air, the locale and CBS's expensive production facilities were used for one of the most successful PI series ever, featuring **Thomas Magnum** (Tom Selleck). Living free on the Oahu beachfront property of wealthy writer Robin Masters (never seen), with the use of his Ferrari, in exchange for guarding the estate, Magnum was in constant conflict with Masters' pompous British manservant Jonathan Quayle Higgins III (Waco born John Hillerman). Two Vietnam vet buddies, helicopter pilot T.C. (Roger E Mosley) and Rick (Larry Manetti) became increasingly prominent in the last two series which moved away from earlier traditional PI themes. Selleck won a 1983-84 Leading Actor Emmy. During the last season of The **ROCKFORD FILES** he played **Lance White**, a PI with all the answers much resented by Rockford. **Joe GORES** wrote an episode, "Animal Crackers." Novelizations: **Roger BOWDLER** and **Dan ZADRA**.

MAN AGAINST CRIME (October 1949-July 1955; July-August 1956). Ralph Bellamy played **Mike Barnett**, a tough, hard-boiled, loner New York PI who never carried a gun but used his wits and his fists. In the summer of 1951, Robert Preston filled in for Bellamy as Mike's brother **Pat Barnett**. Gun-toting Frank Lovejoy took over for the live 1956 program. The series, shot live for its first two years then on film to ease production and location problems, was, perhaps uniquely, regularly scheduled at the same time on the same day by two different networks (NBC and DuMont), ranking 13th in the 1950/51 ratings with a 37.4 share. Syndicated as **FOLLOW THAT MAN**. See **Radio: MAN AGAINST CRIME**.

MAN FROM BLACKHAWK (October 1959-September 1960). An employee of the Blackhawk Insurance Company of Chicago, **Sam Logan** (Robert Rockwell) investigated insurance frauds in the late 1880s West, though also traveling to New Orleans and San Francisco. A city slicker with string tie and briefcase, Logan almost never carried a gun but often had to use his fists. Distinguished from more modern PIs only by clothes and transportation.

MAN IN A SUITCASE (May-September 1968). Like most 'loner' serials of the 60s, that about disgraced American Intelligence officer turned PI, **McGill** (Richard Bradford), was filmed in England. Falsely accused of a treasonous offence, McGill takes on cases while combing Europe for proof of his innocence.

MAN ON THE OUTSIDE = GRIFF

MAN WITH A CAMERA (October 1958-February 1960). As Jack Casey of *Crime Photographer* counts as a PI, so presumably does a straight lift of that series with freelance ex-combat photographer **Mike Kovak** (Charles Bronson). Taking assignments from newspapers, insurance companies, the police and private individuals, the tough Kovak constantly got into fights with villains and, though he didn't carry a gun, could usually kill them with their own weapons.

MANHUNTER (September 1974-April 1975). Set during the Depression, **Dave Barrett** (Ken Howard), an ex-Marine whose best friend was killed during a bank robbery, gave up his Idaho farm to become a PI with a mission, to bring gangsters like the ones who killed his friend to justice, and he traveled constantly in pursuit of them.

MANNIX (September 1967-August 1975). After first working for Intertect, a bureaucratic Los Angeles detective agency with which he was constantly at odds, unconventional, athletic **Joe Mannix** (Mike Connors) set up his own agency in the second season, working mainly in the Los Angeles area but accepting assignments anywhere. His secretary-Girl Friday, Peggy Fair, was played by Gail Fisher who won a 1970 Best Supporting Actress Emmy (the first award won by any PI series). One of the longest-running PI shows, it invariably had a major brawl and the body count, even in the opening minutes, could be staggering. Novelizations: **Michael AVALLONE** and **J.T. MacCARGO**.

MARGIN FOR MURDER = MICKEY SPILLANE' MIKE HAMMER (1984)

MARKHAM (May 1959-September 1960). Developed from an original story, *Eye For Eye*, shown in the anthology *Suspicion*, suave, well-educated **Roy Markham** (Ray Milland), a lawyer with a PI licence, carried out investigations world-wide thanks to his lucrative practice and inherited wealth, working more for excitement than money and charging very flexible fees, sometimes exorbitant, sometimes gratis. Though he has a house in New York, he lived out of a suitcase and had an answering service instead of an office. For the first two months Markham had a legman assistant, **John Riggs** (Simon Scott), but thereafter worked alone. Novelization: **Lawrence BLOCK**.

MARK SABER = SABER OF LONDON

MARTIN KANE, PRIVATE EYE (September 1949-June 1954). The original TV private eye series lasted for five years with the lead role, easy-going but tough and determined New Yorker **Martin Kane**, taken first by William Gargan (who was once a Brooklyn PI), in whose hands a smooth, wise-cracking Kane co-operated with the police, then by Lloyd

Nolan and Lee Tracy with the series getting more hard-boiled, Kane and the police often at odds. In August 1953 the title was shortened to **MARTIN KANE** and the emphasis shifted to mystery and suspense with Mark Stevens in the title role. The series ranked 12th in the 1950/51 Neilsen ratings with an all-time PI series high 37.8 share. Sponsored by the US Tobacco Corporation, smoking featured heavily, Kane using Happy MacMann's tobacco shop as an HQ until 1953, with Gargan smoking Model pipe tobacco, Nolan and Stevens puffing Sano cigarettes and Tracy Old Briar pipe tobacco. See **The NEW ADVENTURES OF MARTIN KANE** and **Radio: MARTIN KANE, PRIVATE DETECTIVE.**

MASK OF MARCELLA = COOL MILLION

A MASTERPIECE OF MURDER (1986). In his first TV film, Bob Hope played an over the hill PI, **Dan Dolan**, who teams up with a retired master thief (Don Ameche) to solve a string of art thefts and murders. Leonard Maltin describes it as a tired walk-through by Hope and below average.

MATT HELM (September 1975-January 1976). With a swinging, opulent LA background (luxury bachelor pad, fancy foreign sports car, sexy girlfriend) taken from the Bond-spoofing film, in which he was a secret super-agent, **Matt Helm** (Anthony Franciosa) was transformed into a PI taking only 'high-level' cases around the world. The series had little connection with **Donald HAMILTON's** books in which Helm was an outdoorsy adventurer and counterspy.

MATT HOUSTON (September 1982-July 1985). In the first year, **Matt Houston** (Lee Horsley), son of a Texan oil millionaire managing his father's Californian operations, sleuthed as a hobby, barely making enough to cover his license fee. Thereafter he became a full-time PI in a series distinguished, in the network's words, by "beautiful women, stunning sets and freewheeling action."

A MATTER OF WIFE . . . AND DEATH (1976). A spin-off of Burt Reynolds' film *Shamus*, a failed pilot for a prospective series featuring freewheeling PI **Shamus**, with Rod Taylor in the lead.

MEET McGRAW (July 1957-October 1959). A tough, wandering PI, who had served time in prison before moving to the other side of the law, **McGraw** (Frank Lovejoy) was a snappy dresser who avoided fights and did not carry a gun. Accepting any job, no matter how dangerous, for pay, loner McGraw usually had to leave a good-looking woman behind. Switching networks in 1958, the title was changed to **The ADVENTURES OF McGRAW.**

MIAMI UNDERCOVER (Syndicated 1961). Lee Bowman, a former TV Ellery Queen in his fifties, played **Jeff Thompson**, a PI who worked for the Miami Beach hotel association who paid the $100,000 involved in setting up his playboy front. "I keep trouble out of the Collins Avenue glitter strip so that the tourists will stay tucked in, safe and spending." Muscle was provided by former middleweight champion of the world turned restaurateur and self-appointed sidekick Rocky (Rocky Graziano). Thompson worked almost exclusively on hunches, Graziano was virtually inarticulate and the low budget series was short-lived. Novelization: **Evan Lee HEYMAN**.

MICHAEL SHAYNE (September 1960-September 1961). Though Davis Dresser (**Brett HALLIDAY**), author of the original novels, served as technical consultant and writer, the series about the popular PI only lasted one season, pulled after complaints about excessive violence. Suave, debonair Miami Beach PI **Michael Shayne** (Richard Denning) tended to solve bizarre murders, and though he had a girlfriend, Lucy Hamilton (Patricia Donahue, later Margie Regan), his roving eye often got him into trouble. See **Radio: MICHAEL SHAYNE**.

MICKEY SPILLANE'S MIKE HAMMER (1957-1959). Described by *TV Guide* as "easily the worst show on TV" and *Variety* as "a mixture of blood, violence and sex," the syndicated 78 episodes of the first **Mike Hammer** (Darren McGavin) series were, despite the Television Code, almost as violent and sexist as the novels, featuring at least one fist fight, one shooting, one knifing and one apparently successful pass by Hammer at a married woman each episode. Author **Mickey SPILLANE** defended the violence at the time but later claimed minimal involvement, saying "I just took the money and went home." **Bill S. BALLINGER** and **Frank KANE** wrote scripts for this show. See **Radio: THAT HAMMER GUY**.

MICKEY SPILLANE'S MIKE HAMMER (January 1984-September 1987). 25 years after the first series, another violent, sexist, wisecracking incarnation of **Mickey SPILLANE's Mike Hammer** caused less controversy. The first pilot, **MARGIN FOR MURDER** (1981), featuring Kevin Dobson as Hammer and Cindy Pickett as Hammer's secretary Velda, not included in the earlier series, failed to sell, but two others, **MURDER ME, MURDER YOU** (1983), with Stacy Keach as Hammer, Tanya Roberts as Velda and Don Stroud as NYPD Capt. Pat Chambers, and **MORE THAN MURDER** (1984), with Keach, Stroud and Lindsay Bloom as Velda (the final casting) did. **Joe GORES** wrote the episode, "Seven Dead Eyes." The series successfully relaunched in 1986, after Keach's British drug bust with **The RETURN OF MIKE HAMMER.**

MISSING PIECES (1983). Adapted from **Karl ALEXANDER**'s novel *A Private Investigation*, Elizabeth Montgomery starred as **Sara Scott** in what Leonard Maltin rated as an engaging above average thriller.

The MISSING 24 HOURS = RICHIE BROCKELMAN, PRIVATE EYE

The MITERA TARGET = ROGER & HARRY

The MONK (1969). Busted pilot featuring George Maharis as **Gus Monk**, a stereotyped contemporary PI plagued by poor dialogue, unrealistic villains and a predictable outcome, rated below average by Leonard Maltin.

The MONKEY MISSION = JOE DANCER

MOONLIGHTING (March 1985-?). Billed by the network as "a romantic comedy," with failed film actress Cybill Shepherd as **Maddie Hayes**, who inherits and takes over a failing PI business run by **David Addison** (Bruce Willis), more attention has been given to the interplay between the two stars, culminating in the enormous ballyhoo that attended their becoming lovers, than to the detective business.

MORE THAN MURDER = MICKEY SPILLANE'S MIKE HAMMER (1984)

The MOST DEADLY GAME (October 1970-January 1971). A whodunit series created by Eric Ambler, about an expensive agency of trained criminologists which dealt only with unusual murders. Despite its pedigree and cast, veteran Ralph Bellamy, who was in MAN AGAINST CRIME, as urbane, cerebral **Ethan Arcane**, George Maharis as handsome ex-Military Intelligence officer **Jonathan Croft**, and Yvette Mimieux as criminology graduate **Vanessa Smith**, the show died after 11 episodes due mainly to appalling, would-be 'mod' scripts. Novelizations: **Ed FRIEND** and **Richard GALLAGHER**.

MURDER IN MUSIC CITY (1979). Buying a detective agency as a tax shelter, Nashville songwriter **Sonny Hunt** (Sonny Bono) found himself and his model wife involved in murders in a pilot condemned with unusual venom by Maltin for desecrating the memory of Nick & Nora Charles. Also shown as **The COUNTRY MUSIC MURDERS.**

MURDER ME, MURDER YOU = MICKEY SPILLANE'S MIKE HAMMER (1984)

MURDER 1 DANCER 0 = JOE DANCER

MURHY'S LAW (December 1988-?). George Segal stars as down on his luck insurance investigator and recovering alcoholic **Daedelus**

Murphy beset by Murphy's Law which says that everything that can go wrong will. His flatmate is a Eurasian model (Maggie Han). Created by REMINGTON STEELE writers, with fairly obvious debts to Warren MURPHY, the series is routine; Segal walks through without creating any depth to the character and with an off and on Irish accent, and the comedy is labored.

MY FRIEND TONY (January-September 1969). Only 16 episodes, a half-season, were made of this series in which UCLA criminology professor **John Woodruff** (James Whitmore) became a partner in a PI agency with **Tony Novello** (Enzio Cerusico), a former Italian street urchin whom he had befriended during WW2. Stolid, conservative Woodruff was the forensic brains, carefree, romantic Novello the legs and muscle. Novelization: **William JOHNSTON.**

MY PARTNER THE GHOST (UK 1973). British series, shown there as **RANDALL & HOPKIRK (DECEASED)**, this one season late-night show featured **Jeff Randall** (Mike Pratt) as a British PI assisted by the ghost, that only he can see, of his murdered associate **Marty Hopkirk** (Kenneth Cope).

NERO WOLFE (January-August 1981). A pilot, **The DOORBELL RANG**, based on **Rex STOUT**'s novel, with Thayer David as **Nero Wolfe** and Tom Mason as **Archie Goodwin**, was made in 1977 but David's death delayed the making of a series for four years. It was not until 1981 that the idea was revived with William Conrad in the lead. Though faithfully adapted from Stout's concept, with Lee Horsley as Goodwin, the presence of Conrad, fresh from playing portly, food-loving **CANNON**, did tend to make Wolfe seem like a semi-retired version of that PI. See **Radio: The ADVENTURES OF NERO WOLFE.**

NEW ADVENTURES OF CHINA SMITH = CHINA SMITH

The NEW ADVENTURES OF MARTIN KANE (1957). Filmed in Europe, William Gargan, the first actor to play Kane in **MARTIN KANE, PRIVATE EYE**, was based in London in this revival. With greatly reduced violence, Kane himself not carrying a gun, the criminals were always turned over to the law once apprehended and Kane assisted Scotland Yard and Interpol while tracking down suspects for his clients. 39 episodes were made.

NICE NIGHT FOR A HANGING = CHARLIE COBB

NICK AND NORA (1975). Misconceived update of the famous **Dashiell HAMMETT** characters with Craig Stevens as **Nick Charles**, Jo Ann Pflug as **Nora**, screened late-night to allow free (or, rather freer) rein to the Charles' drinking habits and sexual innuendoes.

NICK DERRINGER, P.I. (1988). A single spinoff of *Hooperman* featured the well-known dwarf actor David Rappaport as sleazy, diminutive San Francisco PI **Nick Derringer**. Producer Stephen Bochco, creator of *Hill Street Blues* and *L.A.Law*, has announced his desire to make a series based on the character.

ONE SHOE MAKES IT MURDER (1982). Robert Mitchum made his TV acting debut in an adaptation of **Eric BERCOVICI**'s novel *So Little Cause For Caroline*, as has-been ex-cop PI Harold Shilling, renamed **Harold Shillman** in the film. Leonard Maltin complains that the adaptor failed to give the part "that extra edge for Mitchum to hone."

The OUTSIDER (September 1968-September 1969). Los Angeles PI **David Ross** (Darren McGavin) was an orphan, a high-school drop-out and ex-con, framed for a crime he didn't commit, constantly followed by the police because of his record, which precluded him from carrying a gun. Cynical and embittered, he was poorly-paid and drove an old car, but was a thorough and proficient professional nonetheless, capable of looking after himself with any weapon that came to hand when necessary. Edited episodes are shown as TV films, described by Leonard Maltin as above average with excellent performances and off-beat point of view, under the titles **The FORTY-EIGHT HOUR MILE** and **ANATOMY OF A CRIME**. Novelization: **Lou CAMERON**.

PARTNERS IN CRIME (1973). A second attempt at the premise of The JUDGE & JAKE WYLER with Lee Grant as retired **Judge Meredith Leland**, Lou Antonio as her ex-con associate **Sam Hatch** setting up a PI agency.

PARTNERS IN CRIME (September-December 1984). The two beautiful ex-wives of a murdered San Francisco PI, prim photographer and heiress **Carole Stanwyck** (Lynda Carter) and jazz bass player and amateur pickpocket **Sydney Kovak** (Loni Anderson), team up to solve the murder and his last case. Finding themselves joint heirs of his fine old Victorian house and thriving agency, they go into business together. Glamorous clothes and bitchy backchat.

PETER GUNN (September 1958-September 1961). One of the essential PI TV shows and model for many that followed. Suave, aggressive ladykiller PI **Peter Gunn** (Craig Stevens) spent much of his time at a Los Angeles waterfront bar, Mother's, where his girlfriend Edie Hart (Lola Albright) was a singer, and met clients and underworld contacts there. His police force buddy, Lt. Jacoby, was played by Herschel Bernadi and Mother first by Minerva Urecal, later Hope Lange. During the third season Gunn started to travel abroad on assignments. Blake Edwards'

Film: GUNN was poorly received partly because of the absence of Albright and Bernadi. Novelization: **Henry KANE.**

PHILIP MARLOWE (October 1959-March 1960). In his first TV incarnation **Raymond CHANDLER's** quintessential PI **Philip Marlowe** (Philip Carey) lost his reluctance to carry, or use, a gun and became an executioner as well as an investigator. Set in Los Angeles, naturally, the show lasted only one season. See **Radio: The** ADVENTURES OF PHILIP MARLOWE.

PHILIP MARLOWE, PRIVATE EYE (1983 & 1986). Made in the same manner as 40s films rather than modern TV shows, quickly and cheaply by current film standards but with more time, care and panache than TV episodes, this Canadian produced series starring Powers Boothe as **Philip Marlowe** was far and away the best version of **Raymond CHANDLER's** work since the early films and, indeed, many of the episodes were taken directly from Chandler short stories—"Blackmailers Don't Shoot," "Pick-Up On Noon Street," "Smart-Aleck Kill," "Spanish Blood," etc, with Jo Eisinger's script for "The Pencil" winning an MWA Edgar. Five episodes appeared in 1983 and a further six in 1986.

The PIGEON (1969). A TV comedy with Sammy Davis Jr. as **Larry Miller**, an eager PI who insists on protecting a woman who doesn't want his help.

PRIVATE EYE (September 1987-January 1988). From the creators of *Miami Vice*, with the same production values. **Jack Cleary** (Michael Woods) is a 50s LA cop, dismissed on trumped up charges, naturally, who sinks into alcoholism before inheriting his murdered brother's PI business and, reluctantly, his assistant **Johnny Betts**, whom he describes as a "thrill crazy rock and roll delinquent." Novelizations: **David ELLIOTT, Max LOCKHART** and **T.N. ROBB.**

POWDERKEG = BEARCATS!

The PROTECTORS (1972-1973). Having ruled out another TV series after *The Man From UNCLE*, Robert Vaughn accepted a not dissimilar role as **Harry Rule**, the American branch of an elite trio of international PIs, with Nyree Dawn Porter as the aristocratic British widow of an Italian nobleman, **Contessa Caroline di Contini** and Tony Anholt as Frenchman **Paul Buchet**. The glossy series was strong on expensive cars and exotic, fashionable European locales in the fight against high-level crime. Novelization: **Robert MIALL.**

PUBLIC EYE (dates not known). An excellent British PI series, featuring the small-time adventures of seedy Birmingham Inquiry Agent **Frank Marker**, played by the fine British actor Alfred Burke. In my experience, this was the least glamorous, most realistic TV PI show. Novelizations: **Audley SOUTHCOTT** and **Anthony MARRIOTT**.

The RACING GAME (1980-81). Adapted from **Dick FRANCIS'** novels, with Mike Gwilyn as ex-jockey **Sid Halley** turned PI after an accident in which he lost his hand, specializing, naturally, in horse racing cases. Six episodes were shown in America.

RANDALL & HOPKIRK (DECEASED) = MY PARTNER THE GHOST

REMINGTON STEELE (October 1982-?). After setting up an agency, smart, attractive **Laura Holt** (Stephanie Zimbalist) found that being a woman was driving away business, so she invented a male supersleuth boss, **Remington Steele**, and the agency flourished. When wealthy clients insisted on meeting Steele, she hired a handsome, suave, mysterious stranger (Pierce Brosnan), whose real name is never revealed, to act the part. He quickly picked up the trade and became a real partner, though given to playing out scenes from classic movies during a case.

The RETURN OF FRANK CANNON = CANNON

The RETURN OF MIKE HAMMER = MICKEY SPILLANE'S MIKE HAMMER (1984)

The RETURN OF SHERLOCK HOLMES (1987). Dr Watson's great-granddaughter **Jane Watson** (Margaret Colin), a modern-day Boston PI, found the body of the great detective **Sherlock Holmes** (Michael Pennington) suspended in frozen animation and restored him to life in a lighthearted piece of fluff, made "with apologies to the late Sir Arthur Conan Doyle," that involved the Victorian master with such things as a plane-hijacking, counterfeit money, the FBI and a '40s style vamp female client.

REWARD (1980). A failed pilot starring Michael Parks as **Michael Dolan**, a disgruntled policeman who quits the force and sets out to solve the murder of his former colleague and best friend. The title, and the fact that a series was intended, make it eligible.

RICHARD DIAMOND, PRIVATE DETECTIVE (July 1957-September 1960). Tough ex-cop **Richard Diamond** (David Janssen) was based on the role Dick Powell created and made famous on radio, but which he decided he was too old to play on television. Originally based in New York, ex-NYPD policeman Diamond moved to Los Angeles in early 1958, where he became a pioneer of the now ubiquitous car telephone and one of the show's most famous ingredients was the sultry-voiced Sam, Diamond's answering service, though only her legs were ever shown. Sam was actually Mary Tyler Moore who quit the show in disgust at the low pay ($80 an episode) she received. Syndicated as **CALL MR D.** See **Radio: RICHARD DIAMOND, PRIVATE DETECTIVE.**

RICHIE BROCKELMAN, PRIVATE EYE (March-April & August 1978). An unsuccessful spinoff from **The ROCKFORD FILES**, in which 23-year old, college educated PI **Richie Brockelman** (Dennis Dugan) first appeared and to which he returned when the first few episodes about his own small agency failed to win an audience, a second try having no greater success. His youthful looks were Brockelman's trump card because nobody took him seriously and he was able to talk his way into and out of situations. The pilot was subtitled, and also shown as **The MISSING 24 HOURS.**

RIPTIDE (January 1984-April 1986). Two Southern California beach bums, **Cody Allan** (Perry King) and **Nick Ryder** (Joe Penny) decide to become PIs, working from Cody's cabin cruiser *Riptide*, moored at Pier 56, King's Harbor. They also had a speedboat, *Ebbtide*, and an aging Sikorsky helicopter, *Screaming Mimi*. Thoroughly modern, they enlisted an army buddy, electronics whiz **Murray 'Boz' Bozinsky** (Thom Bray). High-speed chases, explosions and beautiful girls in bikinis, particularly the all-girl crew of the neighboring charter boat *The Barefoot Contessa*, were standard features.

The ROCKFORD FILES (September 1974-July 1980). Perhaps the best loved and most respected PI series of all starred James Garner as dogged, sly **Jim Rockford**. Imprisoned for a crime he did not commit, then exonerated and pardoned when new evidence came up, Rockford lived in and worked from a trailer on a Los Angeles beach—The Rockford Agency, Specializing in Closed Cases Since 1964, Criminal Only, 24-Hour Service, Licensed and Bonded, One Ocean Lane, nr. Marineland, Los Angeles—Rockford had no secretary, only the famous telephone (555 2368) answering machine that opened each episode with a new message, and charged $200 a day plus expenses. The program's strongest suit, apart from its sense of humor, was Garner himself, one of those actors who disarm and charm simply by playing themselves. A strong supporting cast, including Jim's father Rocky (Noah Beery), Lt. Dennis Becker (Joe Santos) and the appalling Angel Martin (Stuart Margolin), Rockford's ex-cellmate, lent further depth. Garner won an Emmy in 1977, the series itself won one in 1978, with Rita Moreno receiving another for her role in the episode "The Paper Palace," while Margolin was voted Best Supporting Actor in 1979 and 1980. In the last season an insufferable PI, **Lance White** (Tom Selleck, later **MAGNUM, P.I.**) enraged Rockford by knowing all the answers. Another guest PI, **R I C H I E**

BROCKELMAN (Dennis Dugan) had an unsuccessful spinoff show. For syndication the show was retitled **JIM ROCKFORD, PRIVATE INVESTIGATOR**. Novelizations: Mike **JAHN**.

ROGER & HARRY: The MITERA TARGET (1977). A failed pilot for a proposed TV series featuring freewheeling PIs **Roger Quentin** (John Davidson) and **Harry Jaworsky** (Barry Primus), who specialize in recovering lost and stolen property,missing or kidnaped people. Also shown as **LOVE FOR RANSOM**.

SABER OF LONDON (1957). A police show, called, at various times, *Mystery Theatre*, *The Vise*, *Uncovered*, *Detective's Diary* and *Inspector Mark Saber*, but best known simply as **MARK SABER**, featuring Tom Conway as a suave New York cop, changed abruptly into a PI show with Donald Gray as a one-armed, London-based former Scotland Yard Chief Inspector turned sleuth, who carries a very unBritish gun.

77 SUNSET STRIP (October 1958-September 1964). Based, loosely, on **Roy HUGGINS'** novel *The Double Take*, the PI firm located at 77 Sunset Strip originally consisted of **Stuart Bailey** (Efrem Zimbalist Jr.) and **Jeff Spencer** (Roger Smith). Assisting them was **Gerald Lloyd Kookson III** (Edd Byrnes), better known as 'Kookie,' parking lot attendant at the next-door restaurant who was constantly combing his hair. Eventually Byrnes used his popularity to gain a larger part as a full partner and licensed investigator. In the fifth and final season Bailey worked alone, the others being dropped from the cast, as an international freelance investigator, the season opening with a five-part chase across two continents featuring two dozen big-name guests. The series was the prototype for a rash of very similar glamorous PI shows including BOURBON STREET BEAT, after whose collapse Rex Randolph (Richard Long) was brought in as fourth partner for one season, SURFSIDE 6 and HAWAIIAN EYE, Bailey making occasional guest appearances on the latter. **Robert Leslie BELLEM** and **Howard BROWNE** wrote scripts for the show.

SHAFT (October 1973-August 1974). After the successful films featuring **John Shaft**, who has been described as a "black Mike Hammer," themselves based on novels by **Ernest TIDYMAN**, star Richard Roundtree featured in a toned-down TV series in which he was just another PI, cut off from the black community. Producer William Woodfield demonstrated his incomprehension of Tidyman's original concept when he said "We thought the American public would accept this man as a friend."

SHANNON (Syndicated 1961). 39 half-hour episodes were made of this show about **Joe Shannon** (George Nader), an insurance investigator assigned to protect the Transport Bonding & Surety Company's clients from hijackings and thefts anywhere on the continental United States. Shannon had an electronically equipped car which was a crime lab on wheels and boasted a wrist tape-recorder like Dick Tracy's.

SHOESTRING (1978-?). British series featuring Trevor Eve as Bristol PI **Eddie Shoestring**, a former computer whiz who cracked up and got hooked on mysteries while convalescing. Perpetually broke, romantic, self-indulgent and cocksure, he has a phone-in program on Radio West. Novelizations: **Paul ABLEMAN.**

SHOOTING STARS (1983). After being fired from a TV PI series, because the star (Efrem Zimbalist Jr.!) was jealous of them, **Douglas Hawke** (Billy Dee Williams) and **Bill O'Keefe** (Parker Stevenson) thought that 58 episodes had qualified them to set up as real life PIs in the pilot for a proposed series.

SHOTGUN SLADE (Syndicated 1959-1961). Sporting a unique two-in-one shotgun, **Shotgun Slade** (Scott Brady) was an Old West detective on horseback, working for Wells Fargo, insurance companies, banks and private individuals who wanted crimes solved. The show had a jazz score and Slade was very successful with women, giving it a contemporary feel, though the Western style action—one episode featured an ambush, a mine explosion, a saloon bar brawl, a hanging and plenty of gunplay—was abundant. Celebrity guests included Ernie Kovacs, Johnny Cash, Tex Ritter, football stars, golfers, baseball players and heavyweight boxers. 78 episodes were made. Created by **Frank GRUBER.**

SIMON & SIMON (November 1981-?). Though **Andrew Jackson 'A.J.' Simon** (Jameson Parker) and **Rick Simon** (Gerald McRaney) were brothers, the former was conservative, clean-cut, house-proud and ambitious, driving a pristine convertible, the latter eccentric, grubby and laid-back with a beat-up pickup truck, living on a scruffy houseboat and more interested in playing guitar than working. Nonetheless they were partners in a small, struggling San Diego agency. Across the street was another agency run by crabby **Myron Fowler** (Eddie Barth), whose daughter **Janet** annoyed him by helping the brothers until she became an assistant DA. After retiring, Myron got bored and started working for them himself as a legman. **Howard BROWNE** writes scripts for it.

SLOW BURN (1986). A TV adaptation of **Arthur LYONS'** novel *Castles Burning*, with Eric Roberts as **Jacob Asch**, described by Leonard Maltin as below average.

SMALL & FRYE (March-June 1983). A PI situation comedy with **Nick Small** (Darren McGavin) as an old style hard-nosed, trench-coated PI who refused to adjust to the modern world and his young partner **Chip Frye** (Jack Blessing) who, as the result of a laboratory accident, could shrink to six inches in height by using a special ring, though the process could be set off by things like lightning, some foodstuffs or even hiccups. Chip's ability enabled the partners to get into places nobody else could.

SMILE JENNY, YOU'RE DEAD = HARRY-O

SONNY SPOON (February 1988-?). Unorthodox, savvy, big city black PI **Sonny Spoon** (Mario Van Peebles) operates out of a telephone booth on which he's hung an "out of order" sign. A slick con artist, with good street connections, Spoon is a talented imitator and can pass for male or female, black or white. The series is marked by pace, energy and coincidences.

SPENSER: FOR HIRE (September 1985-?). Robert Urich, previously a PI in VEGA$, plays the part of **Spenser**, the tough but sensitive Boston PI. Author **Robert B. PARKER** serves as consultant, and occasional scriptwriter while accepting the many changes made to his original concept. When poor audience figures threatened the series in 1987, Massachusetts Governor, soon to be Democratic Party Presidential candidate, Michael Dukakis and other Boston figures campaigned on the show's behalf.

SPRAGGUE (1984). Oddly, this threadbare TV film, a pilot for a proposed series, supposedly based on **Linda J. BARNES'** books and characters, transformed **Michael Spraggue** into wealthy science teacher and amateur detective called Nicholas, though his aunt, for unexplained reasons, called him Michael.

The SPY KILLER (1969). British made TV film starring Robert Horton as **John Smith**, spy turned London PI, forced back into service, based on **Jimmy SANGSTER**'s novel *Private i*. Confused and over-complex with a would-be cynical point of view. Followed by a sequel, FOREIGN EXCHANGE, also from a Sangster 'John Smith' novel.

STACCATO = JOHNNY STACCATO

STEVE RANDALL (November 1952-January 1953). A tough PI who wouldn't hesitate to hit a woman if she pulled a gun on him, suave, mustachioed **Steve Randall** (Melvyn Douglas) was a bitter, cynical former Intelligence officer and disbarred lawyer who used his skills to track down runaway wives and criminals while working for the reinstatement at the bar which concluded the short run. The show was syndicated locally in some places as **HOLLYWOOD OFF-BEAT**.

STONESTREET: WHO KILLED THE CENTERFOLD MODEL? (1977). Failed pilot for a proposed TV series featuring female PI **Liz Stonestreet** who goes undercover posing as a porno actress.

SURFSIDE 6 (October 1960-September 1962). One of the spin-offs of *77 Sunset Strip*, a tongue-in-cheek show with an affluent, bachelor lifestyle designed to attract a young audience. Operating from a Miami houseboat (the title refers to the telephone exchange), were **Ken Madison** (Van Williams), brought in from the failed **BOURBON STREET BEAT, Dave Thorne** (Lee Patterson) and **Sandy Winfield III** (Troy Donahue). Donahue also had a role in HAWAIIAN EYE and for a period was starring in two private eye shows at the same time. Novelization: **J.M. FLYNN.**

SWITCH (September 1975-September 1978). Retired bunco cop **Frank McBride** (Eddie Albert) and former conman **Pete Ryan** (Robert Wagner) formed a PI agency that specialized in pulling switches on conmen, bilking them out of the money they had swindled by persuading them to swindle themselves. Based in Los Angeles, they travelled far and wide, recruiting small-time thief and conman gone straight **Malcolm Argos** (Charlie Callas) to help them. During the second season the storylines featured fewer of the elaborate confidence tricks and more traditional detective plots. Novelizations: **Mike JAHN.**

T.H.E. CAT (September 1966-September 1967). A professional body-guard who fought crime on behalf of clients usually marked for death, **Thomas Hewitt Edward Cat**, alias The Cat (Robert Loggia), wore all-black clothes and, because of his circus acrobat and aerialist training, could scale the tallest building and relied on his reflexes and agility instead of weapons. He operated out of a San Francisco night club called Casa del Gato, where well-known jazz musicians were often seen in the cast.

TAKE A PAIR OF PRIVATE EYES (1968?). British TV play by Peter O'Donnell, known only from a novelization by **J.T. McINTOSH.** Featuring husband and wife, **Ambrose & Dominique Frayne** (cast not known), as 'working partners' in a detective agency, an arrangement viewed with particular scorn by Klein as using "the implied collaboration of partnership as a device rather than an integral part of the plot and structure," and therefore something of a disappointment from the creator of Modesty Blaise.

TENAFLY (October 1973-August 1974). A family man and black, LA PI **Harry Tenafly** (James McEachin) was an unusual TV eye on both counts. The show was divided between his home life and business, which was strictly a job with no girl-chasing (or being chased by girls).

TENSPEED AND BROWN SHOE (January-June 1980). A cult show featuring odd couple black **E.L. 'Tenspeed' Turner** (Ben Vereen), a hustler and master of disguise who needed legitimate employment as a parole requirement, and well-to-do, white, somewhat naive **Lionel Whitney** (Jeff Goldblum), known as 'Brown Shoe,' an expression for other straight business types, whose idea of being a PI was taken from 40s novels (an in-joke had producer Stephen Cannell's name on the covers as author of the 'Mark Savage' books Whitney read for inspiration) and Bogart movies. Teaming up in their own agency, two blocks from Sunset Boulevard, Los Angeles, they did well with cases, less well with ratings despite a huge promotional campaign.

The THIN MAN (September 1957-June 1959). After successful films and a radio show, **Dashiell HAMMETT**'s retired PI had yet another lease of life with Peter Lawford as **Nick Charles**, Phyllis Kirk as **Nora**, and, of course, Asta in attendence. See **NICK AND NORA** and **Radio: The ADVENTURES OF THE THIN MAN**.

THIS GIRL FOR HIRE (1983). Pilot taking off '40s detective films, with Bess Armstrong as flippant, klutzy **B.T. Brady**. Described by Leonard Maltin as clever but ultimately too cute.

TRAVIS McGEE (1983). Adapted from **John D. MacDONALD**'s *The Empty Copper Sea*, this pilot, described by Maltin as below average, suffered from a confused plotline and a lifeless performance by Sam Elliott in the title role.

TRIPLECROSS (1986). Lighthearted but tedious pilot for a proposed series about ex-cops, **Elliot Taffle** (Ted Wass), **Delia Langtree** (Markie Post) and **Cole Donovan** (Gary Swanson), who made a coup and became millionaire PIs, competing with each other to be first to solve complex murder cases, charging a standard rate of $1. Strained humor, juvenile pranks and inane witticisms, rated below average by Maltin.

TUCKER'S WITCH (October 1982-August 1983). A PI series crossed with *Bewitched*, **Rick & Amanda Tucker** (Tim Matheson and Catherine Hicks) were husband and wife partners in a PI agency with Rick as a conventional detective and Amanda relying on intuition, which, as she was a witch and could cast spells to solve cases, wasn't to be sniffed at. Unfortunately the spells didn't always work out as planned.

TURNOVER SMITH (1980). Pilot for a proposed post-*Cannon* series for William Conrad as **Thaddeus Smith**, a San Francisco criminology professor who uses scientific methods, advanced computer technology and his students' legwork to solve crimes.

21 BEACON STREET (July 1959-March 1960). Operating out of an office at that address in an unspecified city, **Dennis Chase** (Dennis Morgan) and his assistants, sexy Lola who could beguile information, law school graduate Brian and handyman Jim, who had a knack for dialects, didn't appear until the crime situation was developed, preferring to let the police apprehend the culprits after he had determined who they were by deduction.

TWIN DETECTIVES (1976). A failed pilot for a proposed series featuring identical twin PIs who capitalize on a seeming ability to be in two places at once. *Hee Haw* stars Jim and Jon Hager starred as **Tony & Shep Thomas**.

TWO FOR THE MONEY (1972). Two cops, one black, one white, quit the force to become PIs. Robert Hooks as **Larry Dean** and Stephen Brooks as **Chip Bronx** starred in this failed pilot.

The UNDERGROUND MAN = ARCHER

VEGA$ (September 1978-September 1981). On retainer to the owner of several big Las Vegas casino-hotels, including the Desert Inn where he had his office/apartment, handsome, wisecracking **Dan Tanna** (Robert Urich, who went on to become **SPENCER: FOR HIRE**) wore blue jeans, drove a vintage red Thunderbird convertible and had a sexy show girl receptionist and a sexy show girl secretary. Novelization: **Max FRANKLIN**.

The VISE = SABER OF LONDON

The VIEW FROM DANIEL PIKE (dates not known). British, or rather Scottish, series known only from a 1974 book by **Bill KNOX** & **Edward BOYD**, in which the author of the well-known Thane-Moss Glasgow police procedurals, adapted Boyd's scripts about tough, pugnacious, slum-born Glasgow private investigator and debt collector **Daniel Pike** as four short stories.

WHEN THE BOUGH BREAKS (1986). Ted Danson (of *Cheers*) starred as **Jonathan KELLERMAN**'s child psychologist/PI hero **Alex Delaware** in a TV film that was faithful to the book and, therefore, gripping, but for a very confused climax. Winner of an MWA award.

WHO KILLED THE CENTERFOLD MODEL? = **STONESTREET**

FILMS

ACCOMPLICE (1946). Based on **Frank GRUBER**'s novel *Simon Lash, Private Detective*, directed by Walter Colmes, script by Irving Elman and Gruber, starring Richard Arlen as **Simon Lash**, Tom Dugan as **Eddie Slocum**, in a mediocre whodunit with occasional high spots.

AFTER THE THIN MAN (1936). **Dashiell HAMMETT**s original story (serialized in A1 #5 & 6), a sequel to **The THIN MAN**, again directed by W.S. Van Dyke, script by Frances Goodrich and Albert Hackett and starring William Powell and Myrna Loy as **Nick & Nora Charles**, initiated the odd misnomer of the Thin Man, originally the villain, now identified with the hero of the film, radio and TV series.

AGAINST ALL ODDS (1984). Remake of **OUT OF THE PAST**, itself based on **Geoffrey HOMES'** novel *Build My Gallows High*, directed by Taylor Hackford and starring Jeff Bridges and Rachel Ward, with Jane Greer playing the mother of her character in the original. The hero was no longer a PI but hard-up pro football player **Terry Brogan**.

ANGEL HEART (1987). Based on **William HJORTSBERG**'s novel *Falling Angel*, directed (very badly) by Alan Parker, who also wrote the incomprehensible, florid and heavy-handed script, starring Mickey Rourke as **Harry Angel**, a 50s PI with *Miami Vice* designer stubble, Robert De Niro, Lisa Bonet and Charlotte Rampling. While opinions on the original book vary, Parker telegraphs everything so crudely that none of its admitted shock value remains.

ANOTHER THIN MAN (1939). The third of the Thin Man films, once again directed by W.S. Van Dyke, script by Frances Goodrich and Albert Hackett and starring William Powell and Myrna Loy as **Nick & Nora Charles**. **Dashiell HAMMETT**, author of the original novel, provided the story on which the film was based.

345

ARMED RESPONSE (1986). Directed by Fred Olen Ray, script by T.L. Lankford, starring Ross Hagen as greedy PI **Cory Thorton** who double-crosses his partner **Clay Roth** (David Goss) when they're hired by a Japanese gangster to recover a stolen jade antique, leading to his death which incurs the wrath of ex-cop Burt Roth (Lee Van Cleef) and Vietnam vet Jim Roth (David Carradine). A formula action-revenge film with an above par cast, corny dialogue and a strong performance in the Gig Young mold by Hagen.

ASESINATO EN EL COMITE CENTRALE (Spain 1982). **Manual Vazquez MONTALBAN**'s novel *Murder In The Central Committee*, featuring gourmet, Catalalonian ex-Communist PI **Pepe Carvalho**, was filmed in Spain, scripted and directed by Vicente Aranda. No other details.

ASSIGNMENT TO KILL (1968). Directed and written by Sheldon Reynolds, starring Patrick O'Neal as **Richard Cutting**, Joan Hackett, John Gielgud, Herbert Lom, Eric Portman and Oscar Homolka in a dull thriller about a PI investigating shady corporate goings-on in Switzerland. Much talk, little action.

BERMUDA MYSTERY (1944). Directed by Benjamin Stoloff, script by Scott Darling from a story by John Larkin, starring Preston Foster as **Steve Carromond**, investigating an insurance merry-go-round of murder in an obvious whodunit whose distinguishing feature has been described as its mediocrity.

The BIG BOODLE (1957). Based on **Robert SYLVESTER**'s novel, directed by Richard Wilson, script by Jo Eisinger, starring Errol Flynn as **Ned Sherwood**, transformed from a PI into a Havana casino croupier, in "a seedy programmer emphasizing Flynn's career decline. Tame caper of gangsters and counterfeit money." Released in Britain as **A NIGHT IN HAVANA**.

The BIG FIX (1978). Based on **Roger L. SIMON**'s novel, directed by Jeremy Paul Kagan, starring Richard Dreyfuss whose screen persona is well suited to the part of **Moses Wine**. A hopelessly tangled whodunit, due largely to Simon, who himself wrote the muddled script.

The BIG SLEEP (1946). From the novel by **Raymond CHANDLER,** directed by Howard Hawks with a screenplay by William Faulkner, **Leigh BRACKETT** and Jules Furthman, the best known of all the **Philip Marlowe** films starred, of course, Humphrey Bogart, with Lauren Bacall and Martha Vickers as the Sternwood sisters, John Ridgely, Dorothy Malone, Elisha Cooke Jr. and Bob Steele. A witty film, so complicated that nobody could figure it out, with one murder, that of the chauffeur, remaining totally unexplained. Hawks sent Chandler a telegram querying this and Chandler replied that the butler did it! So entertaining that nobody cared about this off-hand treatment of plot.

The BIG SLEEP (UK 1978). Based on the novel by **Raymond CHANDLER**, directed by Michael Winner, who also wrote the script, starring Robert Mitchum as **Philip Marlowe**, Sarah Miles, Oliver Reed, Richard Boone, James Stewart, John Mills, Edward Fox, Joan Collins, Harry Andrews and Richard Todd. Mitchum again (see **FAREWELL, MY LOVELY**) played an aging, world-weary Marlowe in this textually faithful, though updated and set in London, British-made version of the novel which was terminally etiolated by Winner's turgid script and lifeless direction.

BIG ZAPPER (UK 1973). Directed by Lindsay Shonteff, starring Linda Marlowe as **Harriet Zapper**, a tough, violent, blonde PI with a trusty, masochistic sidekick named Rock Hard in a low-grade comic strip sex adventure also released as **The PRIVATE LIFE OF A FEMALE PRIVATE EYE**.

The BLACK BIRD (1975). Directed by David Giler, with a script by Giler, Don Mankiewicz and Gordon Cotler. A misconceived comic-nostalgic sequel to, and parody of, **The MALTESE FALCON**, starring George Segal as **Sam Spade Jr.**, with Lee Patrick and Elisha Cook Jr. reprising their roles as Effie Perine and Wilmer Cook. Segal and Patrick, as a fat, bitter and bitchy Effie, gave good performances but the script, about the continuing search for the famous fowl, was incoherent and grimly unfunny. One charitable critic remarked, "a mish-mash which will infuriate the Hammett purists and mildly entertain some filmgoers." Novelization: **Alexander EDWARDS**

BLACK EYE (1974). Based on **Jeff JACKS'** novel *Murder On The Wild Side*, directed by Jack Arnold, script by Mark Haggard and Jim Martin, starring Fred Williamson, here an LA cop (Shep?) **Stone**, first suspended, then reinstated in an action-mystery investigation of drug-related murders in Venice, California. Episodic with tacky, expoitative forays into Jesus freaks, drugs, lesbianism and porno movies.

BLADE RUNNER (1982). Based on **Philip K. DICK**'s novel *Do Androids Dream Of Electric Sheep?*, directed by Ridley Scott, script by Hampton Fancher and David Peoples, starring Harrison Ford as (Rick) **Deckard,** a 21st century LA ex-cop who tracks down androids passing themselves off as human. TV ad director Scott sacrificed everything to production values, with astonishing sets of a decaying, futuristic LA, but the script was hopelessly muddled and the acting non-existent.

BLONDE FOR A DAY (1946). Based on the **Brett HALLIDAY** series, though not on any specific title, the 10th **Michael Shayne** film was directed by Sam Newfield with a script by Fred Myton and starred Hugh Beaumont. Shayne hunts the killers of a journalist friend shot for exposing a gambling ring.

BLUE, WHITE & PERFECT (1941). Based on the **Brett HALLIDAY** series, and on an original story by Borden Chase, the 4th **Michael Shayne** film was directed by Herbert I. Leeds, screenplay by Samuel G. Engel, and starred Lloyd Nolan in a 'topical' story in which he works in an aircraft factory as a cover to expose Axis agents, getting to Hawaii before he thwarts them.

The BRASHER DOUBLOON (1947). From **Raymond CHANDLER**'s novel *The High Window*, directed by John Braham, script by Dorothy Hannah, adapted by Dorothy Bennett and Leonard Praskins, with George Montgomery as **Philip Marlowe**. A neglected, but tough and faithful, version and the last *noir* film based on a Chandler novel. See **TIME TO KILL** for another version of *The High Window*.

CALLING MR CALLAGHAN (? 1960). Curious as it may seem, the existence of this film, based apparently on a **Slim Callaghan** short story, "The Amazing Mr. Callaghan," by **Peter CHEYNEY**, cannot be confirmed by available reference sources. Hubin was equally baffled.

The CARIBBEAN MYSTERY (1945). Based on the novel *Murder in Trinidad* by John W. Vandercook, directed by Robert Webb, script by W. Scott Darling, starring James Dunn as **Mr Smith**, an ex-Brooklyn cop and special investigator for an oil company in a short, taut, jungle island set action thriller.

The CASE OF THE MISSING BLONDE = The LADY IN THE MORGUE

CHANDLER (1972). Directed by Paul Magwood, script by John Sacret Young, starring Warren Oates as **Chandler**, a PI who falls in love with the ex-mistress of a racketeer in a sub-standard programmer, that also featured Leslie Caron and Gloria Grahame. Mediocre script and direction let down good performances.

The CHEAP DETECTIVE (1978). Directed by Robert Moore, screenplay by Neil Simon, starring Peter Falk as **Lou Peckinpaugh** of Peckinpaugh & Merkle, Private Investigators, whose office is in San Francisco's Private Detective Center (Merkle, whose wife Peckinpaugh is having an affair with, is shot at the outset). Peckinpaugh is short, narrow-eyed and gravel voiced, with a shabby trenchcoat, a Mauser and an inexhaustible supply of ready-mixed cocktails. A funny, if often obvious film, blending the hoods of *The Maltese Falcon* with the Nazis of *Casablanca,* that also featured Ann-Margaret, Eileen Brennan, Sid Caesar, Stockard Channing, James Coco, Dom DeLuise, Madelaine Kahn and Phil Silvers. Novelization: **Robert GROSSBACH.**

CHEAPER TO KEEP HER (1980). Directed by Ken Annakin, screenplay, very disappointingly, by **Timothy HARRIS** and Herschel Weingrad, with Mac Davis as **Bill Dekkar,** hired by a lawyer to check out husbands delinquent with their alimony checks and taking advantage of their wives. Described as sexist, racist and obnoxious.

CHINATOWN (1974). Directed by Roman Polanski, Oscar winning screenplay by Robert Towne, starring Jack Nicholson as **J.J. Gittes,** 30s LA PI in a complex, volatile case based on true events, also featuring Faye Dunaway, John Huston and Polanski himself as a hood who mutilates Gittes. A bleak film in which the divorce specialist ex-cop's career is ruined in a case he could never solve or be allowed to solve.

CITY AFTER MIDNIGHT (UK 1957). Based on John Dickson Carr's *The Emperor's Snuff Box,* directed and written by Compton Bennett, starring Dan O'Herlihy as insurance investigator **Dermot Kinross** in a tame, talky inquiry into an antique dealer's death. Released in Britain as **THAT WOMAN OPPOSITE.**

COAST OF SKELETONS (UK 1964). Very, very loosely based on Edgar Wallace's *Sanders Of The River,* directed by Robert Lynn, script by Anthony Scott Veitch, based on a story by Peter Welbeck 'inspired' by Wallace (phew!), starring Richard Todd as **Harry Sanders,** an ex-officer insurance investigator hired to investigate the sabotaging of an American tycoon's African diamond mining operations. Or possibly to foil a plot to loot valuables from sunken ships. Plot summaries differ radically.

The CONVERSATION (1974). Written and directed by Francis Ford Coppola, a brilliant, disturbing thriller, probing questions about violation of privacy and personal responsibility, starring Gene Hackman as **Harry Caul,** an obsessive surveillance expert who becomes involved in a case.

COSMO JONES, CRIME SMASHER (1943). Directed by James Tinling, script by Michael L. Simmons, starring Frank Graham as **Cosmo Jones,** a correspondence school detective who has to turn theory into practice when he witnesses a gangland killing.

CRIME BY NIGHT (1944). Based on **Geoffrey HOMES'**s novel *Forty Whacks,* directed by William Clemens, script by Richard Weil and Joel Malone, starring Jerome Cowan as **Sam** (rather than Humphrey) **Campbell.** A slow-moving, low budget mystery undermined by early revelation of whodunit. See **NO HANDS ON THE CLOCK.**

CRY UNCLE! (1971). Based on **Michael BRETT**s novel *Lie A Little, Die A Little*, directed by John G. Avildsen, script by David Odell, starring Allen Garfield as **Jacob Masters** (Pete McGrath in the novel), getting involved with murder, sex and blackmail in an often hilarious X-rated spoof in wonderfully taste that has a minor cult following.

The **DAIN CURSE** (1978). Shown as a mini-series in America (see **TV: The DAIN CURSE**), this long, complex version of **Dashiell HAMMETT**'s novel, starring James Coburn as **Hamilton Nash**, was released as a feature film in Europe.

DANGEROUS FEMALE = The MALTESE FALCON (1931)

The **DARK CORNER** (1946). From a novel by **Leo ROSTEN**, published in the US as by **Leonard Q. ROSS**, directed by Henry Hathaway, script by Jay Dratler and Bernard Schoenfeld. Mark Stevens starred as PI **Bradford Galt**, with Lucille Ball and William Bendix co-starring. Framed by his ex-partner, Galt is jailed and on his release finds himself caught up in machinations surrounding the ex-partner's affair with a married woman. Described as one of the most important *noir* films of 1946, with the emphasis on the psychological anguish and confusion of a tough but emotionally vulnerable protagonist.

DARKER THAN AMBER (1970). Based on **John D. MacDONALD**'s novel, directed by Robert Clouse, script by Ed Waters, starring Rod Taylor as **Travis McGee**, Suzy Kendall, Theodore Bikel (as Mayer) and Jane Russell in a reasonably faithful, but very violent, overlong and confusing film depiction.

DEAD MEN DON'T WEAR PLAID (1982). Directed by Carl Reiner, script by Reiner, George Gipe and Steve Martin, starring Steve Martin as inept 40s PI **Rigby Reardon** and Rachel Ward in a one-joke, cute idea comedy-mystery in which Martin interacts with clips from vintage 40s *noir* melodramas, notably *The Bribe*. Amusing at first, but the lack of story and characterization make it of more interest to the film buff than anyone else.

DEAD PIGEON ON BEETHOVEN STREET (1972). Fast paced, tongue in cheek thriller written and directed, without his usual intensity, by **Sam FULLER**, financed by German TV, with Glenn Corbett as an American PI known only as **Sandy**. Novelization: **Sam FULLER**.

DEADLY CIRCUIT = MORTELLE RANDONEE

DEADLY ILLUSION (1987). Directed by Larry Cohen, who also wrote the script, completed by William Tanned, starring black actor Billy Dee Williams as **Hamberger**, an unlicenced operative in an entertaining, low budget tongue-in-cheek homage to *film noir*, spotlighting a charming and funny performance by Williams whose habit of causing accidental deaths is the source of much black humor. Hired to kill a man's wife, he instead warns her but then discovers that both are imposters.

DETECTIVE (France 1985). Directed by Jean-Luc Godard, script by Godard, Alain Sarde, Philippe Setbon, Ann-Marie Mieville, starring Laurent Terzieff as **William Prospero**, house dick of the Hotel Concorde, Saint Lazare, Paris, still trying to solve a two year old murder. Godard's themes, the commercialization of sex, the threat of the multinationals and the mystique of film itself, are aired in a loose yet complex framework filled with asides, jokes and anecdotes. *Variety* commented "those expecting a neat plot will, of course, be bitterly disappointed; the final resolution, involving a shoot-out and several bodies, is so offhand as be quite obscure."

The **DETECTIVE** (1968). Based on the novel by **Roderick THORP**, directed by Gordon Douglas, script by Abby Mann, starring Frank Sinatra as **Joe Leland**, here transformed into a top-flight NYPD homicide cop with problems.

DETECTIVE SCHOOL DROPOUTS = DUMB DICKS

The **DEVIL'S MASK** (1946). Directed by Henry Levin, script by Charles O'Neal and Dwight V. Babcock, based on Carleton E Morse's radio program, starring Jim Bannon as **Jack Packard** and Barton Yarborough as **Doc Long**, hired to find the murderer of an explorer. Intriguing if far-fetched, with an all too obvious suspect. See **I LOVE A MYSTERY** below and **Radio: I LOVE A MYSTERY**.

DRESSED TO KILL (1941). Based on the **Brett HALLIDAY** series, though actually taken from **Richard BURKE**'s PI novel *The Dead Take No Bows*, the 3rd **Michael Shayne** film was directed by Eugene Ford, script by Stanley Rauh and Manning O'Connor and starred Lloyd Nolan. Leaving a marriage licence bureau, Shayne and his fiancée hear a shot from an adjacent theater. Shayne gets involved, solving the case but losing the girl (Mary Beth Hughes).

The **DROWNING POOL** (1976). Based on the novel by **Ross MACDONALD**, directed by Stuart Rosenberg, script by Tracy Keenan Wynn, Lorenzo Semple and Walter Hill, starring Paul Newman returning to the role of **Harper** (as Lew Archer was renamed, see **HARPER**), co-starring Joanne Woodward, in a slickly made but stagnant whodunit, good performances vitiated by sloppy, unimaginative and predictable direction.

DUMB DICKS (1986). Directed by Filippo Ottoni, script by David Landsberg and Lorin Dreyfuss who also starred as **Donald Wilson**, a pint-sized, job-losing nebbish obsessed by detective stories who signs up as a student of hard-up hardboiled PI **Paul Miller**. Mostly set in Italy, where the duo get involved with feuding Mob families, this comedy-thriller features slapstick and running gags in the Bob Hope mode. Also shown as **DETECTIVE SCHOOL DROPOUTS**.

EIGHT MILLION WAYS TO DIE (1986). Based on the novel by **Lawrence BLOCK**, directed by Hal Ashby, script by Oliver Stone and David Lee Henry, starring Jeff Bridges as (Matt) **Scudder**, with Rosanna Arquette, in what is described as a slow, arid film populated by unpleasant and uninteresting characters and whose title *NYT* decided was a reasonable epitaph for anybody foolish enough to watch it.

The EMPTY BEACH (Australia 1985). Based on the novel by **Peter CORRIS**, directed by Chris Thomson, script by Keith Dewhurst, starring Bryan Brown as **Cliff Hardy** in a faithful and atmospheric translation of Corris' distinctly Australian ambience.

EYES IN THE NIGHT (1942). Based on **Baynard KENDRICK**'s novel *The Odor Of Violets*, directed by Fred Zinneman, script by Guy Trosper and Howard Emmett Rogers, starring Edward Arnold as the blind PI **Captain Duncan Maclain** in what is described as an above-average mystery. See also **The HIDDEN EYE**.

The FALCON TAKES OVER (1942). Having paid $2000 for the rights to **Raymond CHANDLER**'s *Farewell, My Lovely*, RKO made it a vehicle for their series about adventurer Gay Lawrence, alias The Falcon, played by George Sanders. Irving Reis directed, Lynn Root and Frank Fenton wrote a script that closely followed the original Chandler story with Ward Bond as Moose Molloy, Helen Gilbert as "little Velma."

FAREWELL, MY LOVELY (UK 1975). Based on the novel by **Raymond CHANDLER**, directed by Dick Richards, script by David Zelag Goodman, starring Robert Mitchum as **Philip Marlowe**, Charlotte Rampling, John Ireland, Sylvia Miles, Harry Dean Stanton and Sylvester Stallone in the third, British-made, version (see **The FALCON TAKES OVER** and **MURDER, MY SWEET**). Tries hard to evoke the period, with some very effective Edward Hopperish visual effects but Mitchum's performance as a tired, aging, world-weary Marlowe, a role he repeated in **The BIG SLEEP** (1975), appeals more as an expression of the Mitchum film persona than as a portrait of Chandler's hero.

FAT CHANCE = PEEPER

The FAT MAN (1951). Loosely based on the character of **Dashiell HAMMETT**'s Continental Op, directed by William Castle, script by Harry Essex and Leonard Lee, starring J. Scott Smart, star of the popular

40s **Radio: The FAT MAN** show, as rotund, gourmet PI **Brad Runyan**. Described as unremarkable and occasionally listed on TV as starring Rock Hudson who made his debut in it.

FIND THE BLACKMAILER (1943). Based on a story by **G.T. FLEMING-ROBERTS**, "Blackmail With Feathers," directed by Ross Lederman, script by Robert E. Kent, starring Jerome Cowan as **D.L. Trees**, a PI hired to find a talking blackbird that can incriminate a mayoral candidate. A mild take-off of the *The Maltese Falcon* with twists and turns neatly tied together.

FORBIDDEN (1954). Directed by Rudolph Maté, script by William Sackheim and Gil Doud. Tony Curtis played **Eddie Darrow,** hired by a Chicago mobster to find a woman he once knew (Joanne Dru) who traces her to Macao where numerous complications arise when he falls for her.

FOXTRAP (1986). Directed by, and starring, Fred Williamson, a low-budget US-Italian production with Williamson as **Thomas Fox**, hired to bring a runaway back to her family from Europe and described as little more than a fashion parade for the director/star.

The FRENCH KEY (1946). Based on the novel by **Frank GRUBER**, who wrote the screenplay, directed by Walter Colmes, starring Albert Dekker as **Johnny Fletcher** and Mike Mazurki as **Sam Cragg** in a convoluted, and never clearly resolved story, in which the duo must find the murderer when the victim winds up dead in their locked hotel room.

The GIRL HUNTERS (1963). Based on the novel by **Mickey SPILLANE**, who wrote the script with Roy Rowland and Robert Fellows, and played the part of his own detective, **Mike Hammer**. Directed by Roy Rowland, co-starring Lloyd Nolan (who made seven films as Brett Halliday's Michael Shayne) and Shirley Eaton, this rugged murder mystery was made in Britain.

GIRL IN ROOM 13 (1961). Directed by Richard Cunha, script by Cunha and H.E. Barrie, starring an aging Brian Donlevy as **Steve Marshall** in a low-grade Brazil-set story, tracking down a murder and counterfeiting gang. This US-Brazilian quickie production made an inelegant wind down for Donlevy's career.

GRAND CENTRAL MURDER (1942). Based on the novel by **Sue MacVEIGH**, directed by S. Sylvan Simon, script by Peter Ruric, with Van Heflin as **Rocky Custer** (Andy MacVeigh in the original book) in what is described as "a slick, fast-moving B whodunit," blessed with a strong, moody performance by Van Heflin, a solid cast, a good script and tight direction. Peter Ruric was the screenwriting name of **Paul CAIN**

who, according to film historian Don Miller, "toughened it up, disposed of the husband-and-wife sleuthing team from the novel, and re-wrote the role of Van Heflin as a private investigator."

The GRISSOM GANG (1971). Based on the novel *No Orchids For Miss Blandish* by **James Hadley CHASE**, directed by Robert Aldrich, script by Leon Griffiths, starring Kim Darby as the kidnapped heiress, Scott Wilson as the member of the gang of grotesque degenerates who falls for her, and Robert Lansing as **Dave Fenner**, the PI in pursuit. Outlandish, very violent, comic-book thriller set in the 1930s and very funny if you appreciate Aldrich's self-indulgent sense of humor. See **NO ORCHIDS FOR MISS BLANDISH** for another version.

GUILTY BYSTANDER (1950). From the novel by **Wade MILLER**, directed by Joseph Lerner, script by Don Ettlinger, starring Zachary Scott as **Max Thursday**. An alcoholic ex-cop searches for his former wife's kidnapped son. Notable low-life settings pervade this sleazy *noir* thriller.

GUMSHOE (UK 1972). Directed by Stephen Frears, script by **Neville SMITH**, starring Albert Finney as small-time Liverpool Bingo caller **Eddie Ginley** who acts out his hardboiled private eye fantasies on his 31st birthday by placing an ad in the local paper, "Ginley's the name, Gumshoe's the game. Private Investigations. No Divorce Work," and gets involved in serious crime. Half *Secret Life of Walter Mitty*, half *The Maltese Falcon*. Novelization: **Neville SMITH**.

GUNN (1967). Based on **TV: PETER GUNN**, directed by Blake Edwards, who wrote the script with William Peter Blatty, starring the TV show's lead Craig Stevens as, of course, **Peter Gunn**, but not the essential characters of Lola Albright and Herschel Bernardi, nor the literate scripts that characterized the show and created a dynamic tension with the violence that here, unmitigated, becomes tasteless and repugnant.

HAMMETT (1983). Based on the novel by **Joe GORES**, directed by Wim Wenders, screenplay by **Ross THOMAS**, Dennis O'Flaherty and Thomas Pope, starring Frederic Forrest as **Dashiell Hammett**, Marilu Henner, Peter Boyle, Elisha Cook Jr. and Samuel Fuller. Set in the late 1920s, with Hammett making the transition from hardboiled Pinkerton detective to writer of hardboiled crime fiction, Wenders' first American film, based on the same true events which Hammett used in various stories, was years in the making, much of it had to be reshot (the script has been referred to as "the stuff that nightmares are made of"), but is still a powerful evocation of the period, with a fine performance by Forrest.

HARPER (1966). Based on **Ross MACDONALD**'s novel *The Moving Target*, directed by Jack Smight, screenplay by William Goldman, starring Paul Newman as **Harper**, Lauren Bacall, Julie Harris, Shelley Winters and Robert Wagner. With Lew Archer renamed at the whim of the star, who thought that film titles beginning with H (such as *Hud* and *The Hustler*) were lucky for him, it's hardly surprising that this lavish production was flat and simplistic, though Harris shone in her role when most characterization was throttled by plot convolutions. However, it was superior to the sequel, **The DROWNING POOL**.

HAZARD (1948). Based on the novel by **Roy CHANSLOR**, directed by George Marshall, script by Chanslor and Arthur Sheekman, starring Macdonald Carey as **J.D. Storm**, a PI hired to track down Paulette Goddard who falls in love with her in a routine comedy.

HERE'S FLASH CASEY (1937). Based on a story by **George Harmon COXE**, directed by Lynn Sholes, script by John Krafft, starring Eric Linden as newspaper photographer, and accepted PI, **Jack 'Flash' Casey**. The weak plot appears to have no crime content at all. See also **WOMEN ARE TROUBLE**.

HICKEY & BOGGS (1972). Directed by Robert Culp, who also co-starred as **Franklin Boggs**, script by Walter Hill, with Bill Cosby as **Albert Hickey**. After the duo's success in the spoofy TV series *I Spy* came this contrasting, tough, downbeat, very violent melodrama about two down-and-out PIs with personal problems, Hickey a nagging wife, Boggs incipient alcoholism, who get caught up in a bloody clash between gangsters and political guerrillas in which they're so thoroughly out of their depth that, in an ironic sunset finale, they survive simply because they're too unimportant to kill. Novelization: **Philip ROCK**.

The HIDDEN EYE (1945). Based on **Baynard KENDRICK**'s character, though not on any particular novel, this follow-up to **EYES IN THE NIGHT** was directed by Richard Whorf, with a screenplay by **George Harmon COXE** and Harry Ruskin, and again starred Edward Arnold as **Captain Duncan Maclain**, the blind PI. Described as a fast-moving, entertaining mystery.

The HOUSE OF FATE = MUSS 'EM UP

I LOVE A MYSTERY (1945). Directed by Henry Levin. starring Jim Bannon as **Jack Packard** and Barton Yarborough as **Doc Long**, described by Maltin as "Bizarre, entertaining whodunnit based on popular radio show . . . involves strange Oriental cult, and a prophecy of doom for bewildered (George) Macready." See **Radio: I LOVE A MYSTERY** and **The DEVIL'S MASK** above.

I LOVE TROUBLE (1948). Based on *The Double Take* by **Roy HUGGINS**, who also wrote the screenplay, directed by S. Sylvan Simon, starring Franchot Tone as **Stuart Bailey** in a flippant mystery.

I, THE JURY (1953). From **Mickey SPILLANE**s novel, directed by Harry Essex who also wrote the script. Biff Elliott was the first film incarnation of **Mike Hammer**, going after the murderer of his best friend in a 3-D *noir* movie with muted sex and violence, though matching Spillane in crudity. Preston Foster (Jonathan Latimer's Bill Crane in three films), Peggie Castle and Elisha Cook Jr. co-starred.

I, THE JURY (1982). Based on the novel by **Mickey SPILLANE**, directed by Richard T. Heffron, script by Larry Cohen, starring Armand Assante, as a sullen, though still violent, **Mike Hammer** in the second, updated, version whose plot line is full of holes. Taking advantage of modern times to match Spillane's levels of graphic violence and nudity, this cartoon strip was to have been directed by Larry Cohen who was fired and replaced by Heffron who, unable to fully grasp either the hardboiled ethos, Spillane's original concept or Cohen's parodic script, combined elements of all three uneasily together.

IT STARTED IN TOKYO = TWENTY PLUS TWO

IT'S ONLY MONEY (1962). Directed by Frank Tashlin, script by John Fenton Murray, starring Jerry Lewis as **Lester March**, aspiring PI who goes after an advertised reward for finding the missing heir to a billion-dollar fortune and finds himself the target of ever more ingenious murder attempts, discovering that he himself is the long lost nephew. Welcomed by fans as a return to the inspired slapstick of his earlier films.

JUST OFF BROADWAY (1942). Based on the **Brett HALLIDAY** series, though not on any specific title, the 6th **Michael Shayne** film was directed by Herbert I. Leeds, script by Arnaud d'Usseau and starred Lloyd Nolan. One of the weaker films, apart from comic relief provided by Phil Silvers, with Shayne on jury duty which he leaves to investigate the case being tried and proves the accused woman's innocence, drawing a short jail term for contempt in the process.

The KEYHOLE (1933). Directed by Michael Curtiz, script by Robert Presnell, based on a story, "Adventuress," by Alice D.G. Miller, starring George Brent as private detective **Neil Davis**, hired by a millionaire to follow Kay Francis to Havana where she is trying to get a quick divorce from a blackmailing husband from whom she thought she was already divorced. Not knowing that she is the millionaire's wife, Brent falls for her and they end up together in a soap opera distinguished by Francis' exceptional comic talent.

KISS ME DEADLY (1955). From **Mickey SPILLANE**'s novel, directed by Robert Aldrich, script by A.I. Bezzerides, with Ralph Meeker as a self-centred, brutish **Mike Hammer** following a series of leads in search of "the great whatsit." The ultimate *noir* detective film which never ceases to amaze and by far the most successful (artistically) of the Spillane films. Interestingly, Bezzerides was blacklisted as a result of the House UnAmerican Activities Committee's investigation of Hollywood.

LADY ICE (1973). Directed by Tom Gries, script by Alan Trustman and Harold Clemens, starring Donald Sutherland as insurance investigator **Andy Hammond** and Jennifer O'Neill as a wealthy fence's daughter in a dull caper wasting good cast including Robert Duvall and Patrick Magee. Novelization: **Malcolm BRALY**

LADY IN CEMENT (1968). Based on the novel by **Anthony ROME**, pseudonym of **Albert MARVIN** who wrote the now dated script with Jack Guss, directed by Gordon Douglas, starring Frank Sinatra repeating the role of Miami PI **Tony Rome** (see **TONY ROME**), with Richard Conte, Raquel Welch, Dan Blocker and Joe E. Lewis in a complicated story that lacked the first film's humor. Talk of a TV series was scotched by the film's box-office failure.

The LADY IN THE LAKE (1947). From the novel by **Raymond CHANDLER**, directed by Robert Montgomery who also played the lead role of **Philip Marlowe**, script by **Steve FISHER**, co-starring Lloyd Nolan (Mike Shayne in several Brett Halliday films). The subjective camera technique, entirely as seen by Marlowe, has inspired cheers and jeers in equal quantities, but the film remains one of the most unusual and humorous of all hardboiled *noir* thrillers.

The LADY IN THE MORGUE (1938). Based on **Jonathan LATIMER**'s novel, directed by Otis Garrett, screenplay by Eric Taylor, starring Preston Foster as **Bill Crane**, Frank Jenks as **Doc Williams**. Filmed as part of Universal's Crime Club and, like the other two Bill Crane films (**The WESTLAND CASE** and **The LAST WARNING**), a fast, action-packed and thoughtful version with all the virtues, vitality and humor of a good B picture. Released in Britain as **The CASE OF THE MISSING BLONDE**.

LARCENY IN HER HEART (1946). Based on the **Brett HALLIDAY** series, though no specific title, the 9th **Michael Shayne** film was directed by Sam Newfield, script by Raymond L. Strock and starred Hugh Beaumont in a complicated story. Good production values.

The LAST WARNING (1938). Based on **Jonathan LATIMER**'s novel *The Dead Don't Care*, directed by Albert Rogell, screenplay by

Edmund L. Hartmann, with Preston Foster as **Bill Crane**, Frank Jenks as **Doc Williams**. Third and last of the entertaining, fast-moving Universal Crime Club Crane films (see **The LADY IN THE MORGUE** and **The WESTLAND CASE**).

The LATE SHOW (1977). Directed by Robert Benton, who also wrote the script, starring Art Carney as aging PI **Ira Wells** trying to solve the murder of his ex-partner in the face of the "help" of a flaky, aimless young woman, Lily Tomlin. Benton's script echoes Hammett and Chandler and the chemistry between the two stars is remarkable.

The LEAGUE OF FRIGHTENED MEN (1937). Based on **Rex STOUT**'s novel, directed by Alfred E. Green, script by Eugene Solow and Guy Endore, starring Walter Connolly as **Nero Wolfe** and Lionel Stander as **Archie Goodwin**. The second of only two Wolfe/Goodwin films (see **MEET NERO WOLFE**), plans for more being shelved because of Connolly's ill-health.

LEAVE IT TO THE IRISH (1944). Directed by William Beaudine, script by Tim Ryan and Eddie Davis, starring James Dunn as **Terry Moran** and Wanda McKay as **Nora O'Brien**, PIs who team up to solve a murder. Low-budget comedy short on laughs.

LEND ME YOUR EAR = The LIVING GHOST

The LIVING GHOST (1942). Directed by William Beaudine, starring James Dunn, hamming outrageously as **Nick Trayne** in a low-budget comedy-mystery, with the detective trying to find out which of a houseful of suspects is giving Gus Glassmire brain paralysis. Released in the UK as **LEND ME YOUR EAR**.

LOCKER SIXTY-NINE (UK 1962). From a story by Edgar Wallace, directed by Norman Harrison, script by Richard Harris, starring Eddie Byrne as **Simon York**, a PI framed for his boss's murder in a typically far fetched Wallace plot.

The LONG GOODBYE (1973). Based on, or rather bastardized from, the novel by **Raymond CHANDLER**, misdirected by Robert Altman, script by Leigh **BRACKETT** (who also worked on the 1946 version of **The BIG SLEEP**), starring a hopelessly miscast Elliott Gould as **Philip Marlowe** in a shoddy, updated, contemptuous and contemptible piece of loathsome rubbish much admired by cinéastes, which says it all. Leigh Brackett's credit for the script should not be held against her, given Altman's disjointed and unintelligable approach. The video version, apparently, lacks the original ending which is a definite plus.

A LOVELY WAY TO GO = A LOVELY WAY TO DIE

A LOVELY WAY TO DIE (1968). Directed by David Lowell Rich, script by A.J. Russell, starring Kirk Douglas as tough, likeable ex-cop PI **Jim Schuyler**, hired by the DA (Eli Wallach) to protect Sylva Koscina pending her trial for murdering her husband. Odd suspense film with a somewhat improbable and predictable plot, but a good cast, deft direction and offbeat pacing that gloss over the script's weaknesses. Released in the UK as **A LOVELY WAY TO GO**.

MALIBU EXPRESS (1985). Directed by Andy Sidaris, starring Darby Hinton as country boy PI **Cody Abilene** working on a complex espionage and blackmail case, but mainly a vehicle for the physical charms of numerous *Playboy* centerfold models plus a sprinkling of Mr. Universe beefcake. A loose remake of Sidaris' earlier **STACEY (AND HER GANGBUSTERS)**.

The MALTESE FALCON (1931). From the novel by **Dashiell HAMMETT**, directed by Roy Del Ruth, screenplay by Maude Fulton, Lucien Hubbard and Brown Holmes, with some uncredited dialogue by Hammett, starring Ricardo Cortez as **Sam Spade**, Bebe Daniels as Ruth Wonderley (a renamed Brigid O'Shaughnessy), Dudley Diggs as Casper Gutman and Otto Matiesen as Joel Cairo. The working title was *Woman Of The World*. Silent movie star Cortez was an effective Spade, Una Merkel as Effie Perine and Dwight Frye as the degenerate gunsel Wilmer Cook were outstanding, and the story stayed close to the original except for a softer ending, with Spade probably going to work for the DA's office and Brigid likely not to have to serve much time in prison. Well received at the time, this little seen version, available on TV as **DANGEROUS FEMALE**, holds up well with its tough guy dialogue and verisimilitude. See below and **SATAN MET A LADY**.

The MALTESE FALCON (1941). The credits of this version of **Dashiell HAMMETT**'s novel, directed by John Huston, who also wrote the script, with a working title of *The Gent From Frisco*, hardly need repeating; Humphrey Bogart as **Sam Spade** (George Raft turned the part down!), Mary Astor as Brigid O'Shaughnessy, Sydney Greenstreet making his film debut as Casper Gutman, Peter Lorre as Joel Cairo, Gladys George as Iva Archer, Lee Patrick as Effie Perine, Barton MacLane as Lt. Detective Dundy, Ward Bond as Detective Tom Polhaus, Walter Huston as Captain Jacobi and, of course, Elisha Cook Jr. as Wilmer Cook. A classic movie in any context. Plans for *The Further Adventures Of The Maltese Falcon* with the same line-up, were shelved because of the war. Patrick and Cook reprised their roles in **The BLACK BIRD**. See **Radio: The MALTESE FALCON**.

The MAN INSIDE (UK 1958). Based on **M.E.CHABER**'s novel, directed by John Gilling, script by Gilling, Richard Maibaum and David Shaw, starring Jack Palance as **Milo March**, with Anita Ekberg, Nigel Patrick and Anthony Newley in a shoddy robbery caper with comic interludes, with Milo hunting jewel thieves across Europe.

MAN KILLER = PRIVATE DETECTIVE 62

The MAN WHO WOULDN'T DIE (1942). Based on the **Brett HALLIDAY** series, though actually taken from Clayton Rawson's Great Merlini novel *No Coffin For The Corpse*, the 5th **Michael Shayne** film was directed by Herbert I. Leeds, script by Arnaud d'Usseau, starring Lloyd Nolan in a horror-mystery, made in the Baskerville Hall set of the 1939 *The Hound Of The Baskervilles*.

The MAN WITH BOGART'S FACE (1980). Based on the novel by **Andrew FENADY**, who adapted it and produced the film, directed by Robert Day, starring Robert Sacchi as the modern day PI who undergoes plastic surgery and changes his name legally to **Sam Marlow**. An offbeat mystery with light touches, it also features Michelle Phillips, Olivia Hussey, Franco Nero, Victor Buono, Herbert Lom, George Raft (in his last film), Mike Mazurki and Yvonne DeCarlo. Also released as **SAM MARLOW, PRIVATE DETECTIVE**.

The MANCHU EAGLE MURDER CAPER MYSTERY (1973). Directed by Dean Hargrove, starring Gabriel Dell as novice PI **Malcolm**, investigating the death of his milkman, in a low-budget but occasionally quite successful satire of tough 40s PI melodramas with good performances helping offseat the clichés.

MANHANDLED (1949). Directed by Lewis R. Foster, script by Foster and **Whitman CHAMBERS** from a story by L.S. Goldsmith, "The Man Who Stole A Dream," starring Dan Duryea as underhanded, cynical, lowlife, indeed downright crooked PI **Karl Benson** who tries to pin a robbery-murder rap on innocent Dorothy Lamour. Described as a turgid, over-complicated drama that a reliable cast that also included Sterling Hayden and Irene Harvey couldn't salvage.

MARLOWE (1969). Based on the novel *The Little Sister* by **Raymond CHANDLER**, directed by Paul Bogart, script by Stirling Silliphant, starring James Garner as an updated **Philip Marlowe**, with Gayle Hunnicut, Carroll O'Connor, Rita Moreno and Bruce Lee, who, in the film's most memorable scene, made his film debut by destroying Marlowe's office with his bare hands. Superficial but engaging, with Garner simply too relaxed and amiable to make a convincing Marlowe.

La MAZETTA (Italy 1978). Based on the novel *The Payoff* by **Attilio VERALDI**, directed by Sergio Corbucci, script by Dino Maiuri, Massima De Rita, Luciano De Crescenzo and Elvio Porta, starring Nino Manfredi as **Sasa Iovine**, Neapolitan operator whose life gets turned upside down in a comedy-thriller.

MEET NERO WOLFE (1936). Based on **Rex STOUT**'s novel *Fer De Lance*, directed by Howard Biberman, screenplay by Howard J. Green, starring Edward Arnold as **Nero Wolfe** and Lionel Stander as **Archie Goodwin** in the first of only two Wolfe & Goodwin films (see **The LEAGUE OF FRIGHTENED MEN**). Arnold was not used in the second film but went on to play Captain Duncan Maclain in two films based on Baynard Kendrick's hero.

MICHAEL SHAYNE, PRIVATE DETECTIVE (1940). Based on **Brett HALLIDAY**'s novel *Dividend On Death* (the only one of the 12 **Michael Shayne** films to be directly based on one of the original stories), directed by Eugene Ford, script by Stanley Rauh and Manning O'Connor, with Lloyd Nolan as the Miami detective, a role he would play seven times. Described by the *New York Times* as "pretty good fun," the comic dialogue and plot made this a good start to the series and initiated its trademark of depicting the police as dullards.

The MIDNIGHT MAN (1974). Loosely based on **David ANTHONY**'s novel *The Midnight Lady & The Mourning Man*, directed by Roland Kibbee and Burt Lancaster, who also co-wrote the script, Lancaster starring as **Jim Slade** (Morgan Bass in the novel), an ex-police detective, jailed for killing his wife's lover, released on parole and working as a college security officer. Involved and overlong mystery.

MORTELLE RANDONEE (France 1983). Based on the novel *The Eye Of The Beholder* by **Marc BEHM**, directed by Claude Miller, script by Michel and Jacques Audiard, starring Michel Serrault and Isabel Adjani. Released in Britain and America as **DEADLY CIRCUIT** and hailed in certain cinéaste circles as marking the ne plus ultra of PI movies.

MR DYNAMITE (1935). Little was left in the final production of Dashiell **HAMMETT**'s 90 page treatment, "On The Make," about a corrupt, hardbitten antihero PI. Rewritten by Doris Malloy and Harry Clork, **T.N. 'Mr Dynamite' Thompson**, played by Edmund Lowe, was a dapper charmer in the Nick Charles mold and the picture was reviewed as "a comedy, with homicidal interruptions."

MURDER BY DEATH (1976). Directed by Robert Moore, script by Neil Simon, starring Peter Falk as **Sam Diamond** (Sam Spade), David Niven and Maggie Smith as **Dick & Dora Charleston** (Nick & Nora

Charles), Peter Sellers (Sidney Wang), James Coco (Milo Perrier), Alec Guinness (The Butler), Elsa Lanchester (Jessica Marbles), Eileen Brennan (Tess Skeffington). Truman Capote invites the world's greatest detectives to his home for a baffling whodunit. Myrna Loy, then 72, was offered the Dora Charleston part but declined it. Novelization: **Henry KEATING**.

MURDER GOES TO COLLEGE (1937). By far the better of two different 1937 versions of **Kurt STEEL's** novel (see **PARTNERS IN CRIME**). Directed by Charles Riesner, script by Brian Mallow, Robert Wyler and Eddie Welch, starring Lynne Overman as **Hank Hyer** in a well-balanced comedy-mystery, the killer's identity well concealed.

MURDER IS MY BUSINESS (1946). Based on the **Brett HALLIDAY** series, and loosely on Halliday's novel of the same title, directed by Sam Newfield, script by Fred Myton, starring Hugh Beaumont in the first of four appearances as **Michael Shayne**. He was praised as an affable, easy-going Shayne backed by a capable cast and production.

MURDER, MY SWEET (1944). From the novel *Farewell, My Lovely* by **Raymond CHANDLER**, directed by Edward Dymtryk, script by John Paxton, starring Dick Powell as **Philip Marlowe**, with Claire Trevor, Ann Shirley, Otto Kruger and Mike Mazurki (as Moose Molloy). The first true Chandler film, and in many people's opinion, including that of Chandler himself, the most successful. A *noir* classic which won the MWA's first ever film Edgar.

MUSS 'EM UP (1936). Based on **James Edward GRANT's** novel *The Green Shadow*, directed by Charles Vidor, script by Erwin Gelsey, starring Preston Foster as hardboiled PI **Tip O'Neil**, who was much reviled by Bill Pronzini in his book incarnation, but the film is described as funny and imaginative if over-long, face-paced direction balancing comedy and drama. Released in the UK as **The HOUSE OF FATE**.

MY GUN IS QUICK (1957). Based on the novel by **Mickey SPILLANE**, directed by George White, script by Richard Collins and Richard Powell, with Robert Bray as **Mike Hammer** in a film more than usually distinguished by senseless violence and gratuitous sex.

A NIGHT IN HAVANA = The BIG BOODLE

NIGHT INVADER (1943). Based on **John BENTLEY's** novel *Rendezvous With Death*, directed by Herbert Mason, script by Brock Williams, Edward Dryhurst and Roland Pertwee, starring David Farrar as British PI **Dick Marlow** parachuting into Occupied Europe.

NIGHT MOVES (1975). Based on the novel by **Alan SHARP** who also wrote the script, directed by Arthur Penn, starring Gene Hackman as Los Angeles PI **Harry Moseby**, putting aside his marital woes to find a missing nymphet in the Florida Keys, Very complex and psychological and, for Hackman, a weak follow-up to **The CONVERSATION.**

NIGHTKILL (1980). Directed by Ted Post, filmed on location in Arizona by a German company, starring Jaclyn Smith, Mike Connors, James Franciscus and Robert Mitchum in a confused suspense drama involving a cat-and-mouse game between a wealthy widow and a mysterious investigator. According to a biography of Mitchum, the film was eventually sold to NBC-TV but appears never to have been shown.

NINE LIVES ARE NOT ENOUGH (1941). Based on the novel by **Jerome ODLUM,** directed by A. Edward Sutherland, script by Fred Niblo Jr., starring Ronald Reagan as **Matt Sawyer** (rather than John Steele), an aggressive reporter who solves a murder after getting fired for treading on powerful toes in an enjoyable, fast-paced B film so clichéd and stereotyped that it ends with a wealthy girl-friend buying the paper and reinstating the hero.

NO HANDS ON THE CLOCK (1941). Based on **Geoffrey HOMES**'s novel, directed by Frank McDonald, script by Maxwell Shayne, starring Chester Morris (star of the *Boston Blackie* films) as **Humphrey Campbell** in a nifty thriller, breezily paced and directed, though with many loose ends, most notably the failure to resolve the fate of the kidnap victim whose predicament interrupts Campbell's honeymoon and starts the whole story. See **CRIME BY NIGHT** for another Campbell film.

NO ORCHIDS FOR MISS BLANDISH (UK 1948). Based on **James Hadley CHASE**'s novel, directed by John Leigh Clowes, who also wrote the script, starring Hugh McDermott as **Fenner** in a sick exercise in sadism, with senseless and gratuitous violence, an inane script and dialogue, comic book characterizations and quite unbelievable 'New York' sets. "As wretched as they come" was one critic's summary.

NO PLACE FOR A LADY (1943). Directed by James Hogan, script by Eric Taylor, starring William Gargan as **Jess Arno,** a PI who solves the murder of a wealthy widow and recovers some stolen car tires! Good performances off-set by lifeless direction and dialogue. Taylor used the name Jess Arno for a PI in a 1936 *Black Mask* story, "Murder To Music."

OH HEAVENLY DOG! (1980). Directed by **Joe CAMP,** who also wrote the script with Rod Browning, starring Chevy Chase as **Benjamin Browning,** a PI who returns to earth in the shape of a dog, Benji, to solve his own murder. Jane Seymour, Omar Sharif and Robert Morley co-starred in this silly, slow moving reversal of Dick Powell's 1951 *You*

Never Can Tell which misfires in trying to combine a kiddy film with adult humor. Novelization: **Joe CAMP.**

ONE BODY TOO MANY (1944). Directed by Frank McDonald, script by Winston Miller and Maxwell Shayne, starring Jack Haley as **Albert Tuttle**, a carefree insurance salesman mistaken for a PI and forced to solve a caper in a spoof comedy that also starred Bela Lugosi.

OUT OF THE PAST (1947). From the novel *Build My Gallows High* by **Geoffrey HOMES**, directed by Jacques Tourneur, script by Homes himself and Frank Fenton, starring Robert Mitchum as **Jeff** (rather than Red) **Bailey**, with Jane Greer as Kathie Moffat, Kirk Douglas as Whit Sterling and Rhonda Fleming. Considered by many critics to be the most powerful and important *noir* film ever made, with one-time New York PI Bailey's errors of judgment returning inexorably to haunt him and drag him to his fate in a classic of betrayal and revenge. Forgettably remade as **AGAINST ALL ODDS.**

P.J. (1968). Directed by John Guillermin, script by Philip Reisman Jr., starring George Peppard as **P.J. Detweiler**, a PI supposedly bodyguarding the mistress (Gayle Hunnicut) of a tycoon (Raymond Burr) but actually set up to murder the tycoon's business partner. Very violent, muddled and unmemorable.

PARTNERS IN CRIME (1937). Based on the novel *Murder Goes to College* by **Kurt STEEL**, the second of two versions of which, both made in 1937 (see **MURDER GOES TO COLLEGE**), was directed by Ralph Murphy, script by Garnett Weston, and again starred Lynne Overman as **Hank Hyer** in an inept and incomprehensible plot.

PEEPER (1975). Based on **Keith LAUMER**'s novel *Deadfall*, directed by Peter Hyams, script by W.D. Richter, starring Michael Caine as circa 1947 Los Angeles PI **Tucker** (Joe Shaw in the original book) and Natalie Wood in a tepid and blasé take-off of 40s detective dramas, with Caine getting involved with a weird family while trying to find a client's long-lost daughter. The credits, recited by Bogart impersonator Jerry Lacy, are the best part, after which the film goes rapidly downhill. Also released as **FAT CHANCE.**

The **PINK CHIQUITAS** (1986). Known only from a cable TV listing. Frank Stallone (Sylvester's brother) starred with Claudia Udy as "a private eye in a white convertible" who "saves the world from women excited by a meteorite." You think I'm making this up, don't you?

PLUNDER OF THE SUN (1953). Based on the novel by **David DODGE**, directed by John Farrow, script by **Jonathan LATIMER**, and starring Glenn Ford as **Al Colby**, an adventurer-PI operating in

Latin America. Adequate performances, with flashbacks weakening the suspense but Mexican temples making striking backdrops.

PORTRAIT IN SMOKE (UK 1957). Based, though very loosely, on the novel by **Bill S. BALLINGER**, directed by Ken Hughes, script by Hughes, Robert Westerby and Sigmund Miller. The film tells the story of a ruthless woman determined to escape from poverty but I cannot determine if the PI of the original book, certainly there is no character called Danny April, survived the scriptwriters who moved the story to Europe. Released in the UK as **WICKED AS THEY COME**.

PRIVATE DETECTIVE (1939). Directed by Noel Smith, script by Earle Snell and Raymond Schrock, based on the story "Invitation To Murder" by Kay Krausse, starring Jane Wyman as **Myrna Winslow** who shows up Dick Foran as **Jim Rickey** by solving the case they're both working on, but this brings them together and they decide to marry.

PRIVATE DETECTIVE 62 (1933). Based on a treatment by **Raoul WHITFIELD**, directed by Michael Curtiz, script by Rian James, starring William Powell as **Donald Free** who accepts a job with a shady PI (Arthur Hohl) and agrees to dupe wealthy Margaret Lindsay, falling for her instead. Picks up after a slow start and Powell carries it off despite gaping holes in the plot. Nothing remained of **HAMMETT**'s involvement at an early stage. Also shown as **MANKILLER**.

PRIVATE EYES (1953). Directed by Edward Bernds, script by Elwood Ullman, starring Leo Gorcy as **Terrence Aloysius 'Slip' Mahoney** who opens the Eagle Eye Detective Agency after acquiring, through a punch on the nose, the ability to read minds. Slapstick comedy in the mode of the Three Stooges with whom Bernds and Ullman often worked.

The PRIVATE EYES (Hong Kong 1976). Written and directed by Michael Hui who also starred as **Joseph Wong**, owner of Hong Kong's Manix Detective Agency, with his brother Sam Hui as ne'er-do-well Lee who comes to work for him. A Chinese comedy, taking off the *Mannix* TV show among many other things, the film was a South-East Asian box-office smash, raved about by *Variety*'s man in Hong Kong, but appears never to have been adapted for a non-Cantonese-speaking audience.

The PRIVATE LIFE OF A FEMALE PRIVATE EYE = BIG ZAPPER

PUBLIC EYE (UK 1972). Adapted from his stage play by Peter Shaffer, directed by Carol Reed, starring Topol as **Julian Cristoforou**, a London PI entangled in the marital skirmishes of an Anglo-American couple. The original play was thin enough and was blown up into a trite and footling film, with Israeli actor Topol almost unbelievably hammy.

RADIOACTIVE DREAMS (1986). Written and directed by Albert Pyun, described by *Variety* as "Raymond Chandler meets Mad Max." **Phillip** (sic, John Stockwell) and **Marlowe** (Michael Dudikoff) spend 15 years in a fall-out shelter with Chandler's novels. Emerging to a richly stylized 2010 post-nuclear war world, they have, jointly, taken on Philip Marlowe's personality. With period narrative style, *Variety* adds "alternatively silly and daringly ingenious."

RENTADICK (UK 1972). Directed by Jim Clark, script by John Cleese and Graham Chapman, starring James Booth, Julie Ege, Ronald Fraser, Donald Sinden, Michael Bentine and Spike Milligan. A secret gas which paralyzes from the waist down has been stolen and the incompetent PIs of **Rentadick Inc.** must recover it in this hit-or-miss spoof by two of the giants of *Monty Python's Flying Circus*. Goes off at odd tangents.

ROADBLOCK (1951). From a story by Richard Landau and **Geoffrey HOMES**, directed by Harold Daniels, script by **Steve FISHER** and George Bricker, starring Charles McGraw as **Joe Peters**, an insurance investigator who, to please his ambitious girlfriend, gets involved in a robbery. Well-paced, fatalistic *noir* thriller with a strong performance by McGraw.

ROADHOUSE NIGHTS (1930). Based on **Dashiell HAMMETT**'s novel *Red Harvest*, in theory, at least, directed by Hobart Henley, script by Ben Hecht, starring Charles Ruggles as newspaperman **Willie Bindbugel** investigating municipal corruption in more or less the Continental Op part. Best remembered as Helen Morgan's film debut, with Jimmy Durante as her piano accompanist.

The RUNAROUND (1946). Directed by Charles Lamont, script by Arthur T. Horman and Sam Hellman, starring Rod Cameron as **Eddie Kildane** and Broderick Crawford as **Louis Prentice**, two competing PIs who are both hired, supposedly, to find an industrialist's runaway daughter, the one who brings her back getting $15,000. Battling with each other from San Francisco to New York and back, they discover that things are not what they seem.

ST. IVES (1976). Based on the novel *The Procane Chronicles* by **Oliver BLEECK** (Ross THOMAS), directed by J. Lee Thompson, script by Barry Beckerman, starring Charles Bronson as **Raymond St. Ives** (Philip St Ives in the books—why change it?), transformed from Bleeck's tough professional go-between into a former crime reporter turned novelist roped into a boring, plodding, muddled, stupid plot.

SAM MARLOW, PRIVATE EYE = The **MAN WITH BOGART'S FACE**

SATAN MET A LADY (1936). The dire second version of **Dashiell HAMMETT**'s novel *The Maltese Falcon*, directed by William Dieterle, script by Brown Holmes, starring Warren William as **Ted Shayne** (Sam Spade), Bette Davis as Valerie Purvis (Brigid O'Shaughnessy). Holmes, who worked on the script of the 1931 version of **The MALTESE FALCON**, mutilated the story, changing all the names, transforming Casper Guttman into a woman (Madame Barabbas played by Alison Skipworth) and the Falcon itself into a gem-filled horn. John Baxter, in *Hollywood In The Thirties*, noted that the film was "hopelessly written and acted, though blessed with a nutty logic."

SCREAM IN THE DARK (1943). Based on **Jerome ODLUM**'s novel *The Morgue Is Always Open*, directed by George Sherman, script by Gerald Schnitzer and Anthony Coldeway, starring Robert Lowery as **Mike Brooker** (compressed down from the original duo of Sam Booker and Jimmy Webb) in a well-handled mystery with a touch of humor.

SECRET FILE: HOLLYWOOD (1962). Directed by Ralph Cushman, script by Jack Lewis, starring Robert Clarke as out of work PI **Maxwell Carter**, who reluctantly becomes photographer for a sleazy Hollywood tabloid and gets mixed up in a blackmailing ring, which he breaks. Also released as **SECRET FILE OF HOLLYWOOD**.

SHADOW OF THE THIN MAN (1941). The 4th of the series tenuously based on **Dashiell HAMMETT**'s novel *The Thin Man*, directed, for the last time, by W.S. Van Dyke, script by Irving Brecher and Harry Kurnitz, with, as always, William Powell and Myrna Loy as **Nick & Nora Charles**. Centered round a racetrack, one of the best scenes has Nick pretending to read the comics and his now six year old son Nick Jr. being quite aware that he's studying form.

SHAFT (1971). Based on the novel by **Ernest TIDYMAN**, directed by Gordon Parks, script by Tidyman and John D.F. Black, starring Richard Roundtree as black PI **John Shaft** in the first of three of the best, of the cycle of blaxploitation films. Roundtree also appeared in the limp, misconceived TV series

SHAFT IN AFRICA (1973). Based on an **Ernest TIDYMAN** story, directed by John Guillermin, script by Stirling Silliphant, starring Richard Roundtree in the third and last **John Shaft** film, the black PI helping an African nation stop latter-day slave trading. Very violent.

SHAFT'S BIG SCORE! (1972). Based on the novel by **Ernest TIDYMAN**, directed by Gordon Parks, script by Tidyman, starring Richard Roundtree for the second time as black PI **John Shaft** in a sexy, violent film with a hair-raising finale.

SHAMUS (1973). Directed by Buzz Kulik, script by Barry Beckerman, starring Burt Reynolds as Brooklyn pool-hustler and PI **Shamus McCoy**. Kulik never decides whether it's a hardboiled drama, a comedy or a send-up, and, trying to do too much, ends up looking witless, with loose ends and pointless episodes. Novelization: **Raymond GILES**.

The SKIP TRACER (Canada 1979). Directed by Zale Dalen, starring David Petersen as a specialist in recovering goods on which the payments have defaulted who suddenly finds his life in danger. Slow paced, with well built suspense, moody sense of style and a good central performance.

SLEEPERS WEST (1941). Based on the **Brett HALLIDAY** series, though actually taken from **Frederick NEBEL**'s novel *Sleepers East*, directed by Eugene Ford, screenplay by Lou Breslow and Stanley Rauh and starring Lloyd Nolan as **Michael Shayne** protecting a witness on a Denver to San Francisco train. The 2nd Shayne film, not as well received as the the first, **MICHAEL SHAYNE, PRIVATE DETECTIVE**.

SONG OF THE THIN MAN (1947). The unsuccessful last film of the series, very tenuously based on **Dashiell HAMMETT**'s novel *The Thin Man*, directed by Edward Buzzell, screenplay by **Steve FISHER**, Nat Perrin, James O'Hanlon and Harry Crane and starring William Powell and Myrna Loy as **Nick & Nora Charles**. In the post-war era the Thin Man concept was anachronistic, while Powell and Loy, on whose team work the series relied, were becoming too old for the parts. Loy was, reportedly, reluctant to make it at all, so it is hardly surprising that, at 72, she turned down the part satirizing Nora in **MURDER BY DEATH**.

SPEEDTRAP (1978). Directed by Earl Bellamy, script by Stuart A. Segal and Walter M. Spear, starring Joe Don Baker as **Pete**, a PI called in to help the police catch an elusive car thief. Good performances, with Tyne Daly as Baker's police liaison, are undermined by a poor script and a childish enthusiasm for car chases.

The SQUEEZE (1987). Directed by Roger Young, script by Daniel Taplitz, a "hapless comedy" (*Variety*) starring Rae Dawn Chong as **Rachel Dobs**, bill-collector and would-be detective in a nonsensical story, full of holes about Lotto fixing. "Combination of dull personalities and leaden script adds up to boredom."

The SPIDER (1945). From a play by Charles Fulton Oursler and Lowell Brentano, directed by Robert D. Webb, script by Jo Eisinger and W. Scott Darling. Richard Conte, supported by Faye Marlowe, Kurt Kreuger, John Harvey and Martin Kosleck, is **Chris Conlon**, a PI pursued both by the police, who think he's a killer, and a mysterious murderer trying to cover up an old crime.

STACEY (AND HER GANGBUSTERS) (1973). Directed by Andy Sidaris, script by William Edgar, starring former *Playboy* Playmate Anne Randall as **Stacey Hansen**, a superwoman PI in an absurdly complicated sexploiter involving murder, blackmail and a religious cult. Very sexy and violent. See **MALIBU EXPRESS**.

STAR OF MIDNIGHT (1935). Directed by Stephens Roberts, script by Howard J. Green, Anthony Veiller and Edward Kaufman from a novel by Arthur Somers Roche (in which the hero was an amateur), this mystery comedy starred William Powell as sauve, urbane attorney **Clay Dalzell**, who doubles as a detective. Asked to look into the disappearance of a Broadway star, Powell and his chic drinking companion (Ginger Rogers) are very much in the Nick & Nora Charles mold in a funny film that combines wit, sophistication and gunplay.

SUNBURN (1979). Based on **Stanley ELLIN**'s novel *The Bind,* directed by Richard C. Serafian, script by Daly Stephen Oliver and James Booth, starring Charles Grodin as New York PI **Jake** (the Dekker of the book omitted) investigating a murder in Florida, with Art Carney as local PI Marcus and Farrah Fawcett (-Majors) as Grodin's hired 'wife' doing little but working on her tan and making trouble about her billing.

SUPER SLEUTH (1937). Directed by Ben Stoloff, script by Gertrude Purcell and Ernest Pagano, based on a play by Harry Segall, starring Jack Oakie as **Willard Martin**, an egocentric movie detective who starts taking his roles too seriously, believing himself capable of sleuthing in real life. A clever script, good direction and fine performances from Oakie, Ann Sothern as the studio publicist trying to curb his fantasies, and Edgar Kennedy as a policeman in a fine mix of comedy and suspense.

SYLVIA (1965). From the novel by **E.V. CUNNINGHAM**, directed by Gordon Douglas, script by Sidney Boehm, starring George Maharis as **Alan Macklin**, a PI hired by Peter Lawford to investigate his fiancée, Carroll Baker, whom he falls for. He refuses to reveal her murky past and goes off with her.

THAT WOMAN OPPOSITE = CITY AFTER MIDNIGHT

THEY ALL LAUGHED (1981). Written and directed by Peter Bogdanovitch, starring Ben Gazzara as **John Russo**, John Ritter as **Charles Rutledge** and Blaine Novak as **Arthur Brodsky**, very differing detective agency operatives who become romantically involved with wives they've been assigned to follow. A romantic-comedy with an odd history involving Bogdanovich's relationship with ex-Playmate Dorothy Stratten, who appeared in the film and was murdered by her husband, who had had her followed by PIs during the making of the film.

The **THIN MAN** (1934). Based on **Dashiell HAMMETT**'s novel, directed by W.S. Van Dyke, script by Alfred Hackett and Frances Goodrich, with the inspired casting of William Powell and Myrna Loy as **Nick & Nora Charles**, accompanied, of course, by their wire-haired terrier Asta. Made in two weeks with a then large budget of $2 million, the film was an enormous critical and popular success whose sophisticated screenplay and comic strength spawned a carefully spaced out string of very slowly declining sequels, transferring the Thin Man soubriquet from the villain of the original story to Nick Charles.

The **THIN MAN GOES HOME** (1944). The 5th in the series tenuously based on **Dashiell HAMMETT**'s novel *The Thin Man*, directed by Richard Thorpe, script by Robert Riskin, Dwight Taylor and Harry Kurnitz, starring, of course, William Powell and Myrna Loy as **Nick & Nora Charles**. Made on a much smaller budget than the first four, the series was beginning to show its age with the penultimate film, though it still had much to offer.

THREE ON A TICKET (1947). Based on the **Brett HALLIDAY** series, though no actual title, the 11th, penultimate, **Michael Shayne** film, directed by Sam Newfield, script by Fred Myton and starring Hugh Beaumont, centers round a baggage ticket delivered to Shayne's office by a dying man and sought by the agents of a foreign power.

TIME TO KILL (1942). Based on **Raymond CHANDLER**'s novel *The High Window*, adapted into a vehicle for **Brett HALLIDAY**'s **Michael Shayne**, directed by Herbert I. Leeds, script by Clarence Upson Young and starring, for the 7th and last time, Lloyd Nolan. One of the strongest in the series, mainly because it kept close to Chandler's story, many Chandler fans consider it a superior version of the story than the 'official' Marlowe film **The BRASHER DOUBLOON**.

TIMETABLE (1956). From a story by Robert Angus, directed by Mark Stevens, script by Aben Kandel, with Stevens also starring as **Charlie**, an insurance investigator assigned to look into a train robbery he himself masterminded. The script fails to hold the various elements together.

TONY ROME (1967). Based on the novel *Miami Mayhem* by **Anthony ROME**, directed by Gordon Douglas, script by Richard Breen, starring Frank Sinatra as Miami PI **Tony Rome** in a diverting comedy-thriller with a witty script. The sequel was **LADY IN CEMENT**.

TOO LATE FOR TEARS (1949). Based on the novel by **Roy HUGGINS**, who also wrote the script, directed by Byron Haskin, starring Lizabeth Scott as the money-hungry woman without a conscience who is determined to keep the $60,000 she and her husband accidentally acquire from gangsters. Dan Duryea is a crooked but weak PI, **Danny Fuller**, who helps her rob and murder but is himself killed by her.

TOO MANY WINNERS (1947). The 12th and last film based on the **Brett HALLIDAY** series, though not on any actual title, directed by William Beaudine. script by Fred Myton and Scott Darling, with Hugh Beaumont as **Michael Shayne** in a racetrack set story favorably mentioned by *Variety*.

TRUCK TURNER (1974). Directed by Jonathan Kaplan, script by Leigh Chapman, Oscar Williams and Michael Allin, based on a story by Jerry Wilkes, starring Isaac Hayes as **Truck Turner**, a black skip-tracer/bounty hunter in a very violent quickie blaxploitation film with little plot and a director weak at action sequences.

TWENTY PLUS TWO (1961). Based on the novel by **Frank GRUBER**, who also wrote the script, directed by Joseph M. Newman, starring David Janssen as **Tom Alder**, in a potentially good story undermined by poor production values that still manages to be good, pulp fun much of the time with an edge of self-parody. Released in the UK as **IT STARTED IN TOKYO**.

An UNSUITABLE JOB FOR A WOMAN (UK 1981). Based on the novel by **P.D. JAMES**, directed by Chris Petit, script by Petit, Elizabeth McKay and Brian Scobie, starring Pippa Guard as London PI **Cordelia Gray** in a moody, neo-noir film.

The WESTLAND CASE (1937). Based on **Jonathan LATIMER's** novel *Headed For A Hearse*, directed by Christy Cabanne, script by Robertson White, with Preston Foster as **Bill Crane** and Frank Jenks as **Doc Williams**, roles both played in all three Crane films (see **The LADY IN THE MORGUE** and **The LAST WARNING**). A fast-moving, faithful adaptation in Universal's Crime Club series.

WHO DONE IT? (1942). Directed by Erle C. Kenton, script by Stanley Roberts, Edmund Joseph and John Grant, starring Bud Abbott as **Chick Larkin** and Lou Costello as **Mervyn Milgrim**, would be radio mystery writers working as soda jerks in a radio station building who pass themselves off as PIs when the network president is killed, even the killer believing them. William Bendix was an even more incompetent cop. One of the best Abbott & Costello films, according to connoisseurs.

WHO DONE IT? (1956). Directed by Basil Dearden, script by T.E.B. Clarke, starring Benny Hill as **Hugo Dill**, an ice-rink sweeper who wins big money and a bloodhound in a contest and opens a detective agency. Hill, a British comic far more popular in America, confines himself to slapstick rather than his later brand of smut and sniggering innuendo.

WHO FRAMED ROGER RABBIT? (1988). Based on Gary Wolf's rather dire novel *Who Censored Roger Rabbit?*, film was a more appropriate medium for the basic idea of mixing humans and animated cartoon characters. Bob Hoskins starred as **Eddie Valiant**, a standard 40s down at heel gumshoe working for the title character, an over-the-hill "Toon" star. The 40s ambience is poorly handled and the movie is thick with Hollywood and LA in-jokes but the combination of live action and animation is superb.

WHO'S HARRY CRUMB? (1989). Directed by Paul Flaherty, starring comedian John Candy as a fat, stupid and inept PI with a penchant, but no skill or flair, for disguises, who gets called in after a kidnaping. Apparently the film relies totally on Candy's physical attributes and is massively unfunny.

WICKED AS THEY COME = PORTRAIT IN SMOKE

WOMEN ARE TROUBLE (1936). Based on a story by **George Harmon COXE**, directed by Errol Taggart, script by Michael Fessier, starrring Stuart Erwin as **Jack 'Flash' Casey** in a better mix of comedy and action than **HERE'S FLASH CASEY**.

WORLD FOR RANSOM (1954). Directed by Robert Aldrich, script by Lindsay Hardy and (uncredited) Hugo Butler, starring Dan Duryea reprising a TV role (see **TV: CHINA SMITH**) as **Mike Callahan**, a world-weary WW2 veteran turned Singapore PI who tries to prevent a nuclear scientist from being murdered. Heavily censored, this was the first of several late *noir* films which Aldrich imbued with magnified style and meaning.

RADIO

ABBOTT MYSTERIES (1945-1947). Attempting to emulate MR. & MRS. NORTH and The ADVENTURES OF THE THIN MAN, a series adapted by Ed Adamson from **Frances CRANE**'s novels, starred Charles Webster and Julie Stevens (for a time Les Tremayne and Alice Reinheart) as **Pat & Jean Abbott**, had irregular summertime runs.

ADVENTURES BY MORSE (1944). The versatile Morse created this high adventure series when his famous I LOVE A MYSTERY was dropped. San Francisco detective **Captain Bart Friday** (Elliott Lewis, David Ellis and Russell Thorson at different times) and his Texan sidekick **Skip Turner** (Barton Yarborough), much in the Doc Long mold, roamed the world solving mysteries often bordering on the supernatural, though with Morse, there was invariably a semi-logical explanation.

ADVENTURES OF BILL LANCE (1947). Gerald Mohr starred as an LA PI.

The ADVENTURES OF NERO WOLFE (1943-1944). Santos Ortega was the first, sardonic, radio **Nero Wolfe**, with John Gibson as **Archie Goodwin**, in an ABC series sponsored by Elgin watches, with scripts by Louis Vittes which did not use any **Rex STOUT** material, and to which the author never listened. See **The AMAZING NERO WOLFE** and **NEW ADVENTURES OF NERO WOLFE**.

The ADVENTURES OF PHILIP MARLOWE (1947-1950). **Raymond CHANDLER**'s PI first aired as *The Bob Hope Show*'s summer replacement, Van Helfin starring in Milton Geiger's adaptations. In 1948 Gerald Mohr took over as the toughest Marlowe so far heard, opening the show with "Get this and get it straight; crime is a sucker's road, and those who travel it wind up in the gutter, the prison or an early grave." The radio Marlowe stressed his co-operation with the police.

The ADVENTURES OF SAM SPADE (1946-1950). Editor, producer and director William Spier gave the fast and funny radio version of **Dashiell HAMMETT's Sam Spade** a parodic edge, with the tough, streetcar riding, Old Grandad drinking (glass was heard clinking when Sam sat at his desk) San Francisco PI, license number #137596, presenting each case as a report dictated to Effie Perine (Lurene Tuttle), the two exchanging much suggestive banter. Many Continental Op plots were used in the series. Howard Duff was the original Spade but quit when CBS dropped the show after Hammett's name came up in the House UnAmerican Activities hearings in 1949, replacing it with the virtually identical CHARLIE WILD, PRIVATE DETECTIVE. NBC took it over, still with the support of Wildroot Cream Oil, Speir and Tuttle, casting Stephen Dunne, but audiences decided he sounded too young.

The ADVENTURES OF THE THIN MAN (1941-1947). Sponsored by General Foods, later Post Toasties, the first radio series of **Dashiell HAMMETT's Nick & Nora Charles** set out to reproduce the spirit of the William Powell and Myrna Loy films and many thought Les Damon and Claudia Morgan were actually the film stars themselves. In 1944 Damon joined the armed forces, replaced by David Gothard, then Les Tremayne, returning for the 1946-1947 seasons. Hammett, who received $500 a week for the use of his name and characters, stipulated in his contract that he would have no personal involvement. See **The NEW ADVENTURES OF THE THIN MAN.**

The AFFAIRS OF ANN SCOTLAND (1946). Arlene Francis starred as a satin-tongued cutie gumshoe, quick on the uptake, who worked independently of the police and solved crimes her own way. Only aired on the West Coast.

The AFFAIRS OF PETER SALEM (1949). Santos Ortega starred as a sauve, sophisticated small-town PI, using deductive abilities rather than brawn, with Jack Grimes as his assistant Marty.

AGAIN—CALLAGHAN = The CALLAGHAN TOUCH

The AMAZING NERO WOLFE (1946). **Rex STOUT's** heroes were resurrected (see **The ADVENTURES OF NERO WOLFE**) by Mutual with Francis X. Bushman as a pontifical **Nero Wolfe**, and Elliott Lewis as **Archie Goodwin**. See **The NEW ADVENTURES OF NERO WOLFE.**

BARRY CRANE, CONFIDENTIAL INVESTIGATOR (1951-1955). William Gargan starred as a private detective who undertook cases on behalf of people unable to go to the police.

The BIG GUY (1950). John Calvin starred as a hard-hitting PI.

BOSTON BLACKIE (1944/1945). Jack Boyle's one-time jewel thief was transformed for radio into a PI with a flair for smart comments who was on such good terms with the police that in one program he helped them raise funds for underprivileged children. Billed as "enemy to those who made him an enemy, friend to those who have no friends," he was played first by Chester Morris, star of the films, then by Richard Kollmar. See **TV: BOSTON BLACKIE.**

CALLAGHAN COME-BACK = The CALLAGHAN TOUCH

THE CALLAGHAN TOUCH (1941). I can discover nothing about three radio series broadcast during the war, featuring London PI **Slim Callaghan**, with scripts by author **Peter CHEYNEY**. The others were **AGAIN-CALLAGHAN** (1942) and **The CALLAGHAN COME-BACK** (1943).

CANDY MATSON, YUkon 2-8209 (1949-1952). Described as one of the brightest, most unusual radio detective shows, featuring Natalie Masters as a chic, beautiful PI, feminine without being squeamish. Operating out of her San Francisco apartment, murder was always the main motif. The character was unusually well developed, possibly because of the star's producer-writer husband, Monte Masters, but still portrayed as a pin-up ("Figure? She picks up where Miss America leaves off. Clothes? She makes a peasant dress look like opening night at the opera. Hair? Blonde, of course. And eyes? Just the right shade of blue to match the hair.") In the manner noted by Klein (see Bibliography), her career ended with a proposal of marriage from the series' regular policeman.

CASEY, CRIME PHOTOGRAPHER (1943/1946-1950/1953-1955). An on and off series known variously as FLASHGUN CASEY; CASEY, PRESS PHOTOGRAPHER and CRIME PHOTOGRAPHER, based on the work of **George Harmon COXE**, who wrote scripts for the show, and, uniquely, novelized by **Paul AYRES**, starred Matt Crowley, then Staats Cotsworth as **Jack Casey** of *The Morning Express* who hung out in the Blue Note Café.

CHARLIE WILD, PRIVATE DETECTIVE (1950-1951). CBS' replacement for The ADVENTURES OF SAM SPADE, dropped after Hammett refused to answer Joe McCarthy's questions, was a close copy, starring George Petrie, which was converted into the TV show, see **TV: CHARLIE WILD, PRIVATE DETECTIVE.**

CHRISTOPHER LONDON (1950). A character created by **Erle Stanley GARDNER**, London, played by Glenn Ford, would go anywhere and do anything for a price.

CRIME AND PETER CHAMBERS (1954). Dane Clark starred as Henry KANE's PI.

The CRIME FILES OF FLAMOND (1953). Everett Clark played a master PI who used psychological methods.

A CRIME LETTER FROM DAN DODGE (1952). Myron McCormick played the part of a PI who dictated the facts relating to each case to his secretary, Shirley Eggleston, the story being told in flashbacks.

DETECTIVES BLACK AND BLUE (1931). An early comedy-mystery series, primitively produced, without sound effects, the action revealed through the heroes' dialogue, about two Duluth shipping clerks who take a criminology correspondence course and open an agency, with the motto "Detec-a-tives Black and Blue, good men tried and true," and, according to one source, helped set criminology back 40 years.

DYKE EASTER, DETECTIVE (1949). Cited by J. Fred MacDonald in *Don't Touch That Dial* (1979) as an example of the existential detective, quoted as saying of himself, "Dyke Easter—whip him, shoot him, tear his heart out. He got paid for it, didn't he?"

EASY MONEY (1946). Willard Waterman starred as a magician turned private detective who used magic to catch criminals.

The FAT MAN (1946-1950). One of the top radio detective thrillers, starring J. Scott Smart in a role created for radio by **Dashiell HAMMETT** and sharing many of the characteristics of his Continental Op. Sponsored by Pepto Bismol, the show had a famous opening sequence: "His name: **Brad Runyan**. There he goes now, into that drugstore. He's stepping on the scale." (Sound effects) "Weight? 239 pounds. Fortune? Danger! Whoooooooo is it? The Fat Man!" Smart actually weighed 270 pounds. **Richard ELLINGTON** was chief scriptwriter and **Frank KANE** wrote scripts for the show. See **Films: The FAT MAN**.

The GENTLEMAN ADVENTURER = SPECIAL AGENT HANNIBAL COBB (1949). Starring Santos Ortega, the show announced "as you will find him in the Photocrime pages of *Look* magazine. Here is a dramatic story of human conflict vividly told from from the point of view of someone closely involved."

HAVE GUN, WILL TRAVEL (1958-1960). One of the last radio dramas and an oddity in that it was adapted from the already successful TV show of the same title. John Dehner provided a contrasting interpretation of the part of **Paladin** and the series was notable for libertarian politics and anti-racism. Virginia Gregg appeared as Hey Boy's girlfriend.

I DEAL IN CRIME (1946). William Gargan starred as private detective **Ross Dolan.**

I LOVE A MYSTERY (1939-1943/1949-1952). Many collectors of old radio shows consider this the finest adventure series ever. Veterans of the Sino-Japanese War, **Jack Packard, Doc Long** and **Reggie York** became partners in the A-1 Detective Agency, "just off Hollywood Boulevard and one flight up," whose motto was "No job too tough, no mystery too baffling." Packard, who was thrown out of medical school after getting a girl into trouble, avoided and distrusted women, big, redheaded Texan Doc was a two-fisted womanizer, York a cool Britisher. Originally played by Michael Raffetto, Barton Yarborough and Walter Patterson, each of the 15-20 chapters of their fast-moving, often bizarre adventures was introduced by Sibelius' *Valse Triste* and the chimes of a clock. One episode, "Temple of Vampires," was so creepy that the Nicaraguan government lodged a protest. Carlton E. Morse wrote, with a globe of the world at his side, and produced a 15 minute script every day. After Patterson's death the York character was dropped for a time and the agency's curvy secretary **Jerri Booker** (Gloria Blondell, sister of Joan) was given a larger and more active part. In 1949 a new series, using Morse's original scripts, was aired with Russell Thorson, Jim Bowles and Tony Randall in the leads. See TV: **I LOVE A MYSTERY** and Films: **I LOVE A MYSTERY/The DEVIL'S MASK.**

IT'S A CRIME, MR. COLLINS (1956). The cases of "infamous private eye" **Greg Collins** were followed through the eyes of his beautiful wife Gail, who barely concealed her jealousy of inevitable curvaceous clients.

JEFF REGAN, INVESTIGATOR (1948-1950). The last of Jack Webb's anti-social PIs (see **PAT NOVAK, FOR HIRE** and **JOHNNY MODERO, PIER 23**) was introduced each week with the words "My name's Jeff Regan. I get ten a day and expenses from a detective bureau run by a guy named Lyon—**Anthony J. Lyon.** They call me 'The Lion's Eye.'" Wilms Herbert played the part of Lyon. After Webb left for *Dragnet*, Frank Graham took the role, with Frank Nelson as Lyon, taking the typical Webb anti-cop chip off Regan's shoulder and showing him as a champion of the underdog.

JOHNNY MODERO, PIER 23 (April-September 1947). This show marked Jack Webb's first significant appearance, showcasing the famous staccato style. One source remarked "To call Modero similar to Novak (**PAT NOVAK, FOR HIRE**) is like casually describing the similarities of Siamese twins." Praised by *Variety* as "a hard-hitting, fast moving item that carries a good deal of punch in its dialog," it was cancelled by the network because Richard Breen, the writer, could not, or would not, tone down the characterizations.

KITTY KEENE, INC. (1937-1941). A soap opera heroine from the tragedy mill of Frank and Anne Hummert, Keene has been described as an "honest-to-bubbles female detective complete with a mysterious past and a beautiful face." All that is revealed of her past is that she was once a Follies showgirl. Beverly Younger, Gail Henshaw and Fran Carlon had stints as Kitty in a daytime show whose theme was Tchaikovsky's *None But The Lonely Heart*.

LET GEORGE DO IT (1950). Bob Bailey, later in YOURS TRULY, JOHNNY DOLLAR, starred as a brains not brawn PI whose cases came from his newspaper ad: "Personal notice—danger's my stock-in-trade. If the job's too tough for you to handle, you've got the job for me, **George Valentine**. Write full details." Virginia Gregg was Valentine's secretary-girlfriend-sidekick **Claire 'Brooksie' Brooks**.

The LONE WOLF (1948-1949). Based on Louis Joseph Vance's novels, despite the superhero sounding name, **Michael Lanyard**, was just a gumshoe, so-called because he worked alone and was single. The reformed thief could often be found sipping highballs in the Silver Seashell Bar & Grill. Gerald Mohr (1948) and Walter Coy (1949) played the lead. See **TV: The LONE WOLF**.

The McCOY (1950). Howard Duff played **Mike McCoy, LA PI**.

The MALTESE FALCON (1946). Humphrey Bogart, Mary Astor and Sydney Greenstreet were reunited for a 30 minute capsule radio version of the film shown in the *Academy Award Theatre* series.

MAN AGAINST CRIME (1947). Ralph Bellamy starred as **Mike Barnett**, unarmed New York PI, a role he also played in the TV series. In the summer of 1951, Robert Preston deputized for him. See **TV: MAN AGAINST CRIME**.

MARTIN KANE, PRIVATE DETECTIVE (1949). While New York PI Kane, played first by William Gargan, wanted a quiet life, *Radio Life* pointed out in 1950 that, so far, he'd been "drugged, beaten, locked in a chamber with poison gas seeping in, thrown in the river, stabbed, shot, tied up in a burning building and locked unarmed in a room with a homicidal maniac bearing a meat cleaver." When the show made its effortless transition to TV with the same sponsor, US Tobacco, Gargan handpicked Lloyd Nolan as his replacement, as he was to do again with the TV role, see **TV: MARTIN KANE, PRIVATE EYE**.

MICHAEL SHAYNE (1944). Originally shown on the West Coast, with Wally Maher as **Brett HALLIDAY's** redheaded Irish PI, the series went national with Cathy Lewis replacing Louise Arthur as his secretary-girlfriend-sidekick **Phyllis Knight.** Transplanted to New York, Jeff Chandler, a considerably more hardboiled Shayne in a syndicated version, and Robert Sterling, in ABC's, both starred with Judith Parrish.

MIKE MALLORY (1953). Steve Brodie starred.

MISS PINKERTON, INC. (1941). Joan Blondell (then Mrs. Dick Powell) starred as a young woman attempting to run an agency inherited from an uncle.

MR. & MRS. NORTH (1942/1950). Adapted from **Richard & Frances LOCKRIDGE's** books, Joseph Curtin and Alice Frost first starred as ex-PI turned book publisher, **Jerry North** and his wife **Pamela**, with Richard Denning and Barbara Britton taking over in 1950. Both couples appeared in TV series, the first (1949) very shortlived, the second running for two years, with the Norths cast as amateurs in both.

MYSTERY WITHOUT MURDER (1947). Luther Adler starred as **Peter Gentle**, a private detective opposed to violence.

The NEW ADVENTURES OF NERO WOLFE (1950-1951). The third radio incarnation of **Rex STOUT's** heroes (see **The ADVENTURES OF NERO WOLFE** and **The AMAZING NERO WOLFE**) featured Sydney Greenstreet as a wry Wolfe, casting of which Stout himself warmly approved, though preferring the scripts of the second series. A succession of actors played **Archie Goodwin** in different ways, gushing (Gerald Mohr), angry (Herb Ellis), needling (Larry Dobson), earnest (Wally Maher) and assured (Everett Sloane).

The NEW ADVENTURES OF THE THIN MAN (1948-1950). Pabst Blue Ribbon sponsored this series (see **The ADVENTURES OF THE THIN MAN**) and **Dashiell HAMMETT** was offered so much money that he agreed to act as script supervisor. Claudia Morgan, reputedly one of the most beautiful, though of course unseen, actresses on radio, again played **Nora**, Les Tremayne, then Joseph Curtin appeared as **Nick Charles.**

PAT NOVAK, FOR HIRE (1946/1949). "That's what the sign outside my office says. Down on the waterfront in San Francisco, you don't get prizes for being subtle. You want to make a living down here, you got to get your hands in the till any way you can. You rob Peter to pay Paul, and then you put it on the cuff." Originally heard only on the West Coast, **Pat Novak** propelled Jack Webb to national prominence as radio's prime tough guy. When Webb left for Hollywood, Ben Morris replaced him but public outcry led first to **JOHNNY MODERO, PIER 23**, a carbon copy, also written by Richard Breen, and then to a national Novak series with Webb back in the lead, Tudor Owen as ex-doctor and boozehound sidekick **Jocko Madigan** and Raymond Burr as Inspector Hellman, who beats Novak up from time to time just for the hell of it. Famed for its purple dialogue, it was, like all Webb's PI shows (see also **JEFF REGAN, INVESTIGATOR**) primarily a showcase for caustic quips and one liners.

PETER QUILL (1940). Marvin Miller starred in the exploits of a mysterious scientist-detective-adventurer.

RESULTS, INC. (1944). A lively comedy-mystery-adventure series with Lloyd Nolan as **Johnny Strange** and Claire Trevor as his partner **Theresa 'Terry' Travers**, who answered his ad saying "Secretary wanted; blonde, beautiful, between 22 and 28 years, unmarried, with the skin you love to touch and a heart you can't," and gets 25% commission, with hospital bills and bail money paid. Their business comes from another ad that reads: "Results, Inc.; your problem is our problem. Will locate your long-lost uncle, work your crossword puzzle, hold your baby. Where others fail, we succeed."

RICHARD DIAMOND, PRIVATE DETECTIVE (1949-1952). After fighting the studios to get away from glamor boy roles and play parts like Marlowe in *Murder, My Sweet*, Dick Powell seemed to relax into this series which combined slick sophistication and two-fisted action. A happy-go-lucky OSS-trained PI, Diamond enjoys the free life, ribbing the cops and relaxing with his girlfriend Helen Asher (Virginia Gregg), even singing in their romantic moments. A take-off of Jack Webb's Pat Novak, Pat Cosak, featured as Diamond's funny-rude rival. When the series transferred to TV, Powell considered himself too old for the part. See **TV: RICHARD DIAMOND, PRIVATE EYE**.

ROCKY FORTUNE (1953). During a career slump—after the bobbysoxers but before his acting success in *From Here To Eternity*—Frank Sinatra appeared on radio as a footloose and fancy free adventurer-PI who would undertake any commission for money.

ROGUE'S GALLERY (1945/1947/1950-1952). Dick Powell's float through warm-up for **RICHARD DIAMOND** in which he played **Richard Rogue**, trailing luscious blondes and other lightweight PI activities. The series was revived in 1947 with Barry Sullivan in the lead and in 1950 with Chester Morris.

SECRET CITY (1941). Bill Idelson starred as **Ben Clark**.

SPECIAL AGENT (1948). Originally aired as **The GENTLEMAN ADVENTURER**, James Meighan starred as **Alan Drake**, an investigator working for his father's firm and specializing in marine insurance cases.

THAT HAMMER GUY (1953). Starring Larry Haines as **Mickey SPILLANE's Mike Hammer**, the undistinguished basis for the TV series.

TWO ON A CLUE (1944). Dramatizing actual case histories, Ned Weaver and Louise Fitch starred as husband and wife PI team **Jeff & Debby Spencer**. A short-lived daytime series.

YOURS TRULY, JOHNNY DOLLAR (1949-1962). The last major dramatic series on network radio, and in its last days one of the best detective shows ever, featured an insurance investigator with an "action-packed expense account" which provided the basis for each episode. As Johnny itemised his expenses, he narrated the story behind each outgoing, ending with "yours truly, **Johnny Dollar**." Dollar's character was as developed as the medium allowed, though early in the show his generosity was rather ostentatiously manifested by a habit of tossing silver dollars as tips. A confirmed bachelor, his best girl was Virginia Gregg. The role was played successively by Charles Russell, Edmund O'Brien, John Lund, Bob Bailey, Robert Readick and Mandel Kramer. One source claims that Bailey was "far and away" the best and toughest Johnny Dollar; Kramer, with a low-key sense of humor, second.

YELLOW PAGES

AUSTRALIA
Sydney	Peter Fleck
	Cliff Hardy

CANADA
Balmoral	Johnny Canuck
Grantham	Benny Cooperman
Montreal	Mike Garfin
	Philip Kaufman
	Bill Yates
Toronto	John Jantarro
	John Locke
Vancouver	Helen Keremos
	Meg Lacey

CHINA
Peking	Li Kao & Lu Yu

FRANCE
Paris	B.F. Cage
	Guy Roland
	Pierre-Ange Sawyer

GERMANY
Nurnberg	Karl Jaeger

HOLLAND
Amsterdam	Tim Parnell

ITALY
Naples	Alessandro Iovine

JAPAN
Tokyo	Burns Bannion
	Curt Stone

MEXICO
Mexico City	Al Colby

PHILIPPINES
Manila	Jo Gar

SPAIN
Barcelona	Pepe Carvalho
	Lonia Guiu

VENEZUELA
Punto Fijo	Bernardo Thomas

OTHER PLANETS
Carinthia	Stefan Vynalek
Cassander	Miro Hetzel
Ja-Lur	Kamus of Kadizar
Mars	Sam Space

GREAT BRITAIN
Belfast	Bernard Holland
Birmingham	Frank Marker
	Norman Pink
Bristol	Eddie Shoestring
Glasgow	Clutha
	Daniel Pike
Liverpool	Eddie Ginley
London	Bill Banning
	Nick Bellamy
	Miriam Birdseye
	& Natasha Nevkorina
	Rupert Bradley
	Steve Bradshaw
	Chico Brett
	Rickard Britton
	Slim Callaghan
	Harry Cambert
	Mike Cardby
	Rex Carver
	Clive Conrad
	Nick Duffy
	Joe Dust
	John Earlstone
	Ian Firth & John Smith
	Eric Fisher
	Adam Flute
	Brad Ford
	Pete Fry
	Nicholas Gale
	Dirk Gently
	Cordelia Gray

London	Sid Halley	UNITED STATES	
(cont)	Willie Halliday	ARIZONA	
	John Harley	Phoenix	Mike & Bob Brannigan
	James Hazell		Daniel Falconer
	Hooky Hefferman	Tucson	Henry Dyer
	James Helder	Yavapai	Dallas Webster
Ron Hoggett & Dave Baxter		CALIFORNIA	
	Barney Huggins	Bay City	Doan & Carstairs
	Joe Hussey	Berkeley	Dan Brodsky
	Barney Hyde	Carmel	Pat Riordan
	Jimmy Jenner		Samuel Clemens Tucker
	Harry Kent	Crystal Cove	Fiddler
	Tom Langley	Long Beach	Jim Sader
	Anna Lee		Honey West
	Johnny Macall	Los Angeles	Lew Archer
	Frank MacAllister		Jacob Asch
	Vicki McBain		Stuart Bailey
	James Malcolm		Miles Banyon
	Nick Marshall		Pete Bayliss
	Buddy Mustard		Otis Beagle & Joe Peel
	Terence O'Day		Fred Bennett
	Cary O'Hara		Arthur Blake & Dan Wheeler
	Jim Piron		Jim Blaney
	Johnny Preston		Leo Bloodworth
	Francis Quarles		Silas Booth
	Mark Raeburn		David Brandstetter
	Bob Ross		Pete Brass
	John Samson		Nathan Brightlight
	Ned Sanderson		Mark Brill
	Mark Savage		Fritz Brown
	Maud Silver		Brock Callahan
	John Smith		Humphrey Campbell
	Harry Somers		Ace Carpenter
	William A. Tempest		Steve Cash
	Philip Tolefree		Antonio Cervantes
	Johnny Vallon		Bart Challis
	Lee Vaughan		Edmond Clive
	Brendan Wallace		Elvis Cole
Newton Lauder	Keith Calder		Bertha Cool & Donald Lam
Rogate-On-Sands	Harry Thompson		Roger Dale

Los Angeles (cont)

Elton Dancey
Jeffrey Dean
Alex Delaware
Red Diamond
Eli Donovan
John Easy
Mike Faraday
Mark Foran
Mike Garrett
Roger Garrison
Tony Garrity
Alison B Gordon
Avery Gregg & Tony Ellis
Wade Griffin
& S. Michael Murdoch
Peter Gunn
Aaron Gunner
Lucas Hallam
Harry Herbold & Warren Hearst
Albert Hickey &Franklin Boggs
Rick Holman
Sam Hunter
John Baron Hyde
Ben Jardinn
Sam King
Thomas Kyd
Alexander L'Hiboux
Johnny Lamb
Simon Lash & Eddie Slocum
Jake Lieberman
Mark Logan
Tom Logan
Jimmy Lujack
Rex McBride
Pete McCoy
Steve Mallory
Erik March
Sam Marlow
Philip Marlow
Johnny Marshall

Paul Marston & Angel Cantini
Anthony Martin
Steve Midnight
Al Mooney
Fergus O'Breen
Toby Peters
John P Phelan
Duke Pizzatello
Jay Pletcher
Duncan Pride
Charlie Quinlan
Corey Raleigh
Lamaar Ransom
Ray Ripley
Jim Rockford
Howie Rook
Saxon
Pete Schofield
Shell Scott
Mavis Seidlitz & Johnny Rio
John J Shannon
Joe Shaw
Cellini Smith
Jake Spanner
John Steele
Nichole Sweet
Fritz Thieringer
& Maggie McGuane
Terry Traven
Dan Turner
Eddie Valiant
Sam Welpton
Whistler
Moses Wine

James Woodruff & Tony Novello
(2019)
LA Island City
Monkton City
Newport Beach
Oakland

Rick Deckard
Charlie Case
Mark Preston
Matt Murdock
Jake Samson

Oakland	Eliza Pirex	(cont)	Dan Kearny Associates
Orange County	Delilah West		Riley Kovacs
Orchid City	Vic Malloy		Tommy Lee
Pacific City	Steve Bryant		Paul MacDonald
Peninsula City	Steve Summers		Manx McCatty
San Diego	Sydney Bryant		Sharon McCone
Matt Doyle & Carter Winfield			Amos McGuffin
	Harold Shilling		Lou Peckinpaugh
	Max Thursday		Nick Polo
San Felice	Steve Pinata		Johnny Powers
San Francisco	Pat Abbot		Jason Prophet
	Carver Bascombe		Jay Rogers
	Stan Bass		Catherine Sayler
	Alan Bernhardt		Sam Spade
	Arthur Bironico		Jeremiah St John
	Mike Blair		John Marshall Tanner
	Jacob Blake		Derek Thompson
	Al Bocca		Cassandra Thorpe
	Walter Brackett		Timothy Wilde
	Pete Bragg		Martin Windrow
	Mike Brennan		Trygve Yamamura
	C. Card		Joe Zanca
	Rocco Conigliaro	San Vicente	Ed Gray
	Sean Connell	Santa Barbara	Kane Jackson
	Continental Op	Santa Monica	Steve Craig
	Jerry Cool		Evan Paris
	Simon Crole		Max Roper
	Elmer Dodd	Santa Teresa	Kinsey Millhone
Aileen Douglass& Sharon Atwood		Venice	Sara Scott
	Maggie Elliott	Vista Beach	Max London
	Neil Fargo	**COLORADO**	
	Tom Farley	Aurora	Phil Kramer
	Peter Flynn		Vince Latimer
	Joe Gaylord	Denver	Jim Bannerman
	Joe Goodey	Zebulion Buck & Jim Dunn	
	Hector Gronig		Nick Caine
	Jim Haley		Devlin Kirk
	Mike Haller		Jacob Lomax
	Mick Halsey		Joe Reddman
San Francisco	Ben Henry	Colorado Springs	Carl Heller

CONNECTICUT

	P. Moran
Greenwich	Chris Rockwell
	& Sarah Saber
Redding Ridge	Jake & Hildy Pace
Worcester	Griff Hughes

FLORIDA

Castile	Clay MacKinnon
Fort Lauderdale	Cam McCardle
	Travis McGee
Key West	T.D. Stash
Miami	Roman Cantrell
	R.J. Decker
	Brain Keyes
	Miles Standish Rice
	Tony Rome
	Michael Shayne
Quin St James & Mike McCleary
Miami Beach	Pete Draco
	Jeff Thompson
Orlando	Fred Carver
Paradise City	Dirk Wallace
Sarasota	Anna Peters
Sun City	Nathan Hawk
Tampa	Ed Rivers

GEORGIA

Atlanta	Jim Hardman
	& Hump Evans
	Hank Prince

HAWAII

Honolulu	Johnny Aloha
Oahu	Thomas Magnum

ILLINOIS

Boone	Charles Horne
Cedar Rapids	Jack Dwyer
Chicago	Danny April
	Big Bull Benson
	Calvin Bix
	Mark Brandon
	Barr Breed

Barney Burgess
Marty Cole
Kelly J Deckard
Frank Dragovic
Rusty Forbes
Murray Glick
Carl Good
Marcus Greene
Carl Guard
Madge Hatchett
Nate Heller
Rush Henry
Ed & Ambrose Hunter
Mike James
Morocco Jones
Max Keene
Phil Keene
Birch Kirby
Dan Kruger
Luke Lassiter
Lacy Lockington
Mac (Robinson)
Micah McCall
Arnold Magnuson
Johnny Maguire
Tip O'Neil
Bridget O'Toole & Harry Garnish
Paul Pine
Chance Purdue
Max Raven
Jim Rehm
Leo Roi
Bob Ruff
Jerry Todd
V.I. Warshawski
Tuthill Willow

Rockford	Joe Hannibal
Springfield	Robert Miles

INDIANA

Indianapolis	Albert Samson

KANSAS		MINNESOTA	
Wichita	Mitch Roberts	Minneapolis	Nathan Phillips
KENTUCKY			Chet Johnson
Louisville	Jamie MacRae	**MISSISSIPPI**	
	Michael Rhineheart	Gulfport	Wayne Temple
Rough River	Warren Stone	**MISSOURI**	
LOUISIANA		Kansas City	Johnny April
New Orleans	Johnny Bordelon		Larry Crystal
	Micah Dunn		Mike Saxon
	Frank Le Roux	St Louis	Clio Brown
	Neal Rafferty		Steve Cardigan
	Jerry Roe & Stuart Worth		Karl Craven
MARYLAND			Alo Nudger
Baltimore	Jim Pierce		John Shields
MASSACHUSETTS		**MONTANA**	
Boston	Harvey Blissberg	Meriwether	Milo Milodragovitch
	Carlotta Carlyle		C.W. Sughrue
	Jack Casey	**NEBRASKA**	
	John Francis Cuddy	Omaha	Nebraska
	Brian Desmond	**NEVADA**	
	Jack Fenner	Carson Valley	Dakota
	Max C. Hale	Las Vegas	Julian Burroughs
	J.D. Hawkins		Barney Conroy
	John Kincaid		Zachariah Rolfe
	Knightsbridge		Devlin Tracy
	Marmaduke McCale	Reno	Pogy Rogers & Beau Smith
	James Maxfield Mallory		Jack Ross
	James Marley	**NEW JERSEY**	
	Kent Murdock	Jersey City	Malone
	Jason T. O'Neil	Newark	Ezell Barnes
	Spenser		Nash Kanzler
	Michael Spraggue	Trenton	Nick Magaracz
MICHIGAN		**NEW MEXICO**	
	John Bent	Santa Fe	Rita Mondragon
Ann Arbor (?)	Fred Crockett		& Joshua Croft
Birmingham	Jane Mulroy	**NEW YORK**	
Detroit	Ben Perkins	Albany	Don Strachey
	Frank Ryan	Long Island	Patrick Bray
	Amos Walker		J.C.K. Masters

New York City

Squire Adams	Paul Damian
Russell Ames	Timothy Dane
Sid Ames	Hal Darling
Harry Angel	Jan Darzek
Berkeley Barnes & Larry Howe	Tyger Decker
Gerry Barnes	Biff Deegan
Jake Barrow	Jake Dekker
Charity Bay	Johnny Dekker
Lutie & Amanda Beagle	Nick Delvecchio
Joe Binney	Frank De Nardo
Jana Blake	Red Diamond
Blue	Willy Diaz
Marty Bond	Dick Donahue
Glenn Bowman	Pat Doyle
Peter Braid	Steve Drake
Al Bressio	Mark East
Sam Briscoe	Fortune Fanelli
Brody	Harry Fannin
Vee Brown	Kevin Fitzgerald
Burke	Johnny Fletcher & Sam Cragg
Huntingdon Cage	Virgil Fletcher
David Calder	Dan Fortune
Charles Camelot & Philip Revere	Dr Robert Frederickson
Curt Cannon	Gale Gallagher
Tony Cassella	Steve Gant
Pete Chambers	Ben Gates
Joe Cinquez	Barney Glines
Frank Clemons	Alexander & Nora Gold
Daniel J. Cluer	Angel Graham
Schyler Cole & Luke Speare	Victor Grant
Steve Conacher	Edwin Green
Bart Condor	Jeffrey Green
Timothy Cone	Leo Haig & Chip Harrison
Steve Considine & Mike Zacharias	Arthur Halstead
Tony Costaine & Norbert McCall	Barney Hamet
Robert Craig	Mike Hammer
Bill Crane	Chess Hanrahan
Steve Crane	Angela Harpe
Sam Crombie	Barney Harris
Peter Cross	Kirby Hart

New York City (cont)

Bump Harwell
Stanley Hastings
Cyrus Hatch
Amos Hatcher
Ben Helm
George Herbert Henry
Steve Hershey
Quinny Hite
Pete Holland
Larry Hornblower
Anthony Hunter
Hank Hyer
Miles Jacoby
Quentin Jacoby
Michael Dane James
Wood Jaxon
Sam Kelly
Johnny Killian
Tom Kincaid
Murray Kirk
Max Klein
PaPa LaBas
Louis Lait
Lou Largo
Roger Levin
Jack LeVine
Johnny Liddell
Wylie Lincoln & Russ Turner
Ben Lomax
Ed London
Bill Lockwood
Philip Macadam
Shamus McCoy
Pete McGrath
Inspector McGregor
Kevin MacInnes
Ross McKellar
Duncan Maclain
Harry MacNeil
John Justin Mallory

Eddie Margolis
Jason Marr
Johnny Midas
Johnny Milano
Toussaint Moore
Jigger Moran
Ruff Morgan
Jerry Nelson
Billy Nevers
Ed Noon
Joe Noonan
Nick Palladino
Bryce Patch
Sidney Pincus & Mike Clancy
Henry Po
Hilary Quayle & Gene
Ellery Queen & Beau Rummell
Glen Ransom
Matt Ranzino
Pete Reno
Mark Renzler
Slots Reznick
Sampson Roach
George Robin
Terry Rooke
John Thomas Ross
Johnny Saxon
William Schaefer & Ann Lang
Matt Scudder
John Shaft
Dale Shand
Desmond Shannon
James Shaw
Paul Shaw
Pete Shay
Ned Sherwood
Ben Shock & Charity Tucker
Mac Slade
Benjamin Smoke
J.T. Spanner

New York City	Johnny Staccato		Mark Corrigan
(cont)	Rocky Steele		Mike Dime
	Shep Stone		Jerry Mooney
	John Storm		Carney Wilde
	Clem Talbot	(1899)	Kyra Keaton
	Mitch Tobin	Pittsburgh	Casey Carmichael
	Marla Trent		Matt Gregg
	Steve Tyner		Yuri Nevsky
	Rick Vanner	**TENNESSEE**	
	Val Vernon	Memphis	Steve Lee
	William Wallace	**TEXAS**	
	Clint Walsh	Austin Clayton Yankee Taggart	
	Sheridan Wesley	Brownsville	Cheney Hazzard
	Race Williams	Dallas	Steve Dart
Nero Wolfe & Archie Goodwin		Jackson Fury & Jillian Fletcher	
	Russel Wren		Rafferty
	Eve Zabriskie		Dan Roman
(1999)	Jack Hughes	El Paso	Houston McIver
	George Sandford		Gregory Quist
(1923)	William Edmondson	Fort Worth	Cody
Saratoga Springs	Charlie Bradshaw	Jacinto City	Mike Cavanaugh
Sparta .	Ron Gentry	Yellow	Deuce Ramsey
Winston	Tim Smith	**UTAH**	
NORTH DAKOTA		Salt Lake City	Moroni Traveler
Corden	Carl Wilcox		Gabriel Utley
OHIO		**VIRGINIA**	
Cincinnati	Harry Stoner	Charlottesville	Loren Swift
Cleveland	Jim Bennett	**WASHINGTON**	
	Gil Disbro	Puget Sound	Jonas Duncan
	Milan Jacovich	Seattle	Thomas Black
	David Stuart		Hank Bradford
Jordan	Morgan Butler		Peter Cory
OKLAHOMA			John Denson
Oklahoma City	Steve Cranmer		Clifford Grant
	& Butch Maneri		Guinevere Jones
OREGON			Bert Norden
Holliday Beach	Conan Flagg	**WASHINGTON DC**	
PENNSYLVANIA			Steve Bentley
Philadelphia	Bill Canilli		Dan Cronyn
	Peter Congdon		Chester Drum

CHECK LIST

ABBOTT, Keith
Rhino Ritz
ABLEMAN, Paul
Shoestring
Shoestring's Finest Hour
ABRAHAMS, Robert D.
Death After Lunch
Death In 1-2-3
Sabotage = Death Before Breakfast
   = Death At The Dam
Decoy
Up Jumped Devil = Murder All Over
Crooking Finger
Shady Lady
Private Eye
No Wings On A Cop
What Price Murder
ADAMS, Douglas
Dirk Gently's Holistic Detective
   Agency
Long Dark Tea-Time Of The Soul
ADAMS, Harold
Murder
Paint The Town Red
Missing Moon
Naked Liar
Fourth Widow
Barbed Wire Noose
Man Who Met The Train
Man Who Missed The Party
When Rich Men Die
ALBERT, Marvin
Tony Rome = Miami Mayhem: **ROME**
Stone Angel
Back In The Real World
Long Teeth
Get Off At Babylon
Last Smile
ALEXANDER, David
Murder In Black & White
Most Men Don't Kill
   = Corpse In My Bed
ALEXANDER, Karl
Private Investigation

ALLAN, Dennis
Brandon Is Missing
ALLAN, Francis
First Come, First Kill
ALLEGRETTO, Michael
Death On The Rocks
Blood Stone
ALLEN, Leslie
Murder In The Rough = as **BROWN, H**
ALLEN, Steve
Talk Show Murders
ALLYSON, Alan
Do You Deal In Murder?
Don't Mess With Murder
Lady Said No
ALVERSON, Charles
Fighting Back
Goodey's Last Stand
Not Sleeping, Just Dead
ANDERSON, M.
Her Mother's Husband
ANDERSON, Poul
Perish By The Sword
Murder In Black Letter
Murder Bound
ANTHONY, David
Midnight Lady & Mourning Man
Blood On A Harvest Moon
Long Hard Cure
Organization
Stud Game
ANTHONY, Evelyn
Poellenberg Inheritance
ARD, William
Perfect Frame
.38 = You Can't Stop Me
   = This Is Murder
Diary
Private Party = Rogue's Murder
Don't Come Crying To Me
Mr Trouble
Hell Is A City = Naked & Innocent
Cry Scandal
Root Of His Evil = Deadly Beloved >

393

All I Can Get
Like Ice She Was
Babe In The Woods
Make Mine Mavis
And So To Bed
Give Me This Woman
When She Was Bad
You'll Get Yours = as WILLS
ARDEN, William
Dark Power
Deal In Violence
Goliath Scheme
Die To Distant Drum
    = Murder Underground
Deadly Legacy
ARRIGHI, Mel
Alter Ego
ARTHUR, Robert
Somebody's Walking Over My Grave
AUSTER, Paul
City Of Glass = NY Trilogy
Ghosts = NY Trilogy
AVALLONE, Michael
Spitting Image
Tall Dolores
Dead Game
Violence In Velvet
CoT Bouncing Betty
CoT Violent Virgin
Crazy Mixed-Up Corpse
Voodoo Murders
Meanwhile Back At Morgue
Alarming Clock
Bedroom Bolero = Bolero Murders
Living Bomb
There Is Something About A Dame
Lust Is No Lady = Brutal Kook
Fat Death
February Doll Murders
Assassins Don't Die In Bed
Horrible Man
Flower-Covered Corpse
Doomsday Bag = Killer's Highway
Death Dives Deep
Little Miss Murder
    = Ultimate Client
Shoot It Again, Sam
    = Moving Graveyard >

Girl In The Cockpit
London, Bloody London
    = Ed Noon In London
Kill Her—You'll Like It!
Hot Body
Killer On The Keys
X-Rated Corpse
Big Stiffs
Dark On Monday
High Noon At Midnight
Mannix
AYRES, Paul
Dead Heat
BABULA, William
St John's Baptism
BAILEY, Hilea
What Night Will Bring
Give Thanks To Death
Smiling Corpse
Breathe No More, My Lady
BAKER, Sidney J
Time Is An Enemy
BALLARD, Willis Todhunter
Say Yes To Murder
    = Demise of A Louse: SHEPHERD
Murder Can't Stop
Dealing Out Death
Hollywood Troubleshooter
Murder Las Vegas Style
BALLINGER, Bill S
Body In The Bed
Body Beautiful
Heist Me Higher
Portrait In Smoke = Deadlier Sex
BANDY, Eugene Franklin
Deceit & Deadly Lies
Blackstock Affair
Farewell Party
BANKS, Oliver
Rembrandt Panel = Rembrandt File
Caravaggio Obsession
BANKS, Raymond
Meet Me In Darkness
Computer Kill
BARNAO, Jack
Hammer Locke
Lockestep

BARNES, Linda J
Blood Will Have Blood
Bitter Finish
Dead Heat
Cities Of The Dead
Trouble Of Fools
Snake Tattoo
BARNS, Glenn M
Murder Is A Gamble
Murder Walks The Stairs
Murder Is Insane
BARRY, Joe
Third Degree
Fall Guy
Triple Cross
Clean Up
Pay-Off
BAYNE, Spencer
Murder Recalls Van Kill
Turning Sword
BAYNES, Jack
Meet Morocco Jones
CoT Syndicate Hoods
Hand Of The Mafia
Peeping Tom Murders
Morocco Jones In CoT Golden Angel
BEAL, M.F
Angel Dance
BEAR, David
Keeping Time
BECK, K.K
Unwanted Attentions
BEHM, Marc
Eye Of The Beholder = Thrillers
BEINHART, Larry
No One Rides For Free
You Get What You Pay For
BELLEM, Robert Leslie
Blue Murder
Dan Turner, Hollywood Detective
Three Dan Turner Stories
BENJAMIN, Paul
Squeeze Play
BENSON, O.G
Cain's Woman = Cain's Wife
BENTLEY, John
Dangerous Waters
   = Mr Marlow Takes To Rye >

Prelude To Trouble
   = Mr Marlow Chooses Wine
Front Page Murder
   = Mr Marlow Stops For Brandy
Rendezvous With Death
Macedonian Mixup
Dead Do Talk
BERCOVICI, Eric
So Little Cause For Caroline
BERGER, Thomas
Who Is Teddy Villanova?
Nowhere
BERGMAN, Andrew
Big Kiss-Off Of 1944
Hollywood & LeVine
BERNARD, Trevor
Brightlight
BESTOR, Clinton
Corpse Came Calling
BEYER, William Gray
Eenie, Meenie, Minie Murder
   = Murder By Arrangement
   = Murder Secretary
BIGGLE, Lloyd Jr
All The Colors Of Darkness
Watchers Of The Dark
This Darkening Universe
Silence Is Deadly
Whirligig Of Time
Interface For Murder
BILGREY, Marc
Private Eye Cartoon Book
BILLANY, Dan
Opera House Murders = It Takes A Thief
BIRKETT, John
Last Private Eye
BLACK, Thomas
3-13 Murders
Whitebird Murders
Pinball Murders
Four Dead Mice = Million $ Murder
BLAINE, Richard
Silver Setup
Tainted Jade
BLAKE, William Dorsey
My Time Or Yours
BLANKENSHIP, William D
Programmed Man

BLEECK, Oliver
Brass Go-Between
Protocol For A Kidnapping
Procane Chronicle = Thief Who
    Painted Sunlight = St Ives
Highbinders
No Questions Asked
BLOCH, Robert
Shooting Star
BLOCHMAN, Lawrence G
Wives To Burn
BLOCK, Lawrence
Five Little Rich Girls = Make Out
    With Murder: **HARRISON**
Topless Tulip Caper = by **HARRISON**
In The Midst Of Death
Sins Of The Fathers
Time To Murder & Create
Stab In The Dark
Eight Million Ways To Die
When Sacred Ginmill Closes
Death Pulls A Doublecross
    = Coward's Kiss
CoT Pornographic Photos
    = You Could Call It Murder
BLOOMFIELD, Robert
From This Death Forward
BLUMENTHAL, John
Tinseltown Murders
CoT Hardboiled Dicks
BOCCA, Al
Blonde Dynamite
City Limit Blonde
Curves For Danger
Dame Ain't Safe
Dead On Time
It's Your Funeral
Long Sleep
She Was No Lady
Sinner Takes All
Slaughter In Satin
Coffin Fits
Deadly Ernest
Easy Come, Easy Go
Harder They Fall
Let's Face It
No Dice!
Sudden Death >

Wait For It, Pal
Any Minute Now
Dressed To Kill
Black Morning
Gun For Company
Let's Not Get Smart
Sorry You've Been Shot
All Or Nothing
Double Trouble
Requiem For A Redhead
Slick & The Dead
Ticket To San Diego
Trouble Calling
Corner In Corpses
No Room At The Morgue
BOGART, William
Hell On Friday = Murder Man
Murder Is Forgetful
Queen City Murder
BONNEY, Joseph L
Death By Dynamite
Murder Without Clues = No Man's Hand
BOOTH, Louis F
Bank Vault Mystery
Brokers' End
BOSTON, Charles K
Silver Jackass = as **GRUBER**
BOUCHER, Anthony
CoT Crumpled Knave
CoT Solid Key
CoT Seven Sneezes
BOWDLER, Roger
Magnum PI
BOWEN, Robert Sidney
Make Mine Murder
Murder Gets Around
BOWERS, Elizabeth
Ladies' Night
BOWMAN, Robert
House Of Blue Lights
BOYD, Frank
Johnny Staccato
BRACKEEN, Steve
Delfina
BRACKETT, Leigh
No Good From A Corpse
BRADFORD, Kelly
Footprints

BRALY, Malcolm
Master
BRANDON, William
Dangerous Dead
BRANSON, H.C
I'll Eat You Last = I'll Kill You Last
Pricking Thumb
Fearful Passage
CoT Giant Killer
Last Year's Blood
Leaden Bubble
Beggar's Choice
BRAUTIGAN, Richard
Dreaming Of Babylon
BRENT, Nigel
Scarlet Lily
Blood In The Bank
Motive For Murder
Dig The Grave Deep
Murder Swings High
Leopard Died Too
Golden Angel
Badger In The Dusk
No Space For Murder
Spider In The Web
BRETT, Martin
Hot Freeze
Darker Traffic
    = Blondes Are My Trouble
Dum-Dum For The President
BRETT, Michael
Kill Him Quickly, It's Raining
Another Day, Another Stiff
Dead, Upstairs In A Tub
Ear For Murder
Flight Of The Stiff
Turn Blue, You Murderers
We, The Killers
Death Of A Hippie
Lie Little, Die Little = Cry Uncle
Slit My Throat Gently
BREWER, Mike
Man In Danger
Man On The Run
BROCK, Stuart
Death Is My Lover
Just Around The Coroner
Killer's Choice

BROWN, Carter
Honey, Here's Your Hearse
Bullet For My Baby
Good Morning, Mavis
Murder Wears A Mantilla
Loving & The Dead
None But Lethal Heart = Fabulous
Tomorrow Is Murder
Lament For A Lousy Lover
Bump & Grind Murders
(Seidlitz &) Super-Spy
Murder Is So Nostalgic
And The Undead Sing
So Deadly, Sinner= Walk Softly, Witch
Wayward Wahine = Wayward
Dream Is Deadly
(Sad-Eyed) Seductress
Savage Salome= Murder Is My Mistress
Ice-Cold Nude
Lover, Don't Come Back!
Nymph To The Slaughter
Passionate Pagan
Silken Nightmare
Catch Me A Phoenix!
Sometime Wife
Black Lace Hangover
House Of Sorcery
Mini-Murders
Murder Is The Message
Only The Very Rich
Coffin Bird
Sex Clinic
Angry Amazons
Manhattan Cowboy
So Move The Body
Pipes Are Calling
Savage Sisters
Rip-Off
Strawberry Blonde Jungle
Death To A Downbeat
Kiss Michelle Goodbye
Real Boyd
Death Of A Doll = Ever-Loving Blues
Zelda 1961
Murder In Harem (Key) Club
Murder Among Us
Blonde On The Rocks
Jade-Eyed Jinx = Jade-Eyed Jungle >

Ballad Of Loving Jenny = White Bikini
Wind-Up Doll
Never-Was Girl
Murder Is A Package Deal
Who Killed Dr Sex?
Nude - With A View
Girl From Outer Space
Blonde On A Broomstick
Play Now—Kill Later
No Tears From The Widow
Deadly Kitten
No Time For Leola
Die Anytime, After Tuesday
Flagellator
Streaked-Blonde Slave
Good Year For Dwarfs?
Hang-Up Kid
Where Did Charity Go?
Coven
Invisible Flamini
Pornbroker
Master
Phreak-Out!
Negative In Blue
Star-Crossed Lover
Ride The Roller Coaster
Remember Maybelle
See It Again, Sam
Phantom Lady
Swingers
Myopic Mermaid
BROWN, Fredric
Fabulous Clipjoint
Dead Ringer
Bloody Moonlight
    = Murder By Moonlight
Compliments Of A Fiend
Death Has Many Doors
Late Lamented
Mrs Murphy's Underpants
BROWN, Gerald
Murder On Beacon Hill
Murder In Plain Sight
BROWN, Horace
Penthouse Killings
Murder In The Rough = as Allen, L
BROWN, Hosanna
I Spy, You Die >

Death Upon A Spear
BROWN, R.D
Hazzard
Villa Head
BROWNE, Howard
Halo In Blood = as EVANS
Halo In Brass = as EVANS
Taste Of Ashes
Paper Gun
BROWNER, John
Death Of A Punk
BRUCCOLI & LAYMAN
(eds) New Black Mask
(eds) Matter Of Crime
BUCHANAN, Patrick
Murder Of Crows
Parliament Of Owls
Requiem Of Sharks
Sounder Of Swine
BUNN, Thomas
Closet Bones
BURKE, J.F
Location Shots
Death Trick
Kelly Among The Nightingales
BURKE, Richard
Dead Take No Bows
Chinese Red
Here Lies The Body
Fourth Star
Sinister Street
BURNS, Charles
Hard-Boiled Defective Stories
BURNS, Rex
Suicide Season
BUSBY, Roger & HOLTHAM
Main Line Kill
BYERS, Charles Alma
Inverness Murder
BYRD, Max
California Thriller
Fly Away, Jill
Finders Weepers
CAGNEY, Peter
No Diamonds For A Doll
Hear The Stripper Scream
Grave For Madam
CAIN, Paul
Seven Slayers

CAINE, Hamilton T
Carpenter, Detective
Hollywood Heroes
CAKE, Patrick
Pro-Am Murders
CALIN, Hal Jason
Rocks & Ruin = Payoff In Blood
CAMERON, Lou
Outsider
CAMP, Joe
Oh Heavenly Dog
CAMPBELL, Harriette R
String Glove Mystery
Porcelain Fish (Mystery)
Moor Fires Mystery
Three Names For Murder
Murder Set To Music
Magic Makes Murder
Crime In Crystal
CAMPBELL, Hazel
Olga Knaresbrook: Detective
CAMPBELL, Robert
In La-La Land We Trust
Alice In La-La Land
Plugged Nickel
Red Cent
CANNING, Victor
Venetian Bird = Bird Of Prey
Whip Hand
Doubled In Diamonds
Python Project
Melting Man
Fall From Grace
CANNON, Curt
I'm Cannon For Hire
I Like 'Em Tough
CARLO, Philip
Stolen Flower
CARLTON, Mitchell
Hot Oil
CARMICHAEL, Harry
Death Leaves A Diary
Vanishing Track
Deadly Night-Cap
School For Murder
Death Counts Three
    = Screaming Rabbit
Why Kill Johnny? >

Noose For A Lady
Money For Murder
Justice Enough
Dead Of Night
Emergency Exit
Put Out That Star = Into Thin Air
James Knowland, Deceased
Or Be He Dead
Stranglehold = Marked Man
Seeds Of Hate
Requiem For Charles= Late Unlamented
Alibi
Link
Of Unsound Mind
Vendetta
Flashback
Safe Secret
Post Mortem
Suicide Clause
Murder By Proxy
Remote Control
Death Trap
Most Deadly Hate
Quiet Woman
Naked To The Grave
Too Late For Tears
Candles For The Dead
Motive
False Evidence
Grave For Two
Life Cycle
CARR, Joseph B
Death Whispers
Man With Bated Breath
CARR, Kirby
Girls Who Came To Murder
Let Me Kill You Sweetheart!
Who Killed You, Cindy Castle?
You Die Next, Jill Baby!
You're Hired;You're Dead
Don't Bet On Living, Alice!
They're Coming To Kill You, Jane!
CARSON, Robert
Quality Of Mercy
CASSIDAY, Bruce
Brass Shroud
Buried Motive
While Murder Waits

CASTLE, Frank
Hawaiian Eye
CASTLE, Jayne
Desperate Game
Chilling Deception
CHABER, M.E
Hangman's Harvest = Don't Get Caught
No Grave For March = All Way Down
As Old As Cain = Take 1 For Murder
Man Inside = Now It's My Turn
Splintered Man
Lonely Walk
Gallows Garden = Lady Came To Kill
Hearse Of Another Color
So Dead The Rose
Jade For A Lady
Softly In The Night
Six Who Ran
Uneasy Lies The Dead
Wanted:Dead Men
Day It Rained Diamonds
Man In The Middle
Wild Midnight Falls
Flaming Man
Green Grow The Graves
Bonded Dead
Born To Be Hanged
CHAMBERS, Peter
Murder Is For Keeps
Big Goodbye
Wreath For A Redhead
Down-Beat Kill
Lady, This Is Murder
Dames Can Be Deadly
Nobody Lives Forever
This'll Kill You
Always Take The Big Ones
You're Better Off Dead
Don't Bother To Knock
No Gold When You Go
Bad Die Young
Blonde Wore Black
No Peace For The Wicked
Speak Ill Of The Dead
They Call It Murder
Somebody Has To Lose
Day Of The Big Dollar
Deader They Fall >

Deep Blue Cradle
Nothing Personal
Beautiful Golden Frame
Female - Handle With Care
Lady Who Never Was
Long Time Dead
Murder Is Its Own Reward
Highly Explosive Case
Moving Picture Writes
Vanishing Holes Murder
Dragons Can Be Dangerous
Jail Bait
CHAMBERS, Whitman
Dead Men Leave No Fingerprints
Dog Eat Dog = Murder In The Mist
CHANDLER, A Bertram
Bring Back Yesterday
CHANDLER, Raymond
Big Sleep
Farewell, My Lovely
High Window
Lady In The Lake
Five Murderers
Five Sinister Characters
Finger Man & Other Stories
Red Wind
Spanish Blood
Little Sister = Marlowe
Simple Art Of Murder = Trouble Is My
        Business + Pick-Up On Noon Street
        + Simple Art Of Murder
Long Goodbye
Smart Aleck Kill
Pearls Are A Nuisance
Playback
Raymond Chandler Speaking
Killer In The Rain
Smell Of Fear
Midnight Raymond Chandler
Unknown Thriller
CHANSLOR, Roy
Hazard
CHANSLOR, Torrey
Our First Murder
Our Second Murder
CHASE, Elaine Raco
Dangerous Places
Dark Corners

CHASE, James Hadley
No Orchids For Miss Blandish
  = Villain & Virgin
12 Chinks & Woman = 12 Chinamen &
  A Woman = Doll's Bad News
Double Shuffle
There's Always A Price Tag
Shock Treatment
Tell It To The Birds
You're Lonely When You're Dead
Figure It Out For Y'self=Marijuana Mob
Lay Her Among Lilies
  = Too Dangerous To Be Free
You Never Know With Women
Hit Them Where It Hurts
CHASTAIN, Thomas
Pandora's Box
Vital Statistics
High Voltage
CHESBRO, George
Shadow Of A Broken Man
City Of Whispering Stone
Affair Of Sorcerers
Beasts Of Valhalla
Two Songs This Archangel Sings
Cold Smell Of Sacred Stone
CHESTER, Peter
Killing Comes Easy
Murder Forestalled
CHETWYND, Bridget
Death Has 10,000 Doors
Rubies, Emeralds & Diamonds
CHEYNEY, Peter
Urgent Hangman
Dangerous Curves = Callaghan
You Can't Keep The Change
Mr Caution—Mr Callaghan
It Couldn't Matter Less
  = Set-Up For Murder
Sorry You've Been Troubled
  = Farewell To The Admiral
Unscrupulous Mr Callaghan
They Never Say When
Uneasy Terms
Calling Mr Callaghan
G Man At The Yard
You Can Call It A Day
  = Man Nobody Saw >

Lady, Behave! = Lady Beware
Dark Bahama = I'll Bring Her Back
1 Of Those Things = Mistress Murder
Dance Without Music
Try Anything Twice=Undressed To Kill
Another Little Drink = Trap For
  Bellamy = Premeditated Murder
CHRISTOPHER, Constance
Dead Man's Flower
CHUTE, Verne
Wayward Angel = Blackmail
CLAPPERTON, Richard
No News On Monday
  = You're A Long Time Dead
Sentimental Kill
CLARK, Dale
Red Rods = Blonde, Gangster & PI
CLAYFORD, James
Man Crazy = Passion Pulls The
  Trigger: A Wallace
CLINE, Edward
First Prize
COBB, Irvin S
Murder Day By Day
COBDEN, Guy
Murder Was My Neighbour
My Guess Was Murder
Murder Was Their Medicine
Murder For His Money
Murder For Her Birthday
Murder Inherited
CODY, Liza
Dupe
Bad Company
Stalker
Head Case
Under Contract
COE, Tucker
Kinds Of Love, Kinds Of Death
Murder Among Children
Wax Apple
Jade In Aries
Don't Lie To Me
COGGINS, Paul
Lady Is The Tiger
COHEN, Barney
Taking Of Satcon Station
Blood On The Moon

COHEN, Stephen Paul
Island Of Steel
COLE, G.D.H & Margaret
Mrs Warrender's Profession
Knife In The Dark
COLLINS, Max Allan
True Detective
True Crime
Million Dollar Wound
Neon Mirage
COLLINS, Max & BEATTY
Cold Dish
Files Of Ms Tree
Mike Mist Case Book
Ms Tree
COLLINS, Michael
Act Of Fear
Brass Rainbow
Night Of The Toads
Walk A Black Wind
Shadow Of A Tiger
Silent Scream
Blue Death
Blood-Red Dream
Nightrunners
Slasher
Freak
Minnesota Strip
Red Rosa
Castrato
COLTER, Eli
Gull Cove Murders
Cheer For The Dead
CONAWAY, Jim
Deadlier Than The Male
They Do It With Mirrors
CONTERIS, Hiber
Ten Percent Of Life
COOK, Bruce
Mexican Standoff
COOK, Glen
Sweet Silver Blues
Bitter Gold Hearts
Cold Copper Tears
COOK, Thomas H
Flesh & Blood
COOMBS, Murdo
Moment Of Need

COOPER, Will
Death Has 1000 Doors
COPPER, Basil
Dark Mirror
Night Frost
No Flowers For The General
Scratch On The Dark
Die Now, Live Later
Don't Bleed On Me
Marble Orchard
Dead File
No Letters From The Grave
Big Chill
Strong-Arm
Great Year For Dying
Shock-Wave
Breaking Point
Voice From The Dead
Feedback
Ricochet
High Wall
Impact
Good Place To Die
Lonely Place
Crack In The Sidewalk
Tight Corner
Year Of The Dragon
Death Squad
Murder One
Quiet Room In Hell
Big Rip-Off
Caligari Complex
Flip-Side
Long Rest
Empty Silence
Dark Entry
Hang Loose
Shoot-Out
Far Horizon
Trigger-Man
Pressure-Point
Hard Contract
Narrow Corner
Hook
You Only Die Once
Tuxedo Park
Far Side Of Fear
Snow Job >

Jet-Lag
Blood On The Moon
Heavy Iron
Turn Down An Empty Glass
Print-Out
House Dick
CORDER, Eric
Bite
CORMANY, Michael
Lost Daughter
Red Winter
CORRIGAN, Mark
Bullets & Brown Eyes
Sinner Takes All
Wayward Blonde
Golden Angel
Lovely Lady
Madame Sly
Shanghai Jezebel
Lady Of China Street
Baby Face
All Brides Are Beautiful
Sweet & Deadly
I Like Danger
Naked Lady
Love For Sale
Madam & Eve
Big Squeeze
Big Boys Don't Cry
Sydney For Sin
Cruel Lady
Dumb As They Come
Honolulu Snatch
Menace In Siam
Girl From Moscow
Singapore Downbeat
Sin Of Hong Kong
Lady From Tokyo
Riddle Of Double Island
Danger's Green Eyes
Why Do Women . . . ?
Riddle Of The Spanish Circle
CORRIS, Peter
Dying Trade
White Meat
Marvelous Boy
Empty Beach
Heroin Annie >

Make Me Rich
Winning Side
Big Drop
Deal Me Out
Greenwich Apartments
Cliff Hardy Collection
January Zone
COX, Irving E
Murder Among Friends
COX, William R
Hell To Pay
Murder In Vegas
Death On Location
COXE, George Harmon
Murder With Pictures
Barotique Mystery=Murdock's Acid Test
Camera Clue
(Four) Frightened Women
Glass Triangle
Mrs Murdock Takes A Case
Charred Witness
Jade Venus
Fifth Key
Hollow Needle
Lady Killer
Eye Witness
Widow Had A Gun
Crimson Clue
Focus On Murder
Murder On Their Minds
Big Gamble
Last Commandment
Hidden Key
Reluctant Heiress
Easy Way To Go
Murder For The Asking
Lady Is Afraid
Silent Are The Dead
Murder For Two
Flash Casey, Detective
Error Of Judgment= 1 Murder Too Many
Man Who Died Too Soon
Deadly Image
Alias The Dead
Frightened Fiancée
Impetuous Mistress
Fenner
Silent Witness
No Place For Murder

CRAIS, Robert
Monkey's Raincoat
Hagakure
CRANE, Frances
Turquoise Shop
Golden Box
Yellow Violet
Applegreen Cat
Pink Umbrella
Amethyst Spectacles
Indigo Necklace
Cinnamon Murder
Shocking Pink Hat
Murder On The Purple Water
Black Cypress
Flying Red Horse
Daffodil Blonde
Murder In Blue St = Death In Blue Hour
Polkadot Murder
Murder In Bright Red
13 White Tulips
Coral Princess Murders
Death In Lilac Time
Horror On The Ruby X
Ultraviolet Widow
Buttercup Case
Man In Gray = Gray Stranger
Death-Wish Green
Amber Eyes
CREIGHTON, John
Half Interest In Murder
Blonde Cried Murder
CRONIN, George
Answer From A Dead Man
Death Of A Delegate
CROSBY, Lee
Terror By Night
Too Many Doors = Doors To Death
CROWE, John
Crooked Shadows
CRUMLEY, James
Wrong Case
Dancing Bear
Last Good Kiss
CULLEN, Carter
Deadly Chase
CUNNINGHAM, E.V
Sylvia >

Lydia
Cynthia
DALE, William
Terror Of The Handless Corpse
DALY, Carroll John
Snarl Of The Beast
Hidden Hand
Tag Murders
Tainted Power
Third Murderer
Amateur Murderer
Murder From The East
Better Corpses
Adventures Of Race Williams
Man In The Shadows
Murder Won't Wait
Emperor Of Evil
DANIEL, Roland
Crawshay Jewel Mystery
Evil Shadows
Lady In Scarlet
Dead Man Sings
Murder At A Cottage
Arrow Of Death
Three Sundays To Live
Murder Gang
Man From Paris
Missing Body
Big Shot
Hangman Waits
Gangster's Daughter
Frightened Eyes
Kidnappers
Brunettes Are Dangerous
Red-Headed Dames & Murder
Women—Dope—And Murder
Murder In Ocean Drive
DATESH, John Nicholas
Janus Murders
DAVIS, Frederick C
Coffins For 3= One Murder Too Many
He Wouldn't Stay Dead
Poor, Poor Yorick
    = Murder Doesn't Always Out
Graveyard Never Closes
Let The Skeletons Rattle
Detour To Oblivion
Thursday's Blade >

Gone Tomorrow
Deadly Miss Ashley
Lilies In Her Garden Grew
Tread Lightly, Angel
Drag The Dark
Another Morgue Heard From
    = Deadly Bedfellows
Night Drop
DAVIS, Gordon
House Dick
    = Washington Payoff: HUNT
DAVIS, Kenn
Dark Side
Forza Trap
Words Can Kill
Melting Point
Nijinsky Is Dead
As October Dies
DAVIS, Means
Chess Murders
DAVIS, Norbert
Mouse In Mountain = Dead Little Rich
    Girl = Rendezvous With Fear
Sally's In The Alley
Oh, Murderer Mine
Adventures Of Max Latin
DAVIS, Tech
Terror On Compass Lake
Full Fare For A Corpse
Murder On Alternate Tuesdays
DEAN, Robert George
What Gentleman Strangles A Lady?
Three Lights Went Out
Sutton Place Murders
Murder On Margin
Murder Makes Merry Widow
Murder Of Convenience
Murder Through The Looking Glass
Murder By Marriage
Murder In Mink
On Ice
Layoff
Body Was Quite Cold
Case Of Joshua Locke
Affair (Death) At Lover's Leap
DEAN, Spencer
Frightened Fingers
Scent (Smell) Of Fear >

Marked Down For Murder
Murder On Delivery
Dishonor Among Thieves
Merchant Of Murder
Price Tag For Murder
Murder After A Fashion
Credit For Murder
DeANDREA, William L
Killed In The Ratings
Killed In The Act
Killed With A Passion
Killed On The Ice
Killed In Paradise
HOG Murders
DEKKER, Carl
Woman In Marble
DEKKER, Johnny
Dolls & Dollars
Siamese Cat
Singapore Set-Up
Hex Marks The Spot
Manhunt In Manhattan
Streetcar To Hell
DELANCEY, Roger
Murder Below Wall Street
DeMARCO, Gordon
October Heat
Canvas Prison
Frisco Blues
Murder At The Fringe
DEMARIS, Ovid
Gold-Plated Sewer
DEMING, Richard
Gallows In My Garden
Tweak Devil's Nose
    =Hand-Picked To Die
Whistle Past Graveyard= Give Girl Gun
Juvenile Delinquent
Hit & Run
DENBOW, Richard
Chandler
DENNIS, Ralph
Atlanta Deathwatch
Charleston Knife's Back In Town
Down Among The Jocks
Golden Girl & All
Pimp For The Dead
Murder's Not An Odd Job >

Working For The Man
Deadly Cotton Heart
Hump's First Case
One-Dollar Rip-Off
Last Of Armageddon Wars
Buy Back Blues
DENVER, Paul
Golden Bullet
Falling Blonde
DE PUY, E Spence
Long Knife
Hospital Homicides
DESMOND, Hugh
Hand Of Vengeance
Viper's Sting
Death Walks In Scarlet
Clear Case Of Murder
Calling Alan Fraser
Pact With The Devil
Deliver Us From Evil
Night Of The Crime
Death Parade
Destination—Death
She Met Murder
Appointment At Eight
Lady, Where Are You?
Poison Pen
Doorway To Death
In Fear Of The Night
CoT Blue Orchid
Fanfare For Murder
Stay Of Execution
Bodies In A Cupboard
Silent Witness
Slight Case Of Murder
Condemned
Hostage To Death
Someday I'll Kill You
Dark Shadow
Murder Strikes At Dawn
Not Guilty, My Lord
Lady Has Claws
Murder On The Moor
Horror At The Moated Mill
Mask Of Terror
We Walk With Death
DEWEY, Thomas B
Draw Curtain Close = Dame In Danger⟩

Prey For Me = CoT Murdered Model
Mean Streets
Brave, Bad Girls
You've Got Him Cold
CoT Chased & Unchaste
Girl Who Wasn't There
    = Girl Who Never Was
How Hard To Kill
Sad Song Singing
Don't Cry For Long
Portrait Of A Dead Heiress
Deadline
Death & Taxes
King-Killers = Death Turns Right
Love-Death Thing
Taurus Trip
And Where She Stops = IOU Murder
Go To Sleep Jeannie
Too Hot For Hawaii
Golden Hooligan = Mexican Slayride
Go, Honeylou
Girl With Sweet Plump Knees
Girl In The Punchbowl
Only On Tuesdays
Nude In Nevada
DE WITT, Jack
Murder On Shark Island
DiCHIARA, Robert
Hard-Boiled
DICK, Philip K
Do Androids Dream Of Electric Sheep?
    = Blade Runner
DICKENSON, Fred
Kill 'Em With Kindness
DICKINSON, Weed
Dead Man Talks Too Much
DICKSON, Arthur
Death Bids For Corners
DIETRICH, Robert
Murder On The Rocks
House On Q Street
End Of A Stripper
Mistress To Murder
Murder On Her Mind
Angel Eyes
Curtains For A Lover
Steve Bentley's Calypso Caper
My Body = as **HUNT**

DILLON, Walter
Deadly Intrusion
DISNEY, Doris Miles
Dark Road = Dead Stop
(CoT) Straw Man
Trick Or Treat = Halloween Murder
Method In Madness = Quiet Violence
    = Too Innocent To Kill
Did She Fall Or Was She Pushed?
Find The Woman
Chandler Policy
Here Lies
DOBSON, Margaret
Soothsayer
DOBYNS, Stephen
Saratoga Swimmer
Saratoga Headhunter
Saratoga Longshot
Saratoga Snapper
Saratoga Bestiary
DODGE, David
Death & Taxes
Shear The Black Sheep
Bullets For The Bridegroom
It Ain't Hay = Drug On Market
Long Escape
Plunder Of The Sun
Red Tassel
DOLD, Gaylord
Hot Summer, Cold Murder
Snake Eyes
Cold Cash
Bonepile
DOUGLAS, John
Blind Spring Rambler
DOUGLAS, Malcolm
Deadly Dames
DOWNING, Warwick
Player
Gambler, Minstrel & Dance Hall Queen
DOYLE, James T
Deadly Resurrection
Epitaph For A Loser
DOZOIS & EFFINGER
Nightmare Blue
DREW, Bernard (ed)
Hard-Boiled Dames
DUFF, James >

Some Die Young
Who Dies There?
DUNCAN, W Glenn
Rafferty's Rules
Rafferty:Last Seen Alive
Rafferty:Poor Dead Cricket
DUNDEE, Robert
Pandora's Box
DUNDEE, Wayne D
Burning Season
DUNNE, Colin
Ratcatcher
Hooligan
EARLY, Jack
Creative Kind Of Killer
EASTON, Nat
Always The Wolf
One Good Turn
Bill For Damages
Mistake Me Not
Book For Banning
Quick Tempo
Right For Trouble
Forgive Me, Lovely Lady
EBY, Lois & FLEMING
CoT Malevolent (Wicked) Twin
Hell Hath No Fury
EDGELEY, Leslie
Fear No More
EDWARDS, Alexander
Black Bird
EFFINGER, George Alec
When Gravity Fails
ELLIN, Stanley
Eighth Circle
Bind = Man From Nowhere
Star Light, Star Bright
Dark Fantastic
ELLINGTON, Richard
Shoot The Works
It's A Crime
Stone Cold Dead
Exit For A Dame
Just Killing Time = Shakedown
ELLIOTT, David
Blue Movie
ELLROY, James
Brown's Requiem

EMERSON, Earl W
Rainy City
Poverty Bay
Nervous Laughter
Fat Tuesday
Deviant Behaviour
ENEFER, Douglas
Deadly Quiet
Long Chance
Dark Kiss
Shining Trap
Painted Death
Long Hot Night
Girl Chase
Girl In Arms
Gilded Kiss
Farewell, Little Sister
Shoot-Out
ENGEL, Howard
Suicide Murders
Ransom Game
Murder On Location
Murder Sees The Light
City Called July
Victim Must Be Found
ENGLEMAN, Paul
Dead In Center Field
Catch A Fallen Angel
Murder-In-Law
ERNST, Paul
Bronze Mermaid
ESTLEMAN, Loren D
Motor City Blue
Angel Eyes
Midnight Man
Glass Highway
Sugartown
Every Brilliant Eye
Lady Yesterday
Downriver
General Murders
ESTOW, Daniel
Moment Of Fiction
Moment Of Silence
ETHAN, John B
Black Gold Murders
Call Girls For Murder
Murder On Wall Street

EVANS, John
Halo In Blood = as BROWNE
Halo For Satan
Halo In Brass = as BROWNE
EVERSON, David
Recount
EVERSZ, Robert
Bottom Line Is Murder
FAIR, A.A
Bigger They Come
 = Lam To The Slaughter
Turn On The Heat
Gold Comes In Bricks
Spill The Jackpot
Double Or Quits
Owls Don't Blink
Bats Fly At Dusk
Cats Prowl At Night
Give 'Em Axe = Axe To Grind
Crows Can't Count
Fools Die On Friday
Bedrooms Have Windows
Top Of The Heap
Some Women Won't Wait
Beware The Curves
You Can Die Laughing
Some Slips Don't Show
Count Of Nine
Pass The Gravy
Kept Women Can't Quit
Bachelors Get Lonely
Shills Can't Cash Chips
 = Stop At Red Light
Try Anything Once
Fish Or Cut Bait
Up For Grabs
Cut Thin To Win
Widows Wear Weeds
Traps Need Fresh Bait
All Grass Isn't Green
FAIRLIE, Gerard
Winner Take All
No Sleep For Macall
Deadline For Macall
Double The Bluff
Macall Gets Curious
Please Kill My Cousin
FAIRMAN, Paul
Glass Ladder

FANTONI, Barry
Mike Dime
Stickman
FARJEON, J Jefferson
Judge Sums Up
FARREN, Mick
Long Orbit
FEIFFER, Jules
Ackroyd
FENADY, Andrew
Man With Bogart's Face
Secret Of Sam Marlow
FERGUSON, W.B.M
Escape To Eternity
Shayne Case
FICKLING, G.G
This Girl For Hire
Gun For Honey
Girl On The Loose
Honey In The Flesh
Girl On The Prowl
Kiss For A Killer
Dig A Dead Doll
Blood & Honey
Bombshell
Stiff As A Broad
Honey On Her Tail
Naughty But Dead
CoT Radioactive Redhead
Crazy Mixed-Up Nude
FIELDING, A
Murder In Suffolk
FINE, Peter
Troubled Waters
FISCHER, Bruno
Dead Men Grin
More Deaths Than One
Restless Hands
Angels Fell = Flesh Was Cold
Silent Dust
Paper Circle = Stripped For Murder
FISHER, Steve
Winter Kill
FLEMING, Robert
Night Freight Murders
    = Bullet In His Cap
    = Death Comes To Dinner
    = And Death Drove On

FLYNN, Jay/J.M
Bannerman
Border Incident
Terror Tournament
SurfSide 6
FOOTE-SMITH, Elizabeth
Gentle Albatross
Never Say Die
FORD, Leslie
Strangled Witness
Ill Met By Moonlight
Simple Way Of Poison
Reno Rendezvous
    = Mr Cromwell Is Dead
False To Any Man
    =Snow-White Murder
Old Lover's Ghost
Murder Of 5th Columnist
    = Capital Crime
Murder In OPM = Priority Murder
Siren In The Night
All For Love Of Lady = Crack Of Dawn
Philadelphia Murder
Honolulu (Murder) Story
    = Honolulu Murders
Woman In Black
Devil's Stronghold
Washington Whispers Murder
    = Lying Jade
Three Bright Pebbles
FORWARD, Robert
Owl
FOSTER, Richard
Bier For A Chaser
Too Late For Mourning
FOX, James M
Lady Regrets
Death Commits Bigamy
Inconvenient Bride
Gentle Hangman
Wheel Is Fixed
Aleutian Blue Mink = Fatal In Furs
Iron Virgin
Scarlet Slippers
Shroud For Mr Bundy
Bright Serpent = Rites For A Killer
FOXX, Jack
Freebooty

FRANCIS, Dick
Odds Against
Whip Hand
FRANCIS, William
Rough On Rats = IOU Murder
Kill Or Cure
Bury Me Not
Don't Dig Deeper
FRANKLIN, Eugene
Murder Trapp
Money Murders
Bold House Murders
FRANKLIN, Max
Angels In Chains
Angels On A String
Charlie's Angels
Killing Kind
Angels On Ice
Vega$
FRAY, Al
Dame's The Game
FRAZER, Andrew
Find Eileen Hardin—Alive
Fall Of Marty Moon
FRAZER, Robert Caine
Mark Kilby Solves Murder = RISC
    = Timid Tycoon
(Mark Kilby &) Miami Mob
(Mark Kilby &) Secret Syndicate
Hollywood Hoax
Mark Kilby Takes A Risk
Mark Kilby Stands Alone
    = Mark Kilby & Manhattan Murders
FREDMAN, John
Fourth Agency
False Joanna
Epitaph To A Bad Cop
FREDMAN, Mike
You Can Always Blame The Rain
Kisses Leave No Fingerprints
FREEMAN, Martin J
CoT Blind Mouse
Scarf On The Scarecrow
FREY, James N
Long Way To Die
Killing In Dreamland
FRIEND, Ed
Corpse In Castle

FRY, Pete
Long Overcoat
Scarlet Cloak
Grey Sombrero
Black Beret
Purple Dressing Gown
Green Scarf
Red Stockings
Yellow Trousers
Thick Blue Sweater
Paint-Stained Flannels
Bright Green Waistcoat
Orange Necktie
Brown Suede Jacket
White Crash Helmet
Black Cotton Gloves
FULLER, Samuel
Dead Pigeon On Beethoven Street
FURST, Richard
Your Day In The Barrel
Paris Drop
Caribbean Account
GAGE, Edwin
Phoenix No More
GAINES, Audrey
Old Must Die
While The Wind Howled
Voodoo Goat
GAIR, Malcolm
Sapphires On Wednesday
Long Hard Look
Burning Of Troy
Bad Dream
Schultz Money
Snow Job
GALLAGHER, Gale
I Found Him Dead
Chord In Crimson
GALLAGHER, Richard
Murder By Gemini
Stewardess Strangler
One-Armed Murder
GALLISON, Kate
Unbalanced Accounts
Death Tape
GALLOWAY, David
Lamaar Ransom, Private Eye

GARRETT, Robert
Run Down
Spiral
GARRISON, Christian
Paragon Man
GARRITY, Dave J
Dragon Hunt
GAT, Dimitri
Nevsky's Return
Nevsky's Demon
GAULT, William Campbell
Ring Around Rosa = Murder In Raw
Day Of The Ram
Convertible Hearse
Come Die With Me
Vein Of Violence
County Kill
Dead Hero
Bad Samaritan
Cana Diversion
Death In Donegal Bay
Dead Seed
Chicano War
Cat & Mouse
End Of Call Girl = Don't Call Tonight
Night Lady
Sweet Wild Wench
Wayward Widow
Million Dollar Tramp
Hundred-Dollar Girl
GELLER, Michael
Heroes Also Die
Major League Murder
GEORGE, Peter
Come Blonde, Come Murder
GIBSON, William
Count Zero
GILBERT, Dale L
Black Star Murders
Mother Murders
GILES, Guy Elwyn
Three Died Variously
Target For Murder
GILES, Raymond
Shamus
GILLIGAN, Roy
Chinese Restaurants Never Serve
    Breakfast

GILLIS, Jackson Clark
Killers Of Starfish
Chain Saw
GLAZNER, Joseph Mark
Smart Money Doesn't Sing Or Dance
Fast Money Shoots From The Hip
Dirty Money Can't Wash Both Hands
    At Once
Big Apple Money Is Rotten To The Core
Hot Money Can Cook Your Goose
GLICK, Carl
Death Sits In
GOLDMAN, Lawrence
Fall Guy For Murder
Tiger By The Tail
GOLDSBOROUGH, Robert
Murder In E Minor
Death On Deadline
Bloodied Ivy
GORDON, Russell
Dead Level = She Posed For Murder
GORES, Joe
Dead Skip
Final Notice
Gone, No Forwarding
Interface
Hammett
GORMAN, Ed
Murder Straight Up
New Improved Murder
Murder In The Wings
Autumn Dead
(ed) Black Lizard Anthology of Crime
    Fiction
(ed) 2nd Black Lizard Anthology Of
    Crime Fiction
GOTTLIEB, Nathan
Stinger
GOULART, Ron
After Things Fell Apart
Ghost Breaker
If Dying Was All
Too Sweet To Die
Same Lie Twice
One Grave Too Many
Odd Job #101
Calling Dr Patchwork
Hail Hibbler >

Big Bang
Brainz, Inc.
Enormous Hour Glass
Suicide, Inc.
Daredevils Ltd.
Wisemann Originals
(ed) Hardboiled Dicks
GRAAF, Peter
Dust & Curious Boy
    = Give Devil His Due
Daughter Fair
Sapphire Conference
GRADY, James
Runner On The Streets
Hard Bargains
GRAFTON, Sue
A Is For Alibi
B Is For Burglar
C Is For Corpse
D Is For Deadbeat
E Is For Evidence
F Is For Fugitive
GRAHAM, Anthony
No Sale For Halos
GRAHAM, Neill
Play It Solo
Murder Makes A Date
Say It With Murder
You Can't Call It Murder
Salute To Murder
Hit Me Hard
Murder Rings A Bell
Killers Are On Velvet
Murder Is My Weakness
Murder On The 'Duchess'
Make Mine Murder
Label It Murder
Graft Town
Murder Makes It Certain
Murder Made Easy
Murder Of A Black Cat
Murder On My Hands
Murder Always Final
Money For Murder
Murder On Demand
Murder Makes The News
Murder Has Been Done
Pay Off >

Candidates For A Coffin
Death Of A Canary
Murder Lies In Waiting
Blood On The Pavement
One For The Book
Matter For Murder
Murder, Double Murder
Frame-Up
Cop In A Tight Frame
Murder In A Dark Room
Assignment, Murder
Murder On The List
Search For A Missing Lady
Motive For Murder
GRANT, Ben
Alice Dies Twice
GRANT, James Edward
Green Shadow
GRANT, Linda
Random Access Murder
GREENLEAF, Stephen
Grave Error
Death Bed
State's Evidence
Fatal Obsession
Beyond Blame
Toll Free
GREGORICH, Barbara
Dirty Proof
GREX, Leo
Man From Manhattan
GRIBBLE, Leonard
Stand-In For Murder
GROSSBACH, Robert
Cheap Detective
GRUBER, Frank
French Key (Mystery)
    = Once Over Deadly
Laughing Fox
Hungry Dog (Murders) = Die Like A Dog
Navy Colt
Talking Clock
Gift Horse
Mighty Blockhead
    = Corpse Moved Upstairs
Silver Tombstone (Mystery)
Honest Dealer
Whispering Master >

Scarlet Feather = Gamecock Murders
Leather Duke = Job Of Murder
Limping Goose = Murder One
Simon Lash, (Private) Detective
Buffalo Box
Murder '97 = Long Arm Of Murder
Swing Low, Swing Dead
Silver Jackass = as BOSTON
Beagle Scented Murder
   = Market For Murder
Lonesome Badge = Mood For Murder
Twenty Plus Two
Yellow Overcoat (as ACRE)
   = Fall Guy For A Killer
Gold Gap
Etruscan Bull
GUNN, James
Magicians
GUTHRIE, Al
Private Murder
GUY, David
Man Who Loved Dirty Books
HAIBLUM, Isidore
Murder In Yiddish
HALL, Parnell
Detective
Murder
Favor
HALLAHAN, William H
Ross Forgery
HALLERAN, Tucker
Cool, Clear Death
Sudden Death Finish
HALLIDAY, Brett
Dividend On Death
Private Practice Of Michael Shayne
Uncomplaining Corpses
Tickets For Death
Bodies Are Where You Find Them
Michael Shayne Takes Over
Corpse Came Calling
   = CoT Walking Corpse
Murder Wears A Mummer'sMask
   = In A Deadly Vein
Blood On Black Market
   = Heads You Lose
Michael Shayne Investigates
Michael Shayne Takes A Hand >

Michael Shayne's Long Chance
Murder & The Married Virgin
Murder Is My Business
Marked For Murder
Dead Man's Diary/Dinner At Dupré's
Blood On Biscayne Bay
Counterfeit Wife
Blood On Stars = Murder Is A Habit
Michael Shayne's Triple Mystery
Taste For Violence
Call For Michael Shayne
This Is It, Michael Shayne
Framed In Blood
When Dorinda Dances
What Really Happened
One Night With Nora
   = Lady Came By Night
She Woke To Darkness
Death Has Three Lives
Stranger In Town
Blonde Cried Murder
Weep For A Blonde
Shoot The Works
Murder & Wanton Bride
Fit To Kill
Date With A Dead Man
Die Like A Dog
Target: Mike Shayne
Dolls Are Deadly
Homicidal Virgin
Murder Takes No Holiday
Careless Corpse
Killers From The Keys
Murder In Haste
Murder By Proxy
Never Kill A Client
Pay Off In Blood
Body Came Back
Corpse That Never Was
Too Friendly, Too Dead
Michael Shayne's 50th Case
Redhead For Mike Shayne
Shoot To Kill
Nice Fillies Finish Last
Violent World Of Mike Shayne
Armed . . . Dangerous . . .
Murder Spins The Wheel
Guilty As Hell
Mermaid On The Rocks >

So Lush, So Deadly
Violence Is Golden
Lady Be Bad
Fourth Down To Death
Six Seconds To Kill
Count Backwards To Zero
I Came To Kill You
Caught Dead
Blue Murder
Kill All The Young Girls
At The Point Of A .38
Last Seen Hitchhiking
Million Dollar Handle
HAMILL, Pete
Dirty Laundry
Deadly Piece
Guns Of Heaven
HAMMETT, Dashiell
Red Harvest
Dain Curse
$106, 000 Blood Money = Blood
    Money = Big Knockover
Continental Op
Return Of The Continental Op
Hammett Homicides
Dead Yellow Woman
Nightmare Town
Creeping Siamese
Dashiell Hammett Omnibus
Woman In The Dark
Big Knockover = Hammett Story
Omnibus = Big Knockover +
    Continental Op
Continental Op
Maltese Falcon
Adventures Of Sam Spade
    = They Can Only Hang You Once
    = Man Called Spade
Thin Man
Man Named Thin
HAMMOND, Gerald
Fred In Situ
Loose Screw
Mud In His Eye
Dead Game
Reward Game
Revenge Game
Fair Game >

Game
Cousin Once Removed
Sauce For The Pigeon
Pursuit Of Arms
Silver City Scandal
Executor
Worried Widow
Adverse Report
Stray Shot
HANSEN, Joseph
Fadeout
Death Claims
Troublemaker
Man Everybody Was Afraid Of
Skinflick
Gravedigger
Nightwork
Brandstetter & Others
Little Dog Laughed
Early Graves
Obedience
HANSEN, Vern
Whisper Of Death
HARPER, David
Hanged Men
HARRIS, Timothy
Kyd For Hire
Goodnight & Goodbye
HARRISON, Chip
Make Out With Murder
    = Five Little Rich Girls: BLOCK
Topless Tulip Caper = as BLOCK
HAYES, William Edward
Black Doll
Before The Cock Crowed
Black Chronicle
HAYS, Lee
Harry-O
Harry-O #2 = High Cost Of Living
HAYWOOD, Gar Anthony
Fear Of The Dark
HEALY, Jeremiah
Blunt Darts
Staked Goat = Tethered Goat
So Like Sleep
Swan Dive
HEARN, Daniel
Bad August

HEATH, Eric
Death Takes A Dive
Murder In The Museum
HEBERDEN, M.V
Death On The Doormat
Fugitive From Murder
Subscription To Murder
Aces, Eights & Murder
Lobster Pick Murder
Murder Follows Desmond Shannon
Murder Makes A Racket
Murder Goes Astray
Murder Of A Stuffed Shirt
Vicious Pattern
Drinks On The Victim
They Can't All Be Guilty
CoT Eight Brothers
Exit This Way
     = You'll Fry Tomorrow
That's The Spirit = Ghosts Can't Kill
Tragic Target
Murder Unlimited
Murder Cancels All Debts
Engaged To Murder
HELGERSON, Joel
Slow Burn
HELSETH, Henry Edward
Brothers Brannigan
HERBER, William
King-Sized Murder = Some Die Slow
Live Bait For Murder
HERSHMAN, Morris
Guilty Witness
HEYES, Douglas
Kiss-Off = Goodbye Stranger
12th Of Never
Kill
HEYMAN, Evan Lee
Miami Undercover
HIAASEN, Carl
Tourist Season
Double Whammy
HILARY, Richard
Snake In The Grasses
Pieces Of Cream
Pillow Of The Community
HIMMEL, Richard
Chinese Keyhole >

I Have Gloria Kirby
Two Deaths Must Die
Cry Of Flesh = Name's Maguire
I'll Find You = It's Murder, Maguire
Rich & The Damned
HINKLE, Vernon
Murder After A Fashion
HIRSCHFELD, Burt
Verdugo Affair
HITCHENS, Bert & Dolores
FOB Murder
One-Way Ticket
End Of The Line
Man Who Followed Women
Grudge
HITCHENS, Dolores
Sleep With Strangers
Sleep With Slander
HJORTSBERG, William
Falling Angel
HOBSON, Hank
Gallant Affair
Death Makes A Claim
Big Twist
Mission House Murder
Beyond Tolerance
HOCH, Edward D
Shattered Raven
HODGES, Carl G
Murder By The Pack
HOLDEN, Genevieve
Deadlier Than The Male
HOLT, Deben
Circle Of Shadows
HOLT, Gavin
Theme Is Murder
Swing It, Death
Give A Man Rope
Green For Danger
Ladies In Ermine
Begonia Walk = Send No Flowers
HOMES, Geoffrey
Man Who Murdered Himself
Then There Were Three
No Hands On The Clock
Finders Keepers
Forty Whacks
     = Stiffs Don't Vote >

Six Silver Handles
= CoT Unhappy Angels
Build My Gallows High
HOPKINS, A.T
Have A Lovely Funeral
HOPPENSTAND & BROWNE (eds)
Defective Detective In The Pulps
HOPPENSTAND et al (eds)
More Tales Of Defective Detective
HORNIG, Doug
Foul Shot
Hardball
Dark Side
Deep Dive
HOWARD, Hartley
Last Appointment
Last Deception
Last Vanity
Death Of Cecilia
Other Side Of The Door
Bowman Strikes Again
Bowman On Broadway
Bowman At A Venture
Sleep For The Wicked
No Target For Bowman
Bowman Touch
Hearse For Cinderella
Long Night
Key To The Morgue
Big Snatch
Sleep, My Pretty One
Deadline
Armitage Secret
Fall Guy
Extortion
Time Bomb
I'm No Hero
Count Down
Portrait Of A Beautiful Harlot
Routine Investigation
Secret Of Simon Cornell
Cry On My Shoulder
Room 37
Million Dollar Snapshot
Murder One
Epitaph For Joanna
Nice Day For A Funeral
Highway To Murder >

Dead Drunk
Treble Cross
Payoff
One-Way Ticket
Sealed Envelope
HOWIE, Edith
Murder For Xmas
Cry Murder
HOYT, Richard
Decoys
30 For A Harry
Siskiyou Two-Step
Siskiyou
Fish Story
HUGGINS, Roy
Double Take
77 Sunset Strip
Too Late For Tears
HUGHART, Barry
Bridge Of Birds
Story Of The Stone
HUGO, Richard
Death & The Good Life
HUME, David
Bullets Bite Deep
Crime Unlimited
Murders Form Fours
= Foursquare Murders
Below The Belt
They Called Him Death
Too Dangerous To Live
Dangerous Mr Dell
Gaol (Jail) Gates Are Open
Bring 'Em Back Dead
Meet The Dragon
Cemetery First Stop!
Halfway To Horror
Corpses Never Argue
Goodbye To Life
Death Before Honour
Heads You Live
Make Way For The Mourners
Eternity, Here I Come!
Return Of Mike Cardby
Destiny Is My Name
Dishonour Among Thieves
Get Out Of The Cuffs
Mike Cardby Works Overtime >

Toast To A Corpse
Come Back For The Body
They Never Came Back
Heading For A Wreath
HUNT, E Howard
Washington Payoff
    = House Dick: **DAVIS**
HUNTER, John
Three Die At Midnight
HURLEY, Gene
Have You Seen This Man?
HUSTON, Fran
Rich Get It All
IRVINE, Robert R
Baptism For The Dead
ISRAEL, Peter
Hush Money
French Kiss
Stiff Upper Lip
I'll Cry When I Kill You
If I Should Die Before I Die
JACKS, Jeff
Murder On The Wild Side
Find The Don's Daughter
JAEDIKER, Kermit
Tall, Dark & Dead
JAFFE, Michael
Death Goes To A Party
JAHN, Mike
Unfortunate Replacement
Deadliest Game
Switch
Switch #2
JAKES, John
Johnny Havoc
Johnny Havoc Meets Zelda
Johnny Havoc & Doll Who Had It
JAMES, P.D
Unsuitable Job For A Woman
Skull Beneath The Skin
JEFFERS, H Paul
Rubout At The Onyx Club
Murder On Mike
Rag Doll Murder
JENKINS, Will F
Man Who Feared
JERINA, Carol
Tall Dark Alibi >

Sweet Jeopardy
JEROME, Oscar Fox
Corpse Awaits =Night At Club Baghdad
JOHNSON, Philip
Hung Until Dead
JOHNSTON, William
Banyon
My Friend Tony
JONES, James
Touch Of Danger
KAMINSKY, Stuart M
Bullet For A Star
Murder On Yellow Brick Road
You Bet Your Life
Howard Hughes Affair
Never Cross A Vampire
High Midnight
Catch A Falling Clown
He Done Her Wrong
Fala Factor
Down For The Count
Man Who Shot Lewis Vance
Smart Moves
Think Fast, Mr Peters
Buried Caesars
KANE, Frank
About Face = Death About Face
    = Fatal Foursome
Green Light For Death
Slay Ride
Bullet Proof
Dead Weight
Bare Trap
Poisons Unknown
Grave Danger
Red Hot Ice
Real Gone Guy
Johnny Liddell's Morgue
Living End
Trigger Mortis
Short Bier
Time To Prey
Due Or Die
Mourning After
Stacked Deck
Crime Of Their Life
Dead Rite
Ring-A-Ding-Ding >

Johnny Come Lately
Hearse Class Male
Barely Seen
Final Curtain
Fatal Undertaking
Guilt-Edged Frame
Esprit De Corpse
Two To Tangle
Maid In Paris
Margin For Terror
KANE, Henry
Halo For Nobody = Martinis & Murder
Armchair In Hell
Report For A Corpse
   = Murder Of Park Avenue Playgirl
Hang By Your Neck
Corpse For Xmas = Deadly Doll
   = Homicide At Yuletide
Until You Are Dead
My Business Is Murder
Trinity In Violence
Trilogy In Jeopardy
Too French & Too Deadly
   = Narrowing Lust
CoT Murdered Madame
   = Triple Terror
Who Killed Sweet Sue? = Sweet Charlie
Death On The Double
Name Is Chambers
Fistful Of Death = Dangling Man
Death Is Last Lover
   = Nirvana Can Also Mean Death
Death Of A Flack
Dead In Bed
Death Of A Hooker
Kisses Of Death = Killer's Kiss
Death Of A Dastard
Never Give A Millionaire An Even
   Break = Murder For Millions
Nobody Loves A Loser
Snatch An Eye
Devil To Pay = Unholy Trio
   = Better Wed Than Dead
Don't Call Me Madame
Shack Job
Bomb Job
Don't Go Away Dead
Kiss! Kiss! Kill! Kill! >

Glow Job
Tail Job
Come Kill With Me
Escort Job
Kill For The Millions
Private Eyeful
Peter Gunn
Midnight Man
   = Other Sins Only Speak
Conceal & Disguise
Laughter In The Alehouse
KANTNER, Rob
Back Door Man
Harder They Hit
Dirty Work
KAPLAN, Arthur
Killing For Charity
KARLINS & ANDREWS
Gomorrah
KATZ, Michael J
Murder Off The Glass
Last Dance In Redondo Beach
KAUFMAN, Wolfe
I Hate Blondes
KAVANAGH, Dan
Duffy
Fiddle City
Putting The Boot In
Going To The Dogs
KAYE, Marvin
Lively Game Of Death
Grand Ole Opry Murders
Laurel & Hardy Murders
Bullets For Macbeth
Soap Opera Slaughters
KAYE, William
Wrong Target
KEATING, Henry
Murder By Death
KEENE, Day
Dead In Bed
Payola
KEITH, Carlton
Diamond-Studded Typewriter
   = Gem Of A Murder
Missing, Presumed Dead
Rich Uncle
Crayfish Dinner = Elusive Epicure
Taste Of Sangria= Missing Bookkeeper

Puzzle In Petticoats
KRAFT, Gabrielle
Bullshot
Screwdriver
KRUGER, Paul
Bullet For A Blonde
Weep For Willow Green
Weave A Wicked Web
If The Shroud Fits
Bronze Claws
Cold Ones
KYLE, Robert
Blackmail, Inc.
Model For Murder
Kill Now, Pay Later
Some Like It Cool
Ben Gates Is Hot
LA FRANCE, Marston
Miami Murder-Go-Round
LACY, Ed
Strip For Violence
Best That Ever Did It = Visa To Death
Men From The Boys
Room To Swing
Moment Of Untruth
Sin In Their Blood = Passport To Death
Bugged For Murder
LAMB, J.J
Nickel Jackpot
Chinese Straight
Losers Take All
LAND, Myrick
Search (The Dark Woods)
LANDON, Christopher
Stone Cold Dead In The Market
Shadow Of Time = Unseen Enemy
LANG, Brad
Crockett On The Loose
Brand Of Fear
Perdition Express
LARIAR, Lawrence
Friday Is For Death
You Can't Catch Me
Death Is Confidential
LARSEN, Gaylord
Paramount Kill
LARSON, Russell W
Death Stalks A Marriage

LATHAM, Brad
Gilded Canary
Sight Unseen
Hate Is Thicker Than Blood
Death Of Lorenzo Jones
Corpses In The Cellar
LATIMER, Jonathan
Murder In The Madhouse
Headed For A Hearse = Westland Case
Lady In The Morgue
Dead Don't Care
Red Gardenias
  = Some Dames Are Deadly
Solomon's Vineyard = Fifth Grave
LAUMER, Keith
Deadfall = Fat Chance
LAUNAY, Droo
She Modelled Her Coffin
New Shining White Murder
Corpse In Camera
Death & Still Life
Two-Way Mirror
Scream
LAURENCE, Gerald
One Bang-Up Job
LAW, Janice
Shadow Of The Palms
Death Under Par
LAWRENCE, Hilda
Blood Upon The Snow
Time To Die
Death Of A Doll
LAWRENCE, James D
Dream Girl Caper
Emerald Oil Caper
Gilded Snatch Caper
Godmother Caper
LAWRENCE, Kelly
Gone Shots
LEE, Austin
Sheep's Clothing
Call In Miss Hogg
Miss Hogg & Bronte Murder
Miss Hogg & Squash Club Murder
Miss Hogg & The Dead Dean
Miss Hogg Flies High
Miss Hogg & Covent Garden
  Murders >

Miss Hogg & Missing Sisters
Miss Hogg's Last Case
LEE, Babs
Model Is Murdered
Passport To Oblivion
Measured For Murder
LEE, Edward
Needle's Eye
Fish For Murder
= Death Goes Fishing
= Lust To Kill
LEITFRED, Robert H
Corpse That Spoke
Man Who Was Murdered Twice
Death Cancels The Evidence
= Murder Is My Racket
LEONARD, Charles L
Stolen Squadron
Deadline For Destruction
Fanatic Of Fez = Assignment To Death
Secret Of The Spa
Expert In Murder
Pursuit In Peru
Search For A Scientist
Fourth Funeral
Sinister Shelter
Secrets For Sale
Treachery In Trieste
LEONARD, Elmore
Unknown Man #89
Cat Chaser
LEWIN, Michael Z
Ask The Right Question
Way We Die Now
Enemies Within
Night Cover
Missing Woman
Silent Salesman
Out Of Season = Out Of Time
And Baby Will Fall
LEWIS, Elliott
Two Heads Are Better
Dirty Linen
People In Glass Houses
Double Trouble
Here Today, Dead Tomorrow
Bennett's World
Death & The Single Girl

LEWIS, Stephen
Cowboy Blues
LINDSAY, R Howard
Fowl Murder
LINGO, Ade E
Murder In Texas
LINKLATER, J Lane
Black Opal
Shadow For A Lady
(And) She Had Little Knife
Bishop's Cap (Murder)
Odd Woman Out
Green Glove
Tisket, A Casket
LINZEE, David
Discretion
Belgravia
LIVINGSTON, Jack
Piece Of The Silence
Die Again, Macready
Nightmare File
Hell-Bent For Election
LIVINGSTON, Nancy
Trouble At Aquitane
Fatality At Bath & Wells
Incident At Pargeta
Death In A Distant Land
LOCHTE, Dick
Sleeping Dog
Laughing Dog
LOCKE, Robert Donald
Taste Of Brass
LOCKHART, Max
Nobody Dies In Chinatown
LOGAN, Carolynne & Malcolm
One Of These Seven
LORE, Phillips
Who Killed The Pie Man?
Murder Behind Closed Doors
Looking Glass Murders
LOUIS, Joseph
Madelaine
Trouble With Stephanie
LOVELL, B.E
And Incidentally, Murder!
Rage To Kill
LUTZ, John
Buyer Beware >

Nightlines
Right To Sing The Blues
Ride The Lightning
Dancer's Debt
Tropical Heat
Scorcher
Kiss
LYALL, Gavin
Blame The Dead
LYNCH, Jack
Bragg's Hunch
Missing & The Dead
Pieces Of Death
Sausalito
San Quentin
Monterey
Seattle
LYNNE, James Broome
Rogue Diamond
LYON, Dana
It's My Own Funeral
LYONS, Arthur
Dead Are Discreet
All God's Children
Killing Floor
Dead Ringer
Castles Burning
Hard Trade
At The Hands Of Another
Three With A Bullet
Fast Fade
Other People's Money
McBAIN, Ed
Where There's Smoke
McCALL, John J
Is Money Everything?
McCALL, Wendell
Dead Aim
MacCARGO, J.T
Faces Of Murder
Round Trip To Nowhere
Walk On The Blind Side
Fine Day For Dying
McCONNELL, Frank
Murder Among Friends
Blood Lake
McCONNOR, Vincent
Man Who Knew Hammett

McCURTIN, Peter
Minnesota Strip
McCUTCHEON, Hugh
Angel Of Light = Murder At The Angel
Cover Her Face
MacDONALD, John D
Drowner
Deep Blue Goodbye
Nightmare In Pink
Purple Place For Dying
Quick Red Fox
Deadly Shade Of Gold
Bright Orange For The Shroud
Darker Than Amber
One Fearful Yellow Eye
Pale Grey For Guilt
Girl In Plain Brown Wrapper
Dress Her In Indigo
Long Lavender Look
Tan & Sandy Silence
Scarlet Ruse
Turquoise Lament
Dreadful Lemon Sky
Empty Copper Sea
Green Ripper
Free Fall In Crimson
Cinnamon Skin
Lonely Silver Rain
MACDONALD, Ross
Moving Target = Harper
Drowning Pool
Way Some People Die
Ivory Grin
   = Marked For Murder
Find A Victim
Name Is Archer
Barbarous Coast
Doomsters
Galton Case
Zebra-Striped Hearse
Wycherly Woman
Chill
Far Side Of The Dollar
Black Money
Instant Enemy
Goodbye Look
Underground Man
Sleeping Beauty >

Blue Hammer
Lew Archer, Private Investigator
MacDONALD, William Colt
Law & Order, Unlimited
Mascarada Pass
Destination Danger
Comanche Scalp
Devil's Drum
Action At Arcanum
Tombstone For A Troubleshooter
Osage Bow
McDOUGALD, Roman
Deaths Of Lora Karen
Whistling Legs
Blushing Monkey
MacDOUGALL, James
Weasel Hunt
Death & The Maiden
McDOWELL, Emmett
Switcheroo
McDOWELL, Rider
Mercy Man
McGIRR, Edmund
Funeral Was In Spain
Hearse With Horses
Here Lies My Wife
Lead-Lined Coffin
Entry Of Death
Death Pays The Wages
No Better Fiend
Bardel's Murder
Murderous Journey
McGOWN, Jill
Evil Hour
McGRAW, Lee
Hatchett
McGREGOR, Don & COLAN
Detectives Inc.
MacGREGOR, T.J
Dark Fields
Kill Flash
Death Sweet
On Ice
McINTOSH, J.T
Take A Pair Of Private Eyes
Coat Of Blackmail
MacKENZIE, Donald
Kyle Contract

McKNIGHT, Bob
Downwind
Murder Mutuel
Bikini Bombshell
Swamp Sanctuary
Kiss The Babe Goodbye
Running Scared
Slice Of Death
Drop Dead, Please
Flying Eye
Stone Around Her Neck
Homicide Handicap
MacLEAN, Katherine
Missing Man
MacNEIL, Neil
Death Takes An Option
Third On A Seesaw
Two Guns For Hire
Hot Dam
Death Ride
Mexican Slay Ride
Spy Catchers
McNEILE, H.C
Tiny Carteret = as SAPPER
Bulldog Drummond Strikes Back
    = Knock-Out: SAPPER
Bulldog Drummond At Bay
    = as SAPPER
Challenge = as SAPPER
McQUAY, Mike
Hot Time In Old Town
When Trouble Beckons
Deadliest Show In Town
Odds Are Murder
McRAE, Diana
All The Muscle You Need
McSHANE, Mark
Girl Nobody Knows
Night's Evil
MacVEIGH, Sue
Murder Under Construction
Grand Central Murder
Streamlined Murder
Corpse & Three Ex-Husbands
MADDREN, Jerry
CoT Johannisberg Reisling
MAHANNAH, Floyd
Yellow Hearse = No Luck For A Lady
Golden Goose = Broken Body

MALING, Arthur
Lover & Thief
MANDELKAU, Jamie
Leo Wyoming Caper
MANER, William
Image Killer
MANN, Jack
Gees' First Case
Grey Shapes
Nightmare Farm
Kleinart Case
Maker Of Shadows
Her Ways Are Death
Ninth Life
Glass Too Many
MANOR, Jason
(Girl In) The Red Jaguar
Pawns Of Fear = No Halo For Me
MARBLE, M.S
Everybody Makes Mistakes
Die By Night
MARCUS, A.A
Widow Gay = Post-Mark Homicide
Walk The Bloody Boulevard
Make Way For Murder
MARKSON, David
Epitaph For A Tramp = Fannin
Epitaph For A Dead Beat
Miss Doll, Go Home
MARLOWE, Dan J
Doorway To Death
Killer With A Key
Doom Service
Fatal Frails
Shake A Crooked Town
MARLOWE, Derek
Somebody's Sister
MARLOWE, Stephen
Second Longest Night
Mecca For Murder
Killers Are My Meat
Murder Is My Dish
Trouble Is My Name
Violence Is My Business
Terror Is My Trade
Double In Trouble (& PRATHER)
Homicide Is My Game
Danger Is My Line >

Death Is My Comrade
Peril Is My Pay
Manhunt Is My Mission
Jeopardy Is My Job
Francesca
Drum Beat - Berlin
Drum Beat - Dominique
Drum Beat - Madrid
Drum Beat - Erica
Drum Beat - Marianne
MARRIOTT, Anthony
Marker Calls The Tune
MARSHALL, Lovat
Sugar For The Lady
Sugar On The Carpet
Sugar Cuts The Corners
Sugar On The Target
Sugar On The Cuff
Sugar On The Kill
Sugar On The Loose
Sugar On The Prowl
Murder In Triplicate
Murder Is The Reason
Ladies Can Be Dangerous
Death Strikes In Darkness
Dead Are Silent
Dead Are Dangerous
Murder Of A Lady
Blood On The Blotter
Money Means Murder
Death Is For Ever
Murder's Out Of Season
Murder's Just For Cops
Death Casts A Shadow
Moment For Murder
Loose Lady Death
Date With Murder
Strangler
Key To Murder
Murder Mission
Murder To Order
MARSHALL, Raymond
Blondes' Requiem
Mallory
Why Pick On Me?
MARTELL, Charles
Halsey & The Dead Ringer

MARTIN, James E
Mercy Trap
MARTIN, Robert
Sleep, My Love
Tears For The Bride
Widow & The Web
Catch A Killer
Hand-Picked For Murder
Killer Among Us
Key To The Morgue
Just A Corpse At Twilight
To Have & To Kill
Coffin For Two
She, Me & Murder
Bargain For Death
MASON, Clifford
When Love Was Not Enough
Jamaica Run
MASTERSON, Whit
Dead, She Was Beautiful
MASUR, Harold Q
Bury Me Deep
Suddenly A Corpse
You Can't Live Forever
So Rich, So Lovely & So Dead
Big Money
Tall, Dark & Deadly
Last Gamble = Last Breath
    = Murder On Broadway
Send Another Hearse
Name Is Jordan
Make A Killing
Legacy Lenders
Mourning After
MATHIS, Ed
From A High Place
Dark Streaks & Empty Places
Natural Prey
Another Path, Another Dragon
MAXWELL, A.E
Just Another Day In Paradise
Frog & The Scorpion
Gatsby's Vineyard
Just Enough Light To Kill
MAXWELL, Thomas
Kiss Me Twice
MEEK, M.R.D
Hang The Consequences >

Split Second
MEYER, Nicholas
Target Practice
MEYNELL, Laurence
Frightened Man
Danger Round The Corner
Too Clever By Half
Death By Arrangement
Little Matter Of Arson
Fatal Flaw
Thirteen Trumpeters
Fairly Innocent Little Man
Don't Stop For Hooky Hefferman
Hooky & The Crock Of Gold
Lost Half Hour
Hooky Gets The Wooden Spoon
Papersnake
Hooky & Villainous Chauffeur
Hooky & The Prancing Horse
Hooky Goes To Blazes
Silver Guilt
Open Door
Affair At Barwold
Hooky Catches A Tartar
Hooky On Loan
Hooky Hooked
MIALL, Robert
Protectors
MICHAELS, Melisa C
Through The Eyes Of The Dead
MICHEL, M Scott
Sweet Murder = House In Harlem
X-Ray Murders = Sinister Warning
MILES, John
Dally With A Deadly Doll
MILLAR, Margaret
Listening Walls
Stranger In My Grave
How Like An Angel
MILLER, Geoffrey
Black Glove
MILLER, J.M.T
Weatherby
MILLER, Victor B
Fernanda
MILLER, Wade
Deadly Weapon
Guilty Bystander >

Fatal Step
Uneasy Street
Calamity Fair
Murder Charge
Shoot To Kill
MILNE, John
Dead Birds
Shadowplay = Moody Man
Daddy's Girl
MITCHAM, Gilroy
Full Stop
Man From Bar Harbour
Dead Reckoning
MITCHELL, James
Dead Ernest
Dying Day
MODIANO, Patrick
Missing Person
MOFFATT, James
Time For Sleeping
Blue Line Murder
Blood Is A Personal Thing
Eighth Veil
Twisted Thread
Curtain Of Hate
Course Of Villainy
Terror-Go-Round
MONIG, Christopher
Burned Man = Don't Count The Corpses
Abra-Cadaver
Once Upon A Crime
Lonely Graves
MONMOUTH, Jack
Donovan Case
Lonely, Lovely Lady
Sleepy-Eyed Blonde
Lightning Over Mayfair
Not Ready To Die
MONTALBAN, Manuel V
Murder In Central Committee
Southern Seas
MORGAN, D Miller
Money Leads To Murder
Lovely Night To Kill
MORRISON, Henry (ed)
Come Seven, Come Death
MORROW, J.T
Prophet

MORSE, Larry
Old Dick
Big Enchilada
Sleaze
MULKEEN, Thomas P
Honor Thy Godfather
My Killer Doesn't Understand Me
MULLEN, Clarence
Thereby Hangs A Corpse
Good Place For Murder
MULLER, Marcia
Edwin Of The Iron Shoes
Ask The Cards A Question
Cheshire Cat's Eyes
Games To Keep Dark Away
Leave A Message For Willie
Double (& **PRONZINI**)
There's Nothing To Be Afraid Of
Eye Of The Storm
There's Something In A Sunday
MULLER, Paul
Make Mine Mayhem
You Kill Me!
Lady Is Lethal
Danger—Dame At Work
Hasty Heiress
Finders, Losers
Slay Time
Why Pick On Me?
Goodbye Shirley
Don't Push Your Luck
Some Dames Don't
This Is Murder
Wistful Wanton
Friendly Fiends
MUNRO, Hugh
Who Told Clutha?
Clutha Plays A Hunch
Clue For Clutha
Clutha & The Lady
Get Clutha
MURPHY, Robert
Murder In Waiting
MURPHY, Warren
Smoked Out
Fool's Flight
Dead Letter
Lucifer's Weekend >

Trace
Trace & 47 Miles Of Rope
When Elephants Forget
Pigs Get Fat
Once A Mutt
Too Old A Cat
Getting Up With Fleas
Ceiling Of Hell
NASH, Anne
Said With Flowers
Death By Design
NEBEL, Frederick
Six Deadly Dames
Adventures Of Cardigan
NELSON, Hugh Lawrence
Ring The Bell At Zero
Murder Comes High
Gold In Every Grave
Season For Murder
Sleep Is Deep
Fence
Kill With Care
Suspect
NEVINS, Francis M Jr
120-Hour Clock
Ninety Million Dollar Mouse
NEWMAN, G.F
Men With The Guns
NEWMAN, Joel
Dead Man's Tears
NISBET, Jim
Gourmet = Damned Don't Die
NIXON, Allan
Get Garrity = Garrity
Goodnight Garrity
Go For Garrity
NOEL, Atanielle Annyn
Murder On Usher's Planet
NOLAN, William F
Death is For Losers
White Cad Cross-Up
Space For Hire
Look Out For Space
(ed) Black Mask Boys
NORMAN, Earl
Kill Me In Tokyo
Kill Me In Shimbashi
Kill Me In Yokohama >

Kill Me In Shinjuku
Kill Me In Yoshiwara
Kill Me On The Ginza
Kill Me In Atami
Kill Me In Roppongi
NYLAND, Gentry
Mr South Burned His Mouth= Run For
    Your Money= Hot Bullets For Love
O'CALLAGHAN, Maxine
Death Is Forever
Run From Nightmare
Hit & Run
ODLUM, Jerome
Nine Lives Are Not Enough
Night & No Moon
Morgue Is Always Open
Mirabilis Diamond
O'DONOHOE, Nick
April Snow
Wind Chill
Open Season
OGAN, George
To Kill A Judge
Murder In The Wind
Murder By Proxy
O'HARA, Kevin
Customer's Always Wrong
Exit & Curtain
Sing, Clubman, Sing!
Always Tell The Sleuth
It Leaves Them Cold
Keep Your Fingers Crossed
Pace That Kills
Women Like To Know
Danger:Women At Work!
Well, I'll Be Hanged!
And Here Is The Noose!
Taking Life Easy
If Anything Should Happen
Don't Tell The Police
Don't Neglect The Body
It's Your Funeral
OLIVER, Maria-Antonia
Study In Lilac
O'MALLEY, Frank
Best Go First
O'NEIL, Kerry
Mooney Moves Around >

PAYNE, Laurence
Take The Money & Run
Malice In Camera
Dead For A Ducat
Vienna Blood
Late Knight
PECK, Winifred
Warrielaw Jewel
PEEBLES, Nile
See The Red Blood Run
Blood Brother, Blood Brother
PENDLETON, Don
Ashes To Ashes
Eye To Eye
Hand To Hand
Life To Life
Heart To Heart
Mind To Mind
Copp For Hire
Copp On Fire
PENDOWER, Jacques
Perfect Wife
Operation Carlo
Master Spy
Sinister Talent
Traitor's Island
PENFIELD, Cornelia
After The Widow Changed Her Mind
PEPPE, Frank
Riddle In Wax
PEROWNE, Barry
Arrest These Men!
I'm No Murderer
They Hang Them In Gibraltar
Raffles & The Key Man
PERRY, Ritchie
Presumed Dead
PETERS, Bill
Blondes Die Young
PETERS, Ellis
House Of Green Turf
PETERS, Ludovic
Snatch Of Music
Tarakian
Two Sets To Murder
Out By The River
Two After Malic
Riot '71

PHILBRICK, W.R
Slow Dancer
Shadow Kills = Slow Grave
Ice For The Eskimo
Neon Flamingo
Crystal Blue Persuasion
Tough Enough
PHILIPS, Judson
Death Syndicate
Death Delivers A Postcard
PHILLIPS, R.B
Gun Play
PIPER, H Beam
Murder In The Gunroom
PLATT, Kin
Pushbutton Butterfly
Kissing Gourami
Princess Stakes Murder
= Pride Of Women
Giant Kill
Match Point For Murder
Body Beautiful Murder
Screwball King Murder
PLUM, Mary
Killing Of Judge McFarlane
Dead Man's Secret
Murder At The Hunting Club
Murder At The World's Fair
= Broken Vase Mystery
POPKIN, Zelda
Death Wears White Gardenia
Time Off For Murder
Murder In The Mist
Dead Man's Gift
No Crime For A Lady
POTTER, Jerry Allen
Talent For Dying
If I Should Die Before I Wake
POWELL, Talmage
Killer Is Mine
Girl's Number Doesn't Answer
With A Madman Behind Me
Start Screaming Murder
Corpus Delectable
PRATHER, Richard S
CoT Vanishing Beauty
Bodies In Bedlam
Everybody Had A Gun >

Find This Woman
Way Of A Wanton
Darling, It's Death
Ride High Horse = Too Many Crooks
Always Leave 'Em Dying
Strip For Murder
Wailing Frail
Have Gat—Will Travel
Three's A Shroud
Slab Happy
Take A Murder, Darling
Scrambled Yegg
   = Pattern For Murder: KNIGHT
Over Her Dead Body
Double In Trouble (& MARLOWE)
Dance With The Dead
Dig That Crazy Grave
Shell Scott's 7 Slaughters
Pattern For Panic
Kill The Clown
Dead Heat
Joker In The Deck
Cockeyed Corpse
Trojan Hearse
Kill Him Twice
Dead Man's Walk
Meandering Corpse
Kubla Khan Caper
Gat Heat
Cheim Manuscript
Kill Me Tomorrow
Shell Scott Sampler
Shell Scott's Murder Mix
Dead-Bang
Sweet Ride
Sure Thing
Amber Effect
Shellshock
Dagger Of Flesh
PREISS, Bryon (ed)
Raymond Chandler's Marlowe
PRONZINI, Bill
Snatch
Vanished
Undercurrent
Blowback
Twospot (& WILCOX)
Labyrinth >

Hoodwink
Scattershot
Dragonfire
Bindlestiff
Casefile
Cat's Paw
Quicksilver
Nightshades
Double (& MULLER)
Bones
Graveyard Plots
Deadfall
Shackles
(ed) Arbor House Treasury Of Detective
   & Mystery Stories From The Great
   Pulps
PRONZINI & GREENBERG (eds)
Mammoth Book Of Private Eye Stories
QUARRY, Nick
Trail Of A Tramp
Hoods Come Calling
Girl With No Place To Hide
No Chance In Hell
Till It Hurts
Some Die Hard
QUARTERMAIN, James
Diamond Hook
Man Who Walked On Diamonds
Rock Of Diamonds
Diamond Hostage
QUEEN, Ellery
Dragon's Teeth = Virgin Heiresses
Kiss & Kill
Campus Murders
Black Hearts Murder
Blue Movie Murders
QUINN, E Baker
One Man's Muddle
Death Is A Restless Sleeper
QUINN, Patrick
Once Upon A Private Eye
Twice Upon A Crime
Thrice Upon A Killing Spree
Fatal Complaint
Big Game
RALSTON, Gilbert
Dakota Warpath
Red Revenge >

Cat Trap
Murder's Money
Chain Reaction
RAND, Lou
Gay Detective = Rough Trade
RANDISI, Robert J
Disappearance Of Penny
Eye In The Ring
Steinway Collection
Full Contact
No Exit From Brooklyn
(ed) Eyes Have It
(ed) Mean Streets
(ed) Eye For Justice
RANSOME, Stephen
Shroud For Shylock
Sin File
RAY, Robert
Cage Of Mirrors
Murdock For Hire
Bloody Murdock
Dial M For Murdock
RAYTER, Joe
Victim Was Important
Asking For Trouble
REAMY, Tom
San Diego Lightfoot Sue
REASONER, James
Texas Wind
REAVES, Michael J
Darkworld Detective
REED, Christopher
Big Scratch
REED, Harlan
CoT Crawling Cockroach
Swing Music Murder
REED, Ishmael
Mumbo Jumbo
Last Days Of Louisiana Red
REESE, John
Texas Gold
Sequoia Shootout
Dead Eye
REEVES, Robert
Dead & Done For
No Love Lost
   = Come Out Killing
Cellini Smith:Detective

RESNICK, Mike
Stalking The Unicorn
RESNICOW, Herbert
Gold Solution
Gold Deadline
Gold Frame
Gold Curse
Gold Gamble
REYNOLDS, Mack
CoT Little Green Men
REYNOLDS, William J
Nebraska Quotient
Moving Targets
Money Trouble
RICHARDS, Nat
Otis Dunn, Manhunter
RIDER, J.W
Jersey Tomatoes
Hot Tickets
RIEFE, Alan
Lady Killers
Bullet-Proof Man
Conspirators
Killer With A Golden Touch
Silver Puma
Tyger At Bay
RIFKIN, Shepard
Murderer Vine
RIGSBY, Howard
Kill & Tell
RILEY, Dick
Rite Of Expiation
RING, Adam
Killers Play Rough
RING, Raymond H
Telluride Smile
RITCHIE, Jack
New Leaf & Other Stories
RITCHIE, Simon
Hollow Woman
RIVERA, William L
Panic Walks Alone
ROBB, T.N
Private Eye
Flip Side
ROBBINS, Clifton
Dusty Death
Man Without Face= Mystery Of Mr X >

Death On The Highway
Smash & Grab
Methylated Murder
ROBERTS, Garyn G (ed)
Cent A Story!
ROBERTS, Lee
Little Sister
CoT Missing Lovers
Pale Door
ROBERTS, Les
Infinite Number Of Monkeys
Not Enough Horses
Carrot For The Donkey
Pepper Pike
ROBERTSON, Colin
Tiger's Claws
You Can Keep The Corpse
Venetian Mask
Eastlake Affair
Who Rides A Tiger?
Golden Triangle
Threatening Shadows
Murder Sits Pretty
ROBINSON, Abby
Dick & Jane
ROBINSON, David
Confessions Of Andrew Clare
ROCHE, Arthur Somers
Case Against Mrs Ames
ROCK, Philip
Hickey & Boggs
RODEN, H.W
You Only Hang Once
Too Busy To Die
One Angel Less
Wake For A Lady
RODERUS, Frank
Oil Rig
Rain Rustlers
Video Vandal
Turn-Out Man
Coyote Crossing
Dead Heat
ROEBURT, John
Jigger Moran = CoT Tearless Widow
  = Wine,Women & Murder
There Are Dead Men In Manhattan
  = Murder In Manhattan >

  = Triple Cross
Corpse On The Town
  = CoT Hypnotized Virgin
Hollow Man
ROFFMAN, Jan
Daze Of Fears
ROHDE, William L
High Red For Dead
  = Murder On Line
ROMANO, Deane
Banacek
ROME, Anthony
Miami Mayhem
  = Tony Rome: ALBERT
Lady In Cement
My Kind Of Game
RONALD, E.B
Cat & Fiddle Murders
Death By Proxy
Sort Of Madness
RONNS, Edward
Corpse Hangs High
ROOS, Kelley
Murder On Martha's Vineyard
ROPER, L.V
Red Horse Caper
Emerald Chicks Caper
Hookers Don't Go To Heaven
ROSCOE, Mike
Death Is A Round Black Ball
Riddle Me This
Slice Of Hell
One Tear For My Grave
Midnight Eye
ROSEN, R.D
Strike Three, You're Dead
Fadeaway
Saturday Night Dead
ROSENBLUM, Robert
Good Thief
ROSENTHAL, Erik
Calculus Of Murder
Advanced Calculus Of Murder
ROSS, Albert
If I Knew What I Was Doing
ROSS, Leonard Q
Dark Corner = as ROSTEN

ROSS, Philip
Blue Heron
White Flower
ROSS, Z.H
Three Down Vulnerable
One Corpse Missing
ROSTEN, Leo
Silky!
King Silky
Dark Corner; as ROSS, L.Q
ROTH, Holly
Crimson In The Purple
Shadow Of A Lady
ROVIN, Jeff
Hollywood Detective: Garrison
Hollywood Detective: The Wolf
RUBEL, James L
No Business For A Lady
RUD, Anthony M
Rose Bath Riddle
House Of The Damned
Stuffed Men
RUHM, Herbert (ed)
Hard-Boiled Detective
RUNYON, Charles
Black Moth
RUSSELL, Richard
Paperbag
Reunion
Point Of Reference
RYAN, Conall
Black Gravity
SABER, Robert O
Dove = Chicago Woman
Deadly Lover
Scented Flesh
Murder Doll
Too Young To Die
Sucker Bait
Dame Called Murder
Time For Murder
SADDLER, K Allen
Great Brain Robbery
Gilt Edge
Talking Turkey
SADLER, Mark
Falling Man
Here To Die >

Mirror Image
Circle Of Fire
Touch Of Death
Deadly Innocents
ST CLAIR, Dexter
Lady's Not For Living
SANDERS, Daphne
To Catch A Thief
SANDERS, Lawrence
Timothy Files
Timothy's Game
SANGSTER, Jimmy
Private i
Foreign Exchange
Snowball
Blackball
SAPIR, Richard
Bressio
SAPPER
Tiny Carteret = as McNEILE
Knock-Out = Bulldog Drummond
    Strikes Back: McNEILE
Ronald Standish
Bulldog Drummond At Bay
    = as McNEILE
Ask For Ronald Standish
Challenge = as McNEILE
SARRANTONIO, Al
Cold Night
SATTERTHWAIT, Walter
Wall Of Glass
SAXON, John A
Liability Ltd = This Was No Accident
Half-Past Mortem
SCHOENFELD, Howard
Let Them Eat Bullets
SCHOPEN, Bernard
Big Silence
SCHORR, Mark
Red Diamond: Private Eye
Ace Of Diamonds
Diamond Rock
SCHUTZ, Benjamin M
Embrace The Wolf
All The Old Bargains
Tax In Blood
Things We Do For Love
SCOTT, Denis
Murder Makes A Villain >

Beckoning Shadow
SCOTT, Roney
Shakedown
SEARLS, Hank
Adventures Of Mike Blair
SEWARD, Jack
Cave Of Chinese Skeletons
Assignment: Find Cherry
Chinese Pleasure Girl
Frogman Assassination
Eurasian Virgins
SHAND, William
Man Called Tempest
Tempest Weaves A Shroud
Tempest In A Tea Cup
SHANNON, Jimmy
Devil's Passkey
SHARKEY, Jack
Murder, Maestro Please
Death For Auld Lang Syne
SHARP, Alan
Night Moves
SHAW, Joseph T (ed)
Hard-Boiled Omnibus
SHELLEY, Mike
Terror Of Her Ways
Madame Eddie's Chamber Of Horrors
Last Private Eye In Belfast
SHEPHERD, John
Lights, Camera, Murder
Demise Of Louse
    = Say Yes To Murder: BALLARD
SHERMAN, Steve
Maple Sugar Murders
White Mountain Murders
SHIRLEY, John
Black Hole Of Carcosa
SHORE, Julian
Rattle His Bones
SHUMAN, M.K
Mayo Stone Murders
SILER, Jack
Triangles Of Fire
SIMON, Roger L
Big Fix
Wild Turkey
Peking Duck
California Roll >

Straight Man
Raising The Dead
SINGER, Shelley
Samson's Deal
Free Draw
Full House
Spit In The Ocean
Suicide King
SLESAR, Henry
Thing At The Door
SLOVO, Gillian
Death Comes Staccato
SMITH, Don
Man Who Played Thief
Padrone
Payoff
Corsican Takeover
SMITH, J.C.S
Jacoby's First Case
Nightcap
SMITH, Julie
True-Life Adventures
Huckleberry Fiend
SMITH, Mark
Death Of The Detective
SMITH, Neville
Gumshoe
SMITH, Richard C
Secret Singing
SMITH, Richard N
Death Be Nimble
SMOKE, Stephen
Trick Of The Light
SOLOMON, Brad
Gone Man
Open Shadow
SOUTHCOTT, Audley
Cross That Palm When I Come To It
SPAIN, John
Dig Me A Grave
Death Is Like That
SPAIN, Nancy
Poison For Teacher
Death Goes On Skis
Cinderella Goes To The Morgue
R In The Month
Not Wanted On Voyage
Out, Damned Tot!

SPARLING, Joyce
North Of Delhi, East Of Heaven
SPENCER, John
Case For Charley
Charley Gets The Picture
SPENCER, Ross H
DADA Caper
Reggis Arms Caper
Stranger City Caper
Abu Wahab Caper
Radish River Caper
Missing Bishop
Monastery Nightmare
Kirby's Last Circus
Death Wore Gloves
Fifth Script
SPICER, Bart
Dark Light
Blues For The Prince
Golden Door
Black Sheep, Run
Long Green = Shadow Of Fear
Taming Of Carney Wilde
Exit, Running
SPILLANE, Mickey
I, The Jury
My Gun Is Quick
Vengeance Is Mine!
Big Kill
One Lonely Night
Kiss Me, Deadly
Girl Hunters
Snake
Twisted Thing
Body Lovers
Survival . . . Zero!
Tomorrow I Die
SPROUL, Kathleen
Birthday Murder
Death & Profs= Death Among Profs
Murder Off Key
Mystery Of The Closed Car
SQUERENT, Will
Your Golden Jugular
STAFFORD, Marjorie
Death Plays The Gramophone
STANFORD, Donald K
Slaughtered Lovelies >

Bargain In Blood
STARK, Michael
Run For Your Life = Kill-Box
STARRETT, Vincent
Case Book Of Jimmie Lavender
STEEL, Kurt
Murder Of Dead Man
    = Traveling Corpses
Murder For What?
Murder Goes To College
Murder In G-Sharp = Stranglers Holiday
Crooked Shadow
Judas Incorporated
Dead Of Night
Madman's Bluff
Ambush House
STEINER, Susan
Murder On Her Mind
STEPHENS, Reed
Man Who Killed His Brother
Man Who Risked His Partner
STEPHENSON, Neal
Zodiac
STERANKO
Red Tide
STERLING, Stewart
Dead Wrong
Dead Sure
Dead Of Night
Alibi Baby
Dead Right = Hotel Murders
Dead To World = Blonde In Suite 14
Body In The Bed
Dead Certain
STEVENS, Frank
She Left A Silver Slipper
STEVENSON, Richard
Death Trick
On The Other Hand, Death
Ice Blues
STEWART, Gary
Tenth Virgin
Zarahemla Vision
STEWART, Sam
Big Rip-Off
STOCKWELL, Gail
Death By Invitation
Embarrassed Murderer

STOKES, Manning Lee
Crooked Circle = Too Many Murderers
Wolf Howls Murder
Green For A Grave
Murder Can't Wait
STOUT, Rex
Fer De Lance = Meet Nero Wolfe
League Of Frightened Men
Rubber Band = To Kill Again
(CoT) Red Box
Too Many Cooks
Some Buried Caesar = Red Bull
Over My Dead Body
Where There's A Will
(CoT) Black Orchids
Cordially Invited To Meet Death
Invitation To Murder
Not Quite Dead Enough
Silent Speaker
Too Many Women
And Be A Villain
    = More Deaths Than One
Second Confession
Trouble In Triplicate
(Even In) In The Best Families
Three Doors To Death
Door To Death
Curtains For Three
Murder By The Book
Triple Jeopardy
Prisoner's Base = Out She Goes
Golden Spiders
Black Mountain
Three Men Out
Before Midnight
Might As Well Be Dead
Three Witnesses
If Death Ever Slept
Three For The Chair
And Four To Go = Crime & Again
Champagne For One
Plot It Yourself = Murder In Style
Too Many Clients
Three At Wolfe's Door
Final Deduction
Homicide Trinity
Gambit
Mother Hunt >

Right To Die
Trio For Blunt Instruments
Doorbell Rang
Death Of A Doxy
Father Hunt
Death Of A Dude
Please Pass The Guilt
Family Affair
Corsage
Death Times Three
Hand In Glove = Crime On Her Hands
Double For Death
Bad For Business
Broken Vase
Alphabet Hicks = Sound Of Murder
STRAHAN, Kay Cleaver
Desert Moon Mystery
Footprints
Death Traps
October House
Meriwether Mystery
Hobgoblin Murder
Desert Lake Mystery
SUCHER, Dorothy
Dead Men Don't Give Seminars
SUTTON, Tom & PREISS
Raven
SWAN, Phyllis
Trigger Lady
You've Had It Girl
Find Sherri
Death Inheritance
SWIGGETT, Howard
Corpse In Derby Hat
    = Stairs Lead Nowhere
Most Secret . . . Most Immediate
SYLVESTER, Robert
Big Boodle = Night In Havana
SYMONS, Julian
Murder! Murder!
Francis Quarles Investigates
TACK, Alfred
Selling's Murder!
Interviewing's Killing
Prospect's Dead
Death Takes A Dive
TAYLOR, Elizabeth Atwood
Murder At Vassar

TAYLOR, H Baldwin
Trouble With Tycoons
  = Missing Tycoon
TAYLOR, Sam S
Sleep No More
No Head For Her Pillow
So Cold, My Bed
THOMAS, Jim
Cross Purposes
THOMAS, Ross
Money Harvest
THOMPSON, Jim
Wild Town
THOREAU, David
Good Book
THORNBURG, Newton
Dreamland
THORP, Roderick
Detective
Nothing Lasts Forever
TIDYMAN, Ernest
Shaft
Shaft Among The Jews
Shaft's Big Score
Shaft Has A Ball
Goodbye, Mr Shaft
Shaft's Carnival Of Killers
Last Shaft
TONE, Teona
Lady On The Line
Full Cry
TOPOR, Tom
Bloodstar
Coda
TORREY, Roger
42 Days For Murder
TRACY, Don
Flats Fixed—Among Other Things
High, Wide & Ransom
Death Calling—Collect
Big X
TREAT, Lawrence
Lady, Drop Dead
TREYNOR, Blair
Widows's Pique
TRIMBLE, Louis
Cargo For The Styx
Dead & Deadly >

Love Me & Die
Anthropol
Noblest Experiment In The Galaxy
TRIPP, Miles
Obsession
Once A Year Man
Wife-Smuggler
Cruel Victim
Frightened Wife
Death Of A Man-Tamer
TROY, Simon
Road To Rhuine
TUCKER, Wilson
Chinese Doll
To Keep Or Kill
Stalking Man
Dove
Red Herring
Man In My Grave
TURNER, William Price
Another Little Death
ULLMAN, James Michael
Neon Haystack
UPTON, Roger
Who'd Want To Kill Old George?
Fade Out
Dead On The Stick
Fabergé Egg
USHER, Jack
Fix = Girl In The White Mercedes
VACHSS, Andrew
Flood
Strega
Blue Belle
VALIN, Jonathan
Lime Pit
Final Notice
Dead Letter
Day Of Wrath
Natural Causes
Life's Work
Fire Lake
Extenuating Circumstances
VAN ATTA, Winfred
Good Place To Work & Die
VANCE, Jack
Galactic Effectuator

VANCE, William E
Homicide Lost
VERALDI, Attilio
Payoff
WADE, Harrison
So Lovely To Kill
WAGER, Walter
Blue Leader
Blue Moon
Blue Murder
WAINWRIGHT, John
Blind Brag
WALKER, Harry
CoT Missing Gardener
WALKER, Walter
Two Dude Defense
Rules Of The Knife Fight
WALL, William
Wake Up Dead = Quiet Terror
WALLACE, Arthur
Passion Pulls The Trigger
    = Man Crazy: CLAYFORD
WALLACE, F.L
Three Times A Victim
WALLACE, Patricia
Small Favors
WALLING, R.A.J
Fatal Five Minutes
Follow Blue Car = In Time For Murder
VIII To IX = Bachelor Flat Mystery
Tolliver Case = Prove It, Mr Tolefree
Cat & Corpse
    = Corpse In Green Pajamas
Five Suspects = Legacy Of Death
Corpse In Crimson Slippers
Corpse With Dirty Face
    = Crime In Cumberland Court
Mr Tolefree's Reluctant Witnesses
    = Corpse In Coppice
Bury Him Deeper
    = Marooned With Murder
Mystery Of Mr Mock
    = Corpse With Floating Foot
Coroner Doubts= Corpse w/Blue Cravat
More Than One Serpent
    = Corpse With Grimy Glove
Dust In Vault
    = Corpse With Blistered Hands >

They Liked Entwhistle
    = Corpse With Red-Headed Friend
Why Did Trethewy Die? = Spider & Fly
By Hook Or (By) Crook
Castle-Dinas = Corpse With Eerie Eye>
Doodled Asterisk
    = Corpse By Any Other Name
Corpse Without A Clue
Corpse With Missing Watch
WALSH, Maurice
Man In Brown
    = Nine Strings To Your Bow
WALSH, Paul E
Murder Room
WARDEN, Mike
Death Beat
Dead Ringer
Bitter Homicide
Model For Murder
Topless Corpse
WARGA, Wayne
Hardcover
Fatal Impressions
WARREN, Charles Marquis
Deadhead
WARREN, James
Runaway Corpse
    = Disappearing Corpse
Cold Steel
Brush Of Death
WARREN, Vernon
Brandon Takes Over
Brandon In New York
Brandon Returns
Brandon:The Blue Mauritius
No Bouquets For Brandon
Bullets For Brandon
Appointment In Hell
Back-Lash
Farewell By Death
Invitation To Kill
WARRINER, Thurman
Method In His Murder
Ducats In Her Coffin
Death's Dateless Night
Doors Of Sleep
Death's Bright Angel
She Died, Of Course
Heavenly Bodies

WASHBURN, L.J
Wild Nights
WAUGH, Hilary
Madam Will Not Dine Tonight
   = If I Live To Dine
Hope To Die
Odds Run Out
Rich Man, Dead Man
   = Rich Man, Murder
   = Cot Brunette Bombshell
Run When I Say Go
Girl Who Cried Wolf
Glenna Powers Case
Doria Rafe Case
Billy Cantrell Case
Nerissa Claire Case
Veronica Dean Case
Priscilla Copperwaite Case
WAYE, Cecil
Figure Of Eight
End Of The Chase
Murder At Monk's Barn
Prime Minister's Pencil
WEISS, Mike
No Go On Jackson Street
WELCH, Timothy
Tennis Murders
WELLMAN, Manly Wade
Find My Killer
WELLS, Anna Mary
Murderer's Choice
WELLS, Charlie
Last Kill
WENTWORTH, Patricia
Grey Mask
Case Is Closed
Lonesome Road
In The Balance = Danger Point
Chinese Shawl
Miss Silver Deals With Death
   = Miss Silver Intervenes
Key
Clock Strikes Twelve
She Came Back = Traveller Returns
Pilgrim's Rest = Dark Threat
Latter End
Wicked Uncle = Spotlight
Case Of William Smith >

Eternity Ring
Miss Silver Comes To Stay
Catherine Wheel
Brading Collection
Through The Wall
Anna, Where Are You?
   = Death At Deep End
Ivory Dagger
Watersplash
Ladies' Bane
Vanishing Point
Out Of The Past
Benevolent Treasure
Silent Pool
Poison In The Pen
Listening Eye
Gazebo = Summerhouse
Fingerprint
Alington Inheritance
Girl In The Cellar
WERRY, Richard R
Casket For A Lying Lady
WEST, Elliott
Killing Kind
WEST, John B
Eye For An Eye
Cobra Venom
Taste For Blood
Bullets Are My Business
Death On The Rocks
Never Kill A Cop
WESTLAKE, Donald
Killing Time = Operator
Enough!
WEVERKA, Robert
Griff
WHALLEY, Peter
Robbers
Bandits = Crooks
Villains = Rogues
WHEELER, Benson & PURDY
Riddle Of The 8th Guest
WHELTON, Paul
Call The Lady Indiscreet
WHITFIELD, Raoul
Death In A Bowl
WHITTINGTON, Harry
Lady Was A Tramp

WILCOX, Collin
Bernhardt's Edge
WILDE, Percival
Rogues In Clover
P. Moran, Operative
WILHELM, Kate
Hamlet Trap
Smart House
WILLEFORD, Charles
Wild Wives
WILLIAMS, Louis
Tropical Murder
WILLIAMS, Philip Lee
Slow Dance In Autumn
WILLIAMSON, Chet
McKain's Dilemma
WILLS, Thomas
You'll Get Yours = as ARD
WILMOT, Robert Patrick
Blood In Your Eye
Murder On Monday
Death Rides A Painted Horse
WILSON, Gahan
Eddy Deco's Last Caper
Everybody's Favorite Duck
WILTZ, Chris
Killing Circle
Diamond Before You Die
WINTER, Bevis
Redheads Cool Fast
Darker Grows The Street
   = Noose Of Emeralds
Dead Sleep For Keeps
Next Stop—The Morgue
Let The Lady Die
Night Was Made For Murder
Sleep Long, My Lovely
Blondes End Up Dead
Dark & Deadly
WISE, Arthur
Death's-Head
WOHL, James P
Nirvana Contracts
Blind Trust Contracts
WOLF, Gary
Who Censored Roger Rabbit?
WOLFF, Benjamin
Hyde & Seek >

Hyde In Deep Cover
WOOD, Ted
Live Bait
When The Killing Starts
WOODFIN, Henry
Virginia's Thing
WOODY, William
Mistress Of Horror House
WREN, M.K
Curiosity Didn't Kill The Cat
Multitude Of Sins
Oh, Bury Me Not
Nothing's Certain But Death
Seasons Of Death
Wake Up, Darlin' Corey
WRIGHT, Wade
Blood In The Ashes
Suddenly You're Dead
Hearse Waiting
Until She Dies
Blonde Target
Shadows Don't Bleed
Two Faces Of Death
YARDLEY, James A
Kiss The Boys & Make Them Die
Kiss A Day Keeps The Corpses Away
YOUNG, David
Agent Provocateur
YUILL, P.B
Hazell Plays Solomon
Hazell & Three Card Trick
Hazell & Menacing Jester
ZACKEL, Fred
Cocaine & Blue Eyes
Cinderella After Midnight
ZADRA, Dan
Magnum PI
ZAHAVA, Irene (ed)
Woman Sleuth Anthology
ZAREMBA, Eva
Reason To Kill
Work For A Million
ZELAZNY, Roger
My Name Is Legion
ZOCHERT, Donald
Another Weeping Woman
Man Of Glass

TITLE INDEX

441

Ladies In Ermine	Holt, G
Ladies' Night	Bowers
Lady Be Bad	Halliday
Lady, Behave!	Cheyney
Lady Beware	Cheyney
Lady Came By Night	Halliday
Lady Came To Kill	Chaber
Lady, Drop Dead	Treat
Lady From Tokyo	Corrigan
Lady Has Claws	Desmond
Lady In Cement	Rome
Lady In Scarlet	Daniel
Lady In The Lake	Chandler, R
Lady In The Morgue	Latimer
Lady Is Afraid	Coxe
Lady Is Lethal	Muller, P
Lady Is The Tiger	Coggins
Lady Killer	Coxe
Lady Killers	Riefe
Lady Of China Street	Corrigan
Lady On The Line	Tone
Lady Regrets	Fox
Lady Said No	Allyson
Lady, This Is Murder	Chambers, P
Lady Was A Tramp	Whittington
Lady, Where Are You?	Desmond
Lady Who Never Was	Chambers, P
Lady Yesterday	Estleman
Lady's Not For Living	St Clair
Lam To The Slaughter	Fair
Lamaar Ransom, Private Eye	
	Galloway
Lament For A Lousy Lover	Brown, C
Last Appointment	Howard
Last Breath	Masur
Last Commandment	Coxe
Last Dance In Redondo Beach	Katz
Last Days Of Louisiana Red	Reed, I
Last Deception	Howard
Last Express	Kendrick
Last Gamble	Masur
Last Good Kiss	Crumley
Last Kill	Wells, C
Last Of The Armageddon Wars	Dennis
Last Private Eye	Birkett
Last Private Eye In Belfast	Shelley
Last Seen Alive	Duncan
Last Seen Hitchhiking	Halliday

Last Shaft	Tidyman
Last Smile	Albert
Last Vanity	Howard
Last Year's Blood	Branson
Late Knight	Payne
Late Lamented	Brown, F
Late Unlamented	Carmichael
Latter End	Wentworth
Laughing Dog	Lochte
Laughing Fox	Gruber
Laughter In The Alehouse	Kane, H
Laurel & Hardy Murders	Kaye, M
Law & Order, Unlimited	
	MacDonald, WC
Lay Her Among The Lilies	Chase, JH
Layoff	Dean, RG
Lead-Lined Coffin	McGirr
Leaden Bubble	Branson
League Of Frightened Men	Stout
Leather Duke	Gruber
Leave A Message For Willie	
	Muller, M
Legacy Lenders	Masur
Legacy Of Death	Walling
Leo Wyoming Caper	Mandelkau
Leopard Died Too	Brent
Let Me Kill You Sweetheart!	Carr, K
Let The Lady Die	Winter
Let The Skeletons Rattle	Davis, FC
Let Them Eat Bullets	Schoenfeld
Let's Face It	Bocca
Let's Not Get Smart	Bocca
Lew Archer, Private Investigator	
	Macdonald, R
Liability Limited	Saxon
Lie A Little, Die A Little	
	Brett, Michael
Life Cycle	Carmichael
Life To Life	Pendleton
Life's Work	Valin
Lightning Over Mayfair	Monmouth
Lights, Camera, Murder	Shepherd
Like Ice She Was	Ard
Lilies In Her Garden Grew	Davis, FC
Lime Pit	Valin
Limping Goose	Gruber
Link	Carmichael
Listening Eye	Wentworth

STOP PRESS

INTRODUCTION

WOMEN DETECTIVES
Note new totals: 174 women PIs, 124 women writers.
Colorado, Kat — **Karen KIJEWSKI**
Davis, Mavis — **Susan BAKER**
Horowitz, Helen — **DELMAN, David**
McGarron, Claire — **TV: LEGWORK**
Noonam, Rita — **HENDRICKS, Michael**
O'Shaughnessy, Kiernan — **DUNLAP, Susan**
Reece, Caitlin — **DOUGLAS, Lauren Wright**
Tramwell, Hyacinth & Primrose — **Dorothy CANNELL**
Wilder, Johanna & Ruth Wilson — **BUSHNELL, Agnes**

ETHNIC DETECTIVES
Dean, Sam — **PHILLIPS, Mike** (Black British)
Horowitz, Helen — **DELMAN, David** (part Apache)

THE GOLDEN AGES
DiCHIARA, Robert — Los Angeles, 1949
KERR, Philip — Berlin, Germany, 1936
STEED, Neville — Torquay, England, 1930s
WRIGHT, Stephen — NYC/Hollywood, 1945

A—Z
* indicates new entry

*ABSHIRE, Richard
A Dallas police officer who stole **Jack Kyle**'s wife and had him thrown off the force is his first, murder suspect, client in a debut *Booklist* describes as having "atmosphere in spades but suffers from some lackadaisical plotting." Abshire, an ex-cop PI himself, "writes with authority, his tale laced with dark wit amid much death and confusion."
     Dallas Drop (1989)
ALBERT, Marvin
     The Last Smile (UK 1989)

ALLEGRETTO, Michael
>   Dead Of Winter (1989)

*AMBLER, Dail

Ambler's ultra-prolific paperback output of more than usually feeble British ersatz featured New York PI **Danny Spade**, also written as by **Danny SPADE**.

>   Duet For Two Guns (UK 1952)
>   Hold That Tiger (UK 1952)
>   Johnny Gets His! (UK 1952)
>   The Lady Says When (UK 1952)
>   What's With You (UK 1952)
>   Danny Spade Spells Danger (UK 1953)
>   A Curtain Of Glass (UK 1954)
>   Danny Spade Sees Red (UK 1954)
>   Someone Falling (UK 1954)

ANTHOLOGIES

*A22 Mason, Tom (ed): Spicy Detective Stories (1989) Robert Leslie BELLEM, Arthur HUMBOLT, Carl MOORE, Huntley PALMER.

BABULA, William
>   According To St. John (1989)

*BAKER, Susan

PW remarked "etherizing readers with clichés and slack writing, Baker fails to impress in this introduction of PI **Mavis Davis** of Houston . . . to succeed, she'll have to do better than this mediocrity."

>   My First Murder (1989)

Baron, Lee — BREWER, Gil

Bartells, Clifford — MacDONALD, John D.

BELLEM, Robert Leslie

Dan Turner short story "Temporary Corpse" (*Spicy Detective Stories*, 1935) in **A22**.

Black, Johnny — STEED, Neville

BRACKETT, Leigh
>   No Good From A Corpse (UK 1989)

*BREWER, Gil 1922-1983

Prolific pulpster who set many hardboiled books in Florida, one featuring St Petersberg PI **Bill Maddern**. Second generation PI **Lee Baron** returns to Florida's Gulf Coast to take over his dead father's agency. James REASONER (*Paperback Parade #9*) commented, "The plot is muddled to the point of incoherence in places, the characters unlikeable (even the narrator and nominal hero comes off as a jerk most of the time) and the overall theme is extremely bleak. However, these things can be considered mere examples of Brewer's technique. The plot may not make much sense, he may be saying, because life itself usually doesn't. This novel has headlong pace, a lot of brutal but well-done action scenes and a fine sense of place. Brewer makes Florida a hellish, nightmare place to live."

Maddern: So Rich, So Dead (1951, UK 1952)
Baron: Wild (1958, UK 1959)

*BROD, D.C.
Harking back to an almost vanished sub-genre, Brod's hero is middle-aged ex-cop **Quint McCauley**, security head of Chicago department store Hauser's. *PW* found the settings and dialogue of this hardboiled first-in-a-series realistic, "solid, satisfying fare."

      Murder In Store (1989)

Buntz, Norman — TV: BEVERLY HILLS BUNTZ
*BUSHNELL, Agnes
Portland, Maine, PI partners **Johanna Wilder** and **Ruth Wilson** feature in a WomanSleuth mystery involving Russian emigres, ballet stars and radical feminists.

      Shadow Dance (1989)

CAMPBELL, Robert
      Sweet La-La Land (1989, UK 1989)

*CANNELL, Dorothy
A British born author, now a US resident, whose blurb boasts of two of the most cunning and unlikely private eyes, **Hyacinth & Primrose Tramwell**, of the Flowers Detective Agency whose (first?) case is set among murderous ladies in the English "village" of Chitterton Fells.

      The Widows Club (1989, UK 1989)

CHESBRO, George
      Second Horseman Out Of Eden (1989)

Colorado, Kat — KIJEWSKI, Karen
COOK, Glen
      Old Tin Sorrows (1989)

CRUMLEY, James
Whores (1988) contains an excerpt from a forthcoming **C.W. Sughrue** novel, *The Mexican Tree Duck*.

*DAVIS, Lindsey
In 70 A.D. Imperial Rome, young republican **M. Didius Falco** is hired to investigate the murder of a senator's niece, uncovering a plot to overthrow Emperor Vespasian. "Wisecracking in ancient idiom, Falco seems, nevertheless, a recognizably up-to-date young man, one whose

honor, humor and humanity work him quickly into reader's affection. Davis's story, though couched in period detail, rewards as much for deft handling of plot and depth of charactization as for its historicity" (*PW*).

Silver Pigs (1989)

Davis, Mavis — BAKER, Susan

Dean, Sam — PHILLIPS, Mike

*DELMAN, David

An ex-cop, part-Apache **Helen Horowitz**, married to NYPD Homicide Lieutenant Jacob Horowitz, sets up as a PI.

The Liar's League (UK 1989)

DiCHIARA, Robert

LAPD patrolman Jonathan Harding sells his soul to the devil to become 1949 LA PI **Johnny Hard** and investigates his father's murder. As Hard, with the devil as his partner, his father hires him to tail his own mother. *PW* found it an enjoyable and offbeat debut even though the conclusion did not quite come up to the story's premise.

The Dick And The Devil (1989)

*DOUGLAS, Lauren Wright

S&W .375 Magnum toting Victoria PI **Caitlin Reece** is hired by a prominent closet lesbian whose orientation is about to be exposed.

The Always Anonymous Beast (1989)

*DUNLAP, Susan

A young medical examiner turned PI, **Kiernan O'Shaughnessy** investigates religious murder in Phoenix, Ariz. *PW* remarked "Feisty Kiernan has appeal, but her debut is overburdened with subplots, complaints about the weather and hard-to-credit emotional conflicts."

Pious Deception (1989)

ESTLEMAN, Loren D.

Silent Thunder (1989)

EVERSON, David

Rebound (1989)

Falco, M. Didius — DAVIS, Lindsey

FREY, James N.

The Long Way To Die (UK 1989)

Garland, Stan - McDOWELL, Paul

GILBERT, Dale L. (deceased)

Murder Begins At Home (1989)

Grist, Simeon — HALLINAN, Timothy

Gunther, Bernhard — KERR, Philip

HALL, Parnell
>Strangler (1989)

*HALLINAN, Timothy

A former UCLA English professor, **Simeon Grist** is now a novice LA PI. "Televangelism, brainwashing, research into the early 19th century diaspora of new American religions and a most unusual ally lead Grist to the denouement of this very satisfying mystery" (*PW*).
>The Four Last Things (1989)

Hammer, Mike — SPILLANE, Mickey & Ed ROBBINS
Hammett, Dashiell — WRIGHT, Stephen
HANSEN, Vern
>Murder With Menaces (UK 1962)

Hard, Johnny — DiCHIARA, Robert
HEALY, Jeremiah
>Yesterday's News (1989)

*HENDRICKS, Michael

After 7 years with NYC agency Ortner & Lloyd, **Rita Noonan** wants a partnership. *PW* found her a "tough, tender and thoroughly likeable heroine, more important, a credible detective," in a "promising" novel with "crisp prose and an interesting plot enlivened by several surprises."
>Money To Burn (1989)

HILARY, Richard
>Behind The Fact (1989)

Horowitz, Helen — DELMAN, David
*HUMBOLT, Arthur

A *Spicy Detective Stories* (1935) short story, "Killer's Cut" in **A22** features **Herbert Todd**. "Five years with the Bell Agency had taught him that private dicks make enemies." In a classic Spicy moment, he remarks towards the end of the story that the obligatory cutie looks funny with a dress on - this being the first time he's seen her fully clothed.

IRVINE, Robert R.
>The Angels' Share (1989)

KENNEALY, Jerry
>Polo In The Rough (1989)

*KERR, Philip

WW1 Turkish Front veteran and former policeman, **Bernhard Gunther** is a PI specializing in missing persons, his first case taking place in Nazi-ruled Berlin in 1936, when missing persons were commonplace. A follow-up will be set in the Harry Lime territory of post-war Vienna.
>March Violets (UK 1989, 1989)

*KIJEWSKI, Karen
Winner of the 3rd PWA Best First Novel competition with a story featuring **Kat Colorado** of Sacramento. A spunky lady, "sure to win the hearts of mystery fans," *PW* felt the story successfully combined stark terrors, comedy and even pathos."
   Katwalk (1989, UK 1989)
Kyle, Jack — ABSHIRE, Richard
LARIAR, Lawrence
   Friday Is For Death features **Steve McGrath**
*LINDSAY, Frederic
Former Glasgow, Scotland, policeman turned Glaswegian PI, **Murray Wilson** investigates a spate of killings and mutilations of men marking the 100th anniversary of the Jack the Ripper murders in London.
   Jill Rips (UK 1987, 1989)
LUTZ, John
   Kiss (UK 1989)
   Time Exposure (1989) Nudger
McCauley, Quint — BROD, D.C.
MacDONALD, John D.
Resigning from the Florence City, Florida, police after being busted down from Lieutenant to patrolman for exposing corruption, **Clifford Bartells** stays in town investigating for Security Theft & Accident Insurance Co.
   The Brass Cupcake (1950)
*McDOWELL, Paul
Redundant art teacher and martial arts student **Stan Garland** is an "Alternative" PI, "heavy on karma and light on luck," in a novel that appeared in a British crime series with a left-wing emphasis.
   Dope Opera (UK 1987)
McGarron, Claire — TV: LEGWORK
McGrath, Steve — LARIAR, Lawrence
Maddern, Bill — BREWER, Gil
MARTELL, Charles
   Halsey And The Fine Art Of Murder (1989)
MASON, Tom (ed) — see A22
MATHIS, Edward
   The Burned Woman (1989, UK 1989)
MAXWELL, A.E.
   The Art Of Survival (1989)

MILNE, John
>Daddy's Girl (1989)

*MOORE, Carl
With a reputation as "the toughest dick west of New York," **Victor Strawn** has the usual problems with his libido and gorgeous, willing women in "An Eye For An Eye" (*Spicy Detective Stories* 1937; **A22**).

Noonan, Rita — HENDRICKS, Michael
Nowak, Tommy — Film: PINK CADILLAC
OLIVER, Maria-Antonia
>Study In Lilac (UK 1987)

O'Shaughnessy, Kiernan — DUNLAP, Susan
*PALMER, Huntley
House dick of the Hotel Demerest, "a cross between a dime-a-dance spot and Madame Sophie's. Not a night goes by when I don't have to drag some potted floozie out by the neck and dunk her under a cold shower," **Eddie Riley** features in "A Shamus And A Sheba" (*Spicy Detective Stories* 1937; **A22**).

PENDELTON, Don
>Copp In Deep (1989)

*PETERSON, Geoff
A reformed alcoholic, ex-sportswriter and would-be PI, **Boyd Sherman** investigates horse theft and murder in modern Wyoming. "Atmospheric but contrived . . . Though the dialogue has the feel of real conversation and Peterson's spare style skillfully evokes the dreary winter Wyoming landscape, coincidences and expediency mar the resolution," said *PW*.
>Medicine Dog (1989)

PHILBRICK, W.R.
Hawkins: Paint It Black (1989)

*PHILLIPS, Mike
Black Guyanan author whose black Londoner hero **Sam Dean** is actually a hard-up reporter who accepts a sleuthing job from a University friend. Described by a British critic as having "a cool eye for the ironies of life in the White world . . . Dean moves effortlessly - at times even innocently - through what amounts to a black London underworld, and while Phillips is no Chester Himes, he instills a ring of real truth to his characters and locations. Mercifully short on polemic." A TV series is projected.
>Blood Rights (UK 1989, 1989)

Reece, Caitlin — DOUGLAS, Lauren Wright
REYNOLDS, William J.
>Things Invisible (1989)

Riley, Eddie — PALMER, Huntley
RITCHIE, Simon
    Work For A Dead Man (1989)
ROSEN, R.D.
    Saturday Night Dead (UK 1989)
SANGSTER, Jimmy
    Snowball (UK 1989)
    Blackball (UK 1989)
Sherman, Boyd — PETERSON, Geoff
*SPADE, Danny = AMBLER, Dail
Breathtakingly mediocre British ersatz series featuring NYC PI **Danny Spade**. *Spades Are Trumps!* and all undated titles are unlisted in Hubin.
    She Liked It That Way (UK 1950?)
    The Dame Plays Rough (UK 1950)
    You Slay Me (UK 1950)
    Silks And Cordite (UK 1951) In Hubin as Silk And Cordite
    The Lady Holds A Gun (UK 195?)
    Waterfront Rat (UK 1951)
    Move Fast, Brother (UK 195?)
    Count Me Out (UK 195?)
    You'll Play This My Way (UK 1951)
    Hi-Jack (UK 195?)
    San Francisco By Night (UK 195?)
    Dial Death (UK 195?)
    Spades Are Trumps! (UK 1951)
    'Frisco Rock (UK 1951)
    Not Killed—Just Dead (UK 1952)
    A Gun For Sale (UK 1952)
    Twice As Dead (UK 1952)
    Kiss Me As You Go (UK 1953)
    Lady Likes To Sin (UK 1953)
    Nothing To Hide (UK 1953)
    Story Of A Killer (UK 1953)
    That's All I Need (UK 1954)
*SPILLANE, Mickey & Ed ROBBINS
Spillane wrote the words, Robbins drew the pictures, for a **Mike Hammer** comic strip for newspaper syndication. Hammer originated as an unrealized comic book project under the name Mike Danger.
    The Sudden Trap & Other Stories (1982)
    The Dark City & Other Stories (1985)

*STEED, Neville
Set in Torquay, on the South Coast of England, in the 1930s, **Johnny Black** runs the Black Eye Detective Agency.
> Black Eye (UK 1989)

*STRASSER, Todd
Novelization of **Films: PINK CADILLAC** featuring skip-tracer **Tommy Nowak.**
> Pink Cadillac (1989)

Strawn, Victor — MOORE, Carl
SUCHER, Dorothy
> Dead Men Don't Marry (1989)

Todd, Herbert — HUMBOLT, Arthur
Tramwell, Hyacinth & Primrose — CANNELL, Dorothy
TRIPP, Miles
> The Chords Of Vanity (UK 1989)

VACHSS, Andrew
> Blue Belle (UK 1989)
> Hard Candy (1989)

WASHBURN, L.J.
> Dead-Stick (1989)

West, Sandy — WRIGHT, Stephen
Wilder, Johanna — BUSHNELL, Agnes
Wilson, Murray — LINDSAY, Frederic
Wilson, Ruth — BUSHNELL, Agnes
*WRIGHT, Stephen
Post-WW2, **Sandy West** meets **Dashiell Hammett** who, suffering from writer's block, intends to open an NYC detective agency. Impressed, for no obvious reason, Hammett takes West on as an apprentice. Episodic, claiming to be both spoof and whodunit.
> The Adventures Of Sandy West, Private Eye (198?)

ZAREMBA, Eve
> Beyond Hope (Can 1987, UK 1989)

TV

*BEVERLY HILL BUNTZ (November 1987 - ?). *Hill Street Blues* refugees **Norman Buntz** (Dennis Franz), tough guy ex-cop, and Sid the Snitch (Peter Jurasik), one of his informants, move to Beverly Hills where Buntz gets a PI license. An odd couple anyway, both are fish out of water in glossy California.

*LEGWORK (October-December 1987). Quitting the DA's office, capable, assertive, but ever-so-vulnerable **Claire McGarron** (Margaret Colin) becomes an NYC PI, struggling to make ends meet despite driving a drop-top Porsche. Entertaining, beautifully made hokum with many one-liners and plots of Rockford-esque complexity, studious avoidance of excess clichés and a well-sustained ambience, axed after only 10 episodes.

FILMS

PINK CADILLAC (1989). Directed by Buddy Van Horn, script by John Eskow, starring Clint Eastwood as **Tommy Nowak**, the best skip tracer in the business, the one sent after bail jumpers nobody else could catch. Bernadette Peters is his quarry, last seen in the eponymous vehicle. Novelization: **Todd STRASSER**.

YELLOW PAGES

GERMANY
Berlin	Bernhard Gunther

ITALY
Rome (70AD)	M Didius Falco

UNITED KINGDOM
Glasgow	Murray Wilson
London	Sam Dean
Torquay	Johnny Black

UNITED STATES
California
Sacramento	Kat Colorado

Florida
St Petersberg	Bill Maddern

Texas
Dallas	Jack Kyle
Houston	Mavis Davis

CHECK LIST

*ABSHIRE, Richard
Dallas Drop
ALLEGRETTO, Michael
Dead Of Winter
*AMBLER, Dail
Duet For Two Guns
Hold That Tiger
Johnny Gets His!
Lady Says When
What's With You
Danny Spade Spells Danger
Curtain Of Glass
Danny Spade Sees Red
Someone Falling
BABULA, William
According To St John
*BAKER, Susan
My First Murder
*BREWER, Gil
So Rich, So Dead
Wild
BROD, D.C.
Murder In Store
BUSHNELL, Agnes
Shadow Dance
CAMPBELL, Robert
Sweet La-La Land
*CANNELL, Dorothy
Widows Club
CHESBRO, George
Second Horseman Out Of Eden
COOK, Glen
Old Tin Sorrows
*DAVIS, Lindsey
Silver Pigs
*DELMAN, David
Liar's League
DiCHIARA, Robert
Dick & The Devil
DOUGLAS, Lauren Wright
Always Anonymous Beast
*DUNLAP, Susan
Pious Deception
ESTLEMAN, Loren D.
Silent Thunder

EVERSON, David
Rebound
GILBERT, Dale L.
Murder Begins At Home
HALL,Parnell
Strangler
*HALLINAN, Timothy
Four Last Things
HANSEN, Vern
Murder With Menaces
HEALY, Jeremiah
Yesterday's News
*HENDRICKS, Michael
Money To Burn
HILARY, Richard
Behind The Fact
IRVINE, Robert
Angels' Share
KENNEALY, Jerry
Polo In The Rough
*KERR, Philip
March Violets
*KIJEWSKI, Karen
Katwalk
*LINDSAY, Frederic
Jill Rips
LUTZ, John
Time Exposure
MacDONALD, John D.
Brass Cupcake
*McDOWELL, Paul
Dope Opera
MARTELL, Charles
Halsey & The Fine Art Of Murder
*MASON, Tom (ed)
Spicy Detective Stories
MATHIS, Edward
Burned Woman
MAXWELL, A.E.
Art Of Survival
PENDLETON, Don
Copp In Deep
*PETERSON, Geoff
Medicine Dog
PHILBRICK, W.R.
Paint It Black
*PHILLIPS, Mike
Blood Rights

TITLES

March Violets	Kerr, P
Medicine Dog	Peterson
Money To Burn	Hendricks
Move Fast, Brother	Spade
Murder Begins At Home	Gilbert
Murder In Store	Brod
Murder With Menaces	Hansen, V
My First Murder	Baker, S
Not Killed—Just Dead	Spade
Nothing To Hide	Spade
Old Tin Sorrows	Cook, G
Paint It Black	Philbrick
Pink Cadillac	Strasser
Pious Deception	Dunlap
Polo In The Rough	Kenneally
Rebound	Everson
San Francisco By Night	Spade
Second Horseman Out Of Eden	
	Chesbro
Shadow Dance	Bushnell
She Liked It That Way	Spade
Silent Thunder	Estleman
Silks And Cordite	Spade
Silver Pigs	Davis, L
So Rich, So Dead	Brewer, G
Someone Falling	Ambler
Spades Are Trumps!	Spade
Spicy Detective Stories	Mason (ed)
Story Of A Killer	Spade
Strangler	Hall
Sudden Trap & Other Stories	
	Spillane & Robbins
Sweet La-La Land	Campbell, R
That's All I Need	Spade
Things Invisible	Reynolds,WJ
Time Exposure	Lutz
Twice As Dead	Spade
Waterfront Rat	Spade
What's With You	Ambler
Widows Club	Cannell
Wild	Brewer, G
Work For A Dead Man	Ritchie, S
Yesterday's News	Healy
You Slay Me	Spade
You'll Play This My Way	Spade